THE

BABYLONIAN TALMŪD:

TRACTATE *B^{e}RĀKŌT*

CAMBRIDGE
UNIVERSITY PRESS

University Printing House, Cambridge CB2 8BS, United Kingdom

Published in the United States of America by Cambridge University Press, New York

Cambridge University Press is part of the University of Cambridge.

It furthers the University's mission by disseminating knowledge in the pursuit of education, learning and research at the highest international levels of excellence.

www.cambridge.org
Information on this title: www.cambridge.org/9781107676954

First published 1921
First paperback edition 2013

A catalogue record for this publication is available from the British Library

ISBN 978-1-107-67695-4 Paperback

THE

BABYLONIAN TALMŪD: TRACTATE *B^E^RĀKŌT*

TRANSLATED INTO ENGLISH FOR THE FIRST TIME, WITH INTRODUCTION, COMMENTARY, GLOSSARY AND INDICES

BY

THE REV. A. COHEN, M.A.
Sometime Scholar of Emmanuel College, Cambridge
Author of *Ancient Jewish Proverbs*

CAMBRIDGE
AT THE UNIVERSITY PRESS
1921

TO

DR ISRAEL ABRAHAMS

READER IN TALMUDIC TO THE UNIVERSITY OF CAMBRIDGE

A PUPIL'S TRIBUTE OF GRATITUDE

PREFACE

ONE frequently meets with references to, or quotations from, the Talmūd; but to most readers "Talmūd" is merely a name for a branch of ancient literature remote, esoteric and inaccessible. The Jews who produced it, impressed by its vastness, speak of "The Sea of the Talmūd"; but except to the comparative few who are willing to spend years in the study of the difficult language and intricate style in which it is composed, it is a sea uncharted and hazardous to navigate.

The mystery which enshrouds this important section of Jewish literature is deepened by the diametrically opposite valuations which have been placed upon it. On the one hand, there are they who regard it as the greatest production of the Jewish genius after the Bible—a mine of the richest lore, an unfailing well of wisdom. Even fables and legends which, read superficially, sound but childish fancies are invested with a deep meaning and made the source of wholesome instruction. On the other hand, there are the critics who can discover only a few grains of corn hidden away in a huge heap of chaff. To them, the discussions of *Hᵃlākāh* are nothing more than dry casuistry and hair-splitting, and the *Aggādāh*, with rare exceptions, examples of extreme puerility.

In a conflict of opinion of this kind, the truth is usually to be sought midway between the two extremes. Even eminent Jewish authorities of the Talmūd have admitted that not every sentence in that work is to be regarded as the quintessence of wisdom. See, for instance, the opinion of Naḥmanides quoted in § 4 of the Introduction. As for the unfriendly critics, it is impossible to consider their judgment as altogether unbiassed and disinterested. There is undoubted truth in what R. T. Herford writes: "If learned men like Lightfoot, Wagenseil, and especially Eisenmenger, explored the Rabbinical literature well-nigh from end to end, it was mainly for the purpose of reviling what they found there. And, in our own day, though there is no longer to be found amongst Talmudic scholars the scurrilous rancour of an Eisenmenger, there is still the inveterate habit of regarding Rabbinical Judaism as a means of exalting Christianity; there is nearly always the criticism of Judaism from the Christian point of view, and judgment given upon premises which it never recognised. There is scarcely any attempt to learn what it really meant to those who held it as their religion, who lived by it, and who died by it, and have done for two thousand years" (*Pharisaism*, p. 332).

Whatever be the merits or demerits of the Talmūd, in it are enshrined the intellectual activity and the spiritual aspiration of the leaders of Jewish thought during many centuries; and such a work cannot with fairness be rudely dismissed with scorn. It deserves respectful study.

The difficulty of making the Talmūd intelligible to the general reader is very great indeed. It is sometimes said that it defies translation. Certain it is that a bald, literal rendering would not convey its meaning. This is due principally to the fact that the *Gᵉmārā* is not a literary composition, but a compilation of *précis* notes which were intended to be amplified and explained *by oral teaching*. The Talmūd re-echoes the Schools of Palestine and Babylon and has been preserved in the Jewish *Schools* of subsequent generations. The translator is therefore compelled to fill up gaps to obtain the proper sequence of thought, and for this purpose I have resorted to the use of square brackets to mark off what is not in the text. I have endeavoured to keep as close to the original as possible, so that the student may be helped who wishes to read the Tractate by the aid of the translation. In the notes I have deemed it necessary to include the kind of comment with which the teacher would furnish his pupil. Although abundance of footnotes is distracting, it could not be avoided in the present work without sacrificing necessary guidance. But the warning must be uttered that no translation, however excellent, and no Commentary, however lucid, can make the Talmūd easy reading. The reasoning is usually so acute and the style so concise, that to follow the drift of a discussion demands the closest attention.

The reader who is new to Rabbinic literature is advised to study the Introduction before proceeding to the text and to use the Glossary of technical terms until these become familiar. Attention is also drawn to the Index of Rabbis cited in the Tractate, where I have, as far as possible, stated the School—Palestinian or Babylonian—and the century to which they belong. This information is necessary in any attempt to trace back a practice or teaching to its source or follow up its development. For this purpose I have also noted the variants of the names of the Rabbinic authorities as collated by Rabbinovicz in his *Variae Lectiones*.

Finally, the reader should throughout bear in mind that the Talmūd cannot and should not be judged by the canons of modern literature. It reflects a mode of life and thought, and is based on a methodology, utterly foreign to the Western culture of this age. In many matters it indicates conditions rather Oriental than specifically Jewish, and for that reason I have occasionally quoted parallels from Eastern life as described by Lane in his *Modern Egyptians*. Large sections, especially of the *H^{a}lākāh*, will no doubt prove quite uninteresting to many; but for the legist and archaeologist it is just these passages which have the greatest value. The Talmūd, however, touches on such a variety of topics that few will fail to find in its pages points of interest and instruction.

It is a pleasure for me to acknowledge my indebtedness to my friends, the Rev. A. Newman of Leicester, and Mr H.

Loewe, M.A., of Exeter College, Oxford, who kindly undertook the laborious task of proof-reading, despite the pressure of their official duties. Their revision has been most helpful, and their suggestions of great value. The former, in particular, often saved me from falling into traps which lie in wait for the unwary who venture into the paths of Rabbinic literature. A word of appreciation is also due to the Staff of the Cambridge University Press for the painstaking manner in which they have done their work.

A. COHEN.

BIRMINGHAM.
February, 1921.

TABLE OF CONTENTS

PAGE

PREFACE v

SUMMARY OF THE TRACTATE . . . xi

INTRODUCTION:

I. The Talmūd. xxiii

II. The Tractate *Beᵉrākōt* . . . xxviii

III. *Hᵃlākāh* xxix

IV. *Aggādāh* xxxii

V. The Use of the Bible in the Talmūd xxxv

LIST OF ABBREVIATIONS xxxviii

TRANSCRIPTION OF HEBREW AND ARAMAIC WORDS xl

TRANSLATION AND COMMENTARY . . 1

GLOSSARY. 427

INDEX I. RABBINICAL AUTHORITIES . 431

II. SCRIPTURAL AND LITURGICAL 440

III. GENERAL 452

SUMMARY OF THE TRACTATE

CHAPTER I (PAGES 1–81)

MISHNĀH I (1–54)

On the time of the evening Sh^{e}ma‘.

Why the evening *Sh^{e}ma‘* is treated before that of the morning . . 1
The *terminus a quo* for the reading of the evening *Sh^{e}ma‘* . . . 2
The watches of the night 6
R. Josē's encounter with Elijah 7
Why ruins should be avoided 8
The number of night-watches 9
David's praise of God 10
The harp above his bed 11
His claim to godliness 13
The *terminus ad quem* for the reading of the evening *Sh^{e}ma‘* . . 15
The relative order of the *Sh^{e}ma‘* and the *T^{e}fillāh* 16
Psalm cxlv. to be recited thrice daily 17
Omission in this Psalm of a verse commencing with N . . . 18
The *Sh^{e}ma‘* to be read on lying down 18
Its protective power against evil spirits 19
Teachings concerning suffering 20
Narratives about R. Ḥiyya b. Abba, R. Johanan, R. Ḥannina, R. Eleazar, Rab Huna and *Abbā* Benjamin 24
Concerning evil spirits 27
Importance of congregational worship 28
Digression on God's *T^{e}fillīn* 29
Subject of congregational worship resumed 30
The three statutory services 33
Some teachings of Rab Huna 33
Prayer offered by God 34
The wrath of God 35
Problem of reward and punishment 38
Moses and God 38
Some teachings of R. Simeon b. Johai 40
Explanation of the names Reuben and Ruth 40
Why Psalm iii. is entitled "A Psalm (not Lament) of David" . . 41
On contending with the wicked 41
Importance of praying with the Congregation 43
Explanations of "in the time of finding" (Ps. xxxii. 6) . . . 45
Importance of the study of *H^{a}lākāh* 46
Some teachings of ‘Ulla 46
Honouring the Scroll of the *Tōrāh*, and the weekly lections . . 47
Raba's advice to his sons 48
Praiseworthy habits of the Medes and Persians 49

Reading the *Sh^ema'* twice in a night or day sometimes legitimate . 50
Incident of Rabban Gamaliel and his sons explained 51
The Paschal offering 51
The Exodus from Egypt 53
Explanation of "I am that I am" 54

MISHNĀH II (55–66)

On the time of the morning Sh^ema'.

The *terminus a quo* 55
On uniting the *G^e'ullāh* with the *T^efillāh* 56
The numbering of the Psalms 57
R. Meir's wife, B^eruriah 57
Law of juxtaposition in the Bible 58
David's songs 58
God's attributes 59
God and the soul 60
Hezekiah and Isaiah 60
Hezekiah's six acts 62
The Shunammite woman and Elisha 64
Proper to pray in a lowly place and before eating 65
Reading the *Sh^ema'* not in its proper time 66

MISHNĀH III (67–70)

On the posture for reading the Sh^ema'.

Bēt Shammai's view explained 67
The performance of a religious duty exempts the reading of the *Sh^ema'* 68
Bēt Hillel's view confirmed 68

MISHNĀH IV (70–79)

On the benedictions of the Sh^ema'.

The first benediction before the morning *Sh^ema'* 70
The second benediction 71
The benediction before the study of *Tōrāh* 71
Ritual used in the Temple 72
Reading of the Decalogue before the *Sh^ema'* abolished 73
Benediction used in the Temple for the outgoing guard 74
Validity of a benediction depends upon the nature of its conclusion . 74
Some teachings of Rabbah b. Ḥinnana regarding the ritual . . . 76
Why the *Pārāshāh* of Balak was not included in the *Sh^ema'* . . 78
Why the *Pārāshāh* of Fringes was included 79

MISHNĀH V (79–81)

On referring to the Exodus from Egypt in the evening Sh^ema'.

Exodus will be remembered in the days of the Messiah . . . 80
The names Abram and Abraham, Sarai and Sarah explained . . 81

CHAPTER II (PAGES 82–115)

MISHNĀH I, II (82–95)

On greeting a person during the reading of the Sh^e^ma'; *its sections.*

Whether the *Sh^e^ma'* must be read in Hebrew only 83
How it must be read: the law of *Kawwānāh* 84
How R. Judah the Prince read it 86
First sentence of the *Sh^e^ma'* sufficient at night 87
Returning a salutation while reading the *Sh^e^ma'* 87
Permissible to give greeting while reading *Hallēl* or the *M^e^gillāh* . 88
Prayer should precede the salutation of one's friends 89
Prayer must precede attendance to personal concerns 90
On reading the third section of the *Sh^e^ma'* in the evening: Palestinian custom 91
The sequence of paragraphs in the *Sh^e^ma'* 92
T^e^fillīn must precede the *Sh^e^ma'* 93
How to receive upon oneself the yoke of the Kingdom of Heaven. . 94
Hands may be cleansed with pebbles, etc. when water not available . 95

MISHNĀH III (95–102)

On how the Sh^e^ma' *must be read.*

Whether it must be read audibly 95
Prov. xxx. 15 teaches the resurrection of the dead 100
First two paragraphs of the *Sh^e^ma'* included in the *T^e^fillīn in extenso* . 100
Distinct enunciation of the words required 101
If mistake is made while reading the *Sh^e^ma'* 102

MISHNĀH IV, V (103–105)

On workmen reading the Sh^e^ma' *and the exemption of a bridegroom.*

Regulations referring to workmen 103
Exemption of a bridegroom 105

MISHNĀH VI–VIII (105–115)

On bathing before the burial of a relative, receiving condolence on the death of a slave, and the omission of the Sh^e^ma' *on the first night of marriage.*

Rabban Gamaliel's action explained 106
Burial customs for slaves 106
Prayers composed by some of the Rabbis 107
Favourite sayings of some Rabbis 111
Farewell benedictions pronounced by the disciples of R. Ammi and Rab Ḥisda 112
On the bridegroom who wishes to read the *Sh^e^ma'* 114

CHAPTER III (PAGES 116–171)

MISHNĀH I, II (116–131)

On the exemption of mourners from the Sh^e^ma' *and other commandments.*

Is the presence of the corpse necessary to give exemption? 116
The watcher of the body also exempt 117
Respectful treatment of the dead. 118
Exposition of Eccles. ix. 15 119
Do the dead know what transpires on earth? 120
Speaking evil of the dead 123
Honouring teachers 123
Reading the *Sh^e^ma'* during a funeral oration and after burial of the dead 126
Honouring God is man's principal duty 127
Superiority of former generations 130
Rab Giddel and R. Joḥanan unafraid of temptation 131

MISHNĀH III (131–134)

On the exemptions and obligations of women, slaves and minors.

Women exempt from commands which depend upon a definite point of time 132
Ḳiddūsh obligatory upon women 133
Are women commanded by the *Tōrāh* to say Grace after meals? . . 133
Why God has regard for Israel 134

MISHNĀH IV (134–147)

On a polluted person (Ba'al Ḳ^e^rī) *and the* Sh^e^ma' *and Grace.*

Whether meditation is the equivalent of speech 134
Authority for Grace and the benediction over the *Tōrāh* . . . 135
Procedure when one is in doubt about having read the *Sh^e^ma'* and its benedictions. 136
On saying the *T^e^fillāh* a second time in error or in Synagogue . . 137
Whether a *Ba'al Ḳ^e^ri* may study *Tōrāh* 139
Discussion on the need for immersion by polluted persons . . . 140
Restrictions imposed upon a *Ba'al Ḳ^e^ri* 141
Words of *Tōrāh* cannot contract defilement. 142
The purification of a *Ba'al Ḳ^e^ri* 143

MISHNĀH V (148–171)

On prayer in an unclean environment.

Saying the *T^e^fillāh* amidst defiling circumstances 148
Laws regulating *T^e^fillin* with reference to a privy 150
Respectful treatment of the *T^e^fillīn* 151
On reading the *Sh^e^ma'* in bed when not alone 155
Views on nakedness as applied to a woman. 157
Habits of R. Judah the Prince 158

Praying aloud denounced 159
Praying in unclean places 159
When urine and excrement lose their defiling power for one reading the *Sh^ema'* 164
Reading the *Sh^ema'* when the naked body is immersed in water . . 166
Nullifying urine by the addition of water 168
Scroll of *Tōrāh* must not be left lying in a bedroom 169
Reading the *Sh^ema'* facing excrement or a privy 170

MISHNĀH VI

On immersion for polluted persons (171)

CHAPTER IV (PAGES 172–201)

MISHNĀH I (172–186)

On the terminus ad quem *of the* T^efillōt.

The morning *T^efillāh* 172
If the afternoon *T^efillāh* has been omitted, is there reparation? . . 172
Omission of a Sabbath *T^efillāh* and its reparation 173
T^efillōt instituted by the Patriarchs and to correspond with the sacrifices 174
R. Judah's view on the *terminus ad quem* discussed 175
The afternoon *T^efillāh* 178
Ḳiddūsh and *Habdālāh* to be recited in addition to the references in the *T^efillāh* 179
The evening *T^efillāh* 180
Quarrel between Rabban Gamaliel and R. Joshua 180
Rabban Gamaliel deposed 181
He conciliates R. Joshua and is partially re-installed 183
The additional *T^efillāh* 185

MISHNĀH II (187–188)

On the prayers to be said in the House of Study.

The wording 187
R. Eliezer's exhortation to his disciples 187
Death of Rabban Joḥanan b. Zakkai 188

MISHNĀH III–VI (188–198)

On the Eighteen Benedictions, praying in a place of danger or on a journey.

To what the Eighteen Benedictions correspond 189
The added benediction relating to the *Minim* 189
The benedictions of the Sabbath and New Year *T^efillōt* 191
Abstract of the Eighteen Benedictions 192
Omission of special references in the *T^efillāh* and its reparation . . 194
Prayer must not be "a fixed task" 194

Prayer to be offered in a place of danger 195
Prayer for a journey 196
Saying the *Tᵉfillāh* when riding upon an ass 197
The direction in which one must pray. 197
Saying the *Tᵉfillāh* before the *Shᵉma'* when setting out on a journey . 198

MISHNĀH VII (199–201)

On omitting the additional Tᵉfillāh *where there is no Congregation.*

The *Hᵃlākāh* discussed 199
Mechanical prayer prohibited 200
Reference to the New Moon in the *Tᵉfillāh* 200

CHAPTER V (PAGES 202–232)

MISHNĀH I (202–219)

On the requisite frame of mind for saying the Tᵉfillāh.

Biblical authority for the teaching of the *Mishnāh* 202
Excessive merriment deprecated 203
Tᵉfillāh must not be said when the mind is disturbed 203
The heart must be directed to Heaven. 205
Procedure of prayer based on the practice of Daniel 205
Where personal supplications may be introduced 206
Deductions from the Biblical narrative of Hannah 206
Moses' plea for Israel 211
Some teachings of R. Eleazar 214
Prayer deliberately lengthened not acceptable to God 215
Homily on Is. xlix. 14 f. 216
Meditation before and after prayer 217
Tᵉfillāh must not be interrupted to respond to a greeting from an Israelite king or from a nobleman 218
It may be interrupted when there is danger from a scorpion or wild ox 219
R. Ḥannina b. Dosa and the lizard 219

MISHNĀH II (220–224)

On the inclusion of the prayer for rain in the Tᵉfillāh.

Reason for the location of the reference 220
Greatness of knowledge 220
Inclusion of the *Habdālāh* in the *Tᵉfillāh* 221
Its wording on a Festival 224

MISHNĀH III (225–227)

On exaggerated prayers.

Objection to the prayers cited in the *Mishnāh* 225
Example of exaggerated praise of God 226
The fear of Heaven 226
The wording of a prayer must not be duplicated 226

MISHNĀH IV (227–230)

On the regulations concerning the Precentor and the Tᵉfillāh.

How to treat an invitation to act as Precentor 227
If the Precentor erred in the *Tᵉfillāh* 228
On long and short prayers 228
Where one bows in the *Tᵉfillāh* 229
Bowing, bending and prostrating defined 229

MISHNĀH V (230–232)

To err in the Tᵉfillāh *a bad omen. R. Ḥannina b. Dosa's prayers.*

Error in the first benediction only a bad omen 230
Teachings of R. Joḥanan concerning the prophets 231
R. Ḥannina b. Dosa prays for the son of Rabban Gamaliel and of Rabban Joḥanan b. Zakkai 232

CHAPTER VI (PAGES 233–290)

MISHNĀH I (233–264)

On the benedictions over fruits, bread and vegetables.

Necessity of the benediction discussed. 233
To enjoy anything without uttering a benediction is sacrilege . . 236
Duty of earning a livelihood 237
Benediction over wine 238
When a benediction is necessary over olive-oil 240
Benediction over wheaten-flour 241
Benediction over the palm-heart 242
Whether caper-berries and buds are fruit 243
What constitutes "protection of the fruit" 244
Benediction over pepper 246
Benediction over boiled *Ḥābîṣ* 247
Benediction over a dish which contains one of the five species . . 247
Benediction over rice and millet 247
Benediction after partaking of dates 249
Benediction after partaking of the seven species 250
Benediction over *Rihᵃṭā* 250
Benediction over *Ḥābîṣ* which contains large pieces of bread . . 251
Ṭroḳnīn, *Ṭāritā*, and *Ḳuttāḥ* 252
Benediction over date-honey 253
Benediction over *Ṭrimmā* 253
Benediction over *Shattīt* 253
Form of benediction over bread—*Mōṣî'* or *hammōṣî'*? 254
Benediction over vegetables 255
Benediction over turnip-tops 259
Broth of beet beneficial 260
Benediction over soaked bread 260
Saying the benediction and breaking the bread 260
Foods which are beneficial to health 263

MISHNĀH II (265–267)

On saying the wrong benediction.

The tree from which Adam ate 265
Whether the form of the benediction as fixed by the Rabbis must be adhered to 266
Is the benediction valid if not in Hebrew? 266
Whether a benediction must contain a reference to God as King . . 267

MISHNĀH III, IV (268–275)

On the benediction over things which do not grow from the earth and when there is a choice of several articles of food.

Benediction over food which does not grow from the earth . . . 268
Discussion on the meaning of *nōbelōt* 268
Giving preference to an article of food for the purpose of the benediction 270
Exposition of Deut. viii. 8 271
Whether a benediction is required over food brought in the course of a meal 273
Whether bread-dessert requires *hammōṣī'* 274
When a meal may be considered as finished 274
Anointing the hands with oil before saying Grace 274

MISHNĀH V, VI (275–284)

On the benediction which makes another unnecessary; and on the Grace after meals.

Benediction over each cup of wine not necessary on Sabbaths and Festivals 275
One can say Grace for the whole company 277
Reclining at a meal 278
Use of perfume at a meal, and its benediction 280
Benediction over balsam-oil, fragrant woods and flowers . . . 280
Some teachings of Rab 281
Order of benedictions over oil, myrtle and wine 282
Eight things that disgrace a disciple of the wise 282

MISHNĀH VII (284–285)

On the benediction for several articles of food eaten together.

The fruits of Gennesareth 284
Two wonderful cities in Palestine 285

MISHNĀH VIII (285–290)

On the benedictions after food.

Why Rabban Gamaliel requires three benedictions after grapes, etc. . 286
Benedictions over the five and seven species 286
Wording of the one benediction which is an abstract of three . . 286
Benediction over eggs and meat 287
Nourishment in an egg 288
Foods beneficial and harmful 288

CHAPTER VII (PAGES 291–330)

MISHNĀH I, II (291–318)

On who may and may not be included for Zimmūn.

Biblical basis for *Zimmūn* 291
Tone of voice in which responses and the translation of the lections should be uttered 292
Whether two may arrange *Zimmūn* 292
On including an absent person for *Zimmūn* 294
Response to be made by one who has not joined in the meal . . 295
Response "Amen" in the Grace 295
Who has the privilege of saying Grace before and after the meal . . 295
Extent of the *Zimmūn*-benediction 296
The fourth benediction of the Grace not ordained by the *Tōrāh* . . 297
Form of Grace to be said in the house of a mourner 298
Etiquette of a meal among the Persians and Jews 299
Reason why the persons named in the *Mishnāh* are included for *Zimmūn* 302
Definition of the *'Am hā'āreṣ* 303
Reason why the persons named in the *Mishnāh* are excluded from *Zimmūn* 304
Inclusion of a slave to make a quorum in Synagogue 306
Meritorious to be among the first ten in Synagogue 306
When a minor may be included for *Zimmūn* 307
King Jannaeus and Simeon b. Sheṭaḥ 308
What constitutes a meal for the purpose of Grace 309
Who instituted the benedictions of the Grace after meals . . . 309
Order of the benedictions 310
Basis for the Grace in the Pentateuch 310
Basis for the benediction over *Tōrāh* 312
God must be blessed for the bad as well as the good 312
The proper wording of the Grace 312
Whether the conclusion of a benediction may contain two references . 314
Omission of reference to the Sabbath in the Grace: its reparation . 316
If error is made in the Grace 316
Minimum quantity of food which qualifies one for *Zimmūn* . . . 317

MISHNĀH III (318–322)

On the form of Zimmūn *with different numbers of diners.*

Wording of the *Zimmūn*-benediction 319

MISHNĀH IV, V (322–330)

On parties of diners separating and uniting and the law of Zimmūn; *and whether the benediction may be pronounced over undiluted wine.*

Three who eat together may not separate before Grace is said . . . 322
Benediction over undiluted wine 323
Foodstuffs must be carefully handled 324
If one placed food in his mouth without a benediction. 325
The asparagus-beverage 326
Supernatural communications to R. Ishmael b. Elisha and R. Joshua b. Levi 327
Cup of wine used for Grace 328
Rab Naḥman's wife and the cup of Grace 329
The cup of ill-luck 329
Grace must be said sitting 330

CHAPTER VIII (PAGES 331–347)

MISHNĀH I–VIII (331–347)

On the points of variance between the Schools of Hillel and Shammai in connection with the meal.

Order of the benedictions over the wine and the Sabbath or Festival . 332
Procedure when there is only one cup of wine 334
Order of washing the hands and filling the cup 334
Where the napkin is to be placed 335
Order of clearing the room and washing the hands before Grace . . 336
Order of the benedictions 337
Wording of the benediction over the *Habdālāh* light 338
Light and spices of gentiles may not be used for *Habdālāh* . . . 338
Light which may and may not be used for *Habdālāh* 339
Whether one can say the benediction for all in Synagogue . . . 341
Benediction not to be said over the light or spices of the dead . . 342
When a benediction is not said over a fragrant odour 342
When a light is regarded as illumination for the purpose of the benediction 343
How near one must be to the light 343
Whether one must return to the place where he had eaten to say Grace 344
How long it takes for food to be digested 345
Responding to a benediction the whole of which has not been heard . 345
Anointing the hands with oil before Grace 346

CHAPTER IX (PAGES 348–426)

MISHNĀH I–V (348–426)

On benedictions for various occasions.

Benediction on beholding a place where a miracle had been wrought . 350
Miracle at the fords of Arnon 351
Miracle of the hail-stones 351
Fate of Og, king of Bashan 352
Pillar of Lot's wife 352
Four classes of people from whom thanksgiving is due 353
Three things which it is meritorious to prolong 355
Three things which shorten life 356
Three things for which one should pray 356
Three things which God proclaims 356
The wisdom of Beṣalel 357
On dreams 358
How the Evil Eye may be averted 361
Dream-lore continued 362
Things which do and do not benefit the body 378
Things which do and do not benefit an invalid 378
Benediction over a place from which idolatry had been uprooted. . 379
Benedictions to be said in Babylon 379
Benediction on beholding a crowd of Israelites 380
Adam's toil to supply his wants 380
Difference between a good and bad guest 381
Benedictions on beholding Sages and Kings 381
Rab Sheshet and the *Mīn* 382
Story of R. Shela 382
On beholding the houses of Israelites and idolaters 384
Philanthropy of Rab Ḥanna b. Ḥanilai 384
On beholding the graves of Israelites 385
Benediction on seeing a friend after a lapse of time 385
Beholding men with deformities 386
Shooting stars 386
Orion and the Pleiades 387
Legend about the constellation of the Bear 387
What is an earthquake? 388
Concerning thunder, storms and lightning 389
On seeing the rainbow. 390
Seeing the firmament in its purity and the heavenly bodies. . . 390
The Euphrates and Tigris 391
Benediction for rain 392
Form of benediction when the good is shared with others . . . 393
When a benediction is necessary on acquiring new vessels . . . 393
Prayer in connection with an unborn child 395
Hillel's confidence 396
Prayers on entering and leaving a town 396
Prayers on entering and leaving a bath-house 397
Prayer before cupping 397
Prayers on entering and leaving a privy 398

Prayer on retiring to sleep 398
Prayers to be said on rising 399
Resignation to the Divine Will 400
Example of R. 'Aḳiba 401
Man's two impulses 401
Creation of Eve 402
A man should not walk behind a woman 404
Functions of the human organs 405
The love of God 406
R. 'Aḳiba and Pappos b. Judah 406
Martyrdom of R. 'Aḳiba 407
Respectful conduct necessary in the direction of the Temple . . 407
Regulations concerning behaviour in a privy 408
Saul's modesty 413
Why David could get no heat 413
His sin in numbering the people 413
Using a Synagogue as a short cut 414
Expectoration in the Synagogue 415
"Amen" not used in the Temple 416
Form of greeting 416
Some teachings of Bar Ḳappara 417
Some teachings of Rabbi 418
Fate of the man who withholds his Temple dues. 418
Ḥᵃnanyah and the Palestinian Rabbis 419
Expositions of *Tōrāh* by Rabbis who visited Jabneh 420
Tōrāh only acquired by collective study 422
One must be prepared to suffer in the cause of the *Tōrāh* . . . 422
Meritorious to entertain disciples of the wise 423
The blessing of Obed-Edom 423
"Sinai" and "The uprooter of mountains" 424
Eating with a disciple of the wise like partaking of the *Shᵉkīnāh*. . 425
The phrases "Go in peace" and "Go to peace". . . . 425
From the Synagogue to the House of Study. 425
Disciples of the wise have no rest in both worlds. 425
Prayer for peace 425

INTRODUCTION

I. THE TALMŪD[1]

AROUND a written code of law there gradually accumulates a mass of interpretations, amplifications and precedents. No code is able to cover all the varied circumstances of human life, and the gaps are filled by decisions and customs which in course of time come to have the force of law.

Thus Judaism, from an early period, recognised two authoritative sources—the *Written Law* as contained in the Scriptures, and the *Oral Law* which was preserved by word of mouth and transmitted from generation to generation. "Moses," it was said, "received the *Tōrāh* on Sinai, and handed it down to Joshua; Joshua to the Elders; the Elders to the Prophets; and the prophets handed it down to the men of the Great Assembly[2]." By *Tōrāh* is here intended much more than the legislation found in the Pentateuch. It includes also teachings explanatory of, and complementary to, that legislation.

That there is a substantial basis of truth in this tradition is very probable. The laws of the Pentateuch do not embrace all the affairs of life, nor are they complete in themselves. They usually lay down general principles, and make no mention of the details which would be required in actual practice. For instance, Exod. xx. 10 declares: "The seventh day is a Sabbath unto the Lord thy God; in it thou shalt not do any manner of work"; but there is no attempt to define what is to be understood by "work." From Jeremiah xvii. 21 f. it is seen that the carrying of a burden was regarded a breach of the Sabbath, though there is no mention of this in the Mosaic code. Moreover, the penalty for the desecration of the day of rest was omitted from the enactment; and when a case occurred, a difficulty arose "because it had not been declared what should be done to him" (Num. xv. 34). It cannot be doubted

[1] For a fuller account of the growth of the Talmūd, the reader is referred to the articles by Bacher in *J. E.* Vol. XII., S. A. Cook in *Encyclopedia Britannica* (11th ed.), Vol. XXVI., and Schechter in *Hastings' Dictionary of the Bible*, Vol. V.; also to the valuable Introductions by Strack and Mielziner.

[2] Ābōt I. 1, Singer, p. 184.

that complicated questions must soon have presented themselves for consideration as to what kind of work constituted a breach of the Sabbath, and the decisions became part of the traditional teaching. This is one of many examples which might be cited to show the necessity for an Oral Law to make the Written Law workable[1].

From the nature of the Oral Law, it would necessarily be of gradual development, growing larger in the course of centuries as new conditions demanded fresh enactments or modifications of the written code. As time passed, the distinction between what was written and what was oral would tend to become obliterated, and both would have equal authority.

This was the standpoint of the Pharisaic party in Judaism; but it was not accepted by all Jews even in pre-Christian times. Josephus writes: "What I would now explain is this, that the Pharisees have delivered to the people a great many observances by succession from their fathers, which are not written in the law of Moses; and for that reason it is that the Sadducees reject them, and say that we are to esteem those observances to be obligatory which are in the written word, but are not to observe what are derived from the tradition of our forefathers; and concerning these things it is that great disputes and differences have arisen among them[2]." It is in this opposition of the Sadducees to the Oral Law that we may trace the motive force of the movement which culminated in the compilation of the Talmūd.

The denial of the authority of the Oral Law by the Sadducees compelled its upholders to defend its validity. The Pharisees sought to refute their opponents by demonstrating that the Oral Law is an integral part of, and is inseparable from, the written code. In our Tractate[3] we have the statement: "What means that which is written, 'And I will give thee the tables of stone, and the law and the commandment, which I have written, that thou mayest teach them' (Exod. xxiv. 12)? 'Tables of stone,' i.e. the Decalogue; 'law,' i.e. the Pentateuch; 'commandment,' i.e. the *Mishnāh*; 'which I have written,' i.e. the Prophets and Hagiographa; 'that thou mayest teach them,' i.e. the *Gᵉmārā*. The verse teaches that all of them were given to Moses on Sinai."

[1] The subject has been fully treated by I. H. Weiss in his monumental work (composed in Hebrew) *Dōr Dōr wᵉDōrᵉshāw*. See Schechter's review of it in *Studies in Judaism* (First Series), pp. 222 ff., reprinted from *J.Q.R.* IV.

[2] *Antiquities*, XIII. x. 6.

[3] Fol. 5 *a*, p. 19.

Here we have the main defence of the authority of the Oral Law—that it goes back to the time of the Revelation. It was not contended that every part of the Oral Law originated then. Only forty-two enactments outside the Pentateuch are described as *Hªlākāh lᵉMōshéh mi-Sīnai* "a law given to Moses on Sinai[1]." What the Talmūd here intends to teach is that the Oral Law is *contained in* the Written Law. As the full-grown oak may be said to be potentially in the acorn, so the whole corpus of Jewish traditional teaching was considered the natural growth from the seed planted at Sinai.

The next step would be to endeavour to prove that the Oral Law was *deducible* from the Written Law, and consequently the distinction drawn by the Sadducees untenable. That was the principal task undertaken by the Jewish Schools. For this purpose exegetical rules had to be devised whereby inferences might be drawn from the text of the Scriptures. Hillel the Elder was the author of seven such rules, which were added to by R. 'Aḳiba and others, and finally reached the total of thirteen, systematised by R. Ishmael and generally adopted[2]. With the aid of these hermeneutical laws, the study of the *Tōrāh* entered upon a new phase. Seminaries were established and disciples multiplied rapidly.

It was soon found necessary for the purpose of study to have the mass of traditional lore reduced to a systematic arrangement. The first attempt to do this was made by Hillel who formulated six main divisions. His work was continued by R. 'Aḳiba and R. Meïr; but their classification did not meet with general approval. It was R. Judah the Prince who, about the end of the second century, finally succeeded in preparing a code which commanded universal acceptance by the Rabbis. His codification is known as the *Mishnāh*. It consists of six Orders, subdivided into sixty-three Tractates[3].

The question whether R. Judah the Prince committed the *Mishnāh* to writing or merely arranged it for verbal transmission has long been debated, but not yet decided[4]. However that may be, the style in which it is composed is very concise as though the thought of condensation were constantly in the mind of the

[1] They are enumerated in Weiss, *Dōr* (1904 ed.) I. pp. 69 f.

[2] They are enumerated in Singer, pp. 13 f., and expounded by Mielziner, Part II. See also *J.E.* XII. 30 ff.

[3] For an enumeration, see Mielziner, pp. 9–14; Oesterley and Box, Appendix.

[4] See Mielziner, note on pp. 5 f.

Redactor. This brevity often resulted in obscurity, with the consequence that the teaching of the *Mishnāh* seemed sometimes to contradict traditions on the same subject as contained in the *Bārāitā*[1]. Hence the *Mishnāh* became the subject of critical study in the Schools of Palestine and Babylon[2]. Its wording was minutely scrutinised, its meaning and scope fully debated, the authority for its teaching sought in the Bible, and contradictions with the *Bārāitā* harmonised. For nearly three centuries it remained the principal theme of study and discussion in the Jewish Seminaries, until a vast mass of teaching had accumulated which called for systematisation and a permanent form of record.

The proceedings of the Palestinian Schools were probably first collected by R. Johanan, the famous *Āmōrā* of the third century; but the Palestinian (usually, but less correctly, called Jerusalem) Talmūd as we now possess it belongs to the end of the fourth, or the beginning of the fifth, century. Who was its later Redactor is not known.

The main work of compiling the proceedings of the Babylonian Schools was undertaken by Rab Ashē, the Principal of the renowned Academy in Sura, who is said to have spent thirty years on the task. He died in 427, leaving the work unfinished. It was resumed by Rabina II who presided over the same Seminary from 488 to 499, and apart from some later additions, he left the Babylonian Talmūd substantially as we now have it.

Neither Talmūd is a complete work, in the sense that it covers the whole of the *Mishnāh*. The Palestinian extends over thirty-nine Tractates, and of these some are defective, while the Babylonian extends only over thirty-seven; but the *G^emārā* of the latter is both longer and of greater importance than that of its Palestinian rival.

"The Talmūd must not be regarded as an ordinary book, composed of twelve volumes; it possesses absolutely no intrinsic similarity with any other literary production, but forms without any figure of speech, a world of its own which must be judged by its peculiar laws." So writes a Jewish historian[3]. The main difficulty in viewing the Talmūd from the correct standpoint is the fact that it is a work strictly *sui generis*. There have been no Schools comparable to those of the Jews in Babylon and Palestine,

[1] See Glossary, *s.v.*

[2] The principal Schools were: in Palestine—Caesarea, Sepphoris, Tiberias and Usha; in Babylon—Nehardea, Sura and Pombedita.

[3] Graetz, *History of the Jews* (Eng. trans.) II. p. 639.

and the type of study pursued there was likewise unique. Moreover, the Talmūd is not a literary production. The object of the Redactor was merely to collect in a convenient form the innumerable expositions of the Scriptures, and the teachings and *obiter dicta* of the Rabbis. Deterred by the injunction that the saying of a teacher must be transmitted *verbatim*[1], he made no attempt to put his material into literary shape. For that reason his work appears scrappy and disjointed; but it should be regarded as a collection of reporters' notebooks rather than a connected book.

The lack of system, as we understand it, in the Talmūd has often been commented upon. When one first approaches it, its contents appear formless and chaotic. Sentences are strung together with no apparent connection. The sharp transition from one subject to another is bewildering. But a fuller acquaintance will reveal method and order where a superficial reading gives the impression of chaos. It should be remembered that no text-books were used in the Jewish Schools. The teachings had to be memorised by the pupil. We are, e.g., informed in our Tractate[2] that R. Ḥiyya b. Abba used to revise his study in the presence of R. Joḥanan his master every thirty days; i.e. he repeated the names of the Rabbinic authorities and their opinions before his teacher to test the accuracy of his memory. In such circumstances a different methodology is required from that which would be used in a written book. Advantage was taken of whatever aided the memory. A number of teachings emanating from the same source or reported by the same Rabbi were gathered together and learnt together; for that reason they follow in sequence in the text of the Talmūd, although there is no connection of subject-matter. A word in a Biblical verse is expounded, and another word in the same verse suggests a comment of quite a different nature. The casual reference to a subject will be made the starting-point of a long disquisition. All such tendencies account for the lack of cohesion in the material. Delitzsch has aptly described the Talmūd as "an enormous theatre, in which thousands and thousands of voices, from at least five centuries, speak in confusion[3]"; but by dint of perseverance, the student of Rabbinic literature is able to make the clamour coherent and understand its message.

[1] Cf. fol. 47*a*, p. 301.
[2] Fol. 38*b*, p. 257.
[3] *Jewish Artisan Life*, Chap. III.

II. THE TRACTATE *BᴱRĀKŌT*

Bᵉrākōt, "Benedictions," is the first Tractate of the first Order. It is thus the opening Tractate of the Talmūd. Maimonides, in his Commentary on the *Mishnāh*, attempts an explanation of the sequence of the Orders and Tractates, and gives the following reason why the Talmūd opens with this Tractate: "[The Redactor of the *Mishnāh*] commences with the Order *Zᵉrā'īm* ['Seeds'], because it contains the precepts that apply to the cultivation of the land, upon which depends the living of all creatures....The reason which induced him to open with the Tractate *Bᵉrākōt* is this: The expert physician who wishes to preserve a healthy person in good health first arranges his diet. Therefore the Sage [R. Judah the Prince] thought it proper to begin with the subject of 'Benedictions' because nobody is allowed to eat without first pronouncing a benediction....On that account he deals with the various benedictions which a person is obliged to say with different articles of food and the commandments relating thereto. The only commandment which a man is obliged to perform daily is the reading of the *Shᵉma'*, and as it would not be proper to treat of the benedictions of the *Shᵉma'* before treating of the *Shᵉma'* itself, he opens with the question, 'From what time may the *Shᵉma'* be read?' and all that is connected therewith."

Stripped of extraneous matter, the theme of the Tractate is the daily prayers of the Jew which it is his duty to offer either with a Congregation or in private, and the benedictions which should be uttered on various occasions. The first three Chapters are devoted to the consideration of the *Shᵉma'* and the next two to the *Tᵉfillāh*, these being the principal parts of the Jewish statutory Service. The remaining four deal with the benedictions over food and special circumstances. This Tractate is accordingly one of the main sources of information relative to the growth of the Jewish ritual. Another interesting feature is the abundance of Aggadic material, which is in larger proportion than in any other Tractate.

The Talmūd is quoted by folio, which remains uniform in the printed editions. Each folio consists of a double page, denoted *a* and *b* respectively. The pagination commences with 2*a*. *Bᵉrākōt* contains 62½ folios, 2*a*–64*a*. Each Chapter is named after the opening word or words; e.g. the first Chapter is known as "From what time?"

The text of the Talmūd was guarded with loving care by the Jews until the age of printing; but it has not altogether escaped the consequences of copyists' errors. The immense task of preparing a critical edition has yet to be undertaken. Numerous MSS of the Talmūd, in its entirety or in parts, are extant in European and American libraries. The work of collation was begun by Raphael Rabbinovicz, who minutely examined the MS in the Royal Library of Munich and commented upon its variants. His results were published in a Hebrew work *Diḳdūḳē Sōf^{e}rīm*, with the Latin title: *Variae lectiones in Mishnam et in Talmūd Babylonicum* (Munich, 1868–86). He died before completing his undertaking, only having covered three and a half of the six Orders. The more important variants in our Tractate which occur in the Munich MS have been included in the Notes.

The first complete printed edition of the Babylonian Talmūd was published in Venice by Daniel Bomberg in 1520–23 and is named after him "The Bomberg Talmūd." But several Tractates had already appeared in print, having been published by Gershom of Soncino. The subsequent editions have usually been based on that of Bomberg, and its text is that which the present Translation follows except where otherwise stated.

III. *H^{A}LĀKĀH*

The Rabbis were not only theologians; they were principally ecclesiastical lawyers. This was necessarily so, because Rabbinic Judaism aimed at controlling the whole life of its adherents. Even the Pentateuchal code touches upon many matters which are usually excluded from the sphere of religion; and Judaism, in its later developed form, drew no sharp line of demarcation between the secular and religious. If God is omnipresent, every phase of human existence must be influenced by that idea. There could be nothing in the life of man which was outside the sphere of Judaism. "Which is a brief Scriptural passage," asks a Rabbi[1], "upon which all the principles of the *Tōrāh* depend? '*In all thy ways* acknowledge Him, and He will direct thy paths'" (Prov. iii. 6).

That is the theory which underlies the *H^{a}lākāh*. It attempts to offer guidance for every experience of life. Nothing that pertains to human existence is beyond its purview. It enters into the privacy of the home and into man's most intimate relationships. With such a purpose in view, it is perhaps inevitable that the *H^{a}lākāh* should present to the onlooker the appearance of an in-

[1] See fol. 63 *a*, p. 417.

tolerable incubus, a load of crushing weight. And it is usually so described by non-Jewish critics. "It was a fearful burden," writes Schürer[1], whose opinion may be taken as typical, "which a spurious legalism had laid upon the shoulders of the people. Nothing was left to free personality, everything was placed under the bondage of the letter. The Israelite, zealous for the law, was obliged at every impulse and movement to ask himself, what is commanded? At every step, at the work of his calling, at prayer, at meals, at home and abroad, from early morning till late in the evening, from youth to old age, the dead, the deadening formula followed him. A healthy moral life could not flourish under such a burden, action was nowhere the result of inward motive, all was, on the contrary, weighed and measured. Life was a continual torment to the earnest man, who felt at every moment that he was in danger of transgressing the law; and where so much depended on the external form, he was often left in uncertainty whether he had really fulfilled its requirements."

This is purely subjective criticism, and is based on imagination rather than facts. No evidence is advanced to prove that life was so hard to the Jew who lived under the régime of the *Halākāh.* All that Schürer and the other critics can fairly assert is that it appears to them so, and if they had been living under the Rabbinic system they would have found it intolerable. Schechter has summed up the position in his characteristic way: "Here, again, there is a fresh puzzle. On the one side, we hear the opinions of so many learned professors, proclaiming *ex cathedra* that the Law was a most terrible burden, and the life under it the most unbearable slavery, deadening body and soul. On the other side we have the testimony of a literature extending over about twenty-five centuries, and including all sorts and conditions of men, scholars, poets, mystics, lawyers, casuists, schoolmen, tradesmen, workmen, women, simpletons, who all, from the author of the 119th Psalm to the last pre-Mendelssohnian writer—with a small exception which does not even deserve the name of a vanishing minority—give unanimous evidence in favour of this Law, and of the bliss and happiness of living and dying under it—and this, the testimony of people who were actually living under the Law, not merely theorising upon it, and who experienced it in all its difficulties and inconveniences[2]." "Somebody," he concludes, "either the

[1] II. ii. 124 f.

[2] *Studies in Judaism* (First Series), pp. 296 f.

learned professors, or the millions of the Jewish people, must be under an illusion[1]."

More important than the question whether the *Tōrāh* was a crushing weight upon those who adopted it is the allegation "Action was nowhere the result of inward motive; all was, on the contrary, weighed and measured." We may test the accuracy of this criticism by the example of Prayer, which figures so prominently and is dealt with so exhaustively in our Tractate. We find long and intricate discussions on how and when one's devotion to God should be offered. The externals of the Services are treated with such minuteness, every conceivable contingency being anticipated and provided for, that the conclusion seems justified that to the Rabbis prayer was nothing more than a mechanical act. But when one looks deeper, one realises that such a conclusion is far from the truth. The Rabbis understand full well that true prayer is the communion of the human soul with God. They denounce mechanical prayer. Prayer, they say, must not be *ḳĕba'*, a matter of routine[2]; the heart must be directed to Heaven[3]. They commend the practice of the pious men who spent an hour in silent meditation before and after prayer[4]. And it was they who defined prayer as "the service which is *in the heart*[5]."

The *Hªlākāh* does not legislate on that aspect of prayer, because it is a matter on which legislation is impossible. The outpouring of the human soul to its Maker is the sacred concern of the individual with which the *Hªlākāh* does not deal. That the Rabbis did not confine their conception of prayer to the daily recital of fixed forms of supplication is proved by the personal petitions which are preserved in our Tractate[6].

What the *Hªlākāh* does deal with is the statutory Services in which the individual should participate *as a member of the Jewish Community*. The prayers he then offered were quite apart from the expression of his personal needs. They were his daily act of devotion as a unit in the body of Israel. In connection with such Services, questions arise similar to those of any other organised religious brotherhood. There must of necessity be a limit to the time in which the morning, afternoon and evening Services can

[1] *Op. cit.* p. 301. See also his *Aspects of Rabbinic Theology*, Chap. XI., and Montefiore, Hibbert Lectures, Lect. IX.

[2] Fol. 29 *b*, p. 194. [3] Fol. 31 *a*, p. 205. [4] Fol. 32 *b*, p. 217.

[5] Ta'ănīt 2 *a*. See the article on "Some Rabbinic Ideas on Prayer" by I. Abrahams in *J.Q.R.* xx. 272 ff.

[6] See fol. 17 *a*, pp. 107 ff.

be rendered, and their *termini* have to be fixed. Errors occur in the rendition of the liturgy, and such a contingency must be provided for.

It must further be borne in mind that the conditions of life were in those days very different from what they are now and gave rise to questions which would no longer apply. In particular, sanitary arrangements were very defective; and the presence of defiling matter in the house had necessarily to be considered in connection with the saying of prayers. How were religious acts to be performed when the surroundings were unclean? The Rabbis in their Halakic discussions deal with questions which the facts of life presented for consideration. The people looked to them for guidance in their practical difficulties; and the debates of the Schools were attempts to solve them. The discussions may be casuistical, but not more so than those of lawyers—ecclesiastical or civil—in other branches of legislation. The *Haॱlākāh* may deal with things external; but the refreshing springs of religion were not blocked as a consequence. The mystical and spiritual elements of Faith obviously find no place in the records of discussions on ritual, but it by no means follows that they were non-existent. The *Haॱlākāh* represents only one aspect of the Judaism of the Rabbis, as it forms only one part of their literature.

IV. *AGGĀDĀH*

"Is it thy desire to know Him Who spake and the world came into being? Learn the *Aggādāh*; for from it wilt thou come to know the Holy One, blessed be He, and cleave to His ways[1]." That is the fundamental purpose of the *Aggādāh* according to the Rabbis. If the *Haॱlākāh* only be taken into consideration, the strictures passed by the critics upon the religion of the Talmūd seem justified; but the spirit of the *Aggādāh*, which is so important an element in its composition, will help to rectify the error into which they have fallen. Rabbinic Judaism was never identical with pure legalism. It had its spiritual, poetical and mystical side, and this is enshrined in the *Aggādāh*.

But the Aggadic portions of the Talmūd need to be read with caution, because it is ever essential carefully to distinguish between the form and the thought it contains. It is passing strange that the critics who are always eager to condemn the Rabbis as strict literalists should themselves assume that rôle when dealing with

[1] Sifrē to Deut. xi. 22; ed. Friedmann, p. 85 *a*.

the *Aggādāh*. It must be steadily borne in mind that the *Aggādāh* comes from the Orient, where the imagination is permitted unrestricted flight. Exaggeration of language is the rule, and unless allowance is made for this tendency, it is easy to misjudge the thoughts which are given such unusual expression. Statements which in their crude form shock the Westerner sound perfectly natural to the Oriental who instinctively strips them of their verbal covering and penetrates through to the idea that is contained therein.

Some of the most beautiful Aggadic material in the Rabbinic literature treats of the conception of God[1]. And yet, the Talmūd has been charged with blasphemy, although it always uses a paraphrase—such as, the Holy One, blessed be He; the All-merciful; the All-present—in order to avoid taking His name in vain! The error is due to the failure to distinguish between letter and spirit. In our Tractate, for instance, we are told that God prays[2], that He wears the phylacteries[3], that He begged a blessing of a mortal[4]. It is surely impossible to suppose that the Rabbis believed in the existence of a corporeal God[5]. What, then, did they intend by such statements?

The explanation seems to lie in the idea of *Imitatio Dei* which plays an important part in Rabbinic theology[6]. God is perfection, and man can only strive after perfection by imitating His ways. He is the Pattern upon which human life should be modelled.

Starting from this principle, it is a natural step to regard God as the *complete* exemplar of conduct, and the ideal life demanded by Judaism but a reflection of His. Not only are the divine attributes of holiness, justice, charity and mercy to become human attributes, but if God has commanded the Israelite to obey the precepts of the *Tōrāh*, He Himself shows the way by submitting to them. He has enjoined the sacred act of prayer; therefore He too must pray, so that His creatures should do as He does. He has ordained the wearing of the phylacteries; He obeys His ordinances, and His people must follow in His ways.

Such a thought as this, strange though it be to us, added an authority to the teachings of Judaism which they otherwise could

[1] See Schechter, *Aspects*, Chapters II–VII.

[2] Fol. 7*a*, p. 34. [3] Fol. 6*a*, p. 29. [4] Fol. 7*a*, p. 35.

[5] See the interesting article by R. T. Herford on "The Talmudic Doctrine of God" in *J.Q.R.* II. pp. 454 ff., although the explanation there given differs from that offered above.

[6] See Abrahams in *Jewish Addresses*, pp. 44 ff., and Schechter, *op. cit.* pp. 199 ff.

never have possessed for its adherents. More than that, it hallowed the ceremonies prescribed by religion, and saved them from becoming mechanical and meaningless rites. It brought the spirit of God into man's daily life, so that it is true to say: "The Presence of God was everywhere to the Rabbinic Jew, and life must be lived with this unchanging consciousness. God's will must be fulfilled at every turn, and the Rabbinic Jew felt that he was fulfilling it, and that he was being inwardly illumined at every step, by a kinship and communion with the Divine[1]."

If the *Aggādāh* enshrines the religious conceptions of the Rabbis, it also reflects the popular superstitions of their age. That the people were credulous and ready to believe tales dealing with the supernatural need occasion no surprise, and the *Aggādāh* has preserved much material of this class. But it is folklore and nothing more. It never had binding force for the people. The attitude of the enlightened Jew of the Middle Ages towards the *Aggādāh* is thus stated by Moses b. Naḥman (13th century): "We [Jews] possess three kinds of [religious] literature. The first is the Bible, the contents of which we accept with perfect faith. The second is called the Talmūd[2], which is a commentary on the commandments of the *Tōrāh*. In the *Tōrāh* are 613 commandments, and every one of them is expounded in the Talmūd. That exposition of the commandments we likewise accept. There is still a third branch, called *Midrāsh*, which means 'Sermons'....As for this literature, if one believe it, well and good; but if not, he does no wrong[3]."

Like all other peoples, the Jews of old lived in a world inhabited by evil spirits, and felt themselves constantly exposed to the attack of the Evil Eye. There is much Demonology in the *Aggādāh*, as in all popular literature; and the lover of the Talmūd feels no need to apologise for its presence. One does not think any the less of Luther for flinging his ink-pot at the devil. Demonology is the peculiar possession of no one people or religion. All ancient peoples, not to speak of modern times, were steeped in it, and it coloured the thoughts of even the learned. The contagion was widespread throughout the Jewish, Christian and pagan world. Church Father as well as Rabbi was infected[4].

[1] Abelson, *Immanence of God in Rabbinic Literature*, p. 297.

[2] "Talmūd" is here used loosely to denote the *Hᵃlākāh* and "Midrāsh" the *Aggādāh*.

[3] *Naḥmanidis Disputatio publica pro fide Judaica*, ed. Steinschneider, p. 10.

[4] See Conybeare's articles on Demonology in *J.Q.R.* Vols. VIII. and IX.

Another superstition which figures very prominently in the *Aggādāh* of *B^erākōt* is Dream-lore. Several folios are entirely devoted to the subject. Many Rabbis believed in the serious reality of dreams. This, however, seems to have been due to the influence of the Orient; for Lane writes of the Muhammadans: "The Egyptians place great faith in dreams, which often direct them in some of the most important actions of life. They have two large and celebrated works on the interpretations of dreams....These books are consulted, even by many of the learned, with implicit confidence[1]."

Nevertheless, if one reads the passage on Dream-lore in our Tractate carefully, there is evidence of an attempt to discredit the importance attached to dreams. Such teachings as: A dream follows its interpretation[2]; a man only dreams of what he has been thinking about during the day[3]; a bad dream is preferable to a good dream[4]; it is impossible for a dream to be without something that is vain[5]—would tend to destroy one's reliance upon "the children of the night." There is also wise counsel in the statement "An uninterpreted dream is like an unread letter[6]," which is clearly intended as an inducement for people not to try and learn its meaning. Even the story of Abbai and Raba's dealings with Bar Hedja, the interpreter of dreams[7], reads like an attempt to lower that profession in the eyes of the people, by exposing the mercenary basis upon which the interpretations were founded.

The Rabbis, we are told, were fond of relieving the strain of Halakic discussion by occasional excursions into the lighter realm of the *Aggādāh* with its humour, parables and anecdotes. It enriches, as well as enlivens, the pages of the Talmūd. The modern reader of Rabbinic literature turns with no less delight to the quaint ideas and startling expressions which await him in the passages of the *Aggādāh*.

V. THE USE OF THE BIBLE IN THE TALMŪD

The teaching of the Talmūd is based on the Hebrew Scriptures. Almost every idea and every practice is explicitly derived from that source. The Rabbis constantly refer to a Scriptural passage for confirmation of their teaching. The Bible is made to bear the

[1] *Modern Egyptians*, p. 268.
[2] Fol. 55 *b*, p. 362. [3] p. 363. [4] Fol. 55 *a*, p. 358.
[5] *Ibid.* [6] *Ibid.* [7] Fol. 56 *a*, pp. 364 ff.

weight of the immense mass of Rabbinic doctrine. But the use which is made of the Scriptures in the Talmūd is so different from modern exegesis that attention must be drawn to this subject.

The purpose of the modern commentator is to interpret the mind of the author. He is careful not to read into the words his own ideas, and endeavours only to expound the writer's message. This type of Biblical exegesis was also recognised by the Rabbis, to which they gave the name *P^eshāṭ*, "the simple," i.e. literal interpretation. But we find comparatively few references to it in the Talmūd. Instead we usually have the *D^erāsh*, "the derived interpretation"—the thoughts which are extracted from, or imposed upon, the Scriptures.

To the Rabbis the Bible was an inexhaustible mine. The saying "Turn it and turn it over again, for everything is in it[1]" well describes their standpoint. The words of *Tōrāh*, they declared, were exceedingly fruitful and many-sided; and they discovered in them hidden meanings which were not visible on the surface. More important to them than what the Bible actually taught was what they could make it teach. As a consequence, in the Rabbinic literature one constantly meets with interpretations which are poles asunder for the simple meaning.

It has already been explained that the exigencies of theological controversy gave an impetus to new methods of Biblical study and created new rules of exposition. The Rabbis searched the Scriptures for authority for time-honoured religious practices. They sought in the Bible a "support" (*Asmaktā*) for the Oral Law[2]; and to discover such a basis they had necessarily to go outside the *P^eshāṭ* and have recourse to *D^erāsh*.

The *Tōrāh*, being a divine revelation and therefore perfect as its Inspirer is perfect, could not contain a single word, or even letter, which was superfluous. There were no needless repetitions, and not a syllable was without meaning. Such a phrase as "Thou shalt die and not live" was not tautology. Each clause taught something; hence the comment: "Thou shalt die" in this world, "and not live" in the world to come[3]. Even grammatical idioms, such as the addition of the infinitive to the finite verb to give it emphasis, were pressed to yield teachings. Very interesting is the protest against the excessive use of this method which occurs in our Tractate, viz. "The *Tōrāh* speaks according to the language of the sons of man[4]."

[1] Ābōt v. 25, Singer, p. 204.
[2] Cf. fol. 41 *b*, p. 272.
[3] Fol. 10 *a*, p. 61.
[4] Fol. 31 *b*, p. 208.

The reader will also meet with frequent plays on words. The Rabbis did not hesitate to resort to punning and even to distortion for the purpose of making the Bible fruitful of teaching. "Read not—but—" is a common phrase in the Talmūd. These alterations of the text are not to be treated seriously. The high reverence which the Rabbis paid to every word of the *Tōrāh*—they even counted the number of words and letters in the Hebrew Bible—would make it unthinkable that any deliberate change could be intended.

However strange the treatment of the Bible by the Rabbis may appear to modern conceptions, it can hardly be denied that the method proved in their hands an instrument of infinite possibility, by means of which they reaped a rich harvest. The words of *Tōrāh* were made adaptable to the varying conditions of life, and produced ever fresh streams of thought. The Rabbis were preachers as well as teachers, and the Midrashic interpretation of a text often summarises the homily which, as a result of their licence, they based upon the passage. Their method of exposition did much to popularise the Sacred Writings, and for centuries it has been an intellectual pastime of the learned among the Jews to discover *Ḥiddūshīm*, *novellae*, new ideas in the Biblical text. The treatment of the Scriptures was certainly peculiar, but it was reverent and prompted by the same spirit that permeates the 119th Psalm: "Open Thou mine eyes, that I may behold wondrous things out of Thy Law" (*v.* 18).

LIST OF ABBREVIATIONS

A.B.A. ....*Agada der babylonischen Amoräer* by Prof. W. Bacher, 1878. Reprinted with additions, 1913.

ABRAHAMS ......Historical and Explanatory Notes to Singer's edition of the Hebrew Prayer Book, 1914.

A.P.A. ....*Agada der palästinensischen Amoräer* by Prof. W. Bacher, Vol. I. 1892, Vol. II. 1896, Vol. III. 1899.

'Ărūk ....Talmudical Lexicon by R. Nathan b. Jeḥiel (11th cent.). Edited with considerable additions under the title *'Ărūk Completum* by A. Kohut, 1878–92.

A.T. ....*Agada der Tannaiten* by Prof. W. Bacher; Vol. I. (revised in 1903), Vol. II. 1890.

b. ....Hebrew *ben*, or Aramaic *bar*, "son of."

D.C.A. ....*Dictionary of Classical Antiquities* by O. Seyffert, revised by H. Nettleship and J. E. Sandys.

D.S. ....*Diḳdūḳē Sōpherīm, Variae lectiones in Mishnam et in Talmud Babylonicum*, by R. Rabbinovicz, 1868–86.

EDD. ....The printed editions of the Talmūd.

GOLDSCHMIDT...*Der babylonische Talmud* übersetzt von L. Goldschmidt, Vol. I. 1897.

HYMAN ....*Tōledōt Tannāīm waĂmōrāīm* by A. Hyman, 3 vols. 1910.

JASTROW ....*Dictionary of the Targumim*, etc. by M. Jastrow, 2 vols. 1903.

J.E. ....*Jewish Encyclopedia.*

J.Q.R. ....*Jewish Quarterly Review.* (Unless otherwise stated, the Old Series is referred to.)

J.R. ....*Jewish Review.*

J.T. ....The Jerusalem (or Palestinian) Talmūd to the Tractate *Berākōt*. An English version from the French translation of M. Schwab appeared in 1886.

KRAUSS ....*Griechische und Lateinische Lehnwörter im Talmud*, etc. by S. Krauss, 1898–9.

LANE ....*Manners and Customs of the Modern Egyptians* by E. W. Lane. (Quotations are made from the reprint in Everyman's Library.)

M. ....Reading of the Munich MS of the Talmūd collated by Rabbinovicz; see *D.S.* above.

M.G.W.J. ......*Monatsschrift für Geschichte und Wissenschaft des Judentums.*

MIELZINER......*Introduction to the Talmud* by M. Mielziner, 2nd ed. 1903.

NEUBAUER......*La géographie du Talmud* by A. Neubauer, 1868.

OESTERLEY AND BOX...*The Religion and Worship of the Synagogue* by W. O. E. Oesterley and G. H. Box; 2nd ed. 1911.

R..................Rabbi.

RASHI ....The Commentary of *R*abbi *Sh*ᵉlōmōh *I*ṣḥāḳī (1040–1105) on the Talmūd.

R.E.J. ....*Revue des Études Juives.*

R.V. ....Revised Version of the Bible. R.V. marg. denotes the marginal reading. The translation of Biblical verses which has been adopted is usually that issued by the Jewish Publication Society of America in 1917. The verses are always numbered according to the Hebrew text.

SC. ....*scilicet* "to be understood."

SCHÜRER ......*A History of the Jewish People* by E. Schürer. English Translation in 5 vols. (2nd ed.) 1890–91.

SINGER ....*Authorised Daily Prayer Book* edited and translated by the Rev. S. Singer.

T.A. ....*Talmudische Archäologie* by S. Krauss, 3 vols. 1910–12.

TŌSĀFŌT ....“Additions”—annotations on the Talmūd by glossarists of the 12th and 13th centuries.

WIESNER ......*Scholien zum babylonischen Talmud* by I. Wiesner, Vol. I. 1859.

WÜNSCHE ......*Der babylonische Talmud in seinen haggadischen Bestandtheilen* by A. Wünsche, Vol. I. 1886.

TRANSCRIPTION OF HEBREW AND ARAMAIC WORDS

א is represented by ' or a diæresis in the middle of the word, but is omitted when it is the initial letter.

בּ and ב are both represented by *b*.

ח is transcribed *ḥ*.

ט is transcribed *ṭ*.

כּ and כ are both represented by *k*.

ע is indicated by ʻ.

צ is transcribed *ṣ*.

ק is transcribed *ḳ*.

תּ and ת are both represented by *t*.

Long vowels are marked by a stroke over the letter, and the accented *s^{e}gōl* by *é*. (*ā* as in 'father,' *ī*=*ee* in 'seem,' *ē*=*a* in 'bathe,' *ū*=*oo* in 'boon'.)

The *Sh^{e}wā mobile* is indicated by ^{e} (=*er* in 'perhaps'), and half-vowels by ^{a}, ^{e}, ^{o}, except at the beginning of a word when they are transcribed *ă*, *ĕ*, *ŏ*.

CHAPTER I

MISHNĀH I

From what time may the Sh^{e}ma'[1] *be read in the evening? From the time the priests*[2] *enter [the Temple] to partake of their* T^{e}rūmāh, *until the end of the first watch*[3]. *These are the words of R. Eliezer; but the Sages*[4] *say: Until midnight. Rabban Gamaliel says: Until the rise of dawn*[5]. *It once happened that his sons returned from a feast [after midnight] and said to him, "We have not read the* Sh^{e}ma'*!" He told them, "If the dawn has not yet risen, you are still under the obligation of reading it. And not only in this connection do they so decide; but wherever the Sages use the expression 'Until midnight,' the obligation continues until the rise of dawn." The duty of burning the fat and parts of the animal*[6] *continues until the rise of dawn. Likewise with all offerings which have to be eaten the same day [they are sacrificed]*[7], *the duty continues until the rise of dawn. If so, why do the Sages say "Until midnight"? In order to keep a man far from transgression.* fol. 2 a.

G^{E}MĀRĀ

What authority has the *Tannā* [that the *Sh^{e}ma'* is to be read at all] that he raises the question: *From what time?*[8] Further, on what ground does he first deal with the evening? Let him first deal with [the *Sh^{e}ma'*] of the morning! The *Mishnāh* criticised.

[1] For the meaning of Hebrew and Aramaic terms, see Glossary.

[2] Who had become ritually unclean and, after bathing, waited until the evening before they could eat "of the holy things" (cf. Lev. xxii. 4–7).

[3] Whether the night is divisible into three or four watches will be discussed in the *G^{e}mārā* below: see pp. 6, 9 f.

[4] The majority of the Rabbis.

[5] According to Maimonides, in his Commentary on the *Mishnāh*, this refers to the first light which becomes visible in the East, about 1$\frac{1}{5}$ hours before actual sunrise. Cf. P^{e}sāḥ. 93 b.

[6] Cf. Leviticus vi. and vii.

[7] Cf. *ibid.* vii. 15 ff.

[8] Lit. Where does the *Tannā* stand that he teaches, *From what time?*

Alternative answers.

The *Tannā* bases his authority on Scripture; for it is written, "When thou liest down and when thou risest up" (Deut. vi. 7)[1]. His statement in the *Mishnāh* is to be understood thus: When is the time for reading the *Sh^{e}ma‘* which is to be recited when lying down? From the time the priests enter [the Temple] to partake of their *T^{e}rūmāh.* Or if thou wilt, I can say that he derives [his reason for commencing with the evening] from the account of the Creation; for it is written: "It was evening and it was morning, one day" (Gen. i. 5)[2].

An objection to the answer removed.

If this be so, in the sequel where he teaches: *In the morning [the reading of the* Sh^{e}ma‘*] is preceded by two benedictions and followed by one; in the evening it is preceded by two and followed by two*[3], let him likewise treat of the evening first! The *Tannā* commenced with the evening and then treats of the morning[4]; but while on the subject of the morning, he explains matters connected with the morning, and afterwards explains matters connected with the evening.

Why the Mishnāh mentions criterion of priests and T^{e}rūmāh.

The teacher stated: *From the time the priests enter [the Temple] to partake of their* T^{e}rūmāh. Yes, but when do the priests partake of their *T^{e}rūmāh*? From the time the stars appear. Then let him explicitly teach: "From the time of the appearance of the stars"! He wishes to tell us something incidentally: When do the priests partake of their *T^{e}rūmāh*? From the time the stars appear[5]. He thereby informs us that [the omission of] the sin-offering does not prevent [the priest from partaking of the *T^{e}rūmāh*]. This is in agreement with the teaching: "When the sun is down and it is clean" (Lev. xxii. 7)[6]—i.e. the setting of the sun[7] prevents him from partaking of the *T^{e}rūmāh*, but not [his failure to bring] his sin-offering.

[1] Two deductions are drawn from the verse: (1) The law of reading the *Sh^{e}ma‘*, since the Israelite is commanded "to talk of them" (viz. "these words which I command thee this day") on lying down and rising up; (2) The right order is "lying down" and "rising up," i.e. evening and morning.

[2] Hence the Jews reckon the day as commencing with the evening that precedes. See *T. A.* II. p. 418.

[3] See below, p. 70.

[4] In *Mishnāh II* of this chapter, p. 55.

[5] By defining the time for reading the evening *Sh^{e}ma‘* as the time when the priests partake of their *T^{e}rūmāh*, the *Mishnāh* wishes it to be understood that the priests who have been unclean regain their privilege at sunset (when the *Sh^{e}ma‘* is read) whether they bring their sin-offering or not.

[6] The *G^{e}mārā* requires the translation "it (the day) is clean," i.e. ended, and not "he (the man) shall be clean" from his impurity.

[7] Meaning, the fact that the sun had not set.

The meaning of Lev. xxii. 7 discussed. fol. 2 b.

How is it to be known, however, that the phrase "When the sun is down" means the [complete] setting of the sun[1], and the phrase "It is clean" means the *day* is clean? Perhaps the former signifies the setting of its light[2], and the latter the *man* shall be clean! Rabbah b. Rab Shela answered: In that case the text should have read *w^{e}yiṯhar*[3]; what means *w^{e}ṭāhēr*? The day is clean [of light]; as people commonly say, "When the sun has set, the day is *cleansed*."

Its interpretation confirmed in Palestinian Schools.

In the West[4], this explanation of Rabbah b. Rab Shela had not been heard by them, and they raised the question: The phrase "When the sun is down" means the [complete] setting of the sun, and the phrase "It is clean" means the day is clean; but perhaps the former signifies the setting of its light, and the latter the man shall be clean! They then solved it from a *Bārāitā*; for it is taught in a *Bārāitā*: The sign for the matter[5] is the appearance of the stars. Conclude from this that the [complete] setting of the sun is intended; and what means "It is clean"? The day is clean.

A *Bārāitā* quoted against the *Mishnāh*.

The teacher stated: *From the time the priests enter* [*the Temple*] *to partake of their* T^{e}rūmāh. Against this I quote: From what time may the *Sh^{e}ma'* be read in the evening? From the time when the poor man[6] goes home to eat his bread with salt, until such time as he usually stands up to leave his meal! The latter part of this passage is certainly at variance with our *Mishnāh*[7]; but is it to be said that the first part is also at variance with it? No; the poor man and the priest have the one standard of time.

Another *Bārāitā* contrasted with the *Mishnāh*.

I quote the following against our *Mishnāh*: From what time may we begin to read the *Sh^{e}ma'* in the evening? From the time

[1] I.e. the appearance of the stars.

[2] I.e. the disappearance of the sun below the horizon, but not the appearance of the stars. So Tōsāfōt; Rashi, less probably, refers Lev. xxii. 7 to the dawn of the eighth day.

[3] I.e. "then he *shall be* clean," whereas *w^{e}ṭāhēr* means "it (or he) *is* clean."

[4] The Palestinian Schools, from the geographical standpoint of Babylon.

[5] When the priests may partake of the *T^{e}rūmāh*.

[6] On account of his poverty, he cannot afford artificial light; therefore he takes his evening meal while there is yet sufficient light. See fol. 3 *a* (p. 7) for a reference to sleeping in a dark room; and on fol. 5 *b* (p. 24) it is mentioned that R. Eleazar, who was very poor, was lying in a dark room. According to Lane, p. 145, Orientals have their supper "shortly after sunset." In *J. T.* it is mentioned that the inhabitants of villages leave the fields before nightfall for fear of wild beasts.

[7] The *terminus ad quem* does not agree with any of the views stated in the *Mishnāh*.

that people go home to eat their bread on the Sabbath-eve[1]. These are the words of R. Meïr; but the Sages say: From the time the priests[2] are entitled to partake of their *Tᵉrūmāh*. A sign for the matter is the appearance of the stars, and although there is no proof of this[3], yet is there some indication; as it is said, "So we wrought in the work: and half of them held the spears from the rising of the morning till the stars appeared" (Neh. iv. 15), and it continues "That in the night they may be a guard to us, and may labour in the day" *(ibid. v.* 16). What is the meaning of this latter verse? Shouldest thou say that immediately the sun set it was reckoned to be night, but they worked late and started early[4]—come and hear[5]: "That in the night they may be a guard to us, and may labour in the day."

Conclusion that the poor and the priest have same standard of time.

The thought has occurred to thee that the poor man and people generally have the same standard of time[6]. Shouldest thou, however, maintain that the poor man and the priest have the same standard of time, then the opinion of the Sages and R. Meïr would be identical[7]! Is it then to be concluded that the poor man and the priest have each a different standard of time? No; the poor man and the priest have the same standard of time, but the poor man and people generally have a different standard.

[1] The meal would be earlier on the Sabbath-eve, everything having been prepared before the advent of the Sabbath.

[2] See p. 1 n. 2.

[3] Viz. that the day ends with the appearance of the stars.

[4] *M.* reads: but on account of the building of the Temple they started early and worked late.

[5] "Come and hear" introduces a quotation or illustration, often with the object of refuting an argument. Its use in the present instance is as follows: According to Neh. iv. 15, the day-shift of workers laboured from "the rising of the morning" (i.e. dawn) until "the stars appeared." These two points of time may be regarded as defining the beginning and end of a day. But should it be objected that no such inference can be drawn, inasmuch as the workmen in their enthusiasm may have exceeded the normal hours of the day, the objection is met by *v.* 16, where it is explicitly stated "and may labour in the day." The conclusion, therefore, is that a normal day is intended in *v.* 15.

[6] I.e. the poor man (mentioned in the first *Bārāitā*) who has his evening meal early through lack of artificial light, and people generally (mentioned in the second) on the Sabbath-eve who have their supper early.

The reasoning may be simplified by calling the meal-time of the poor man A, that of people on the Sabbath-eve B, and that of the priest for partaking of the *Tᵉrūmāh* C. In this paragraph A is assumed to equal B. If, then, A is said to equal C, then B=C. But R. Meïr, who adopts B, is *contrasted* with the Sages who adopt C, so these cannot be identical.

The poor man and the priest have the same standard of time! Against this I quote: From what time do we begin to read the *Sh^e^ma'* in the evening? From the time that the day becomes hallowed on the Sabbath-eve. These are the words of R. Eliezer. R. Joshua says: From the time the priests become ritually clean to partake of their *T^e^rūmāh.* R. Meïr says: From the time the priests bathe so as to be able to partake of their *T^e^rūmāh.* (R. Judah asked him, "But do not the priests bathe while it is yet day[1]?") R. Hannina says: From the time the poor man goes home to eat his bread with salt. R. Aḥai (another version: R. Aḥa) says: From the time when the majority of people go home to have their evening repast. Shouldest thou maintain that the poor man and the priest have the same standard of time, then R Hannina and R. Joshua hold the same opinion[2]! Must it not therefore be concluded that each of them has a different standard? Yes, draw that conclusion.

This conclusion refuted by a *Bārāitā*.

Which of the two[3] is later[4]? It is more probable that the poor man is later; for shouldest thou maintain that he is earlier, then R. Ḥannina and R. Eliezer would hold the same opinion[5]! Must it not therefore be concluded that the poor man is later? Yes, draw that conclusion.

The poor man is later than the priest.

The teacher stated above: "R. Judah asked him, 'But do not the priests bathe while it is yet day?'" R. Judah's question to R. Meïr is a forcible one! But R. Meïr answered him thus: Dost thou think that I agree with thy opinion of "twilight[6]"? I agree with R. Josē's opinion. For R. Josē said: The twilight is like a flicker of the eye; the night comes on and the day passes without anyone being able to perceive it[7].

R. Judah's question to Meïr answered.

[1] And it is agreed by all that the evening *Sh^e^ma'* must not be read in the daytime. This question is dealt with below.

[2] R. Ḥannina adopts A and R. Joshua adopts C. According to the hypothesis A=C; but that cannot be, since these two Rabbis hold divergent views.

[3] The time-standards of the poor man and the priest.

[4] *M.* inserts: Rab Naḥman b. Isaac said.

[5] There is not sufficient data in the *G^e^mārā* to account for this conclusion. Tōsāfōt note the difficulty.

[6] In Shab. 34 *b* R. Judah defines "twilight" thus: From the time the sun sets and so long as the sky in the East is coloured red. When the lower horizon is pale but not the upper horizon, it is still twilight; but when the upper horizon is pale like the lower, it is night. Cf. Lane, p. 74 n. 2.

[7] Should, therefore, the priest bathe about the time of twilight (according to R. Josē's view), although it is still day, it is legitimate to read the *Sh^e^ma'* then, since it is practically night.

fol. 3 a. R. Meïr has contradicted himself[1]! There are two *Tannāīm* in the sense of R. Meïr[2]. R. Eliezer has contradicted himself[3]! There are two *Tannāīm* in the sense of R. Eliezer. Or if thou wilt, I can say that the first part of the Mishnaic statement is not R. Eliezer's[4].

Until the end of the first watch.

The night divided into three watches.

What is R. Eliezer's view? If he holds that the night is divided into three watches, let him say explicitly [in the *Mishnāh*] "until the end of the fourth hour[5]." If, on the other hand, he holds that the night is divided into four watches[6], let him say explicitly "until the end of the third hour." His opinion is certainly that there are three watches in the night; but his intention is to inform us that there are watches in heaven as on earth[7]. For there is a teaching[8]: R. Eliezer says: There are three watches in the night, and at each watch, the Holy One, blessed be He, sits enthroned and roars like a lion; as it is said, "The Lord doth roar from on high, and utter His voice from His holy habitation; He doth mightily roar[9] because of His fold" (Jer. xxv. 30). A sign for the matter [of the three earthly night-watches] is: at the first watch, the ass brays; at the second, dogs bark; and at the third, the babe sucks at the breast of its mother and a woman converses with her husband.

[1] In the first *Bārāitā* quoted, R. Meïr's view is that the *Sh*ᵉ*ma'* may be read from the time people go home for their meal on the Sabbath-eve (i.e. after twilight); but in the second *Bārāitā* his view is from the time the priest bathes (i.e. before twilight).

[2] R. Meïr's teaching is reported by two later Rabbis; hence the discrepancy.

[3] In the *Mishnāh*, R. Eliezer's time-standard is when the priests enter to eat the *T*ᵉ*rūmāh* (i.e. the appearance of the stars); in the *Bārāitā*, it is when the Sabbath is hallowed (i.e. sunset).

[4] According to this explanation, only "until the end of the first watch" in the *Mishnāh* are the words of R. Eliezer.

[5] The division of the day was reckoned as follows: From sunrise to sunset consisted of twelve "hours," which would be longer in Summer and shorter in Winter. The sixth hour ended at noon; hence it is convenient to speak of the day as commencing at 6 a.m., and the night (which was similarly divided into twelve hours) at 6 p.m. "Until the end of the fourth hour" would accordingly be 10 p.m.

[6] The Romans divided the night into four *vigiliae*. So also Matt. xiv. 25, Mark vi. 48.

[7] The ministering angels are formed into three bands, each doing duty a part of the night.

[8] See Glossary, s.v. *Bārāitā*.

[9] "Mightily roar" is literally in the Hebrew "roaring He doth roar." Hence the word "roar" occurs three times in the verse, and is referred to the *three* night-watches.

R. Eliezer's statement explained.

Of what is R. Eliezer thinking? If he is thinking of the commencement of the watches, what need is there for a sign of the beginning of the first watch, since it is dusk? Should he be thinking of the end of the watches, what need is there for a sign of the end of the last watch, since it is day? Nay, he must be thinking of the end of the first watch, the beginning of the last watch, and the middle of the central watch. Or if thou wilt, I can say that in every case he is thinking of the end of the watches; and shouldest thou urge that a sign of the end of the last watch is unnecessary, and ask what is its purpose? It is for the reading of the *Sh^ema'* on the part of one who sleeps in a dark room[1] and does not know when is the time for reading the *Sh^ema'*. Therefore, when the woman converses with her husband and the child sucks at the breast of its mother, let him get up and read it.

The divine lament.

R. Isaac b. Samuel[2] said in the name of Rab[3]: The night is divided into three watches[4], and at each watch the Holy One, blessed be He, sits enthroned, roars like a lion and exclaims, "Alas for My children, for whose iniquities I destroyed My house, burnt My Temple, and exiled them among the nations of the world!"

R. José and Elijah.

There is a teaching: R. José said: Once I was journeying by the way, and I entered one of the ruins of Jerusalem to pray. Elijah[5]—may he be remembered for good!—came, waited at the entrance for me, and stayed until I had concluded my prayer[6]. After I had finished my prayer he said to me, "Peace be to thee, my master." I responded, "Peace be to thee, my master and teacher." Then he said to me, "My son, why didst thou enter this ruin?" I answered, "To pray." He said to me, "Thou shouldest have prayed by the roadside." I said, "I feared lest passers-by interrupt me." Then said he to me, "Thou shouldest

[1] Windows were rare in houses, especially of the poor. Cf. *T. A.* I. p. 42, and p. 347 n. 539.

[2] *M.:* Rab Isaac b. R. Samuel b. Marta.

[3] It will be noted that the Talmūd is careful to trace a teaching to its source; hence the frequent occurrence of the phrase "in the name of." Cf. Ābōt vi. 6: "Whoever reports a thing in the name of him that said it brings deliverance into the world; as it is said, 'And Esther told the king in the name of Mordecai' (Esth. ii. 22)" (Singer, p. 207).

[4] The Greeks divided the night into three *φυλακαί*.

[5] Elijah is frequently represented in Rabbinic Literature as appearing on earth. See *A. T.* II. p. 163 n. 1, and the article in *J. E.* v. pp. 122 ff.

[6] By "prayer" is usually, as here, meant the Eighteen Benedictions (see Glossary, s.v. *T^efillāh*). This prayer must be said with the feet in a fixed position (see fol. 10 *b*, p. 65 n. 6) and without interruption.

have offered an abbreviated prayer[1]." On that occasion I learnt three things from him: first, one should not enter ruins; second, it is permissible to pray by the roadside; third, one who prays by the roadside should offer an abbreviated prayer.

Then he said to me, "My son, what sound didst thou hear in that ruin?" I answered, "I heard a *Bat Ḳōl* moaning like a dove[2], crying, 'Alas for My children for whose iniquities I destroyed My house[3], burnt My Temple, and exiled them among the nations!'" He said to me, "By thy life and the life of thy head, not only at this hour does it so cry, but thrice daily it exclaims thus. Moreover, whenever the Children of Israel enter their Synagogues and Houses of Study and respond 'Let His great Name be blessed[4],' the Holy One, blessed be He, shakes His head[5] and exclaims, 'Happy the King Who is so praised in His house! Alas[6] for the Father Who has banished His children! And alas for the children who have been banished from their Father's table!'"

Why ruins should be avoided.

Our Rabbis have taught: For three reasons one should not enter ruins: on account of suspicion[7], of falling fabric and evil spirits[8]. [Why mention] on account of suspicion, since thou canst

fol. 3 b.

derive [a sufficient reason] from the danger of falling fabric? They might be new ruins[9]. Then derive it from the danger of evil spirits! This would not apply when two men entered a ruin. But should there be two men, there would likewise be no ground for suspicion[10]! There would be in the case of two men of ill-repute. [Why mention] on account of falling fabric, since thou canst derive

[1] I.e. the prayer "Give us understanding" (Singer, p. 55); see below fol. 29 *a*, p. 192.

[2] For the bearing of this passage on Matt. iii. 16, see Abrahams, *Studies in Pharisaism* (First Series), p. 47.

[3] The original reading was probably, "Woe to Me that I have destroyed," etc. See *D. S. ad loc.* The alteration was made for the purpose of euphemism.

[4] This is the response in the important feature of the Synagogue Service, known as the *Ḳaddīsh*. Cf., e.g., Singer, p. 37, and p. 86 for the form used in the House of Study. On the *Ḳaddīsh*, see *J. E.* VII. pp. 401 ff.

[5] To denote regret or meditation; cf. *T. A.* III. p. 245 n. 65.

[6] Reading אוי; see *D. S. ad loc.* The text has מה which means "What is there for the Father?"

[7] Of immoral intent.

[8] The Evil Spirits of Jewish Folklore correspond to the *Jinn* of the Arabs. Among the places they are supposed to frequent are "ruined houses" (Lane, p. 229). On Jewish Demonology, see *J. E.* IV. pp. 514 ff.

[9] In which this danger is not so great.

[10] According to *Mishnāh* Ḳiddūshīn iv. 12, a woman may be accompanied by two men.

[a sufficient reason] from the grounds of suspicion and evil spirits? No, not in the case of two men of good repute. [Why mention] on account of evil spirits, since thou canst derive [a sufficient reason] from the grounds of suspicion and falling fabric? No, not in the case of new ruins and two men of good repute. Is there no fear of evil spirits also when there are two men? In such places where evil spirits resort there is occasion for fear. Or if thou wilt, I can say that even in the case of a person alone and new ruins situated in a wild place[1] there is no ground for suspicion, because a woman does not frequent such a spot; but the fear of evil spirits remains.

On the number of night-watches. Argument in favour of three.

Our Rabbis have taught: The night is divided into four watches. These are the words of Rabbi[2]. R. Nathan says: Three. What is R. Nathan's reason? Because it is written, "So Gideon, and the hundred men that were with him, came unto the outermost part of the camp in the beginning of the middle watch" (Judges vii. 19). Hence he teaches that there cannot be a "middle watch" unless one precedes and follows. How does Rabbi explain the phrase "middle watch"? He takes it to mean one of the middle watches. What reply does R. Nathan make to this? He asks, Does Scripture state "one of the two middle watches"? No; the "middle watch" is explicitly mentioned[3].

Argument in favour of four.

What is Rabbi's reason [for declaring there are four watches]? R. Z^{e}riḳa stated that R. Ammi said in the name of[4] R. Joshua b. Levi: One verse states, "At midnight I will rise to give thanks unto Thee because of Thy righteous ordinances" (Ps. cxix. 62) and another verse states, "Mine eyes forestalled the night-watches" (*ibid.* v. 148). How is this? There must be four watches in the night[5]. How does R. Nathan answer this argument? He agrees with the opinion of R. Joshua; for there is a Mishnaic teaching[6]: R. Joshua says: *Until the third hour* [in the day may the morning *Sh^{e}ma'* be read], *for so is the custom of kings to rise at the third hour.* Six hours of the night and two of the day make two

Its refutation.

[1] Rashi "field" and it is so usually rendered; but cf. *T. A.* II. p. 470 n. 382.

[2] "Rabbi," without any name following, refers to R. Judah the Prince, the redactor of the *Mishnāh.*

[3] In *J. T.*, R. Nathan is answered: There are four watches, but the first is not counted because people are generally still awake.

[4] *M.*: R. Simeon b. Laḳish. Bacher adopts this as correct; see *A. P. A.* I. p. 131 n. 5.

[5] If by rising "at midnight" David forestalled "night-watches" (the plural signifying two), there must be four watches in the night.

[6] See below fol. 9 *b*, p. 55.

watches[1]. Rab Ashē said: A watch and a half are also referred to as "watches[2]."

Another teaching reported by R. Z^e^rika.

R. Z^e^riḳa also stated that R. Ammi said in the name of[3] R. Joshua b. Levi: In the presence of the dead, we should only speak of matters relating to the dead. R. Abba b. Kah^a^na said: This applies only to words of *Tōrāh*; but as for worldly matters we can have no objection[4]. Another version is: R. Abba b. Kah^a^na said: This applies even to words of *Tōrāh*; how much more so to worldly matters!

How David passed the night.

David rose at midnight! He rose at eventide; as it is written, "I arose early *b^e^nēshef*[5] and cried" (Ps. cxix. 147). Whence is it learnt that *nēshef* means evening? Because it is written, "In the twilight [*b^e^nēshef*], in the evening of the day, in the blackness of night and the darkness" (Prov. vii. 9). R. Osha'ya said in the name of R. Aḥa[6]: Thus declared David, "Midnight never passed me by in my sleep[7]." R. Zera said: Until midnight David used to slumber like a horse[8], but from thence he grew strong like a lion[9]. Rab Ashē said: Until midnight he was occupied with words of *Tōrāh*, but from thence with psalms and praises.

The meaning of *nēshef*.

Nēshef means evening! Lo, it means the morning; for it is written, "And David smote them from the *nēshef* even unto the

[1] If the day of royal personages commences with the beginning of the third hour (i.e. 8 a.m.), by rising at midnight David forestalled them by eight hours. Therefore a "watch" consists of four hours and there are three in the night.

[2] This is an alternative answer to uphold R. Nathan's view. By "watches" is not necessarily to be understood two *complete* periods of time.

[3] *M.*: R. Simeon b. Laḳish. Bacher adopts this as correct; see *A.P.A.* i. p. 131 n. 5.

[4] To be an auditor of a discussion on *Tōrāh* and not take part in it was a mark of ignorance and one incurred shame thereby. The dead, being unable to participate, although for other reasons, would thus be disgraced. The idea will not seem so fantastic in view of the belief that the corpse was conscious of what transpired in its presence. Cf. the discussion on pp. 120 ff.

[5] R.V. "at dawn"; but the Talmūd wishes to give it the meaning of "evening." See the discussion in this and the following paragraphs.

[6] In place of "in the name of R. Aḥa," *M.* reads: Another version: R. Eleazar said in the name of R. Osha'ya.

[7] This is taken to be the meaning of Ps. cxix. 62, and therefore David rose *before* midnight.

[8] The horse was known to be a light sleeper. According to Sukkāh 26 *b* its sleep consisted of only 60 respirations.

[9] Cf. Ābōt v. 23: "Judah b. Tema said: Be strong as a leopard, light as an eagle, fleet as a hart, and strong as a lion, to do the will of thy Father Who is in heaven" (Singer, p. 203).

evening [*'éreb*] of the next day" (I Sam. xxx. 17). Is this not to be understood to mean from the morning unto the evening? No, from evening unto evening. If so, the text should have read "from the *nêshef* unto the *nêshef*" or "from the *'éreb* unto the *'éreb*"! But, says Raba[1], there are two occasions in the day called *nêshef*; there is the *nêshef* of the night followed by day, and the *nêshef* of the day followed by night.

How David knew when it was midnight.

Did David know when it was [exactly] midnight, since even Moses our teacher was not certain; as it is written, "*About* midnight will I go out into the midst of Egypt" (Exod. xi. 4)? What means "*about* midnight"? Are we to suppose that the Holy One, blessed be He, used the phrase "*about* midnight" to Moses? Can there be any doubt in the mind of God? Nay; God told him "*At* midnight[2]"; but Moses came and said "*about* midnight." Hence it is to be understood that Moses was in doubt, but David did know it! He had a sign. For R. Ḥannah b. Bizna[3] said in the name of R. Simeon Ḥᵃsida: There was a harp hanging above David's bed, and when the time of midnight arrived a North wind came and blew upon it, so that it produced melody[4]. He used immediately to rise and occupy himself with *Tōrāh* until the break of dawn.

His interview with the wise men at dawn.

At the rise of dawn, the wise men of Israel entered his presence and said to him, "Our lord, the king, thy people Israel are in need of sustenance." He answered them, "Go, let each sustain himself from the other[5]." They said to him, "A handful cannot satisfy a lion, nor can a pit be filled with its own clods[6]." He said to them, "Go, stretch forth your hands with the army[7]." At once they took counsel with Ahitophel, consulted the *Sanhedrin*[8], and

1 *M.:* Rab Ashē.

2 This is the reading of *M.* The edd. read: To-morrow at midnight, the same time as now. See *D. S. ad loc.*

3 So *M.* correctly. Edd.: R. Aḥa b. Bizna. In *J. T.* the reference to the harp is in the name of R. Levi; cf. *A. P. A.* ɪɪɪ. p. 697.

4 A reminiscence of the Aeolian harp.

5 Let the rich help the poor.

6 The poor cannot remain satisfied with charitable doles, any more than a handful will satisfy a hungry lion. Moreover a nation needs external sources of supply. It cannot live on itself, just as the soil taken out of a pit will not completely fill the cavity. Others render the proverb: "A grasshopper cannot satisfy a lion; nor can a cistern be filled by rain-water [but must also depend upon drawn water]"; cf. *T. A.* ɪ. p. 419 n. 17.

7 Send out soldiers to obtain plunder.

8 The Jewish Senate, one of whose duties was to decide war. See *J. E.* xɪ. p. 41.

inquired of the *Ūrīm* and *Tummīm*[1]. Rab Joseph asked: What is the Scriptural authority for this? "And after Ahitophel was Benaiah the son of Jehoiada[2], and Abiathar; and the captain of the king's host was Joab" (I Chron. xxvii. 34)—"Ahitophel" was the counsellor, for thus it is stated, "Now the counsel of Ahitophel, which he counselled in those days, was as if a man inquired of the word of God" (2 Sam. xvi. 23). "Benaiah the son of Jehoiada" refers to the *Sanhedrin*; for so the Scriptures declare, "And Benaiah the son of Jehoiada was over the Cherethites and over the Pelethites" (2 Sam. xx. 23). "Abiathar[3]" denotes the *Ūrīm* and *Tummīm*[4]. Why were the members of the *Sanhedrin* called *K^e^rētī* and *P^e^lētī*? They were called *K^e^rētī* because they were concise [*kōr^e^tīm*] with their words, and *P^e^lētī* because they were "distinguished" [*muflāīm*] with their words[5]. After them came "the captain of the king's host, Joab[6]."

fol. 4 a.

Authority of Scripture for story of David's harp.

Rab Isaac b. Adda[7] (another version: Rab Isaac b. Rab Iddi) said: What Scriptural authority is there for the story of David's harp? "Awake, my glory; awake, psaltery and harp; I will awake the dawn" (Ps. lvii. 9).

Moses also knew when it was midnight.

R. Zera said: Moses certainly knew [the exact time of midnight], and David also knew it. Since David knew it, why did he require a harp? In order that he may be aroused from his sleep. And since Moses knew it, what object had he in saying "*About* midnight"? Moses thought that perhaps Pharaoh's astrologers would err[8] and say, "Moses is a liar." For a teacher has said: Teach thy tongue to say, "I do not know," lest thou be led to falsehoods

1 Objects connected with the High Priest's breastplate, used as a divine oracle by means of which questions were answered. See *J. E.* XII. p. 384.

2 This reading of edd. "Benaiah the son of Jehoiada" agrees with II Sam. xx. 23. The Hebrew text of Chronicles reads "Jehoiada the son of Benaiah" which is also the reading of *M.* here.

3 He being the High Priest.

4 The text of *M.* has been followed, which is supported by the Tosafist, Rabbēnū Tam. Edd. insert "Abiathar denotes the *Ūrīm* and *Tummīm*" after the word "Sanhedrin"; and accordingly the explanation of the *K^e^rētī* and *P^e^lētī* is referred to the *Ūrīm* and *Tummīm*.

5 *M.* adds: Why are they called *Ūrīm* and *Tummīm*? They are called *Ūrīm* because they give their answers *clearly*, and *Tummīm* because they *fulfil* their words; i.e. what they foretell comes to pass. This explanation is given in Jōmā 73 *b*.

6 To lead the marauding expedition.

7 *M.*: Rab Isaac b. Rab.

8 As to the precise time of midnight, and if Moses did not appear according to their reckoning bring discredit upon him.

and be apprehended. Rab Ashē said: It[1] happened in the middle of the night of the thirteenth [of the first month] which is the beginning of the fourteenth; and thus spake Moses to Israel, "The Holy One, blessed be He, said, 'To-morrow, like the time of midnight, as it is now, I will go forth in the midst of Egypt.'"

David's claim to godliness.

David prayed, "Keep my soul, for I am godly" (Ps. lxxxvi. 2). [R.] Levi[2] and R. Isaac differ in their interpretation. One explains: Thus spake David before the Holy One, blessed be He, "Lord of the Universe, am I not godly, seeing that all the kings of the East and West sleep unto the third hour of the day, but as for me, 'At midnight I rise to give thanks unto Thee' (Ps. cxix. 62)?" The other explains: Thus spake David before the Holy One, blessed be He, "Lord of the Universe, am I not godly, seeing that all the kings of the East and West sit in companies[3] in all their pomp, whereas my hands are stained with the blood of a *foetus* or with the *placenta*[4] in order to pronounce a woman clean to her husband? Moreover, whatever I do I discuss with my teacher Mephibosheth[5], saying to him, 'Mephibosheth, my teacher, have I decided well? Have I convicted correctly or acquitted correctly? Did I rightly pronounce unclean or rightly pronounce clean?' And I was not ashamed [so to do]." R. Joshua b. Rab Iddi[6] asked: What is the Scriptural authority for this? "I will also speak of Thy testimonies before kings, and will not be ashamed" (Ps. cxix. 46).

The name of David's teacher.

It has been taught: His name was not Mephibosheth but Ishbosheth. Why, then, was he called Mephibosheth? Because he used to put David to shame[7] on questions of *Hᵃlākāh*. On that account David merited that Chileab[8] should issue from him; and

[1] The incident of Exod. xi. 4, and the preposition *k* is taken to mean "like," not "about."

[2] This is the Palestinian *Āmōrā* and not the *Tannā* of that name; cf. Hyman, III. p. 862 *a–b*.

[3] Making merriment.

[4] So *M*. Edd. read "stained with [menstrual] blood, with *foetus* and *placenta*." In certain cases an abortive embryo would not make a woman liable to the restrictions of Lev. xii. 2 ff., and David is represented as deciding such a question as this instead of feasting.

[5] Cf. II Sam. ix. 13 where it is stated, "But Mephibosheth dwelt in Jerusalem; for he did eat continually at the king's table." This is the only reference to intimate relations existing between them.

[6] *M.*: R. Shesha b. Iddi.

[7] Mephibosheth is explained as *mippī* "from my mouth" *bōshet* "is shame."

[8] Cf. II Sam. iii. 3.

R. Johanan said: His name was not Chileab but Daniel[1]. Why, then, was he called Chileab? Because he put Mephibosheth to shame[2] on questions of *Halākāh*; and concerning him Solomon said in his wisdom, "My son, if thy heart be wise, my heart will be glad, even mine" (Prov. xxiii. 15), and "My son, be wise, and make mine heart glad, that I may answer him that taunteth me" (*ibid.* xxvii. 11).

David's doubt about his godliness.

But how could David describe himself as "godly[3]"? For behold it is written, "If I had not [*lūlē'*] believed to look upon the goodness of the Lord in the land of the living" (Ps. xxvii. 13); and it has been taught in the name of R. Josē: Why are there dots over the word *lūlē'*[4]? David spake before the Holy One, blessed be He, "Lord of the Universe, I am confident that Thou repayest a good reward to the righteous in the hereafter, but I know not whether I have a portion among them or not[5]. Perhaps my sin will cause [me not to[6]]." This is like the teaching of R. Jacob b. Iddi who asked: It is written, "Behold, I am with thee, and will keep thee whithersoever thou goest" (Gen. xxviii. 15), and then it is written, "Jacob was greatly afraid" (*ibid.* xxxii. 8)! But Jacob said, "Perhaps sin will cause [His protection to be withheld]." This is like the teaching: "Till Thy people pass over, O Lord, till the people pass over that Thou hast gotten" (Exod. xv. 16).—"Till Thy people pass over, O Lord" refers to the first entry [into Canaan]; "till the people pass over that Thou hast gotten" refers to the second entry[7]. Hence the Sages said: The Israelites were worthy that a miracle should be performed for them in the days of Ezra

[1] See I Chron. iii. 1, as compared with II Sam. iii. 3. In a very interesting article in *R. E. J.* XXVIII. pp. 60 ff., Büchler suggests that under the guise of Biblical names (cf. Dryden's *Absalom and Achitophel*) we have an echo of the quarrel between the Patriarch, Rabban Simeon b. Gamaliel and R. Nathan and R. Meïr. These two Rabbis (i.e. Mephibosheth) attempted to belittle the Halakic knowledge of Rabban Simeon (i.e. David); but his adversaries found more than their match in R. Judah his son (i.e. Chileab). On the quarrel, see Weiss, *Dōr* (ed. 1904), II. p. 157.

[2] The name is explained as *maklīm* "putting to shame" *āb* "a father," i.e. a teacher, Mephibosheth.

[3] In Ps. lxxxvi. 2 quoted above.

[4] In the Hebrew text.

[5] Therefore David was doubtful whether he deserved to be included with the righteous, so how could he describe himself as "godly"?

[6] The answer is he felt himself to be "godly," but feared that the sins he had committed would more than counterbalance the general righteousness of his life.

[7] Under the leadership of Zerubbabel and then of Ezra.

in the same way that it was performed for them in the days of Joshua, the son of Nun; but sin caused [the miracle to be withheld][1].

But the Sages say: Until midnight.

With whose opinion do the Sages agree? If with R. Eliezer's, let them express themselves like R. Eliezer; if with Rabban Gamaliel's, let them express themselves like Rabban Gamaliel[2]! They certainly agree with Rabban Gamaliel, and the reason they say *Until midnight* is to keep a man far from transgression. **fol. 4 b.**

The "fence" of the Sages.

This is like the teaching: The Sages made a "fence[3]" to their words, so that a man shall not come from the field[4] in the evening and say, "I will go home, eat a little, drink a little, sleep a little, and after that I will read the *Sh^ema'* and say the *T^efillāh*"; for slumber may overcome him and as a result he may sleep through all the night[5]. Rather should a man come from the field in the evening and enter a Synagogue; if he is accustomed to read [the Scriptures], let him read; if he is accustomed to study[6], let him study. Then let him read the *Sh^ema'* and say the *T^efillāh*; after that he should eat his meal and say Grace. Whosoever transgresses the words of the Sages [in this matter] is worthy of death.

Why is it not stated in any other place that whosoever transgresses the words of the Sages is worthy of death, but here a distinction is made and it is so stated? If thou wilt, I can say

[1] Their return depended upon the permission of Cyrus and not divine intervention.

[2] R. Eliezer's view "Until the end of the first watch" is based upon the following interpretation of "when thou liest down," viz. the *Sh^ema'* is to be read about the time a person thinks of retiring to bed. Rabban Gamaliel's view, "Until the rise of dawn" follows from a different interpretation, viz. the *Sh^ema'* may be read any time during the period given over to sleep. Which interpretation is adopted by the Sages? Their view "Until midnight" seems to follow neither. It must be remembered that in the Orient, people retire to rest at a rather early hour. Lane says, "The Egyptian is a very early riser, and he retires to sleep at an early hour" (p. 137), and this may be taken to be typical of Orientals.

[3] Cf. Ābōt i. 1: Make a fence round the *Tōrāh* (Singer, p. 184), i.e. "impose additional restrictions so as to keep at a safe distance from forbidden ground" (Taylor, *Sayings of the Fathers, in loc.*).

[4] The antiquity of many a *Bārāitā* may be seen from the fact that by a labourer is usually intended an agricultural workman. Cf. also fol. 17 *a*, p. 111.

[5] Fortified by the thought that the *Sh^ema'* may be read any time before dawn, he will put it off and in this way come to omit it altogether.

[6] The *Tōrāh* as expounded in the Schools.

that here there is the danger of the overpowering force of sleep[1]; or if thou wilt, I can say that it is intended to exclude the opinion of those who maintain that the evening prayer is voluntary[2]; and hence we are informed that it is an obligation.

The order of the *Sh^e^ma'* and *T^e^fillāh.*

The teacher stated above: "Then let him read the *Sh^e^ma'* and say the *T^e^fillāh.*" This supports the view of R. Joḥanan who declared: Who will inherit the world to come? He who joins the *G^e^'ullāh* to the evening *T^e^fillāh*[3]. R. Joshua b. Levi said: The *T^e^fillōt* were arranged in the middle[4].

What is the point on which they differ? If thou wilt, I can say [they differ in the interpretation of] a Scriptural passage; or if thou wilt, I can say [they differ] in their reasoning. If thou wilt, I can say [they differ] in their reasoning: for R. Joḥanan holds that the deliverance [from Egypt] began also at night[5], but the complete deliverance did not take place until the morning. R. Joshua b. Levi holds that since the deliverance did not take place until the morning, [what happened in the night] is not to be considered a proper deliverance. Or if thou wilt, I can say [they differ in the interpretation of] a Scriptural passage; and they both expound the same verse, viz. "When thou liest down and when thou risest up" (Deut. vi. 7). R. Joḥanan holds that an analogy is here to be drawn between "lying down" and "rising up" in this sense: as with "rising up" the order is the reading of the *Sh^e^ma'* and then the *T^e^fillāh*, so also with "lying down" the order is the reading of the *Sh^e^ma'* and then the *T^e^fillāh*. R. Joshua b. Levi, however, thinks that the analogy is to be drawn between "lying down" and "rising up" in this sense: as with "rising up" the reading of the *Sh^e^ma'* is nearer to his contact with the

[1] Therefore the Sages deemed it necessary to emphasise the warning, because his transgression might otherwise be involuntary.

[2] This question is referred to below, fol. 27 *b*, p. 180.

[3] That is to say, the benediction "Blessed...Who hast redeemed Israel" (Singer, p. 99) should be immediately followed by the Eighteen Benedictions (*ibid.* pp. 44-54). This order is supported by the quotation "Then let him read the *Sh^e^ma'* and say the *T^e^fillāh*," as against R. Joshua b. Levi's opinion that in the evening the *Sh^e^ma'* should follow the *T^e^fillāh*. On the idea of joining the *G^e^'ullāh* and the *T^e^fillāh*, see below fol. 9 *b*, p. 56 n. 7.

[4] I.e. between the morning and evening recital of the *Sh^e^ma'*; hence in the evening, the *T^e^fillāh* would come first.

[5] Therefore we should have the prayers referring to the deliverance (Singer, pp. 98 f.) and then the benedictions. But R. Joshua b. Levi only regards the deliverance as having taken place after midnight; consequently R. Joḥanan's reason does not apply.

bed[1], so with "lying down" the reading of the *Shᵉma'* must be nearer to his contact with the bed.

Mar b. Rabina quoted in objection: *In the evening* [*the reading of the* Shᵉma'] *is both preceded and followed by two benedictions*[2]. If, then, thou sayest that the *Gᵉ'ullāh* must be joined to the *Tᵉfillāh*, behold that condition is not fulfilled because one is required to say the prayer "Cause us, O Lord our God, to lie down[3]!" They answer: Since the Rabbis instituted the prayer "Cause us, etc.," it is to be considered part of the *Gᵉ'ullāh*[4]. If thou dost not admit this, how is it possible to affect the same union in the morning service; for lo, R. Johanan has said: Before the *Tᵉfillāh* one says, "O Lord, open Thou my lips" (Ps. li. 17)[5], and at its conclusion, "Let the words of my mouth...be acceptable" (*ibid.* xix. 15)! In this case, since the Rabbis instituted the saying of "O Lord, open Thou my lips," it is considered part of the *Tᵉfillāh*; so likewise in the evening prayer, the Rabbis having instituted the saying of "Cause us, etc.," it is considered part of the *Gᵉ'ullāh*.

An objection to R. Johanan's view answered.

R. Eleazar b. R. Abina[6] said: Whoever recites Psalm cxlv. thrice[7] daily may be assured that he is a son of the world to come. What is the reason? Is it to be supposed because the initial letter of the verses follows the alphabetical order? Then let him recite Psalm cxix. which contains an eight-fold alphabetical order! No, the reason is that it contains the verse, "Thou openest Thy hand and satisfiest every living thing with favour" (Ps. cxlv. 16)[8]. Then let him say the Great *Hallēl*[9] which includes "Who giveth food to all flesh" (*ibid.* cxxxvi. 25)! But [Psalm cxlv. is selected] because it contains both features.

Ps. cxlv. to be recited thrice daily.

[1] The order being: leaving the bed, *Shᵉma'*, *Tᵉfillāh*; so at night the order must be reversed: *Tᵉfillāh*, *Shᵉma'*, retiring to bed.

[2] See below, p. 70.

[3] Singer, p. 99. This prayer interrupts the connection of "Who hast redeemed Israel" and the Eighteen Benedictions. The prayer, "Blessed be the Lord for evermore" (*ibid.* p. 100) is a later addition to the Service. See Elbogen, *Der jüdische Gottesdienst*, pp. 102 f.

[4] Lit. a long *Gᵉ'ullāh*.

[5] Singer, p. 44. These words might be regarded as constituting an interruption.

[6] So *M.* Edd.: R. Eleazar said in the name of R. Abina.

[7] Twice in the morning service and once in the afternoon. See Abrahams, p. xxxvi.

[8] Hence the meaning is: a man should thrice daily acknowledge his dependence upon the divine mercy.

[9] See Glossary, s.v. *Hallēl*.

Omission in the Psalm of verse commencing with N. R. Johanan[1] said: Why is there no verse beginning with the letter N in that Psalm? Because it would refer to the downfall of Israel's enemies[2]; as it is written, "Fallen (*Nāphᵉlāh*] is the virgin of Israel, she shall no more rise" (Amos v. 2). In the West[3] they interpret the verse thus: "She is fallen, but she shall no more fall; rise, O virgin of Israel." Rab Naḥman b. Isaac said: Even so, David refers to it and finds support for Israel in the Holy Spirit; as it is said, "The Lord upholdeth all that fall" (Ps. cxlv. 14).

Another teaching of R. Eleazar b. Abina. R. Eleazar b. Abina [also] said: What is declared of [the angel] Michael is greater than what is declared of Gabriel; for of Michael it is written, "Then flew unto me one of the Seraphim" (Is. vi. 6), but of Gabriel it is written, "The man Gabriel whom I had seen in the vision at the beginning, being caused to fly swiftly[4], approached close to me about the time of the evening offering" (Dan. ix. 21). How is it to be inferred that "one of the Seraphim" means Michael? R. Johanan said: By comparing the occurrence of the word "one"[5] in the following passages: In Isaiah it is written, "Then flew unto me *one* of the Seraphim," and elsewhere it is written, "But, lo, Michael, *one* of the chief princes, came to help me" (*ibid.* x. 13). It has been taught: Michael flew in one flight, Gabriel in two, Elijah in four, and the Angel of Death in eight; but in the time of plague [the Angel of Death flies] in one.

The Shᵉma' to be read on lying down. R. Joshua b. Levi said: Although a man has read the *Shᵉma'* in the Synagogue, it is a pious act to read it again upon his bed. R. Assi[6] said: What is the Scriptural authority for this? "Tremble and sin not; commune with your own heart *upon your bed*, and

fol. 5 a. be still. Selah" (Ps. iv. 5). Rab Naḥman added: In the case of a disciple of the wise[7], this is not necessary. But Abbai said: Even the disciple of the wise should recite a verse of supplication; for instance, "Into Thy hand I commit my spirit. Thou hast redeemed me, O Lord, Thou God of truth" (*ibid.* xxxi. 6).

1 *M.*: R. Ḥanin.

2 A euphemism for Israel.

3 See p. 3 n. 4.

4 Lit. "being caused to fly in a flight," the word for "flying" occurring twice. This is interpreted that he covered the distance in two flights, resting in between; whereas the verse in Isaiah speaks only of one flight.

5 This argument is known as *Gᵉzērāh Shāwāh*, "analogy of expression." See Mielziner, pp. 142 ff., especially pp. 148 ff. where the safeguards against the exorbitant use of the argument are explained.

6 So *M.* correctly. Edd.: R. Josē.

7 Title of a student of *Tōrāh*. He need not read the *Shᵉma'* on his bed because his mind is constantly bent on his religious studies.

R. Levi b. Ḥamma[1] said in the name of R. Simeon b. Laḳish: A man should always oppose [*yargīz*] the good impulse to the evil impulse[2]; as it is said: "Tremble [*rigzū*] and sin not" (*ibid.* iv. 5). If he conquer it, well and good; but if not, let him occupy himself with *Tōrāh*; as it is said, "Commune with your own heart" (*ibid.*)[3]. Should this gain him the victory, well and good; but if not, let him read the *Shema'*; as it is said, "Upon your bed[4]." If he conquer it, well and good; but if not, let him reflect upon the day of death; as it is said, "And be still[5]. Selah." Ps. iv. 5 further expounded.

R. Levi b. Ḥamma also said in the name of R. Simeon b. Laḳish: What means that which is written, "And I will give thee the tables of stone, and the law and the commandment, which I have written, that thou mayest teach them" (Exod. xxiv. 12)? "Tables of stone," i.e. the Decalogue: "law," i.e. the Pentateuch; "commandment," i.e. the *Mishnāh*; "which I have written," i.e. the Prophets and Hagiographa; "that thou mayest teach them," i.e. the *Gemārā*[6]. The verse teaches that all of them were given to Moses on Sinai[7]. Another teaching reported by R. Levi b. Ḥamma.

R. Isaac[8] said: Whoever reads the *Shema'* upon his bed is as though he holds a two-edged sword in his hand[9]; as it is said, "Let the high praises of God be in their mouth, and a two-edged sword in their hand" (Ps. cxlix. 6). How is this inferred? Mar Zoṭra (another version: Rab Ashē) said: From what precedes; for it is written, "Let the saints exult in glory, let them sing for joy *upon their beds*" (*ibid. v.* 5), and this is followed by "Let the high praises of God be in their mouth, and a two-edged sword in their hand." Protective power of recital of the *Shema'*.

R. Isaac also said: Whoever reads the *Shema'* upon his bed, the evil spirits flee from him; as it is said, "And the sons of Puts evil spirits to flight.

[1] *M.*: b. Laḥma.

[2] On the *Jēṣer Ṭōb* and *Jēṣer Ra'*, the tendency towards good and evil, see *J. E.* XII. p. 601. To the literature there cited may now be added, Schechter, *Aspects of Rabbinic Theology*, Chaps. XV, XVI, and Abelson, *Immanence of God*, Chap. XXIII.

[3] Of the *Tōrāh* it is said, "And these words, which I command thee this day, shall be upon thy *heart*" (Deut. vi. 6).

[4] The *Shema'* was to be read "when thou liest down" (Deut. vi. 7).

[5] Stillness being a symbol of death. Cf. "The dead praise not the Lord, neither any that go down into silence" (Ps. cxv. 17).

[6] *M.*: *Talmūd.*

[7] On the significance of this passage, see Introduction, § I.

[8] *M.*: R. Eleazar.

[9] To ward off the evil spirits.

Rêshef[1] fly upwards [*'ūf*]" (Job v. 7). *'Ūf* means nothing else than *Tōrāh*; as it is said, "Wilt thou set [*ha'tā'īf*][2] thine eyes upon it? It is gone" (Prov. xxiii. 5). And *Rêshef* means nothing else than "evil spirits"; as it is said, "The wasting of hunger, and the devouring of the fiery bolt [*Rêshef*] and bitter destruction" (Deut. xxxii. 24)[3].

Study of *Tōrāh* removes sufferings.

R. Simeon b. Laḳish said: Whoever occupies himself with *Tōrāh*, sufferings depart from him; as it is said, "And the sons of *Rêshef* fly upwards [*'ūf*]." *'Ūf* means nothing else than *Tōrāh*; as it is said, "Wilt thou set thine eyes upon it? It is gone." And *Rêshef* means nothing else than "sufferings"; as it is said, "The wasting of hunger, and the devouring of the fiery bolt." R. Joḥanan said to him: Why, even school-children know that[4]; as it is stated, "And He said, If thou wilt diligently hearken to the voice of the Lord thy God, and wilt do that which is right in His eyes, and wilt give ear to His commandments, and keep all His statutes, I will put none of the diseases upon thee, which I have put upon the Egyptians; for I am the Lord that healeth thee" (Exod. xv. 26)! But[5], everyone who is able to occupy himself with *Tōrāh* and does not do so, the Holy One, blessed be He, brings upon him dreadful sufferings to stir him; as it is said, "I was dumb with silence, I held my peace, had no comfort [*ṭōb*]; and my pain was stirred" (Ps. xxxix. 3). "Comfort" means nothing else than *Tōrāh*; as it is said, "For I give you good [*ṭōb*] doctrine; forsake ye not My teaching" (Prov. iv. 2).

God rejoiced on giving *Tōrāh* to Israel.

R. Zera (another version: R. Ḥannina b. Pappa)[6] said: Come and see that the attribute of a human being differs from that of the Holy One, blessed be He. What is the attribute of a human

[1] "Sons of *Rêshef*" in the English version is "sparks." The ancient Jewish Aramaic version, the Targūm, renders it "the sons of evil spirits."

[2] The root of this word is *'ūf*, "to fly." The verse is applied to *Tōrāh*: "Wilt thou cause thine eyes to fly upon it [i.e. neglect it]? It is gone [from thy mind]."

[3] The Targūm here renders *Rêshef* by "birds"; so LXX in Job v. 7. But "bitter destruction" is rendered by "attacked by evil spirits." According to a statement in P^e^sāḥīm 111 *b*, *Ḳeṭeb m^e^rīrī* "bitter destruction" is the name of an evil spirit which is active about the time of noon. It is probably heat personified; cf. *T. A.* III. p. 346 n. 131.

[4] The teaching is explicitly inculcated in the *Tōrāh* in a passage known to school-children. Why, then, derive it from obscure verses?

[5] This is what R. Simeon meant to teach, and it cannot be deduced from Exod. xv. 26.

[6] *M.* adds: Another version in the West: in the name of R. Abba b. Mari. This is probably an error for Raba b. Mari; cf. D.S. *ad loc.*

being? When a man sells a valued article to his fellow, the seller grieves[1] and the purchaser rejoices. But with the Holy One, blessed be He, it is not so. He gave the *Tōrāh* to Israel and rejoiced[2]; as it is said, "For I give you good doctrine; forsake ye not My teaching."

Discipline under suffering.

Raba (another version: Rab Ḥisda)[3] said: Should a man see sufferings come upon him, let him scrutinise his actions; as it is said, "Let us search and try our ways, and return unto the Lord" (Lam. iii. 40). If he has scrutinised his actions without discovering the cause, let him attribute them to neglect of *Tōrāh*; as it is said, "Happy is the man whom Thou chastenest, and teachest out of Thy law" (Ps. xciv. 12). If he attributed them to neglect of *Tōrāh* without finding any justification, it is certain that his sufferings are chastenings of love; as it is said, "For whom the Lord loveth He correcteth" (Prov. iii. 12)[4].

Submission under suffering.

Raba stated that Rab Saḥorah said in the name of Rab Huna: Him in whom the Holy One, blessed be He, delighteth He crusheth with sufferings; as it is said, "Yet it pleased the Lord to crush him by disease" (Is. liii. 10). It is possible to think that this is so even with one who does not receive the chastenings in a spirit of love: therefore there is a teaching to say, "To see if his soul would offer itself in restitution" (*ibid.*). Just as the trespass-offering[5] is brought voluntarily, so are the sufferings voluntarily received. If he accept them, what is his reward? "He will see his seed, prolong his days" (*ibid.*). More than that, his study [of *Tōrāh*] will endure with him; as it is said, "The purpose of the Lord will prosper in his hand" (*ibid.*).

What are chastenings of love?

R. Jacob b. Iddi and Rab Aḥa b. Ḥannina [differ in opinion]. One of them says: Those are to be considered chastenings of love which do not involve neglect of *Tōrāh*; as it is said, "Happy is the man whom Thou chastenest, O Lord, and teachest him out of Thy law" (Ps. xciv. 12). The other declares: Those are to be considered chastenings of love which do not involve neglect of prayer;

[1] At parting with the article.

[2] He rejoiced inasmuch as He "gave" it, willingly and without price.

[3] Instead of "another version: Rab Ḥisda," *M.* reads: in the name of R. Saḥorah, in the name of Rab Huna.

[4] On the Rabbinic doctrine of Retribution, see Schechter, *Studies in Judaism* (First Series), pp. 259 ff.

[5] The work for "restitution" is *āshām* which also means "trespass-offering." Before the *āshām* was offered, confession had to be made (Lev. v. 5), and therefore the sacrifice was a voluntary act. Hence the inference is drawn that the sufferings are voluntarily endured.

as it is written, "Blessed be God, Who hath not turned away my prayer, nor His mercy from me" (Ps. lxvi. 20)[1]. R. Abba the son of R. Ḥiyya b. Abba said to them: Thus declared R. Ḥiyya b. Abba in the name of R. Joḥanan: Both of them are to be considered chastenings of love; as it is said, "For whom the Lord loveth He correcteth" (Prov. iii. 12). But what does the phrase "and teachest him out of Thy law" (Ps. xciv. 12) intend to convey to us? Read not *t^elamm^edĕnnū* "and teachest *him*" but *t^elamm^edēnū* "and teachest *us*[2]"; i.e., Thou teachest us this matter out of Thy law as a deduction[3] from the ordinance concerning "the tooth and eye[4]." Should the tooth or eye of a slave be injured, which is only one of the members of a man's body, he thereby obtains his freedom, how much more so with the sufferings which afflict the whole body of a man[5]!

R. Joḥanan's view supported.

This is in accord with the statement of R. Simeon b. Laḳish who said: The word *b^erīt* "covenant" is mentioned in connection with salt and also with chastenings. With salt, as it is written, "Thou shalt not suffer the salt of the covenant of Thy God to be lacking" (Lev. ii. 13); and with chastenings, as it is written, "These are the words of the covenant" (Deut. xxviii. 69)[6]. As with the "covenant" mentioned in connection with salt, it is salt which sweetens meat, so with the "covenant" mentioned in connection with chastenings, they are chastenings which purge all the iniquities of man.

Divine gifts through suffering.

There is a teaching: R. Simeon b. Joḥai said: Three precious gifts did the Holy One, blessed be He, give to Israel, and all of them He gave only through the medium of suffering; they are: *Tōrāh*, the land of Israel, and the world to come. Whence is it deduced that *Tōrāh* [was given through the medium of suffering]? As it is said: "Happy is the man whom Thou chastenest, O Lord, and teachest him out of Thy law" (Ps. xciv. 12). And the land of

[1] The preceding verses (cf. *vv.* 10-12) speak of sufferings.

[2] The Rabbis frequently suggest an alteration of the Scriptural text for homiletic purposes. In the present instance, a slight change in the vowels is required. See Introduction, § v.

[3] The argument here used is called *Ḳōl wāḥōmer*, lit. "light and heavy," i.e. *a fortiori* or *a majore ad minorem*. See Mielziner, pp. 130 ff.

[4] See Exod. xxi. 26 f.

[5] If God ordained that a slave should be set free whose eye or tooth had been damaged, will He not show His mercy to His creatures who suffer more than that!

[6] The verse occurs at the end of the chapter containing the penalties threatened to Israel if disobedient to the word of God.

Israel? For it is written, "As a man chasteneth his son, so the Lord thy God chasteneth thee" (Deut. viii. 5), which is followed by "For the Lord thy God bringeth thee into a good land" (*ibid. v.* 7). And the world to come? For it is written, "For the commandment is a lamp, and the teaching is light, and reproofs of instruction[1] are the way of life" (Prov. vi. 23).

The expiation of sins.

fol. 5 b.

A *Tannā* taught in the presence of R. Joḥanan: Whoever occupies himself with *Tōrāh* and benevolent acts, or who buries his children, all his sins are forgiven him. R. Joḥanan said to him: It is quite right with *Tōrāh* and benevolent acts; for it is written, "By mercy and truth iniquity is expiated" (Prov. xvi. 6)—"mercy" means benevolent acts, as it is said, "He that followeth after righteousness and mercy findeth life, prosperity and honour" (*ibid.* xxi. 21), and "truth" means *Tōrāh*, as it is said, "Buy the truth, and sell it not" (*ibid.* xxiii. 23); but how know we that this is true of one who buries his children? A certain Elder taught in the name of R. Simeon b. Joḥai[2]: It is to be derived from the occurrence of the same word *'āwōn* "iniquity" in the following passages: "By mercy and truth *iniquity* is expiated" (*ibid.* xvi. 6) and "Who recompensest the *iniquity* of the fathers into the bosom of their children" (Jer. xxxii. 18)[3].

Plagues and childlessness not chastenings of love.

R. Joḥanan said: Plagues and childlessness are not to be considered chastenings of love. Are not plagues to be so considered? Lo, there is a teaching: Whoever is afflicted with any of four plague-symptoms[4] is to regard them as nothing but an altar of atonement[5]! Yes, they may be considered an altar of atonement, but not chastenings of love. Or if thou wilt, I can say this is our teaching and that is theirs[6]. Or if thou wilt, I can say the

[1] The word for "instruction," *mūsār*, comes from the same root as *jisūr* "suffering." "The way of life" is referred to the life eternal.

[2] *M.*: A certain Elder of the school of R. Simeon b. Joḥai taught.

[3] On this mode of reasoning, see p. 18 n. 5. The early death of children is declared to be due to the wrongdoing of the parents, and the pain of their bereavement brings expiation.

[4] Enumerated in *Mishnāh* N^e^gā'īm i. 1.

[5] A medium of expiation.

[6] Declining to draw the fine distinction between "an altar of atonement" and "chastenings of love," an alternative answer is suggested, viz. "our," i.e. the teaching of the Babylonian Schools regards plagues as "chastenings of love," because a more lenient view was taken of them than by the Palestinian Schools, to which R. Joḥanan belonged. In Palestine, a plague-infected person had to be isolated outside the city (cf. Lev. xiii. 46), and therefore the consequences were too severe for the plague to be regarded as "chastenings of love."

latter teaching refers to when the plague affects a hidden part of the body and the other to the case where an exposed part is affected[1]. Is not childlessness to be considered [chastenings of love]? What is meant [by childlessness]? Is it to be supposed to refer to a man who had children but they died? Lo, R. Joḥanan himself said, "This is the bone of my tenth son[2]!" Nay, the latter teaching refers to one who never had children, the other to one who has been bereft of his children.

R. Joḥanan visits R. Ḥiyya b. Abba in illness and heals him.

R. Ḥiyya b. Abba was ill and R. Joḥanan went in to visit him. He said to him, "Are thy sufferings dear to thee?" "No," he replied, "neither they nor the reward they bring." R. Joḥanan said to him, "Give me thy hand." He gave him his hand and R. Joḥanan raised him[3].

R. Ḥannina acts likewise towards R. Joḥanan.

R. Joḥanan was ill and R. Ḥannina went in to visit him. He said to him, "Are thy sufferings dear to thee?" "No," he replied, "neither they nor the reward they bring." R. Ḥannina said to him, "Give me thy hand." He gave him his hand and R. Ḥannina raised him. Why did not R. Joḥanan raise himself? They answer: A prisoner does not release himself from the dungeon.

R. Joḥanan and R. Eleazar.

R. Eleazar[4] was ill and R. Joḥanan went in to visit him. He saw that he was lying in a dark room, so he bared his arm and a brightness was radiated therefrom[5]. He then noticed that R. Eleazar was weeping. He said to him, "Why weepest thou? Is it because thou hast not applied thyself sufficiently to the study of *Tōrāh*? We have learnt that it matters not whether one does much or little, so long as he directs his heart to Heaven! Is it because of [the lack of] food[6]? Not everyone has the merit of two tables[7]! Is it because of childlessness? This is the bone of my

[1] When the plague affects a part of the body which is normally covered by clothing, it may be regarded as "an altar of atonement"; but when in addition to discomfort there is disfigurement visible to all, the teaching of R. Joḥanan applies.

[2] By "bone" the commentators understand a tooth. Ten children of R. Joḥanan died, and he preserved a tooth of the last to show to people who had suffered bereavement, for the purpose of inducing them to evidence the same spirit of resignation as himself. Consequently it would seem that R. Joḥanan regarded the loss of children, but not sterility, as "chastenings of love."

[3] Cured him of his ailment by the healing touch. Cf. *T. A.* I. p. 267.

[4] So *M.* correctly. Edd.: Eliezer.

[5] R. Joḥanan was famed for the beauty of his person. Cf. Bābā Mᵉṣīa' 84 a.

[6] R. Eleazar was very poor, as may be inferred from the mention of the dark room in which he was lying. See p. 3 n. 6.

[7] To enjoy prosperity in this world and the bliss of the hereafter.

tenth son!" R. Eleazar answered him, "I weep because of this beauty[1] which will decay in the earth." R. Joḥanan said to him, "Well dost thou weep on that account"; and they both wept. After a while, he said to him, "Are thy sufferings dear to thee?" He replied, "Neither they nor the reward they bring." He said to him, "Give me thy hand." He gave him his hand and R. Joḥanan raised him.

Rab Huna and the Rabbis.

It happened to Rab Huna that four hundred flasks of wine turned sour. There visited him Rab Judah the brother of Rab Sala Ḥasida and other Rabbis. (Another version: Rab Adda b. Ahaba and other Rabbis.) They said to him, "The master[2] should look into his actions[3]." He answered them, "Have I aroused suspicion in your eyes?" They retorted, "Is the Holy One, blessed be He, to be suspected of passing an unjust judgment?" He said to them, "If there be anyone who has heard aught against me, let him speak out." They replied, "Thus have we heard, that our master has not given the vine-tendrils to his labourer[4]." He said to them, "Has he left me any of them? He has stolen the lot!" They replied, "That is what the proverb tells: 'Steal from a thief and thou also hast a taste of it'[5]." He said to them, "I undertake to give him what is due." Some declare that thereupon the vinegar turned back into wine, but others say that vinegar became very dear and was sold at the price of wine.

***Abbā* Benjamin's acts of piety.**

There is a teaching: *Abbā* Benjamin said: Throughout my life I was most anxious about two things, viz., that my *Tefillāh* should be recited before my bed, and that my bed should be placed between North and South. "That my *Tefillāh* should be recited before my bed." What means "before my bed"? Is it to be supposed that it was actually in front of the bed? But Rab Judah has said in the name of Rab (another version: R. Joshua b. Levi)[6]: Whence do we learn that when one prays, there should be nothing intervening between him and the wall? As it is said, "Then Hezekiah turned his face to the wall and prayed" (Is. xxxviii.

[1] The beautiful person of R. Joḥanan. [2] See p. 43 n. 5.

[3] The misfortune that had befallen him must be due to some wrong he had done.

[4] The law allowed the labourer a proportion of the wine and also of the vine-cuttings.

[5] To rob even a thief is also stealing.

[6] *M.* adds: Another version: it was taught in a tradition: *Abbā* Benjamin says.

2)[1]! Do not read "before my bed" but "near my bed[2]." "And that my bed should be placed between North and South[3]"; for R. Ḥamma b. R. Ḥannina said in the name of[4] R. Isaac: Whoever places his bed between North and South will have male children[5] born to him; as it is said, "And whose belly Thou fillest with Thy treasure[6], who have *sons* in plenty" (Ps. xvii. 14). Rab Naḥman b. Isaac said: Also, his wife will not miscarry; for it is here written, "Thou *fillest* with Thy treasure," and elsewhere it is written, "And when her days to be delivered were *fulfilled*, behold, there were twins in her womb" (Gen. xxv. 24).

One must not leave the Synagogue without his companion.

There is a teaching: *Abbā* Benjamin said: Should two enter a Synagogue[7] to pray, and one of them finishing before the other does not wait for him but goes out, his prayer is torn in his face; as it is said, "Thou tearest thy soul[8] in thine anger, shall the earth be forsaken for thee?" (Job xviii. 4). More than that, he causes the *Sh^e^kīnāh* to depart from Israel; as it is said, "Shall the Rock be removed out of its place?" (*ibid.*) "Rock" means nothing else than the Holy One, blessed be He; as it is said, "Of the Rock that begat thee thou wast unmindful" (Deut. xxxii. 18)[9].

fol. 6 a. Should he, however, wait for him, what is his reward? R. Josē b. Ḥannina answered: He is worthy of the following blessings; as it is said, "Oh that thou wouldst hearken to My command-

[1] If *Abbā* Benjamin prayed "before his bed" in this sense, he acted contrary to the quoted teaching. The reason why it is recommended to face the wall with nothing intervening is to avoid distraction.

[2] He used the word "before" in the sense of time, not place. Immediately on rising, he offered his prayers.

[3] To avoid facing East, the direction of the Temple and of prayer.

[4] Instead of "in the name of," *M.* reads: Another version.

[5] It is well known that, in the Orient, males are more valued than females. Lane, p. 58, mentions that Muhammadan women often dress their boys as girls when taking them into the street so that envious glances be not cast upon them and to avert the Evil Eye. See also Frazer, *Folklore of the Old Testament*, I. p. 550 and *T. A.* II. p. 434 n. 89.

[6] The word for "treasure" is *ṣāfūn*, and by the change of a vowel, *ṣāfōn*, we get the meaning "North." Cf. also fol. 61 *b*, where it is forbidden to perform the functions of nature towards East or West, to prevent the exposure of the body in the direction of the Temple.

[7] "A Synagogue" does not occur in edd., but is added by *M.*

[8] "Soul" is here used in the sense of the outpouring of the soul, prayer. The commentators compare I Sam. i. 15.

[9] Synagogues in Babylon were usually situated in a field, near a river, at some distance from the town. See *J. E.* XI. p. 623, Schürer, II. ii. p. 69. It was because of the danger of being attacked by footpads if alone that this regulation was made.

ments! Then would thy peace be as a river, and thy righteousness as the waves of the sea; thy seed also would be as the sand, and the offspring of thy body like the grains thereof; his name would not be cut off nor destroyed from before Me" (Is. xlviii. 18 f.).

The human being surrounded by evil spirits.

There is a teaching: *Abbā* Benjamin said: Had the human eye been given the power of seeing them, no person could endure because of the evil spirits. Abbai[1] said: They outnumber us, and surround us like the ridge round a field. Rab Huna said: Every one of us has a thousand on his left hand and myriads on his right[2]. Raba[3] said: The crush at the public discourses[4] is due to them; the knees grow fatigued because of them; the wearing out of the clothes of the Rabbis is the consequence of their rubbing against them; the feet are bruised by them.

How to detect their footprints.

Who wishes to perceive their footprints[5] should take sifted ashes and sprinkle them around his bed. In the morning he will see something resembling the footprints of a cock[6].

How to see them.

Who wishes to see them should take the after-birth of a black she-cat[7], the offspring of a black she-cat, the first-born of a first-born, roast it in the fire, pulverise it, then fill his eyes with it, and he will see them. He must pour the powder into an iron tube and seal it with an iron signet, lest the evil spirits steal it. He must also seal its mouth, lest he come to harm. Rab Bebai b. Abbai did this; he saw the evil spirits and was injured. The Rabbis prayed for him and he was cured.

[1] *M.*: Rab Joseph. [2] Cf. Mark v. 9. [3] *M.*: Abbai.

[4] On the Sabbath, expositions of *Tōrāh* were given in the Synagogues and Houses of Study. The name given to such an assembly is *Kallāh* "the bride," because "court was paid to the *Tōrāh*, and fresh declarations of love and devotion and loyalty were made to her" (Schechter, *Seminary Addresses*, p. 54). Wünsche (p. 12 n. 2) considers that the name is connected with the Sabbath, the day on which the gathering was held, the Sabbath being frequently referred to as a bride (cf. Singer, p. 111 bot.). The word has also been connected with σχολή, *schola*, with elision of the first letter. Other suggested explanations are given by Abrahams, p. clix. For a description of the *Kallāh*, see *J. E.* I. pp. 146 f. Although the hall was not overcrowded, yet the audience would feel crushed. This was due to the evil spirits who wished to make them uncomfortable and induce people to stay away.

[5] So *M.* Edd.: Who wishes to know them.

[6] Orientals regard the cock as a power of darkness, possibly because it crows in the dark. Cf. Sanh. 63 *b* where "Succoth Benoth" (II Kings xvii. 30) is identified with the hen, and "Nergal" (*ibid.*) with the cock. Note also the reference to the cock's comb on fol. 7 *a*, p. 37.

[7] Cf. R. C. Thompson, *Semitic Magic*, p. 61, "The ashes of a black cat are a popular form of magician's stock-in-trade in the modern Arabic books of sorcery."

Prayer heard only in Synagogue.

There is a teaching: *Abbā* Benjamin said: A man's prayer is only heard [by God] when offered in a Synagogue[1]; as it is said, "To hearken unto the song and to the prayer" (I Kings viii. 28)—where there is song, let there be prayer.

The *Sh^ekīnāh* in the Synagogue, Court of Justice and Study-circle.

Rabin b. Adda said in the name of R. Isaac: Whence is it that the Holy One, blessed be He, is found in the Synagogue? As it is said, "God standeth in the godly congregation" (Ps. lxxxii. 1). And whence is it that when ten assemble for prayer, the *Sh^ekīnāh* is in their midst? As it is said, "God standeth in the godly congregation[2]." And whence is it that when three sit and judge, the *Sh^ekīnāh* is in their midst? As it is said, "In the midst of the judges[3] He judgeth" (*ibid.*). And whence is it that when two sit and occupy themselves with *Tōrāh*, the *Sh^ekīnāh* is in their midst? As it is said, "Then they that feared the Lord spoke one with another[4]; and the Lord hearkened and heard, and a book of remembrance was written before Him for them that feared the Lord and that thought upon His name" (Mal. iii. 16). What means "and that *thought* upon His name"? Rab Assi[5] said: If a man contemplated fulfilling a commandment, and through compulsion did not perform it, the verse ascribes it to him as though he had done it. And whence is it that even if an individual sits and occupies himself with *Tōrāh*, the *Sh^ekīnāh* is with him? As it is said, "In every place where I cause My name to be remembered I will come unto thee and will bless thee" (Exod. xx. 24).

Some questions answered.

Since [the *Sh^ekīnāh* is] even with one, why mention two? With two, their words are written in the book of remembrance, but the words of an individual are not so recorded. Since [the *Sh^ekīnāh* is] even with two, why mention three? Thou mightest argue that since the act of judging is merely for the sake of peace[6], the *Sh^ekīnāh* does not come [in their midst], therefore he informs us that the administration of justice is equal to being occupied with

1 The prayer referred to here is not private devotion, but the statutory service which is congregational in character. Cf. fol. 7 *b*–8 *a*, pp. 43 f.

2 That "congregation" signifies at least ten is derived from Num. xiv. 27 where the word is applied to ten of the spies. A minimum of ten adult males is required to constitute a quorum for the Service in Synagogue. See Oesterley and Box, p. 340.

3 *Ĕlōhīm* means "God or gods" but also "judges." See Exod. xxi. 6, R.V. marg. According to Jewish law, a case was tried by at least *three* judges.

4 "One with another" denotes two; and since they are "fearers of the Lord," it is presumed their conversation would be regarding *Tōrāh*.

5 So *M.* correctly. Edd.: Rab Ashē.

6 Consequently not like occupation with *Tōrāh*.

Tōrāh. Since [the *Shkīnāh* is] even with three, why mention ten? With ten, the *Shkīnāh* precedes them[1]; with three, it waits until they are seated [to try cases].

Rab Abin b. Rab Adda said in the name of R. Isaac[2]: Whence is it that the Holy One, blessed be He, lays *Tfillīn*[3]? As it is said, "The Lord hath sworn by His right hand, and by the arm of His strength" (Is. lxii. 8). "By His right hand" means *Tōrāh*; as it is said, "At His right hand was a fiery law unto them" (Deut. xxxiii. 2); "by the arm of His strength" means *Tfillīn*, as it is said, "The Lord will give strength unto His people" (Ps. xxix. 11). But whence is it that the *Tfillīn* are a strength to Israel? As it is written, "And all the peoples of the earth shall see that the name of the Lord is called upon thee, *and they shall be afraid of thee*" (Deut. xxviii. 10); and there is a teaching: R. Eliezer the Elder says: This refers to the *Tfillīn* worn on the head[4]. God's *Tfillīn*.

Rab Naḥman b. Isaac asked Rab Ḥiyya b. Abin: What is written in the *Tfillīn* of the Lord of the Universe? He answered, "And who is like Thy people Israel, a nation one in the earth?" (I Chron. xvii. 21). Does, then, the Holy One, blessed be He, glory in the praises of Israel? Yes, for it is written, "Thou hast avouched the Lord this day" (Deut. xxvi. 17) and "The Lord hath avouched thee this day" (*ibid. v.* 18). The Holy One, blessed be He, said to Israel, "You have made Me the only object of your love[5] in the world, so I shall make you the only object of My love in the world." "You have made Me the only object of your love in the world"—as it is said, "Hear O Israel, the Lord our God, the Lord is *one*" (*ibid.* vi. 4). "I shall make you the only object of My love in the world"—as it is said, "And who is like Thy people Israel, a nation *one* in the earth?" (I Chron. xvii. 21). What they contain.

Rab Aḥa b. Raba said to Rab Ashē: This is all very well with one case of the *Tfillīn*; what, however, of the other[6]? He answered: Subject continued.

[1] To the Synagogue and does not wait until they are assembled.

[2] *M.*: in the name of Rab.

[3] See Introduction, § IV, on this paragraph.

[4] The arm-*Tfillīn* would be covered by the sleeve, but that of the head would be visible. Also, the latter is inscribed with a symbol of the divine Name; see Oesterley and Box, p. 448.

[5] So Jastrow, p. 449 *b*, correctly, and with this meaning of *ḥṭībāh* may be compared the Arabic *ḥṭb* "to ask in marriage." Goldschmidt renders, "You proclaimed Me the one Ruler in the world, so I shall proclaim you the one ruling [nation] in the world"—an improbable translation.

[6] Granted that I Chron. xvii. 21 is contained in the case worn on the arm, what is contained in the case worn on the head?

[It contains the following[1]:] "For what great nation is there," etc. (Deut. iv. 7), "And what great nation is there," etc. (*ibid. v.* 8), "Happy art thou, O Israel" etc. (*ibid.* xxxiii. 29), "Or hath God assayed to go" etc. (*ibid.* iv. 34), and "To make thee high above all nations" etc. (*ibid.* xxvi. 19). If so, it will have too many partitions[2]! Nay, "For what great nation is there" and "And what great nation is there," which are very similar, are in one partition; "Happy art thou, O Israel" and "Who is like Thy people Israel" in one; "Or hath God assayed to go" in one; and "To make thee high above all nations" in one[3].

fol. 6 b. On regular attendance at Synagogue.

Rabin b. Rab Adda said in the name of R. Isaac: If one is accustomed to attend the Synagogue regularly and absents himself one day, the Holy One, blessed be He, makes inquiry about him; as it is said, "Who is among you that feareth the Lord, that obeyeth the voice of His servant, that walketh in darkness and hath no light?" (Is. l. 10). If [his absence is because] he went to perform a religious duty, he will have light; but if he went to attend to some secular business, he will have no light. "Let him trust in the name of the Lord" (*ibid.*). For what reason [is the light denied him][4]? Because he should have trusted in the name of the Lord, but did not[5].

God angry at absence of quorum.

R. Joḥanan said: When the Holy One, blessed be He, enters a Synagogue and does not find there ten[6], He is immediately filled with wrath; as it is said, "Wherefore, when I came, was there no man? When I called, was there none to answer?" (*ibid. v.* 2)[7].

One should fix a place for prayer.

R. Ḥelbo said in the name of Rab Huna: Whoever fixes a place for his prayer has the God of Abraham for his help; and on his death, it is said of him, "Where is the humble and pious man,

[1] In addition to I Chron. xvii. 21 which is included in both cases.

[2] The case of the head-*Tᵉfillīn* consists of *four* partitions, in each of which is a strip of parchment containing a prescribed Scriptural passage. But here Rab Ashē enumerates *six* passages!

[3] Edd. add: and all these verses are written in [the *Tᵉfillīn* of] His arm. The words are omitted in *M.* and read like a marginal note inserted unnecessarily into the text.

[4] The words "is the light denied him" do not occur in edd., but are added by *M.*

[5] He should not allow his private concerns, i.e. probably the earning of his livelihood, to interfere with his religious obligations, but should trust that God will provide. Cf. Matt. vi. 34.

[6] See p. 28 n. 2.

[7] When there is no quorum in the Synagogue, certain parts of the Service, including important responses (cf. "none to *answer*") for the Congregation, are omitted. See Oesterley and Box, p. 344.

of the disciples of our father Abraham!" Whence do we learn that our father Abraham fixed a place for his prayer? For it is written, "And Abraham got up early in the morning to the place where he had stood" (Gen. xix. 27). "Stood" means nothing else than prayer; as it is said, "Then stood up Phineas and prayed" (Ps. cvi. 30)[1].

R. Ḥelbo [also] said in the name of Rab Huna: When leaving the Synagogue, one should not take large steps[2]. Abbai said: This refers only to leaving; but to enter a Synagogue it is praiseworthy to hasten; as it is said, "Let us *eagerly* strive to know the Lord" (Hos. vi. 3). One should not hurry from the Synagogue,

R. Zera said: At first when I saw the Rabbis hastening to the study-session on the Sabbath, I thought they were desecrating the holy day[3]; but when I heard the statement of R. Tanḥum, in the name of R. Joshua b. Levi: A man should always run to hear the *Hªlākāh* discussed, even on the Sabbath, as it is said, "They shall walk after the Lord, who shall roar like a lion, for He shall roar, and the children shall come *hurriedly* from the West" (*ibid.* xi. 10), I also hastened. but may hasten to the study-session, even on the Sabbath.

R. Zera said: The merit of attending the study-session lies in hastening thereto[4]. Abbai said: The merit of attending the discourse lies in the crush[5]. Raba said: The merit of studying [*Tōrāh*] lies in the reasoning thereon[6]. Rab Pappa said: The merit of attending a house of mourning lies in maintaining silence[7]. Mar Zoṭra said: The merit of a fast consists in dispensing charity[8]. Rab Sheshet[9] said: The merit of listening to a funeral oration lies in raising [the voice in lamentation][10]. Rab Ashē[11] said: The Wherein lies the merit of certain pious acts.

[1] *Wayyᵉfallēl* ["and wrought judgment" R.V.] is taken to be identical with *wayyitpallēl* "and he prayed."

[2] It would then appear that he was eager to leave.

[3] It is forbidden to take large steps on the Sabbath; cf. Shab. 113 *b*.

[4] Thus showing eagerness for the *Tōrāh*.

[5] Although one may not be sufficiently learned to understand the address given in the Synagogue or House of Study, yet one can acquire merit by hastening thereto and enduring the discomfort of the crush.

[6] It was meritorious to reason about the *Tōrāh* and discover therein new teachings. See Introduction, § v.

[7] Silent sympathy is better than profuse words of consolation. Cf. Job ii. 13.

[8] "The giving of charity on fast days was much encouraged," Oesterley and Box, p. 434.

[9] *M.*: Ashē.

[10] The funeral oration was an address in honour of the deceased, and the heirs could be compelled to defray the cost of hiring an orator for the purpose. Loud wailing was also a feature of funerals in the Orient. See *J.E.* v. p. 529, Lane, Chap. XXVIII, *T. A.* ɪɪ. pp. 68 ff.

[11] *M.*: Rabina.

merit of attending a wedding lies in addressing words [of felicitation to the bride and bridegroom].

Forbidden to pray at the rear of a Synagogue.

Rab Huna said[1]: Whoever prays at the rear of a Synagogue is called wicked; as it is said, "The wicked walk on every side" (Ps. xii. 9). Abbai said: This applies only to one who does not turn his face towards the Synagogue[2]; but if he does that, we can have no objection. Once a man prayed at the rear of a Synagogue and did not turn his face in its direction. Elijah passed by, and seeing him thought that he was an Arab[3]. He said to him, "With thy back [to the Synagogue][4] standest thou before thy Master?" And drawing his sword, he slew him.

Ps. xii. 9 expounded.

One of the Rabbis said to Rab Bebai b. Abbai (another version: Rab Bebai said to Rab Naḥman b. Isaac)[5]: What means, "When vileness is exalted [*kerūm*] among the sons of men" (*ibid.*)? He answered: This refers to the things that stand in the height [*rūm*] of the world[6] which are despised by men. R. Joḥanan and R. Eleazar [offer another explanation]. They both say: As soon as a man stands in need of the help of his fellow-creatures, his face changes like a *Kerūm*; as it is said, "*Kerūm* is vileness to the sons of men." What is *Kerūm*? When Rab Dimai came [from Palestine] he said[7], "There is a bird in the coast-towns[8] called *Kerūm*[9], and when the sun shines, it changes into many colours." R. Ammi and R. Assi both say: [The man who needs help from his fellow-creatures] is as though he were sentenced to two penalties,

[1] *M.* adds: in the name of R. Ḥelbo.

[2] Wiesner, p. 18, finds here an attack on sun-worshippers (cf. fol. 7 *a*, p. 37). Rab Huna, being a Babylonian, the Ark in his Synagogue would be in the West (see fol. 30 *a*, p. 197); therefore to pray with the back to the Synagogue would be praying towards the rising sun. Cf. Ezek. viii. 16.

[3] In place of "Elijah...Arab," *M.* reads: An Arab saw him. On Elijah, see p. 7 n. 5.

[4] The text has כדו בר which Rashi explains to mean "as if there were two divine Powers." *M.* has בדו בר which yields no sense. Jastrow, p. 139, rightly reads as one word בדובר.

[5] *M.*: "Another version: to Rab Bebai b. Rab Naḥman." According to Hyman, I. p. 264 *b*, the correct reading is "Rab Bebai to Rab Naḥman" or "to Rab Naḥman b. Jacob."

[6] E.g. prayer which *ascends* to God.

[7] *M.* adds: R. Joḥanan said.

[8] "Coast-towns" corresponds very much with our phrase "foreign parts."

[9] The word is a transcription of χρῶμα "colour," which is used in Hebrew and Aramaic in the sense of "a precious stone of reddish hue"; Krauss, p. 296. Lewysohn, *Zoologie des Talmuds*, p. 183, identifies the bird with the "bird of Paradise," and compares the Spanish name for it, *pajaro del sol*.

viz., fire and water; as it is said, "Thou hast caused men to ride over our heads, we went through fire and water" (*ibid.* lxvi. 12)[1].

Importance of the afternoon prayer. R. Ḥelbo also said in the name of Rab Huna: A man should always be careful with the afternoon prayer, for behold, Elijah was only answered in the afternoon[2] prayer; as it is said, "And it came to pass at the time of the offering of the afternoon offering, that Elijah the prophet came near and said, O Lord, the God of Abraham....Hear me, O Lord, hear me" (I Kings xviii. 36 f.). The first "Hear me" means: that fire may descend from heaven; the second "hear me" means: that they may not say it is due to sorcery.

Importance of evening prayer. R. Joḥanan[3] said: Also with the evening prayer [must a man be careful]; as it is said, "Let my prayer be set forth as incense before Thee, the lifting up of my hands as the evening sacrifice" (Ps. cxli. 2).

Importance of morning prayer. Rab Naḥman b. Isaac said: Also with the morning prayer [must a man be careful]; as it is said, "O Lord, in the morning shalt Thou hear my voice; in the morning will I order my prayer unto Thee, and will look forward" (*ibid.* v. 4).

One must felicitate a bridegroom. R. Ḥelbo also said in the name of Rab Huna: Whoever partakes of the festivity of a bridegroom without felicitating him transgresses the five "voices"; as it is said, "The voice of joy and the voice of gladness, the voice of the bridegroom and the voice of the bride, the voice of them that say, Give thanks to the Lord of Hosts" (Jer. xxxiii. 11). If he does felicitate him, what is his reward? R. Joshua b. Levi said: He is worthy of *Tōrāh* which was given amidst five "voices"; as it is said, "And it came to pass on the third day, when it was morning, that there were thunders[4] and lightnings and a thick cloud upon the mount, and the voice of a horn exceeding loud...and when the voice of the horn waxed louder and louder, Moses spoke, and God answered him by a voice" (Exod. xix. 16 ff.). But it is not so; for it is

[1] The Grace after meals includes the petition, "We beseech Thee, O Lord our God, let us not be in need either of the gifts of flesh and blood or of their loans, but only of Thy helping hand,...so that we may not be ashamed nor confounded for ever and ever" (Singer, p. 281). Cf. "Make thy Sabbath [table] like that of a week-day, but be not dependent upon others" (Shab. 118*a*); and "Flay a carcase in the street and earn a living, and say not, I am a great man and the work is beneath my dignity" (Pᵉsāḥ. 113 *a*).

[2] R.V. "evening"; but the *Minḥāh* was brought in the afternoon. See Schürer, II. i. pp. 286 f.

[3] *M.*: Nathan. Another reading is Jonathan.

[4] *Lit.* "voices," and the plural, when not otherwise specified, means two.

written, "And all the people perceived the thunderings" (Exod. xx. 18)[1]! The "voices" referred to are those before the giving of the *Tōrāh*. R. Abbahu said: [If he felicitates the bridegroom] it is as though he had brought a thanksgiving offering; as it is said, "Even of them that bring offerings of thanksgiving into the house of the Lord" (Jer. *l.c.*). Rab Naḥman b. Isaac said: It is as though he had rebuilt one of the ruins of Jerusalem; as it is said, "For I will cause the captivity of the land to return as at the first, saith the Lord" (*ibid.*).

Prayer of God-fearing man heard.

R. Ḥelbo also said in the name of Rab Huna: Every man in whom is the fear of God, his words are heard; as it is said, "The end of the matter, all having been heard, fear God, and keep His commandments, for this is the whole man" (Eccles. xii. 13). What means "for this is the whole man"? R. Eleazar[2] answered: The Holy One, blessed be He, said, The whole universe was only created for his sake. R. Abba b. Kahana said: Such a man is equal in worth to the whole world. R. Simeon b. 'Azzai (another version: R. Simeon b. Zoma) said: The whole world has only been created to be subservient[3] to him.

On greeting a fellow-man.

R. Ḥelbo also said in the name of Rab Huna: Whoever is in the habit of greeting his neighbour, and omits to do so a single day, transgresses the injunction "Seek peace and pursue it" (Ps. xxxiv. 15)[4]. Should his neighbour greet him and he does not respond, he is called a robber; as it is said, "It is ye that have eaten up the vineyard; the spoil of the poor is in your houses" (Is. iii. 14).

fol. 7 a. God's prayer.

R. Joḥanan said in the name of R. Josē[5]: Whence is it that the Holy One, blessed be He, prays[6]? As it is said, "Even them will I bring to My holy mountain, and make them joyful in My house of prayer [*lit.* the house of My prayer]" (*ibid.* lvi. 7). It is not said "their prayer" but "My prayer"; hence we infer that the Holy One, blessed be He, prays. What does He pray? Rab Zoṭra b. Ṭobiah said in the name of Rab: "May it be My will

[1] Add these "thunderings" (*lit.* "voices") and we have seven, not five!

[2] The parallel passage in Shab. 30 *b* reads Eliezer.

[3] Reading לצבות "to be subservient" in place of the unintelligible לצוות. See Jastrow, p. 1260.

[4] The reading of *M.* is adopted in preference to edd.: "Whoever knows that his neighbour is in the habit of greeting him should greet him first; as it is said, 'Seek peace and pursue it'." "To greet" is literally "to give peace," the form of salutation being "Peace upon you."

[5] According to Hyman, II. p. 722 *b*, we should read Josē b. Zimra.

[6] See Introduction, § IV, and also Abelson, *Immanence of God*, p. 70 note.

that My mercy may subdue My wrath; and may My mercy prevail over My attributes[1], so that I may deal with My children in the quality of mercy and enter on their behalf within the line of strict justice."

R. Ishmael b. Elisha's experience in the Temple.

There is a teaching: R. Ishmael b. Elisha said: Once I entered [the Holy of Holies][2] to offer incense in the innermost part of the Sanctuary, and I saw Okteriēl[3], Jah, the Lord of Hosts, seated upon a high and exalted throne. He said to me, "Ishmael, My son, bless Me." I replied, "May it be Thy will that Thy mercy may subdue Thy wrath; and may Thy mercy prevail over Thy attributes, so that Thou mayest deal with Thy children in the quality of mercy and enter on their behalf within the line of strict justice." And He nodded His head towards me[4]. We are thus informed that the blessing of a common person should not be esteemed lightly in thine eyes[5].

Not to appease a wrathful man.

R. Joḥanan also said in the name of R. Josē: Whence is it that we should not try to appease a man in the time of his wrath[6]? As it is written, "My face shall go[7] and I will give thee rest" (Exod. xxxiii. 14). The Holy One, blessed be He, said to Moses, "Wait for Me until My wrathful countenance shall have passed away, then I will give thee rest."

The Divine wrath: its duration.

Is there ever anger before the Holy One, blessed be He? Yes; as there is a teaching: "A God that hath indignation every day" (Ps. vii. 12). But how long does His anger last? A moment.

[1] Of justice.

[2] "The Holy of Holies" added by *M*. According to the Jewish sources, he was one of the last of the High Priests and suffered martyrdom (see fol. 57 *b*) with Rabban Simeon b. Gamaliel the Elder. He is accordingly identified by some with Ishmael b. Phabi who held the Office about 60 C.E. This identification, however, is very uncertain, and there are scholars who doubt whether there was a High Priest of that name. They think that the person referred to here is the *Tannā* Ishmael, who was the son of a High Priest, and that the theosophical passages where he is mentioned (see fol. 51 *a*) are later legendary additions to the Talmūd. See *A. T.* I. pp. 259–263.

[3] A divine appellation usually explained as a combination of *kĕter* "throne" and *ēl* "God." Schorr (quoted by Goldschmidt) connects it with ὀχθηρός, Heb. עליון "Most High."

[4] See p. 8 n. 5.

[5] Since God asked for the blessing of a mortal. An instance of the doctrine of *Imitatio Dei*; see Introduction, § IV.

[6] Cf. "R. Simeon b. Eleazar said: Do not appease thy fellow in the hour of his anger, and comfort him not in the hour when his dead lies before him, and question him not in the hour of his vow, and strive not to see him in the hour of his disgrace." Ābōt iv. 23, Singer, pp. 197 f.

[7] So the Hebrew literally.

And how long is a moment? A moment is one 58,888th[1] part of an hour; and nobody has ever been able to fix upon just that moment with the exception of the wicked Balaam, of whom it is written, "He knoweth the knowledge of the Most High" (Num. xxiv. 16).

Balaam and the wrath of God.

Was Balaam, then, ignorant of the mind of his ass, and yet acquainted with the knowledge of the Most High? Nay; it teaches that he knew how to fix upon that moment in which the Holy One, blessed be He, is wrathful. This is the intention of the statement which the prophet made to Israel: "O My people, remember now what Balak king of Moab devised, and what Balaam the son of Beor answered him...that ye may know the righteous acts of the Lord" (Micah vi. 5). What means "that ye may know the righteous acts of the Lord"? R. Eleazar answered: The Holy One, blessed be He, said to Israel, "Know ye how many are the righteous acts which I have wrought on your behalf, that I was not wrathful in the days of the wicked Balaam; for had I been wrathful, there would not have been left any remnant of the enemies of Israel[2]." That is the meaning of what Balaam said to Balak, "How shall I curse, whom God hath not cursed? And how shall I execrate, whom the Lord hath not execrated?" (Num. xxiii. 8). This teaches that during all those days He did not execrate.

The Divine execration.

How long does His execration last? A moment. And how long is a moment? R. Abin (another version: R. Abina) said: The moment lasts as long as it takes to utter the word. Whence do we know that He is angry but for a moment? As it is said, "For His anger is but for a moment, His favour is for a life-time" (Ps. xxx. 6). Or if thou wilt, I can say it may be deduced from the following: "Hide thyself for a moment until the indignation be overpast" (Is. xxvi. 20). When is God angry? Abbai said: During the first three hours of the day when the comb of the cock is white and it stands on one foot. But[3] the comb is white at all times! During the rest of the day there are many red streaks in it, but not at the afore-mentioned time.

When God is angry.

[1] The number is corrupt, and there are numerous variants ranging from 88,888 to 8,888. *J. T.* reads 56,848. The correct number is 82,080; see Brodetsky in *J. R.* II. p. 173.

[2] Euphemism for Israel.

[3] So *M.* Edd.: But it stands on one foot at all times! During the rest of the day, it has red streaks [in its white comb], but not during the afore-mentioned hours.

A certain *Mīn*[1], who lived in the neighbourhood of R. Joshua b. Levi, used to plague him with questions about [the interpretation of] the Scriptures. One day R. Joshua took a cock and placed it between the feet of his bed and watched [the comb] closely. His intention was to curse the heretic when the moment arrived [in which God was wrathful]; but when the moment arrived, he was sleeping. On waking up[2] he said: Learn from this that it is not proper to act thus; for it is written, "His tender mercies are over all His works" (Ps. cxlv. 9), and "To punish is also not good for the righteous" (Prov. xvii. 26).

R. Joshua b. Levi and the heretic.

It has been taught in the name of R. Meïr: At the hour when the sun shines forth and all the kings of the East and West place their crowns upon their heads and worship it, at once the Holy One, blessed be He, is filled with wrath.

God angry when sun is worshipped.

Further said R. Joḥanan in the name of R. Josē: One chastisement in the heart of a man[3] is better than many lashes; as it is said, "And she shall run after her lovers, but she shall not overtake them, and she shall seek them, but shall not find them; then shall she say [in her heart], I will go and return to my first husband; for then was it better with me than now" (Hos. ii. 9). R. Simeon b. Laḳish said: It is better than a hundred lashes; as it is said, "A rebuke entereth deeper into a man of understanding than a hundred stripes into a fool" (Prov. xvii. 10).

Rebuke more effective than a blow.

R. Joḥanan also said in the name of R. Josē: Three things Moses sought of the Holy One, blessed be He, and He granted them. He sought that the *Shᵉkīnāh* should rest upon Israel, and He granted it; as it is said, "Is it not in that Thou goest with us?" (Exod. xxxiii. 16). He sought that the *Shᵉkīnāh* should not rest upon the other peoples of the world[4], and He granted it; as it is said, "So that we are distinguished, I and Thy people" (*ibid.*). He sought that God should show him His ways, and He granted it; as it is said, "Show me now Thy ways" (*ibid. v.* 13).

Three requests of Moses granted.

[1] Edd.: Sadducee; an alteration to satisfy the scruples of the mediaeval Censor who regarded every reference to the *Mīn* as an attack on Christianity.

[2] "On waking up" occurs in *M.* but is wanting in edd.

[3] I.e. self-reproach.

[4] This is the reading of *M.* and the earliest edd. Subsequently it was altered to "that the *Shᵉkīnāh* should rest only upon Israel" for fear of the Censor. Bacher detects in the words a polemic against the aspirations of Christianity; *A. T.* II. p. 179, n. 8.

His question about the Divine scheme of reward and punishment.

Moses said before Him[1], "Lord of the Universe, why is there a righteous man enjoying prosperity and a righteous man afflicted with adversity? Why is there a wicked man enjoying prosperity and a wicked man afflicted with adversity?" He answered him, "Moses, the righteous man who enjoys prosperity is the son of a righteous father; the righteous man who is afflicted with adversity is the son of a wicked father; the wicked man who enjoys prosperity is the son of a righteous father; the wicked man who is afflicted with adversity is the son of a wicked father."

A criticism of the answer.

The teacher stated above: "The righteous man who enjoys prosperity is the son of a righteous father; the righteous man who is afflicted with adversity is the son of a wicked father." But it is not so; for lo, it is written, "Visiting the iniquity of the fathers upon the children" (Exod. xxxiv. 7) and it is also written, "The children shall not be put to death for the fathers" (Deut. xxiv. 16)! We set these verses one against the other and conclude there is no contradiction; because the former passage refers to those children who continue in their fathers' ways[2], and the latter to those who do not continue in their fathers' ways. But [we may suppose that] God answered Moses thuswise, "The righteous man who enjoys prosperity is perfectly righteous; the righteous man who is afflicted with adversity is not perfectly righteous; the wicked man who enjoys prosperity is not perfectly wicked; the wicked man who is afflicted with adversity is perfectly wicked[3]."

R. Meïr teaches that God did not enlighten Moses on this problem.

This[4] is opposed to the teaching of R. Meïr; for R. Meïr said that God granted two of Moses' requests and refused one. As it is said, "I will be gracious to whom I will be gracious" (Exod. xxxiii. 19), i.e. although he may not be deserving; "And I will show mercy on whom I will show mercy" (*ibid.*), i.e. although he may not be deserving[5].

Moses' wish to see God's face.

"And He said, Thou canst not see My face" (*ibid. v.* 20). It has been taught in the name of R. Joshua b. Ḳarḥah: Thus spake the Holy One, blessed be He, to Moses, "When I was willing

[1] What follows is the purport of Moses' request, "Show me now Thy ways."

[2] *Lit.* hold the deed of their fathers in their hands.

[3] Against this attempt to solve the problem, cf. "R. Jannai said: It is not in our power to explain either the prosperity of the wicked or the afflictions of the righteous"; Ābōt iv. 19, Singer, p. 197.

[4] R. Josē's statement that God granted the *three* requests of Moses.

[5] The third request "to know God's ways," according to R. Meïr, remained unanswered, Exod. xxxiii. 19 teaching that prosperity and its opposite are solely dependent upon the will of God.

[that thou shouldest see My face] thou wert not willing[1]; so now that thou art willing, I am not willing." This disagrees with the teaching of R. Samuel b. Naḥmani in the name of R. Jonathan[2], viz. By virtue of three [meritorious acts] Moses became worthy of three [favours]. By virtue of "Moses hid his face" (Exod. iii. 6), he was granted the shining of his countenance (cf. *ibid.* xxxiv. 29 f.). By virtue of "For he was *afraid*" (*ibid.* iii. 6), he merited "And they were *afraid* to come nigh him" (*ibid.* xxxiv. 30). By virtue of "[He was afraid] to *behold* God" (*ibid.* iii. 6), he merited "The similitude of the Lord doth he *behold*" (Num. xii. 8).

Explanation of God's "back."

"And I will take away My hand, and thou shalt see My back" (Exod. xxxiii. 23). Rab Ḥanna[3] b. Bizna said in the name of R. Simeon Ḥasida: This teaches that the Holy One, blessed be He, showed Moses the knot of the *Tefillīn*[4].

God never retracts a propitious utterance.

R. Joḥanan also said in the name of R. Josē: Any propitious utterance which issues from the mouth of the Holy One, blessed be He, though it be conditional, He does not retract [though the condition be not fulfilled]. Whence do we learn this? From Moses our teacher; as it is said, "Let Me alone, that I may destroy them, and blot out their name from under heaven; and I will make of thee a nation mightier and greater than they" (Deut. ix. 14). Although Moses supplicated God against this decree and averted it, nevertheless He fulfilled [the blessing contained therein] in his seed; as it is said, "The sons of Moses: Gershom and Eliezer" (I Chron. xxiii. 15), and then "And the sons of Eliezer were: Rehabiah the chief. And Eliezer had no other sons; but the sons of Rehabiah were very [*lema'alāh*] many" (*ibid.* v. 17). On this Rab Joseph taught: They were upwards of [*lema'alāh*] sixty myriads. One draws an analogy from the occurrence of the word *rābāh* "many" in the following passages: here it is written, "they were very many," and elsewhere it is written, "And the children of Israel were fruitful, and increased abundantly, and became very many" (Exod. i. 7)[5].

[1] At the burning bush where Moses hid his face: Exod. iii. 6.

[2] These Rabbis explain the act of "hiding the face" as meriting reward not punishment.

[3] *M.*: Ḥannina; but this is doubtful. There is another variant: Huna. See *D. S. ad loc.*

[4] What feature in the "back" of God had an interest for Moses? This could only be the peculiar shape of the knot of the head-*Tefillīn* which resembles the Hebrew letter *dālet* or *mēm*.

[5] According to Exod. xii. 37 the number of Israelites who left Egypt was 600,000. This number is described as "many," the same term being applied

Abraham the first to call God "Lord."

R. Joḥanan said in the name of R. Simeon b. Joḥai: From the day that the Holy One, blessed be He, created the Universe, nobody called Him "Lord[1]" until Abraham came and so called Him; as it is said, "And he said, O Lord God, whereby shall I know that I shall inherit it?" (Gen. xv. 8). Rab said: Also, Daniel was only answered because of Abraham; as it is said, "Now therefore, O our God, hearken unto the prayer of Thy servant, and to his supplications, and cause Thy face to shine upon Thy sanctuary that is desolate, for the Lord's sake" (Dan. ix. 17). It should have read "for Thy sake"! But [he means] "for the sake of Abraham, who called Thee 'Lord'."

Do not appease a wrathful man.

R. Joḥanan also said in the name of R. Simeon b. Joḥai: Whence is it that we should not try to appease a man in the time of his wrath? As it is said, "My face shall go, and I will give thee rest" (Exod. xxxiii. 14)[2].

Leah the first to praise God.

R. Joḥanan also said in the name of R. Simeon b. Joḥai: From the day that the Holy One, blessed be He, created the Universe, nobody praised Him until Leah came and praised Him; as it is said, "This time will I praise the Lord" (Gen. xxix. 35).

Explanation of name Reuben.

"Reuben"—[what means "Reuben"][3]? R. Eleazar answered: Leah said, "See the difference-between[4] my son and the son of my father-in-law; for the son of my father-in-law, although he voluntarily sold his birthright—as it is written, 'And he sold his birthright unto Jacob' (*ibid.* xxv. 33)—see what is written of him, 'And Esau hated Jacob' (*ibid.* xxvii. 41) and 'Is not he rightly called Jacob? for he hath supplanted me these two times' (*ibid.* v. 36). But as for my son, although Joseph forcibly deprived him of his birthright—as it is written, 'But, forasmuch as he defiled his father's couch, his birthright was given unto the sons of[5] Joseph' (I Chron. v. 1)[6]—nevertheless he was not jealous of him; for it is written, 'And Reuben heard it, and delivered him out of their hand' (Gen. xxxvii. 21)."

to the descendants of *one* of Moses' sons. Hence a greater nation issued from Moses, although God's promise was conditional on the destruction of Israel, a threat which was not carried out.

[1] I.e. *Ādōn* not *JHWH*.   [2] Cf. fol. 7 *a*, p. 35.

[3] "What means Reuben?" is wanting in edd. but occurs in *M*.

[4] The name is explained as a combination of *rᵉʾū* "see" *bēn* "between."

[5] Edd. omit "the sons of"; but *M*. adds it in agreement with the Biblical text.

[6] From the standpoint of the *Ăggādāh*, there is nothing strange in Leah quoting Chronicles. Cf. Sanh. 7 *a*, where Aaron quotes the Book of Lamentations. To the Rabbis, the Bible was an organic whole.

"Ruth"—what means "Ruth"? R. Joḥanan said: Because she was worthy that David should issue from her, who *delighted*[1] the Holy One, blessed be He, with songs and praises.

Explanation of name Ruth.

Whence do we learn that the name of a person affects his life[2]? R. Eleazar[3] said: Because the Scriptures declare, "Come, behold the works of the Lord, Who hath made *shammōt* ['desolations'] in the earth" (Ps. xlvi. 9). Read not *shammōt* but *shēmōt* "names."

Name shapes destiny.

R. Joḥanan also said in the name of R. Simeon b. Joḥai: More painful is filial impiety in a man's house than the wars of Gog and Magog[4]; as it is said, "A Psalm of David, when he fled from Absalom his son" (*ibid.* iii. 1), after which it is written, "Lord, how many are mine adversaries become! Many are they that rise up against me" (*ibid. v.* 2). But in connection with the wars of Gog and Magog it is written, "Why are the nations in an uproar? And why do the peoples mutter in vain?" (*ibid.* ii. 1); but it is not written, "How many are mine adversaries become!"

Pain of filial impiety.

"A Psalm of David, when he fled from Absalom his son" (*ibid.* iii. 1). "A *Psalm* of David"! Rather should we have expected "A *Lament* of David"! R. Simeon b. Abishalom said: A parable: To what is it like? To a man to whom it is said, "To-morrow a bill of debt will be issued against thee." Before he sees it, he worries; but having seen it, he rejoices[5]. So was it likewise with David. When the Holy One, blessed be He, said to him, "Behold, I will raise up evil against thee out of thine own house" (II Sam. xii. 11), he grieved; for he said, "Perhaps it refers to a slave or illegitimate child who will have no pity on me." When, however, he found that it was Absalom, he rejoiced; and therefore he uttered a Psalm.

Why Ps. iii is entitled "A *Psalm* of David."

R. Joḥanan also said in the name of R. Simeon b. Joḥai: It is permissible to contend with the wicked[6] in this world; as it is said,

Permissible to contend with the wicked.

[1] Ruth is here derived from the root *rāwāh* "to delight."

[2] This question is raised to anticipate the objection against the interpretations of the names Reuben and Ruth, that the name *preceded* the event which is said to explain it.

[3] Not Eliezer, as some edd. read.

[4] The wars of Gog and Magog figure prominently in Jewish Eschatology. The Messianic Era will be preceded by a final combat between Israel and the heathen nations led by Gog and Magog. See *J. E.* v. p. 212.

[5] The claim is not as heavy as he anticipated. I have adopted the reading of *M.* which is preferable to that of edd., viz.: "To a man against whom a bill for debt has been issued. Before he has settled it, he worries; but having settled it, he rejoices." The point of the comparison is the anxiety caused by uncertainty.

[6] There is probably here an allusion to the tyrannical power of Rome; see *A. T.* II. p. 12, n. 3.

"They that forsake the law praise the wicked, but such as keep the law contend with him" (Prov. xxviii. 4). There is a teaching to the same effect: R. Dostai b. R. Mattun said: It is permissible to contend with the wicked in this world; as it is said, "They that forsake the law praise the wicked," etc. Should a man try to mislead thee, saying, Lo, it is written, "Contend not with evil-doers, neither be thou envious against them that work unrighteousness" (Ps. xxxvii. 1), answer him, Only he whose conscience pricks him[1] speaks thus. Nay, "Contend not with evil-doers" means, to emulate them; "be not envious against them that work unrighteousness" means, to be like them. And so it is stated, "Let not thy heart envy sinners, but be in the fear of the Lord all the day" (Prov. xxiii. 17).

A contrary opinion.

But it is not so! For behold, R. Isaac has said: If thou seest a wicked man upon whom fortune smiles[2], do *not* contend with him; as it is said, "His ways prosper at all times" (Ps. x. 5). More than that, [if thou contendest with him] he will be justified in judgment; as it is said, "Thy judgments are far above out of his sight" (*ibid.*). More even than that, he will see his desire on his enemies[3]; as it is said, "As for his enemies, he puffeth at them" (*ibid.*)!

The contradiction removed.

There is no contradiction: R. Isaac speaks of one who is wicked in his personal affairs, the other[4] of one who is wicked in religious matters[5]. Or if thou wilt, I can say that both refer to religious matters, and still there is no contradiction; for R. Isaac may be taken to mean the wicked upon whom fortune smiles, and the other the wicked upon whom fortune does not smile. Or if thou wilt, I can say that both refer to the wicked upon whom fortune smiles, and still there is no contradiction; for R. Joḥanan may be understood as speaking of a perfectly righteous man [contending with the wicked], and the other of one who is not perfectly righteous. For Rab Huna said: What means that which is written, "Wherefore lookest Thou, when they deal treacherously, and holdest Thy peace, when the wicked swalloweth up the man that is more righteous than he"? (Hab. i. 13). Does, then, the wicked swallow up the righteous? And lo, it is written, "The Lord will not leave him in his hand" (Ps. xxxvii. 33) and "There shall no mischief befall the righteous" (Prov. xii. 21)! Nay; "the wicked swalloweth up the man that is more righteous than

[1] *Lit.* whose heart knocks him.
[2] *Lit.* the hour laughs.
[3] Although they be righteous.
[4] R. Joḥanan in the name of R. Simeon b. Joḥai.
[5] *Lit.* things of Heaven.

he," but a perfectly righteous man he doth not swallow up. Or if thou wilt, I can say that when fortune smiles upon him, it is different[1].

To fix a place for prayer brings triumph over enemies.

R. Joḥanan also said in the name of R. Simeon b. Joḥai: Whoever fixes a place for his prayer[2], his enemies fall beneath him; as it is said: "And I will appoint a place for My people Israel, and will plant them, that they may dwell in their own place, and be disquieted no more; neither shall the children of wickedness afflict them any more as at the first" (II Sam. vii. 10). Rab Huna asked: It is written here "to afflict them," but in the parallel passage (I Chron. xvii. 9) it is written "to exterminate them[3]"! The answer is: At first "to afflict them" and finally "exterminate them."

Service of *Tōrāh* greater than study.

R. Joḥanan also said in the name of R. Simeon b. Joḥai: Greater is the service of *Tōrāh*[4] than its study; as it is said, "Elisha the son of Shaphat is here, who poured water on the hands of Elijah" (II Kings iii. 11). It is not mentioned that he studied [with Elijah] but that he poured water. That teaches that its service is greater than its study.

Importance of praying with the congregation.

Rab Isaac asked Rab Naḥman, "Why does not the master[5] come to the Synagogue to pray?" He answered, "I am not able [through indisposition]." He said to him, "Then the master should gather ten together and pray [with a quorum]." He replied, "It is too great a trouble for me." "Then the master should tell the messenger of the congregation at the time when the congregation prays to come and inform him[6]." He asked him, "But why all this?" He answered, "Because R. Joḥanan said in the name of R. Simeon b. Joḥai: What means that which is written, 'But as for me, let my prayer be unto Thee, O God, in an acceptable time' (Ps. lxix. 14)? When is an 'acceptable time'? At the time when the congregation prays." R. José b. R. Ḥannina derived it from the following: "Thus saith the Lord, In an acceptable time have I answered thee" (Is. xlix. 8). R. Aḥa b. R. Ḥannina[7] derived it from the following: "Behold, God despiseth not the mighty" fol. 8 a.

1 At such a time, the wicked can swallow up even the perfectly righteous.

2 Cf. fol. 6 *b*, pp. 30 f.

3 Edd. read *lᵉkallōtō* "to exterminate them," but the Biblical text has *lᵉballōtō* "to waste them."

4 By attending upon and associating with the Rabbis.

5 It was respectful to address a person in the third person with the title "master," not in the second person.

6 So that Rab Naḥman should say his prayers simultaneously with them.

7 *M.*: Rab Naḥman b. Isaac.

(Job xxxvi. 5)[1]; and it is written, "He hath redeemed my soul in peace so that none came nigh me; for they were many with me" (Ps. lv. 19)[2]. There is a teaching to the same effect: R. Nathan said: Whence is it that the Holy One, blessed be He, does not reject the prayer offered by many[3]? As it is said, "Behold, God despiseth not the mighty"; and it is written, "He hath redeemed my soul in peace so that none came nigh me; for they were many with me." The Holy One, blessed be He, said, "Whoever occupies himself with *Tōrāh*, practises benevolent acts and prays with the congregation, I ascribe it to him as though he had redeemed Me and My son [Israel] from [exile] among the peoples of the world."

Evil not to attend the Synagogue.

R. Simeon b. Laḳish said: Whoever has a Synagogue in his town, and does not enter it to pray, is called "an evil neighbour"; as it is said, "Thus saith the Lord, As for all Mine evil neighbours, that touch the inheritance which I have caused My people Israel to inherit" (Jer. xii. 14). More than that, he causes exile to come upon himself and his sons; as it is said, "Behold, I will pluck them up from off their land, and will pluck up the house of Judah from among them" (*ibid.*).

Attendance at Synagogue prolongs life.

It was said to R. Joḥanan[4], "There are old men to be found in Babylon." He was astonished and exclaimed, "It is written 'that your days may be multiplied, and the days of your children, *upon the land*' (Deut. xi. 21); but not outside the land [of Israel]!" When they told him that [the old men] are in the Synagogue early and late, he said, "It is this which helps them [to live long]." This is like what R. Joshua b. Levi said to his sons: Rise early and stay up late to enter the Synagogue, so that you may prolong your life. R. Aḥa b. R. Ḥannina[5] asked, What is the Scriptural authority for this? "Happy is the man that hearkeneth to Me, watching daily at My gates, waiting at the posts of My doors" (Prov. viii. 34), after which it is written, "For whoso findeth me findeth life" (*ibid. v.* 35). Rab Ḥisda said: A man should always enter two doors in the Synagogue and then pray; as it is said,

[1] "The mighty" means the many assembled for prayer. This rendering of the verse is based on a slightly different reading of the Hebrew text; viz. the *wāw* of *w^e^lō'* is omitted, so that *kabbīr* is taken to be the object of the verb and not an adjective qualifying *ēl*. R.V. "Behold, God is mighty, and despiseth not any."

[2] I.e. many joining with me in prayer, and for that reason I was delivered. R.V. "for there were many [that strove] with me." The reference to Ps. lv. 19 is out of place here and has been wrongly inserted from the *Bārāitā* which follows; cf. *A. P. A.* III. p. 542, n. 5.

[3] I.e. a Congregation. [4] He was a Palestinian. [5] *M.*: R. Aḥa b. Adda.

"Waiting at the posts of My doors[1]." "Two doors" [literally], dost imagine! But say [the meaning is], A man should penetrate into the Synagogue a distance which equals the width of two doors, and then offer prayer[2].

"For this let every one that is godly pray unto Thee in the time of finding" (Ps. xxxii. 6). R. Ḥannina said: "In the time of finding" refers to [the choice of] a wife; as it is said, "Whoso findeth a wife findeth a great good" (Prov. xviii. 22). In the West[3], when a man marries, they say to him, "*Māṣā'* or *Mōṣē'*?" —*Māṣā'*, as it is written, "Whoso findeth [*māṣā'*] a wife findeth a great good"; *Mōṣē'*, as it is written, "And I find [*mōṣē'*] more bitter than death the woman" etc. (Eccles. vii. 26). Ps. xxxii. 6 applied to marriage,

R. Nathan[4] said: "In the time of finding" refers to *Tōrāh*; as it is said, "For whoso findeth me findeth life, and obtaineth favour of the Lord" (Prov. viii. 35). to *Tōrāh*,

Rab Naḥman b. Isaac said: "In the time of finding [*meṣō'*]" refers to death; as it is said, "The issues [*tōṣā'ōt*] of death" (Ps. lxviii. 21). There is a teaching to the same effect: Nine hundred and three varieties of death have been created in the world; as it is said, "The issues of death." *Tōṣā'ōt* has that numerical value[5]. The severest of them all is croup, and the lightest is the kiss of death. Croup is like a thorn in a ball of clipped wool which tears backwards[6]. Others say it is like the whirling waters at the entrance of a canal[7]. The kiss of death is like taking a hair out of milk[8]. to death,

1 "Doors"—the unspecified plural signifying two. "And then pray," etc. is added by *M.*

2 By praying near the door, he makes it appear as though he were eager to leave.

3 I.e. Palestine.

4 *M.*: Jonathan, which is probably correct; cf. *A. P. A.* I. p. 64, n. 1.

5 The Hebrew letters are also used as numbers, each having a numerical value. The word *tōṣā'ōt* [$t=400$, $o=6$, $ṣ=90$, $a=1$] totals 903. By a process known as *Gēmaṭriyyā* (Krauss, p. 171, γεωμετρία; but Jastrow, p. 239, and Bacher, *Terminologie*, I. p. 127, a transposition of γραμμάτια), words are changed into others of a similar numerical total to yield an interpretation. See *J. E.* v. p. 589.

6 When one tries to pull it out. Similarly croup tears the membranes of the throat.

7 When the sluice-bars are raised; so Jastrow. Rashi explains, "Like ropes pulled through loop-holes in the boards of a ship." Cf. *T. A.* II. p. 682, n. 234.

8 Metaphorically to describe an easy and painless process. Aaron (Num. xxxiii. 38) and Moses (Deut. xxxiv. 5), it is said, died "at the command (*lit.* mouth) of the Lord," which is explained to mean as by the divine kiss. B. Bat. 17 *a*.

to burial, R. Joḥanan said: "In the time of finding" refers to burial. R. Ḥannina[1] said: What is the Scriptural authority for this? "Who rejoice unto exultation and are glad, when they can *find* the grave" (Job iii. 22). Rabbah b. Rab Shela said: Hence the popular saying: "Let a man pray for peace even to the last shovelful of earth[2]."

to a privy. Mar Zoṭra said: "In the time of finding" refers to a privy[3]. In the West, they said that the interpretation of Mar Zotra was the best of all.

Study of *Hªlākāh* greater than service of Synagogue. Raba said to Rafram b. Pappa: Let the master tell us some of those excellent things which thou reportest in the name of Rab Ḥisda, relating to the Synagogue. He replied, Thus said Rab Ḥisda: What means that which is written, "The Lord loveth the gates of Zion [*Ṣiyyōn*] more than all the dwellings of Jacob" (Ps. lxxxvii. 2)? The Lord loveth the gates distinguished [*mᵉṣuyyānīm*] for *Hªlākāh* more than Synagogues and Houses of Study. That agrees with what R. Ḥiyya b. Ammi said in the name of 'Ulla: Since the day the Temple was destroyed, there is left to the Holy One, blessed be He, in His Universe the four cubits of *Hªlākāh* alone[4]. And Abbai said: At first I used to study at home and pray in Synagogue, but after hearing the statement of R. Ḥiyya b. Ammi in the name of 'Ulla—"Since the day the Temple was destroyed, there is left to the Holy One, blessed be He, in His Universe the four cubits of *Hªlākāh* alone"—I only pray where I study. R. Ammi and R. Assi, although there were thirteen[5] Synagogues in Tiberias[6], used to pray only between the pillars where they studied.

Dignity of labour. R. Ḥiyya b. Ammi said in the name of 'Ulla: Greater is he who enjoys the fruit of his labour than the fearer of Heaven; for with regard to the fearer of Heaven it is written, "Happy is the man that feareth the Lord" (*ibid.* cxii. 1), but with regard to him who enjoys the fruit of his labour it is written, "When thou

[1] *M.*: Ḥanin. [2] *Sc.* thrown upon his coffin.

[3] In the Babylonian towns, the privy was very rare owing, as Rashi points out, to the marshy character of the soil which caused the pits to be soon filled with water. Consequently the privies were to be found outside the city, often at a considerable distance, which was not only a great inconvenience but a danger to health. This fact had its effect on the *Hªlākāh*; and we shall find many references to it, meaningless under modern conditions, but a serious matter in ancient times.

[4] The meaning is: the study of *Tōrāh* has taken the place of the Temple Service as a medium of communion with God. So Bacher, *A. B. A.* p. 96, n. 32.

[5] *M.*: twelve. [6] A city in Galilee, on the W. shore of Lake Gennesaret.

eatest the labour of thy hands, happy shalt thou be, and it shall be well with thee" (*ibid.* cxxviii. 2)—"happy shalt thou be" in this world, "and it shall be well with thee" in the world to come[1]. It is not written, "and it shall be well with thee" about the fearer of Heaven.

Well to reside in same place as one's teacher.

R. Ḥiyya b. Ammi also said in the name of 'Ulla: A man should always reside in the same place as his teacher, for so long as Shimei the son of Gera[2] lived, Solomon did not marry the daughter of Pharaoh. But there is a teaching: A man should not reside [in the same place as his teacher]! There is no contradiction; the former referring to the pupil who submits to his master, the latter to him who does not[3].

Wrong to leave the Synagogue with Scroll unrolled.

Rab Huna b. Judah stated that R. Menaḥem said in the name of R. Ammi: What means that which is written, "They that forsake the Lord shall be consumed" (Is. i. 28)? This refers to one who leaves a Scroll of the Law [unrolled][4] and goes out [from the Synagogue]. R. Abbahu used to go out between man and man[5]. Rab Pappa asked: How is it between verse and verse—[may one go out]? The question remains [unanswered]. Rab Sheshet used to turn his face [away from the Scroll] and study, saying, "We with ours, they with theirs[6]."

The weekly lection of Pentateuch.

Rab Huna b. Judah stated that R. Menaḥem said[7] in the name of R. Ammi: A man should always finish his *Pārāshāh* with the congregation, twice the Hebrew text and once the *Targūm*[8]—

[1] The dignity of labour is a favourite theme of the Rabbis. Cf. Delitzsch, *Jewish Artisan Life*, Chap. II and my *Ancient Jewish Proverbs*, Chap. v.

[2] He is supposed to have been Solomon's tutor. The notice of his death (I Kings ii. 46) is immediately followed by the mention of Solomon's marriage with Pharaoh's daughter.

[3] The teacher would have more opportunities of noticing the conduct of his pupil and correcting him if they dwelt together. But should the pupil be unwilling to have his faults pointed out to him, it were better they lived apart.

[4] For a description of the Scroll, see Oesterley and Box, p. 338. The reference is here to the time when it is being used for the Scriptural reading.

[5] The lection is divided between a number of persons (*op. cit.* pp. 380 f.); and the Rabbi considered it permissible to go out during the interval of "calling up" another to the *Tōrāh*.

[6] The Reading was intended to instruct the people; but scholars could spend the time better by devoting it to more advanced study.

[7] "That R. Menaḥem said" is added by *M.*

[8] In addition to hearing the recital of the weekly lection from the Pentateuch in the Synagogue, it was a pious act to read through the *Pārāshāh* at home, twice in the original and once in the Aramaic translation, the *Targūm*. It is here recommended that the home-reading should cover the same portion of Scripture as the Synagogue-reading.

fol. 8 b. even "Ataroth and Dibon" (Num. xxxii. 3)[1]—for whoever finishes his *Pārāshāh* with the congregation, his days and years are prolonged. Rab Bebai b. Abbai thought to complete the *Pārāshōt* of the whole year on the eve of the Day of Atonement; but Ḥiyya b. Rab of Difti[2] taught him: It is written, "Ye shall afflict your souls, in the ninth day of the month at even" (Lev. xxiii. 32). Do we fast on the ninth? Surely it is on the tenth that we fast! But the intention is to tell thee that whoever eats and drinks on the ninth, the Scriptures ascribe it to him as though he fasted on the ninth and tenth[3]. He then thought to anticipate [the reading of the *Pārāshōt*]; but a certain Elder said to him: We have learnt that one should neither anticipate nor postpone [the reading of the *Pārāshāh*]; as R. Joshua b. Levi said to his sons, "Finish your *Pārāshōt* with the congregation, twice the Hebrew text and once the *Targūm*; and also be careful to sever the jugular vein [of a bird when slaughtering] in accord with the opinion of R. Judah—for there is a Mishnaic teaching: R. Judah says: [One must cut] until he severs the jugular vein—and be careful [to honour] an old man, who has forgotten his learning involuntarily[4]; for we say that both the whole tables of stone and the pieces of the broken tables were placed in the Ark[5]."

Raba's advice to his sons. Raba said to his sons: When you cut meat, do not cut it upon your hand—some say, on account of danger[6], others, on account of spoiling the meal[7]—and do not sit upon the bed of an Aramaean[8] woman; and do not pass behind a Synagogue[9] at the time when the congregation is at prayer. [He advised them] not to sit upon

[1] Place-names which have no Targūm, but should still be read in the Aramaic version.

[2] Difti is identified with Dibitach on the lower Tigris; Neubauer, p. 390.

[3] It is consequently wrong to devote the eve of the Day of Atonement to the reading of the entire Pentateuch. It must be observed as a normal day.

[4] Through old age, sickness or trouble, but not through wilful neglect.

[5] According to B. Batra 14 *b*, the statement in Deut. x. 2 is intended to teach that reverence should be shown even to the fragments of the first tables of stone. Similarly one must respect the old, though they be broken by years or trouble.

[6] Of cutting the hand.

[7] Some blood may drip on to the table and make the meal repugnant to the diners.

[8] It is probable that "Aramaean" has been substituted for "Roman" for fear of the Censor.

[9] It is disrespectful not to enter and join in the Service. Blau, *Das altjüdische Zauberwesen*, p. 150, n. 4, suggests as the original reason for the prohibition: "der Weg soll nicht gekreuzt werden."

the bed of an Aramaean woman[1]. Some say he meant, Do not lie down to sleep without first reading the *Sh^e^ma'*[2]; others explain he meant, Do not marry a proselyte; but others declare that he really meant an Aramaean woman, because of what happened to Rab Pappa. For Rab Pappa went to the house of an Aramaean woman, who brought out a couch for him and told him to be seated. He said to her, "I will not sit down until thou raisest up the couch." They lifted it up and found a dead child there. On this account the Sages say: It is forbidden to sit upon the bed of an Aramaean woman. [His advice] "Do not pass behind a Synagogue at the time when the congregation is at prayer" supports the teaching of R. Joshua b. Levi who said[3]: It is forbidden a man to pass behind a Synagogue at the time when the congregation is at prayer. Abbai said: This only applies when the building has no other entrance; but should it have another entrance, we can have no objection; further it applies only when there is no other Synagogue [in the town], but should there be another Synagogue, we can have no objection; further it applies only to one who is not carrying a load, or is not running, or is not wearing *T^e^fillīn*; but in any of such cases, we can have no objection[4].

Praiseworthy actions of the Medes.

There is a teaching: R. 'Aḳiba said: For three things I admire the Medes: When they cut up meat, they only do so upon the table; when they kiss, they only kiss on the hand; and when they hold a consultation, they only do so in a field[5]. R. Adda b. Ah^a^bah said: What Scriptural authority is there for this? "And Jacob sent and called Rachel and Leah *to the field*" (Gen. xxxi. 4).

Praiseworthy actions of Persians.

There is a teaching: Rabban Gamaliel[6] said: For three things I admire the Persians: They are temperate with their food, modest in the privy, and modest in another matter[7]. "I have commanded My consecrated ones" (Is. xiii. 3). Rab Joseph taught: These are the Persians who are consecrated and destined for *Gēhinnōm*[8].

[1] Blau, *op. cit.* pp. 47 f., thinks that a reference to witchcraft is here intended, and the "dead child" mentioned below was the medium through which the sorceress worked.

[2] The bed would then be like that of a heathen who never reads the *Sh^e^ma'*.

[3] See fol. 61 *a*.

[4] Because in these circumstances it would not appear disrespectful.

[5] Because "walls have ears"; Levit. *R.* XXXII. § 2.

[6] *M.*: Rabban Simeon b. Gamaliel.

[7] Sexual intercourse.

[8] This bitter outburst is due to the persecution of the Persian Jews under Shapor II. See S. Funk in *M. G. W. J.* XLIX. p. 539.

Rabban Gamaliel said: Until the rise of dawn.

To read the Sh^{e}ma‘ twice in a night sometimes legitimate.

Rab Judah said in the name of Samuel: The *H^{a}lākāh* is in accord with Rabban Gamaliel. There is a teaching: R. Simeon b. Joḥai said: There are times when a man reads the *Sh^{e}ma‘* twice in a night, once before the rise of dawn and once after the rise of dawn, and thereby fulfils his obligation both for the day and night. This is self-contradictory! Thou sayest, "There are times when a man reads the *Sh^{e}ma‘* twice in a *night*"; consequently, after the rise of dawn is still night! And it continues, "The man thereby fulfils his obligation both for the *day* and night"; consequently, it is day! No; it is certainly still night; and that he calls it "day" is because there are people who rise at that early hour[1]. Rab Aḥa b. Ḥannina said in the name of R. Joshua b. Levi: The *H^{a}lākāh* is in accord with R. Simeon b. Joḥai.

To read the Sh^{e}ma‘ twice in a day sometimes legitimate.

There are some who apply the statement of Rab Aḥa b. Ḥannina to the following: There is a teaching: R. Simeon b. Joḥai said in the name of R. ‘Aḳiba: There are times when a man reads the *Sh^{e}ma‘* twice in a day, once before sunrise and once after sunrise, and thereby fulfils his obligation both for the day and night. This is self-contradictory! Thou sayest, "There are times when a man reads the *Sh^{e}ma‘* twice in a *day*"; consequently, before sunrise is day! And it continues, "The man thereby fulfils his obligation both for the day and *night*"; consequently it is still night! No; (fol. 9 a.) it is certainly day, and that he calls it "night" is because there are people who retire to rest at that hour[2]. Rab Aḥa b. R. Ḥannina said in the name of R. Joshua b. Levi: The *H^{a}lākāh* is in accord with R. Simeon who spoke in the name of R. ‘Aḳiba. R. Zera said: This is so, only one does not say, "Cause us, O Lord our God, to lie down[3]."

Teaching of R. Simeon confirmed.

When Rab Isaac b. Joseph came [from Palestine], he said: The statement of Rab Aḥa b. R. Ḥannina in the name of R. Joshua b. Levi was not explicitly said but was inferred. For it happened that two Rabbis became intoxicated at the marriage feast of R. Joshua b. Levi's son, and they omitted to read the *Sh^{e}ma‘*[4]. They came before R. Joshua b. Levi who said: R. Simeon is worthy that one should rely upon his opinion in a time of emergency.

1 Although it is before dawn, "when thou risest up" applies.

2 Consequently "when thou liest down" applies.

3 Singer, p. 99, since that is essentially a *night* prayer.

4 "and they omitted," etc. added by *M*.

It once happened that his sons returned from a feast, etc.

Before then, had they never heard this teaching of Rabban Gamaliel? But they spoke to him thus: The Rabbis differ from thee, and where an individual differs from the many, the *Halākāh* is in accord with the many. Or perhaps, the Rabbis agree with thee, and the reason that they declare [that the evening *Shema'* may be read] "Until midnight" is in order to keep a man far from transgression? He answered them, The Rabbis hold the same view as myself, and you are under the obligation [to read the *Shema'*]; and the reason they say "Until midnight" is to keep a man far from transgression.

Question of Gamaliel's sons explained.

And not only in this connection do they so decide.

But did Rabban Gamaliel say "Until midnight" that he teaches "and not only in this connection do they so decide[1]"? Nay, thus spake Rabban Gamaliel to his sons: Even according to the Rabbis who say "Until midnight," the obligation continues until the rise of dawn; and the reason they say "Until midnight" is to keep a man far from transgression.

Gamaliel's answer explained.

The duty of burning the fat, etc.

But he does not mention the eating of the Paschal offering[2]! And I quote against the *Mishnāh*: The reading of the evening *Shema'*, and *Hallēl* on the Passover night, and the eating of the Paschal offering—their obligation continues until the rise of dawn! Rab Joseph said: There is no contradiction; the statement of the *Mishnāh* being the view of R. Eleazar b. 'Azariah, the other the view of R. 'Akiba. For there is a teaching: "And they shall eat the flesh in that night" (Exod. xii. 8). R. Eleazar b. 'Azariah said, "Here it is stated, 'in that night' and the same phrase occurs in 'For I will go through the land of Egypt in that night' (*ibid.* v. 12); as in the latter passage it means 'until midnight', so also in the former it means 'until midnight'." R. 'Akiba said to him, "But has it not already been stated, 'Ye shall eat it in haste' (*ibid.* v. 11)—i.e. until the time of hastening[3]?" R. Eleazar b. 'Azariah asked[4], "If so, why is there a teaching to state 'in

Bārāitā quoted against the *Mishnāh*.

Contradiction removed.

Divergence of views concerning the Paschal offering.

[1] The continuation of the *Mishnāh* is "but wherever the Sages use the expression 'Until midnight,' the obligation continues until the rise of dawn." Since Rabban Gamaliel holds that the obligation continues until the rise of dawn, it might be supposed that he also teaches "until midnight."

[2] To which the same law applies.

[3] I.e. until the time of hastening out of Egypt, viz. dawn; cf. "And none of you shall go out of the door of his house *until the morning*" (Exod. xii. 22). Therefore R. 'Akiba rejects the other's argument which makes "in that night" mean "until midnight."

[4] Added by *M*.

that night'?" R. 'Aḳiba answered¹, "One might otherwise have thought that the Paschal offering could be eaten like the other holy offerings during the day; therefore there is a teaching to state 'in that night,' meaning it must be eaten at night, not during the day." According to R. Eleazar b. 'Azariah who uses the argument of *Gᵉzērāh Shāwāh*², it is quite right that it was necessary to state "in *that* night"; but how does R. 'Aḳiba explain the word "that³"? [He declares] that its purpose is to exclude the following night; for it might have occurred to thee to say that since the Paschal offering belongs to the class of things holy in a minor degree⁴, and peace offerings are in the same category, as the peace offerings might be eaten within two days and a night, so also the Paschal offering might be eaten two nights instead of two days, and therefore might be eaten any time during two nights and one day! Therefore it informs us "in *that* night," i.e. it must be eaten that night and no other. And R. Eleazar b. 'Azariah⁵? He deduces that from "And ye shall let nothing of it remain until the morning" (Exod. xii. 10). And R. 'Aḳiba⁶? If one deduced it from this passage, I might have said, Which "morning"? The second morning! And R. Eleazar⁷? He would answer thee, "Morning," used generally, means only the first morning.

A similar divergence of views.   These *Tannāīm* are like those other *Tannāīm*⁸; for there is a teaching: "There shalt thou offer the Passover-offering at even, at the going down of the sun, at the season that thou camest forth out of Egypt" (Deut. xvi. 6). R. Eliezer said: "At even" thou shalt sacrifice; "at the going down of the sun" thou shalt eat it; "at the season that thou camest forth out of Egypt" thou shalt burn [the remainder]⁹. R. Joshua said: "At even" thou shalt

---

¹ Added by *M*.   ² See p. 18, n. 5.

³ Since he only deduces from the phrase that the Paschal offering was not to be eaten in the daytime, it would be sufficient for the text to state "in the night."

⁴ See *Mishnāh* Zᵉbāḥīm, v. 8 (Singer, p. 13), and for the peace offering, *ibid.* § 7.

⁵ How does he know that the Paschal offering may not be eaten two nights and a day? He cannot derive it from "in *that* night," since he has used the phrase for the purpose of drawing the analogy.

⁶ Why does he not use this verse?

⁷ How does he meet R. 'Aḳiba's objection?

⁸ The point of variance between R. Eleazar b. 'Azariah and R. 'Aḳiba also divides R. Eliezer and R. Joshua.

⁹ This is in agreement with R. Eleazar b. 'Azariah's view above; for according to R. Eliezer, the right of eating the Paschal offering did not continue until the morning when the remainder was burnt.

sacrifice; "at the going down of the sun" thou shalt eat it; and how long mayest thou continue eating it? Until "the season that thou camest forth out of Egypt[1]."

The time of the Exodus.

R. Abba[2] said: Everybody admits that the Israelites were only redeemed from Egypt at even; as it is said, "The Lord thy God brought thee forth out of Egypt by night" (*ibid. v.* 1); but they actually left Egypt by day; as it is said, "On the morrow after the Passover, the children of Israel went out with a high hand" (Num. xxxiii. 3). What is the point of disagreement? The time of "hastening." R. Eleazar b. 'Azariah holds that it refers to the haste of the Egyptians[3]; but R. 'Aḳiba holds that it refers to the haste of the Israelites[4]. There is a teaching to the same effect: "The Lord thy God brought thee forth out of Egypt by night" (Deut. xvi. 1). Was it in the night they went out? Surely they went out during the day; as it is said, "On the morrow after the Passover the children of Israel went out with a high hand" (Num. xxxiii. 3)! But this teaches that the redemption began for them at even.

God had to request Israel to take the gold of the Egyptians. fol. 9 b.

"Speak now [*nā'*] in the ears of the people" etc. (Exod. xi. 2). In the school of R. Jannai they said: The word [*nā'*] always expresses a request. The Holy One, blessed be He, said to Moses, "I request thee, Go and say to the Israelites: I beg of you to ask of the Egyptians vessels of silver and vessels of gold, so that the righteous one[5] shall not say, 'And they shall serve them, and they shall afflict them' (Gen. xv. 13) He did fulfil in them, but 'and afterward shall they come out *with great substance*' (*ibid. v.* 14) He did not fulfil in them." They answered Moses, "Would that we could escape with our lives!" A Parable: [It may be likened] to a man who was imprisoned in a dungeon, and people came to tell him, "To-morrow thou wilt be released from the dungeon and be presented with a large sum of money." He replies to them, "I beg of you to release me to-day, and I ask for nothing more."

Two interpretations of Exod. xii. 36.

"They let them have what they asked" (Exod. xii. 36). R. Ammi said: This teaches that they let them have what they asked against their will. Some explain: Against the will of the

[1] This opinion agrees with R. 'Aḳiba's, that the eating may continue until daybreak.

[2] *M.*: Raba, which is probably correct.

[3] Cf. Exod. xii. 33, "And the Egyptians were urgent upon the people, to send them out of the land in haste"; this was at midnight, see *v.* 29.

[4] I.e. the hastening of the Israelites out of Egypt, which did not occur until the morning.

[5] Abraham.

Egyptians; but others explain: Against the will of the Israelites. Those who say it was against the will of the Egyptians, because it is written, "And she that tarrieth at home divideth the spoil" (Ps. lxviii. 13)[1]. Those who say it was against the will of the Israelites, because of the burden[2].

Egypt left bare.

"And they despoiled Egypt" (Exod. xii. 36). R. Ammi said: This teaches that they made it like a fort without provisions[3]. R. Simeon b. Laḳish said: They made it like a pond without fish.

Explanation of "I am that I am."

"I am that I am" (*ibid.* iii. 14). R. Ammi said[4]: The Holy One, blessed be He, spake to Moses, "Go, say to the Israelites, I was with you in this servitude, and I will be with you in the servitude of the kingdoms[5]." He said before Him, "Lord of the Universe, sufficient is the evil in its time[6]." The Holy One, blessed be He, said to him, "Go say to them, *I am*[7] hath sent me unto you" (*ibid.*).

Why Elijah said "Hear me" twice.

"Hear me, O Lord, hear me" (I Kings xviii. 37)[8]. R. Abbahu said: Why did Elijah exclaim "Hear me" twice? This teaches that Elijah spake before the Holy One, blessed be He, "Lord of the Universe, hear me, that fire may descend from heaven and consume all that is upon the altar; and hear me, that Thou mayest divert their mind so that they say not it was the effect of sorcery; as it is said, 'For Thou didst turn their heart backward' (*ibid.*)."

[1] *vv.* 7 f. of the Psalm refer to the release from Egypt; accordingly "she that tarrieth at home" means the Egyptians, and "spoil" implies that it was taken from them by force.

[2] The Israelites were reluctant to load themselves with burdens for the journey.

[3] Rashi translates, "Like a trap [for birds] in which was no corn [wherewith to catch them]." The text is uncertain; see *D. S. ad loc.* and *A. P. A.* II. p. 170, n. 4. *M.* reads: "Like husks without grain (cf. Jastrow, p. 824 *b*) ...like a net without fish."

[4] Added by *M.* correctly. See *D. S. ad loc.*

[5] This is the interpretation of the two "I am." The second foretells the captivity of Assyria and Babylon.

[6] Cf. Matt. vi. 34, "Sufficient unto the day is the evil thereof." Why should Moses have to tell the Israelites of the trials that were in store for their descendants?

[7] Not "I am that I am"; thus the reference to the Captivity was to be omitted.

[8] The explanation of I Kings xviii. 37 occurs also on fol. 6 *b*, p. 33.

MISHNĀH II

From what time may the Sh^e^ma' *be read in the morning? From the time that one can distinguish between blue and white*[1]. *R. Eliezer says: Between blue and green. And he may finish it any time until sunrise. R. Joshua says: Until the third hour, for so is the custom of kings to rise at the third hour. He who reads from that time onward incurs no loss, for he is to be regarded as one reading in the* Tōrāh[2].

GEMĀRĀ

What is to be understood by "between blue and white"? Is it to be supposed between a lump of white wool and a lump of blue wool? That can be distinguished also at night! But it means, between the blueness in it and the whiteness in it[3]. A question answered.

There is a teaching: R. Meïr says: [The morning *Sh^e^ma'* is to be read] from the time one can distinguish between a wolf and a dog. R. 'Aḳiba says: Between an ass and a wild ass. Others say: When he can see an associate of his at a distance of four cubits[4] and recognise him. Rab Huna said: The *H^a^lākāh* is in accord with the "others." Abbai said: [The *H^a^lākāh* is] in accord with the "others" with respect to the *T^e^fillāh*[5]; but with respect to the *Sh^e^ma'* it is in accord with the *W^e^tīḳīn*[6]. For R. Joḥanan said: The *W^e^tīḳīn* used to conclude it with the sunrise. There is a teaching to the same effect: The *W^e^tīḳīn* used to conclude it with the sunrise in order to unite the *G^e^'ullāh* with the *T^e^fillāh*[7], *Terminus a quo* of the morning *Sh^e^ma'*.

[1] Similarly the Koran ii. 183 regards the day as commencing for the purpose of a fast when one "can plainly distinguish a white thread from a black thread by the daybreak."

[2] He will earn merit by reading it after the prescribed time, but not as much.

[3] I.e. the wool is partly dyed blue, and one can distinguish the undyed parts. *J. T.* explains it as referring to the "Fringes" which are used when reading the *Sh^e^ma'* and contain "a thread of blue" (Num. xv. 38).

[4] A little over two yards.

[5] The Bomberg edition reads: *T^e^fillīn.*

[6] *Lit.* pious. They were a sect who paid scrupulous care to the fulfilment of the religious ordinances. They are sometimes identified with the Essenes; cf. *J. E.* v. p. 226. Blau in *R. E. J.* XXXI. pp. 184 f. regards them as a community of *priests* who held a service in common, and identifies them with "the Holy Congregation of Jerusalem" mentioned below.

[7] See Singer, p. 44. The prayer "O Rock of Israel" is part of the benediction connected with the *Sh^e^ma'*. But the Eighteen Benedictions which follow may not be said until sunrise; so as to be able to unite the two, the *W^e^tiḳin* took care to conclude the reading of the *Sh^e^ma'* at that time.

and consequently pray in the day. R. Zera said: What is the Scriptural authority for this? "They shall fear Thee *with the sun*[1], and before the moon, throughout all generations" (Ps. lxxii. 5).

Meritorious to unite *G^e'ullāh* with *T^efillāh*.

R. Josē b. Eliakim testified in the name of the Holy Congregation of Jerusalem[2]: Whoever unites the *G^e'ullāh* with the *T^efillāh* will meet with no mishap all that day. R. Zera exclaimed, "But it is not so! For lo, I united them but mishap befel me!" He asked him, "What was the mishap? That thou didst carry myrtle into the king's palace[3]? Why, thou shouldest even have offered some reward to be privileged to behold a king. For R. Johanan has said: A man should always be eager to run to meet a king of Israel; and not only to meet an Israelite king, but even a king of the other nations, for if he be worthy, he will distinguish[4] between the kings of Israel and the kings of other peoples."

Rab B^erona did so.

R. El'ai[5] said to 'Ulla: When thou goest up there [to Palestine], make inquiries about the welfare of my brother, Rab B^erona, in the presence of the whole college; for he is a great man and rejoices in [the performance of] the commandments. On one occasion he united the *G^e'ullāh* with the *T^efillāh*, and laughter did not cease from his mouth all that day.

A criticism removed.

How was he able to unite them? For lo, R. Johanan has said: At the commencement of the *T^efillāh* one should say "O Lord, open Thou my lips" (Ps. li. 17) and at the conclusion "Let the words of my mouth etc." (*ibid.* xix. 15)[6]! R. Eleazar said: [R. Johanan's statement] refers to the *T^efillāh* of the evening. But R. Johanan has said: Who will inherit the world to come? He who unites the *G^e'ullāh* of the evening to the *T^efillāh* of the evening[7]! R. Eleazar said: Then it must refer to the *T^efillāh* of the afternoon service. Rab Ashē[8] said: Thou mayest even

[1] I.e. they will pay their devotions at sunrise.

[2] Probably a survival of an Essene Community; see *J. E. loc. cit.*, and p. 55, n. 6.

[3] This refers to the incident mentioned in *J. T.* On the day that R. Zera was careful to unite the two prayers, he was pressed into the king's service to carry myrtle into the palace.

[4] In the Messianic Era. [5] *M.*: Eleazar. [6] See fol. 4 *b*, p. 17.

[7] Therefore R. Johanan's teaching cannot apply to the evening *T^efillāh*, because "O Lord, open Thou my lips" would constitute an interruption. The importance which this Rabbi attached to uniting the two prayers in the evening is accounted for by Elbogen (*J. Q. R.* xix. pp. 711 ff.) on the theory that it was intended to abolish the custom of introducing prayers of a personal nature after the *Sh^ema'* which was likely to destroy the congregational character of the Service. Cf. fol. 31 *a*, p. 206.

[8] *M.*: Assi; but the reading of edd. is to be preferred. See *D. S. ad loc.*

suppose that it refers to all of them; for, since the Rabbis instituted it[1] in the *Tefillāh* it is to be considered as part thereof. If thou dost not admit this, how could one unite them in the evening, since one has to say the prayer "Cause us, O Lord our God, to lie down[2]"! But since the Rabbis instituted that prayer, it is considered part of the *Ge'ullāh*; and so here also, since the Rabbis instituted "O Lord, open etc." in the *Tefillāh*, it is to be considered part thereof.

The numbering of the Psalms.

Since the verse: "Let the words of my mouth be acceptable before Thee" might with equal propriety be said at the conclusion or the commencement [of the *Tefillāh*], why did the Rabbis institute it at the end of the Eighteen Benedictions? Let it be said at the commencement! R. Judah, the son of R. Simeon b. Pazzi, answered: Since David only says this verse after eighteen Psalms, therefore the Rabbis arranged it at the end of the Eighteen Benedictions. How so eighteen Psalms—there are nineteen[3]! "Happy is the man" (Ps. i. 1) and "Why are the nations in an uproar" (*ibid.* ii. 1) form one Psalm[4]. For R. Judah, the son of R. Simeon b. Pazzi, has said: David composed one hundred and three Psalms, and did not say Hallelujah until he had seen the overthrow of the wicked; as it is said, "Let sinners cease out of the earth, and let the wicked be no more. Bless the Lord, O my soul. Hallelujah" (*ibid.* civ. 35). How so one hundred and three Psalms—there are one hundred and four! But infer from this that "Happy is the man" and "Why are the nations in an uproar" are one Psalm. For R. Samuel b. Naḥmani said in the name of R. Jonathan[5]: Every Psalm which was dear to David he opened **fol. 10 a.** with "Happy" and concluded with "Happy." He opened with "Happy" as it is written, "Happy is the man" (*ibid.* i. 1) and concluded with "Happy" as it is written, "Happy are all they that take refuge in Him" (*ibid.* ii. 12).

R. Meïr and Beruriah.

There were some lawless men[6] living in the neighbourhood of R. Meïr, and they used to vex him sorely. Once R. Meïr prayed that they should die. His wife, Beruriah[7], exclaimed, "What

[1] The introductory sentence, "O Lord, open Thou my lips."

[2] See p. 17.

[3] The verse concludes the 19th Psalm.

[4] In Acts xiii. 33 where Ps. ii. 7 is quoted, Codex Bezae and other authorities read "In the *first* Psalm."

[5] So *M.* which is to be preferred to edd.: Joḥanan, since R. Jonathan was his teacher.

[6] *Barjōni* which Krauss, p. 165, identifies with φρούριον. But this is doubtful.

[7] Equivalent of the Latin name, Veluria; Krauss, p. 165.

thinkest thou? Is it because it is written, 'Let sinners cease out of the earth'? But has the text *ḥōṭe'īm*? It is written *ḥaṭā'īm*[1]. Glance also at the end of the verse, 'And let the wicked be no more'—i.e. when 'sins will cease,' then 'the wicked will be no more.' Rather shouldest thou pray that they repent and they be no more wicked." R. Meïr offered prayer on their behalf and they repented.

Beruriah and the heretic. A *Mīn* said to Beruriah: It is written, "Sing, O barren, thou that didst not bear" (Is. liv. 1). Is the woman to sing because she did not bear? She answered him, "Fool, glance at the end of the verse; for it is written, 'For more are the children of the desolate than the children of the married wife, saith the Lord[2].' But what means, 'barren woman, thou that didst not bear'? Sing, O community of Israel, who art like a barren woman that hath not borne children for *Gēhinnōm*—like you."

The law of juxtaposition. A *Mīn* said to R. Abbahu: It is written "A Psalm of David, when he fled from Absalom his son" (Ps. iii. 1) and also "Of David, Michtam; when he fled from Saul, in the cave" (*ibid*. lvii. 1). Which incident happened first? Surely the incident of Saul happened first; then he should record it first! He replied: For you who do not use the rule of juxtaposition[3] it is a difficulty, but not for us who do make use of it. For R. Joḥanan[4] said: Whence is the rule of juxtaposition derived from the *Tōrāh*? As it is said: "*Semūkīm*[5] for ever and ever, they are done in truth and righteousness" (*ibid*. cxi. 8). Why, then, is the Psalm concerning Absalom (Ps. iii) next to the Psalm concerning Gog and Magog (Ps. ii)[6]? So that should anybody ask thee, "Is there a slave that rebels against his master[7]?" do thou ask him, "Is there a son who rebels against his father?" The latter has happened, and similarly will the former happen.

David's songs. R. Joḥanan said in the name of R. Simeon b. Joḥai: What means that which is written, "She openeth her mouth with wisdom, and the law of kindness is on her tongue" (Prov. xxxi. 26)? Of

---

[1] The text reads חט‎ם‎ ‎יום‎ not חוטאים; so instead of pointing חַטָּאִים "sinners," she pointed חֲטָאִים "sins."

[2] Wünsche, p. 25, explains "the desolate" to refer to devastated Jerusalem and "the married wife" to Rome. See also *A. P. A.* III. p. 84 n.

[3] See Glossary, *s.v. Semūkīn*.

[4] M.: Eleazar, perhaps correctly; cf. *A. P. A.* II. p. 38, n. 3.

[5] Anglice: "they are established." But the word is here taken in its later technical sense.

[6] See p. 41.

[7] Is it at all possible that the nations will rise in revolt against God?

whom does Solomon say this? He said it of no one else than David his father, who dwelt in five worlds and composed songs [in each]. He dwelt in the womb of his mother and composed a song; as it is said, "Bless the Lord, O my soul, and all that I am within[1], bless His holy name" (*ibid.* ciii. 1). He issued forth into the air of the world, gazed at the stars and planets, and composed a song; as it is said, "Bless the Lord, ye angels of His, ye mighty in strength, that fulfil His word, hearkening unto the voice of His word. Bless the Lord, all ye His hosts, etc." (*ibid. vv.* 20 f.). He sucked at his mother's breast, gazed at her nipples, and composed a song; as it is said, "Bless the Lord, O my soul, and forget not all His benefits" (*ibid. v.* 2). What means "all His benefits[2]"? R. Abbahu said: [It means] that He placed her breast in the place of understanding[3]. For what reason? Rab Judah said: So that [the child] may not gaze at the place of nakedness. Rab Matt^e^na said: So that it should not have to suck from a part of the body which is foul. David looked upon the overthrow of the wicked and composed a song; as it is said, "Let sinners cease out of the earth, and let the wicked be no more. Bless the Lord, O my soul. Hallelujah" (*ibid.* civ. 35). He reflected on the day of death and composed a song; as it is said, "Bless the Lord, O my soul; O Lord my God, Thou art very great, Thou art clothed with glory and majesty" (*ibid. v.* 1). How is it understood that this verse speaks of the day of death? Rabbah b. Rab Shela answered: From the continuation; as it is written, "Thou hidest Thy face, they vanish; Thou withdrawest their breath, they perish, and return to the dust" (*ibid. v.* 29).

God's attributes.

Rab Shimi b. 'Uḳba (another version: Mar 'Uḳba) was frequently in the company of R. Simeon b. Pazzi who[4] used to arrange the *Aggādāh* in the presence of R. Joshua b. Levi[5]. He asked him: What means that which is written, "Bless the Lord, O my soul, and all that is within me, bless His holy name" (*ibid.* ciii. 1)? He replied: Come and see that the attribute of man is not like the attribute of the Holy One, blessed be He. It is an attribute

[1] R.V. "all that is within me."

[2] The root of the word for "benefits," *g^e^mūl*, also has the meaning of "to wean."

[3] Over against her heart, not as with the lower animals.

[4] Reading with *M.* דהוה "who used" instead of edd. והוה "and he used"; i.e. the subject of the verb is Simeon b. Pazzi.

[5] In the Rabbinical Schools, the lecturer used to give the gist of his discourse to the *Āmōrā* who then expounded it in fuller detail to the disciples.

of man to draw a figure on a wall, but he is unable to endow it with breath and soul, with inward parts and bowels. But with the Holy One, blessed be He, it is not so. He draws a figure within a figure, and endows it with breath and soul, with inward parts and bowels. That is what Hannah said, "There is none holy as the Lord, for there is none beside Thee; neither is there any rock like our God" (I Sam. ii. 2). What means "there is no rock [*ṣūr*] like our God"? [It means] "there is no designer [*ṣayyār*] like our God." What means "for there is none beside Thee"? R. Judah b. Menasya said: Read not *ēn biltĕkā* "there is none beside Thee," but *ēn l^eballōt^ekā* "there is none to outlast Thee." For not like the attribute of the Holy One, blessed be He, is the attribute of the human being. With the human being, his works outlast him; but the Holy One, blessed be He, outlasts His works.

God and the soul.

He said to him[1]: I tell thee as follows: These five "Bless the Lord, O my soul"—with reference to whom did David compose them? He composed them with reference to none other than the Holy One, blessed be He, and the soul. As the Holy One, blessed be He, fills the whole world, so also the soul fills the whole body. As the Holy One, blessed be He, sees but cannot be seen, so also the soul sees but cannot be seen. As the Holy One, blessed be He, nourishes the whole world, so also the soul nourishes the whole body. As the Holy One, blessed be He, is pure, so also the soul is pure. As the Holy One, blessed be He, dwells in the inmost part [of the Universe], so also the soul dwells in the inmost part [of the body][2]. Let him in whom are these five qualities come and praise Him Who possesses these five qualities.

Hezekiah and Isaiah.

Rab Hamnuna said: What means that which is written, "Who is as the wise man? and who knoweth the interpretation [*pêsher*] of a thing?" (Eccles. viii. 1)? [It means], Who is like the Holy One, blessed be He, Who knows how to make a reconciliation [*p^eshārāh*] between the two righteous men, Hezekiah and Isaiah. Hezekiah said, "Let Isaiah come to me, for so we find that Elijah went to Ahab; as it is said, 'And Elijah went to show himself unto Ahab' (I Kings xviii. 2)." Isaiah said, "Let Hezekiah come to me, for so we find that Jehoram, son of Ahab, went to Elisha"

[1] Rab Shimi to R. Simeon b. Pazzi. What follows is an alternative explanation of the fivefold "Bless the Lord, O my soul" as given in the last paragraph but one.

[2] On the theological import of this passage, see Abelson, *Immanence of God*, p. 109 n.

(II Kings iii. 12). What did the Holy One, blessed be He, do? He brought sufferings upon Hezekiah and said to Isaiah, "Go and visit the sick[1]"; as it is said, "In those days was Hezekiah sick unto death. And Isaiah, the prophet, the son of Amoz came to him and said to him, Thus saith the Lord, Set thy house in order; for thou shalt die, and not live" (Is. xxxviii. 1). What means "For thou shalt die, and not live"?—"for thou shalt die" in this world, "and not live" in the world to come. He asked him, "Why all this [severe punishment]?" He replied, "Because thou hast not performed the duty of begetting children[2]." Hezekiah said to him, "The reason is that I have seen by the aid of the Holy Spirit[3], that worthless children will issue from me." Isaiah asked him, "What hast thou to do with the secrets of the All-merciful? What thou hast been commanded thou shouldest perform, and let the Holy One, blessed be He, do whatever is pleasing to Him." Hezekiah said to him, "Then give me thy daughter; perhaps my merit and thine will have effect, and worthy children will issue from me." He replied, ["Lo, I have brought thee the message 'Set thy house in order' and thou sayest to me 'Give me thy daughter'!][4] The verdict [of death] has already been decreed against thee!" He said to him, "Son of Amoz, end thy prophecy and go! For thus has it been handed down to me from my forefather[5]: Even if a sharp sword be laid upon a man's neck, let him not despair of [the divine] mercy." It has been similarly reported: R. Joḥanan and R. Eleazar[6] both said: Even if a sharp sword be laid upon a man's neck, let him not despair of [the divine] mercy, as it is said, "Though He slay me, yet will I trust in Him" (Job xiii. 15). R. Ḥanan said: Even if the lord **fol. 10 b.**
of dreams[7] inform a man that he will die on the morrow, he should not despair of [the divine] mercy; as it is said, "For through the multitude of dreams and vanities there are also many words; *but*

[1] To visit the sick is a religious obligation.

[2] "Be fruitful and multiply" (Gen. i. 28) was held in high esteem as the first commandment given to man.

[3] I.e. the prophetic gift.

[4] The sentence in brackets is added by *M.*

[5] David who prayed even in the presence of the destroying angel; II Sam. xxiv. 17.

[6] So *M.* correctly; edd. Eliezer.

[7] The phrase used here is identical with that in Gen. xxxvii. 19 applied to Joseph. More usually we have "The master of the dream," which merely represents the personification of the dream. See Bacher in *R. E. J.* xxxv. p. 238, n. 2.

fear thou God" (Eccles. v. 6)[1]. Immediately, "Then Hezekiah turned his face to the wall [*ḳīr*] and prayed unto the Lord" (Is. xxxviii. 2). What means *ḳīr*? R. Simeon b. Laḳish said: [He prayed][2] from the chambers [*ḳīrōt*] of his heart; as it is said, "My bowels, my bowels! I writhe in pain! the chambers of my heart, etc." (Jer. iv. 19). R. Levi[3] declared: [He prayed][2] in connection with the "wall," saying before Him, "Lord of the Universe, if Thou didst bring back to life the child of the Shunammite woman who but made 'a little chamber on the roof[4],' how much more so [shouldest Thou spare my life], seeing that my forefather Solomon overlaid the whole Temple with silver and gold!"

Hezekiah's prayer.

"Remember now, O Lord, I beseech Thee, how I have walked before Thee in truth and with a whole heart, and have done that which is good in Thy sight" (Is. xxxviii. 3). What means "I have done that which is good in Thy sight"? Rab Judah said in the name of Rab: He joined the *Ge'ullāh* to the *Tefillāh*[5]. R. Levi said: He hid the Book of Remedies[6].

Hezekiah's six acts.

The Rabbis have taught: Six acts did King Hezekiah perform; of three [the Rabbis] approved, and of three they disapproved. Of three they approved, viz. he hid the Book of Remedies, and they approved; he broke the brazen serpent[7], and they approved; he dragged his father's bones upon a bed of ropes[8], and they approved. But of three of his acts they disapproved, viz. he stopped up the waters of Giḥon[9], and they disapproved; he cut down the doors of the Temple and sent them to the King of Assyria[10], and they

[1] *M.* adds: Finally Isaiah gave him his daughter in marriage, and there issued from him Manasseh and Rabshakeh. One day Hezekiah carried them on his shoulder to the Synagogue; and one of them said, "Father's bald head would be fine for breaking nuts on," while the other said, "[It would be fine] to roast fish on." He threw them to the ground, and Rabshakeh was killed, but not Manasseh. He applied to them the verse, "The instruments also of the churl are evil; he deviseth wicked devices" (Is. xxxii. 7).

[2] Added by *M.*

[3] *M.*: Joḥanan.

[4] II Kings iv. 10, *lit.* "chamber of a *wall*."

[5] See p. 56.

[6] King Solomon was reputed to have compiled a book containing infallible prescriptions for almost all ailments. Josephus, *Antiq.* VIII. ii. 5, mentions that he was skilled in expelling demons and "composed incantations by which distempers are alleviated." Hezekiah destroyed the book so that people in times of sickness should pray to God and not depend upon these cures.

[7] Cf. II Kings xviii. 4.

[8] He had his father's body borne to burial on a common pallet, because of his wickedness, instead of giving him royal honours.

[9] II Chron. xxxii. 30.

[10] II Kings xviii. 16.

disapproved; he intercalated *Nīsān* in *Nīsān*[1], and they disapproved. Did not Hezekiah know of the teaching, "This month shall be unto you the beginning of months" (Exod. xii. 2), i.e. this month and none other shall be *Nīsān*[2]? But he erred in the teaching of Samuel who said: We do not intercalate the year on the 30th day of *Ădār*, since that day may possibly be fixed as *Nīsān*. Hezekiah thought that we do not say "since that day may possibly be fixed as *Nīsān*[3]."

One should not rely on one's own merit in prayer.

R. Johanan said in the name of R. Josē b. Zimra: Whoever refers to his own merit [when praying], the merit of others is referred to [in the answer to the petition]; and whoever refers to the merit of others, his own merit is referred to. Moses referred to the merit of others; as it is said, "Remember Abraham, Isaac and Israel, Thy servants" (*ibid.* xxxii. 13), and his own merit was referred to; as it is said, "Therefore He said that He would destroy them, had not Moses His chosen stood before Him in the breach, to turn back His wrath, lest He should destroy them" (Ps. cvi. 23). Hezekiah referred to his own merit; as it is written, "Remember now, O Lord, I beseech Thee, how I have walked before Thee" (Is. xxxviii. 3), and the merit of others was referred to; as it is said, "For I will defend this city, for Mine own sake, and for My servant David's sake" (*ibid.* xxxvii. 35). This agrees with the statement of R. Joshua b. Levi who said: What means that which is written, "Behold, for my peace I had great bitter-

[1] This is a reference to II Chron. xxx. 2 where it is mentioned that he observed the Passover in the second month. According to the Talmūd, he had made a mistake in intercalation. The Hebrew month is lunar and lasts 29 or 30 days. Whether the 30th day was to be regarded as the last day of the month or the first of the new month depended upon observation of the New Moon (cf. Lane, p. 478). For the purpose of periodically adjusting the lunar and solar year (so that, e.g., the Passover which must be observed in the Spring should not occur in the Summer), an extra month was intercalated between *Ădār* and *Nīsān* seven times in nineteen years. On the Jewish Calendar, see *J. E.* III. p. 498, Oesterley and Box, pp. 346 ff.

[2] I.e. the month having once been proclaimed *Nīsān*, it cannot be intercalated.

[3] By "Samuel" is meant the *Ămōrā* of that name. He taught that if the year is to be intercalated, it must be announced before the 30th of *Ădār*, since witnesses might come to testify that the New Moon had been observed on that day, and it would accordingly be reckoned as the 1st of *Nīsān*. Hezekiah, however, thought that the 30th of *Ădār* could never be reckoned as the 1st of *Nīsān*. He therefore intercalated the year on that day, which afterwards proved to be the New Moon, with the consequence that he observed the Passover in the second month instead of in the first.

ness" (Is. xxxviii. 17)? Even when the Holy One, blessed be He, sent him peace, it was bitter for him[1].

Elisha's accommodation.

"Let us make, I pray thee, a little chamber on the roof" (II Kings iv. 10)[2]. Rab and Samuel [discuss its meaning]. One says: It was an open chamber which they roofed in; the other says: It was a large verandah[3] which they divided into two [by erecting a wall]. This is all very well according to him who says it was a verandah, since it is written *ḳīr* "a wall"; but for him who says it was an upper chamber, what means *ḳīr*? He takes it to mean "they roofed it." It is all very well according to him who says it was an upper chamber, since it is written *'ăliyyāh* "upper chamber"; but for him who says it was a verandah, what means *'ăliyyāh*? He takes it to mean the finest [*m^e'ullāh*] of the rooms.

Offer of hospitality need not be accepted.

"And let us set for him there a bed, and a table, and a stool and a candlestick" (*ibid.*). Abbai (another version: Rab Isaac[4]) said: Whoever wishes to take advantage [of an offer of hospitality] may do so like Elisha; and whoever does not wish to accept may do so[5] like Samuel of Ramah; as it is said, "And his return was to Ramah, for there was his house" (I Sam. vii. 17)[6], and R. Joḥanan[7] said: Wherever he went, he took his house with him.

Woman's discernment.

"And she said to her husband, Behold now, I perceive that this is a holy man of God" (II Kings iv. 9). R. Josē b. R. Ḥannina said: From here [we learn] that a woman can better estimate [the character of] a guest than a man.

Elisha's godliness perceived.

"A man of God[8]." How did she know it? Rab and Samuel [offer explanations]. One says: She never saw a fly pass over his

[1] Because having prayed for it in his own name, it was granted in the name of another.

[2] *Lit.* "chamber of a wall [*ḳīr*]."

[3] On the various meanings of *aksedrā* (the Greek ἐξέδρα) see Krauss, pp. 44 f.

[4] *M.*: Raba b. Isaac which *D.S.* corrects to Rabbah b. Isaac.

[5] He can refuse the invitation without being thought proud. To offer and accept such invitations belongs to the ordinary courtesy of Oriental life. Cf. Lane, p. 296.

[6] Why mention "for there was his house," a fact well known? Since the preceding verse speaks of his circuit, these words are taken to apply not only to Ramah but also to the places there named.

[7] In the parallel passage, N^e^dārīm 38*a*, the teaching is ascribed to Raba.

[8] So *M.* Edd.: "a holy man"; but those words are commented upon below.

table[1]; the other says: She spread a linen sheet upon his bed and never found it stained with seminal emission.

Gehazi condemned.

"A holy man." R. Josē b. R. Ḥannina said: *He* is holy, but not his servant; as it is said, "Gehazi came near to thrust her away" (*ibid.* *v.* 27). R. Simeon b. Laḳish[2] said: He seized her by the breast[3].

Meritorious to entertain a disciple of the wise.

"That passeth by us *continually*" (*ibid.* *v.* 9). R. Josē b. R. Ḥannina said in the name of R. Eliezer b. Jacob: Whoever invites a disciple of the wise as a guest to his house and lets him enjoy his possessions, the Scriptures ascribe it to him as though he had brought *continual* offerings[4].

Proper to pray in a lowly place.

R. Josē b. R. Ḥannina also said in the name of R. Eliezer b. Jacob: Let not a man stand on an elevated place and pray, but let him pray in a lowly place[5]; as it is said, "Out of the depths have I called Thee, O Lord" (Ps. cxxx. 1). There is a teaching to the same effect: Let not a man stand upon a chair, or a stool, or any elevated place to pray, but let him pray in a lowly place, because there can be no haughtiness before the Omnipresent; as it is said, "Out of the depths have I called Thee, O Lord," and it is said, "A prayer of the afflicted, when he fainteth" (*ibid.* cii. 1).

Attitude of prayer.

R. Josē b. R. Ḥannina also said in the name of R. Eliezer b. Jacob: Whoever prays must direct his feet; as it is said, "And their feet were straight feet" (Ezek. i. 7)[6].

Prayer must precede meal.

[7]R. Josē b. R. Ḥannina also said in the name of R. Eliezer b. Jacob: What means that which is written, "Ye shall not eat

[1] That his food did not attract flies was evidence of his being a man of God. Cf. Ābōt v. 8 where it is stated that one of the ten miracles wrought in the Temple was "no fly was seen in the slaughter-house" (Singer, p. 200).

[2] So *M.*; edd.: R. Josē b. Ḥannina.

[3] *Lit.* "the splendour of her beauty." להוד יפיה is read in להדפה "to thrust her away."

[4] Cf. fol. 63 *b*.

[5] Hence in Babylon it was customary to have the reading desk, where the Precentor stood, at a lower level than the floor of the Synagogue. In modern Synagogues the Precentor's platform is raised; see Oesterley and Box, p. 338. But according to Elbogen, the recommendation of the Talmūd to pray in a lowly place is intended to apply to the individual, not the Precentor. Cf. *J. Q. R.* xix. p. 705 n.

[6] *Lit.* "a straight *foot*," i.e. they were placed together so as to appear like one foot. That is the correct posture for the *T^efillāh*. *J. T.* offers two reasons: (1) to imitate the angels; (2) to imitate the priests in the Temple.

[7] *M.* omits "R. Isaac said in the name of R. Joḥanan" which some edd. insert here.

with the blood" (Lev. xix. 26)? [It means], Ye shall not eat before you have prayed for your life[1]. There are some who declare that R. Isaac stated that R. Joḥanan said[2] in the name of R. Eliezer b. Jacob: Whoever eats and drinks and afterwards offers his prayers, concerning him the Scriptures say, "Thou hast cast Me behind thy back" (I Kings xiv. 9). Read not *gēwēkā* "thy back," but *gēēkā* "thy pride." The Holy One, blessed be He, says, "After this person has exalted himself, he receives upon himself the kingdom of Heaven[3]."

R. Joshua said: Until the third hour.

Rab Judah said in the name of Samuel: The *Hᵃlākāh* is in accord with R. Joshua.

He who reads from that time onward incurs no loss.

Reading the *Shᵉmaʻ* not in proper time.

Rab Ḥisda said in the name of Mar ʻUḳba: Provided he does not say "Blessed...Who formest light[4]." Against this view I quote: He who reads [the *Shᵉmaʻ*] from that time onward incurs no loss; he is regarded as one reading in the *Tōrāh*, but he must precede it with two benedictions and follow it with one! This refutation of Rab Ḥisda's view remains unshaken. Some declare: Rab Ḥisda said in the name of Mar ʻUḳba: What means *he incurs no loss*? He loses none of the benedictions[5]. There is a teaching to the same effect: He who reads [the *Shᵉmaʻ*] from that time onward incurs no loss; he is regarded as one reading in the *Tōrāh*, but he must precede it with two benedictions and follow it with one. R. Manni said: Greater is he who reads the *Shᵉmaʻ* in its proper time than one who occupies himself with *Tōrāh*; for the *Mishnāh* states: *He who reads from that time onward incurs no loss, he is regarded as one reading in the* Tōrāh; hence it is to be deduced that he who reads [the *Shᵉmaʻ*] in its proper time is superior.

[1] *Lit.* "for your blood"—your life having been restored after the night's sleep.

[2] *M.* here omits "in the name of R. Josē b. R. Ḥannina," rightly so because he was a *disciple* of R. Joḥanan.

[3] "To receive upon oneself the Kingdom of Heaven" is the technical expression for reading the *Shᵉmaʻ*; cf. fol. 13 *a*, p. 82.

[4] The first of the two benedictions introductory to the *Shᵉmaʻ*. See Singer, p. 37.

[5] The benedictions have to be read with the *Shᵉmaʻ* even after the third hour; and this version of Rab Ḥisda's statement agrees with the *Mishnāh* and *Bārāitā*.

MISHNĀH III

Bēt *Shammai say: In the evening a man should recline and read* [*the* Sh^ema'], *and in the morning he should stand up* [*to read it*]; *as it is said, "When thou liest down and when thou risest up"* (*Deut.* vi. 7). *But* Bēt *Hillel say: A man reads it after his own manner*[1]; *as it is said, "And when thou walkest by the way"* (*ibid.*). *If so, why is it said, "When thou liest down and when thou risest up"?* [*That means*], *At the* time *when people lie down and rise up. R. Ṭarphon said: I was once journeying by the way and I reclined to read* [*the* Sh^ema'], *according to the view of* Bēt *Shammai, and I placed myself in danger on account of robbers. They said to him: Thou didst justly incur a penalty for thyself, in that thou didst transgress the view of* Bēt *Hillel.*

GEMĀRĀ

fol. 11 a.

The ground of *Bēt* Shammai's view.

It is all very well that *Bēt* Hillel explain their reasons and the reason of *Bēt* Shammai; but why do not *Bēt* Shammai agree with *Bēt* Hillel? *Bēt* Shammai would tell thee: In that case[2], the text should read, "In the morning and at even"; what means "When thou liest down and when thou risest up"? At the time of lying down, there should be actual lying down [to read the *Sh^ema'*], and at the time of rising up, there should be actual rising up. What, then, do *Bēt* Shammai make of the phrase "and when thou walkest by the way"? This is required in accordance with the teaching: "When thou sittest in thy house" excludes one occupied with a religious duty; "and when thou walkest by the way" excludes a bridegroom[3]. Hence they say: He who takes a virgin to his house as wife is exempt [from the obligation of reading the *Sh^ema'* on the night of his marriage]; but if he marry a widow, he has that obligation. How is this demonstrated[4]? Rab Pappa said: Because [the text uses the word] "way" [we argue], Just as the way is voluntary, so all is voluntary[5].

[1] As he pleases, standing or reclining or walking.

[2] If, as *Bēt* Hillel say, "When thou liest down and risest up" means the *time* when people lie down and rise up.

[3] *M.* applies the bridegroom to "when thou sittest in thy house"; but the reference to "way" later on is against this reading.

[4] That one engaged upon a religious duty is exempt from reading the *Sh^ema'*.

[5] One has the choice of which road he will take; similarly he can choose to engage himself in the fulfilment of a religious duty and consequently be freed from the obligation of the *Sh^ema'*.

Performance of religious duty exempts reading of the *Shema'*.

Are we not here dealing with one who is on his way to perform a religious duty, and even so, the All-merciful requires of him the reading [of the *Shᵉma'*][1]? In that case, the All-merciful should have written "when sitting and when walking." What means "when *thou* sittest and when *thou* walkest"? When sitting for thine own purpose and when walking for thine own purpose, thou art under the obligation [to read the *Shᵉma'*]; but when it is the performance of a religious duty, thou art exempt. If so, even one who takes a widow as wife should also [be exempt][2]! The man [who marries a virgin] is anxious[3]; the other is not. Should the reason [of exemption] be on account of anxiety, then it ought also to apply to one whose ship has sunk at sea! Shouldest thou say that he likewise is exempt, why does R. Abba b. Zabda declare in the name of Rab: A mourner[4] is under the obligation to observe all the commandments mentioned in the *Tōrāh* except *Tᵉfillīn*, because they are called an adornment; as it is said, "Bind thine adornment upon thee" (Ezek. xxiv. 17)? [No, there is a difference]; the former is troubled by the anxiety of a religious duty; but as for the latter, his anxiety is caused by some voluntary affair. And *Bēt* Shammai[5]? They require it for the exclusion of messengers sent out in connection with a religious duty[6]. And *Bēt* Hillel[7]? They answer that it is self-evident that they may read [the *Shᵉma'*] while even on a journey.

Bēt Hillel's view confirmed.

The Rabbis have taught: *Bēt* Hillel say: When standing they may read [the *Shᵉma'*], when sitting they may read, when reclining they may read, when walking by the way they may read, when doing work they may read. It once happened that R. Ishmael and R. Eleazar b. 'Azariah were dining in a certain place, the

[1] The Bible ordains that we should "speak of them" when walking by the way; does this not mean even when on the way to perform a religious duty?

[2] To marry, whether a widow or a virgin, is a religious duty. Why, then, the distinction in the matter of reading the *Shᵉma'*?

[3] Whether she has signs of virginity, an important matter in the Orient. See Deut. xxii. 13 ff., Burckhardt, *Arabic Proverbs* (2nd ed.), p. 140.

[4] An example of one labouring under mental anguish.

[5] What explanation do they offer of "When thou walkest" as distinct from "when walking"? *Bēt* Shammai had explained "when thou walkest" as excluding one occupied with a religious duty; but, according to the *Gᵉmārā*, "when walking" implies that.

[6] For instance, the couriers of the Sanhedrin who, while not actually engaged in a religious duty, are for all that occupied with a task of religious import. According to *Bēt* Shammai they need not interrupt their journey to read the *Shᵉma'*.

[7] What is their opinion of such messengers with reference to the *Shᵉma'*?

former reclining and the latter sitting upright. When the time for reading the *Shema'* arrived, R. Eleazar reclined[1] and R. Ishmael sat up. R. Eleazar b. 'Azariah said to R. Ishmael, "My brother, I will narrate a parable for thee. To what is this like? To one who is told 'Thy beard is well grown[2]' and he answers, 'Then it shall be taken in hand by the barbers[3].' So art thou; all the time that I was sitting up thou wert reclining, but now that I have reclined[4] thou hast sat up!" He replied, "I have acted according to the teaching of *Bēt* Hillel, and thou according to the teaching of *Bēt* Shammai. Not only that, [I sat up] lest the disciples see this[5] and fix the *Halākāh* for future generations." What means "not only that"? Shouldest thou say, "*Bēt* Hillel also hold [that the *Shema'* may be read] in a reclining position!" that is so, but only when one was reclining from the first; but in thy case, since hitherto thou has been sitting up and now thou reclinest, they will say, "We have to infer that [our teachers] agree with the opinion of *Bēt* Shammai," and there is a fear, that the disciples seeing this, will fix the *Halākāh* accordingly for future generations.

Rab Ezekiel taught: If a man acted in accordance with the view of *Bēt* Shammai, he has done [rightly]; if in accordance with the view of *Bēt* Hillel, he has done [rightly]. Rab Joseph said: If he acted in accordance with the view of *Bēt* Shammai, he has done nothing at all. For there is a Mishnaic teaching: If the head and greater part of a man's body be in a *Sukkāh* and his table inside his house[6], *Bēt* Shammai pronounce it invalid, but *Bēt* Hillel declare it valid. *Bēt* Hillel said to *Bēt* Shammai, "It once happened that the Elders of *Bēt* Shammai and the Elders of *Bēt* Hillel went to visit R. Joḥanan b. ha-Ḥoranit and they found him with his head and the greater part of his body in the *Sukkāh* and his table inside his house, but they said nothing to him." They asked them[7], "Is proof to be drawn from this? They certainly told him, 'If this be thy practice, never hast thou in thy life-time properly observed the commandment of *Sukkāh*!'"

Further confirmation.

[1] Acting according to *Bēt* Shammai; but why did R. Ishmael sit up?

[2] A compliment in the East; cf. Lane, p. 29.

[3] So Rashi. Another possible rendering is: "It is only in opposition to those who destroy [their beard by shaving]." Cf. *T.A.* I. p. 648 n. 853. The point of the parable is perverseness in doing the opposite of what is expected.

[4] Out of deference to R. Ishmael.

[5] That we both read the *Shema'* reclining.

[6] During the Feast of Tabernacles when the Israelite is commanded to dwell in a booth.

[7] *Bēt* Shammai replied.

Rab Naḥman b. Isaac said: If one acted according to the view of *Bēt* Shammai, he is worthy of death; for we have learnt in our *Mishnāh*: *R. Ṭarphon said: I was once journeying by the way and I reclined to read [the* Shᵉma'] *according to the view of* Bēt *Shammai, and I placed myself in danger on account of robbers. They said to him: Thou didst justly incur a penalty for thyself, in that thou didst transgress the view of* Bēt *Hillel.*

MISHNĀH IV

In the morning [the reading of the Shᵉma'] *is preceded by two benedictions and followed by one*[1]; *in the evening it is preceded by two and followed by two*[2], *one long and one short. Where [the Rabbis] order to say a long benediction, it is not permissible to say a short one; [where they order] to say a short benediction, it is not permissible to say a long one. [Where they order] to "seal" a benediction*[3], *it is not permissible not to "seal"; [where they order] not to "seal," it is not permissible to "seal."*

GᴱMĀRĀ

The first benediction before the morning *Shᵉma'*. fol. 11 b. Which benedictions does one say [in the morning]? R. Jacob[4] said in the name of R. Osha'ya: "[Blessed]....Who formest light and createst darkness[5]." Surely one ought rather to say: "Who formest light and createst *brightness*"! As it is written[6], so we say it. But in the case of the words "I make peace and create evil" (Is. xlv. 7), do we say them as they are written? It is written "evil," but [in the prayer] we say "all things[7]"! It is an euphemism. Then in the former instance, let us [in the prayer] also use "brightness" [instead of "darkness"] as an euphemism! Raba[8] answered: The purpose is to mention the characteristic of day at night and the characteristic of night in the day. It is quite right [about mentioning] the characteristic of night in the day,

[1] See Singer, p. 37, "Blessed...Who formest light" and p. 39, "With abounding love"; and p. 42, "True and firm."

[2] See Singer, p. 96, "Blessed...Who at Thy word" and "With everlasting love"; and p. 98, "True and trustworthy" and p. 99, "Cause us...to lie down."

[3] I.e. to conclude with the formula "Blessed art Thou, O Lord...."

[4] *M.*: R. Jacob b. Iddi.

[5] Singer, p. 37.

[6] In the Biblical text, Is. xlv. 7.

[7] Singer, *ibid.*

[8] *M.*: Raba b. 'Ulla. On fol. 12 *a*, p. 75, the saying is quoted as the teaching of Rabbah b. 'Ulla, which is the correct form of the name.

since we say "Who formest light and createst *darkness*"; but where is [the mention of] the characteristic of day at night? Abbai answered: [We say] "Thou rollest away the light from before the darkness, and the darkness from before the light[1]."

The second benediction.

Which is the other [blessing to be recited before the morning *Sh^ema'*]? Rab Judah said in the name of Samuel: "With abounding love[2]"; and so R. Eleazar taught his son R. Pedat to say "With abounding love." There is a teaching to the same effect: We do not say "With everlasting love[3]," but "With abounding love." But the Rabbis declare that "With everlasting love" [is to be recited]; for so it is said, "Yea, I have loved thee with an everlasting love; therefore with affection have I drawn thee" (Jer. xxxi. 3).

Benediction of *Sh^ema'* makes that for study of *Tōrāh* unnecessary.

Rab Judah said in the name of Samuel: When one rises early to study [*Tōrāh*], if he had not yet read the *Sh^ema'*, he must utter a benediction [prefatory to study]; but should he have read the *Sh^ema'*, it is not necessary to utter a benediction, for he has freed himself from the obligation by having recited "With abounding love[4]."

Benediction before study of *Tōrāh* required.

Rab Huna said: For the study of the Scriptures a benediction is necessary, but not for the study of *Midrāsh*. R. Eleazar said: For the study of the Scriptures and *Midrāsh* a benediction is required, but not for the study of the *Mishnāh*. R. Joḥanan said: For the *Mishnāh* it is also required, but not for the study of *Talmūd*. Raba said: Also for the study of *Talmūd* it is necessary to recite a benediction[5]. For Rab Ḥiyya b. Ashē said: On many occasions have I stood before Rab to study the chapters of the *Sifrā d^ebē Rab*[6]; he first washed his hands, uttered a benediction, and then taught us the chapters.

Wording of the benediction.

What was the benediction? Rab Judah said in the name of Samuel: "[Blessed art Thou, O Lord our God, King of the Universe], Who hast sanctified us by Thy commandments and

1 Singer, p. 96.

2 *Ibid.* p. 39.

3 Which is prefaced to the evening *Sh^ema'*, *ibid.* p. 96.

4 Because this benediction includes: "O put it into our hearts to understand and to discern...and to fulfil in love all the words of instruction in Thy *Tōrāh*. Enlighten our eyes in Thy *Tōrāh*," etc. Singer, p. 39.

5 Even if the *Sh^ema'* with its benedictions had been said. The views of the various Rabbis here mentioned are differently given in *M.* and edd. See *D. S. ad loc.* The aggregate is the same in all the variants, viz. that a benediction is necessary for each branch of study.

6 A Halakic commentary on Leviticus; see *J. E.* XI. p. 330.

commanded us to occupy ourselves with the words of *Tōrāh*[1]." R. Joḥanan used to conclude thus: "Make pleasant, therefore, we beseech Thee, O Lord our God, the words of Thy *Tōrāh* in our mouth and in the mouth of Thy people, the house of Israel, so that we with our offspring and the offspring of Thy people, the house of Israel, may all know Thy name and occupy ourselves with Thy *Tōrāh*. Blessed art Thou, O Lord, Who teachest *Tōrāh* to Thy people Israel[2]." Rab Hamnuna[3] said: "[Blessed]...Who hast chosen us from all nations and given us Thy *Tōrāh*. Blessed art Thou, O Lord, Who givest the *Tōrāh*[4]." Rab Hamnuna said: This is the choicest of benedictions. Rab Pappa said[5]: Therefore let one say them all.

The ritual in the Temple.

We have learnt elsewhere in the *Mishnāh*: The Temple-superintendent[6] said [to the priests] "Utter one benediction," and they did so. They then read the Decalogue, "Hear, O Israel" etc. (Deut. vi. 4 ff.), "And it shall come to pass if ye shall hearken diligently" etc. (*ibid.* xi. 13 ff.), "And the Lord said" etc. (Num. xv. 37 ff.)[7]. After that they uttered with the people three benedictions, viz. "True and firm[8]," "Accept, O Lord our God[9]" and the Priestly Benediction[10]. On the Sabbath they added a benediction for the outgoing guard[11].

The benediction used in the Temple before the *Sh*ema'.

Which is the one benediction[12]? It so happened that R. Abba and R. Josē b. Abba[13] came to a certain place and were asked: Which is the one benediction? They were unable to answer; so they went and questioned Rab Matt^ena, and he could not answer. They thereupon asked Rab Judah. He replied: Thus said Samuel: It is "With abounding love." But R. Z^eriḳa stated that R. Ammi said in the name of R. Simeon b. Laḳish: It is "Who formest light." When Rab Isaac b. Joseph came [from Palestine], he said:

[1] Singer, p. 4. [2] *Ibid.*

[3] *M.* omits Hamnuna, making Rab the teacher.

[4] Singer, *loc. cit.* [5] Added by *M.*

[6] *Lit.* "the appointed one." He is identical with the *S^egan ha-Kōh^anīm*. On this official, see Schürer, ii. i. pp. 257 ff., *J. E.* x. p. 196, and Büchler, *Priester und Cultus*, pp. 103 ff. Cf. also *M. G. W. J.* lxiv. pp. 30 ff.

[7] These are the three paragraphs of the *Sh^ema'*; Singer, pp. 40 ff.

[8] *Ibid.* p. 42. [9] *Ibid.* p. 50. [10] *Ibid.* p. 53.

[11] The priests were divided into twenty-four "guards" or "courses," each doing duty for a week, from one Sabbath to the next. On the functions of the priests in the Sanctuary, see Edersheim, *The Temple*, p. 86, Schürer, ii. i. p. 220.

[12] Referred to above: The Temple-superintendent said to the priests "Utter one benediction."

[13] *M.*: Raba and Rab Joseph.

The statement of R. Z^e^riḳa was not explicitly made but was inferred; for what R. Z^e^riḳa stated that R. Ammi said in the name of R. Simeon b. Laḳish was: This teaches that the benedictions do not invalidate one another[1]. Now it is quite right if thou maintainest that [the priests] recited "Who formest light"; then it would follow that the benedictions do not invalidate one another, for they omitted "With abounding love." Shouldest thou, on the other hand, maintain that they recited "With abounding love," how would it follow that the benedictions do not invalidate one another? Perhaps the reason they omitted "Who formest light" was because it was not yet time for that prayer[2], and when the proper time arrived, they said it! And if this be an inference, what then[3]? It might have been inferred that it was certainly "With abounding love" that [the priests] recited, and when the proper time for reciting "Who formest light" arrived, they said it; and what means "The benedictions do not invalidate one another"? The *order* of the benedictions[4]. **fol. 12 a.**

Reading of the Decalogue before the *Sh^e^ma'* abolished.

[The *Mishnāh* quoted above states:] Then they read the Decalogue, "Hear, O Israel," "And it shall come to pass, if ye shall hearken diligently," "And the Lord said," "True and firm," "Accept, O Lord our God," and the Priestly Benediction. Rab Judah said in the name of Samuel: Also beyond the confines of the Temple they wished to read [the Decalogue with the *Sh^e^ma'*] but it had long been abolished because of the murmuring of the *Mīnīm*[5]. There is a teaching to the same effect: R. Nathan said: Outside the Temple they wished to read [the Decalogue with the *Sh^e^ma'*] but it had long been abolished because of the murmuring of the *Mīnīm*. Rabbah b. Rab Huna[6] thought to establish it in

[1] E.g. two blessings have to precede the recital of the *Sh^e^ma'*. If the first were said but the second omitted, then the omission of the second does not invalidate the first. All that R. Z^e^riḳa said was that the practice of the priests in the Temple illustrated this principle; and from this statement the conclusion was drawn that the benediction recited was "Who formest light."

[2] This Service in the Temple was before daybreak.

[3] Why was Rab Isaac b. Joseph so careful to mention that R. Z^e^riḳa's opinion depended only on an inference and not explicit teaching?

[4] Not the *omission* of a benediction; i.e. the principle "The benedictions do not invalidate one another" might have been taken to mean that the saying of "With abounding love" first (for the reason that it was not yet daybreak) followed by "Who formest light" was not invalidated because of the inverse order. But this inference would be incorrect.

[5] Who declared that only the Decalogue was given on Mt Sinai; so *J. T.*

[6] This reading of *M.* is to be preferred to edd.: Rabbah b. bar Ḥannah. See Hyman, III. p. 1077 *b*.

Sura[1]; but Rab Ḥisda told him it had been previously abolished because of the murmuring of the *Mīnīm*. Amemar thought to establish it in Nehardea[2]; but Rab Ashē told him it had previously been abolished because of the murmuring of the *Mīnīm*.

The benediction for the outgoing guard.

[The *Mishnāh*-quotation continues:] On the Sabbath they added a benediction for the outgoing guard. Which is this benediction? R. Ḥelbo said: The outgoing guard said to the incoming guard, "May He Who caused His name to dwell in this house make love and brotherhood, peace and comradeship, to abide amongst you."

Where [the Rabbis] order to say a long benediction, it is not permissible to say a short one.

Does validity of a benediction depend upon the main theme or the conclusion?

It is evident that one who took a cup of wine, and thinking that it was beer, commenced saying the benediction on the supposition that it was beer, and then concluded the benediction for wine, has complied with the requirements of the law; because even if he had said "[Blessed]...by Whose word all things exist[3]," he would also have complied with the requirements of the law. For there is a Mishnaic teaching: If one has uttered the benediction "By Whose word all things exist" over any kind of liquor, he has fulfilled his obligation. But if one took a cup of beer, and thinking it was wine began the benediction for wine and concluded with the benediction for beer, how is it then? Do we follow the main theme of the benediction or its conclusion?

A case quoted to prove that it depends upon the conclusion.

Come and hear[4]: In the morning service, if one commences with "Who formest light" but concludes with "Who bringest on the evening twilight[5]," he has not complied with the requirements of the law. If he opened with "[Blessed]...Who at Thy word bringest on the evening twilight" and concluded with "Creator of the luminaries[6]," he has so complied. In the evening service, if he opened with "Who at Thy word bringest on the evening twilight" and concluded with "Creator of the luminaries[7],"

[1] A town in S. Babylonia where Rab founded his School; Neubauer, p. 343.

[2] The oldest Jewish settlement in Babylon, situated near the junction of the Euphrates and Nahr Malka. See Neubauer, pp. 350 f., Schürer, II. ii. pp. 224 f., *J. E.* IX. p. 208.

[3] This is the benediction for any beverage except wine; Singer, p. 290. For wine the benediction is: "...Who createst the fruit of the vine"; *ibid.* p. 287.

[4] See p. 4 n. 5.

[5] Instead of concluding "Blessed...Creator of the luminaries" (Singer, p. 39) he wrongly says the formula of the evening prayer (*ibid.* p. 96).

[6] He wrongly commenced with the evening prayer, and when about to conclude it notices the error and ends it with the correct formula.

[7] The benediction is correct but the conclusion wrong.

he has not so complied. If he opened with "Who formest light" and concluded with "Who bringest on the evening twilight[1]," he has so complied. The general rule in this matter is, therefore, that it depends upon the conclusion of the benediction[2]. But it is different here, because he has said "Blessed art Thou, *O Lord*, Creator of the luminaries[3]." That is quite right according to Rab who declares that a benediction which does not contain the Divine Name is no benediction. But, according to R. Johanan who holds that a benediction which does not contain a reference to the Divine Kingship is no benediction, what is there to say[4]? But since Rabbah b. 'Ulla has declared: "The purpose is to mention the characteristic of day at night and the characteristic of night in the day[5]," having uttered the benediction and the reference to the Divine Kingship from the commencement, he said them of both[6].

The quoted *Bārāitā* elucidated.

Come and hear: From the latter clause [of the quoted *Bārāitā*] "The general rule in this matter is that it depends upon the conclusion of the benediction"—what does "the general rule in this matter" intend to include? Is it not to include what we have mentioned[7]? No; it is to include the instance of bread and dates. How is this to be understood? Are we to suppose that it refers to one who ate bread and thinking that it was dates he had eaten, commences the benediction on the supposition it was dates, but concludes with the benediction for bread? This is the same as

[1] The benediction is wrong but the conclusion correct.

[2] Are we, by analogy, to apply this rule to the instance of wine and beer?

[3] The addition of "Blessed art Thou, O Lord" constitutes what follows a complete benediction in itself, quite irrespective of what precedes. For that reason, although the main theme was wrong, so long as the concluding benediction is correct, the requirement of the law has been fulfilled. The instance of wine and beer is different, because he began the benediction for wine and in the middle noticed the error, but the words which followed did not constitute a *complete* benediction.

[4] The formula "Blessed...Creator of the luminaries" contains the divine Name and is, according to Rab, a complete benediction. But according to R. Johanan who requires the inclusion of the words "King of the universe," how can it be considered a complete benediction?

[5] See fol. 11*b*, p. 70.

[6] The morning prayer opens "Blessed art Thou, O Lord our God, *King of the universe*, Who formest light and createst darkness" (Singer, p. 37); the evening prayer "Blessed art Thou, O Lord our God, *King of the universe*... Thou rollest away the light from before the darkness" (*ibid.* p. 96). In either case his benediction refers to the Kingship and can apply to either "light" or "darkness," since both are mentioned. Therefore the objection raised on the score of R. Johanan's requirement is not valid.

[7] The instance of wine and beer.

the last-mentioned case[1]! No, [the "general rule"] is necessary for the following: If, for instance, one ate dates, and thinking it was bread, commenced with the benediction for bread but concluded with the benediction for dates, he has complied with the requirements of the law; for even if he had concluded with the benediction for bread, he would also have so complied. What is the reason? Because dates likewise nourish[2].

Benediction after *Shᵉma'* essential.

Rabbah b. Ḥinnana[3] the Elder said in the name of Rab: Whoever does not recite "True and firm" in the morning and "True and trustworthy[4]" in the evening has not fulfilled his obligation; as it is said, "To declare Thy lovingkindness in the morning and Thy faithfulness in the night-seasons" (Ps. xcii. 3)[5].

On bowing in the course of the *Tᵉfillāh*.

Rabbah b. Ḥinnana [the Elder] also said in the name of Rab: When one prays [the *Tᵉfillāh*] and has to bow[6], he should bow at the word "Blessed"; and when returning to the erect position, he should do so on mentioning the Divine Name. Samuel asked: What is Rab's reason? Because it is written, "The Lord raiseth up them that are bowed down" (*ibid.* cxlvi. 8)[7]. Against this is quoted, "And from before My name he is afraid" (Mal. ii. 5)[8]! Is it written "at My name[9]"? No, "from before My name" is written. Samuel said to Ḥiyya b. Rab: O son of the Law, come and let me tell thee an excellent thing which thy father once said. Thus spake thy father: When one bows, he should do so at the word "Blessed"; and when he returns to the erect position, he

fol. 12 b.

should do so on mentioning the Divine Name. When Rab Sheshet bowed, he did so like a twig[10]; but when he returned to the erect position, he did so like a snake.

[1] The instance quoted is parallel to that of wine and beer; and if the "general rule" includes the former, why not the latter?

[2] The benediction after eating bread contains "Since Thou nourishest and sustainest all beings...Blessed art Thou, O Lord, Who givest food unto all" (Singer, p. 280); this would appropriately apply also to dates.

[3] *M.*: Raba b. Ḥannina; another variant is: Rabbah b. Ḥannina. See *D. S. ad loc.*

[4] Singer, pp. 42, 98.

[5] The morning prayer refers to God's lovingkindness, the evening prayer to His faithfulness in fulfilling His promises.

[6] The regulation is to bow four times: at the beginning and end of the first benediction (Singer, p. 44), "We give thanks unto Thee" (p. 51), "Blessed...Whose name is all-good" (p. 53).

[7] Therefore one should stand erect on mentioning His name.

[8] Therefore he should still be bent on mentioning His name.

[9] I.e. When the Name is mentioned, one should be bowed?

[10] With one sharp bend of the body, but he raised himself gradually and painfully.

Rabbah b. Ḥinnana the Elder also said in the name of Rab: During the whole year, one should in the *T^{e}fillāh* use the phrases "The holy God" and "King Who lovest righteousness and judgment[1]"; except during the ten days from the New Year until the Day of Atonement, when he should substitute "The holy King" for the former and "King of judgment" for the latter. R. Eliezer said: Even if he used the phrase "holy God," he has complied with the requirements of the law; as it is said, "But the Lord of hosts is exalted through justice, and the *holy God* is sanctified through righteousness" (Is. v. 16). When is "the Lord of hosts exalted through justice"? During the ten days from the New Year until the Day of Atonement, and yet it is stated thereby "the holy God"! How is it, then, in this matter? Rab Joseph declared: "The holy God" and "King Who lovest righteousness and judgment" should be said[2]: Rabbah declared: "The holy King" and "King of judgment" should be said; and the *H^{a}lākāh* is in accord with Rabbah's view.

Alteration in wording of *T^{e}fillāh* during the "ten days of repentance."

Rabbah b. Ḥinnana the Elder also said in the name of Rab: Whoever has it in his power to pray on behalf of his neighbour and fails to do so is called a sinner; as it is said, "Moreover as for me, far be it from me that I should sin against the Lord in ceasing to pray for you" (I Sam. xii. 23). Raba[3] said: If [the neighbour] be a disciple of the wise, then it is necessary to grieve on his behalf [should he be in trouble]. What is the reason? Are we to suppose it is because it is written, "There is none of you that is sorry for me or discloseth unto me" (*ibid.* xxii. 8)? Perhaps it is different in the case of a king[4]! Nay, [derive the reason] from the following: "But as for me, when they were sick, my clothing was sackcloth, I afflicted my soul with fasting; and my prayer, may it return into mine own bosom" (Ps. xxxv. 13)[5].

One should pray for his neighbour, and grieve with a disciple of the wise in time of trouble.

Rabbah b. Ḥinnana the Elder also said in the name of Rab: Whoever commits a transgression and is filled with shame thereby, all his sins are forgiven him; as it is said, "That thou mayest remember and be confounded, and never open thy mouth any more, because of thy shame; when I have forgiven thee all that thou hast done, saith the Lord God" (Ezek. xvi. 63). Perhaps it is

Shame expiates transgression.

[1] See Singer, pp. 45, 48.

[2] Even during the days of penitence.

[3] *M.*: Rabbah.

[4] The verse quoted refers to Saul; and it may be argued that one should grieve for the anxieties of a king, but not of a scholar.

[5] This verse is explained as referring to Doeg and Aḥitophel, who were authorities on *Tōrāh*.

different with a community[1]? Nay, [derive the reason] from the following: "And Samuel said to Saul, Why hast thou disquieted me, to bring me up? And Saul answered, I am sore distressed; for the Philistines make war against me, and God is departed from me, and answereth me no more, neither by prophets, nor by dreams; therefore I have called thee, that thou mayest make known unto me what I shall do" (I Sam. xxviii. 15). Saul did not mention [having inquired through] the *Ūrīm* and *Tummīm*[2], because he put Nob, the city of the priests, to the sword[3]. Whence do we know that he was forgiven by God? As it is said, "(And Samuel said unto Saul)[4], Tomorrow shalt thou and thy sons be with me" (*ibid. v.* 19); upon which R. Joḥanan comments, "with me" i.e. in my division[5]. The Rabbis [find that Saul was forgiven] in the following: "We will hang them up unto the Lord in Gibeah of Saul, the chosen of the Lord[6]" (II Sam. xxi. 6). A *Bat Ḳōl* issued forth and proclaimed "The chosen of the Lord."

Why the *Pārāshāh* of Balak was not included in the *Sh^e^ma'*.

R. Abbahu b. Zuṭarti said in the name of R. Judah b. Z^e^bida[7]: It was sought to include the *Pārāshāh* of Balak[8] in the reading of the *Sh^e^ma'*. Why did they not do so? Because of the trouble [its length would cause] to the congregation. On what ground [did they wish to include it]? Was it because it is written therein, "God Who brought them forth out of Egypt" (Num. xxiii. 22)? Then let one say the *Pārāshāh* of usury[9] or of weights[10] which likewise contains a reference to the exodus from Egypt! Nay; R. Josē

[1] The verse quoted refers to the people generally, not an individual.

[2] See p. 12 n. 1.

[3] In I Sam. xxviii. 6 it is stated, "The Lord answered him not, neither by dreams, nor by *Ūrīm*, nor by prophets." Saul omitted to mention the *Ūrīm* because the oracle was worked through the priests, and he had smitten their city (*ibid.* xxii. 19). This is evidence of shame for his crime.

[4] These words do not occur in the Bible text and are omitted in *M.*

[5] I.e. my division in Heaven—evidence of Saul's sins having been forgiven.

[6] These words were spoken by the Gibeonites who wished to vent their hatred on Saul's house; they would accordingly not have referred to Saul as "the chosen of the Lord." The Rabbis therefore explain that these words were uttered by a *Bat Ḳōl*; and if he was proclaimed "the chosen of the Lord," that is evidence that he had received forgiveness.

[7] *M.*: Rabbi b. Zuṭarti in the name of R. Josē b. Z^e^bida. For "Rabbi" read probably "Rabin"; see *D. S. ad loc.*

[8] Num. xxii. 2–xxiv. 25.

[9] Lev. xxv. 35–38. The last verse reads, "I am the Lord your God, Who brought you forth out of the land of Egypt."

[10] Lev. xix. 36, "Just balances, just weights...shall ye have; I am the Lord your God who brought you out of the land of Egypt."

b. Abin said: [The reason is] because it is written therein, "He couched, he lay down as a lion, and as a lioness; who shall rouse him up?" (*ibid.* xxiv. 9)[1]. Then let him say that verse and no more [if the whole is too lengthy]! We have a tradition that any *Pārāshāh* which Moses our teacher divided off, we may divide off; but a *Pārāshāh* which he had not divided off, we may not.

Why the *Pārāshāh* of Fringes was included.

Why was the *Pārāshāh* of Fringes[2] included [in the *Shma'*]? R. Judah b. Ḥabiba[3] said: Because there are five things contained therein: the command of fringes; the exodus from Egypt; the yoke of the commandments; [a warning against] heretical opinions [*Mīnūt*]; lustful imagination and idolatrous longing. Quite right that three of these are explicitly stated therein; viz.: the yoke of the commandments, as it is written, "That ye may look upon it and remember all the commandments of the Lord" (*ibid.* xv. 39); the command of Fringes, as it is written, "That they make for themselves fringes" (*ibid. v.* 38); the exodus from Egypt, as it is written, "I am the Lord your God, Who brought you out of the land of Egypt to be your God; I am the Lord your God" (*ibid. v.* 41). But where is there reference to heretical opinions and lustful imagination and idolatrous longing? There is a teaching[4]: "After your heart" (*ibid. v.* 39) means heresy; for thus the Scriptures state, "The fool hath said in *his heart*, There is no God" (Ps. xiv. 1). "After your own eyes" (Num. *l.c.*) means lustful imagination; as it is said, "And Samson said unto his father, Get her for me, for she is pleasing in *my eyes*" (Judg. xiv. 3). "After which ye use to go astray" (Num. *l.c.*) means idolatrous longing; for thus the Scriptures state, "The children of Israel again went astray after the Baalim" (Judg. viii. 33).

MISHNĀH V

The exodus from Egypt must be mentioned at night[5]. *R. Eleazar b. 'Azariah said: Behold I am like one seventy years old*[6], *and*

[1] It contains a reference to lying down and rising up.

[2] Num. xv. 37–41; Singer, pp. 41 f.

[3] *M.*: Josē b. Zebida.

[4] *M.*: Rab Joseph taught.

[5] Referring to the third paragraph of the *Shema'*. The reason why this paragraph is said at night cannot be because of the reference to the "Fringes," since the regulation concerning them does not apply at night. It is said because of the reference to the Exodus.

[6] The ordinary translation would be "about seventy years old"; but see the narrative on fol. 28 *a*, p. 182. There is a variant "eighty years old" which Bacher considers the truer reading; see *A. T.* I. p. 214 n. 7.

*I have never been worthy [to hear the reason] why the exodus from Egypt should be mentioned at night, until Ben Zoma expounded it [as follows]. It is said, "That thou mayest remember the day when thou camest forth out of the land of Egypt all the days of thy life" (Deut. xvi. 3). [Had the Scriptures stated] "the days of thy life" [it would have meant] the days only; but "*all *the days of thy life" [must be intended to include] the nights. The Sages explain the verse thus: "The days of thy life" signifies [thy lifetime] in this world; "all" is to include the days of the Messiah.*

GᴱMĀRĀ

The Exodus from Egypt will be remembered in the days of the Messiah.

There is a teaching: Ben Zoma said to the Sages: Will the exodus from Egypt be mentioned in the days of the Messiah? Has it not long ago been declared, "Therefore behold, the days come, saith the Lord, that they shall no more say, As the Lord liveth, that brought up the children of Israel out of the land of Egypt; but, as the Lord liveth, that brought up and that led the seed of the house of Israel out of the north country, and from all the countries whither I had driven them" (Jer. xxiii. 7 f.)? They answered him: [This passage does not mean] that the memory of the exodus from Egypt is to be obliterated, but that [the memory of the release from] the servitude of the kingdoms will be fundamental and the exodus of Egypt secondary to it. Take the following as an analogy: "Thy name shall no more be called Jacob, but

fol. 13 a.

Israel shall be thy name" (Gen. xxxv. 10). It is not intended that the name Jacob shall be obliterated[1], but that Israel will be fundamental and Jacob secondary. Similarly the Scriptures state, "Remember ye not the former things, neither consider the things of old" (Is. xliii. 18)—"Remember ye not the former things," i.e. the servitude of the kingdoms, "neither consider the things of old," i.e. the exodus from Egypt.

Later troubles cause the former to be forgotten.

"Behold I will do a new thing; now shall it spring forth" (*ibid. v.* 19). Rab Joseph taught: This refers to the war of Gog and Magog[2]. A parable: to what is this like? To a man walking by the way, when a wolf attacked him and he was rescued from it; then he is fond of relating his adventure with the wolf. [Later on] a lion attacked him and he was rescued from it; so he is fond of relating his adventure with the lion. [After that] a serpent attacked him and he was rescued from it; so he forgets his two

[1] God Himself refers to him by that name, Gen. xlvi. 2.

[2] See p. 41 n. 4.

previous adventures, and relates the incident of the serpent. So is it also with Israel; later troubles cause the former to be forgotten.

Change of name of Abram and Sarai.

"Abram, the same is Abraham" (I Chron. i. 27). At first he was made the father of Aram, but subsequently the father of all the universe[1]. Sarai, the same is Sarah. At first she was made princess of her own people, but subsequently princess of all the universe[2].

Abraham must not be called "Abram."

Bar Ḳappara taught: Whoever calls Abraham "Abram" transgresses a command; as it is said, "Thy name shall be Abraham" (Gen. xvii. 5). R. Eliezer says: He transgresses a prohibition; as it is said, "Thy name shall no more be called Abram" (*ibid.*). But now, can this also apply to one who calls Sarah "Sarai[3]"? In her case the Holy One, blessed be He, said to Abraham, "As for Sarai thy wife, *thou* shalt not call her name Sarai, but Sarah shall her name be" (*ibid. v.* 15)[4]. Does it likewise apply to one who calls Jacob "Jacob"? No; it is different here, because the Scriptures afterwards repeat [his old name]; as it is written, "And God spoke unto Israel in the visions of the night, and said, Jacob, Jacob" (*ibid.* xlvi. 2). R. Josē b. Abin (others declare it was R. Josē b. Zebida) quoted in objection: "Thou art the Lord the God, Who didst choose *Abram*" (Neh. ix. 7)! He was answered: In this passage the prophet narrates the praise of the All-merciful by reviewing what had happened from the beginning[5].

May we return to thee: *From what time*[6].

1 Abram is taken to mean "the father of Aram," whereas Abraham means "father of a multitude of nations" (Gen. xvii. 4).

2 Sarai is taken to mean "my princess," whereas Sarah means "princess" (sc. of all).

3 Would a command and prohibition be transgressed?

4 The command was meant for Abraham only.

5 The verse narrates history and continues "and gavest him the name of Abraham."

6 A prayer inserted at the end of each chapter. On the method of naming the Chapter, see Introduction, § 2.

CHAPTER II

MISHNĀH I, II

I. *Should a man be reading in the* Tōrāh [*the section of the* Sh^{e}ma'] *and the time of reciting the* Sh^{e}ma' *arrived, if he directed his heart*[1], *he has fulfilled his obligation. Between the sections, he may greet a man out of respect for him and return a salutation; but in the middle* [*of the sections*] *he may greet a man because of fear for him*[2] *and return a salutation. These are the words of R. Meïr. R. Judah says: In the middle, he may greet a man because of fear for him, and return a salutation out of respect; and between the sections, he may greet a man out of respect for him and return the salutation of any person.*

II. *The following are "between the sections": Between the first benediction and the second*[3]; *between the second and "Hear, O Israel"; between "Hear, O Israel" and "And it shall come to pass if ye shall hearken"; between "And it shall come to pass if ye shall hearken" and "And the Lord spake"; between "And the Lord spake" and "True and firm." R. Judah says: One must make no interruption between "And the Lord spake" and "True and firm." R. Joshua b. Ḳarḥah said: Why does the section "Hear, O Israel" precede "And it shall come to pass if ye shall hearken"? So that a man shall first receive upon himself the yoke of the kingdom of heaven, and afterwards receive upon himself the yoke of the commandments. And why does "And it shall come to pass if ye shall hearken" precede "And the Lord spake"? Because the former applies both during the day and night, but the latter during the day only*[4].

[1] I.e. intended that his reading of the passage should be the fulfilment of his duty to recite the *Sh^{e}ma'*. But see the explanation in the *G^{e}mārā*.

[2] The reference is to somebody in authority who might resent the omission to salute him.

[3] At the end of "Creator of the luminaries," Singer, p. 39.

[4] The second section of the *Sh^{e}ma'* deals with the duty of studying *Tōrāh* which continues throughout the day and night; cf. Josh. i. 8. But the third paragraph contains the law of "Fringes" which does not apply at night.

GᴱMĀRĀ

A phrase in the Mishnāh explained.

Is the conclusion to be drawn [from the opening sentence of the *Mishnāh*] that the performance of the commandments requires *Kawwānāh*[1]? [No; for] what means *If he directed his heart* to read? Just to read [in the *Tōrāh* for the sake of study]. But he was reading[2]! [It is to differentiate him] from one who is reading [the *Tōrāh*] for the purpose of correcting[3].

Whether the Shᵉmaʻ must be read in Hebrew only.

Our Rabbis have taught: The *Shᵉmaʻ* must be read as it is written[4]: These are the words of Rabbi[5]; but the Sages say: [It may be read] in any language[6]. What is Rabbi's reason? The text states, "And these words *shall be*" (Deut. vi. 6); i.e. as they are, so must they remain. And what is the reason of the Sages? The text states, "*Hear*, O Israel" (*ibid. v.* 4); i.e. in any language which thou hearest. But for Rabbi also it is written "*Hear*, O Israel[7]"! He requires it to establish the rule, Cause thine ear to hear what thou utterest with thy lips[8]. And the Sages? They agree with him who says that if one does not read [the *Shᵉmaʻ*] audibly, he has still fulfilled his obligation. But for the Sages also it is written "And these words *shall be*"! They require it to establish the rule that one must not read [the sentences of the *Shᵉmaʻ*] out of order. Whence does Rabbi find authority for the rule that the *Shᵉmaʻ* may not be read out of order[9]? He derives it from the fact that the text states "*these* words shall be" and not "*the* words shall be." And the Sages [what do they make of this distinction between "*these* words" and "*the* words"]? They draw no conclusion from it at all.

1 That would seem to be implied in the statement "if he directed his heart"; but elsewhere in the Talmūd it is stated that *Kawwānāh* is not required. See Rōsh Hash. 28 *a*.

2 How can it be maintained that "if he directed his heart" means to study and not to prayer, since the *Mishnāh* opens with the statement that he was studying?

3 The man who was reading the *Tōrāh* may have been a corrector of manuscripts and examining a paragraph of the *Shᵉmaʻ*. Of him it is required that his reading shall have been with the intention of fulfilling his duty to recite it.

4 In Hebrew only.

5 See p. 9 n. 2.

6 The *Shᵉmaʻ* was read in Greek in Caesarea; Schürer, II. ii. p. 284.

7 How does he interpret the word "Hear"?

8 I.e. the *Shᵉmaʻ* must be read audibly.

9 He cannot derive it from "and these words *shall be*," since he has already used that to prove that only Hebrew may be employed.

Deductions drawn from preceding paragraph. It is possible to say that Rabbi holds that the whole *Tōrāh* can be read in any language. For if thou maintainest that it may be read only in the holy tongue, what are we to make of the phrase "and these words *shall be*" which the All-merciful wrote? It is necessary because it is written "*Hear*, O Israel[1]." It is likewise possible to say that the Sages hold that the whole *Tōrāh* must be read in the holy tongue. For if thou maintainest that it can be read in any language, what are we to make of the phrase "*Hear*, O Israel" which the All-merciful wrote? It is necessary because it is written "And these words *shall be*."

How the *Sh^ema'* must be read. Our Rabbis have taught: "And these words *shall be*" means that one must not recite [the sentences of the *Sh^ema'*] out of order. "These words...*upon thine heart*"—one might suppose that the whole *Pārāshāh* requires *Kawwānāh*; therefore there is a teaching to state, "*These words*...[shall be upon thine heart]," that is to say, up to this point *Kawwānāh* is required, but from this point onward it is not necessary. These are the words of R. Eliezer.

fol. 13b. R. 'Aḳiba said to him: Behold it states, "Which I *command thee* this day...upon thine heart." Hence thou learnest that the whole *Pārāshāh* requires *Kawwānāh*! Rabbah b. Bar Ḥannah said in the name of R. Joḥanan: The *H^alākāh* is in accord with R. 'Aḳiba.

A variant tradition. There are some who connect [the statement of Rabbah b. Bar Ḥannah] with the following. There is a teaching: Who recites the *Sh^ema'* must direct his heart thereto. R. Aḥa[2] says in the name of R. Judah: If one directed his heart in the first paragraph, it is no longer necessary [in the succeeding paragraphs]. Rabbah b. Bar Ḥannah said in the name of R. Joḥanan: The *H^alākāh* is in accord with the view of R. Aḥa which he reported in the name of R. Judah.

The law of *Kawwānāh*. There is a further teaching: "And these words...*shall be*" means one must not read [the sentences of the *Sh^ema'*] out of order. "Upon thine heart"—R. Zoṭra[3] says: Up to here[4] the law of *Kawwānāh* applies, but from here onward the commandment to recite applies. R. Josiah[5] says: Up to here the commandment to

[1] If Rabbi were of opinion that the *Tōrāh* can only be read in Hebrew, it would necessarily apply to the *Sh^ema'*. Why, then, should he draw a conclusion from "And these words shall be"? His opinion must therefore be that the *Tōrāh* can be read in any language; and he draws the conclusion from "And these words shall be" that the *Sh^ema'* must be read in Hebrew to oppose the inference which the Sages drew from "Hear, O Israel."

[2] *M.*: Aḥai. We must read in the text R. Aḥa, not Rab Aḥa.

[3] *M.*: Eliezer.

[4] The first paragraph of the *Sh^ema'*.

[5] *M.*: Joshua.

recite applies, but from here onward the law requiring *Kawwānāh* applies What is the distinction that from here onward the commandment to recite applies? Because it is written, "talking of them[1]." But in the first *Pārāshāh* it is likewise written "and shalt talk of them"! What he means to say is, Up to here the law of *Kawwānāh* and reciting applies, but from here onward, reciting without *Kawwānāh* is sufficient. And what is the distinction that up to [the end of the first paragraph] the law of *Kawwānāh* and reciting applies? Because it is written "upon thine heart" and "and shalt talk of them." But in the next paragraph it is likewise written "Upon your heart" and "talking of them"! That is required for that which R. Isaac said: "Therefore shall ye lay up these My words upon your heart" (Deut. xi. 18) is necessary [to teach that the *Tᵉfillīn*] must be placed over against the heart[2].

The teacher stated above: "R. Josiah says: Up to here the commandment to recite applies, but from here onward the law requiring *Kawwānāh* applies." What is the distinction that from here onward the law requiring *Kawwānāh* applies? Because it is written "upon your heart." But in the first *Pārāshāh* it is likewise written "upon thine heart"! What he means to say is, Up to here the law of reciting and *Kawwānāh* applies, but from here onward *Kawwānāh* without reciting is sufficient. And what is the distinction that up to [the end of the first paragraph] the law of reciting and *Kawwānāh* applies? Because it is written "upon thine heart" and "thou shalt talk of them." But in the next paragraph it is likewise written "upon your heart" and "talking of them"! That refers to the words of *Tōrāh*[3]; and thus spake the All-merciful, "Teach your children *Tōrāh* so that they can read therein." **The subject continued.**

Our Rabbis have taught: "Hear, O Israel, the Lord our God, the Lord is one" (Deut. vi. 4)—up to here *Kawwānāh*[4] is required. These are the words of R. Meïr. Raba said: The *Hᵃlākāh* is in accord with R. Meïr. **The decision.**

[1] Deut. xi. 19, in the *second* paragraph of the *Shᵉma'*.

[2] The reference to "heart" in the second paragraph does not indicate *Kawwānāh*, but teaches that the arm-*Tᵉfillīn* must be placed over against the heart. It is worn upon the muscle of the left arm, at a point nearest the heart.

[3] The first paragraph contains "and *thou* shalt talk of them," i.e. the command to recite; but the second contains "Ye shall teach them your children to talk of them" (so literally; i.e. so that *your children* may talk of them by studying *Tōrāh*).

[4] So *M.*; edd. *Kawwānāh* of the heart.

Distinct pronunciation of *éḥād* required.

There is a teaching: Symmachus[1] says: Whoever prolongs the pronunciation of the word *éḥād* "one[2]," his days and years are prolonged for him. Rab Aḥa b. Jacob said: Especially the letter D. Rab Ashē said: Only he must not slur over the letter Ḥ. R. Jeremiah was sitting in the presence of R. Ḥiyya b. Abba[3], and noticed that he prolonged [the word *éḥād*] exceedingly. He said to him: So long as thou hast proclaimed His Kingship above and below and the four winds of heaven[4], more than that is not required of thee.

Sh^e^ma' should be read standing.

Rab Nathan b. Mar 'Uḳba said in the name of Rab Judah: "Upon thine heart" [should be recited] standing. Dost thou imagine that applies only to the words "Upon thine heart"? No; but say, [From the commencement of the *Sh^e^ma'*] up to "upon thine heart" is to be recited standing, but not from there onward. R. Joḥanan said: The whole paragraph should be recited standing; and R. Joḥanan hereby follows out his opinion [expressed in the statement:] Rabbah b. Rab Ḥannah said in the name of R. Joḥanan: The *H^a^lākāh* is in accord with the view of R. Aḥa which he reported in the name of R. Judah[5].

How R. Judah ha-Nāsī' recited the *Sh^e^ma'*.

Our Rabbis have taught[6]: "Hear, O Israel, the Lord our God, the Lord is one"—that was the reading of the *Sh^e^ma'* of R. Judah ha-Nāsī'. Rab said to R. Ḥiyya, "I have never seen Rabbi receive the yoke of the kingdom of heaven upon himself[7]." He replied to him, "Son of princes[8], at the time when he passed his hands across

[1] *M.* adds: b. Joseph.

[2] Thereby emphasising the doctrine of the Unity of God.

[3] *M.*: R. Zera.

[4] I.e. dwell on the word while reflecting that God is One everywhere.

[5] See above, at the beginning of the folio. That view is, the whole of the first paragraph requires *Kawwānāh*. R. Joḥanan, in consistency with that opinion, maintains that if one has to stand for the recital of any part of the first paragraph, he should remain standing for the whole of it.

[6] Instead of "Our Rabbis have taught," *M.* reads: Rab Judah said in the name of Samuel.

[7] When in the course of teaching the time of the *Sh^e^ma'* arrived, Rabbi did not stop to recite it.

[8] A form of address used by R. Ḥiyya to Rab, his nephew. See below, fol. 43 *a*. By "princes" must be understood "ancestors great in *Tōrāh*." It has been ingeniously conjectured that for פחתי (an uncertain word) we should read אחתי "son of my sister," that being the relationship in which Rab stood to him; but it is inexplicable how so common a word as אחתי could have been corrupted. The 'Ārūk reads פאתי, which may be connected with πηός or πάος "a relative by marriage"; see Krauss, p. 420.

his face¹, he received upon himself the yoke of the kingdom of heaven." Did he afterwards finish the *Sh^ema‘* or did he not? Bar Ḳappara says: He did not afterwards finish it. R. Simeon b. Rabbi says: He did afterwards finish it. Bar Ḳappara said to R. Simeon b. Rabbi: It is quite right according to me when I declare he did not afterwards finish it, because Rabbi used [every day] to deal with a theme in which the exodus from Egypt was mentioned²; but according to thee who sayest that he did afterwards finish it, why did he [daily] deal with such a theme? [He replied]: For the purpose of mentioning the exodus from Egypt in its proper time³.

R. Ila⁴ b. Rab Samuel b. Marta said in the name of Rab: [If one recited only the verse] "Hear, O Israel, the Lord our God, the Lord is one" and was then overcome by sleep, he has fulfilled his obligation. Rab Naḥman⁵ said to Daro his servant: With the first verse worry me [to keep awake], but do not so after that. Rab Joseph asked Rab Joseph b. Raba⁶, "How used thy father to do?" He replied, "With the first verse he took pains [to keep awake], but he did not so after that." *First sentence of Sh^ema‘ sufficient at night.*

Rab Joseph said: One who lies on his back should not read the *Sh^ema‘*. Is it only he may not read [the *Sh^ema‘* in this position]; but is it right for him to sleep [in this position]? For lo, R. Joshua b. Levi cursed anyone who slept lying on his back⁷! They answered: To sleep thus is right if he incline a little to one side, but to read the *Sh^ema‘* is forbidden, though he incline to one side. But R. Joḥanan inclined to one side and read the *Sh^ema‘*! It is different with him, because he was corpulent. *Sh^ema‘ must not be read when one lies on his back.*

Between the sections he may greet a man out of respect for him and return a salutation.

He may return a salutation; but on what ground? If it is supposed out of respect, since he is allowed to greet, surely he ought to be permitted to respond! But [the meaning is], He greets a man out of respect, and returns a salutation to any person. *On returning a salutation while reading the Sh^ema‘.*

¹ An act which the pious Jew performs when reciting the first sentence of the *Sh^ema‘*, based on Moses' action of hiding his face at the theophany (Exod. iii. 6). This was an indication that Rabbi recited the opening verse.

² And he intended this as a substitute for the remainder of the *Sh^ema‘*.

³ Rabbi dealt with the theme of the Exodus when the time of the *Sh^ema‘* arrived, but afterwards recited what he had omitted.

⁴ *M.*: Isaac.   ⁵ *M.* incorrectly adds: b. Isaac.

⁶ Not Rabbah as in some edd.

⁷ The word פרקיד is derived from πρωκτός by Perles, *J. Q. R.* xvi. p. 355. The objection to this position is it tends to nocturnal pollution.

Consider the sequel: *In the middle [of the sections] he may greet a man because of fear for him and return the salutation.* On what ground may he respond? If it is supposed because of fear, since he is allowed to greet, surely he ought to be permitted to respond! But [the meaning is, He may return the salutation] out of respect. But that is the view of R. Judah[1]! For our *Mishnāh* states: *R. Judah says: In the middle of a section, he may greet a man because of fear for him and return a salutation out of respect; and between the sections, he may greet a man out of respect and return the salutation of any person!* [The text of the *Mishnāh*] is defective and should read thus: "Between the sections, he may greet a man out of respect for him, and there is no need to state that he may return the salutation; and in the middle [of the sections], he may greet a man because of fear for him, and there is no need to state that he may return a salutation. These are the words of R. Meïr. R. Judah says: In the middle, he may greet

fol. 14 a. because of fear and return a salutation out of respect; and between the sections he may greet out of respect and return the salutation of any person."

The conclusion confirmed.

There is a teaching to the same effect: If one is reading the *Sh^ema'*, and his teacher or one greater than himself meet him, between the sections he may greet him out of respect, and there is no need to state that he may return a salutation; and in the middle [of the sections], he may greet one because of fear, and there is no need to state that he may return a salutation. These are the words of R. Meïr. R. Judah says: In the middle, he may greet because of fear and return a salutation out of respect; and between the sections, he may greet out of respect and return the salutation of any person.

Permissible to interrupt the *Hallēl* or *M^egillāh* to give greeting.

Aḥi, a *Tannā* of the school of R. Ḥiyya, asked R. Ḥiyya: May one interrupt the *Hallēl* or the *M^egillāh* [to greet a person]? Do we argue *a fortiori*: If with the reading of the *Sh^ema'*, which is an ordinance of the *Tōrāh*, one may interrupt, how much more so should it be permitted in the case of the *Hallēl* or the *M^egillāh*[2], which is only a Rabbinical ordinance! Or is it perhaps that the proclamation of a miracle[3] is superior [to the reading of the

[1] But R. Meïr's view which has been under consideration so far cannot agree with R. Judah's, since the latter expounds a different opinion in the *Mishnāh*.

[2] "Or the *M^egillāh*" is added by *M*.

[3] The *Hallēl* proclaims the miracle of the Red Sea, and the *M^egillāh* the miracle of the frustration of Haman's plan to destroy the Jews.

Sh^ema']? He replied: One may interrupt, and there is nothing in that [point you raise].

Rabbah[1] said: On those days when the individual[2] completes the *Hallēl*, he may interrupt between the paragraphs, but in the middle of a paragraph he may not interrupt; and on the days when the individual does not complete the *Hallēl*[3], he may interrupt even in the middle of a paragraph. But it is not so! For behold, Raba b. Rab Shaba[4] visited Rabina[5] on one of those days when the individual does not[6] complete the *Hallēl*, and Rabina did not interrupt [to greet him]! It is different with Raba b. Shaba, since he was not highly esteemed by Rabina. On interrupting the *Hallēl* for a greeting.

Ashyan[7], a *Tannā* of the school of R. Ammi, asked R. Ammi: May one who is undergoing a fast[8] taste anything? If he has taken upon himself [to abstain from] eating and drinking, it comes under the heading of neither; or is it that he has taken upon himself [to abstain from] any kind of gratification, and [tasting] is to be so regarded? He replied: He may taste and there is nothing in that [point you raise]. There is a teaching to the same effect: A woman who tastes [her cooking] is not required to utter a benediction, and she who is undergoing a fast may taste and there is nothing in it. What is the maximum quantity [he may taste]? R. Ammi and R. Assi tasted up to a fourth [of a *lōg*]. One may taste food on a fast day.

Rab said: Whoever greets his neighbour before he prays[9] is as though he accounted him as an idolatrous altar [*bāmāh*][10]; as it is said, "Cease ye from man, in whose nostrils is a breath[11]; for how little [*bamméh*] is he to be accounted" (Is. ii. 22). Read not One should not give greeting before prayer.

[1] *M.*: Raba.

[2] In Tōsāfōt it is pointed out that there is no cause to stress the "individual," the rule holding good also of a Congregation.

[3] On the New Moon and the last six days of Passover; see Singer, p. 220.

[4] So *M.* correctly. Edd: Rab b. Shaba.

[5] *M.*: the School (or house) of Rabina.

[6] *M.* omits "not"; but its inclusion emphasises the objection.

[7] *M.*: R. Isaac b. Ashyan.

[8] A voluntary fast is here meant. On a statutory fast there is no question that tasting (e.g. food that is being cooked) is forbidden.

[9] According to one interpretation, the *T^efillāh* is here intended; otherwise it is contradicted by the passage quoted by Rab Sheshet from the *Mishnāh*, which permits one to offer greeting between the sections of the *Sh^ema'*—which is recited *before* the *T^efillāh*. But R. Abba interprets the phrase "before he prays" quite generally.

[10] On the *Bāmāh* was offered what should have been brought to the Temple. Similarly to greet a man before praying is to give him what is due to God.

[11] To pay him honour instead of God.

bamméh but *bāmāh*[1]. But Samuel said[2]: Why do you esteem this person [whom you greet first] and not God? Rab Sheshet[3] quoted the following in objection: *Between the sections one may greet out of respect and return a salutation*[4]! R. Abba explained [the statements of Rab Samuel to refer] to one who goes first to the door of his neighbour[5].

Prayer must precede one's personal concerns.

R. Jonah said in the name of R. Zera: Whoever attends to his personal affairs before offering his prayers is as though he had erected an idolatrous altar. He was asked: Dost thou say "an idolatrous altar"? He answered: No, I only mean it is prohibited[6]; and it is in accordance with the statement of Rab Iddi b. Abin who said in the name of Rab Isaac b. Ashyan: It is forbidden a man to attend to his personal affairs before offering his prayers; as it is said, "Righteousness shall go before him[7], and shall make his footsteps a way" (Ps. lxxxv. 14). Rab Iddi b. Abin also said in the name of Rab Isaac b. Ashyan: Whoever prays and afterwards goes on his way [to attend to his affairs], the Holy One, blessed be He, attends to them for him; as it is said, "Righteousness shall go before him, and He shall make his footsteps a way."

To be without a dream seven nights is evil.

R. Jonah also said in the name of R. Zera: Whoever sleeps for seven nights without a dream is called evil[8]; as it is said, "He shall abide satisfied [*sābēa'*] he shall not be visited with evil" (Prov. xix. 23). Read not *sābēa'*, but *shéba'* "seven[9]." R. Abba[10], son of R. Ḥiyya b. Abba, said to him: Thus declared R. Ḥiyya[11] in the name of R. Joḥanan: Whoever satisfies[12] himself with words

[1] I.e. translate "for as an idolatrous altar is he to be accounted" if honour is paid to him first.

[2] Interpreting the latter part of the verse as it is written, without reading *Bāmāh* for *bamméh*.

[3] *M.*: Rab Naḥman b. Isaac.

[4] See p. 82.

[5] To greet him, intentionally paying him the first honour. Should he meet him casually, he may salute him prior to praying.

[6] Exception was taken to the exaggeration in applying the word *Bāmāh* to such a case. The reply is that to attend to one's personal affairs before offering prayer in the morning is as prohibited as the erection of a *Bāmāh*.

[7] The verse is made to refer to man, not God. "Righteousness" is understood as the morning devotions.

[8] To be vouchsafed a dream was considered evidence of spiritual grace (cf. Joel iii. 1), and to be without a dream was accordingly deemed to be the consequence of gross, materialistic living.

[9] Translating thus: He who abides seven [nights] without being visited [by a dream] is evil.

[10] So *M.* correctly. Edd.: Aḥa.

[11] *M*: Ḥiyya b. Abba.

[12] Retaining the reading *sābēa'* in Prov. xix. 23.

of *Tōrāh* and then sleeps will not receive evil tidings [in a dream]; as it is said, "He shall abide satisfied [with *Tōrāh*], he shall not be visited with evil."

The following are between the sections, etc.

R. Abbahu said in the name of R. Joḥanan: The *Halākāh* is in accord with R. Judah who maintains that one may not interrupt between "I am the Lord your God" and "True and firm[1]." R. Abbahu [also] said in the name of R. Joḥanan: What is R. Judah's reason? Because it is written, "The Lord God is the true God" (Jer. x. 10). Should one repeat the word "true" or not[2]? R. Abbahu said in the name of R. Joḥanan: He must repeat the word "true." Rabbah[3] said: He does not repeat it. Somebody descended[4] in the presence of Rabbah; and when the latter heard him say *ĕmĕt* "true" twice, he exclaimed, "Every *ĕmĕt* has seized hold of this fellow!"

Benediction after the *Shema'* must immediately follow its conclusion.

fol. 14 b.

Rab Joseph said: How excellent is the teaching which, when Rab Samuel b. Judah came [from Palestine], he reported, viz.: In the West they say in the evening, "Speak unto the children of Israel and say unto them I am the Lord your God. True[5]." Abbai said to him: What is there excellent in this? Behold, Rab Kahana has said in the name of Rab: One need not commence [the third paragraph at all]; but if he has commenced it, he must finish it! Shouldest thou argue that [to say the words] "And thou shalt say unto them" is not commencing[6], behold Rab Samuel b. Isaac has declared in the name of Rab[7]: "Speak unto the children of Israel" is not considered a commencement, but "And thou shalt say unto them" is to be so regarded! Rab Pappa replied: In the West they hold that "And thou shalt say unto them" is likewise not considered a commencement, until one adds "And they shall make

On reading the third paragraph of the *Shema'* in the evening: Palestinian custom.

1 Between the end of the third paragraph of the *Shema'* and the beginning of the benediction which follows; Singer, p. 42.

2 It is customary to conclude the *Shema'*, not with the word "God," but with "true" borrowed from the next paragraph. Has the word "true" to be repeated when continuing the prayer?

3 *M.*: "Raba," and so to the end of the paragraph.

4 "To descend" (or "to pass" sc. before the Ark) means to act as Precentor. On "descending," see p. 65 n. 5.

5 I.e. they say the opening and closing words of the third paragraph of the *Shema'*, leaving out all in between, because it refers to the law of "Fringes" which does not apply at night.

6 Since nothing has been mentioned about the "Fringes"—the theme of the paragraph—one cannot be regarded as having commenced it.

7 *M.*: Behold Rab Samuel b. Rab Isaac has declared.

for themselves fringes." Abbai said: Therefore we[1] commence as they commence in the West, and since we have commenced, we also complete it; for Rab Kahᵃna said in the name of Rab: One need not commence it; but if he has commenced it, he must finish it.

When the benediction after the Shᵉmaʻ must be said.

Ḥiyya b. Rab declared: If one has said "I am the Lord your God," he must continue "True"; if he has not said "I am the Lord your God," it is not necessary to add "True[2]." Yes; but he is required to mention the exodus from Egypt[3]! Let him say the following: "We give thanks unto Thee, O Lord our God, that Thou hast brought us forth from the land of Egypt and redeemed us from the house of bondage, and performed miracles and mighty deeds for us by the Red Sea; to thee do we sing[4]."

R. Joshua b. Ḳarḥah said: Why does the section "Hear O Israel" precede "And it shall come to pass if ye shall hearken"?

The sequence of paragraphs in the Shᵉmaʻ.

There is a teaching: R. Simeon b. Joḥai says: It is right that precedence should be given to "Hear O Israel" over "And it shall come to pass," because the former speaks of learning, the latter of teaching; and to "It shall come to pass" over "And the Lord spake," because the former speaks of teaching[5] and the latter of performing. Do you mean to say that in "Hear O Israel" there is a reference to learning, but not to teaching and performing? Behold it is written, "Thou shalt teach them diligently...thou shalt bind them...thou shalt write them"! And further [do you mean to say that] "And it shall come to pass" contains a reference to teaching, but not to performing? Behold it is written, "Ye shall bind...ye shall write"! Nay; but this is what he means to say: It is right that precedence should be given to "Hear O Israel" over "And it shall come to pass," because the former contains a reference to learning, teaching and performing; and to "And it shall come to pass" over "And the Lord spake," because the former contains a reference to teaching and performing, whereas "And the Lord spake" refers only to performing. But derive the reason [for the order of the paragraphs] from the statement of R. Joshua b. Ḳarḥah[6]! [He gave] one reason and now another is added;

[1] In Babylon.

[2] I.e. the benediction commencing "True and trustworthy"; Singer, p. 93. This benediction contains a reference to the Exodus.

[3] Even in his night-prayers; see above fol. 12 *b*, p. 80.

[4] Continuing "Who is like unto Thee, O Lord?" Singer, p. 99.

[5] Some edd. read "learning" in error.

[6] Why is all this argument necessary, since R. Joshua b. Ḳarḥah gives a reason in the *Mishnāh*?

viz.: [the first is] in order that a man shall first receive upon himself the yoke of the kingdom of heaven and afterwards receive upon himself the yoke of the commandments; and the second reason is because the first paragraph contains these other references.

Tefillin must precede the Shema'.

Rab washed his hands, read the *Shema'*, put on the *Tefillīn* and then offered his prayers. How could he act thus[1]? For lo, there is a teaching: One who is digging a cavity for a corpse[2] is exempt from the obligation of reading the *Shema'*, the *Tefillāh*, *Tefillīn* and all the commandments mentioned in the *Tōrāh*[3]; but when the time of reading the *Shema'* arrives, he ascends, washes his hands, puts on the *Tefillīn*, reads the *Shema'* and offers his prayers? Here is a self-contradiction! The first clause declares such a man to be exempt from the obligation, and the latter imposes the obligation upon him! There is no contradiction: the latter clause referring to where there are two[4], the former to one. Nevertheless it presents a difficulty to Rab. [The solution is:] Rab holds the view of R. Joshua b. Ḳarḥah who says: First there must be the yoke of the kingdom of heaven, and afterwards the yoke of the commandments[5]. R. Joshua b. Ḳarḥah certainly said that the *reading* [of the yoke of heaven, i.e. "Hear O Israel"] is to precede the *reading* [of the yoke of the commandments, i.e. "And it shall come to pass"]; but hast thou heard him say that the reading [of the *Shema'*] should precede the performance [of the duty of *Tefillīn*]? Further, how could Rab be considered as holding the same opinion as R. Joshua b. Ḳarḥah? For Rab Ḥiyya b. Ashē has said: On many occasions have I stood before Rab[6], who first washed his hands, uttered the benediction[7], taught us the chapters, laid *Tefillīn*, *and after that read the Shema'*! Shouldest thou argue that the time for reading the *Shema'* had not yet arrived, in that case

[1] To read the *Shema'* before putting on the *Tefillīn*. From the following discussion it will be seen that this was not Rab's regular practice, but he did so on one occasion.

[2] Edd. add בקבר "in a grave," which is probably a gloss. *M.* reads בקיר "in a wall" i.e. of a cave or vault, where graves were often excavated. See *J.E.* III. p. 437, *T.A.* II. pp. 72 ff.

[3] On the principle "One who is occupied with a religious duty is exempt from a religious duty." Cf. the discussion on fol. 11 *a*, p. 68.

[4] Engaged in digging; in which case one continues the work, while the other offers his prayers.

[5] This Rabbi's statement in the *Mishnāh* is interpreted to mean that first the *Shema'* must be read and then the *Tefillīn* laid.

[6] *M.* adds: "to study the Chapters of the *Sifrā debē Rab*" as on fol. 11 *b* p. 71.

[7] Prior to studying *Tōrāh*.

what purpose is there in the testimony of Rab Ḥiyya b. Ashē? [The object was] to refute him who declared that it is unnecessary to utter a benediction over the study of the *Mishnāh*; hence we are informed that likewise for the *Mishnāh* it is necessary to utter a benediction[1]. Still the difficulty against Rab remains! His messenger was at fault[2].

Reading of *Sh^ema'* without *T^efillīn* denounced.

'Ulla said: Whoever reads the *Sh^ema'* without *T^efillīn* is as though he spoke false testimony against himself[3]. R. Ḥiyya b. Abba said in the name of R. Joḥanan: It is as though he had offered a burnt-offering without a meal-offering (cf. Num. xxviii. 5) and a sacrifice without drink-offerings (*ibid. v.* 14).

fol. 15 a. How to receive upon one's self the yoke of the kingdom of heaven.

R. Joḥanan also said[4]: Whoever wishes to receive upon himself the yoke of the kingdom of heaven in perfection should first have evacuation[5], then wash his hands, lay *T^efillīn*, read the *Sh^ema'* and offer his prayers—that is receiving the kingdom of heaven in perfection. R. Ḥiyya b. Abba said in the name of R. Joḥanan: Whoever has evacuation, washes his hands, lays *T^efillīn*, reads the *Sh^ema'* and offers his prayers, the Scriptures ascribe it to him as though he had erected an altar and brought a sacrifice thereon; as it is written, "I will wash my hands in cleanliness; so will I compass Thine altar, O Lord" (Ps. xxvi. 6). Rabbah[6] said to him: Does not the master think that it is as though he had bathed his whole body[7]? [Yes]; for it is written, "I will wash [in cleanliness][8]" not simply "I will cause [mine hands] to be washed."

[1] Rab Ḥiyya b. Ashē's statement has no bearing on the question under discussion. It was quoted to prove that Rab uttered a benediction before lecturing on *Mishnāh*. In fact, this Rabbi's statement quoted in fol. 11 *b*, does not mention "laid *T^efillīn* and after that read the *Sh^ema'*."

[2] He delayed in bringing the *T^efillīn* for which he had been sent. Rab, fearing that the correct time for reading the *Sh^ema'* would pass before he arrived, on that occasion read it and afterwards laid the *T^efillīn*.

[3] An euphemism for "against God." He declares the Unity of God (by reading the *Sh^ema'*) without adducing the evidence as proclaimed by the *T^efillīn*. Rev. A. Newman writes: "Against himself" may be taken literally. The *Sh^ema'* which he is reading enjoins the wearing of *T^efillīn*; therefore the recital without the phylacteries involves an inconsistency. His acts belie his words.

[4] *M.*: Rabbah b. Bar Ḥannah said in the name of R. Joḥanan.

[5] "The cleansing here has nothing to do with priestly ablution; it means simply to prepare oneself in such a way as to be able to concentrate all one's mind during the prayer without any disturbance"; Schechter, *Aspects of Rabbinic Theology*, p. 66 n. 1. On the practice of the Essenes, see Schürer, II. ii. p. 199.

[6] So *M.* correctly; edd. Raba. Cf. Hyman, II. p. 437 *a*.

[7] "His whole body" added by *M.*

[8] Implying that he is *totally* clean.

Hands may be cleansed with pebbles, etc. when water not available.

Rabina said to Raba[1]: Has the master seen the Rabbinical scholar who has come from the West and said, "Who has no water wherewith to wash his hands should rub them with earth or pebbles or sawdust[2]"? He answered: Well has he spoken; for is it written, "I will wash with water"? No; it is written, "I will wash in cleanliness," i.e. with anything that cleanses. And lo, Rab Ḥisda cursed anyone who went about in search of water at the time of prayer[3]. This, however, applies only to the reading of the *Sh^{e}ma‘*, but for the *T^{e}fillāh* one may go for water[4]. How far may one go for it? A *Parsāh*. But this applies only in front of him; in the rear he may not go even a *Mīl*, [from which it is to be deduced] he may not go in the rear a *Mīl*, but less than that distance is permissible.

MISHNĀH III

Who reads the Sh^{e}ma‘ *without making it audible to his ear has complied with the requirements of the law*[5]. *R. Josē says: He has not so complied. If he read it without distinctly pronouncing its letters—R. Josē says: He has complied with the requirements of the law; but R. Judah says: He has not. If one reads it in the wrong order of its paragraphs, he has not complied with the requirements of the law. If one has read it but made a mistake, he returns to the place where he erred.*

G^{E}MĀRĀ

Why the *Sh^{e}ma‘* must be read audibly.

What is R. Josē's reason [for declaring that unless the *Sh^{e}ma‘* is read audibly the requirements of the law have not been fulfilled]? Because it is written, "Hear O Israel," i.e. let thine ear hear what thou issuest from thy mouth. And the first *Tannā*[6]? He holds that "Hear" [means that the *Sh^{e}ma‘* may be read] in any language which thou hearest. And R. Josē [—where does he find a basis in the *Tōrāh* for this regulation]? Both are to be derived from the word "Hear."

[1] *M.*: Raba to Rafram b. Pappa.

[2] There is a similar law among the Muhammadans: "But if...ye find no water, take fine clean sand and rub your faces and your hands therewith"; Koran iv. 46, v. 9; Lane, p. 72.

[3] *M.*: "At the time of the reading of the *Sh^{e}ma‘*." He feared that the right time would pass during the search for water.

[4] The time for *T^{e}fillāh* is not so strictly defined.

[5] Some authorities insert here: "These are the words of R. Judah."

[6] Who allows it to be read inaudibly, how does he explain "Hear"? See fol. 13 *a*, p. 83.

A parallel case cited.

We have learnt elsewhere in the *Mishnāh*: A deaf man who speaks but cannot hear may not separate the *Terūmāh*[1]; but if he has done so, his *Terūmāh* is valid. Who is the authority for the teaching: [The *Terūmāh* separated by] a deaf man who speaks but cannot hear is *post factum* valid, but not *ab initio*[2]? Rab Ḥisda said: It is R. Josē; because we have learnt in our *Mishnāh*: *Who reads the* Shema‘ *without making it audible to his ear has complied with the requirements of the law. These are the words of R. Judah*[3]. *R. Josē says: He has not so complied.* Only in the matter of the reading of the *Shema‘*, which is an ordinance of the *Tōrāh*, does R. Josē say that the man has not fulfilled his obligation; but in the matter of *Terūmāh* [the deaf man would have fulfilled it], because it is a question of saying the benediction and the saying of the benediction is ordained by the Rabbis, and [the validity of the *Terūmāh*] is not dependent upon the benediction[4].

Attempt to break down the parallel refuted.

But how [do we know that the teaching in the quoted *Mishnāh*] is R. Josē's? Perhaps it is R. Judah's, and he means to say with reference also to the reading of the *Shema‘* that having read it inaudibly he has complied with the requirements of the law, but *ab initio* he should not read it so? Thou mayest find proof for this in the fact that he states *Who reads*[5] [the *Shema‘* without making it audible], i.e. *post factum* it is valid, but not *ab initio*! They answer that the fact that our *Mishnāh* states *Who reads* is intended to show how extreme is the view of R. Josē, for he means to say that even *post factum* it is not valid; since were it R. Judah, even *ab initio* it would still be valid.

A second parallel cited.

Having demonstrated that [the *Mishnāh* about *Terūmāh*] is in accord with R. Josē, what, however, of the following? There is

[1] Because the act was accompanied by the saying of a benediction which the deaf man would not be able to hear.

[2] In Rabbinic law a distinction is often drawn between the validity of an act which one contemplates doing and its validity after it has been performed; and it is sometimes decided that though the former (לְכַתְּחִלָּה "as at the beginning," *ab initio*) is illegitimate, nevertheless the accomplished fact (דְּאִיעֲבַד=דִּיעֲבַד "that which has been done," *post factum*) may be considered as complying with the requirements of the law. See Mielziner, p. 197; Bacher, *Terminologie*, II. p. 232.

[3] Omitted by *M.* in conformity with the wording of the *Mishnāh*.

[4] R. Josē's objection to inaudibility does not apply to the benediction of *Terūmāh*, because it is not so essential a feature of the act, that without it the whole would be illegitimate.

[5] This is the equivalent of "who has read"; therefore the first *Tannā* (i.e. R. Judah) agrees with the *Mishnāh* about *Terūmāh*, not R. Josē.

a teaching: A man must not say the Grace after meals in his heart [inaudibly]; but if he has done so, he has fulfilled his obligation. Whose view is this? It can be neither R. Josē's nor R. Judah's. For were it R. Judah's, if the man had said [Grace inaudibly] *ab initio* he would also have fulfilled his duty; if R. Josē's, even *post factum* it cannot be considered that he has done so[1]. How is it then? It must be R. Judah's, and [his opinion is] *post factum* it is allowed, but not *ab initio.*

What, however, of the following? R. Judah, the son of R. Simeon b. Pazzi, taught: A deaf person who can speak but cannot hear may separate the *Terūmāh ab initio.* In accordance with whose view is this? It can be neither R. Judah's nor R. Josē's. If R. Judah's, he permits it *post factum*, but not *ab initio*; if R. Josē's, he does not allow it even *post factum.* It is certainly in agreement with R. Judah, even though it be *ab initio*; and there is no contradiction[2]. The latter[3] is his own opinion, the other[4] the opinion of his teacher. For there is a teaching[5]: R. Judah says in the name of R. Eleazar b. 'Azariah: When one reads the *Shᵉma'*, he must make it audible to his ear; as it is said, "Hear, O Israel, the Lord our God, the Lord is one" (Deut. vi. 4). R. Meïr said to him: Behold the Scriptures state, "And these words which I command thee this day shall be upon thy heart" (*ibid.* *v.* 6), i.e. the words depend on the *Kawwānāh* of the heart[6]. Since thou hast reached so far[7], thou mayest even suppose that R. Judah agrees with his teacher's opinion, and there is no contradiction, one being R. Meïr's view[8] and the other R. Judah's[9]. A contradiction removed.

[1] Because the Grace after meals is a Pentateuchal ordinance (see fol. 21*a*, p. 135), and therefore parallel to the case of the *Shᵉma'* where R. Josē does not admit as valid even the *post factum* reading, if inaudible.

[2] No contradiction in R. Judah agreeing with R. Judah the son of R. Simeon b. Pazzi, although in the matter of the inaudible Grace after meals it was concluded that he allows it only *post factum.*

[3] That even *ab initio* it is permissible for a deaf man to separate *Tᵉrūmāh.*

[4] That only *post factum* is the inaudible Grace after meals valid.

[5] So *M.*; not "there is a Mishnaic teaching" as in edd.

[6] Not on their audibility.

[7] As to introduce R. Meïr's teaching into the discussion.

[8] The teaching of R. Judah the son of R. Simeon b. Pazzi, viz. the deaf person may separate the *Tᵉrūmāh ab initio*, is in agreement with R. Meïr's view that the *Shᵉma'* may be read inaudibly *ab initio.*

[9] R. Judah's view that the act of the deaf person is only allowed *post factum* agrees with the statement of his teacher, R. Eleazar b. 'Azariah, that *post factum* only is the inaudible reading of the *Shᵉma'* permissible.

A third parallel cited.

We have learnt elsewhere in the *Mishnāh*: All are fit and proper persons to read the *M^egillāh*, except a deaf person, a mentally defective, and a minor[1]. R. Judah allows a minor to read. Who is the authority for the teaching that if a deaf person has read it[2], his recital is even *post factum* invalid? Rab Matt^enah declared that it is R. Josē; for we have learnt in our *Mishnāh*: *Who reads the* Sh^ema' *without making it audible to his ear has complied with the requirements of the law. These are the words of R. Judah. R. Josē says: He has not so complied.* How can we know that [this quoted *Mishnāh*] is R. Josē's view [and means that the reading of the *M^egillāh* by a deaf person] is also invalid *post factum*; fol. 15b. perhaps it is R. Judah's view and *ab initio* it is not permitted, but *post factum* it is valid? This cannot enter thy mind; because the *Mishnāh* refers to a deaf person exactly as to the mentally defective and minor; and therefore, as in the case of a mentally defective and minor even *post factum* [the reading of the *M^egillāh*] is invalid, so also if a deaf person has read it, it is likewise invalid. But perhaps the two have to be kept distinct[3]! Still thou canst not possibly maintain that it is in accord with R. Judah; because from what is stated in the sequel, "R. Judah allows a minor to read [the *M^egillāh*]" it is to be inferred that the first part is not R. Judah's view! But perhaps the whole of it is R. Judah's view, there being two kinds of "minor," and [the wording of the *Mishnāh*] is defective and should read thus: "All are fit and proper persons to read the *M^egillāh* except a deaf person, a mentally defective person and a minor. Of whom does this speak? Of a minor who has not yet reached Initiation[4]; but a minor who has reached Initiation is fit to read it even *ab initio*. These are the words of R. Judah, for R. Judah permits a minor to read."

Having demonstrated that [the *Mishnāh* about the reading of the *M^egillāh*] is in accord with R. Judah and *post factum* it is permissible, but not *ab initio*, what, however, of the teaching of R. Judah, the son of R. Simeon b. Pazzi: A deaf person who speaks but cannot hear may separate the *T^erūmāh ab initio*? Whose view is that? It cannot be R. Judah's, nor R. Josē's. If

[1] A boy under the age of 13 years.

[2] The point at issue is the fact that such a recital must be inaudible to the reader.

[3] Viz. the deaf person is in a different category from the mentally defective and minor. The text is literally: Perhaps this as it is and that as it is.

[4] The stage of mental development when he is introduced to the practice of the religious duties—about the age of nine or ten years.

R. Judah's, *post factum* it should be allowed, but not *ab initio*; if R. Josē's, even *post factum* it should be invalid. Whose view is it then? R. Judah's and even *ab initio* it is permissible.

What, however, of the following? There is a teaching: A man must not say Grace after meals in his heart; but if he has done so, he has complied with the requirements of the law. Whose view is that? It is not R. Judah's, nor R. Josē's. If R. Judah's, he would allow that to act thus *ab initio* likewise complies with the requirements of the law; if R. Josē's, even *post factum* it is not valid. It is certainly R. Judah's view, and even *ab initio* it is valid. Nor is there any contradiction[1]; the latter[2] being R. Judah's own opinion, the other that of his teacher[3]. For there is a teaching: R. Judah says in the name of R. Eleazar b. 'Azariah: He who reads the *Sh^ema'* must make it audible to his ear; as it is said, "Hear O Israel." R. Meïr said to him: Behold the Scriptures state, "And these words which I command thee this day shall be upon thy heart," i.e. the words depend upon the *Kawwānāh* of the heart. Since thou hast reached so far, thou mayest even suppose that R. Judah agrees with his teacher's opinion; and there is no contradiction, one being R. Judah's view, the other R. Meïr's[4]. A contradiction removed.

Rab Ḥisda said in the name of Rab Shela[5]: The *Halākāh* is in accord with R. Judah's view which he reported in the name of R. Eleazar b. 'Azariah, and the *Halākāh* is in accord with R. Judah. It is necessary [to state it in this way]; for if he had informed us only that the *Halākāh* is in accord with R. Judah, I might have supposed [the *Shema'* need not be read audibly] *ab initio*; therefore he tells us that the *Halākāh* is in accord with R. Judah's view which he reported in the name of R. Eleazar b. 'Azariah[6]. And if he had informed us only that the *Halākāh* is in accord with R. Judah's view which he reported in the name of R. Eleazar b. 'Azariah, I might have supposed that it is essential [for the *Shema'* to be read audibly *ab initio*] and there was no rectification [if this had not been done]. Therefore he informs us that the *Halākāh* is in accord with R. Judah[7]. The *Halākāh* stated.

[1] As in note 2 p. 97.
[2] As in note 3 p. 97.
[3] As in note 4 p. 97.
[4] As in notes 8 and 9 p. 97.
[5] *M.*: Mar 'Uḳba.
[6] I.e. *ab initio* it should be audible; only *post factum* is it valid if inaudible.
[7] And *post factum* the inaudible reading is valid.

Whether audibility is required with other commandments.

Rab Joseph said: The dispute is only over the reading of the *Sh^e^ma'*, but with other commandments[1] all agree that [if inaudible] he *has not* complied with the requirements of the law; for it is written, "Attend and hear, O Israel" (Deut. xxvii. 9). But it is quoted in objection: One may not say the Grace after meals in his heart; but if he has done so, he *has* complied with the requirements of the law! But if [the statement of Rab Joseph] was reported, it must have been reported as follows: The dispute is only over the reading of the *Sh^e^ma'*; for it is written, "Hear O Israel"; but with other commandments all agree that [if inaudible] he *has* complied with the requirements of the law. But it is written, "Attend and hear, O Israel[2]"! That refers to reading the Scriptures[3].

If he had read it without distinctly pronouncing its letters.

The *H^a^lākāh*.

R. Ṭabi said in the name of R. Josiah: The *H^a^lākāh* is in accord with the more lenient view in both instances[4].

Prov. xxx. 15 teaches the resurrection of the dead.

R. Ṭabi also said in the name of R. Josiah: What means that which is written, "There are three things that are never satisfied... the grave, and the barren womb," etc. (Prov. xxx. 15 f.)—what is the connection between "the grave" and "the barren womb"? Its intention is to tell thee that as the womb receives and yields up, so the grave receives and yields up. And may we not use the *a fortiori* argument? As the womb receives [the seed] in silence and yields up [the child] with loud cries, how much more so will the grave, which receives [the body] with loud cries [of lament], yield up with loud cries! Hence a refutation of those who assert that the resurrection of the dead is not taught in the *Tōrāh*[5].

First two paragraphs of the *Sh^e^ma'* required in the *T^e^fillin* in their entirety.

Rab Josiah[6] taught in the presence of Raba: "And thou shalt write them" (Deut. vi. 9) means that the whole [of the first two paragraphs of the *Sh^e^ma'*] must be written [in the *T^e^fillīn*], even the words of the commands[7]. Raba said to him: Should one ask

1 Which involve the utterance of a benediction.

2 Therefore audibility should be required!

3 The word *haskēt* translated "attend" is rendered in R.V. "keep silence." For some Rabbinic interpretations of the word, see fol. 63*b*.

4 With R. Judah in permitting the inaudible reading to suffice *post factum*, and with R. Josē in allowing the letters to be indistinctly enunciated.

5 Referring to the Sadducees; cf. Schürer, II. ii. p. 38.

6 So *M.* correctly; not Osha'yah as in edd. Rab Josiah is not the same as R. Josiah mentioned in the preceding paragraph.

7 E.g. "Thou shalt write them...thou shalt bind them."

thee whose teaching this is, it is R. Judah's; for he stated with reference to the woman suspected of adultery: One writes the curses but not the words of the command, because in this connection it is written, "And the priests shall write these curses in a scroll" (Num. v. 23), but here [in connection with *T*^{e}*fillīn*] it is written, "And thou shalt write them," i.e. even the words of the command. Dost thou suppose that R. Judah's reason is because the text states, "[And the priest] *shall write*"? His reason is because the text states, "[And the priest shall write] *these curses*," i.e. the curses shall be written, but not the words of the command. It is necessary [to mention this point]; because it might have entered thy mind that I mean we can draw an analogy from the use of the verb "to write" in the former instance, thus: As there [with reference to the woman suspected of adultery] the curses were to be written and not the words of the command, so here likewise [with the *T*^{e}*fillīn*] the words of the command were not to be written[1]! Therefore the All-merciful wrote, "And thou shalt write *them*," i.e. even the words of the command.

Distinct enunciation of words required.

Rab Obadiah taught in the presence of Raba: "And ye shall teach" (Deut. xi. 19), i.e. let thy teaching be perfect[2]—let one make a brief pause between words which are liable to be jumbled together[3]. Raba added to this observation: For instance *'al l*^{e}*bābĕkā* "upon thy heart"; *'al l*^{e}*bab*^{e}*kem* "upon your heart"; *b*^{e}*kol l*^{e}*bāb*^{e}*kā* "with all thy heart"; *b*^{e}*kol l*^{e}*bab*^{e}*kem* "with all your heart"; *'ēseb b*^{e}*sād*^{e}*kā* "grass in thy field"; *wa'*^{a}*badtem m*^{e}*hērāh* "and ye will perish speedily"; *hakkānāph p*^{e}*tīl* "the corner, a thread"; *etkem mē'ereṣ* "you from the land[4]."

Reward for distinct enunciation.

R. Ḥamma b. R. Ḥannina said: Whoever reads the *Sh*^{e}*ma'* with distinct pronunciation of its letters, *Gēhinnōm* is cooled for him; as it is said, "When the Almighty scattereth kings therein, it snoweth in Zalmon" (Ps. lxviii. 15). Read not *b*^{e}*phārēs* "[When the Almighty] scattereth," but read *b*^{e}*phārēsh* "When one uttereth [the name of the Almighty] distinctly"; and read

[1] On this argument, see p. 18 n. 5.

[2] *w*^{e}*limmadtem* "and ye shall teach" is pointed *w*^{e}*limmūd tam* "and the teaching [shall be] perfect."

[3] By reason of a word ending with the same letter as the initial of the next word.

[4] *J. T.* adds the interesting example, *nishba' 'ădōnāi* "The Lord hath sworn," emphasizing the difference in the two guttural letters. It indeed mentions that one who is unable to make a clear pronunciation of the gutturals may not conduct a Service.

not *bᵉZalmōn* "in Zalmon," but *bᵉṣalmāwet* "in the shadow of death[1]."

Homily on Num. xxiv. 6. **fol. 16 a.**

R. Ḥamma b. R. Ḥannina also said: Why are there found associated "tents" and "streams"—for it is written, "As streams stretched out, as gardens by the river-side, as tents[2] planted by the Lord, as cedars beside the waters" (Num. xxiv. 6)[3]? Its intention is to tell thee that as streams bring a man up from impurity to purity, so do "tents" bring a man up from the scale of guilt to the scale of merit.

If one read it in the wrong order of its paragraphs, he has not complied with the requirements of the law.

If mistake is made while reading the *Shᵉma'*.

R. Ammi and R. Assi were once decorating the bridal-chamber for R. Eleazar. He said to them, "In the meanwhile I will go and listen to the teaching in the House of Study, and will come back and report it to you." He went and found a *Tannā* expounding in the presence of R. Joḥanan: Should one have read the *Shᵉma'* and erred without knowing for certain where he made the mistake, if this occurred in the middle of the first paragraph he must return to the commencement; if between two paragraphs, he must return to the first of them; if between "and thou shalt write them" and "ye shall write them[4]," he must return to the first. R. Joḥanan said to him: This latter only applies if he has not started "That your days may be multiplied"; but should he have commenced that sentence, [he may assume that] he followed on from force of habit[5]. [R. Eleazar] returned and reported it to them. They said to him: "If we had come for nothing else than to hear this, it would be sufficient for us."

[1] With these alterations the verse reads, "When one utters the name of the Almighty distinctly in the prayer where the King [majestic plural] is [i.e. which contains a reference to the Kingdom of Heaven, viz. the *Shᵉma'*], it snoweth in the shadow of death." The words *mᵉlākīm bāh* "kings therein" have been connected, with more ingenuity than probability, by Schorr (quoted in Goldschmidt) with ὁμοιόλογος and βοή, making the first clause mean: When one utters the name of the Almighty distinctly, reading the words of similar sound plainly.

[2] The word אהלים may be pointed to mean "aloes" (so R.V. here) or "tents." In the preceding verse, "thy tents" has the same letters; they are consequently given the same meaning here. By "tents" the Rabbis frequently understand "houses of study"; e.g. "And Jacob was a quiet man, dwelling in tents" (Gen. xxv. 27) is explained (cf. the Targūm): attending schools of learning.

[3] "For it is written" etc. is a later addition to the text; cf. *A.P.A.* I. p. 451 n. 4.

[4] Occurring in the first and second paragraphs respectively.

[5] And there is no need to repeat from the beginning.

MISHNĀH IV, V

IV. *Workmen may read the* Sh^e^ma' *on the top of a tree or on top of scaffolding, but this they may not do with the* T^e^fillāh.

V. *A bridegroom is exempt from the obligation of reading the* Sh^e^ma' *on the first night [of his marriage], and until the termination of the ensuing Sabbath, if he has not consummated the marriage. It happened that when Rabban Gamaliel married, he read the* Sh^e^ma' *on the first night. His disciples said to him, "Our teacher! thou hast taught us that a bridegroom is exempt from the obligation of reading the* Sh^e^ma'[1]." *He replied, "I will not hearken to you to annul the kingdom of heaven from myself even a single hour."*

G^E^MĀRĀ

A Bārāitā amplifying the Mishnāh.

Our Rabbis have taught: Workmen may read [the *Sh^e^ma'*] on the top of a tree or on the top of scaffolding. They may likewise say the *T^e^fillāh* on top of an olive-tree or fig-tree[2]; but with all other trees they must descend to the ground to say the *T^e^fillāh.* The employer must in every instance descend to the ground to say the *T^e^fillāh,* because his mind is not settled[3].

Whether workmen must read the *Sh^e^ma'* with *Kawwānāh.*

Rab Mari, the son of Samuel's daughter[4], asked Raba: Our *Mishnāh* states: *Workmen may read [the* Sh^e^ma'*] on the top of a tree or on the top of scaffolding*; hence it is to be inferred that it does not require *Kawwānāh.* I quote in refutation[5]: Who reads the *Sh^e^ma'* must direct his heart; as it is said, "Hear, O Israel" (Deut. vi. 4) and elsewhere, "Attend and hear, O Israel" (*ibid.* xxvii. 9); as here "attention" is required so also there[6]! [Raba] remained silent; so he asked him: Hast thou heard anything on this point? He replied: Thus said Rab Sheshet[7]: [*Kawwānāh* is demanded of workmen] only if they stop their work to read it. But lo, there is a teaching: *Bēt* Hillel say: Workmen may remain at their

1 *M.*: Hast thou not taught us...the *Sh^e^ma'* on the first night?

2 Because these have numerous branches, and the workmen have less fear of falling to disturb their mind; so Rashi. The reason *J. T.* gives is because the fatigue of getting down from these trees is very great.

3 Through fear of falling. The law is stricter with him, because his time is his own.

4 Her name was Rachel. The son is not called by his father's name, which was Isur (Bab. Bat. 149 *a*), because his mother became pregnant while a prisoner of war; and although the father embraced Judaism before the child was born, his name is omitted. See K^e^tūbōt 23 *a*.

5 *M.* adds: R. Simeon b. Joḥai says.

6 With "Hear, O Israel," i.e. the *Sh^e^ma'*, since the word "hear" is common to both.

7 *M.*: Ḥiyya b. Abba in the name of R. Joḥanan.

work and read it! There is no contradiction; the former refers to the first paragraph [of the *Sh^ema'*], the latter to the second.

The Ritual as affecting workmen.

Our Rabbis have taught: Labourers who are working for an employer should read the *Sh^ema'*, say the benedictions before and after, eat their meal with Grace before and after, and then pray the Eighteen Benedictions[1]; but they cannot descend before the Ark[2] nor raise their hands[3]. But lo, there is a teaching: [Such men are to say] an abstract of the Eighteen Benedictions[4]! Rab Sheshet said: There is no contradiction; the first being Rabban Gamaliel's view, the latter R. Joshua's[5]. If it be R. Joshua's view, why does he mention labourers specially, since it holds good of anybody? But [we have to assume that] both are Rabban Gamaliel's, and there is no contradiction; the latter treating of one who works for a wage[6], the former of one who works for his keep. And so there is a teaching: Labourers who are working for an employer should read the *Sh^ema'*, say the *T^efillāh*, then eat their meal, but should not say Grace before it[7], only two benedictions after it. How is this meant[8]? The first benediction as ordained[9]; the second commences with the benediction of "the land," and they include "Who...rebuildest Jerusalem" in the benediction of "the land[10]." To whom does this apply? To those who work for a wage; but should they work for their keep or their employer take his meals with them[11], they say the [entire] Grace after meals as ordained.

[1] Singer, pp. 44 ff.

[2] To act as Precentor, because this would interfere with their duty to their employer.

[3] A *Kōhēn* (see Glossary, *s.v.*) has the privilege to "raise his hands" in the course of the Service to pronounce the priestly benediction (Num. vi. 24–26); but if a labourer, he must not do so. In Talmudical times, this was done daily; but now it is usually reserved for Festivals only, the Precentor pronouncing the benediction in the daily Service (Singer, p. 53). Cf. *J. E.* III. p. 244.

[4] The prayer "Give us understanding"; Singer, p. 55.

[5] Cf. below fol. 28 *b*, p. 188 where Rabban Gamaliel requires the Eighteen Benedictions to be said daily, whereas R. Joshua declares an abstract sufficient.

[6] If he said it in its entirety, it might interfere unduly with his work.

[7] The Grace *before* meals is not a Pentateuchal ordinance, but the Grace after meals is. Cf. fol. 48 *b*.

[8] What are the two benedictions?

[9] Singer, p. 280, "Blessed art Thou...Who givest food unto all."

[10] *Ibid.* "We thank Thee" and p. 282 "And rebuild Jerusalem." These two benedictions are to be condensed into one.

[11] There would then be no opportunity for the labourers to waste time under the pretext of saying the entire Grace.

A bridegroom is exempt from the obligation of reading the Shᵉma'.

Our Rabbis have taught: "When thou sittest in thy house" (Deut. vi. 7) excludes one occupied with a religious duty; "and when thou walkest by the way" (*ibid.*) excludes a bridegroom. Hence they say: He who takes a virgin to his house as wife is exempt; but if he marry a widow, he has that obligation. How is that demonstrated? Rab Pappa said: Because [the text uses the word] "way" [we argue]: Just as the way is voluntary, so all is voluntary[1].

Exemption of a bridegroom.

Are we not here dealing with one who is on his way to perform a religious duty, and even so the All-merciful requires of him the reading [of the *Shᵉma'*]? In that case, the All-merciful should have written "when walking." What means "when *thou* walkest"? Deduce from this, [it means] when walking for thine own purpose thou art under the obligation [to read the *Shᵉma'*]; but when it is the performance of a religious duty, thou art exempt. If so, why especially mention, "He who takes a *virgin* to his house as wife"? Even one who takes a widow to wife should also [be exempt]! The man [who marries a virgin] is anxious; the other is not. Should the reason [of exemption] be on account of anxiety, then it ought to apply also to one whose ship has sunk at sea! Why, then, does R. Abba b. Zabda declare in the name of Rab: A mourner is under the obligation to observe all the commandments mentioned in the *Tōrāh* except *Tᵉfillīn*, because they are called an adornment; as it is said, "Bind thine adornment upon thee" (Ezek. xxiv. 17)? The answer is: [There is a difference]; the latter being troubled by anxiety of some voluntary matter, whereas the former has anxiety in connection with a religious duty.

Performance of a religious duty exempts the reading of the *Shᵉma'*.

fol. 16 b.

MISHNĀH VI—VIII

VI. [*Rabban Gamaliel*] *bathed on the first night of his wife's death. His disciples said to him, "Our master! Thou hast taught us*[2] *that a mourner is forbidden to bathe!" He replied, "I am not like other men; I am in delicate health."*

VII. *When his slave, Ṭabi, died, he accepted condolence on his behalf. His disciples said to him, "Our master! Thou hast taught us that one may not accept condolence on the death of slaves"! He*

[1] See p. 67 n. 5. The remainder of this *Gᵉmārā* is repeated from fol. 11 *a*, p. 68.

[2] *M.*: Hast thou not taught us...?

replied, "My slave, Ṭabi, was not like other slaves; he was a worthy man."

VIII. *If a bridegroom wishes to read the* Shᵉma' *on the first night [of his marriage], he may do so. Rabban Simeon b. Gamaliel says: "Not everybody who wishes to assume the name*[1] *may do so."*

GᴱMĀRĀ

Why Rabban Gamaliel bathed on the first night of his wife's death.

What was Rabban Gamaliel's reason[2]? He was of the opinion that the application of the laws of mourning in the night is a Rabbinical injunction; for it is written, "And the end thereof as a bitter *day*" (Amos viii. 10)[3]; and in the case of a person in delicate health, the Rabbis do not so decree.

When his slave, Ṭabi, died, etc.

Burial customs for slaves.

Our Rabbis have taught: [At the burial of] male and female slaves, we do not stand in a row[4] for them, nor do we pronounce over them the benediction of mourners[5] and the condolence of mourners[6]. It happened that R. Eliezer's female slave died and his disciples went in to comfort him. When he saw them, he ascended to an upper room, but they ascended after him. He went into the court-way[7], but they went after him. He entered the guest-chamber, but they entered after him. He said to them: I imagined you would be scalded with tepid water[8]; but now you are not scalded even with hot water. Have I not taught you: [On the death of] male and female slaves, we do not stand in a row for them, nor do we pronounce over them the benediction of mourners and the condolence of mourners? What, however, do we say over them? As we say to a man on the death of his ox or ass, "May the Omnipresent repair thy loss,"

[1] I.e. a reputation for excessive piety by reading the *Shᵉma'* on such an occasion, which might not be justified by other acts of his.

[2] The laws of mourning (here *ănīnūt*, the mourning before the burial, which is stricter than *ăbēlūt*, mourning after burial) are derived from Deut. xxvi. 14. Being a Pentateuchal ordinance, how could he set them aside for the personal reason he gives?

[3] This verse relates to a time of mourning, and it mentions only "a bitter day"; from this he deduced that the "bitterness" does not apply in the night.

[4] It is still customary for the friends who attend the funeral to form themselves into two rows through which the mourners pass, receiving words of condolence.

[5] Said after the meal on returning from the cemetery.

[6] The formula is: May the Omnipresent comfort you in the midst of the other mourners of Zion and Jerusalem.

[7] So Jastrow; Krauss, p. 74, "the inner-room."

[8] I.e. I gave you a plain hint that I did not wish to receive your condolence.

so do we say to a man on the death of his slaves, "May the Omnipresent repair thy loss."

No funeral oration for slaves.

There is a further teaching: We do not speak a funeral oration over male and female slaves. R. Josē said: If he was a worthy man, we say of him, "Alas, the good and faithful man who derived pleasure from his work!" They said to him, "In that case, what hast thou left to be said over worthy men [who are not slaves][1]?"

Name "Patriarch" restricted to three, "Matriarch" to four.

Our Rabbis have taught: We restrict the name "Patriarch" to three[2], and "Matriarch" to four[3]. Why is the name "Patriarch" [restricted to three][4]? Is it because we are not certain whether we are descended from Reuben or Simeon? If so, in the case of the Matriarchs we are not certain whether we are descended from Rachel or Leah! But up to here they were esteemed sufficiently [to be called "Patriarchs"]; their successors were not so esteemed.

Slaves not addressed "Father" or "Mother."

There is a further teaching: We do not call male and female slaves "Father so-and-so" or "Mother so-and-so." But Rabban Gamaliel's [slaves] used to be called in this manner. This is an actual fact to upset [the teaching just quoted]! [No; it is different with them,] because they were highly esteemed.

Homily on Ps. lxiii. 5.

R. Eleazar said: What means that which is written, "So will I bless Thee as long as I live; in Thy name will I lift up my hands" (Ps. lxiii. 5)? "So will I bless Thee as long as I live" refers to the reading of the *Sh^ema'*; "in Thy name will I lift up my hands" refers to *T^efillāh*. If one act thus, of him the text saith, "My soul is satisfied as with marrow and fatness" (*ibid. v.* 6); and not only that, but he will inherit two worlds, this world and the world to come, as it is said, "And my mouth will praise Thee with joyful lips" (*ibid.*)[5].

R. Eleazar's prayer.

R. Eleazar used to add at the conclusion of his prayer[6]: May it be Thy will, O Lord our God, to cause love and brotherhood, peace and comradeship, to abide in our lot[7], to enlarge our border

[1] What higher praise could be spoken of any man?

[2] Abraham, Isaac and Jacob.

[3] Sarah, Rebecca, Rachel and Leah.

[4] Not given to the sons of Jacob who founded the tribes called by their name.

[5] *Lit.* "with lips of joyful songs" ("songs," being an unspecified plural, equals two), i.e. a song in this world and a song in the world to come. Bacher considers that the derivation is based upon the spelling of the word for "joyful songs," רננות instead of רנות. *A. P. A.* ii. p. 15 n. 3.

[6] I.e. after "Blessed...Who blessest Thy people Israel with peace"; Singer, p. 54.

[7] Bacher would give the word the meaning "our dwelling-place"; *A.P.A.* i. p. 244 n. 7.

with disciples, to prosper our goal with a [happy] end and with hope, to set our portion in the Garden of Eden[1], and fortify us with good companionship and the good impulse in Thy universe, so that we rise up and find the longing of our heart to fear Thy name; and may the satisfaction of our soul come before Thee for good.

R. Joḥanan's prayer.

R. Joḥanan used to add at the conclusion of his prayer: May it be Thy will, O Lord our God, to glance at our shame and look upon our evil plight; and do Thou clothe Thyself in Thy mercy, cover Thyself with Thy might, enfold Thyself with Thy piety and gird Thyself with Thy grace, and may Thy attribute of goodness and gentleness come before Thee[2].

R. Zera's prayer.

R. Zera used to add at the conclusion of his prayer: May it be Thy will, O Lord our God, that we sin not; neither may we be put to shame nor be confounded before our fathers.

R. Ḥiyya's prayer.

R. Ḥiyya[3] used to add at the conclusion of his prayer: May it be Thy will, O Lord our God, that Thy *Tōrāh* be our occupation; and let not our heart grow faint nor our eyes dim.

Rab's prayer.

Rab used to add at the conclusion of his prayer: May it be Thy will, O Lord our God, to grant us long life, a life of peace, a life of good, a life of blessing, a life of sustenance, a life of bodily vigour, a life marked by the fear of sin, a life free from shame and reproach, a life of prosperity and honour, a life in which the love of *Tōrāh* and the fear of Heaven shall cleave to us, a life wherein Thou fulfillest all the desires of our heart for good[4].

Rabbi's prayer.

Rabbi used to add at the conclusion of his prayer: May it be Thy will, O Lord our God and God of our fathers, to deliver me from arrogant men and from arrogance, from a bad man, and from any mishap, from the evil impulse, from a bad companion, from a bad neighbour, and from the adversary that destroyeth; from a hard judgment, and from a hard opponent, whether he be a son of the covenant or be not a son of the covenant[5]. [Thus did Rabbi pray], although eunuchs were standing by him[6].

[1] The Rabbinic name for Paradise.

[2] *M.* adds: and have compassion upon us.

[3] In *J. T.* it is Ḥiyya b. Abba.

[4] This prayer is now included in the Service for the Sabbath before the New Moon; cf. Singer, p. 154.

[5] See Singer, p. 7.

[6] Rabbi Judah the Prince was an intimate friend of the Roman Procurator in Judea. Although the latter placed a number of his men at Rabbi's disposal to protect him, yet he prayed to God for help against his adversaries, not relying upon human aid.

Rab Saphra used to add at the conclusion of his prayer: May it be Thy will, O Lord our God, to grant peace in the household above[1] and the household below, and among the students who occupy themselves with Thy *Tōrāh*, whether they devote themselves thereto for its own sake or not for its own sake[2]; and as for them that devote themselves thereto not for its own sake, may it be Thy will that they do devote themselves thereto for its own sake.

Rab Saphra's prayer. fol. 17 a.

R. Alexander used to add at the conclusion of his prayer: May it be Thy will, O Lord our God, to place us in a corner of light and not in a corner of darkness; and may not our heart grow faint nor our eyes dim. There are some who say this was Rab Hamnuna's prayer; and R. Alexander used to add at the conclusion of his prayer: Lord of the universe! It is revealed and known before Thee that it is our will to perform Thy will; but what stands in the way? The leaven that is in the dough[3] and the servitude of the kingdoms[4]. May it be Thy will to deliver us from their hand[5], so that we may again perform the statutes of Thy will with a perfect heart.

R. Alexander's prayer.

A variant tradition.

Raba used to add at the conclusion of his prayer: O my God, before I was formed I was nothing worth, and now that I have been formed I am but as though I had not been formed. Dust am I in my life; how much more so in my death. Behold I am before Thee like a vessel filled with shame and confusion. O may it be Thy will, O Lord my God, that I may sin no more; and as to the sins I have committed, purge them away in Thine abounding compassion though not by means of affliction and sore diseases. That is the confession of[6] Rab Hamnuna Ẓuṭa on the Day of Atonement[7].

Raba's prayer.

[1] The "household above" is the angelic host whose dissensions lead to quarrels on earth. The "household below" is either mankind generally or the Sages of Israel.

[2] But for the prestige it brings them. Cf. Abōt iv. 7: "Make not of the *Tōrāh* a crown wherewith to aggrandise thyself, nor a spade wherewith to dig. So also used Hillel to say, He who makes a worldly use of the crown of the *Tōrāh* shall waste away. Hence thou mayest infer that whosoever derives a profit for himself from the words of the *Tōrāh* is helping on his own destruction." Singer, p. 196. See Schechter, *Aspects*, pp. 159 ff.

[3] The evil impulse in man; cf. I Corinth. v. 7.

[4] Religious oppression.

[5] Some edd. read: to humble them before and behind us.

[6] *M.* adds: Raba the whole of the year and of.

[7] It figures now in the Service of the Day of Atonement; Singer, p. 263.

Mar b. Rabina's prayer.

Mar b. Rabina used to add at the conclusion of his prayer: O my God! Guard my tongue from evil and my lips from speaking guile; and to such as curse me let my soul be dumb, yea, let my soul be unto all as the dust. Open my heart to Thy *Tōrāh*, and let my soul pursue Thy commandments. And do Thou deliver me from mishap, from the evil impulse, and from an evil woman and all evil which breaks forth to come upon the world[1]. If any design evil against me, speedily make their counsel of none effect, and frustrate their designs[2]. Let the words of my mouth and the meditation of my heart be acceptable before Thee, O Lord my Rock and Redeemer.

Rab Sheshet's prayer on a fast day.

Rab Sheshet, when observing a fast, used to add at the conclusion of his prayer: Lord of the universe! It is revealed before Thee that when the Sanctuary was in existence, a man sinned and brought an offering, of which they sacrificed only the fat and the blood, and atonement was made for him. But now, I observe a fast, and my fat and blood are diminished. May it be Thy will, that my fat and blood which have been diminished may be accounted as though I had offered them before Thee upon the altar, and do Thou favour me[3].

R. Meïr's meditation after reading the Book of Job.

R. Joḥanan said: R. Meïr[4], on concluding the reading of the Book of Job, used to say: It is the fate of man to die and of cattle to be slaughtered, and all are destined to die. Happy is he who has grown in *Tōrāh* and whose labour has been in *Tōrāh*; who has caused tranquillity of spirit to his Creator, advanced in good repute, and departed from the world with a good name. Of him said Solomon, "A good name is better than precious oil, and the day of death than the day of one's birth" (Eccles. vii. 1).

[1] This sentence is omitted in *M.* as well as in the Prayer Book version; see Singer, p. 54.

[2] *M.* inserts here: Return their recompense upon their head; destroy them and humble them before me. And do Thou deliver me from calamities and adverse times, and from all kinds of punishments which are hastening to break forth upon the world.

[3] *M.* inserts here: A certain disciple used to add at the conclusion of his prayer: Close mine eyes from looking on evil, mine ears from hearing idle words, my heart from reflecting on wickedness, and my reins from thinking of transgression. Make my feet to walk to Thy commandments and righteous ways; and may Thy mercies be turned upon me so that I may be of those spared for life in Jerusalem.

[4] "Said: R. Meïr" added by *M.*, probably correctly. See *D.S. ad loc.*, *A.T.* II. p. 13 n. 1. This reference to R. Meïr connects the series of prayers with the series of aphorisms which follows.

It was a favourite saying of R. Meïr: Learn with all thy heart and with all thy soul to know My ways and watch at the doors of My *Tōrāh*. Guard My *Tōrāh* in thy heart and let the fear of Me be before thine eyes. Keep thy mouth from all sin, and purify and sanctify thyself from all guilt and iniquity. Then shall I be with thee everywhere.

R. Meïr's favourite saying.

It was a favourite saying of the Rabbis of Jabneh[1]: I am a creature [of God] and my neighbour is also His creature; my work is in the city and his in the field; I rise early to my work and he rises early to his. As he cannot excel in my work, so I cannot excel in his work. But perhaps thou sayest, "I do great things and he small things"! We have learnt that [it matters not whether] one does much or little, if only he direct his heart to Heaven.

Favourite saying of the Rabbis of Jabneh.

It was a favourite saying of Abbai: A man should always be cunning[2] in the fear [of God], giving the soft answer that turneth away wrath (cf. Prov. xv. 1), increasing peace with his brethren and relatives and with all men[3], even the heathen in the street; so that he may be beloved above and popular on earth, and acceptable to his fellow-creatures. They say of Rabban Joḥanan b. Zakkai that nobody ever greeted him first, not even the heathen in the street.

Abbai's favourite saying.

It was a favourite saying of Raba: The goal of wisdom is repentance and good works; so that a man shall not read [*Tōrāh*] and study [*Mishnāh*] and then contradict his father or mother or teacher or anybody greater than he in knowledge and number [of years]; as it is said, "The fear of the Lord is the beginning of wisdom, a good understanding have all that do thereafter" (Ps. cxi. 10). "All that learn[4]" is not said here, but "all that do thereafter," i.e. they that practise *Tōrāh* for its own sake, but not they that practise *Tōrāh* not for its own sake[5]. As for him who

Raba's favourite saying.

[1] Jabneh (in Greek, Jamnia) is identical with Jabneel (Josh. xv. 11), and is situated in S. Palestine, near the coast. After the destruction of the Second Temple, the town sprang into great prominence, inasmuch as the Great Sanhedrin transferred its sittings there from Jerusalem; and Rabban Joḥanan b. Zakkai founded a School which became famous. See Neubauer, pp. 73 ff., *J. E.* VII. p. 18.

[2] Cunning in devising ways of manifesting his fear.

[3] By greeting them without waiting for their salutation, as Rabban Joḥanan did.

[4] Some edd. read: all that learn thereafter.

[5] He who learns only to display his knowledge by contradicting others is not one who practises *Tōrāh* for its own sake.

does not fulfil the *Tōrāh* for its own sake, it were better had he never been created[1].

Rab's favourite saying.

It was a favourite saying of Rab: Not like this world is the world to come. In the world to come there is neither eating nor drinking; no procreation of children[2] or business transactions; no envy or hatred or rivalry; but the righteous sit enthroned, their crowns on their heads, and enjoy the lustre of the *Sh^ekīnāh*; as it is said, "And they beheld God, and did eat and drink" (Exod. xxiv. 11)[3].

How women acquire merit.

Our Rabbis have taught[4]: Greater is the promise given by the Holy One, blessed be He, to women than to men; as it is said, "Rise up, ye women that are at ease, and hear My voice; ye confident daughters, give ear unto My speech" (Is. xxxii. 9)[5]. Rab asked R. Ḥiyya: Wherewith do women acquire merit[6]? By sending their children to learn [*Tōrāh*] in the Synagogue and their husbands to study in the schools of the Rabbis, and waiting for their husbands until they return from the schools of the Rabbis[7].

Farewell benediction of R. Ammi's disciples.

As the Rabbis departed[8] from the school of R. Ammi[9] (another version: R. Ḥannina's school), they said to him: Mayest thou see thy world in thy life-time[10], and may thine end be in the life of the world to come and thy hope throughout the generations. May thy heart meditate in understanding, thy mouth speak wisdom, thy tongue abound in joyful songs, thine eyelids set thy glance straight before thee[11], thine eyes be illumined with the light of the *Tōrāh*, thy countenance shine like the splendour of the firmament, thy lips utter knowledge, thy reins exult with uprightness, and thy feet run to hear the words of the Ancient of days.

[1] See above p. 109 n. 2.

[2] Cf. Matt. xxii. 30.

[3] I.e. their beholding God was the equivalent of eating and drinking. Thus it is said of Moses that, during his stay on Mt Sinai, he neither ate nor drank (Exod. xxxiv. 28) but was nourished from the lustre of the *Sh^ekīnāh*. See Exod. Rab. III. 1.

[4] "Our Rabbis have taught" is wanting in edd., but added by *M.*

[5] The verse is given a complimentary sense which it does not possess in the context.

[6] Since they are exempted from many religious duties incumbent upon men. See fol. 20 *b*, p. 132.

[7] The reference is to the Schools at a distance from their homes. The classic example is that of 'Aḳiba's wife who induced him to leave her to prosecute his studies, and he remained away twenty-four years. See K^etūbōt 62 *b*.

[8] At the conclusion of their studies.

[9] *M.*: Rabbi.

[10] I.e. enjoy the good things of life.

[11] In the investigation of *Tōrāh*.

As the Rabbis departed from the school of Rab Ḥisda (another version: the school of R. Samuel b. Naḥmani) they said to him: "Our leaders[1] are well laden; with no breach, and no going forth, and no outcry in our broad places" (Ps. cxliv. 14). "Our leaders are well laden"—Rab and Samuel (another version: R. Joḥanan and R. Eleazar) [differ in interpretation]; one says, "Our leaders" in *Tōrāh* "are well laden" with religious duties; the other says, "Our leaders" in *Tōrāh* and religious duties "are well laden" with sufferings. "With no breach"—may not our company be like the company of David from which issued Aḥitophel; "and no going forth"—may not our company be like the company of Saul from which issued Doeg the Edomite; "and no outcry"—may not our company be like the company of Elisha from which issued Gehazi; "in our broad places"—that we may not have a son or disciple who spoiled his food in public, like the Nazarene[2].

Farewell benediction of Rab Ḥisda's disciples.

fol. 17 b.

"Hearken unto Me, ye stout-hearted, that are far from righteousness" (Is. xlvi. 12). Rab and Samuel (another version: R. Joḥanan and R. Eleazar) [differ in interpretation]. One says: The whole world is nourished through righteousness, but the "stout-hearted" are nourished by the arm[3]. The other says: The whole world is nourished through their merit, but they are not nourished even by their own merit. This is like the statement of Rab Judah who says in the name of Rab: Every day a *Bat Ḳōl* issues from Mount Horeb[4] and proclaims: "All the world is nourished for the sake of My son, Ḥannina[5], but My son, Ḥannina, is satisfied with a *Ḳab* of locusts[6] from the Sabbath-eve to the next Sabbath-eve." This contradicts the statement of Rab Judah who says: Who are the

"Stout-hearted" (Is. xlvi. 12) interpreted.

[1] *Allūfīm* means "oxen" (so R.V. here), but also "leaders."

[2] "Like the Nazarene" is omitted in the later editions through fear of the Censor. "Spoiled (or, cooked) food in public" means, laid himself open to suspicion of heresy by his public declarations. See Herford, *Christianity in Talmūd and Midrāsh*, pp. 60 f.

[3] By the "stout-hearted" is here understood the pious who are "far from righteousness" in the sense that they cannot rely upon it for their sustenance, but have to labour with their arm.

[4] "From Mount Horeb" should probably be omitted, being a reminiscence of Ābōt vi. 2 (Singer, p. 205). Cf. Bacher, *A. B. A.* p. 11 n. 58.

[5] I.e. Ḥannina b. Dosa who was renowned as an ascetic and thaumaturgist. See fol. 33 *a*, 34 *b*, pp. 219, 230, 232.

[6] The carob-tree or locust was the food of the poorest and of ascetics (cf. Matt. iii. 4), and despised by the people. The Midrāsh declares: When the Children of Israel are obliged to eat carobs, they become repentant; Levit. Rab. xxxv. 6.

"stout-hearted"? They are the foolish Gobeans[1]. Rab Joseph[2] said: Thou canst know [that the "stout-hearted" are the Gobeans] because not one of them has ever been made a proselyte. Rab Ashē said: [The "stout-hearted" are] the inhabitants of Mata Mᵉḥasya[3], for they beheld the glory of the *Tōrāh* twice yearly, but not one of them has ever been made a proselyte.

If a bridegroom wishes to read the Shᵉma', etc.

Whether the bridegroom who does not wish to be exempted from reading the *Shᵉma'* is to be regarded as presumptuous.

It is to be inferred that Rabban Simeon b. Gamaliel is concerned lest a charge of presumption [be brought against a bridegroom who reads the *Shᵉma'* on the first night of his marriage and therefore forbids it], whereas the Rabbis have no such concern [and permit it]. But we understood just the opposite of them! For there is a Mishnaic teaching: In a place where they are accustomed to work on the ninth of *Āb*[4], we may work; but in a place where they are not accustomed to work, we may not. Disciples of the wise must cease work in every place. Rabban Simeon b. Gamaliel says: Everyone should regard himself as a disciple of the wise[5]. Here is an inconsistency of the Rabbis and an inconsistency of Rabban Simeon b. Gamaliel! R. Joḥanan said: The statement must be reversed[6]; but Rab Shesha b. Rab Iddi said: Thou hast surely no need to reverse the statement, because the Rabbis do not here contradict themselves. In the case of the reading of the *Shᵉma'* which everybody reads, if [the bridegroom] also reads it, it would not seem presumptuous; but in the latter instance, since everybody works [on the ninth of *Āb*] and he does not, it would appear presumptuous. Likewise, Rabban Simeon b. Gamaliel does not contradict himself. In the case of the reading of the *Shᵉma'*, its validity depends on *Kawwānāh*, and we testify

1 The inhabitants of Gobia in Babylon. A tradition identifies them with the *Nᵉtīnīm* of the Bible, the descendants of the Gibeonites (hence, Gobeans) who were made hewers of wood and drawers of water in the days of Joshua. See Ḳiddūshīn 70 *b*.

2 *M.*: Abbai.

3 A town in Babylon. It possessed a famous School of which Rab Ashē was Principal, and twice a year—before the Passover and New Year—crowds came there to hear the *Tōrāh* expounded.

4 *Āb* is the fifth month of the year. On the 9th of this month, both Temples were destroyed and the day is observed as a solemn fast.

5 In this matter and cease work. Consequently Rabban Simeon b. Gamaliel's teaching here contradicts his teaching in our *Mishnāh*.

6 To remove the contradiction, R. Joḥanan suggests that in the quoted *Mishnāh*, it is the Rabbis, not Rabban Simeon, who say "Everyone should regard himself as a disciple of the wise."

that [the bridegroom] would not be able to concentrate his mind; but here, if one saw [a man not working on the ninth of *Āb*] he would merely say "He has no work to do." Go out and see how many idle men there are in the street[1].

May we return to thee: *Who reads.*

[1] Consequently it would not be presumptuous for one who was not a disciple to abstain from work.

CHAPTER III

MISHNĀH I, II

I. *He whose dead is lying before him [unburied] is exempt from the reading of the* Sh^{e}ma', *from* T^{e}fillāh, T^{e}fillīn *and all the commandments mentioned in the* Tōrāh. *The bearers of the bier and they who relieve them, and they who relieve these latter—such as are before the bier*[1] *and such as are behind it*[2]*—they who are before it, whose services will be required, are exempt; but they who are behind it, whose services may still be required, are under the obligation. But both are exempt from the* T^{e}fillāh.

II. *Having buried the dead and returned [from the grave], if they have sufficient time to begin and finish [the* Sh^{e}ma'*] before arriving at the row*[3]*, they should commence it; but if they have not sufficient time, they should not commence it. As for those who stand in the row, the inner line is exempt, the outer line under the obligation*[4].

G^{E}MĀRĀ

Is the presence of the corpse essential to give exemption?

When the body is lying before him, he is exempt; [it is consequently to be inferred that] when it is not lying before him, he is not exempt! I quote in objection: He whose dead is lying before him should eat his meal in another room, and if he has no other room he should eat in a neighbour's house; if such be not available, he should put up a partition and have his meal; if he has nothing wherewith to make a partition, he should turn his face away [from the body] and eat. But he must not have his meal in a reclining position[5], or partake of meat or drink wine; nor does

fol. 18a. he say Grace or arrange *Zimmūn*, nor do others say Grace on his behalf or include him for *Zimmūn*. He is likewise exempt from the reading of the *Sh^{e}ma'*, from *T^{e}fillāh*, *T^{e}fillīn*, and all the commandments mentioned in the *Tōrāh*. On the Sabbath, however,

[1] Waiting to relieve the bearers.

[2] Having already borne the coffin.

[3] See p. 106. The reference in the next sentence is to a row two-deep.

[4] Edd. print here *Mishnāh III* (p. 131) unnecessarily, since it is treated separately.

[5] A meal was taken reclining on the left elbow on a couch as a mark of comfort and ease. Cf. Oesterley and Box, p. 391 n. 1.

he may recline at his meal, eat meat and drink wine, say Grace and arrange *Zimmūn*, and others may say Grace on his behalf and include him for *Zimmūn*; and he is under the obligation of reading the *Shᵉma'* and *Tᵉfillāh*[1], and all the commandments mentioned in the *Tōrāh*. Rabban Simeon b. Gamaliel[2] says: Since he is under the obligation of these[3], he has obviously the obligation of them all! And R. Joḥanan asked: What is the point of divergence between them[4]? The question of connubial intercourse[5].

It is here at any rate taught that [the mourner, although he is not in the same room as the body[6],] is exempt from reading the *Shᵉma'*, from *Tᵉfillāh*, *Tᵉfillīn*, and all the commandments mentioned in the *Tōrāh*! Rab Pappa replied: [The *Bārāitā*] is to be interpreted as referring to one who turns his face from the body and eats[7]. Rab Ashē said: Since the duty of burying rests upon him, it is to be regarded as though the body was lying before him[8]; as it is said, "And Abraham rose up from before his dead" (Gen. xxiii. 3) and it is said "That I may bury my dead from before me" (*ibid.* v. 4)[9], i.e. so long as the duty of burial rested upon him, it was as though the body was actually before him. The question answered.

He whose dead [is lying before him] is exempt, but [so it may be inferred,] not the watcher[10]. But lo, there is a teaching: Who watches the body, although it is not his dead, is exempt from reading the *Shᵉma'*, from *Tᵉfillāh*, *Tᵉfillīn*, and all the commandments mentioned in the *Tōrāh*! "Who watches the body, although The watcher also exempt.

1 "Reading *Shᵉma'* and *Tᵉfillāh*" is added by *M.* and is found in Sᵉmāḥōt x (cf. Mō'ēd Ḳāṭōn 23 *b*) from which this quotation is taken. *Tᵉfillīn* is not mentioned because the phylacteries are not worn on the Sabbath.

2 *M.*: Rabban Gamaliel.

3 *Shᵉma'* and *Tᵉfillāh*.

4 Between Rabban Simeon and the other Rabbis that the former raises this point.

5 When this, as it sometimes does in Jewish law, becomes a duty, then Rabban Simeon does not allow it to be an exception to the rule that all signs of mourning must be discarded on the Sabbath.

6 In contradiction to the inference drawn from our *Mishnāh*.

7 Not to the mourner who eats in another room or in a neighbour's house; thus the *Bārāitā* presents no contradiction.

8 Rejecting Rab Pappa's solution, Rab Ashē declares that "lying before him" is not to be understood literally, but means the duty of burial is still his.

9 When he said "before me," Abraham was addressing the sons of Heth and was not in the actual presence of the body.

10 The Jewish custom is not to leave the body alone until burial, there being somebody always present to "watch." See Oesterley and Box, p. 332. The reason is to protect the body from mice. Cf. below.

it is not his dead" [so stated the *Bārāitā*; therefore it is to be inferred] if it is his dead, although he does not watch the body, [he is exempt]. If it be his dead or if he watches it, he is exempt; but [so it may be inferred] one who walks in a cemetery is not! But lo, there is a teaching: A man must not walk in a cemetery with his *T^{e}fillīn* on his head or holding a scroll of the *Tōrāh* and reading therein; should he do so, he commits a transgression because of the injunction: "Whoso mocketh the poor blasphemeth his Maker" (Prov. xvii. 5)[1]! In this latter case, within four cubits [of the grave] it is forbidden, but beyond that limit, he is under the obligation; for the teacher has said: A dead body affects four cubits with regard to the reading of the *Sh^{e}ma'*. But here [in the case of a mourner or watcher], even beyond the limit of four cubits he is exempt.

If there be two watchers.

It was stated above [in the *Bārāitā*]: "Who watches the body, although it is not his dead, is exempt from reading the *Sh^{e}ma'*, from *T^{e}fillāh*, *T^{e}fillīn*, and all the commandments mentioned in the *Tōrāh*." Should there be two [watchers], they take it in turn to watch and read. Ben 'Azzai says: Should they be bringing the body in a boat, they place it in one corner and they both pray in another corner[2]! What is the point of divergence between them? Rabina said: They differ whether we have fear of mice [gnawing the body]; the former holds there is such fear, the other there is not.

Respectful treatment of the corpse.

Our Rabbis have taught: He who is removing bones from one place to another must not put them into a saddle-bag and set them upon an ass and ride upon them, because this is disrespectful treatment; but if he is afraid of heathens or robbers, he may do so[3]. What they say of bones applies also to a scroll of the *Tōrāh*. To which [clause in this teaching does this last statement refer]? If to the first clause, it is self-evident; for is a scroll of the *Tōrāh* less than bones? Nay; it refers to the second clause[4].

Duty of following the cortege.

Rabbah said in the name of R. Judah: Whoever sees a body [being conveyed to burial] and does not accompany it[5] commits a transgression because of [the injunction] "Whoso mocketh the poor blasphemeth his Maker" (Prov. xvii. 5). If he accompany

[1] There is none so poor as the dead. Cf. fol. 3 *b*, p. 10 n. 4.

[2] They do not take it in turn to watch and pray.

[3] Sit on them to escape on his ass.

[4] In time of danger he may pack the scroll into the saddle-bag and ride on the ass.

[5] *M.* adds: a distance of four cubits.

it, what is his reward? Rab Assi said: Of him the Scriptures state, "He that is gracious to the poor lendeth unto the Lord" (*ibid.* xix. 17) and "he that is gracious unto the needy honoureth Him" (*ibid.* xiv. 31)[1].

R. Ḥiyya and R. Jonathan were conversing as they walked in a cemetery, and the "fringes" belonging to R. Jonathan fell upon the graves[2]. R. Ḥiyya said to him, "Lift them up, so that [the dead] shall not say, 'To-morrow they will come to us, but to-day they revile us'." He asked him, "Do they know all that; for lo, it is written, 'The dead know not anything' (Eccles. ix. 5)?" He answered, "If thou hast read [this verse], thou hast not read it a second time; if a second time, then not a third time; and if a third time, its meaning has not been explained to thee. 'For the living know that they shall die' (*ibid.*)—this refers to the righteous who are called living even in their death; as it is said, 'And Benaiah the son of Jehoiada, the son of a living man[3] of Kabzeel, who had done mighty deeds, he smote the two altar-hearths of Moab; he went down also and slew a lion in the midst of a pit in time of snow' (II Sam. xxiii. 20).—'Son of a living man!' Are there, then, in the whole world sons [born of] dead men? But, 'son of a living man' [means] even in his death he is called 'living.' 'Of Kabzeel, who had done mighty deeds'—[he is so described] because he multiplied and gathered labourers for the *Tōrāh*[4]. 'He smote the two altar-hearths of Moab[5]'—i.e. he left nobody like him, neither [in the time of] the first Temple nor the Second Temple. 'He went down also and slew a lion in the midst of a pit in time of snow'—some say: He cut a hole in the ice into which he descended to bathe[6]; others say: He learnt the *Sifrā dᵉbē Rab*[7] in a winter's day. 'But the dead know not

Eccles. ix. 5 expounded.

fol. 18 b. II Sam. xxiii. 20 expounded.

[1] An act of respect shown to the dead stands in a higher scale, according to Rabbinic teaching, than to the living, because it is disinterested. On the phrase "Deal kindly and truly with me" (Gen. xlvii. 29) the Rabbis comment that "kindness of truth" is that performed to the dead; Gen. Rab. xcvi. 5.

[2] "Upon the graves" is added by *M.* The "fringes" are the *Ṣīṣīt* attached to the corners of the garment.

[3] So literally; R.V.: a valiant man.

[4] Pointing the word *mᵉḳabbēṣ ēl* "the gatherer for God."

[5] By "Moab" is here understood David who was descended from Ruth the Moabitess and provided the site for the Temple.

[6] To harden his body in order the better to master the intricacies of the *Tōrāh* (= slay a lion).

[7] On the *Sifrā* see p. 71 n. 6. It is regarded as the most difficult of the Halakic commentaries on the Pentateuch and is therefore called "a lion." He mastered this work on a winter's day, i.e. in a short space of time.

anything'—this refers to the wicked who are called dead in their life-time; as it is said, 'And thou, O wicked one, thou art slain, the prince of Israel' (Ezek. xxi. 30)[1]." Or if thou wilt, derive it from the following: "At the mouth of two witnesses, or three witnesses, shall the dead be put to death" (Deut. xvii. 6). But he is alive! Nay, he is accounted as dead from the beginning.

Do the dead know what transpires on earth?

The sons of R. Ḥiyya[2] went out on to the land[3]; their studies had been difficult for them, and they had had considerable trouble to remember them. One said to the other, "Does our father[4] know of this trouble?" The other replied, "How should he know? Lo, it is written, 'His sons come to honour him, and he knoweth it not' (Job xiv. 21)!" The first said to him, "But does he not know; for behold it is written, 'But his flesh grieveth for him, and his soul mourneth over him' (*ibid.* v. 22)? And R. Isaac has said: The worm is as painful to the flesh of the dead as a needle in the flesh of the living!" Some answer: The dead know of their own troubles, but not of the troubles of others.

A case cited.

Do they not [know of the troubles of others]? Lo, there is a teaching: It once happened that a pious man gave a denarius[5] to a beggar on the New Year's eve in a time of drought. His wife upbraided him; so he went and spent the night in the cemetery[6]. He heard two spirits conversing. One said to the other, "Come, friend, let us wander in the world and hear behind the curtain[7] what visitation is to come upon the world." The other spirit replied, "I cannot, because I am buried in a matting of reeds[8]; but go thou and report to me what thou hearest." She[9] went, and having wandered about returned. The other asked, "What didst thou hear, friend, behind the curtain?" She replied, "I heard that if one sows in the first rainfall[10], the hail will smite it." This man

[1] *M.* adds: But was he dead? He was living!

[2] They were named Judah and Hezekiah; cf. *A. P. A.* I. pp. 48 f.

[3] To till their inheritance.

[4] Who had died recently.

[5] A Roman coin. The silver denarius is here intended, which was worth a twenty-fourth of the golden denarius, about 7*d*.

[6] It was the New Year's night when God began His annual judgment of the world.

[7] In the heavenly court of justice.

[8] Instead of linen shrouds; cf. Oesterley and Box, p. 333; Lane, p. 518.

[9] They were both spirits of girls.

[10] The first rainfall is from the 17th to the 23rd of the 8th month; the second from the 23rd to the end of the month.

thereupon went and sowed in the second rainfall. [The hail] destroyed everybody's crops but not his.

The following year, he again spent the [New Year's] night in the cemetery, and heard the same two spirits conversing. One said to the other, "Come, let us wander in the world and hear behind the curtain what visitation is to come upon the world." The other spirit replied, "Have I not told thee, friend, that I cannot, because I am buried in a matting of reeds? But go thou and come and tell me what thou hearest." She went, and wandered about and returned. The other spirit asked, "What didst thou hear behind the curtain?" She replied, "I heard that if one sows in the second rainfall, it will be smitten by the blast." This man went and sowed in the first rainfall. What everybody else sowed was smitten by the blast, but not his. His wife asked him, "How is it that last year everybody's crop was destroyed by hail, but not thine; and this year everybody's crop was blasted except thine?" He told her the whole story.

It is related that very soon afterwards a quarrel broke out between the wife of that pious man and the mother of the girl[1]. The former said to the other, "Come, I will show thee that thy daughter is buried in reed-matting." The following year the same man went and spent the [New Year's] night in the cemetery, and he heard those spirits conversing. One said, "Come, friend, let us wander in the world and hear behind the curtain what visitation is to befall the world." The other replied, "Leave me alone, friend; what has passed between me and thee has been overheard by the living." Infer from this that the dead do know! [No;] it is possible that some other person[2] died and went and informed them.

Come and hear: Zeʿiri left a sum of money in charge of his landlady[3]. During the time he went to the school of his master and returned, she died. He followed her to the court of death[4] and asked her, "Where is the money?" She replied, "Go and take it from beneath the door-socket in such and such a place; and tell my mother to send me my comb and tube of eye-paint[5] Another case cited.

[1] Who had been buried in the reed-matting.

[2] Who was acquainted with this story, on passing over into the world of spirits, related the facts to them; but they did not know of it of their own accord.

[3] *M.*: landlord's daughter.

[4] The cemetery.

[5] *Koḥl* as commonly used in the East; Lane, p. 37.

through so-and-so who will arrive here to-morrow." Conclude from this that the dead do know! [No;] perhaps *Dūmāh*[1] informed [the dead] beforehand[2].

A third case cited.

Come and hear: The father of Samuel was entrusted with some money belonging to orphans. At the time that he passed away, Samuel was not with him. People afterwards called him, "Son of the consumer of the orphans' money." He went after his father to the court of death and said to them[3], "I want Abba." They replied, "There are many of that name here." "I want Abba b. Abba." They answered, "There are also many of that name here." He said to them, "I want Abba b. Abba, the father of Samuel; where is he?" They answered, "He has gone up to the heavenly seminary[4]." In the meantime he noticed Levi[5] who was seated apart. He asked him, "Why sittest thou apart? Why hast thou not gone up [to the heavenly seminary]?" He replied, "I was told, 'The number of years thou didst not attend the seminary of R. Aphes and didst grieve him on that account, we will not permit thee to ascend to the heavenly seminary'." In the meantime his father arrived; and Samuel noticed that he wept and laughed. He said to him, "Why weepest thou?" He answered, "Because thou wilt soon come here." "And why dost thou laugh?" "Because thou art very highly thought of in this world." Samuel said to him, "If I am so esteemed, let them allow Levi to enter"; and they permitted him to enter. He asked him, "Where is the orphans' money?" He answered, "Go, take it from the enclosure of the mill. The upper and lower sums of money belong to us, the middle sum belongs to the orphans." He asked his father, "Why didst thou act in this manner?" He replied, "Should thieves come to steal, they would steal ours; should the earth destroy[6], it would destroy ours." Conclude from this that the dead do know[7]! [No;] perhaps it was different with Samuel; being a man so highly esteemed, it may have been announced in advance "Make way for him."

[1] A word meaning "silence" used in the Psalms to describe the silence of the grave; cf. Ps. xciv. 17, cxv. 17. In the Talmūd it is the name of the guardian angel of the departed.

[2] He announces to the disembodied spirits who will soon join them; but otherwise the dead do not know what transpires on earth.

[3] To the dead who appeared to him seated in conclave.

[4] The *Tōrāh* is studied in Heaven as well as on earth. Cf. Bab. Mᵉṣīa' 86*a* (translated by Herford in *J. Q. R.* II. p. 457).

[5] A departed colleague.

[6] Cf. Matt. vi. 19.

[7] What transpires on earth, since Abba knew of his son's impending death.

R. Jonathan likewise retracted[1]; for R. Samuel b. Naḥmani said in the name of R. Jonathan: Whence do we learn that the dead converse one with the other? As it is said, "And the Lord said unto him[2], This is the land which I swore unto Abraham, unto Isaac, and unto Jacob, saying" (Deut. xxxiv. 4). What means "saying"? The Holy One, blessed be He, spake to Moses, "Go, tell Abraham, Isaac and Jacob, The oath which I swore unto you have I fulfilled for your children." If thou shouldest imagine that they were not cognisant [of what transpires on earth], what use would it be to tell them? On the other hand, if they were cognisant, what need was there for him to inform them? To give the credit to Moses.

Conclusion that the dead do know.

fol. 19 a.

R. Isaac said: Whoever speaks [evil] of the dead is as though he spoke it of a stone. Some say that they are not aware [of what is spoken], while others say they are aware but it does not trouble them. But it is not so! For Rab Pappa[3] spoke [evil] of Mar Samuel [after his death], and a pole fell from the roof and split his skull! It is different with a Rabbinical scholar, because the Holy One, blessed be He, defends his honour.

The dead indifferent to what is spoken about them.

R. Joshua b. Levi said: Whoever talks [evil] after the bier of disciples of the wise will fall into *Gēhinnōm*; as it is said, "But as for such as turn aside unto their crooked ways, the Lord will lead them away with the workers of iniquity. Peace be upon Israel" (Ps. cxxv. 5)—i.e. even at a time when "there is peace upon Israel," "the Lord will lead them away with the workers of iniquity."

Punishment of those who speak evil of the disciples of the wise.

It was taught by the school of R. Ishmael: If thou seest a scholar committing an offence at night, do not criticise him for it by day; perhaps he has repented by then. Dost thou imagine *perhaps* he has repented? Nay, he has certainly repented. This refers[4] only to an offence concerned with his person; but in a matter involving money, [he may be criticised] until he refunds it to its owner.

When the actions of scholars may be criticised.

R. Joshua b. Levi also said: In twenty-four places [it is taught] that the *Bēt Dīn* excommunicates a man for [lack of] respect to

Teachers must be honoured.

[1] His opinion, as stated above (fol. 18*a*, p. 119), had been that the dead knew nothing.

[2] To Moses prior to his death.

[3] This is the reading of *M.* and is probably correct. The reading of the edd.: "Rab Pappa said, Somebody spoke evil" is intended to remove the reproach from him.

[4] *M.*: Rab Ḥisda said: This refers.

a teacher, and we learn them all in our *Mishnāh*[1]. R. Eleazar asked him: Where [are they to be found]? He replied: Search and thou wilt find them. He accordingly went and searched and found three—Who despises the washing of the hands[2], who talks [evil] after the bier of the disciples of the wise, and who acts arrogantly towards the Most High. "Who talks after the bier of disciples of the wise"; where is this to be found? There is a Mishnaic teaching: ['Aḳabya b. Mahalalel] used to say: We may not administer the waters of a woman suspected of adultery[3] to a female proselyte or freed woman; but the Sages say: We may do so. And they said to him, "It happened with Karkemit, a freed handmaid of Jerusalem, and Shemayah and Abṭalion did administer the waters to her!" 'Aḳabya said to them, "It was for show that they made her drink[4]." Thereupon the Sages excommunicated him and he died under the ban, and the *Bēt Dīn* stoned his coffin. "Whoever despises the washing of the hands"; where is this found? There is a Mishnaic teaching: R. Judah said: God forbid that we should suppose that 'Aḳabya b. Mahalalel was excommunicated, for the Temple-court[5] was not locked upon any man of Israel equal to him in knowledge, purity and fear of sin. But who was it they excommunicated? It was Eleazar b. Ḥanok, because he made light of the washing of the hands; and when he died the *Bēt Dīn* sent and placed a large stone upon his coffin, to teach that whoever is excommunicated and dies under the ban, the *Bēt Dīn* stones his coffin. "Who acts arrogantly towards the Most High"; where is this to be found? There is a Mishnaic teaching: Simeon b. Shetaḥ sent to Ḥoni *Hamme'aggēl*[6]: "Thou

[1] "Our *Mishnāh*" usually means the paragraph of the *Mishnāh* under discussion. Here it refers to the work as a whole.

[2] The washing of the hands before a meal is a *Rabbinical* ordinance, and to despite it reflects on the honour of the teachers.

[3] Num. v. 11 ff.

[4] They merely pretended to give her the bitter waters. This is the interpretation of many commentators. Rashi renders: "They administered them to one who was like themselves," i.e. despising Shemayah and Abṭalion on the ground that they were not of pure Jewish stock. According to Giṭṭin 57*b* they were descendants of Sennacherib, king of Assyria.

[5] On the Passover festival when the court was thronged with pilgrims.

[6] "The circle-drawer." He was a famous ascetic to whom the people appealed in time of drought to pray for rain. He thereupon drew a circle and declared he would not step outside it until God had sent rain. See Ta'anīt 23 *a*. It has been suggested that the original meaning of Ḥoni's name is not "circle-drawer" (which later legend gave it) but "roof-tiler," his occupation. Cf. *T. A.* I. p. 325 n. 381. The name Ḥoni is more familiar in its Greek form "Onias."

art deserving of excommunication, and wert thou not Ḥoni, I would pronounce the ban against thee; but what can I do seeing that thou art petulant with the Omnipresent, and nevertheless He fulfils thy desires as a father gratifies a petulant child; and concerning thee the Scriptures state, 'Let thy father and thy mother be glad, and let her that bore thee rejoice' (Prov. xxiii. 25)." Is there no other instance [of arrogance towards God]? Yes, there is; for Rab Joseph has taught[1]: Theodosius of Rome accustomed the Jews in Rome to eat kids roasted in their entirety[2] on the Passover night. They[3] sent him [the message]: "If thou wert not Theodosius, I would have issued a ban against thee, for thou hast induced Israelites to eat the holy things outside [Jerusalem][4]." But we are speaking of instances mentioned in our *Mishnāh*; and this is a *Bārāitā*! Is there none in the *Mishnāh*? Yes, there is; for there is a Mishnaic teaching: If one has cut [a portable earthenware oven] into layers and placed sand between each layer[5], R. Eliezer declares it clean, but the Sages declare it unclean; and this is what is known as "the oven of the serpent[6]." Why "serpent"? Rab Judah said in the name of Samuel: This teaches that the Sages wound it round with discussions as a serpent [winds itself round something] and proved that the oven was unclean. And there is a teaching: That day they brought everything that R. Eliezer had proclaimed clean[7] and burnt it in his presence, and finally they excommunicated[8] him. Despite this, we have not learnt a case of excommunication in the *Mishnāh*! And where

[1] *M.*: "There is a teaching: R. Josē said." This reading is adopted by Bacher, *A. B. A.* p. 103 n. 11.

[2] With the head, legs and entrails (cf. Exod. xii. 9). But this should be done only by the pilgrims in Jerusalem, whereas Theodosius introduced the practice into Rome.

[3] According to *M.* the subject is "the Sages." Some edd. make the subject Simeon b. Shetaḥ: but this would be an anachronism. See *A. T.* II. p. 561 n. 1.

[4] Here, then, is another instance of arrogance against the Most High, since Theodosius altered the law.

[5] A portable earthenware oven is like an earthenware vessel and can contract defilement. In the latter instance, the vessel cannot be purified and must be broken to pieces. In the opinion of the Sages, the same rule applies to the oven. R. Eliezer allows the oven to be cut horizontally into layers and sand placed in between and cemented over.

[6] Krauss, p. 251, thinks that the word translated "serpent" is really a proper name, 'Εχῖνος, after whom that sort of oven was called. See his discussion in Part I of *Lehnwörter*, pp. 295 f.

[7] Everything which had been in contact with this oven.

[8] *Lit.* "blessed," an euphemism.

are the twenty-four places to be found[1]? R. Joshua b. Levi compares one thing with another[2], but R. Eleazar does not.

The bearers of the bier and they who relieve them.

Time of burial should not clash with reading of the *Shᵉma'*.

Our Rabbis have taught: We should not carry out a body [for burial] near the time of reading the *Shᵉma'*[3]; but if they have commenced to do so, we should not stop them. But it is not so! For lo, Rab Joseph was borne out near the time of reading the *Shᵉma'*! With a highly esteemed man it is different.

Such as are before the bier and such as are behind it.

Reading the *Shᵉma'* during a funeral oration,

Our Rabbis have taught: Those who are occupied with the funeral oration at the time when the body is lying before them should slip away one by one and read the *Shᵉma'*; but if the body is not present, they sit and read the *Shᵉma'* and the orator sits in silence; they stand and say the *Tᵉfillāh*, and he justifies the divine decree, saying: "Lord of the Universe, I have often sinned before Thee, and Thou hast not exacted punishment from me for one in a thousand. May it be Thy will, O Lord our God, to repair our breaches and the breaches of all Thy people, the house of Israel, in mercy." Abbai said: A man ought not to speak thus; for R. Simeon b. Laḳish said, and it has been similarly taught in the name of R. Josē: A man should not open his mouth to Satan[4]. Rab Joseph said: What is the Scriptural authority for this? As it is said, "We should have been as Sodom" (Is. i. 9); and what did the prophet reply to them? "Hear the word of the Lord, ye rulers of Sodom" (*ibid. v.* 10).

Having buried the dead and returned, etc.

and after burial.

If they are able to begin and finish the whole, yes; but if only one paragraph or one verse, are they not [to commence it]? Against this conclusion I quote: Having buried the dead and returned, if they are able to begin and complete even one paragraph or one verse [they should commence it]! Here likewise[5] it means that if they are able to begin and finish one paragraph or even one verse, before reaching the row, they should begin; but if not, they should not commence it.

1 That the *Bēt Dīn* excommunicates a man for a lack of respect to a teacher.

2 He holds that, as in the *Bārāitā* here quoted, wherever in the *Mishnāh* an individual Rabbi resists the opinion of the majority, it comes under this heading.

3 According to *J. T.*, one hour before.

4 Lay himself open to an imputation.

5 In our *Mishnāh*.

As for those who stand in the row, etc.

fol. 19 b. Who are exempt.

Our Rabbis have taught: The row which looks upon the inner space[1] is exempt [from reading the *Shema‘*]; but the row which does not look upon the inner space is under the obligation. R. Judah says: Those who come out of regard for the mourner are exempt; but those who come on their own account[2] are under the obligation.

Honouring God man's principal duty, and personal dignity must not be considered.

Rab Judah said in the name of Rab: Who finds diverse kinds[3] in his garment must divest himself thereof even in the street. What is the reason? [As it is said,] "There is no wisdom nor understanding nor counsel against the Lord" (Prov. xxi. 30)—i.e. wherever the Divine Name is liable to be profaned, we pay no respect to a teacher. Against this teaching is quoted: Having buried the dead, and on returning there are two paths before them one clean, the other unclean[4], if [the mourner] enters the clean path, they follow him there, and if he enters the unclean path, they follow him there out of respect for him[5]! Why should this be so? Let one say, "There is no wisdom nor understanding nor counsel against the Lord"! R. Abba explained that it speaks here of a *Bēt Perās*[6] which is declared unclean by the Rabbis[7]. For Rab Judah said in the name of Samuel: One may blow upon a *Bēt Perās* [to see whether there are any bones; and if there are none] he may walk on it[8]. And Rab Judah b. Ashē said in the name of Rab[9]: A *Bēt Perās* which has been much trodden under foot is to be regarded as clean.

Some apparent exceptions discussed.

Come and hear: R. Eleazar b. Ṣadoḳ[10] said: We used to leap upon the coffins of the dead to meet the kings of Israel[11], and not only to meet kings of Israel do they so permit, but even to meet

[1] Where the mourner is standing. [2] As spectators, not comforters.

[3] A mixture of wool and linen; cf. Lev. xix. 19, Deut. xxii. 11.

[4] By reason of a grave being there.

[5] Hence out of deference for a human being, they disregard an ordinance of the *Tōrāh*.

[6] A *Bēt Perās* is a field, half a furrow in length and breadth, on to which crushed bones may have been carried by a plough which had passed over a grave. Contact with even a fragment of a bone would cause defilement. *Perās* is of doubtful etymology. It is explained by some to mean "half"; cf. Dan. v. 28. Wiesner, p. 49, connects it with πυρά, because the corpse was usually first burnt. See also *T. A.* II. p. 490 n. 550.

[7] Therefore the deference they show to the mourner does not involve disregard of the *Tōrāh*. [8] Without contracting defilement.

[9] *M.*: Rab Judah b. Ammi in the name of Rab Judah.

[10] He was a *Kōhēn* and consequently forbidden to come into contact with the dead: cf. Lev. xxi. 1–3.

[11] Probably Agrippa I and Herod II; *A. T.* I. p. 47.

the kings of other nations[1]; for if he be worthy, he will discern between the kings of Israel and the kings of other nations. Why should this be so? Let one say, "There is no wisdom nor understanding nor counsel against the Lord"! It is in accord with the opinion of Raba[2], who said: According to the teaching of the *Tōrāh*, "a tent"—i.e. anything which contains a hollow space at least a handbreadth in extent—forms a partition against uncleanness, but if it does not contain a hollow space at least a handbreadth in extent it does not form such a partition; and most coffins have a hollow space a handbreadth in extent. But the Rabbis decreed that even those which have this hollow space [should defile] because of those which have it not; but for the purpose of paying honour to royalty, the Rabbis do not enforce this decree.

Come and hear: Great is the duty of honouring one's fellow-creatures, since it sets aside a prohibition enjoined by the *Tōrāh*. Why should this be so? Let one say, "There is no wisdom nor understanding nor counsel against the Lord"! Rab b. Shaba explained it in the presence of Rab Kah^a^na as referring to the prohibition, "Thou shalt not turn aside from the sentence which they shall declare unto thee" (Deut. xvii. 11). They laughed at him, for is not the prohibition, "Thou shalt not turn aside" enjoined by the *Tōrāh*[3]! Rab Kah^a^na said to them: A great man having expressed an opinion, you should not laugh at him. We base the authority for all the *dicta* of the Rabbis upon the prohibition, "Thou shalt not turn aside"; but for the duty of honouring a fellow-creature the Rabbis give permission[4].

Come and hear: [It is written:] "And hide thyself from them" (*ibid.* xxii. 1)[5]; i.e. there are times when thou mayest hide thyself from them, and times when thou must not hide thyself from them.

[1] In *J. T.* it is recorded that when Diocletian visited Tyre, R. Ḥiyya b. Abba (who was a *Kōhēn*) crossed a cemetery to meet him.

[2] *M.*: Rabbah.

[3] They misunderstood him. He meant the only prohibition of the *Tōrāh* set aside is that implied in the verse quoted, which teaches that the ordinances of the religious leaders of the age must be adhered to. Consequently, in actual practice, it is only Rabbinical injunctions which are set aside by the honouring of one's fellow-creatures.

[4] They allow their authority, though it is based on the *Tōrāh*, to be set aside for this purpose.

[5] In the Hebrew, the negative "not" is attached to the verb "see" and has to be understood with "and hide thyself." According to the Rabbinic interpretation, since there is no negative qualifying "and hide thyself," it is to be deduced that there are times when one may not restore a straying animal.

How can this be? If he was a *Kōhēn*[1] and [the straying animal] was in a cemetery; or he was an Elder and it was derogatory to his dignity [to be seen leading the animal back]; or his work was more important than his neighbour's[2]—therefore it is said, "And hide thyself." Why should this be so? Let one say, "There is no wisdom nor understanding nor counsel against the Lord[3]"! It is different here; for it is written, "And hide thyself from them[4]." May one, then, conclude from this[5]? We cannot draw an inference about a prohibition from a case involving only financial loss[6].

Come and hear: [It is written,] "Or for his sister" (Num. vi. 7)[7]. What has this teaching to tell us? Supposing he[8] were on his way to sacrifice the Paschal lamb or circumcise his son[9], and he heard that one of his relatives had died, it is possible [to think] that he should turn back and render himself unclean; say, then, he shall not make himself unclean. It is possible [to think] that in the same way that [under these conditions] he may not make himself unclean for his relatives, he may not make himself unclean for a *Mēt Miṣwāh*, therefore there is a teaching to tell us "or for his sister"; i.e. "for his sister" he may not render himself unclean, but for a *Mēt Miṣwāh* he must defile himself. Why should this fol. 20 a. be so? Let one say, "There is no wisdom nor understanding nor

[1] Who is forbidden contact with the dead.

[2] I.e. his loss in restoring the animal would be greater than the owner's if it were not restored. *M.* reads "his loss" instead of "his work."

[3] Why should the Elder consider his dignity before the performance of a duty?

[4] The *Tōrāh* expressly makes such an allowance.

[5] By analogy that one need not take off a garment in the street if diverse kinds are found in it out of self-respect (seeing that the Elder is permitted to consider his dignity), but wait until he reaches his home.

[6] The matter of the straying animal involves nothing more than the owner's loss; it is consequently of less seriousness than a matter involving a principle.

[7] A Nazirite may not make himself ritually unclean by contact with the dead. The list of relations is: father, mother, brother, sister; and the Halakic commentary on Numbers and Deuteronomy, the *Sifrē*, discusses the reason why each is mentioned: He may not defile himself for his father, but he must for a *Mēt Miṣwāh* (see Glossary, s.v.); nor for his mother, but even if he be a *Kōhēn* as well as a Nazirite (i.e. doubly prohibited against such contact), he must defile himself for a *Mēt Miṣwāh*; nor for his brother, but even if he be the High Priest as well as a Nazirite, he must defile himself for a *Mēt Miṣwāh*. The explanation of "his sister" is given in the *Gᵉmārā*.

[8] The Nazirite who is a High Priest.

[9] Which had to be performed at a certain time, and he would be precluded from officiating if he were unclean.

counsel against the Lord[1]"! It is different here; because it is written "for his sister[2]." May one, then, conclude from this? Sit and do nothing is different[3].

The superiority of former generations.

Rab Pappa asked Abbai: How were our predecessors different from us that miracles occurred for them but not for us? Is it a question of learning? In the time of Rab Judah, their whole study was limited to the Order "Damages[4]," whereas we study the six Orders; and when Rab Judah reached the paragraph in *Mishnāh 'Uḳṣīn*[5]: "If a woman presses vegetables in a pot" (some declare it was the paragraph: "Olives which are pressed with their leaves are clean"), he said, "We see here the conflicts of Rab and Samuel[6]," whereas we study *'Uḳṣīn* in thirteen lessons[7]! Yet, with respect to Rab Judah, when he took off one of his shoes[8], the rain descended; but we afflict our souls and cry aloud and there is none that takes notice of us! He replied: Our predecessors jeopardised their lives for the sanctification of the Name, but we do not. As it once happened with Rab Adda b. Ah^a^bah who noticed a heathen woman[9] wearing a *karbāltā*[10] in the street; thinking that she was an Israelite, he went up to her and tore it from off her. It was then discovered that she was a heathen, and

1 The duty of burial is to show respect to the body; why should respect for a person set aside the Pentateuchal prohibition against defilement?

2 And (according to the Rabbinic deduction above) the *Tōrāh* gives him permission.

3 No analogy can be drawn between the wearing of mixed stuff and the burial of a *Mēt Miṣwāh*, because they fall into different categories. The former is a prohibition as an act—one has to "arise and do" [קום ועשה] it (by putting on the garment), to commit the transgression. With the *Mēt Miṣwāh*, on the other hand, it is the omission to bury which constitutes the transgression. To "sit and do nothing" [שב ולא תעשה] is what is forbidden.

4 The Fourth Order of the *Mishnāh*. The detailed division of the *Mishnāh* is given in an Appendix by Oesterley and Box.

5 The last Tractate of the Sixth Order.

6 The disputations between Rab and Samuel are proverbial for their complexity.

7 Others explain: with thirteen different methods of interpretation. In either case, the intention is that the superiority of earlier generations could not be on the score of learning.

8 He merely prepared himself to fast and pray for rain. On any occasion of mourning or self-humiliation, the shoes are taken off.

9 Some edd. read "Samaritan," to satisfy the scruples of the Censor.

10 A word of uncertain meaning; either a kind of headgear or a showy mantle worn by disreputable women. The same word occurs in Dan. iii. 21 where R.V. renders "mantle"; but the Oxford Lexicon, ed. Brown, etc., p. 1097*b* prefers "cap."

they fined him four hundred *Zūzīm*. He said to her, "What is thy name?" She replied, "Matun." He said, "Matun, Matun, is worth four hundred *Zūzīm*[1]."

Rab Giddel had the habit of going and sitting at the gate of the baths[2], saying [to the women as they entered], "Bathe thus and thus." The Rabbis said to him, "Is not the master afraid of [the promptings of] the evil impulse?" He replied, "They are in my eyes like white geese." **Rab Giddel's habit.**

R. Joḥanan had the habit of going and sitting at the gates of the baths, saying, "When the daughters of Israel leave, let them gaze upon me, and they will have children as beautiful as I[3]." The Rabbis said to him, "Art thou not afraid of the Evil Eye[4]?" He answered, "I am come from the seed of Joseph against whom the Evil Eye had no power; for it is written, 'Joseph is a fruitful vine, a fruitful vine by a fountain' (Gen. xlix. 22); and R. Abbahu said: Read not *ᵃlē 'ayin* 'by a fountain' but *'ōlē 'ayin* 'overcoming the [Evil] Eye'." R. Josē b. Ḥannina said: From the following passage [did R. Joḥanan derive his reason]: "And let them grow [*wᵉyidgū*] into a multitude in the midst of the earth" (*ibid.* xlviii. 16); i.e. as the fishes [*dāgīm*] in the sea are covered by the water and the Evil Eye has no power over them, in similar manner the Evil Eye has no power over the seed of Joseph. Or if thou wilt, say that the eye which desired not to partake of what did not belong to it[5] cannot be influenced by the Evil Eye. **R. Joḥanan's habit.**

MISHNĀH III

Women, slaves and minors are exempt from reading the Shᵉma' *and from* Tᵉfillīn; *but they are under the obligation of* Tᵉfillāh, Mᵉzūzāh *and Grace after meals.* **fol. 20 b.**

[1] There is a double play of words. Matun means "deliberate"; hence if he had not been hasty, it would have saved him 400 *Zūz*. Matun also resembles the word for "two hundred," which being repeated, totals 400.

[2] The bath of purification, called *Mikwêh*, is here intended. Certain regulations had to be observed, otherwise the act of purification would be invalid.

[3] On the beauty of R. Joḥanan, see fol. 5*b*, p. 24.

[4] The malignant power which bewitches and harms its victims. It is often used, as here, to denote sexual passion. The belief in the Evil Eye was widespread in the Orient; cf. *J. E.* v. p. 280; Lane, pp. 256f.

[5] Joseph who rejected the advances of Potiphar's wife.

GEMĀRA

Women exempt from commands which depend upon a definite point of time.

Why are the reading of the *Shema'* and *Tefillīn* different [from the others]? Because they are commands[1] the observance of which depends upon a certain point of time, and women are exempt from all commands of this class. *Tefillāh*, *Mezūzāh* and Grace after meals, being commands the observance of which does not depend upon a certain point of time, are obligatory upon women[2].

Why the *Mishnāh* specifies the *Shema'*.

That the reading of the *Shema'* [is not obligatory upon women] is self-evident, because it is a command the observance of which depends upon a certain point of time, and women are exempt from all commands of this class! [Why, then, does the *Mishnāh* mention it?] Thou mightest say that since it contains a reference to the Kingdom of Heaven [it should be read by women]; therefore it informs us [they are exempt].

Why *Tefillīn* is specified.

And from Tefillīn. This too is evident! Thou mightest say that since *Tefillīn* are to be compared with *Mezūzāh*[3] [they should be obligatory upon women]; therefore it informs us [they are exempt].

Why *Tefillāh* is specified.

But they are under the obligation of Tefillāh; [obviously] because this is prayer! But thou mightest say that since it is written thereby, "Evening and morning and at noonday" (Ps. lv. 18), it is like a command the observance of which depends upon a certain point of time [and women are exempt]; therefore it informs us [the obligation is theirs].

Why *Mezūzāh* is specified.

And Mezūzāh. This is evident! But thou mightest say that since it is to be compared with the study of *Tōrāh*[4], [being exempt from the latter they are likewise exempt from the former]; therefore it informs us [that women have the duty of fixing the *Mezūzāh*].

Why Grace after meals is specified.

And Grace after meals. This too is evident! But thou mightest say that since it is written thereby, "When the Lord shall give you in the evening flesh to eat and in the morning bread to the full" (Exod. xvi. 8), it is like a command the observance of which depends upon a certain point of time [and women are exempt]; therefore it informs us [that it is obligatory].

[1] "Command" is literally "command of Do" as distinct from a prohibition—"command of Do not."

[2] This paragraph is omitted in some edd.

[3] The law of *Tefillīn* (Deut. vi. 8) is immediately followed by the law of *Mezūzāh* (*ibid. v.* 9); the inference might therefore be drawn that they are identical in scope of obligation.

[4] The command to "teach them diligently unto thy children" (*ibid. v.* 7) might be placed in the same class as the law to "write them upon the doorposts" (*ibid. v.* 9).

Why women must observe the *Kiddūsh.*

Rab Adda b. Ahᵃbah said: Women are under the obligation to recite the Sanctification[1] of the [Sabbath] day by the ordinance of the *Tōrāh.* But why, since it is a command the observance of which is dependent upon a certain point of time, and women are exempt from all commands of this class! Abbai answered: [The Sanctification by women] is a *Rabbinical* ordinance. Rab said to him: But lo, [Rab Adda] mentioned it was "by the ordinance of the *Tōrāh*"! And further, let us make all commands [of this class] obligatory upon women by Rabbinic authority! But, said Raba, [the correct reason why they have to "sanctify" the Sabbath is because] the Scriptures declare, "Remember the Sabbath day to keep it holy" (Exod. xx. 8) and "Observe the Sabbath to keep it holy" (Deut. v. 12)—everyone who has to "observe[2]" must likewise "remember[3]"; and since women must "observe," so must they "remember."

Are women commanded by the *Tōrāh* to say the Grace after meals?

Rabina asked Raba: Is the recital of the Grace after meals by women an ordinance from the *Tōrāh* or the Rabbis? What is the point at issue? It is whether they have the power of exempting others[4]. It is quite right if thou sayest it is from the *Tōrāh*; then one who is enjoined by the *Tōrāh* [to keep the observance] comes and exempts one [whose observance is likewise commanded] by the *Tōrāh.* But if thou sayest it is from the Rabbis, then it is not a compulsory observance, and one who is not under the obligation [to keep the observance] cannot exempt others. How is it then? Come and hear: It has indeed been stated: A son [who is a minor] may say Grace for his father, a slave for his master, and a woman for her husband; but the Sages declare: May a curse alight upon the man for whom his wife or his son says Grace! This[5] is quite right if thou sayest that it is from the *Tōrāh*; then one who is enjoined by the *Tōrāh* [to keep the observance] comes and exempts one [whose observance is likewise commanded] by the *Tōrāh.* But if thou sayest it is from the Rabbis, then one who is enjoined by the Rabbis [to keep the observance] comes and exempts one [whose observance is commanded] by the *Tōrāh*! Also, according to thy reason, is a minor under the obligation [to say Grace][6]? Nay, with what case are we here dealing? With

[1] See Singer, p. 124, Oesterley and Box, pp. 375ff.

[2] The obligation to "observe" belongs to women, because there are several "prohibitions" (see p. 132 n. 1) in connection with the Sabbath.

[3] We "remember" the Sabbath by the *Kiddūsh* (see Glossary, s.v.).

[4] By saying Grace after meals on their behalf.

[5] That a woman may say Grace for her husband and a son for his father.

[6] I.e. ordained by the *Tōrāh,* since that is presupposed in the argument.

one who, for instance, has eaten the minimum quantity ordained by the Rabbis [as making the saying of Grace necessary][1]; and thus one who is enjoined by the Rabbis [to say Grace][2] comes and exempts one [whose observance is likewise commanded] by the Rabbis[3].

Why God regardeth Israel.

Rab ʻAwira expounded (sometimes he said it in the name of R. Ammi and sometimes in the name of R. Assi): The ministering angels spake before the Holy One, blessed be He, "Lord of the universe! It is written of Thee in Thy *Tōrāh*, 'Who regardeth not persons[4] nor taketh reward' (Deut. x. 17); but dost Thou not regard the person of Israel, for it is written, 'The Lord lift up His countenance upon thee' (Num. vi. 26)?" He replied to them, "And should I not regard the person of Israel, for whom I wrote in the *Tōrāh*, 'And thou shalt eat *and be satisfied* and bless the Lord thy God' (Deut. viii. 10), but they are strict with themselves [and bless] even with a quantity of food equal in size to an olive or an egg?"

MISHNĀH IV

A Baʻal Ḳᵉrī *meditates upon [the wording of the* Shᵉmaʻ*] in his heart and says neither the benediction before nor after*[5]*. At his meal, he says the Grace after [in his heart] but not the Grace before. R. Judah declares: He says Grace before and after.*

GᴱMĀRĀ

Meditation is the equivalent of speech.

Rabina said: [The statement of the *Mishnāh*] means to say that meditation is the equivalent of speech; for if it enter thy mind that it is not the equivalent of speech, why should he meditate! How is it then? Meditation is the equivalent of speech. Let him, then, utter the words with his lips! No; it is as we find at Mount Sinai[6].

[1] According to R. Meïr, food the size of an olive; according to R. Judah, the size of an egg. See fol. 45*a*.

[2] The minor.

[3] The father who has eaten only the quantity required by the Rabbis. The question at the head of the paragraph remains unanswered; but the *Hᵃlākāh* regards the woman as being enjoined by the *Tōrāh* to say Grace, as implied in our *Mishnāh*.

[4] *Lit.* "Who lifteth up not the countenance."

[5] I.e. he does not even meditate on the benedictions.

[6] Cf. Exod. xix. 15. The Israelites had to be ritually clean just to *hear* the Divine words. Therefore to hear (and consequently, to meditate upon) *Tōrāh* is the equal of utterance.

But Rab Ḥisda said: Meditation is not the equivalent of speech; for if it enter thy mind that it is the equivalent of speech, let him utter the words with his lips! How is it then? Meditation is not the equivalent of speech. Why, then, should he meditate? R. Eleazar said: So that the whole world should not be engaged upon the reading of the *Sh^ema'*, whereas he sits idle. Then let him read some other chapter! Rab Adda b. Ah^abah replied: With that wherewith the Community is engaged [should he likewise be engaged]. But *T^efillāh* is also a matter with which the Community is engaged, and there is a Mishnaic teaching: *If he was standing in the* T^efillāh *and recollected that he is a* Ba'al Ḳ^erī, *he should not interrupt [his prayer] but shorten it*[1]. The reason is because he had already commenced it; hence, if he had not commenced it, he should not do so! It is different with *T^efillāh*, because it contains no reference to the Kingdom of Heaven. But in the Grace after meals there is also no reference to the Kingdom of Heaven, and yet our *Mishnāh* declares: *At his meal, he says the Grace after but not the Grace before*! Quite so; but the reading of the *Sh^ema'* and the Grace after meals are ordained by the *Tōrāh*, whereas *T^efillāh* is ordained by the Rabbis.

The contrary opinion.

fol. 21 a.

Rab Judah said[2]: Whence is it that Grace after meals is ordained by the *Tōrāh*? As it is said, "And thou shalt eat and be satisfied and bless the Lord thy God" (Deut. viii. 10). Whence is it that the benediction to be uttered before reading the *Tōrāh* is ordained by the *Tōrāh*[3]? As it is said, "For I will proclaim the name of the Lord: ascribe ye greatness unto our God" (*ibid.* xxxii. 3)[4].

Grace after meals and benediction before reading the *Tōrāh* ordained by the *Tōrāh*.

R. Joḥanan said: We derive the injunction to utter a benediction after reading the *Tōrāh* from the Grace after meals by *a fortiori* argument, and the injunction to say Grace before meals from the benediction over the reading of the *Tōrāh* by a similar method of reasoning. We derive the injunction to utter a benediction after reading the *Tōrāh* from the Grace after meals by *a fortiori* argument: If a meal which requires no benediction before it requires one after it, is it not right that the reading of the *Tōrāh*,

Authority for Grace before meals and benediction after reading the *Tōrāh*.

[1] A quotation from the next *Mishnāh*, fol. 22 *b*, p. 148.

[2] *M.* adds: in the name of Rab.

[3] See fol. 11 *b*, p. 71.

[4] In Jōmā 37 *a* this verse is explained as follows: When Moses was about to begin his song, he said to Israel, "I will open with a benediction, viz. 'For I will proclaim the name of the Lord,' and ye will respond with 'Ascribe ye greatness unto our God'."

which does require a benediction before it, should require one after it! And we derive the injunction to say Grace after meals from the benediction over the reading of the *Tōrāh* by a similar method of reasoning: If the reading of the *Tōrāh*, which requires no benediction after it[1], requires one before it, is it not right that a meal, which does require a benediction after it, should require one before it! One can, however, object to this reasoning: Why is Grace required after a meal? Because it has been enjoyed[2]. Why is a benediction required over the reading of the *Tōrāh*? Because it is life eternal. Moreover there is a teaching in our *Mishnāh*: *At his meal, he says the Grace after but not the Grace* before! The refutation [remains unanswered].

An unanswered objection.

Procedure when one is in doubt about having read the *Sh^e^ma'* and its benedictions.

Rab Judah said[3]: If one is in doubt whether he has read the *Sh^e^ma'* or not, he does not repeat it; if he is in doubt whether he said "True and firm[4]" or not, he does repeat it What is the reason? Because the reading of the *Sh^e^ma'* is ordained by the Rabbis, but saying "True and firm" by the *Tōrāh*. Rab Joseph quoted in objection: "When thou liest down and when thou risest up" (Deut. vi. 7)[5]! Abbai answered him: That is written with reference to words of *Tōrāh*[6]. We have a teaching in our *Mishnāh*: *A* Ba'al Ḳ^e^rī *meditates upon [the wording of the* Sh^e^ma'] *in his heart and says neither the benediction before* nor after. *At his meal, he says the Grace after [in his heart] but not the Grace before.* But if it enter thy mind that "True and firm" is ordained by the *Tōrāh*, then he should say the benediction after the *Sh^e^ma'*! And for what reason should he say this benediction? If because it contains a reference to the Exodus from Egypt[7], he has already mentioned that in the *Sh^e^ma'*[8]! Then let him say this benediction and there will be no necessity for the other[9]! The reading of the *Sh^e^ma'* is more important because it contains two things[10].

[1] I.e. it is not ordained by the *Tōrāh*.

[2] No analogy can be drawn between the material gratification derived from a meal and the spiritual gain from studying *Tōrāh*.

[3] *M.* adds: in the name of Samuel.

[4] The opening words of the benediction after the *Sh^e^ma'*; Singer, p. 42.

[5] The words of *Tōrāh* upon which the ordinance to read the *Sh^e^ma'* is based; see fol. 2*a*, p. 2. How, then, can it be said that this ordinance is by the Rabbis?

[6] And not the reading of the *Sh^e^ma'*. See p. 85.

[7] See Singer, p. 43.

[8] In the third paragraph.

[9] I.e. the *Sh^e^ma'*.

[10] Reference to the Kingdom of Heaven and the Exodus from Egypt.

R. Eleazar said: If one is in doubt whether he has read the *Sh^{e}ma'* or not, he should repeat it; but if he is in doubt whether he has said the *T^{e}fillāh* or not, he need not repeat it. But R. Joḥanan said: Would that a man could pray all day[1]. Another opinion.

Rab Judah also said in the name of Samuel: If a man was standing in the *T^{e}fillāh* and recollected that he had already said it, he must stop even in the middle of a benediction. But it is not so! For lo, Rab Naḥman has said: When we were at the school of Rabbah b. Abbuha we asked him, "How is it with those young disciples who made a mistake and said the week-day *T^{e}fillāh* on the Sabbath, should they finish it[2]?" And he replied, "They should finish the whole of that benediction[3]"! Now is this analogy correct? In the latter instance[4], he was at any rate under the obligation [to say the *T^{e}fillāh*] and the Rabbis did not trouble him out of regard for the Sabbath; but in the former case[5], he had already said the prayer. On saying the *T^{e}fillāh* a second time in error.

Rab Judah also said in the name of Samuel: Should one have already said the *T^{e}fillāh* and then enter a Synagogue and find the Congregation saying it, if he is able to add anything new to the prayer, he may repeat it; but if not, he should not repeat it. It was necessary [to have both this and the former teaching of Rab Judah in the name of Samuel]; for if he had given us only the first teaching, [we might have argued,] To whom does this apply? To a person who said the *T^{e}fillāh* alone and is repeating it alone; or to a person who said the *T^{e}fillāh* with the Congregation and is repeating it with the Congregation; but having said it alone, he is like one who has not prayed when he finds himself with a Congregation! Therefore he informs us [that having once said the *T^{e}fillāh* in private, there is no need to say it a second time with a Congregation]. And if he had only given us the latter teaching, [we might have supposed that he does not say the *T^{e}fillāh* a second time with the Congregation] because he has not actually commenced it; but in the former circumstance[6], having commenced it, therefore he should not [interrupt it on discovering his error]! Repeating the *T^{e}fillāh* with a Congregation. fol. 21 b.

[1] Consequently, the uncertainty gives one a reason for saying the *T^{e}fillāh* again.

[2] I.e. the benediction in which they discovered their error.

[3] This opinion apparently contradicts that of Rab Judah who said that the prayer must be interrupted immediately the mistake is discovered.

[4] Of the person who read the week-day *T^{e}fillāh* on the Sabbath.

[5] Of the person who was reading the *T^{e}fillāh* for the second time.

[6] Of saying the *T^{e}fillāh* a second time in error.

Consequently it was necessary [to have the first teaching of Rab Judah][1].

Procedure in a Synagogue with reference to the *T^e^fillāh.*

Rab Huna said: Should one enter a Synagogue and find the Congregation saying the *T^e^fillāh*, if he is able to commence and finish before the Precentor reaches the words "We give thanks unto Thee[2]," he should say the *T^e^fillāh*; but if not, he should not say it[3]. R. Joshua b. Levi said: If he is able to commence and finish before the Precentor reaches the "Sanctification[4]," he should say the *T^e^fillāh*; but if not, he should not say it. In what do they differ? The former is of the opinion that the individual says the "Sanctification[5]," whereas the other is of the opinion that the individual does not say it[6]. And similarly said Rab Adda b. Ah^a^bah: Whence is it that the individual does not say the "Sanctification"? As it is said, "But I will be hallowed among the children of Israel" (Lev. xxii. 32)—i.e. anything which comes under the heading of "Sanctification" cannot be without a minimum of ten. How is this implied? As Rabbanai, the brother of R. Ḥiyya b. Abba, taught: We draw an analogy from the occurrence of the word "among[7]." It is written here, "But I will be hallowed *among* the children of Israel" and it is written elsewhere "Separate yourselves from *among* this congregation" (Num. xvi. 21). As in the latter circumstance there were ten[8], so here also there must be ten. But everybody agrees that a man must not interrupt [the *T^e^fillāh* in order to make the responses to the "Sanctification" or "We give thanks"]. The question was raised: May one interrupt [the *T^e^fillāh*] to respond, "Let His great name be blessed[9]"? When Rab Dimai came [from Palestine] he reported

[1] Which points out that even if the *T^e^fillāh* has been commenced a second time, he must stop as soon as he recalls his mistake.

[2] Singer, p. 51, at which words the Congregation bows and makes a response.

[3] In order to be able to make the necessary response.

[4] Singer, p. 45, "We will sanctify," to which also the Congregation makes responses.

[5] Therefore being able to say it individually, Rab Huna allows him up to "We give thanks unto Thee" in which to say the *T^e^fillāh*.

[6] It must be said with the Congregation; therefore if he cannot say the *T^e^fillāh* before making the responses, he should not commence it.

[7] On the argument, see p. 18 n. 5.

[8] It cannot be deduced from Num. xvi. 21 that there were ten. In the parallel passage (*M^e^gillāh* 23 *b*), a further analogy is drawn between the use of the word "Congregation" here and in *ibid.* xiv. 27 where the reference is to the twelve spies, minus Joshua and Caleb. See p. 28 n. 2.

[9] In the *Ḳaddīsh*; see p. 8 n. 4.

that R. Judah and R. Simeon[1], disciples of R. Joḥanan, said: For no response may we interrupt [the *Tᵉfillāh*] except for "Let His great name be blessed"; for even one engaged with the study of the *Maʿᵃsēh Merkābāh*[2] must interrupt [to make this response]. But the *Hᵃlākāh* is not in accord with their view.

R. Judah declares: He says Grace before and after.

Whether a *Baʿal Ḳᵉrī* may study *Tōrāh*.

That is to say that R. Judah is of the opinion that a *Baʿal Ḳᵉrī* is permitted to study *Tōrāh*[3]. But lo, R. Joshua b. Levi has said: Whence is it that a *Baʿal Ḳᵉrī* is forbidden to study *Tōrāh*? As it is said, "Thou shalt make them known unto thy children and thy children's children" (Deut. iv. 9) and it continues, "The day that thou stoodest before the Lord thy God in Horeb" (*ibid. v.* 10)—as those who were *Baʿal Ḳᵉrī* were forbidden [in the assembly at Horeb][4], so are they forbidden [to occupy themselves with *Tōrāh*]. Shouldest thou say that R. Judah does not draw deductions from juxtaposition[5], but Rab Joseph has said: Even one who does not draw deductions from juxtaposition in any other part of the *Tōrāh* does so in the Book of Deuteronomy; and R. Judah who does not draw deductions from juxtaposition in any other part of the *Tōrāh* does so in the Book of Deuteronomy.

R. Judah and the law of juxtaposition.

How do we know that he does not use this method in any other part of the *Tōrāh*? For there is a teaching: Ben ʿAzzai said: It is stated, "Thou shalt not suffer a sorceress to live" (Exod. xxii. 17)[6] and it continues, "Whosoever lieth with a beast shall surely be put to death" (*ibid. v.* 18); [the Rabbis] connect the two laws to infer that as the one who lieth with a beast is put to death by stoning[7], so also is the sorceress put to death by stoning. R. Judah said to him: Because the two matters are in juxtaposition, shall we inflict stoning upon the person [condemned for sorcery[8]]! [No;] but they that divine by a ghost or a familiar spirit come under

[1] Viz. Judah b. Pazzi and Simeon b. Abba; Hyman, II. p. 664*a*.

[2] *Lit.* "the Work of the Chariot," the theosophical teaching about the Heavenly Chariot, derived from Ezek. i. and x. This was regarded as one of the highest forms of study upon which but a chosen few should venture, after severe mental and physical discipline. See *J. E.* VIII. p. 498; Abelson, *Jewish Mysticism*, Chap. II.

[3] Since he permits the saying of Grace after meals, which is a *Biblical* ordinance; see above p. 135.

[4] See p. 134 n. 6.

[5] See Glossary, s.v. *Sᵉmūkīn*. The deduction just drawn comes under this rule.

[6] But the mode of her death is not mentioned.

[7] This is not stated in the *Tōrāh*; but see Sanh. 54*b*.

[8] I.e. use the *severest* form of execution (viz. stoning) on such flimsy grounds! He therefore proceeds to give a stronger argument.

the category of sorcerers; and why are they particularised[1]? To draw an analogy and teach thee that as these are punished by stoning, so also is the sorceress[2].

Subject continued.

How do we know that R. Judah does draw deductions from juxtaposition in the Book of Deuteronomy? For there is a teaching[3]: R. Eliezer says: A man may marry one outraged or seduced by his father, or one outraged or seduced by his son. R. Judah prohibits a man to marry one outraged or seduced by his father. Rab Giddel asked in the name of Rab: What is R. Judah's reason? Because it is written, "A man shall not take his father's wife and shall not uncover his father's skirt" (Deut. xxiii. 1)—i.e. the skirt which his father had seen shall he not uncover. But how do we know that this refers to one outraged by his father? Because it is written in the preceding verse, "The man that lay with her shall give unto the damsel's father fifty shekels of silver" (*ibid.* xxii. 29). They said: Yes, in the Book of Deuteronomy R. Judah does use this method of deduction[4]; but the consecutive verses [quoted above] are required for another teaching of R. Joshua b. Levi who says: Whoever teaches his son *Tōrāh*, the Scriptures ascribe it to him as though he had received it from Mount Horeb; as it is said, "Thou shalt make them known unto thy children and thy children's children" (Deut. iv. 9) and it continues, "The day that thou stoodest before the Lord thy God in Horeb" (*ibid. v.* 10)[5].

Discussion on the need for immersion by polluted persons.

There is a Mishnaic teaching: A man with a running issue who has experienced emission, a menstruous woman from whom the semen has escaped and a woman who during intercourse experiences the menstrual flow require immersion[6]; but R. Judah

[1] Why is it specially mentioned of them that they shall be stoned? Cf. Lev. xx. 27.

[2] This is an illustration of the eighth of R. Ishmael's exegetical principles by which the *Tōrāh* is expounded: If anything is included in a general proposition [diviners are in the category of sorcerers] and is then made the subject of a special statement [as in Lev. xx. 27], that which is predicated of it [viz. death by stoning] is not to be understood as limited to itself alone, but is to be applied to the whole of the general proposition; Singer, pp. 13 f. It is hereby shown that R. Judah rejected the inference from juxtaposition and based his conclusion upon this rule.

[3] *M.* more accurately: For there is a Mishnaic teaching. What follows is from *Mishnāh* J^ebāmōt xi. 1.

[4] Why, then, does not R. Judah accept the deduction from Deut. iv. 9 f. above that a *Ba'al Ḳ^eri* is forbidden to study *Tōrāh*?

[5] Accordingly, while R. Judah adopts the method in Deuteronomy, he does not accept the deduction which R. Joshua b. Levi drew from the verses quoted.

[6] Before reading the *Sh^ema'* or studying *Tōrāh*.

exempts them therefrom. Only in the case of a man with a running issue who has experienced emission does R. Judah grant exemption, because he was not originally under the obligation to bathe; but [it may be argued] a man who is merely a *Ba'al Ḳ^{e}rī* he does compel [to have immersion][1]. And shouldest thou say that in fact R. Judah even exempts a mere *Ba'al Ḳ^{e}rī*, and the point of variance [between him and the Rabbis] is the man with a running issue who experienced emission, to show thee the extreme view taken by the Rabbis[2], I then quote the latter part of the Mishnaic teaching: "A woman who during intercourse experiences the menstrual flow requires immersion." For whom does he mention this? If it is supposed for the Rabbis, it is surely obvious; since if a man with a running issue who experiences emission and originally was not under the necessity of bathing is compelled by the Rabbis to have immersion, how much more so a woman who experiences the menstrual flow during intercourse and originally was under the necessity of bathing! Must it not be for R. Judah? But the statement is intended to apply to this case exclusively, viz.: a woman who experienced the menstrual flow during intercourse **fol. 22 a.** does not require immersion; but a mere *Ba'al Ḳ^{e}rī* he does place under the obligation[3].

Restrictions imposed upon the *Ba'al Ḳ^{e}rī*.

Do not read *He says Grace* but *He meditates*[4]. But does R. Judah hold that meditation [is sufficient]? For lo, there is a teaching: A *Ba'al Ḳ^{e}rī* who has no water in which to bathe should read the *Sh^{e}ma'*, but without the benediction before and after; and he eats his meal with Grace after but not before, but he meditates [upon the Grace before meals] in his heart without uttering it with his lips. These are the words of R. Meïr; but R. Judah says: He should utter them both[5]! Rab Naḥman b. Isaac said: R. Judah treats the Grace before and after meals like the *H^{a}lākōt* of *Dérek Éreṣ*[6]; for there is a teaching: "Thou shalt make them known unto thy children and thy children's children" (Deut. iv. 9) and it continues, "The day that thou stoodest before the Lord thy

[1] This would be contrary to the lenient view taken by R. Judah in the *Mishnāh* on fol. 20*b*, p. 134.

[2] Who compel even him to have immersion.

[3] But this conclusion leaves the difficulty in note 1 unanswered.

[4] The statement of R. Judah in the *Mishnāh* (fol. 20*b*, p. 134) is altered to harmonise with his opinion as expounded above.

[5] This proves that, according to R. Judah, meditation does not suffice.

[6] The name of an apocryphal Mishnaic Tractate (see Mielziner, p. 64) which has not the authority of the standard *Mishnāh*, and R. Judah permits it to be read by a *Ba'al K^{e}rī*.

God in Horeb" (Deut. iv. 10)—as [the Israelites stood at Horeb] with dread and fear and trembling and shaking, so here [when teaching *Tōrāh*] must it be with dread and fear and trembling and shaking. Hence [the Rabbis] said: Men with a running issue, lepers and those who have had intercourse with menstruous women are permitted to read the Pentateuch, the Prophets and the Hagiographa[1], to study *Mishnāh*, *Midrāsh*[2], *Talmūd*, *Hªlākōt* and *Aggādōt*; but those who are *Ba'al Ḳᵉrī* are forbidden[3]. R. Josē says: The *Ba'al Ḳᵉrī* may study what is familiar to him[4], but he must not expound the *Mishnāh*. R. Jonathan b. Joseph says: He may expound the *Mishnāh* but not the *Talmūd*. R. Nathan b. Abishalom says: Also the *Talmūd* may he expound, but he must not pronounce the name of God when it occurs[5]. R. Joḥanan the Sandal-maker, disciple of R. 'Aḳiba, said in the name of R. 'Aḳiba: Such a man should not enter upon study at all. Another version of this statement is: Such a man should not enter a House of Study at all. R. Judah says: He may study the *Hªlākōt* of *Dérek Éreṣ*.

How R. Judah acted.

It once happened that R. Judah, who had experienced emission, was walking by the river, and his disciples said to him, "Master, teach us a chapter of the *Hªlākōt* of *Dérek Éreṣ*[6]." He descended into the water, bathed, and then taught them. They said to him, "Hast thou not taught us, Master, that such an one may study the *Hªlākōt* of *Dérek Éreṣ*?" He replied, "Although I am lenient by permitting others, I take a stricter view with myself."

Words of *Tōrāh* cannot contract defilement.

There is a teaching: R. Judah b. Batyra used to say: The words of *Tōrāh* do not contract defilement[7]. It happened that a disciple was speaking indistinctly over against R. Judah b. Batyra[8]. He said to him: My son, open thy mouth and let thy words issue forth clearly, because words of *Tōrāh* cannot contract defilement; as it is said, "Is not My word like a fire? saith the Lord" (Jer. xxiii. 29)—as fire does not contract defilement, so also words of *Tōrāh* do not contract defilement.

[1] The three divisions of the Bible.

[2] This word is added by *M*.

[3] Because it is assumed that their experience results from levity of mind.

[4] And consequently will not require the concentration of his thoughts.

[5] *M*. reads: He may expound the *Mishnāh* but not the *Midrāsh*. R. Eleazar b. Shammua' says: Also the *Midrāsh* may he expound, etc. Rashi also reads *Midrāsh* for *Talmūd*.

[6] Without first bathing.

[7] Therefore one who is ritually unclean may occupy himself therewith.

[8] He was *Ba'al Ḳᵉrī*, and for that reason uttered the words of *Tōrāh* hurriedly and in a subdued tone.

The teacher stated above: "He may expound the *Mishnāh* but not the *Talmūd*." This supports the statement of R. El'ai, for R. El'ai declared that Rab Aḥa b. Jacob[1] said in the name of our master[2]: The *Halākāh* is that he may expound the *Mishnāh* but not the *Talmūd*. This is as the *Tannāīm* [taught]: He may expound the *Mishnāh* but not the *Talmūd*; these are the words of R. Meïr. R. Judah b. Gamaliel says in the name of R. Ḥannina b. Gamaliel: Both of them are forbidden; but [the Rabbis] said to him: Both of them are permitted. He who says both are forbidden agrees with R. Joḥanan the Sandal-maker; and he who says both are permitted agrees with R. Judah b. Batyra.

Whether a *Ba'al Ḳeri* may expound.

Rab Naḥman b. Isaac said: The world acts in conformity with the following three Elders[3]: according to R. El'ai in the matter of the first-shorn wool[4]; according to R. Josiah in the matter of diverse seeds; according to R. Judah b. Batyra in the matter of words of *Tōrāh*. According to R. El'ai in the matter of the first-shorn wool—for there is a teaching: R. El'ai says: The law of the first-shorn wool applies only in the [Holy] Land. According to R. Josiah in the matter of diverse seeds—for there is a teaching[5]: R. Josiah says: A man is not guilty [of the infraction of this law] until he sows wheat, barley and kernels with one throw of the hand. According to R. Judah b. Batyra in the matter of words of *Tōrāh*—for there is a teaching: R. Judah b. Batyra says: Words of *Tōrāh* cannot contract defilement. When Ze'iri came [from Palestine] he said: The Rabbis have abolished immersion[6]. Another version is: [he said:] The Rabbis have abolished the washing of the hands. He who says, "The Rabbis have abolished immersion" agrees with the view of R. Judah b. Batyra. He who says, "The Rabbis have abolished the washing of the hands" is in accord with Rab Ḥisda who cursed the man who went looking for water at the time of prayer[7].

The *Halākāh* on three subjects.

Our Rabbis have taught: A *Ba'al Ḳerī* upon whom nine *Ḳabs* of water have been poured becomes clean. Naḥum, the man of

How a *Ba'al Ḳerī* becomes purified.

[1] According to Hyman, I. 15 *a*, we should read Abba b. Aḥa. Cf. *D. S. ad loc.*

[2] I.e. Rab.

[3] Who take the more lenient view.

[4] Due to the priest; cf. Deut. xviii. 4.

[5] In place of these words, some edd. read: As it is written, "Thou shalt not sow thy vineyard with two kinds of seeds" (*ibid.* xxii. 9).

[6] By permitting a *Ba'al Ḳerī* to occupy himself with *Tōrāh*.

[7] See above, fol. 15 *a*, p. 95.

Gam Zu[1], whispered this to R. ʻAḳiba, who whispered it to Ben ʻAzzai. Ben ʻAzzai went out and taught it to his disciples publicly. Two Palestinian *Ămōrāīm*, R. Josē b. Abin and R. Josē b. Zᵉbida, differ on this matter; one stating that Ben ʻAzzai taught it, the other that he whispered it. He who states that he taught it, because of the nullifying of *Tōrāh* and procreation[2]; he who states that he whispered it, so that disciples of the wise should not be constantly found in the company of their wives like cocks [with the hens][3].

The stricter view advocated. R. Jannai said: I have heard that some take a lenient view[4] and others a stricter view; but whoever applies the stricter rule to himself, his days and years will be prolonged for him.

A reason for the stricter view. R. Joshua b. Levi said: What is the purpose of those [who are *Baʻal Ḳᵉrī*] who bathe in the morning? What is their purpose! And it was he who said that a *Baʻal Ḳᵉrī* is forbidden to be engaged with words of *Tōrāh*[5]! Nay, this is what he means to say: What is their purpose in using forty *Sāōt* of water, when it is possible [to become clean] with nine *Ḳabs*? What is their purpose in undergoing complete immersion when it is possible [to become clean] with water poured over one? R. Ḥannina replied: They have erected a great fence[6] thereby; for there is a teaching: Once a man solicited a woman for an immoral purpose, and she said to him, "Thou good-for-nothing[7]! Hast thou forty *Sāōt* of water in which to immerse?" He immediately left her.

Immersion advocated. Rab Huna said to the Rabbis, "My masters, why do you make light of this immersion[8]? Is it because of the cold? It is possible [to fulfil the requirements] in the baths[9]!" Rab Ḥisda asked him,

[1] In Taʻᵃnīt 21*a* it is related that under the most adverse circumstances his usual exclamation was *Gam zū lᵉṭōbāh*, "This also is for good"; hence his name. Others conjecture that the two words should be combined to read Gimzo, a town in Judea; cf. II Chron. xxviii. 18.

[2] He wished it to be generally known that the *Baʻal Ḳᵉrī* could easily restore himself to a state of purity and resume his duties of studying *Tōrāh* and rearing a family.

[3] He did not want the *Baʻal Ḳᵉrī* easily to regain his state of purity.

[4] By allowing the *Baʻal Ḳᵉrī* to be clean after nine *Ḳabs* of water had been poured over him. The stricter view demanded complete immersion in a bath containing a minimum of forty *Sāōt*.

[5] Their obvious purpose is to render themselves fit for the *Shᵉmaʻ* and *Tōrāh*.

[6] On the religious "fence," see p. 15 n. 3.

[7] *Rēḳā*, the equivalent of Raca, Matt. v. 22.

[8] By agreeing with R. Judah b. Batyra.

[9] See Glossary, s.v. *Mikwéh*.

"Is it then right to have immersion in warm water?" He replied, "Rab Adda b. Ahᵃbah is of the same opinion as thou[1]."

R. Zera was sitting in a tub in a bath-house. He said to his attendant, "Go, bring me nine *Ḳabs* of water and dash them over me." R. Ḥiyya b. Abba[2] said to him, "Why does the master require all that when he is sitting in the midst of water?" He replied, "It is like the regulation of forty *Sāōt*. Just as forty *Sāōt* are necessary for immersion but not pouring, so are nine *Ḳabs* necessary for pouring but not immersion." Pouring of water required even in a bath.

Rab Naḥman ordered a pitcher of the capacity of nine *Ḳabs*[3]. When Rab Dimai came [from Palestine], he said: R. 'Aḳiba and R. Judah the locksmith[4] declared: The teaching [that nine *Ḳabs* may be poured over a *Ba'al Ḳᵉrī* to cleanse him] is meant to apply only to a delicate person who experienced the emission involuntarily; but for a delicate person who caused it to happen, forty *Sāōt* are necessary. Rab Joseph said: Rab Naḥman's pitcher is broken[5]. When Rabin came he said: Such a case happened in Usha[6] in the ante-room of R. Osha'ya, and they came and consulted Rab Assi[7]. He said to them: The teaching [about the nine *Ḳabs*] was meant to apply only to a delicate person who caused it to happen; but the delicate person who experienced it involuntarily was exempt therefrom altogether. Rab Joseph said: Rab Naḥman's pitcher is repaired[8]. When the pouring of nine *Kabs* is sufficient. fol. 22 b.

Note that all the *Ămōrāīm* and *Tannāīm* are at variance over the ordinance of Ezra, so let us see how Ezra ordained it. Abbai said: Ezra ordained forty *Sāōt* for a healthy person whose emission was voluntary and nine *Ḳabs* for a healthy person when it was involuntary. Then came the *Ămōrāīm*[9] and differed as to a person Variations of the law of purification.

1 That cold water is essential.

2 *M.*: R. Abba.

3 For the use of his pupils when necessary.

4 So Jastrow and Krauss, reading *gᵉlusṭᵉrā'ā*, identifying the word with *claustrarius*. Krauss, Part I, p. 78, also suggests a connection with *καλοὐαστρος* "of good star," i.e. fortunate.

5 I.e. useless, because in view of this teaching it will very rarely be required, the presumption being that the *Ba'al Ḳᵉrī* is responsible for what happened.

6 The modern el-Uz, a town in Upper Galilee where the Sanhedrin removed from Jabneh after the death of Rabban Gamaliel. It was the *locale* of a famous academy.

7 *M.*: Ammi. Edd. more accurately: R. Assi.

8 It will be required as a consequence of this teaching.

9 *M.*: *Tannāīm* and *Ămōrāīm*.

in delicate health[1]. Some were of the opinion that the delicate person whose emission was voluntary is like the healthy man whose emission was voluntary [and requires forty *Sāōt*], and the delicate person when it was involuntary like the healthy man when it was involuntary [and requires nine *Ḳabs*]. Others, however, were of opinion that the delicate person whose emission was voluntary is like a healthy man whose emission was involuntary [and requires nine *Ḳabs*], and the delicate person when it was involuntary is exempt therefrom altogether.

Subject continued.

Raba said: Granted that Ezra instituted immersion; did he, then, institute the pouring of water? For lo, the teacher said, "Ezra instituted *immersion* for those who are *Ba'al K^{e}rī*[2]"! But, said Raba, Ezra instituted immersion in forty *Sāōt* for a healthy person whose emission was voluntary, and then the Rabbis came and instituted [the pouring of] nine *Ḳabs* for a healthy man when it was involuntary. After that the *Ămōrāīm*[3] came and differed as to what was to be done to a person in delicate health. Some were of opinion that the delicate person whose emission was voluntary was like a healthy man when it was voluntary [and required immersion], and a delicate person when it was involuntary like a healthy person when it was involuntary [and required pouring]. Others, however, were of opinion that the healthy person when it was voluntary required forty *Sāōt*; and the delicate person when it was voluntary, like the healthy man when it was involuntary, required nine *Ḳabs*; but a delicate person whose emission was involuntary was exempt therefrom altogether.

The *H^{a}lākāh*.

Raba said: The *H^{a}lākāh* is—Both the healthy man and the delicate person when it is voluntary require forty *Sāōt*; the healthy man when it is involuntary requires nine *Ḳabs*; but the delicate person when it is involuntary is exempt therefrom altogether.

Purification for the study and teaching of *Tōrāh*.

Our Rabbis have taught: A *Ba'al Ḳ^{e}rī* upon whom nine *Ḳabs* of water have been poured becomes clean. Of what does this speak? [If he wishes to study *Tōrāh*] for himself; but [if he wishes to teach it] to others, forty *Sāōt* are necessary. R. Judah says that in every case forty *Sāōt* [are required]. R. Joḥanan and R. Joshua b. Levi,

[1] *M.*: delicate person whose emission was voluntary and a healthy person when it was involuntary. But *D. S.* gives as the correct reading: delicate person whose emission was voluntary and a delicate person when it was involuntary.

[2] See Bab. Ḳam. 82 *a* where Ezra's ordinances are enumerated.

[3] *M.*: *Tannāīm* and *Ămōrāīm*.

and R. Eleazar[1] and R. Josē b. R. Ḥannina—one of the first pair is at variance with one of the second pair on the interpretation of the first part of this teaching. One says: The statement, "Of what does this speak? [If he wishes to study *Tōrāh*] for himself; but [if he wishes to teach it] to others, forty *Sāōt* are necessary" is intended to apply only to a delicate person whose emission was voluntary, but nine *Ḳabs* suffice him when it was involuntary. The other says: Whoever [wishes to teach *Tōrāh*] to others, even if he be a delicate person whose emission was involuntary, [cannot be regarded as clean] until there have been forty *Sāōt*. And one of the first pair is at variance with one of the second pair on the latter part of the teaching. One says: The statement, "R. Judah says that in every case forty *Sāōt* are required" is intended to apply only [to water found] in the ground[2], but not [to water] in vessels[3]. The other says: It applies even [to water] in vessels. It is quite right for him who says, "It applies even [to water] in vessels," for that is what has been stated, viz.: "R. Judah says that *in every case* forty *Sāōt* are required"; but for him who says, "In the ground, yes, but in vessels, no," what does the phrase "in every case" include? It is to include drawn water[4].

Rab Pappa and Rab Huna b. R. Joshua and Raba b. Samuel dined together. Rab Pappa said to them, "Permit me to say Grace[5], because nine *Ḳabs* have been poured over me." Raba b. R. Samuel said to them, "We have learnt: 'Of what does this speak? [If he wishes to study *Tōrāh*] for himself [nine *Ḳabs* are sufficient]; but [if he wishes to teach it] to others, forty *Sāōt* are necessary[6].' So permit me to say Grace, because forty *Sāōt* have been poured over me" [by means of immersion]. Rab Huna said to them, "Permit me to say Grace, since I have had need neither of the one nor the other." Rab Ḥamma used to bathe on the day preceding Passover[7] in order to exempt others from their obligation. But the *Haläkāh* is not in accord with their view[8].

An incident narrated.

[1] Another reading is: R. Eliezer, but it is incorrect.

[2] In a well or ditch or river.

[3] Drawn water.

[4] I.e. if water is drawn and poured into a hole in the ground, this would suffice.

[5] Since there were three present, Grace would be said with *Zimmūn* (see Glossary, s.v.).

[6] He draws an analogy between studying *Tōrāh* and saying Grace.

[7] In forty *Sāōt*, because he used then to teach *Tōrāh*; but on other days, when studying for himself, he poured nine *Ḳabs* over himself.

[8] I.e. either nine *Ḳabs* suffice even to teach, or as R. Judah b. Batyra said, "Words of *Tōrāh* do not contract defilement" and no purification is necessary.

MISHNĀH V

If he was standing in the Tᵉfillāh *and recollects that he is a* Ba'al Ḳᵉrī, *he should not interrupt [his prayer] but shorten it. If he had gone down to bathe, should he have time to ascend, clothe himself and read [the* Shᵉma'*] before sunrise, he must ascend, clothe himself and read; but if not, he should immerse his body in the water and read. He may not immerse himself in evil-smelling water, nor water of soaking*[1]*, until he has poured [fresh] water therein. To what distance must he remove himself from it*[2] *and excrement [if he wishes to read the* Shᵉma'*]? Four cubits.*

GᴱMĀRĀ

How a *Ba'al Ḳᵉrī* should act in the *Tᵉfillāh* and when reading in the *Tōrāh*.

Our Rabbis have taught: If a man was standing in the *Tᵉfillāh* and recollects that he is a *Ba'al Ḳᵉrī*, he should not interrupt [his prayer] but shorten it. If he was reading in the *Tōrāh*[3] and recollects that he is a *Ba'al Ḳᵉrī*, he should not interrupt and go away, but should continue reading with hurried pronunciation of the words. R. Meïr says: A *Ba'al Ḳᵉrī* is not permitted to read more than three verses in the *Tōrāh*.

Saying the *Tᵉfillāh* near excrement.

There is another teaching: If a man was standing in the *Tᵉfillāh* and saw some excrement opposite him, he should step forward until he has left it behind him a distance of four cubits. There is, however, a teaching [that in these circumstances he should step] sideways! There is no contradiction; [he should step forward] when that is possible, and [sideways] when he cannot do the other. If a man was reciting the *Tᵉfillāh* and found excrement where he was standing, Rabbah said: Even if he himself was responsible for it, his *Tᵉfillāh* is valid. Raba retorted: But lo [it is written], "The sacrifice of the wicked is an abomination" (Prov. xxi. 27)! Therefore, said Raba, since he is responsible [for the excrement], although he has uttered the prayer, his *Tᵉfillāh* is an abomination[4].

[1] Water in which e.g. flax or soiled clothes have been soaked.

[2] I.e. from urine. The text of the *Mishnāh* is defective here, as will be pointed out in the *Gᵉmārā*. See p. 168.

[3] It refers here to reading a portion of the lection in the Synagogue; and the minimum which constitutes a portion is three verses.

[4] Some edd. add: "What remedy is there? Let him repeat the *Tᵉfillāh*"; but this is probably a marginal gloss which was incorrectly incorporated in the text.

Urinating in the time of the Tᵉfillāh.

Our Rabbis have taught: If he was standing in the *Tᵉfillāh* and the urine began to drip upon his knees, he should interrupt [his prayer] until it ceases and then repeat the *Tᵉfillāh*. To what point does he return? Rab Ḥisda and Rab Hamnuna [differ]. One says that he recommences from the beginning; the other says that he goes back only to the place where he stopped. One may suppose that the following is the point of divergence: One is of opinion **fol. 23 a.** that if the man has waited sufficient time to finish the remainder of the *Tᵉfillāh*, he should recommence from the beginning. The other is of opinion that [in any event] he should go back only to the point where he stopped. Rab Ashē said: The phrase "If the man has waited" must be altered to "If the man has *not* waited"; because everybody agrees that if he waited sufficient time to finish the remainder of the *Tᵉfillāh*, he recommences from the beginning; but the point of divergence there [between Rab Ḥisda and Rab Hamnuna] is the case where the man did not wait. One is of the opinion that the man was in an uncomfortable state and unfit [to pray], and therefore his *Tᵉfillāh* is invalid; while the other is of opinion that the man was fit [to pray] and his *Tᵉfillāh* is valid.

Saying the Tᵉfillāh when in an uncomfortable state.

Our Rabbis have taught: If a man feels the need to relieve himself, he should not say the *Tᵉfillāh*; and if he does, his prayer is an abomination. Rab Zᵉbid (another version: Rab Judah) said: This teaching is meant to apply only to one who is unable to contain himself; but if he is able to contain himself, his *Tᵉfillāh* is valid. But for how long [must one be able to contain himself before venturing to say the *Tᵉfillāh*]? Rab Sheshet said: [Sufficient time to enable one to walk] a *Parsāh*. There are some who make [this statement of Rab Zᵉbid] a part of the *Bārāitā* [quoted above; thus:] Of what does this speak[1]? Of a case where a man is unable to contain himself; but if he is able to contain himself, his *Tᵉfillāh* is valid. But for how long [must one be able to contain himself before venturing to say the *Tᵉfillāh*]? Rab Zᵉbid said: [Sufficient time to enable one to walk] a *Parsāh*.

R. Samuel b. Naḥmani said in the name of R. Jonathan: If a man feels the need to relieve himself, he should not say the *Tᵉfillāh*; because it is said, "Prepare to meet thy God, O Israel" (Amos iv. 12).

Exposition of Eccles. iv. 17.

R. Samuel b. Naḥmani also said in the name of R. Jonathan: What means that which is written, "Guard thy foot when thou goest to the house of God" (Eccles. iv. 17)? Guard thyself so that thou sinnest not; but if thou sinnest, bring an offering into My

[1] According to this version, these words follow on "If a man feels the need ...his prayer is an abomination."

presence. "And be ready to hearken" (Eccles. iv. 17)—Raba said: Be ready to hearken to the words of the Sages; for if they sin, they bring an offering and repent. "It is better than when fools give sacrifices" (*ibid.*)—be not like the fools who sin and bring an offering without repenting. "For they know not to do evil" (*ibid.*)[1]—if so, they are righteous! Nay, [the meaning is:] Be not like the fools who sin and bring an offering and know not whether they bring it for the good [they have done] or for the evil [they have committed]. The Holy One, blessed be He, says, "They are unable to discern between good and evil, and they bring an offering into My presence!" Rab Assi[2] (another version: Rab Ḥannina b. Pappa)[3] said: Take heed to thy orifices[4] at the time when thou standest in prayer before Me[5].

Tᵉfillīn must be divested before entering a privy.

Our Rabbis have taught: When one is about to enter a privy, he should divest himself of the *Tᵉfillīn* at a [minimum] distance of four cubits and then enter. Rab Aḥa b. Rab Huna said in the name of Rab Sheshet: This teaching applies only to a regular privy[6], but with an occasional one, he may divest himself [of the *Tᵉfillīn*] and at once proceed to relieve himself; and when he comes out, he walks a distance of four cubits and relays them, because he has [by his use thereof] made it a regular privy.

Subject continued.

The question was raised: May a man, wearing his *Tᵉfillīn*, enter a regular privy for the purpose of urinating? Rabina permitted it; Rab Adda b. Mattᵉna prohibited it. The question was put to Raba, and he replied: It is forbidden, because we are afraid that he may relieve himself otherwise while wearing them. Another version is: [We are afraid] that he may break wind while wearing them.

A further teaching on the subject.

There is a further teaching: When one is about to enter a regular privy, he divests himself of the *Tᵉfillīn* at a [minimum] distance of four cubits, leaves them on the window-sill which is near the public road, and then enters. When he comes out, he walks a distance of four cubits and relays them. These are the words of *Bēt* Shammai. *Bēt* Hillel declare that he may hold them in his

[1] This is the literal rendering of the Hebrew, and it suggests the comment which follows. R.V. "for they know not that they do evil."

[2] This is the reading of *M.* which is preferable to that of edd.: Ashē.

[3] *M.*: Rab Pappa.

[4] This is an alternative explanation of "Guard thy foot"—"foot" being explained as in I Sam. xxiv. 4.

[5] *M.*: before Him.

[6] This means any spot which has already been used for such a purpose; whereas the "occasional" is one which is thus used for the first time.

hand and enter. R. 'Aḳiba says: He holds them in his garment and enters. In his garment, dost thou imagine? He may sometimes forget them and they will fall! But say that he holds them in his garment with his hand and enters, leaving them in a hole near the privy, but not in a hole near the public road, lest some passer-by take them and it lead him into suspicion. For it once happened that a disciple left his *Tᵉfillīn* in a hole near the public road. A harlot came and took them, and then went to the House of Study and said, "Look what so-and-so gave me as my hire." When the disciple heard that, he went to the top of the roof, threw himself therefrom and died. On that occasion it was ordained that a man should hold the *Tᵉfillīn* in his garment with his hand and enter.

Why the law was altered.

Our Rabbis have taught: At first people used to leave the *Tᵉfillīn* in holes near the privy, but mice came and carried them away; therefore it was ordained that they should be left on window-sills near the public road; but because passers-by used to take them, it was ordained that they should hold them in their hand and enter.

The *Hᵃlākāh*.

R. Mᵉyasha, the grandson[1] of R. Joshua b. Levi, said: The *Hᵃlākāh* is—One should roll them up like a book[2] and hold them in his right hand opposite his heart. Rab Joseph b. Minyomi said in the name of Rab Naḥman: This is so, provided that the strap does not protrude from beneath his hand a handbreadth. R. Jacob b. Aḥa said in the name of R. Zera: This teaching only applies when there is still sufficient time left in the day to relay them; but if not, he should make for them a kind of bag, a handbreadth in size, and place them therein[3].

What to do with the *Tᵉfillīn* at night.

Rabbah b. Bar Ḥannah said in the name of R. Joḥanan: During the day he rolls them up like a kind of book and places them in his hand opposite his heart, but at night he makes for them a kind of bag, a handbreadth in size, and places them therein. Abbai said: This teaching only applies when the bag is reserved for that purpose; but if it is not reserved for that purpose, it may be even less than a handbreadth in size. Mar Zoṭra (another version: Rab Ashē) said: Thou mayest infer that this is so from the fact that small vessels[4] protect [the contents from contracting defilement] in the tent of the dead.

[1] This reading of *M.* (instead of "son" in edd.) is confirmed by fol. 24*b*, p. 161.

[2] *M.*: like a Scroll of the Law. In ancient times, books were in scroll form.

[3] A bag of that size would prevent its contents from contracting defilement.

[4] Even less than a handbreadth in size.

R. Johanan's practice.

Rabbah b. Bar Ḥannah also said: At the time that we were following R. Joḥanan[1], on desiring to enter a privy, if he carried a book of *Aggadtā*, he handed it to us; but if he carried *T^efillīn*, he did not hand them to us. He said, "Since the Rabbis permit it, I will retain them[2]."

fol. 23 b.

Rab Nahman's practice.

Raba said: At the time that we were following Rab Naḥman, if he carried a book of *Aggadtā*, he handed it to us before entering a privy; if he carried *T^efillīn*, he did not hand them to us. He said, "Since the Rabbis permit it, I will retain them."

On holding *T^efillīn* or a scroll of the *Tōrāh*.

Our Rabbis have taught: A man should not hold the *T^efillīn* in his hand, or a scroll of the *Tōrāh* on his arm and say his prayers[3]. He may not urinate while holding them, or sleep with them, neither a regular sleep nor a chance sleep. Samuel said: A knife, money, a dish and a loaf come under the same rule.

The *H^alākāh* stated above questioned.

Raba said in the name of Rab Sheshet: The *H^alākāh* is not in accord with the above *Bārāitā*[4] because it emanates from *Bēt* Shammai[5]; for if it emanated from *Bēt* Hillel, since one is allowed to enter a regular privy [holding the *T^efillīn*][6], how much more so a chance one[7]! It is quoted in objection: "What I have permitted thee in one place I have forbidden thee in another, [and this is an argument *a fortiori* which cannot be refuted"][8]—does this not refer to the *T^efillīn*? It is quite right if thou sayest that the above *Bārāitā* emanates from *Bēt* Hillel; for then I have permitted thee elsewhere[6] [to enter] a regular privy [with *T^efillīn*], but here I forbid thee [to enter] a chance privy! On the other hand, if thou sayest that it emanates from *Bēt* Shammai, they do not permit it in either case[9]! To what, then, does the quoted statement refer?

1 As his disciples.

2 Rashi renders "Let them protect me" sc. from evil spirits which frequent such a place. *M.* omits the word altogether.

3 The fear lest they will fall might disturb his ability to concentrate his mind on his prayer. Blau, *Das altjüdische Zauberwesen*, p. 150 n. 7, suggests a different reason for the origin of this law. It is an allusion to a superstitious practice whereby these sacred objects were held in the hand as amulets while reciting incantations. Similarly, passages from the New Testament were used as charms by Christians; see Grenfell and Hunt, *Oxyrhyncus Papyri*, Part VIII.

4 Viz. that a man may not urinate while holding the *T^efillīn*.

5 So above (fol. 23 *a*, p. 150) where *Bēt* Shammai teach that the *T^efillīn* must be left on the window-sill.

6 See above, fol. 23 *a*, p. 150.

7 Since it is solely for the purpose of urinating, it is assumed that the *Bārāitā* refers to an occasional privy.

8 These words are added by *M.* and are quoted in the *G^emārā* below.

9 The conclusion is therefore: either the statement of Raba is wrong, or the quotation "What I have permitted" etc. cannot refer to holding the *T^efillīn* in a privy.

To the question of one handbreadth or two. For one teacher states: When a man relieves himself, he should uncover himself one handbreadth behind[1] and two in front[2]; and there is another teaching: He should uncover himself one handbreadth behind and not at all in front. It may be taken that both these teachings apply to a male[3], and there is no contradiction: the former referring to the major function of nature, the other to the minor. But how canst thou understand it in this way? For if the second teaching refers to the minor function, why uncover a handbreadth behind? Nay; they should both be referred to the major function, and there is no contradiction: the first teaching applying to a male, the other to a female[4]. If this be so, that which is mentioned in the sequel, viz. "This is an argument *a fortiori* which cannot be refuted"—what means it cannot be refuted? It is a natural proceeding[5]! Quite so; [therefore the quoted statement must refer to] the *T^e^fillīn*, and the refutation of Raba in the name of Rab Sheshet remains unanswered.

On exposing the body in a privy.

Nevertheless there is a difficulty: Since it is permitted to enter a regular privy [with *T^e^fillīn*], should it not be all the more permissible to enter a chance privy[6]! But this is what he means to say: They permit a regular privy[7] where there is no splashing [of urine likely to defile the hand which holds the *T^e^fillīn*], but they prohibit a chance privy where there is this likelihood[8]. If so, why does it mention "[This is an argument *a fortiori*] which cannot be refuted"? [What has just been said] is an excellent refutation! But this is what he means to say: This question [of carrying *T^e^fillīn* in a regular privy but not a chance one] thou mayest argue with a reason[9]; but thou must not argue it by means of *a fortiori*

A question answered.

1 Not more, from a sense of modesty.

2 To avoid soiling his clothes.

3 And then the statement "What I have permitted" etc. would hold good here.

4 Then the quoted statement could be taken to mean: What I have permitted thee in the case of a male I have forbidden thee in the case of a female.

5 For a man to uncover in front and a woman behind, and there is no argument *a fortiori* here at all. Consequently we cannot find anything to which the quoted statement "What I have permitted thee" etc. can be made to refer except the *T^e^fillīn*.

6 *Bēt* Hillel permit the former (see fol. 23*a*, p. 150), but according to the result of the reasoning in the former paragraph, they forbid the latter!

7 To which one resorts for the purpose of the major function.

8 Since it is used as a urinal only.

9 Viz. the probability of soiling the hand with urine.

deduction[1], for if thou usest this method of argument, it is an argument which cannot be refuted.

Tefillin should be divested before a meal.

Our Rabbis have taught: Who wishes to partake of a regular meal[2] should walk a distance of four cubits ten times, or a distance of ten cubits four times[3], and relieve himself; after that he should enter [the dining-room]. R. Isaac said: Who is about to partake of a regular meal should first divest himself of his *Tefillīn* and after that enter[4]. This is at variance with the opinion of R. Ḥiyya, who says: He leaves them upon his table, and thus it is becoming of him to do. How long [should he leave them there]? Rab Naḥman b. Isaac said: Until the time of saying Grace.

On tying up the *Tefillin* with money.

One teacher stated: A man may tie up his *Tefillīn* with his money[5] in his underwear[6]. But there is another teaching: A man may not do so! There is no contradiction. The latter refers to one who has assigned [a place in his underwear in which to deposit his *Tefillīn*]; the other refers to a man who has not assigned such a place. For Rab Ḥisda said: In the cloth in which one assigns to tie up his *Tefillīn* one must not tie up coins, if he has already placed the *Tefillīn* therein. If he assigned to tie up his *Tefillīn* in it but has not bound them therein, or if he has bound up his *Tefillīn* in the cloth without such assignment, he may tie up money therein. But according to Abbai who said that the assignment is the criterion, if he assigned to deposit his *Tefillīn* in the cloth, although he has not actually done so—or having bound them therein, if he thereupon assign it for the purpose—then it is forbidden [to tie up money therein]; but if he has not made that assignment, it is not [forbidden].

Whether the *Tefillin* may be placed beneath the pillow at night.

Rab Joseph b. Rab Neḥunyah[7] asked Rab Judah: May a man place his *Tefillīn* beneath his pillow [at night]? About placing them at the foot of the bed is no question, since that would involve disrespectful treatment; but I ask about placing them beneath his

[1] As follows: An occasional privy is not to be treated as strictly as a regular one; if then we are permitted to hold the *Tefillīn* in the latter, how much more so in the former! This is irrefutable as an argument, but it nevertheless leads to a wrong conclusion. We have consequently to base our position on the practical consideration of the possibility of soiling the hand.

[2] It speaks here of a meal at which he will be one of several guests, and it would be deemed impolite if he had to leave the table during the meal.

[3] Each time he should examine himself and see whether he needs relief.

[4] Lest he become intoxicated and behave in an unbecoming manner while wearing them.

[5] Not together, but in two separate parcels.

[6] So Jastrow; others explain the word to mean a head-cloth or turban.

[7] *M.*: Rab Nehemiah.

pillow—how is it? He replied: Thus said Samuel: It is allowed, even if his wife be with him. Against this teaching is quoted: A man may not place his *Tefillīn* at the foot of the bed because it would be disrespectful, but he may place them beneath his pillow. Should, however, his wife be with him, it is forbidden; but if there is a place three handbreadths above or below[1], he may place them beneath his pillow! The refutation of Samuel remains unanswered.

Subject continued.

Raba said: Although it is stated that the refutation of Samuel remained unanswered, nevertheless the *Halākāh* is in accord with his view. What is the reason? The more one guards them [against contemptuous treatment] the better[2]. Where, then, should one place them? R. Jeremiah said: Between the mattress and the bolster, where he does not lay his head. But R. Ḥiyya has taught: He should place them in a bag under his pillow! Yes, if he leaves the top of the bag protruding outside [the pillow]. Bar Ḳappara used to tie them in the bed-curtain, leaving the cases of the *Tefillīn* outside[3]. Rab Shesha b. Rab Iddi used to place them upon a stool and spread a cloth over them. Rab Hamnuna[4] b. Rab Joseph said: On one occasion I was standing before Raba, and he said to me, "Go, bring me my *Tefillīn*"; and I found them between the mattress and the bolster, where he did not lay his head; and I knew that it was the day of bathing[5] and he had done this for the purpose of teaching us the *Halākāh* for practice[6]. fol. 24 a.

On reading the *Shema'* in bed when not alone.

Rab Joseph b. Rab Neḥunyah[7] asked Rab Judah: How is it when two sleep in one bed—does one turn his face away and read the *Shema'* and the other act likewise[8]? He answered: Thus said Samuel: [That is so] even if his wife is with him. Rab Joseph retorted: [Samuel mentions] his wife, but is it not the more necessary to mention [the case when he is with] somebody else? For on the contrary, his wife is like part of himself, whereas another is

[1] I.e. his pillow on which he could place them in case of necessity.

[2] If they were left lying about mice might get at them.

[3] I.e. not facing the bed.

[4] *M.*: Nehemiah.

[5] For Raba's wife after her period of separation.

[6] Viz. as Samuel taught: It is allowed, even if his wife is with him.

[7] *M.*: Nehemiah.

[8] Throughout this discussion it must be remembered that in the Orient it was the general custom in the Summer to sleep quite naked; cf. Lane, p. 158. Even in the Winter people often slept naked because of lack of clothing. See p. 157 n. 1.

not like part of himself[1]! It is quoted in objection: If two sleep in one bed, one turns his face away and reads [the *Sh^ema'*] and the other acts likewise. But there is another teaching: One who sleeps in a bed with his children or members of his household by his side should not read the *Sh^ema'* unless a sheet separates between them; but if his children or the members of his household are minors, then he is permitted [to read the *Sh^ema'* without such separation]! This is quite right according to Rab Joseph and there is no contradiction [between the two teachings], the first referring to his wife, the second to somebody else[2]. But with Samuel's view there is a contradiction[3]. Samuel could reply to thee: Is it right according to Rab Joseph's opinion? For lo, there is a teaching: If a man sleeps in a bed with his children or the members of his household[4], he may not read the *Sh^ema'* unless a sheet separates between them! What, then, is there for thee to say? There are *Tannāīm* [who are at variance] on Rab Joseph's view of the question of the wife, and there are also *Tannāīm* [who are at variance] on my view[5].

Buttocks not considered nakedness for the purpose of prayer.

The master said, "He turns his face away and reads the *Sh^ema'*"—but their buttocks will be in contact! This supports the opinion of Rab Huna who said that with buttocks there is no concern on the score of nakedness. It is possible to say that the following teaching is a support of Rab Huna's opinion, viz.: A woman may sit and cut off the *Ḥallāh* while she is naked, because she is able to cover her nakedness with the ground[6]; but it is not so with a man. Rab Naḥman b. Isaac explained this [as applying

[1] By using the word "even," Samuel implied that the more lenient view is to be taken when he is with somebody else. Rab Joseph retorts that the more lenient view is to be taken when his wife is with him, because she is to be considered part of himself.

[2] Since he holds that his wife is part of himself, he does not require a sheet between them, but with others he does.

[3] For he said "Even if his wife is with him." If, therefore, he does not require a sheet with her, he cannot require one with somebody else.

[4] According to Rashi, "members of his household" must here be understood to include his wife. Later commentators (see Tōsāfōt) reject this, and correct the text to read "with his wife, he may not turn away and read the *Sh^ema'* unless there is a garment separating between them."

[5] I.e. the dispute between Samuel and Rab Joseph goes back to the days of the *Tannāīm*, and there are *Bārāitōt* (irreconcilable with each other) to be quoted in support of both opinions.

[6] Although the posterior parts are exposed; thus supporting Rab Huna's view.

only to a case where] for instance, her nakedness is sunk in the ground[1].

Age limit of children.

The master said above, "If his children or members of his household are minors, it is permitted." Up to what age? Rab Ḥisda said[2]: With females, three years and one day: with a male, nine years and one day. Others declare: With females, eleven years and one day; with a male, twelve years and one day—i.e. with both of them until the age when "the breasts were fashioned and the hair grown" (Ezek. xvi. 7).

Some questions answered.

Rab Kahana asked Rab Ashē: Raba said above, "Although the refutation of Samuel's view remained unanswered, the *Halākāh* is in accord with him"; how is it here[3]? He replied: Wilt thou weave all these things in one web[4]? Nay, where it is said[5], it is said; and where it is not said, it is not said. Rab Mari asked Rab Pappa: How is it if a hair protruded from his garment[6]? The latter exclaimed: Hair is hair[7].

Shema' may not be read in view of a woman not fully clothed.

R. Isaac said: A handbreadth of a woman [if exposed] is nakedness. For what purpose? Is it a question of gazing upon her? Behold Rab Sheshet said: Why do the Scriptures enumerate the female ornaments worn outside together with those worn under the garments[8]? This is to tell thee that whoever gazes upon the little finger of a woman is as though he had gazed at her nakedness! Nay, [the statement of R. Isaac refers] to his wife and for the purpose of reading the *Shema'*[9].

What constitutes nakedness.

Rab Ḥisda said: The calf of a woman's leg is to be regarded as nakedness; as it is said, "Uncover the leg, pass through the rivers" (Is. xlvii. 2) and it continues, "Thy nakedness shall be uncovered,

1 So that even the posteriors are covered; consequently the *Mishnāh* offers no support to Rab Huna. Büchler, *Der galiläische 'Am hā'āreṣ*, p. 252 n. 1, points out that the circumstance here debated is not far-fetched and imaginary; but the extreme poverty into which a section of the people had sunk, so that some of them had actually no clothing, made it a question of practical importance. See also *T. A.* I. pp. 134 ff.

2 *M.*: Rafram b. Pappa said in the name of Rab Ḥisda.

3 Although Samuel's opinion respecting the reading of the *Shema'* when a man is in bed with others is refuted by Rab Joseph, is the *Halākāh* in agreement with him?

4 Class them all together.

5 That the *Halākāh* is in accord with Samuel.

6 If the man's garment was torn so that hair protruded, is this to be deemed nakedness in connection with the reading of the *Shema'*?

7 It is to be ignored.

8 Cf. Is. iii. 18–24.

9 I.e. he may not read the *Shema'* in these circumstances.

yea, thy shame shall be seen" (Is. xlvii. 3). Samuel said: A woman's voice is to be regarded as nakedness; as it is said, "For sweet is thy voice, and thy countenance is comely" (Cant. ii. 14). Rab Sheshet said: A woman's hair is to be regarded as nakedness; as it is said, "Thy hair is as a flock of goats" (*ibid.* iv. 1).

What Rabbi did with his *Tᵉfillin.*

R. Ḥannina said: I have seen Rabbi hang up his *Tᵉfillīn.* Against this is quoted: He who hangs up his *Tᵉfillīn* will himself be hanged! The *Dōrᵉshē Ḥᵃmūrōt*[1] said, "And thy life shall hang in doubt before thee" (Deut. xxviii. 66)—this refers to one who hangs up his *Tᵉfillīn*! There is no contradiction; for this means one who hangs them up by the thongs, whereas Rabbi hung them up by the case. Or if thou wilt I can say that whether to hang them by the thong or case is forbidden; and when Rabbi hung them up it was in a bag. If this be so, what need was there to mention it? Thou mightest have said that the *Tᵉfillīn* require laying down like a scroll of the *Tōrāh*; therefore he informs us[2].

What Rabbi did during the time of prayer. fol. 24 b.

R. Ḥannina also said: I have seen Rabbi belch, yawn, sneeze, expectorate, and put his garment in order[3] [during his prayer], but he would not rewrap himself[4]; and when he yawned, he would place his hand upon his chin. Against this is quoted: He who makes his voice heard during prayer is of the small of faith[5]; he who raises his voice when praying is of the prophets of falsehood[6]; he who belches and yawns [during prayer] is of the proud of spirit; he who sneezes during prayer should regard it as a bad omen, and some say that it is an indication that he is contemptible; he who expectorates during prayer is as though he expectorated in the

[1] *M.*: *Dōrᵉshē Rᵉshūmōt.* Both these terms are the names of ancient Schools of Bible interpreters. See the exhaustive discussion of Lauterbach in *J. Q. R.* (New Series) I. pp. 291–333, 503–531. His conclusion is, "The *Dōrᵉshē Ḥᵃmūrōt* were, therefore, those allegoristic interpreters of the law whose method and tendency were to find the importance and significance of the law, its real meaning and purpose, since it is this, the real meaning and purpose, that gave the law weight and importance; and they considered the importance and significance of the law, its *ḥōmer*, to lie, not in the plain meaning of the letter of the law, but in the spirit of the law and its allegorical meaning, which they would read into it"; *ibid.* p. 509.

[2] That they may hang in a bag.

[3] This is how some of the commentators understand the phrase. According to Rashi, it means "search in his garment (sc. for vermin)" which are unescapable in the East; cf. Lane, p. 3.

[4] In his *Ṭallīt*, if it fell from him during prayer.

[5] He acts as though God were hard of hearing.

[6] Of the prophets of Baal it is said, "And they cried aloud" (I Kings xviii. 28).

presence of the King! It is quite right that there is no difficulty in the matter of belching or yawning, for here[1] it was an involuntary act and [the denunciation just quoted] refers to one who does it deliberately; but there is a difficulty in the matter of sneezing[2]! No; there is no difficulty; for here[1] it was from above, but the latter refers to one who does so from below[3]. For R. Zera said: This thing was taught me in the school of Rab Hamnuna, and is equal in worth to me to all my studies[4].

He who sneezes during prayer may regard it as a good omen; for just as it brings him gratification below [on earth], so will it bring him gratification above[5]. But there is a difficulty in the matter of expectoration! No, there is no difficulty; for it may be [that Rabbi acted] according to the teaching of Rab Judah who said: If one is standing in prayer and his spittle collected in his mouth, he may empty it into his *Ṭallīt*, and if his *Ṭallīt* is costly, he may empty it into his underwear[6]. Rabina was once standing before Rab Ashē [during prayer], and the spittle collected in the latter's mouth, and he expectorated behind him. Rabina said to him, "Does not the master hold the opinion of Rab Judah that one should empty his spittle into his underwear?" He replied, "I am fastidious [in this matter]." Subject continued.

[The teacher stated above[7]:] "He who makes his voice heard during prayer is of the small of faith." Rab Huna said: This teaching applies only to one who is able to direct his heart when whispering [the words of prayer], but if he is unable to do so, he is permitted [to pray aloud]. And this holds good only of one praying alone; but with a congregation it would cause disturbance to others. Praying aloud denounced.

R. Abba was avoiding Rab Judah because he wished to go up to the land of Israel; for Rab Judah declared: Whoever goes up from Babylon to the land of Israel commits a transgression because of [the injunction] which is stated, "They shall be carried to Babylon, and there shall they be, until the day that I remember them, saith the Lord" (Jer. xxvii. 22). R. Abba said: I will go and hear Saying the *Tᵉfillāh* in defiling circumstances.

[1] When Rabbi acted so. [2] Since it is regarded as an involuntary act.

[3] The verb "to sneeze" is also used euphemistically in the sense "to break wind."

[4] He was susceptible to sneezing and experienced it even when praying. Hence this teaching relieved his mind.

[5] It is a sign his prayer will be heard in Heaven. Mr H. Loewe drew my attention to a Latin parallel: "Hoc ut dixit, Amor, sinistra ut ante, dextra sternuit approbationem"; Catullus 45.

[6] See p. 154 n. 6. [7] Added by *M.*

some teaching from him at the seminary and then I will depart. He went and found a *Tannā* teaching the following in the presence of Rab Judah: If one was standing in the *T^efillāh* and broke wind, he should wait until the odour passes off and then resume the prayer [from where he interrupted it]; another version is: If he was standing in the *T^efillāh* and felt the need to break wind, he should step back four cubits and having relieved himself, wait until the odour passes off and then resume his prayer, saying, "Lord of the universe! Thou hast created us with many orifices and vessels. Revealed and known to Thee is our shame and confusion in our lifetime, and in our end we are but worm and vermin"; he then resumes at the place where he interrupted. R. Abba said to him: Had I only come to hear this, it would suffice me.

Reading the *Sh^ema'* in bed when naked.

Our Rabbis have taught: If one is sleeping in his cloak and is unable to put forth his head because of the cold, he makes a sort of partition with his cloak around his neck and reads the *Sh^ema'*. Others declare [that he makes the partition] by his heart. But according to the first *Tannā*, the heart sees the nakedness [during prayer]! He holds that when the heart sees the nakedness, it is permitted [to read the *Sh^ema'*].

How to act in a filthy alley.

Rab Huna said in the name of R. Joḥanan: If one is walking in filthy courtways [and the time for reading the *Sh^ema'* arrives], he should place his hand over his mouth and read the *Sh^ema'*. Rab Ḥisda said to him, "By God! if R. Joḥanan had told me that himself, I would not have listened to him!" Another version is: Rabbah b. Bar Ḥannah said in the name of R. Joshua b. Levi: If one is walking in filthy courtways, he should place his hand over his mouth and read the *Sh^ema'*. Rab Ḥisda said to him, "By God! if R. Joshua b. Levi had told me that himself, I would not have listened to him!" But did Rab Huna really say that? For Rab Huna has said: A disciple of the wise is forbidden to stand in a filthy place, because it is impossible for him to stand anywhere without meditating upon *Tōrāh*! There is no contradiction; the latter refers to standing still, the former to walking. And did R. Joḥanan really say what is attributed to him? For lo, Rabbah b. Bar Ḥannah has said in the name of R. Joḥanan: One is permitted to meditate anywhere upon words of *Tōrāh* except the bath-house and privy! And shouldest thou urge that here also one refers to standing and the other to walking, it cannot be so; because R. Abbahu once followed R. Joḥanan and he was reading the *Sh^ema'*, but when he reached the filthy courtways he lapsed into silence. He said to R. Joḥanan, "Where should I resume [my prayer]?" He replied, "If thou hast waited sufficient time to finish the whole, return to the commencement"! This is what R. Joḥanan meant to say to him, "As for me, I do not hold [that the reading of the *Shᵉma'* should be interrupted]; but as for thee, since thou dost hold that view, if thou hast waited sufficient time to finish the whole, return to the commencement."

Subject continued.

There is a teaching in agreement with Rab Huna and a teaching in agreement with Rab Ḥisda. There is a teaching in agreement with Rab Huna: If he was walking in filthy courtways, he should place his hand over his mouth and read the *Shᵉma'*. There is a teaching in agreement with Rab Ḥisda: If he was walking in filthy courtways, he should not read the *Shᵉma'*; and not only so, but if he was reading it and entered [such a place], he should stop. If he did not stop, what then? R. Mᵉyasha, the grandson of R. Joshua b. Levi, said: Of him the Scriptures state, "Wherefore I gave them also statutes that were not good, and ordinances whereby they should not live" (Ezek. xx. 25). R. Assi said: [Of him the Scriptures state], "Woe unto them that draw iniquity with cords of vanity" (Is. v. 18). Rab Adda b. Ahᵃbah said: From the following, "Because he hath despised the word of the Lord" (Num. xv. 31). But if he does stop, what is his reward? R. Abbahu said: Of him the Scriptures state, "Through this thing ye shall prolong your days" (Deut. xxxii. 47).

Shᵉma' may be read if only the loins are girded.

Rab Huna said: If his cloak was girded about his loins[1], he is permitted to read the *Shᵉma'*. There is a teaching to the same effect: If his cloak of stuff, or skin, or sackcloth was girded about his loins, he is permitted to read the *Shᵉma'*; but for the *Tᵉfillāh* [it is not permitted] until he covers his heart.

fol. 25 a.

If a man entered a privy wearing his *Tᵉfillīn*.

Rab Huna also said: If a man forgot and entered a privy wearing his *Tᵉfillīn*, he should place his hand over them until he finishes. Until he finishes, dost imagine? Nay, it is as Rab Naḥman b. Isaac[2] has said: Until he finishes the first discharge[3]. Let him, then, stop at once and stand up! [No,] because of [the saying of] Rabban Simeon b. Gamaliel; for there is a teaching: Rabban Simeon b. Gamaliel says: If the fecal discharge is kept back it causes dropsy, and if the fluid in the urinary duct is kept back it causes jaundice[4].

[1] And the upper part of his body bare.
[2] *M.* omits: b. Isaac.
[3] I.e. he must take the earliest opportunity to remove them.
[4] Judaism enjoins the duty of maintaining the body in a healthy condition.

Whether *Sh^e^ma'* may be read when the body is defiled.

It has been reported: If there be filth upon his body, or his hand is placed within a privy[1], Rab Huna said: It is permitted to read the *Sh^e^ma'*; Rab Ḥisda said: It is forbidden to read it. Raba asked: What is Rab Huna's reason? Because it is written, "Let everything that hath breath[2] praise the Lord" (Ps. cl. 6). And Rab Ḥisda said: It is forbidden to read the *Sh^e^ma'* [in such circumstances]—what is the reason? Because it is written, "All my bones[3] shall say, Lord who is like unto Thee" (*ibid.* xxxv. 10).

Reading the *Sh^e^ma'* where there is a foul odour.

It has been reported: If there is a foul odour for which there is a cause [present][4], Rab Huna said: A man should remove himself a distance of four cubits[5] and read the *Sh^e^ma'*. Rab Ḥisda said: He should remove himself a distance of four cubits from the place where the odour ceases and read the *Sh^e^ma'*. There is a teaching in agreement with Rab Ḥisda: A man should not read the *Sh^e^ma'* opposite the excrement of a human being, or of dogs, or pigs, or poultry; nor opposite the filth of a dunghill which gives forth a bad odour. If there be a place ten cubits higher or lower[6], he sits down[7] at the side and reads the *Sh^e^ma'*; but if not, he removes himself as far as he can see it. The same rule applies to the *T^e^fillāh*. "If there is a foul odour for which there is a cause [present], he removes himself a distance of four cubits from the place of the odour and reads the *Sh^e^ma'*." Raba said: The *H^a^lākāh* is not in agreement with this teaching in all these cases, but according to the following teaching: A man should not read the *Sh^e^ma'* opposite the excrement of human beings[8], nor opposite that of pigs or dogs when he has placed skins therein[9].

Subject continued.

Rab Sheshet was asked: How is it with a foul odour which has no [material] cause[10]? He replied: Come and behold the mats

[1] Through a hole in the wall or fence, his body being outside.

[2] I.e. the organs through which breath is taken, the mouth and nose. So long as these are not in the unclean place, praise may be offered.

[3] I.e. limbs; they all have to be clean or in a clean place.

[4] I.e. there is filth lying about.

[5] *M.*: remove himself to a place where the smell is imperceptible and read.

[6] In the vicinity of filth.

[7] *M.*: stands.

[8] Under any circumstances.

[9] The excrement of these animals was used for cleaning purposes; cf. *T. A.* I. p. 154 and p. 574 n. 346.

[10] I.e. it is not caused by excrement but breaking of wind. May one read the *Sh^e^ma'*?

in the school of Rab, on which some are sleeping while others are studying[1]. But this refers only to words of *Tōrāh*, not to the reading of the *Shᵉma'*[2]. And even of words of *Tōrāh* this is not said except [when the bad odour is caused] by another; but if he himself is the cause, he must not [even study until the odour has passed off].

Whether *Shᵉma'* may be read while manure is being carried past.

It has been reported: If manure is being carried past a person, Abbai said: It is permitted to read the *Shᵉma'*; Raba said: It is prohibited to read it. Abbai said: Whence do I derive my opinion? For there is a Mishnaic teaching: If a ritually unclean person[3] is standing under a tree and a person who is ritually clean passes by him, the latter also becomes defiled. If, however, a person ritually clean is standing under a tree and an unclean person passes by, the former remains in his state of purity[4]; but should [the unclean person] remain standing there, then the former becomes unclean. The same law holds good with a stone which has become infected[5]. And Raba[6]? He can tell thee: In this latter circumstance the criterion is a fixed place; for it is written, "He shall dwell alone; without the camp shall his *dwelling* be" (Lev. xiii. 46)[7]. But here[8] the All-merciful declared, "Therefore shall the *camp*[9] be holy" (Deut. xxiii. 15), and behold that is not so.

Shᵉma' must not be read near a pig.

Rab Pappa said: A pig's snout is to be regarded as passing manure [for the purpose of reading the *Shᵉma'*]. That is obvious[10]! No; it is necessary [to mention it], because even if it just came up out of the river [it is to be so considered].

[1] Although some of the sleepers may cause a foul odour, others are studying, an indication that the *Shᵉma'* may be read under such conditions.

[2] The cases are not analogous; he must remove himself from the odour before reading the *Shᵉma'*.

[3] E.g. a leper.

[4] According to Abbai, this is analogous to the quoted *Bārāitā*; so if the passing leper does not cause defilement, the passing manure should not interfere with the reading of the *Shᵉma'*.

[5] Cf. Lev. xiv. 37 ff. If the stone is carried past a man, he is not infected; if it is set down where he is, he does contract defilement.

[6] What reply can he make to the reasoning upon which Abbai bases his view?

[7] The analogy is false, because the quoted *Mishnāh* only means to teach that the leper defiles any place where he stands for a while, which thus becomes temporarily his "dwelling."

[8] The circumstance of the passing manure and saying the *Shᵉma'*.

[9] I.e. not only must the spot where he is standing be holy but the surroundings also.

[10] Since the pig constantly pokes its snout amidst filth.

Whether the *Sh^e^ma'* may be read when there is uncertainty whether excrement or urine is present.

Rab Judah said: If one is uncertain whether excrement is present, it is forbidden [to read the *Sh^e^ma'*]. If one is uncertain whether urine is present, it is permitted. Another version is: Rab Judah said: If one is uncertain whether excrement is in the room, it is permitted [to read it], but by an ash-heap it is forbidden[1]. If one is uncertain whether urine is present, even by an ash-heap it is permitted. His opinion agrees with that of Rab Hamnuna who said: The *Tōrāh* only forbids [the *Sh^e^ma'* to be read] by fecal matter. He is also in agreement with R. Jonathan[2] who asked: It is written "Thou shalt have a place also without the camp, whither thou shalt go forth abroad" (Deut. xxiii. 13) and it continues, "And thou shalt have a paddle among thy weapons; and it shall be when thou sittest down abroad, thou shalt dig therewith, and shalt turn back and cover that which cometh from thee" (*ibid. v.* 14)—how is this[3]? The latter verse refers to the major natural function, the former to the minor. Infer, then, that the *Tōrāh* forbids [the *Sh^e^ma'* to be read] near to urine only when it is by fecal matter; but if it has fallen upon the ground, it is permitted [by the *Tōrāh*], but the Rabbis have decreed against it. Have the Rabbis decreed against it? When it is certain [that urine is there]; but if there is a doubt, they do not decree against it.

When urine and excrement may be considered to have lost their defiling power.

Where it is certain [that urine is present], how long [must one wait before it is allowed to read the *Sh^e^ma'* there]? Rab Judah said in the name of Samuel: As long as the ground is sufficiently wet to moisten. The same reply is given by Rabbah b. Bar Ḥannah in the name of R. Joḥanan and by 'Ulla. G^e^niba said in the name of Rab: As long as the trace thereof can be recognised. Rab Judah said: May his teacher forgive G^e^niba[4]; since in the case of excrement Rab Judah said in the name of Rab: When the surface has hardened it is permitted [to read the *Sh^e^ma'* thereby], how much more so with urine[5]! Abbai said to him: What seest thou that thou reliest upon this; rely upon that which Rabbah b. Rab Huna said in the name of Rab[6]: It is forbidden [to read the *Sh^e^ma'* near] excrement even when it is like earthenware.

[1] The presumption being that there is no excrement in the room, but there is in the ash-heap.

[2] *M.*: Joḥanan.

[3] That in *v.* 13 there is no mention of covering as in *v.* 14.

[4] G^e^niba had wrongly reported the teaching of Rab.

[5] That Rab permits the *Sh^e^ma'* when the moisture had dried, and not when all trace had disappeared, as G^e^niba reported him.

[6] *M.*: Rabbah b. Bar Ḥannah said in the name of R. Joḥanan.

What means excrement like earthenware? Rabbah b. Bar Ḥannah said in the name of R. Joḥanan: When one can throw it to the ground without its crumbling to pieces. Others say: When one can roll it without its crumbling to pieces. Rabina said: I was once standing before Rab Jeremiah[1] of Difti; he noticed some excrement, and he said to me, "See whether its surface has hardened or not[2]." Another version is: He said to him, "See whether it has become cracked."

Discussion continued.

How, then, is it with reference to this matter? It has been reported: When the excrement is like earthenware, Amemar said: It is forbidden; Mar Zoṭra said: It is permitted. Raba said: The *H^alākāh* is—when the excrement is like earthenware it is forbidden; and similarly with urine, so long as the ground is sufficiently wet to moisten. It is quoted in objection: With urine, so long as the ground is wet enough to moisten it is forbidden; but if it has been absorbed [in the soil] or dried up[3], it is permitted. But is not soaking into the soil like drying up by the sun? [No;] for as when it dries up, no trace can be recognised, so when it has penetrated into the soil, there must be no trace visible; but if there be such a trace, it is forbidden [to read the *Sh^ema'* thereby] even though the ground be not sufficiently wet to moisten[4]! But against thine own argument, I quote the first clause [of the *Bārāitā* brought in objection, viz.:] "With urine, so long as the ground is wet enough to moisten it is prohibited"; hence if the trace of it be recognisable, it is permitted[5]! No such deduction can be drawn.

A parallel teaching discussed.

It is possible to say that [the question under consideration] is like [the following discussion of] the *Tannāīm*: It is forbidden to read the *Sh^ema'* by a vessel from which urine has been poured; but with urine which has been poured out, if it has been absorbed it is permitted, if it has not been absorbed it is forbidden. R. Jōsē says: So long as the earth is sufficiently wet to moisten [it is forbidden]. What does the first *Tannā* understand by "absorbed" and "not absorbed"? If it is supposed that "absorbed" means that the earth is not sufficiently wet to moisten, and "not absorbed" means that it can moisten, and R. Jōsē comes to declare, "So long as the earth is sufficiently wet to moisten" it is forbidden, but if

1 So *M.*; not as edd.: Judah. On Difti, see p. 48 n. 2.
2 If so, he would be able to read the *Sh^ema'*.
3 By the sun, when it has fallen on stone.
4 This conclusion contradicts Raba's statement of the *H^alākāh*.
5 And thus the quoted *Bārāitā* would be self-contradictory!

the trace thereof can be recognised it is permitted—then he is in agreement with the first *Tannā*[1]! Nay, by "absorbed" he must mean that no trace can be recognised and by "not absorbed" that the trace is recognisable, and then R. Josē comes to declare, "So long as the earth is sufficiently wet to moisten" it is forbidden, but if the trace can be recognised it is permitted. No[2]; everybody agrees that so long as the earth can moisten it is forbidden, and

fol. 25 b.

if the trace can be recognised it is permitted; but here the point at issue is that the earth must be so wet as to moisten something which can moisten something else.

If he had gone down to bathe, should he have time to ascend, clothe himself and read [the Sheᵉma' *] before sunrise, he must ascend, clothe himself and read.*

The *Mishnāh* in agreement with R. Eliezer and R. Joshua.

It is possible to say that the *Mishnāh* states the law anonymously in agreement with R. Eliezer who declares: *He may finish it any time until sunrise*[3]. Thou mayest even say that it is in agreement with R. Joshua[4], and perhaps it is here like the *Wᵉtīḳīn*[5]; for R. Joḥanan said: The *Wᵉtīḳīn* finish it with the sunrise.

But if not, he should immerse his body in the water and read.

Shᵉma' may be read with naked body immersed in turbid water.

But his heart sees his nakedness! R. Eleazar (another version: R. Aḥa b. Abba b. Aḥa in the name of our master[6]) said: The teaching here refers to turbid water which is to be considered like the solid earth, so that his heart does not see his nakedness.

When the water is clear.

Our Rabbis have taught: With clear water, he must sit immersed up to his neck and read [the *Shᵉma'*], while others declare he should stir up the water with his foot. But according to the first *Tannā* his heart sees his nakedness[7]! He holds that when his heart sees his nakedness, it is permitted [to read]. But lo, his heel sees his nakedness[8]! He holds that when his heel sees his nakedness, it is permitted.

[1] But that is impossible, since his opinion must be different, it being mentioned in contrast to that of the first *Tannā*.

[2] This is to be connected with the opening sentence of the paragraph. It denies that the question here discussed is the same as that before considered.

[3] See the *Mishnāh*, fol. 9 *b*, p. 55.

[4] Who permits the *Shᵉma'* to be read until the third hour.

[5] See p. 55 n. 6.

[6] I.e. Rab. *M.* reads: This supports the opinion of R. El'ai; for R. El'ai said in the name of R. Abba b. Aḥa (another version: R. Ḥiyya b. Abba) in the name of our master.

[7] Since he mentions clear water; the second *Tannā* orders the water to be stirred.

[8] Since he would be sitting with his knees bent under him.

Shᵉmaʻ must not be said when the heel touches the naked body.

It has been reported: If his heel sees his nakedness, it is permitted [to read the *Shᵉmaʻ*]. If the heel touches, Abbai says: It is forbidden [to read]; Raba says: It is permitted. So Rab Zᵉbid taught this subject. Rab Ḥinnana b. Rab Iḳa, however, taught it thus: If the heel touches, all agree that it is forbidden [to read]; but if the heel sees [the nakedness], Abbai says: It is forbidden; Raba says: It is permitted, because the *Tōrāh* was not given to the ministering angels[1]. The *Hᵃlākāh* is: If the heel touches, it is forbidden; if it sees, it is permitted.

Reading the Shᵉmaʻ when excrement or nakedness is visible through a transparent medium.

Raba said: If there be excrement in a transparent vessel, it is permitted to read the *Shᵉmaʻ* thereby; if nakedness be in a transparent vessel[2], it is forbidden to read the *Shᵉmaʻ* thereby. "If there be excrement in a transparent vessel, it is permitted to read the *Shᵉmaʻ* thereby"; because with excrement the criterion is whether it is covered; and behold it is covered. "If nakedness be in a transparent vessel, it is forbidden to read the *Shᵉmaʻ* thereby"; because the All-merciful declared, "That He see no unseemly thing[3] in thee" (Deut. xxiii. 15), and behold it is visible.

How a small quantity of excrement may be nullified.

Abbai[4] said: Should the excrement be but a minute quantity, one can nullify it [by covering it] with spittle. Raba said: It must be with thick spittle. Raba said: If excrement be in a hole, he may place his sandal over it and read the *Shᵉmaʻ*. Mar b. Rabina asked: How is it if excrement adheres to his sandal? The question remained unanswered.

Shᵉmaʻ may not be read in presence of a naked gentile.

Rab Judah[5] said: It is forbidden to read the *Shᵉmaʻ* in the presence of a naked gentile. Why is a gentile specified? Even by a naked Israelite it is likewise [forbidden]! [That it is forbidden with an Israelite is obvious][6]; but it was necessary to specify the case of a gentile. For thou mightest have said: Since it is written with reference to the gentiles, "Whose flesh is as the flesh of asses" (Ezek. xxiii. 20), argue that [in this matter the naked gentile is to be considered] only like an ass[7]; therefore he informs us that to them also [when exposed] is "nakedness" attributed; for it is written, "And they saw not their father's nakedness" (Gen. ix. 23)[8].

[1] I.e. to sexless beings.
[2] I.e. behind a transparent screen.
[3] *Lit.* nakedness of a thing.
[4] *M.*: R. Joḥanan.
[5] Raba.
[6] *M.* omits.
[7] And therefore it would be permissible to read the *Shᵉmaʻ*.
[8] Said of Noah who was not an Israelite.

He may not immerse himself in evil-smelling water, nor water of soaking, until he has poured [fresh] water therein.

The *Mishnāh* emended.

How much water must he proceed to add[1]? Nay, the *Mishnāh* must be read thus: He may not immerse himself *at all* in evil-smelling water, nor in water of soaking; nor [may he read the *Sh^ema‘* by a vessel containing] urine, until he has poured [fresh] water therein, and then he may read it.

Nullifying urine by the addition of water.

Our Rabbis have taught: How much water must be poured therein? Any small quantity. R. Zakkai says: A fourth [of a *Lōg*]. Rab Naḥman said: The difference of opinion applies only to [where the vessel contained urine and into which water has been poured] afterwards; but if originally [the vessel contained water, and urine was then poured into it, then all agree] that any small quantity of water will suffice. But Rab Joseph said: The difference of opinion applies only to [where there was water] originally [and urine had afterwards been added]; but where [water has to be added] afterwards, all agree that a fourth [of a *Lōg*] is necessary. Rab Joseph said to his attendant, "Bring me a fourth [of a *Lōg*] in accordance with the opinion of R. Zakkai."

Sh^ema‘ may not be read by an empty bed-pan.

Our Rabbis have taught: It is forbidden to read the *Sh^ema‘* by a bed-pan for excrement or urine, although empty[2]; also by urine[3] until he has poured water therein. How much water should he pour therein? Any small quantity. R. Zakkai says: A fourth [of a *Lōg*], whether it be before or behind the bed. Rabban Simeon b. Gamaliel says: If it be behind the bed, he may read it[4]; if it be before the bed he may not, but he removes himself a distance of four cubits and reads. R. Simeon b. Eleazar says: Even if the room be the size of a hundred[5] cubits, he may not read until he has removed it or placed it under the bed.

Rabban Simeon's statement discussed.

The question was asked: How did [Rabban Simeon b. Gamaliel] mean, "If [the urine] be behind the bed, he may read forthwith; if it be before the bed, he removes himself a distance of four cubits and reads"? Or perhaps he meant this: If it be behind the bed, he removes himself a distance of four cubits and reads; if it be in front of the bed, he may not read at all! Come and hear: For there is a teaching: R. Simeon b. Eleazar says: If it be behind the bed, he may read forthwith; if it be in front of the bed, he

[1] To remove the foulness, so that he can read the *Sh^ema‘*.

[2] Because it is used solely for such a purpose.

[3] Whether it be in a bed-pan or not.

[4] Because the bed forms a partition.

[5] Probably an error for "ten"; cf. Tōsiftā B^erākōt ii. 16, v. 6.

removes himself a distance of four cubits. Rabban Simeon b. Gamaliel says: Even if the room be the size of a hundred[1] cubits, he may not read until he has removed it or placed it under the bed. Our question is solved for us[2]; but the two teachings are contradictory[3]! Reverse [the names of the teachers] in the latter clause[4]. What seest thou to reverse [the names of the teachers] in the latter clause? Reverse them in the former! Whom hast thou heard say that a whole room is to be considered as four cubits[5]? It was R. Simeon b. Eleazar.

The number of handbreadths which constitute a separate stratum.

Rab Joseph said: I asked Rab Huna, "If a bed is less than three [handbreadths] high, it is evident to me that it is to be regarded as solid [with the ground][6]; but how is it with three, four, five, six, seven, eight or nine?" He replied, "I do not know." There was certainly no need for me to ask about ten. Abbai said [to Rab Joseph], "Thou hast done well not to ask [about ten handbreadths]; for every ten constitute a separate stratum." Raba said: The *Hᵃlākāh* is that less than three is regarded as solid [with the ground], and ten constitute a separate stratum; but it is about the height from three to ten that Rab Joseph questioned Rab Huna, and he was unable to explain it. Rab[7] said: The *Hᵃlākāh* is in accord with R. Simeon b. Eleazar; and so declared Bali in the name of Rab Jacob, the son of Samuel's daughter[8]: The *Hᵃlākāh* is in accord with R. Simeon b. Eleazar. But Raba maintained the *Hᵃlākāh* was not in accord with him.

Scroll of *Tōrāh* must not be left lying in a bedroom.

Rab Aḥai[9] contracted a marriage between his son and the house of Rab Isaac b. Samuel b. Marta. He led him under the wedding-canopy, but the marriage was not successfully consummated. Rab Aḥai went to investigate the cause, and he noticed a scroll of the *Tōrāh* lying in the bedroom. He said to them[10], "If I had

[1] Probably an error for "ten"; cf. Tōsiftā Bᵉrākōt ii. 16, v. 6.

[2] Viz. what Rabban Simeon b. Gamaliel's opinion is upon this question.

[3] The statement introduced by "Come and hear" agrees in wording with the *Bārāitā* in the preceding paragraph, except that the opinion of the one Rabbi is attributed to the other.

[4] Make the "Come and hear" quotation agree with the preceding paragraph.

[5] I.e. walking away from the defiling matter any distance (in the same room) does not remove the disqualification.

[6] So that a bed-pan underneath can be ignored for the reading of the *Shᵉma'*.

[7] *M.*: Rabbah.

[8] See p. 103 n. 4.

[9] *M.*: Ahilai, which is probably to be adopted; cf. Hyman, I. p. 136*a*.

[10] To his daughter-in-law's relatives.

not come now, you would have endangered my son's life; for there is a teaching: It is forbidden to have connubial intercourse in a room where a scroll of the *Tōrāh* or *Tᵉfillīn* are lying, until they are taken out or placed in a receptacle within a receptacle." Abbai said: This teaching applies only to a receptacle which is not used expressly for that purpose; but if it is used for that purpose, even ten receptacles are only to be considered as one. Raba said:

fol. 26 a. A cloth spread over a chest [containing sacred books] is regarded as a receptacle within a receptacle.

Partition of ten hand-breadths required for a scroll of *Tōrāh*.

R. Joshua b. Levi said: For a scroll of the *Tōrāh* it is necessary to make a partition of ten [handbreadths][1]. Mar Zoṭra paid a visit to Rab Ashē's house, and saw the sleeping accommodation of Mar b. Rab Ashē, whereby a scroll of the *Tōrāh* was lying and for which he had made a partition of ten handbreadths. He asked him, "According to whose opinion [hast thou done this]?" "According to R. Joshua b. Levi." "Under which circumstances did R. Joshua b. Levi say that? When there is no other room; but the master has another room!" He said to him, "I did not think of that."

To what distance must he remove himself from it and excrement [if he wishes to read the Shᵉma'*]? Four cubits.*

Reading the *Shᵉma'* facing excrement or a privy.

Raba said in the name of Rab Saḥorah in the name of Rab Huna[2]: This teaching applies only to [excrement which is] behind him; but if it is in front of him, he must remove himself as far as the eye can see it. Similarly is it with the *Tᵉfillāh*. But it is not so! For Rafram b. Pappa said in the name of Rab Ḥisda: A man may stand opposite a privy and say the *Tᵉfillāh*! With what are we here dealing? With a privy which does not contain excrement[3]. But that is not so! For Rab Joseph b. Ḥannina said: When they speak of a "privy" they mean even one in which there is no excrement, and when they speak of a "bath-house" they mean even one in which there is no person. But with what are we here dealing? With a new one[4]. And lo, Rabina raised the question: How is it with a place which had been designated to be used as a privy? Do we take account of the designation or not[5]? How is this question of Rabina to be understood? Whether one may stand *in* such a place to pray therein,

[1] Otherwise connubial intercourse is prohibited in that room.
[2] *M.* omits: in the name of Rab Huna.
[3] It had been cleaned out.
[4] And had never been used.
[5] *M.* adds: It was not explained to him.

not to pray *over against* it. Raba said: The privies of the Persians, although they may contain excrement, are to be regarded as closed in[1].

MISHNĀH VI

A man with a running issue who experienced emission, a menstruous woman from whom the semen has escaped, and a woman who during intercourse experiences the flow require immersion; but R. Judah exempts them therefrom.

GᴱMĀRĀ

The question was asked: If a *Ba'al Ḳᵉrī* sees a flow, how is it according to R. Judah's view? For although R. Judah there [in the *Mishnāh*] exempts the man with a running issue who experienced emission—and such a man originally did not require immersion[2]—but a *Ba'al Ḳᵉrī* who experiences a flow—and such a man originally did require immersion—does he compel to have immersion? Or perhaps there is no difference? Come and hear: *A woman who during intercourse experiences the flow requires immersion; but R. Judah exempts her therefrom.* Behold, a woman in these circumstances is identical with a *Ba'al Ḳᵉrī* who experienced a flow; and since R. Judah exempts her, conclude [that he exempts him also]. R. Ḥiyya taught explicitly: A *Ba'al Ḳᵉrī* who experienced a flow requires immersion; but R. Judah exempts him therefrom.

Whether a *Ba'al Ḳᵉrī* who experiences a flow requires immersion.

May we return to thee: *He whose dead!*

[1] And one may say the *Tᵉfillāh* at a distance of four cubits, because their habit was to dig deep holes into which they relieved themselves.

[2] To be able to occupy himself with *Tōrāh*.

CHAPTER IV

MISHNĀH I

The morning Tᵉfillāh [*may be said*] *until midday. R. Judah says: Until the fourth hour. The afternoon* Tᵉfillāh [*may be said*] *until the evening. R. Judah says: Until the middle of the afternoon. As for the* Tᵉfillāh *of the evening, it has no fixed time. The additional* Tᵉfillāh [*may be said*] *at any time in the day. R. Judah says: Until the seventh hour.*

GᴱMĀRĀ

The *terminus ad quem* of the morning *Tᵉfillāh.*

I quote against the *Mishnāh*: The obligation [of the *Shᵉma'*] is at sunrise, so as to unite the *Gᵉ'ullāh* and the *Tᵉfillāh*[1], and consequently one says the *Tᵉfillāh* in the day-time[2]! For whom is this teaching intended? For the *Wᵉtīḳīn*[3]; for R. Joḥanan said: The *Wᵉtīḳīn* used to finish it with the sunrise. As for the rest of the world, [they may say it] until midday. And not beyond that? For Rab Mari b. Rab Huna, the son of R. Jeremiah b. Abba, has said in the name of R. Joḥanan: If a man erred and omitted to say the *Tᵉfillāh* in the evening, he should say it twice in the morning; [if he omitted it] in the morning, he should say it twice in the afternoon. One can therefore say the prayer all day long! Up to midday one receives the reward of having said the *Tᵉfillāh* in its due time; but beyond that, one receives the reward of having said the *Tᵉfillāh*, but not the reward of having said it in its due time.

If the afternoon *Tᵉfillāh* is omitted.

The question was asked: How is it if one erred and omitted the afternoon *Tᵉfillāh*—shall he say it twice in the evening? If thou thinkest thou canst answer [by quoting] "If one erred and omitted the evening *Tᵉfillāh*, he should say it twice in the morning," [that is different] because it is one day; as it is written, "And there was evening and there was morning one day" (Gen. i. 5)[4]. But

[1] Cf. fol. 9 *b*, p. 55.

[2] Just after daybreak; and not until midday, as the *Mishnāh* declares.

[3] See p. 55 n. 6.

[4] The day was considered to commence at dusk. If, therefore, the afternoon *Tᵉfillāh* were omitted, it could not be compensated for the *same* day.

here the *Tefillāh* is the substitute for the sacrifice[1], and the day having passed, the sacrifice becomes void[2]. Or is it perhaps because *Tefillāh* is supplication, and one may pray whenever he wishes? Come and hear: For Rab Huna b. Judah said in the name of R. Isaac, in the name of R. Joḥanan[3]: If one erred and omitted the afternoon *Tefillāh*, he should say it twice in the evening, and the principle "The day having passed, the sacrifice becomes void" does not apply. It is quoted in objection, "That which is crooked cannot be made straight, and that which is wanting cannot be numbered" (Eccles. i. 15)—"that which is crooked cannot be made straight," i.e. one who has omitted the *Shema'* of the evening or morning, or the *Tefillāh* of the evening or morning[4]; "and that which is wanting cannot be numbered," i.e. his companions were numbered for the purpose of a religious duty[5], and he was not numbered among them! R. Isaac said in the name of R. Joḥanan: With whom are we here dealing[6]? With one who *intentionally* omitted [the *Shema'* or *Tefillāh*]. Rab Ashē said: There is confirmation in the fact that he used the term "omitted" and not "erred." Draw that conclusion[7].

fol. 26 b. Omitting a *Tefillāh* on the Sabbath, and its reparation.

Our Rabbis have taught: If one erred and omitted the afternoon *Tefillāh* on the Sabbath-eve, he says the *Tefillāh* twice on the night of the Sabbath. If one erred and omitted the afternoon *Tefillāh* on the Sabbath, he says the week-day *Tefillāh* twice at the conclusion of the Sabbath. In the first he adds the paragraph of "Division[8]," but not in the second[9]. If he added this paragraph in the second and not in the first, then the reading of the first *Tefillāh* counts for him but not the second[10]. One might deduce from this teaching that since he did not add the paragraph of "Division" in the first *Tefillāh*, he is as though he had not prayed at all and we make him repeat it. But against this I quote: If

1 See the discussion in the next folio, p. 174.

2 If a sacrifice is not brought on its appointed day, it lapses. Is it the same with the *Tefillāh*?

3 *M.*: For Rab Judah said in the name of Rab.

4 Cannot repair his omission. This contradicts all that has preceded.

5 The reading of the *Shema'* and the *Tefillāh* with the Congregation.

6 When it is said that the omitted prayer cannot be replaced.

7 That the inference from Eccles. i. 15 applies only to one who intentionally omitted the prayer.

8 See Singer, p. 46.

9 Because it is said only to compensate for the omission.

10 This *Bārāitā* confirms the opinion of Rab Huna b. Judah in the preceding paragraph, that the omitted afternoon *Tefillāh* can be compensated for in the evening.

one erred and did not mention the reference to rain[1] in the benediction "Thou sustainest the living[2]" or the request for rain in the benediction of "the Years[3]," we make him repeat it; but if he omitted the paragraph of "Division" in the benediction "Thou favourest man with knowledge," we do not make him repeat it, because he is able to say it over the cup [of wine][4]! The contradiction [remains unsolved].

Tᵉfillōt instituted by the Patriarchs, and to correspond with the sacrifices.

It has been reported: R. Josē b. R. Ḥannina said: The Patriarchs instituted the *Tᵉfillōt*. R. Joshua b. Levi said: The *Tᵉfillōt* were instituted to correspond with the continual sacrifices. There is a teaching in agreement with both of them. There is a teaching in agreement with R. Josē b. R. Ḥannina: Abraham instituted the morning *Tᵉfillāh*; as it is said, "And Abraham got up early in the morning to the place where he had stood" (Gen. xix. 27)—"standing" means prayer; as it is said, "Then stood up Phineas and prayed" (Ps. cvi. 30)[5]. Isaac instituted the afternoon *Tᵉfillāh*; as it is said, "And Isaac went out to meditate in the field at eventide" (Gen. xxiv. 63)—"meditation" [*sīḥāh*] means prayer; as it is said, "A prayer of the afflicted when he fainteth, and poureth out his complaint [*sīḥāh*] before the Lord" (Ps. cii. 1). Jacob instituted the evening *Tᵉfillāh*; as it is said, "And he lighted [*pāgaʿ*] upon the place, and tarried there all night" (Gen. xxviii. 11)—"alighting" means prayer; as it is said, "Therefore pray not thou for this people, neither lift up cry nor prayer for them, neither make intercession [*pāgaʿ*] to Me" (Jer. vii. 16). There is also a teaching in agreement with R. Joshua b. Levi: Why is it declared: *The morning* Tᵉfillāh [*may be said*] *until midday*? Because the morning continual offering could be brought until midday. *R. Judah says: Until the fourth hour*, because the morning continual offering could be brought until the fourth hour. And why is it declared: *The afternoon* Tᵉfillāh [*may be said*] *until the evening*? Because the twilight continual offering could be brought until the evening. *R. Judah says: Until the middle of the afternoon*, because the twilight continual offering could be brought until the middle of the afternoon. And why is it declared: *As for the* Tᵉfillāh *of the evening, it has no fixed time*? Because the limbs[6]

[1] *Lit.* "might of rain" (cf. Taʿănīt, 2 *a*), i.e. "Thou causest the wind to blow and the rain to fall"; Singer, p. 44 bot. [2] *Ibid.* p. 45.

[3] *Ibid.* p. 47. In the benediction "Bless this year," the words "Give dew and rain" etc. are added during the winter.

[4] The *Habdālāh* (see Glossary, s.v.).

[5] See above, fol. 6 *b*, p. 31. [6] Of the burnt-offerings.

and the fat[1] which had not been consumed by the evening may be offered at any time during the night. And why is it declared: *The additional* Tᵉfillāh [*may be said*] *at any time in the day*? Because the additional offering could be brought at any time during the day. *R. Judah says: Until the seventh hour*, because the additional offering could be brought until the seventh hour[2].

Which is "the greater afternoon"? The time from six and a half hours and onwards[3]. And which is "the lesser afternoon"? The time from nine and a half hours and onwards[4]. Greater and lesser afternoon defined.

The question was asked: Does R. Judah mean[5] the middle of the first afternoon-tide or the middle of the latter afternoon-tide? Come and hear: For there is a teaching: R. Judah says: [The Sages] mean the middle of the latter afternoon-tide, and that is eleven hours less a quarter[6]. We might suppose that this is a refutation of R. Josē b. R. Ḥannina[7]! But he could reply: I certainly maintain that the Patriarchs instituted the *Tᵉfillōt*, but the Rabbis subsequently found a basis for them in the sacrifices. For if thou sayest not so[8], who instituted the additional *Tᵉfillāh*, according to R. Josē b. R. Ḥannina? But the Patriarchs instituted the *Tᵉfillōt*, and the Rabbis subsequently found a basis for them in the sacrifices. R. Judah's view discussed.

R. Judah says: Until the fourth hour.

The question was asked: Is "until" inclusive, or is it perhaps exclusive[9]? Come and hear: R. Judah says: *Until the middle of the afternoon.* That is quite right if thou maintainest that this means "until" but not including—for that is the point of variance between R. Judah and the Rabbis[10]; but if thou maintainest that Does R. Judah use the word "until" to mean inclusive?

[1] Of other sacrifices where the blood had to be sprinkled before sunset.

[2] The additional offerings were brought on the Sabbath, New Moon, Festivals, New Year and Day of Atonement. Corresponding to them are the additional *Tᵉfillōt*; see Singer, pp. 159 ff., 225 f., 233 ff., 245 ff., 264 ff.

[3] See p. 6 n. 5. The greater afternoon would consequently be from 12.30 p.m. until 6 p.m.

[4] From 3.30 p.m. until 6 p.m.

[5] In his statement in the *Mishnāh.*

[6] 4.45 p.m., i.e. midway between 3.30 and 6 p.m.

[7] Who held that the Patriarchs instituted the *Tᵉfillōt*, whereas throughout the discussion the time of the prayers is determined by the time of the sacrifices.

[8] That R. Josē b. R. Ḥannina agrees that a basis was subsequently found in the sacrifices.

[9] Does it mean until the beginning of, or the end of, the fourth hour?

[10] The Rabbis permit the afternoon *Tᵉfillāh* to be read until the evening; R. Judah until the middle of the afternoon. But if "until" here means "until the end of," his *terminus ad quem* would be identical with that of the Rabbis

fol. 27 a. it means "until" and including, then R. Judah would be in agreement with the Rabbis! What, then, does it signify? Until but not including. Let me, then, quote the sequel of the teaching: *The additional* Tᵉfillāh [*may be said*] *at any time in the day. R. Judah says: Until the seventh hour.* But there is a teaching: If there be before a man two *Tᵉfillōt*, one the additional and the other of the afternoon, he should say that of the afternoon and afterwards the additional; because the former is constant, the latter not constant[1]. R. Judah says: He should first recite the additional *Tᵉfillāh* and afterwards that of the afternoon, because [the time of the former] lapses, but the other does not. That is quite right if thou maintainest that "until" means including, and thus the two *Tᵉfillōt* are found together; but if thou maintainest that "until" means excluding, how is it these two *Tᵉfillōt* are found together? For when the time of the afternoon *Tᵉfillāh* has arrived, the time of the additional *Tᵉfillāh* has passed[2]! What, then, does it signify? "Until" and including[3].

A difficulty removed.

Then the difficulty in the first clause remains, viz.: What is the point of variance between R. Judah and the Rabbis[4]? Dost thou hold the opinion that when R. Judah mentioned "The middle of the afternoon" he meant the second half? He meant the first half, and he must be understood to say: When does the first half conclude and the latter half commence? At the expiration of the eleventh hour less a quarter[5]. Rab Naḥman[6] said: We have also learnt so[7].

R. Judah b. Baba's testimony on the question.

R. Judah b. Baba testified to five matters, viz.: We permit a woman to repudiate a marriage which has been contracted for her while she was a minor[8]; we permit a woman to remarry although

[1] It is a principle of the Jewish ritual that what is constant takes precedence of what is not. The afternoon *Tᵉfillāh* is to be said daily, whereas the additional only on special occasions.

[2] Assuming that "until" means excluding, then according to R. Judah the additional *Tᵉfillāh* may be said until noon. But that of the afternoon only commences at 12.30 p.m.; how, then, could the two *Tᵉfillōt* clash?

[3] This conclusion contradicts that arrived at in the preceding paragraph.

[4] See p. 175 n. 10.

[5] I.e. when R. Judah declares the afternoon *Tᵉfillāh* may be read until the middle of the afternoon, he gives "until" the inclusive meaning; but he refers to the first half, which is 4.45. Up to that time he permits it, whereas the Rabbis allow it to be read the whole afternoon. Hence it is shown that although "until" means including, the opinions of R. Judah and the Rabbis differ.

[6] *M.* adds: b. Isaac.

[7] That "until" means including.

[8] Special circumstances of a rather complicated nature are implied here; see Rashi.

there is only one witness[1]; and concerning a cock which was stoned in Jerusalem for having killed a child[2]; and that wine forty days old was poured over the altar[3]; and concerning the morning continual offering that it was brought in the first four hours[4]. Conclude from this that "until" is inclusive; yes, draw that conclusion. Rab Kahᵃna said: The *Hᵃlākāh* is in accord with R. Judah, since there is such a teaching in the *Bᵉḥīrtā*[5].

"And concerning the morning continual offering that it was brought in the first four hours." Who is the authority for the following teaching: "And as the sun waxed hot, it melted" (Exod. xvi. 21)—this refers to the fourth hour of the day? Thou sayest "the fourth hour"; but perhaps it means the sixth hour! When the Bible states "In the heat of the *day*" (Gen. xviii. 1) it means the sixth hour. How, then, am I to understand "As the *sun* waxed hot, it melted"? That refers to the fourth hour[6]. In accordance with whose opinion is this? It can be neither R. Judah's nor the Rabbis'. If it were R. Judah's, up to [and including] the fourth hour is still morning[7]; and if it were the Rabbis', up to midday is still morning! If thou wilt I can say it is R. Judah's view or the Rabbis'. If thou wilt I can say it is the view of the Rabbis—because the Scriptures state, "Morning by morning" (Exod. *l.c.*), thus dividing the morning into two parts[8]. If thou wilt I can say

Exod. xvi. 21 discussed.

[1] To prove her husband's death in a foreign country. For all other matters two witnesses are required.

[2] I.e. the law of the goring ox (Exod. xxi. 29) was extended to all animals.

[3] The wine of the drink-offering must be at least forty days old, otherwise it is not called "strong drink" as required by Num. xxviii. 7.

[4] This is in agreement with R. Judah's view that the morning *Tᵉfillāh* may be said until the fourth hour.

[5] *Lit.* "selected"—the name given to the Tractate 'Eduyyōt in the fourth Order of the *Mishnāh*, containing a collection of legal decisions and opinions of ancient *Tannāīm*.

[6] A distinction is drawn between the phrases "heat of the day" and "heat of the sun." The latter means the places in the sun are hot but those shaded cool; whereas "heat of the day" means that the heat is general, as at noon. "Heat of the sun" refers to the fourth hour, because before 10 a.m. even the sunny places are not excessively hot.

[7] But although the Israelites were commanded to gather the manna "morning by morning," which according to R. Judah means up to 10 a.m., by that time it had already melted. The gathering had therefore to be done in the third hour.

[8] They understood "morning by morning" to mean half the morning was for gathering the manna; and since they consider the morning to be from 6 a.m. to noon, this would mean in the first three hours and the other half would be for melting.

it is R. Judah's view—because one word for "morning" is superfluous, the intention being to anticipate [the time for gathering] by one hour[1]. Everybody agrees "As the sun waxed hot, it melted" means in the fourth hour. How is this proved? Rab Aḥa b. Jacob said: The Scriptures state, "As the sun waxed hot, it melted"—which is the hour when the sun is hot and the shade cool? Say it is the fourth hour.

The afternoon Tefillāh *[may be said] until the evening. R. Judah says: Until the middle of the afternoon.*

Terminus of the afternoon *Tefillāh.*

Rab Ḥisda asked Rab Isaac[2]: Rab Kahana stated above[3] that the *Halākāh* is in accordance with R. Judah since there is such a teaching in the *Beḥīrtā*. How is it here[4]? He was silent and answered him not a word. Rab Ḥisda said: We see from the fact that Rab recited the Sabbath-*Tefillāh* on the Sabbath-eve while it was yet day, it is to be concluded that the *Halākāh* is in agreement with R. Judah[5]! On the contrary, from the fact that Rab Huna and the Rabbis did not say the [Sabbath]-*Tefillāh* until it was night, conclude that the *Halākāh* is not in agreement with R. Judah. Since it has not been reported whether the *Halākāh* accords with either, he who acted in agreement with the one did rightly, and he who acted in agreement with the other did rightly.

How Rab acted.

Rab went on a visit to the house of Geniba and said the Sabbath-*Tefillāh* on the Sabbath-eve. R. Jeremiah b. Abba was praying behind Rab, and when the latter finished his *Tefillāh* he did not interrupt the devotions of R. Jeremiah[6]. Draw three deductions from this: A man may say the Sabbath-*Tefillāh* on the Sabbath-eve[7]; a disciple may pray behind his master; and it is forbidden to pass in front of those who are saying the *Tefillāh*. [This last-mentioned] supports the teaching of R. Joshua b. Levi: It is forbidden to pass in front of those who are saying the *Tefillāh*. But it is not so, seeing that R. Assi and R. Ammi did so pass! It was beyond a distance of four cubits that R. Ammi and R. Assi passed. But how could R. Jeremiah act thus[8]? For lo, Rab Judah

[1] They gathered the manna within the four hours, but they anticipated the commencement by one hour, thus finishing in the third hour of the day.

[2] *M.*: Rab Naḥman b. Isaac.

[3] With reference to the morning *Tefillāh*.

[4] With reference to the afternoon *Tefillāh*.

[5] Because he taught that the afternoon *Tefillāh* may be said until the middle of the afternoon, after which time the evening prayers may be recited.

[6] By passing in front of him to resume his seat.

[7] Although it is not yet dusk.

[8] In praying behind his teacher.

fol. 27 b.

said in the name of Rab: A man should never pray in front of or behind his master! And there is a teaching: R. Eliezer[1] says: He who prays behind his master[2], or greets his master or returns his salutation[3], or opposes [the opinions taught by] his master's school, or reports a teaching [in his master's name] which he had not heard from his master's lips, causes the *Sh^ekīnāh* to depart from Israel! It was different with R. Jeremiah b. Abba, because he was a disciple-colleague, and thus he asked Rab, "Hast thou made the 'division'[4]?" to which he replied, "Yes, I have done so"; and R. Jeremiah did not say, "Did the master make the 'division'?" But had he made the 'division'? For lo, R. Abin[5] said: On one occasion Rabbi said the Sabbath-*T^efillāh* on the Sabbath-eve, and then entered the bath and came out and taught us our chapter; and it was not yet dark! Rab said: He must have gone into the bath-house only to perspire, and that happened before the decree was issued against it. That cannot be correct, because Abbai permitted Rab Dimai b. Liwai[6] to fumigate baskets[7]! That was a mistake. Can a mistake [of this nature] be rectified? For Abidan[8] said: On one occasion the heavens became thick with clouds, so that the people were led to believe that it was dusk. They entered the Synagogue and said the *T^efillāh* for the conclusion of the Sabbath on the Sabbath. Afterwards the clouds dispersed and the sun shone forth; so they came and put the question to Rabbi. His reply was that since they had said the *T^efillāh*, it must stand. It is different with a Congregation, because we do not put them to trouble[9].

Kiddūsh and *Habdālāh* to be recited in addition to the references in the *T^efillāh*.

R. Ḥiyya b. Ashē[10] said: Rab said the Sabbath-*T^efillāh* on the Sabbath-eve[11]; R. Josiah said the *T^efillāh* for the conclusion of the Sabbath on the Sabbath. "Rab said the Sabbath-*T^efillāh* on the Sabbath-eve"—did he recite the "Sanctification[12]" over the cup of wine, or did he omit it? Come and hear: For Rab Naḥman[13] said in the name of Samuel: A man may say the Sabbath-*T^efillāh*

[1] *M.* adds: b. Ḥisma; but the correct form of the name is Eliezer Ḥisma. *D. S.* thinks that R. Eleazar is here intended.

[2] *M.* adds: or in front of his master.

[3] Without giving him his title of respect.

[4] Between the week-days and the Sabbath by laying aside all work, since he had said the Sabbath-*T^efillāh* so early.

[5] *M.*: Abdan.

[6] *M.* omits: b. Liwai.

[7] On the Sabbath-eve, after saying the Sabbath-*T^efillāh*.

[8] *M.*: Abdan.

[9] Hence in the case of an individual, the *T^efillāh* would have to be repeated.

[10] So *M.* correctly. Edd.: Ḥiyya b. Abin.

[11] I.e. before dusk.

[12] See Singer, p. 124.

[13] *M.*: Judah.

on the Sabbath-eve and recite the "Sanctification" over the cup of wine; and the *H^a^lākāh* is in accord with his view. "R. Josiah said the *T^e^fillāh* for the conclusion of the Sabbath on the Sabbath"—did he recite the *Habdālāh* over the cup of wine or did he omit it? Come and hear: For Rab Judah said in the name of Samuel: A man may say the *T^e^fillāh* for the conclusion of the Sabbath on the Sabbath and recite the *Habdālāh* over the cup of wine. R. Zera said in the name of R. Assi[1], in the name of R. Eleazar, in the name of R. Ḥannina, in the name of Rab[2]: At the side of this pillar, R. Ishmael b. R. Josē said the Sabbath-*T^e^fillāh* on the Sabbath-eve. When 'Ulla came he said: It was at the side of this palm-tree, not pillar; it was not R. Ishmael b. R. Josē, but R. Eleazar b. R. Josē; and it was not the Sabbath-*T^e^fillāh* on the Sabbath-eve, but the *T^e^fillāh* for the conclusion of the Sabbath on the Sabbath.

As for the T^e^fillāh *of the evening, it has no fixed time.*

The evening *T^e^fillāh.*

What means it has no fixed time? If we are to suppose that should a man so desire, he can say the *T^e^fillāh* at any time during the night, then let the *Mishnāh* teach explicitly, "The evening-*T^e^fillāh* [may be said] at any time during the night"! What, then, means it has no fixed time? It is in accord with him who declared that the evening-*T^e^fillāh* is voluntary; for Rab Judah said in the name of Samuel: As for the evening-*T^e^fillāh*, Rabban Gamaliel declares it to be obligatory, but R. Joshua declares it to be voluntary. Abbai said[3]: The *H^a^lākāh* is in agreement with him who declares it to be obligatory; but Raba[4] said: The *H^a^lākāh* is in agreement with him who declares it to be voluntary.

Quarrel between Rabban Gamaliel and R. Joshua.

Our Rabbis have taught: It happened that a disciple came before R. Joshua and asked him, "Is the evening-*T^e^fillāh* voluntary or obligatory?" He replied, "It is voluntary." Then he came before Rabban Gamaliel and asked him the same question. He replied, "It is obligatory." He thereupon said to him, "But has not R. Joshua told me it was voluntary!" Rabban Gamaliel said to him, "Wait until the shield-bearers[5] enter the House of Study." When the shield-bearers had assembled, the questioner stood up and asked, "Is the evening-*T^e^fillāh* voluntary or obligatory?"

1 *M.*: Ammi.

2 *M.* omits: in the name of Rab. *D. S.* gives Rabbi as a variant for Rab; but the reading of edd. is preferred by Hyman, I. p. 20 *b*.

3 Some edd. and *M.* omit: Abbai said.

4 *M.* and some edd.: Rab.

5 A name given to the Rabbis who were skilled in dialectical contests.

Rabban Gamaliel replied, "It is obligatory." Rabban Gamaliel said to the Sages, "Is there anyone who has a different opinion on this matter?" R. Joshua said to him, "No[1]." Then Rabban Gamaliel said to him, "But has it not been reported to me in thy name that it is voluntary?" And he added, "Joshua, stand up that it may be testified against thee." R. Joshua stood up and said, "If I were living and he[2] dead, the living would be able to deny the statement of the dead; but seeing that I am alive and he also is alive, how can the living deny the statement of the living!"

Rabban Gamaliel deposed.

Then Rabban Gamaliel sat and commenced his discourse while R. Joshua remained standing[3], until all those present began to murmur and cried to Ḥuspit the interpreter[4], "Stop!" and he stopped. They said, "How long is [Rabban Gamaliel] going to continue heaping indignities upon [R. Joshua]? Last year he slighted him on the question of the New Year[5]; he slighted him on the question of the firstborn in the incident of R. Ṣadoḳ[6]; and here again he has slighted him. Come, let us depose him[7]! Whom shall we appoint in his stead? Shall we appoint R. Joshua? [No;] he is a party in the incident. Shall we appoint R. 'Aḳiba? [No;] perhaps Rabban Gamaliel will plague him because of his lack of ancestral merit[8]. Let us, then, appoint R. Eleazar b. 'Azariah, for he is wise, rich, and he is of the tenth generation from Ezra. He is wise, so if anyone[9] puts difficult questions to him, he will be able to reply to him; and he is rich, so if it be necessary for someone to attend at the palace of the Emperor[10], he will be qualified to do

[1] He probably suspected Rabban Gamaliel of seeking another opportunity to humiliate him. See below.

[2] The witness against him.

[3] Waiting for Rabban Gamaliel's permission to sit.

[4] I.e. the *Āmōrā*; see Glossary, s.v.

[5] These two Rabbis differed on which day the New Year was to commence, and Rabban Gamaliel compelled R. Joshua to visit him with his stick and money (as though it were not a holy day) on the Day of Atonement according to the latter's calculation. See Rōsh Hash. 25 *a*.

[6] See Bekōrōt 36 *a*. A scene similar to that described here occurred over the question whether a distinction is to be drawn between a priest who was a *Ḥābēr* and one who was an *'Am hā'āreṣ* (see Glossary, s.v.) in the matter of judging the blemish of an animal destined as a sacrifice.

[7] From his Office as President.

[8] He was descended from Gentiles.

[9] Some commentators suppose this to refer to Rabban Gamaliel.

[10] *Lit.* "to work for the palace." The meaning of the phrase is not certain. Krauss, *T. A.* II. p. 543 n. 100, (since the root means "to till") suggests "to provide the palace with agricultural supplies."

so; and he is of the tenth generation from Ezra, so he possesses ancestral merit and Rabban Gamaliel will not be able to worry him on that score."

R. Eleazar b. 'Azariah elected.

They attended upon R. Eleazar b. 'Azariah and asked him, "Would the master consent to become the head of the College?" He replied, "I will first go and take counsel with the members of my household." He went and consulted his wife, and she said to

fol. 28 a.

him, "Perhaps they will soon depose thee!" He answered[1] "[Let a man] use the cup of honour[2] for one day, and to-morrow let it be broken." She said to him, "Thou hast no grey hair[3]!" That day he was eighteen[4] years of age; but a miracle was wrought for him, and eighteen rows of hair[5] turned grey. That is what R. Eleazar b. 'Azariah meant when he said, "Behold I am *like* one seventy years old," and not "I am seventy years old[6]."

The College opened to all comers.

It has been taught: That same day, they removed the door-keeper [of the College] and permission was granted to the disciples to enter; for Rabban Gamaliel had issued a proclamation: "A disciple, who is not inwardly the same as outwardly[7], will not be allowed to enter the House of Study." That day many forms had to be added[8]. R. Joḥanan said: *Abbā* Josē[9] b. Dostai and the Rabbis differ as to the number; one declaring four hundred forms were added, the other declaring it was seven hundred. This [vast addition] depressed Rabban Gamaliel who said, "Perhaps, God forbid, I have withheld *Tōrāh* from Israel!" He was shown in a dream white pitchers full of ashes[10]. It was not really so[11]; but he was shown this to relieve his mind.

[1] *M.* and some edd. here insert: "We have the tradition, 'We may raise to a higher degree of sanctity but not degrade to a lower degree'." "But perhaps Rabban Gamaliel will plague thee!" He answered.... Rashi rejects this reading; and the quotation "We may raise to a higher degree" etc. seems out of place, inasmuch as the Rabbis had just degraded Rabban Gamaliel. The passage occurs further on, whence it probably was wrongly copied here.

[2] Or "precious cup." Rashi gives it the meaning "crystal goblet."

[3] One occupying so exalted a position as President should possess the dignity which grey hair brings. The same idea seems to underlie the wearing of a wig by judge and counsel.

[4] *J. T.* reads sixteen.

[5] Referring to his beard.

[6] See fol. 12 *b*, p. 79.

[7] I.e. sincere and of a high moral standard.

[8] To accommodate the crowds that sought admission.

[9] This is the correct form of the name. Edd.: Joseph.

[10] I.e. the new disciples were beautiful outwardly but not inwardly, and he had not prevented any worthy students from studying.

[11] The new disciples were in reality worthy men.

It has been taught: That same day *'Eduyyōt*[1] was learnt, and wherever we find the phrase "on that day" it refers to that occasion. There was not a *Halākāh* which had been left in a state of uncertainty in the House of Study which was not then made clear. Even Rabban Gamaliel did not absent himself from the House of Study[2]. For there is a Mishnaic teaching: On that day an Ammonite proselyte, named Judah, came before them in the House of Study and said to them, "May I enter the Community [of Israel]?" Rabban Gamaliel replied to him, "Thou art forbidden to enter the Community." R. Joshua said to him, "Thou art permitted to enter the Community." Rabban Gamaliel asked R. Joshua, "But has it not been said, 'An Ammonite or a Moabite shall not enter into the assembly of the Lord'?" (Deut. xxiii. 4). R. Joshua answered him, "Do, then, the Ammonites and Moabites still inherit their lands? Did not Sennacherib, king of Assyria, long ago come up and confuse all the nationalities? As it is said, 'I have removed the bounds of the peoples, and have robbed their treasures, and have brought down as one mighty the inhabitants' (Is. x. 13); and whoever issues [from a mixed body] issues from the majority[3]." Rabban Gamaliel said to him, "But has it not been said, 'Afterward I will bring back the captivity of the children of Ammon, saith the Lord' (Jer. xlix. 6)? and therefore they have returned!" R. Joshua retorted, "And has it not been said, 'I will turn the captivity of My people Israel' (Amos ix. 14)? but they have not yet returned!" They immediately permitted him to enter the Community.

Outstanding questions of *Halākāh* settled.

Admission of Ammonite as proselyte.

Rabban Gamaliel thereupon said, "Since it is so, I will go and conciliate R. Joshua[4]." When he arrived at the latter's house, he noticed that the walls of his house were blackened, and said to him, "From the walls of thy house it can be recognised that thou art a charcoal-burner[5]." R. Joshua replied, "Woe to the generation whose leader thou art, for thou knowest not the struggle of the disciples to support and feed themselves!" He

Rabban Gamaliel conciliates R. Joshua.

[1] It is doubtful whether this is to be identified with the Tractate 'Eduyyōt in the fourth Order of the *Mishnāh*. It more probably refers to a collection of legal decisions which has not been preserved.

[2] Some edd. add: for a single hour.

[3] I.e. the real Ammonites form only a minority of the inhabitants of the land of Ammon; it is consequently presumed that the would-be proselyte belonged to the majority who were not Ammonites.

[4] According to *J. T.* he went to conciliate all the members of the Sanhedrin.

[5] Or, a smith. In the version of *J. T.* he was making needles.

said to him, "I beg thy pardon[1]; forgive me." He took no notice of him. "Do it out of regard for my father!" He made peace with him.

Rabban Gamaliel partially re-installed.

They said, "Who will go and tell the Rabbis [that we are reconciled]?" A fuller[2] said to them, "I will go." R. Joshua sent [the following message] to the House of Study, "Let him who has been accustomed to wear the mantle [of honour] still wear it; and shall he who has not been accustomed to wear the mantle say to him who has been accustomed to wear it, 'Take off thy mantle and I shall put it on'[3]?" R. 'Aḳiba said to the Rabbis, "Bolt the doors, so that the slaves of Rabban Gamaliel may not enter and injure the Rabbis[4]." R. Joshua said, "It is better that I should rise and go myself to him[5]." He went and knocked at his door, and said to him, "Let the sprinkler[6] who is the son of a sprinkler sprinkle; for shall one who is not a sprinkler nor the son of a sprinkler say to a sprinkler who is the son of a sprinkler, 'Thy water is cave water and thy ashes the ashes of a stove'[7]?" R. 'Aḳiba said to him, "R. Joshua, thou hast become reconciled! Have we not done this only out of regard for thine honour? To-morrow thou and I will go early to the door of [Rabban Gamaliel's] house[8]." They asked, "What shall we do? Shall we depose [R. Eleazar b. 'Azariah]? We have the tradition, 'We may raise to a higher degree of sanctity but not degrade to a lower degree!' If we ask one of them to give the discourse on one Sabbath and the other on the next Sabbath, it will lead to jealousy. Let, then, Rabban Gamaliel give the discourse three Sabbaths [in the month] and R. Eleazar b. 'Azariah one Sabbath." That is what the teacher meant who asked, "Whose

[1] *Lit.* "I am humbled to thee." The words could also mean, "I agree with thee," i.e. "Thou art quite right"; cf. *A. T.* I. p. 161 n. 2.

[2] Or, a washer; followers of this occupation are often mentioned in the *Talmūd* and seem to have been rather despised.

[3] He meant that Rabban Gamaliel had a *hereditary* claim to the Office of President which should be respected.

[4] He was evidently against re-installing Rabban Gamaliel. *J. T.* mentions that he was grieved at not being appointed to the Office.

[5] To R. Eleazar b. 'Azariah and induce him to stand aside in favour of Rabban Gamaliel.

[6] By "sprinkler" is meant the priest who had the duty of purifying one defiled by contact with the dead, by sprinkling him with the ashes of the "red heifer" mingled with running water; cf. Num. xix. For the sense of the enigmatic message, see note 3 above.

[7] I.e. ordinary well-water and common ashes, not the running water and ashes of the red heifer, as required by the *Tōrāh*.

[8] To convey to him the invitation to resume Office.

Sabbath was it? It was R. Eleazar b. 'Azariah's[1]." And the disciple was R. Simeon b. Joḥai[2].

The additional Tefillāh [*may be said*] *at any time in the day. R. Judah says: Until the seventh hour.*

R. Joḥanan said: If one reads it after the seventh hour, he is called a transgressor.

If additional and afternoon *Tefillōt* clash.

Our Rabbis have taught[3]: If there be before a man two *Tefillōt*, one of the afternoon and the other the additional, he should say that of the afternoon and afterwards the additional, because the former is constant, the latter not constant[4]. R. Judah says: He should first recite the additional *Tefillāh* and afterwards that of the afternoon, because the former is a duty that lapses, but the other is not. R. Joḥanan said: The *Halākāh* is—one first says the afternoon *Tefillāh* and then the additional.

Report of R. Joḥanan's teaching contradicted.

When R. Zera[5] was weary of study, he used to go and sit at the entrance of the school of R. Nathan b. Ṭobi saying, "When the Rabbis pass by, I will stand up before them and receive the reward[6]." He once went out; and when R. Nathan b. Ṭobi came he asked him[7], "Who is stating the *Halākāh* in the House of Study?" He replied, "Thus spake R. Joḥanan: The *Halākāh* is not according to R. Judah who said, 'He should first recite the additional *Tefillāh* and afterwards that of the afternoon'." R. Zera asked him, "Did R. Joḥanan say that?" He replied, "Yes, it was taught us by him forty times." He asked him, "Is this the only one [he expounded] to thee, or was it new to thee[8]?" He replied, "It was new to me, because I was in doubt [whether it was not a teaching] of R. Joshua b. Levi."

The earlier *terminus* of the *Tefillōt* advocated.

R. Joshua b. Levi said: Whoever prays the additional *Tefillāh* after the seventh hour, as taught by R. Judah, of him the Scriptures state, "Those who are smitten [*nūgē*][9] because of the

[1] In Ḥagīgāh 3 *a* this question is asked by R. Joshua.

[2] Who asked, "Is the evening *Tefillāh* voluntary or obligatory?" and caused the scene. The tradition is faulty; R. Simeon b. Joḥai could not chronologically have taken part in this affair. Cf. *A. T.* II. p. 70.

[3] See above, fol. 27 *a*, p. 176.

[4] See p. 176 n. 1.

[5] *M.*: Ze'ira.

[6] Of honouring the Sages.

[7] What follows is uncertain, and there are many variants. *D. S.* prefers the reading of the Soncino edition: "Who stated the *Halākāh* in the House of Study?" He replied, "R. Joḥanan." He asked him, "What was it?" He replied, "One says the afternoon *Tefillāh* and afterwards the additional." R. Zera asked him.

[8] I.e. that R. Joḥanan was the authority for this teaching.

[9] R.V. "Them that sorrow for." R.V. marg. "Them that are removed from."

appointed seasons will I gather, who are of thee" (Zeph. iii. 18). How is it known that *nūgē* is a term of "breaking"? As Rab Joseph translated: "A breach has come upon the enemies of the house of Israel[1] because they delayed the times of the festivals in Jerusalem." R. Eleazar said: Whoever says the morning *T^e^fillāh* after the fourth hour, of him the Scriptures declare, "Those who are troubled [*nūgē*] because of the appointed seasons will I gather, who are of thee." How is it known that *nūgē* is a term for "trouble"? For it is written, "My soul melteth away from heaviness [*tūgāh*]" (Ps. cxix. 28). Rab Naḥman b. Isaac said: From the following: "Her virgins are afflicted [*nūgōt*], and she herself is in bitterness" (Lam. i. 4).

fol. 28 b. Whether food may be eaten before saying the additional *T^e^fillāh*.

Rab Iwya was ill and did not attend Rab Joseph's discourse[2]. The next day when he arrived, Abbai wished to set Rab Joseph's mind at rest[3]; so he said to him, "For what reason did not the master attend the discourse?" He replied, "My heart was faint and I could not." He asked him, "Why didst thou not eat something and come?" He answered, "Does not the master agree with the opinion of Rab Huna who said: It is forbidden a man to eat anything before praying the additional *T^e^fillāh*?" He replied, "Then the master should have said the additional *T^e^fillāh* by himself and eaten something and attended." He said to him, "Does not the master agree with the opinion of R. Joḥanan who declared: A man is forbidden to anticipate the congregational *T^e^fillāh* by praying alone?" He replied, "But has it not been reported in this connection: R. Abba[4] said: This teaching applies only when he is with the Congregation[5]?" The *H^a^lākāh* is in accord neither with Rab Huna nor R. Joshua b. Levi. [It is not] in accord with Rab Huna, as is here mentioned. [Nor is it] in accord with R. Joshua b. Levi who said: When the time of the afternoon *T^e^fillāh* has arrived, it is forbidden to eat anything before praying the afternoon *T^e^fillāh*.

1 Euphemism for Israel.

2 Rab Joseph was the Principal of the Seminary at Pombedita, and used to deliver a discourse every Sabbath morning before the additional *T^e^fillāh*.

3 Who resented Rab Iwya's absence.

4 *M.*: Raba.

5 I.e. a man may say the *T^e^fillāh* at home before the Congregation says it in the Synagogue.

MISHNĀH II

R. N^{e}ḥunya b. Haḳḳanah, on entering and leaving the House of Study, used to offer a short prayer. They said to him: What is the nature of this prayer? He replied: On entering I pray that no offence should occur through me; and when I leave I offer thanksgiving for my portion[1].

G^{e}MĀRĀ

Our Rabbis have taught: What used he to say on entering? "May it be Thy will, O Lord my God, that no offence occur through me; that I stumble not in the matter of H^{a}lākāh; that my colleagues have occasion to rejoice in me; that I pronounce not anything clean that is unclean, or unclean that is clean; that my colleagues stumble not through me in the matter of H^{a}lākāh; and that I may have occasion to rejoice in them." What used he to say on leaving? "I give thanks before Thee, O Lord my God, that Thou hast set my portion with those who sit in the House of Study and not with those who sit at street-corners[2]; for I and they rise early—I to words of Tōrāh, but they to vain matters; I and they labour, but I labour and receive a reward whereas they labour and receive no reward; I and they hasten—I to the life of the world to come, but they to the pit of destruction." Wording of the prayers in the House of Study.

Our Rabbis have taught: When R. Eliezer was ill, his disciples went in to visit him. They said to him, "Master, teach us the ways of life whereby we may be worthy of the life of the world to come." He said to them, "Be careful of the honour of your colleagues; restrain your children from recitation[3], and seat them between the knees of the disciples of the wise; and when you pray, know before Whom ye stand; and on that account will you be worthy of the life of the world to come." R. Eliezer's exhortation to his disciples.

---

[1] As a teacher of Tōrāh.

[2] Either idlers or stall-holders. Wiesner, p. 64, suggests that the word ḳ^{e}rōnōt is connected with the Latin corona and means "a company," sc. of musicians. J. T. reads: with those who frequent theatres and circuses.

[3] Jastrow, p. 331 a, explains: i.e. parading a superficial knowledge of the Bible by verbal memorising. Goldschmidt suggests that the word higgāyōn (lit. meditation), which in medieval Hebrew is used in the sense of "logic," may here mean "philosophical speculation." It has also been explained as referring to the reading of apocryphal literature as against the canonical Scriptures; cf. A. T. I. p. 97 n. 5.

Rabban Joḥanan b. Żakkai on his death-bed.

When Rabban Joḥanan b. Zakkai was ill, his disciples went in to visit him. On beholding them, he began to weep. His disciples said to him, "O lamp of Israel, right-hand pillar[1], mighty hammer! Wherefore dost thou weep?" He replied to them, "If I was being led into the presence of a human king who to-day is here and to-morrow in the grave, who if he were wrathful against me his anger would not be eternal, who if he imprisoned me the imprisonment would not be everlasting, who if he condemned me to death the death would not be for ever, and whom I can appease with words and bribe with money—even then I would weep; but now, when I am being led into the presence of the King of kings, the Holy One, blessed be He, Who lives and endures for all eternity, Who if He be wrathful against me His anger is eternal, Who if He imprisoned me the imprisonment would be everlasting, Who if He condemned me to death the death would be for ever, and Whom I cannot appease with words nor bribe with money—nay more, when before me lie two ways, one of the Garden of Eden and the other of *Gēhinnōm*, and I know not in which I am to be led—shall I not weep?" They said to him, "Our master, bless us!" He said to them, "May it be His will that the fear of Heaven be upon you [as great] as the fear of flesh and blood." His disciples exclaimed, "Only as great!" He replied, "Would that it be [as great]; for know ye, when a man intends to commit a transgression, he says, 'I hope nobody will see me'[2]." At the time of his departure [from the world] he said to them, "Remove all the utensils because of the defilement[3], and prepare a seat for Hezekiah, king of Judah, who is coming[4]."

MISHNĀH III—VI

III. *Rabban Gamaliel says: Every day one should pray the eighteen [benedictions]*[5]. *R. Joshua says: The abstract of the eighteen [benedictions]*[6]. *R. 'Aḳiba says: If his prayer is fluent*

[1] Corresponding to the right-hand pillar in Solomon's Temple; cf. I Kings vii. 21.

[2] If there is a witness, he desists. Remember, then, that God is always a witness; so have the same fear of Him that you have of a human being.

[3] Caused by the presence of a corpse.

[4] To accompany him into the next world.

[5] See Singer, pp. 44–54. There are now nineteen, the addition being explained below. On this important part of the liturgy, see *J. E.* XI. pp. 270–282; and especially Elbogen, *Geschichte des Achtzehngebets* and his *Der jüdische Gottesdienst*, pp. 27–60, 515–519.

[6] This will be explained below.

in his mouth, he should pray the eighteen; but if not, an abstract of the eighteen.

IV. *R. Eliezer says: If one makes his prayer a fixed task, his prayer is not a supplication. R. Joshua says: If one is journeying in a place of danger, he should offer a short prayer, saying: "Save, O Lord, Thy people, the remnant of Israel; in all times of crisis may their needs be before Thee. Blessed art Thou, O Lord, Who hearkenest to prayer."*

V. *If he is riding upon an ass, he should alight and say the* Tᵉfillāh; *but if he is unable to alight, he should turn his face [in the direction of Jerusalem]. If he is unable to turn his face, he should direct his heart towards the Holy of Holies.*

VI. *If he is journeying in a ship or on a raft, he should direct his heart towards the Holy of Holies.*

GᴱMĀRĀ

To what do these eighteen benedictions correspond? R. Hillel, the son of R. Samuel b. Naḥmani, said: They correspond to the eighteen times the Divine Name [*JHWH*] is mentioned by David in the Psalm "Ascribe unto the Lord, O ye sons of might" (Ps. xxix). Rab Joseph said: They correspond to the eighteen times the Divine Name[1] is mentioned in the *Shᵉma'*. R. Tanḥum said in the name of R. Joshua b. Levi: They correspond to the eighteen vertebrae in the spinal column. To what the eighteen benedictions correspond.

R. Tanḥum also said in the name of R. Joshua b. Levi: When one says the *Tᵉfillāh*, he must bow[2] until all the vertebrae in the spine are loosened. 'Ulla said: [He must bow] until he sees a ring [of flesh formed] opposite his heart. R. Ḥannina said: If he lowered his head, more than that is unnecessary. Raba said: That is so, if it gives him pain [to bow low] and he appears like one making obeisance. Bowing in the *Tᵉfillāh*.

As to those eighteen benedictions—there are nineteen! R. Levi said: The benediction relating to the *Mīnīm*[3] was subsequently instituted at Jabneh[4]. Corresponding to what was it instituted? The benediction relating to *Mīnīm*.

[1] Eleven times *JHWH* and seven times *Ĕlōhīm*.

[2] See p. 76 n. 6 and p. 229.

[3] For this benediction, see Singer, p. 48—"And for slanderers," etc. "It was directed against antinomians—those who rejected or neglected the Law—and also against sectarians within the Synagogue. The statement which originated with Justin Martyr that the paragraph is an imprecation against Christians in general has no foundation whatever" (Abrahams, p. lxiv). See also Herford, *Christianity in Midrash and Talmud*, pp. 125 ff.

[4] See p. 111 n. 1.

R. Levi said: According to R. Hillel, the son of R. Samuel b. Naḥmani[1], it corresponds to "The God [*ēl*] of glory thundereth" (Ps. xxix. 3); according to Rab Joseph, it corresponds to "One" in the *Sh^ema*[2]; according to R. Tanḥum in the name of R. Joshua b. Levi, it corresponds to the small vertebra in the spinal column.

Subject continued. Our Rabbis have taught: Simeon the Cotton-dealer[3] arranged the eighteen benedictions in order in the presence of Rabban Gamaliel at Jabneh. Rabban Gamaliel asked the Sages, "Is there anyone who knows how to word the benediction relating to the *Mīnīm*?" Samuel the Small stood up and worded it. In the following year he had forgotten it[4], and reflected for two or three hours[5]; but they did not discharge him[6]. Why did they not discharge him? For lo, Rab Judah said in the name of Rab: If [the Precentor] errs in all the [eighteen] benedictions we do not discharge him; but [if he errs] in the benediction relating to the *Mīnīm* we do discharge him, for fear that he is a *Mīn*! It was different with Samuel the Small, because he had himself worded it. But there may be a fear that perhaps he had apostatized! Abbai said: We have a tradition that a good man does not become bad. He does not? Behold it is written, "But when the righteous turneth away from his righteousness and committeth iniquity" (Ezek. xviii. 24)! That refers to a man who was originally wicked[7]; but the man who is originally righteous does not. He does not? Behold there is a Mishnaic teaching: "Trust not in thyself until the day of thy death[8]"; and Joḥanan the High Priest held the Office of High Priest for eighty years and eventually became a Sadducee! Abbai said: Joḥanan is the same person as Jannaeus[9]. Raba said: They are different persons; and Jannaeus

fol. 29 a.

1 So *M.* correctly. Edd.: R. Levi the son of R. Samuel b. Naḥmani said: According to R. Hillel.

2 "The Lord is *one*," which is taken as an attribute of the Deity.

3 On the word *ha-Pāḳōli* see *T. A.* I. p. 540 n. 138, II. p. 623 n. 39.

4 Derenbourg, *Essai sur l'histoire*, p. 345 n., explains the statement "in the following year he had forgotten it" by conjecturing that the benediction relating to the *Mīnīm* was originally said not daily as now, but on a special annual occasion.

5 Trying to recall the words.

6 From his Office as Precentor.

7 Before becoming righteous. It is possible for such an one to lapse into evil ways.

8 Ābōt ii. 5; Singer, p. 187.

9 There is confusion between Joḥanan, i.e. John Hyrcanus, and Jannaeus (=Jonathan, see Derenbourg, *op. cit.* p. 95 n.), i.e. Alexander Jannaeus. The former was at first favourably disposed towards the Pharisees, but in the latter part of his life opposed them (Schürer, I. i. pp. 288 f.); but the latter was throughout his reign hostile to them and massacred numbers of them; *ibid.* pp. 300 ff.

was originally wicked, but Joḥanan originally righteous. That is quite right according to Abbai[1]; but it is in contradiction with Raba's view[2]. Raba can reply that even with one who was originally righteous there is the possibility of his apostatizing. If so, why did they not discharge [Samuel the Small]? It was different with him, because he had already commenced it[3]. For Rab Judah in the name of Rab (another version: R. Joshua b. Levi) said: This teaching[4] applies only to one who has not commenced it; but if he had commenced it, he may finish it.

The seven benedictions of the Sabbath Tᵉfillāh. Nine of the New Year.

To what do the seven Sabbath-benedictions[5] correspond? R. Ḥªlafta b. Saul said: To the seven "voices" which David mentioned concerning the waters (Ps. xxix.). To what do the nine benedictions in the New Year *Tᵉfillāh*[6] correspond? R. Isaac[7] of Ḳarṭignin[8] said: To the nine references to the Divine Name which Hannah made in her prayer (I Sam. ii. 1–10); for the teacher said: On the New Year's day Sarah, Rachel and Hannah were "visited." To what do the twenty-four benedictions of the fast day[9] correspond? R. Ḥelbo said: To the twenty-four "cries[10]" Solomon mentioned when he brought the Ark into the house of the Holy of Holies (I Kings viii.). In that case, one should say them every day[11]! [No;] when did Solomon say them? On a day of supplication; and so we likewise say them on a day of supplication.

Twenty-four of the fast day.

[1] In holding that Joḥanan and Jannaeus were identical, he assumes that he had been originally wicked and that accounts for his later lapse.

[2] If Joḥanan was originally righteous, how could he have become a Sadducee?

[3] The benediction relating to *Minīm*. He broke down in the middle; consequently there was no suspicion that his heretical views made him hesitate to pronounce the words.

[4] About discharging the Precentor.

[5] See Singer, pp. 136–142.

[6] *Ibid.* pp. 239-242.

[7] *M.*: Raba.

[8] Either Carthage or Carthagène in Spain, where there was a Jewish Community in the 2nd cent. See Neubauer, p. 411. Krauss, p. 572, identifies it with Carthage. Bacher, *A. P. A.* II. p. 218 n. 6, p. 225 n. 1, denies the existence of an *Āmōrā* of this name and suggests as the true reading: R. Abba of Carthage said in the name of R. Isaac.

[9] The additional six benedictions to the eighteen are enumerated in *Mishnāh* Taʿªnīt ii. 3 f. The only addition now made to the *Tᵉfillāh* on a fast day is the paragraph in Singer, p. 50, which is quoted from *J. T.*

[10] Words for prayer and supplication.

[11] Since it was on no special day of the Calendar that this happened.

R. Joshua says: The abstract of the eighteen [benedictions].

Abstract of the eighteen benedictions.

What is the abstract of the eighteen? Rab said: An abstract of each benediction. Samuel said[1]: "Give us understanding, O Lord, our God, to know Thy ways; circumcise our hearts to fear Thee, and forgive us so that we may be redeemed. Keep us far from our pains; satiate us on the pastures of Thy land and gather our scattered ones from the four [corners of the earth]. Let them that go astray be judged according to Thy will, and wave Thy hand over the wicked. Let the righteous rejoice in the rebuilding of Thy city and in the establishment of Thy Temple, and in the flourishing of the horn of David Thy servant, and in the clear-shining light of the son of Jesse, Thine anointed. Even before we call, do Thou answer. Blessed art Thou, O Lord, Who hearkenest unto prayer."

When the abstract may not be said.

Abbai cursed him who says the prayer "Give us understanding[2]." Rab Naḥman said in the name of Samuel: During the whole of the year, one may say the prayer "Give us understanding" except at the conclusion of the Sabbath and Festivals, because then it is necessary to say the "Division" in the benediction "Thou favourest man with knowledge[3]." Rabbah b. Samuel[4] objected: Let him, then, say the fourth benediction separately[5]! Have we not the Mishnaic teaching: R. 'Aḳiba says: One may say the fourth benediction by itself; R. Eliezer says: [One can say the "Division"] in the benediction of thanksgiving[6]? But do we act the whole of the year in accordance with R. 'Aḳiba's view that we should do so now [at the conclusion of the Sabbath and Festivals]? On what ground do we not follow R. 'Aḳiba's view during the whole year? Because eighteen benedictions were instituted, not nineteen; and so here also, seven were instituted, not eight[7]. Mar Zoṭra objected: Let it be included in brief in the [shortened] *T^e fillāh*, thus: "Give us understanding, Thou Who dividest between holy and profane"! The question [remained unanswered].

Subject continued.

Rab Bebai b. Abbai said: The whole of the year one may say the prayer "Give us understanding" except during the rainy

1 See Singer, p. 55. What follows is a summary of the central benedictions of the *T^e fillāh*, *ibid.* pp. 46–50.

2 And not the eighteen benedictions in full.

3 See Singer, p. 46.

4 *M.*: Raba b. Ishmael.

5 And the abstract of the remainder.

6 See Singer, p. 51, "We give thanks." This benediction and what follows are said in full even when the central benedictions are shortened.

7 Viz. the three introductory and three concluding benedictions and "Give us understanding."

season[1], because it is necessary to add the request [for rain] in the benediction of "the Years." Mar Zoṭra objected: Let it be included in brief in the [shortened] prayer thus: "Satiate us on the pastures of Thy land, and give dew and rain"! It would lead to confusion. If so, the inclusion of the "Division" in the benediction "Thou favourest man with knowledge" should likewise lead to confusion! They answered: In this latter case, since it comes at the beginning of the prayer, it would not cause confusion; but in the former, since it occurs in the middle of the prayer, it would. Rab Ashē objected: Let him say it in the benediction "Who hearkenest unto prayer[2]"; for R. Tanḥum declared in the name of R. Assi: If a man erred and omitted the reference to rain in the benediction of "the Revival of the Dead[3]," we make him repeat it; [if he omitted] the request [for rain] in the benediction of "the Years," we do not make him repeat it, because he can include it in "Who hearkenest unto prayer"; but [if he omitted] the "Division" in "Thou favourest man with knowledge," we do not make him repeat it, because he is able to say it over the cup of wine[4]! It is different with one who erred.

R. Assi's teaching disputed.

It was mentioned above: "R. Tanḥum declared in the name of R. Assi: If a man erred and omitted the reference to rain in the benediction of 'the Revival of the Dead,' we make him repeat it; [if he omitted] the request [for rain] in the benediction of 'the Years,' we do not make him repeat it, because he can include it in 'Who hearkenest unto prayer'; but [if he omitted] the 'Division' in 'Thou favourest man with knowledge,' we do not make him repeat it, because he is able to say it over the cup of wine!" Against this is quoted: If one erred and omitted the reference to rain in the benediction of "the Revival of the Dead," we make him repeat it; [if he omitted] the request [for rain] in the benediction of "the Years," we make him repeat it; but [if he omitted] the "Division" in "Thou favourest man with knowledge," we do not make him repeat it, because he is able to say it over the cup of wine! There is no contradiction, the latter referring to one praying alone, the former to one praying with a Congregation. Why should he not repeat it if praying with a Congregation? Because he can hear it from the Precentor[5]. If so [the reason stated above] "because he can include it in 'Who hearkenest unto

[1] See Singer, p. 47.
[2] *Ibid.* p. 49, "Hear our voice."
[3] *Ibid.* p. 44 bot.
[4] *Ibid.* p. 216.
[5] Who repeats the whole *T^e^fillāh* aloud after it has been said silently by the Congregation.

prayer'" should rather be, because he can hear it from the Precentor! Nay, both the teachings refer to one praying alone and there is no contradiction; the statement [of R. Tanḥum] refers to one who reminds himself [that he had omitted the prayer for rain] before reaching the benediction "Who hearkenest unto

fol. 29 b. prayer[1]," whereas the statement [of the *Bārāitā*] refers to one who reminds himself [of the omission] after having said the benediction "Who hearkenest unto prayer."

If reference to the New Moon omitted from the *Tᵉfillāh.*

R. Tanḥum said in the name of R. Assi[2], in the name of R. Joshua b. Levi: If a man erred and omitted the reference to the New Moon in the sixteenth benediction[3], he must repeat it. If he reminded himself thereof in the seventeenth benediction, he goes back to the sixteenth; if in the eighteenth, he goes back to the sixteenth. If he had concluded the *Tᵉfillāh,* he must recommence it. Rab Pappa the son of Rab Aḥa b. Adda said: The statement "If he had concluded the *Tᵉfillāh,* he must recommence it" only applies should he have moved his feet[4]; but if he has not done so, he returns to the sixteenth benediction. He was asked: Whence hast thou obtained this teaching? He replied: From my father my teacher have I heard it, and he from Rab[5]. Rab Naḥman b. Isaac said: The statement that if he had moved his feet he must recommence the *Tᵉfillāh* applies only to one who is not accustomed to offer personal supplications at its conclusion[6]; but if that be his practice, he returns to the sixteenth benediction. Another version is: Rab Naḥman b. Isaac said: The statement that if he had not moved his feet, he returns to the sixteenth benediction applies only to one who is accustomed to offer personal supplication at the conclusion of the *Tᵉfillāh*; but if that be not his practice, he goes back to its commencement.

IV. *R. Eliezer says: If one makes his prayer a fixed task* [ḳéba'], *his prayer is not supplication.*

Meaning of "fixed task" as applied to prayer.

What means *ḳéba'*? R. Jacob b. Iddi said in the name of R. Osha'ya: Anyone whose prayer seems to him a burden. The Rabbis say: Anyone who does not recite it in language of supplication[7]. Rabbah and Rab Joseph both said: Anyone who is not

[1] He thereupon includes it in this benediction.

[2] *M.* omits: in the name of R. Assi.

[3] See Singer, p. 50.

[4] On concluding the *Tᵉfillāh* one steps back three paces, as though retiring from the divine Throne before which the prayer was offered.

[5] *M.* adds: Rab from R. Ḥiyya and R. Ḥiyya from Rabbi.

[6] Cf. the examples quoted fol. 16 *b*, 17 *a*, pp. 107 ff.

[7] I.e. he performs his devotions in a perfunctory manner.

able to add something new thereto[1]. R. Zera said: I am able to add something new, but I am afraid that I may become confused. Abbai b. Abin and R. Ḥannina b. Abin both said: [His prayer is *ḳēba'*] who does not pray at dawn and sunset[2]; for R. Ḥiyya b. Abba said in the name of R. Joḥanan: It is a religious duty to pray at dawn and sunset. R. Zera said: What Scriptural authority is there for this? "They shall fear Thee with the sun and before the moon[3] throughout all generations" (Ps. lxxii. 5). In the West[4], they cursed anyone who prayed at those times. Why? Perhaps the time will be unsuitable for him[5].

R. Joshua says: If one is journeying in a place of danger, he should offer a short prayer, saying: "Save, O Lord, Thy people, the remnant of Israel; in all times of crisis may their needs be before Thee."

Meaning of the word *'ibbūr.*

What means "times of crisis [*'ibbūr*]"? Rab Ḥisda said in the name of Mar 'Uḳba: Even at the time when Thou art full of wrath [*'ebrāh*] against them like a woman big with child [*'ubbéret*], may all their needs be before Thee. Another version is: Rab Ḥisda said in the name of Mar 'Uḳba: Even at the time when they transgress [*'ōb^erīm*] the words of *Tōrāh*, may all their needs be before Thee.

Prayer to be offered in a place of danger.

Our Rabbis have taught: He who journeys in a place of herds of wild beasts or bands of robbers should offer a short prayer. Which is the short prayer? R. Eliezer said: "Do Thy will in Heaven above; grant tranquillity of spirit to those who fear Thee below, and do that which is good in Thy sight. Blessed art Thou, O Lord, Who hearkenest unto prayer." R. Joshua said: "Hear the lament of Thy people Israel, and speedily fulfil their request. Blessed art Thou, O Lord, Who hearkenest unto prayer." R. Eleazar b. Ṣadoḳ said: "Hear the cry of Thy people Israel, and speedily fulfil their request. Blessed art Thou, O Lord, Who hearkenest unto prayer." Others say: "The needs of Thy people Israel are many but their mind short[6]. May it be Thy will, O Lord

[1] I.e. he makes his prayers stereotyped.

[2] *Dimdūmē ḥammāh* has been explained in two ways: (1) "The reddening of the sun," connecting the word with *ādōm*, "red"; (2) "The stillness of the sun" (from the root *dāmam*), i.e. the time in the morning and evening when the sun appears to stand still or be silent; so Jastrow.

[3] I.e. as the sun rises and before the moon appears.

[4] Palestine.

[5] This refers only to the afternoon prayers. If he waited for sunset to say the afternoon *T^efillāh*, something might detain him and the night come on.

[6] I.e. they are unable to give expression to their wants.

our God, to grant each one sufficient for his maintenance, and to every person enough for his want. Blessed art Thou, O Lord, Who hearkenest unto prayer." Rab Huna said: The *H^{a}lākāh* is in accord with the "others."

Elijah's advice to Rab Judah.

Elijah[1] said to Rab Judah, the brother of Rab Sala Ḥ^{a}sida: "Be not wrathful and thou wilt not sin. Be not intoxicated and thou wilt not sin. When thou settest out on a journey, take counsel with thy Creator and go forth." What means, "Take counsel with thy Creator and go forth"? R. Jacob said in the name of Rab Ḥisda: This refers to the prayer to be offered on undertaking a journey.

Prayer for a journey.

R. Jacob also said in the name of Rab Ḥisda: Whoever sets out on a journey should offer the prayer ordained for a journey. What is this prayer? "May it be Thy will, O Lord my God, to conduct me in peace, to direct my steps in peace, to uphold me in peace, and to deliver me from every enemy and ambush by the way. Send a blessing upon the work of my hands, and let me obtain grace, lovingkindness and mercy in Thine eyes and in the eyes of all who behold me. Blessed art Thou, O Lord, Who hearkenest unto prayer[2]."

fol. 30 a. When this prayer is to be offered.

Abbai said: Always should a man associate himself with the Community[3]. How should he pray? "May it be Thy will, O Lord *our* God, to conduct *us* in peace" etc. When should he offer this prayer? R. Jacob said in the name of Rab Ḥisda: From the time he sets forth on his journey. And how long[4]? R. Jacob said in the name of Rab Ḥisda: The distance of a *Parsāh*. And how should he offer it? Rab Ḥisda said: Standing; Rab Sheshet said: Even while journeying. Rab Ḥisda and Rab Sheshet were once on a journey together. Rab Ḥisda stood up and offered the prayer. Rab Sheshet[5] said to his attendant, "What is Rab Ḥisda doing?" He replied, "He is standing and praying." He said to him, "Raise also me up and I too will pray; for if thou canst be good, do not allow thyself to be called evil[6]."

[1] See p. 7 n. 5.

[2] Cf. Singer, p. 310.

[3] In his prayer, i.e. using the plural and not the singular.

[4] The question is capable of two interpretations: (1) Up to what distance may a man go without saying the prayer, and if he exceed it, his prayer becomes invalid? (2) What is the minimum distance which constitutes a journey necessitating the prayer?

[5] Who was blind.

[6] I.e. he will follow Rab Ḥisda's example and say the prayer standing.

Difference between the abstract and the short prayer.

What is the difference between "Give us understanding[1]" and the short prayer[2]? "Give us understanding" requires three benedictions before and three after it[3], and when he reaches his house, he need not again say the *Tefillāh*; whereas with the short prayer there is no necessity to utter the three benedictions before and after, but when he reaches his house, he must say the *Tefillāh*. The *Halākāh* is also that "Give us understanding" must be said standing, but the short prayer can be said either standing or journeying.

V. *If he is riding upon an ass, he should alight and say the* Tefillāh.

Saying the *Tefillāh* when riding upon an ass.

Our Rabbis have taught: If a man is riding upon an ass and the time of the *Tefillāh* arrives, should he have somebody to hold his ass, he must alight and pray; but if not, he sits in his place and prays. Rabbi says: In either case, he should sit in his place and pray, because his mind is unsettled. Raba[4] (another version: R. Joshua b. Levi) said: The *Halākāh* is in agreement with Rabbi.

The direction in which one must pray.

Our Rabbis have taught: A blind man or one who is unable to locate the directions should direct his heart to his Father in Heaven; as it is said, "And they pray unto the Lord" (I Kings viii. 44). If he is standing outside the [Holy] Land, he must direct his heart towards the land of Israel; as it is said, "And pray unto Thee toward their land" (*ibid. v.* 48). If he is standing in the land of Israel, he must direct his heart towards Jerusalem; as it is said, "And they pray unto the Lord toward the city which Thou hast chosen" (*ibid. v.* 44). If he is standing in Jerusalem, he must direct his heart towards the Temple; as it is said, "And pray toward this house" (II Chron. vi. 32). If he is standing in the Temple, he must direct his heart towards the Holy of Holies; as it is said, "And they pray toward this place" (I Kings viii. 35). If he is standing in the Holy of Holies, he must direct his heart towards the mercy-seat[5]. If he is standing behind the mercy-seat, he must imagine himself to be in front of it. Consequently if he is standing in the East, he must turn West; if in the West, he must turn East; if in the South, he must turn North; if in the North, he must turn South. As a result, all Israel will be directing their heart to one spot. R. Abin (another version: R. Abina)

[1] The abstract of the *Tefillāh*.
[2] Mentioned in the *Mishnāh*.
[3] See the directions in Singer, p. 55.
[4] *M.*: Rab.
[5] Cf. Exod. xxv. 17.

said: What Scriptural authority is there for this? "Thy neck is like the tower of David, builded with turrets [*talpiyyōt*]" (Cant. iv. 4), i.e. a heap [*tēl*] for all mouths [*piyyōt*][1].

Saying the *Tᵉfillāh* before reading the *Shᵉma'* when setting out on a journey.

Samuel's father and Levi, when they wished to set out on a journey, used to rise up early[2] and say the *Tᵉfillāh*; and when the time arrived for reading the *Shᵉma'* they read it then[3]. In accord with whose opinion is this? That of the *Tannā* of the teaching: If one rises early to set out on a journey, they may bring him a *Shōfār*[4] which he blows, a *Lūlāb* which he shakes, a *Mᵉgillāh* in which he reads; and when the time arrives for reading the *Shᵉma'* he reads it. If he rose early to sit in a travelling coach or ship, he may say the *Tᵉfillāh*, and when the time arrives for reading the *Shᵉma'* he reads it. R. Simeon b. Eleazar says: In all circumstances, he reads the *Shᵉma'* and then says the *Tᵉfillāh* in order to unite it with the *Gᵉ'ullāh*. In what do they differ? The former holds that to say the *Tᵉfillāh* standing is of greater importance[5]; the latter holds that to unite the *Gᵉ'ullāh* with the *Tᵉfillāh* is of greater importance.

The practice of some Rabbis.

Maremar and Mar Zoṭra used to gather in their house ten men[6] on the Sabbath preceding a Festival[7], say the prayers and then go to the study-session. Rab Ashē used to say the prayers in the presence of the assembly alone and sitting[8], and when he returned to his house, he again said the *Tᵉfillāh* standing. The Rabbis said to him, "The master should act like Maremar and Mar Zoṭra[9]." He replied, "It is too much trouble for me." "Then let the master act like Samuel's father and Levi[10]." He replied, "We have not seen the Rabbis who are older than we acting in this manner."

[1] The building towards which all mouths offer prayer. Some edd. read: a heap towards which all turn [*pōnīm*].

[2] Before daybreak.

[3] I.e. the *Shᵉma'* after the *Tᵉfillāh*. Cf. above, fol. 4 *b*, p. 16.

[4] The ram's horn used on the New Year; Oesterley and Box, pp. 411 ff.

[5] And this may not be possible while travelling.

[6] The quorum required for Congregational prayer.

[7] On this Sabbath they, as Principals of the Seminaries, delivered a public discourse.

[8] I.e. on the Sabbath before the Festival. He gave his *Āmōrā* the gist of the discourse, and while the latter was expounding it, Rab Ashē said his prayers sitting to avoid giving the assembly the trouble of standing up, as they would have to do out of respect for him, if he stood to say the *Tᵉfillāh*.

[9] Who gathered a quorum at their house.

[10] Who said the *Tᵉfillāh* before the *Shᵉma'*.

MISHNĀH VII

R. Eleazar b. 'Azariah says: The additional Tᵉfillāh *is only to be said with the local Congregation. The Sages say: Whether with or without the local Congregation. R. Judah says in his name*[1]*: In any place where there is a local Congregation, the individual is exempt from the additional* Tᵉfillāh[2].

GᴱMĀRĀ

The point of difference in the views contained in the *Mishnāh.*

R. Judah is identical with the first *Tannā's* view! There is a difference between them, viz.: an individual who lives in a place where there is no local Congregation[3]. The first *Tannā* holds that he is exempt [from the additional *Tᵉfillāh*], but R. Judah holds that he is under the obligation. Rab Huna b. Ḥinnana[4] said in the name of Rab Ḥiyya b. Rab[5]: The *Hᵃlākāh* is in agreement with R. Judah as stated in the name of R. Eleazar b. 'Azariah. Rab Ḥiyya b. Abin said to him: Thou hast said well; for Samuel has declared: Never have I said the additional *Tᵉfillāh* alone in Nehardea[6] except on the day when the king's army came to the town[7], and the Rabbis were so troubled that they did not say the *Tᵉfillāh*, and I said it alone, because I was like an individual without a local Congregation. **fol. 30 b.**

The *Hᵃlākāh* discussed.

R. Ḥannina the Bible-teacher sat before R. Jannai; as he sat he said, "The *Hᵃlākāh* is in agreement with R. Judah as stated in the name of R. Eleazar b. 'Azariah." He said to him, "Go out and read thy Bible verses in the street[8], for the *Hᵃlākāh* is not in agreement with R. Judah as stated in the name of R. Eleazar b. 'Azariah." R. Johanan said, "I noticed that R. Jannai said the *Tᵉfillāh* and then said another *Tᵉfillāh*[9]." R. Jeremiah said to R. Zera, "Perhaps he did not at first direct his heart [to his

[1] The name of R. Eleazar b. 'Azariah.
[2] If he prays alone.
[3] Because there are not ten adult males to constitute a quorum.
[4] *M.*: Rab Abba b. R. Ḥannina, which is probably correct.
[5] *M.*: R. Ḥiyya in the name of Rab.
[6] See p. 74 n. 2.
[7] A reference probably to the Roman-Persian Wars.
[8] The meaning is, I do not recognise you as an authority on the *Hᵃlākāh*.
[9] They must accordingly have been the morning and additional *Tᵉfillōt*, and thereby he acted contrary to the view as stated in the *Mishnāh*.

prayer] and finally did so[1]!" He replied, "See how great a man testifies concerning him[2]."

Although there were thirteen Synagogues in Tiberias[3], R. Ammi and R. Assi never said the T^e*fillāh* except between the pillars where they studied[4].

Mechanical prayer prohibited.

If reference to New Moon omitted from the T^e*fillāh*.

It has been reported: Rab Isaac b. Abdemi said in the name of our teacher[5]: The H^a*lākāh* is in agreement with R. Judah as stated in the name of R. Eleazar b. 'Azariah. R. Ḥiyya b. Abba said the T^e*fillāh*[6] and then said another. R. Zera asked him, "Why did the master act so? Is it because the master did not direct his heart [with the first]? But R. Eleazar has said: A man should always examine himself; if he can direct his heart, then let him pray, but if not, he should not pray! Or is it because the master did not include the reference to the New Moon [in the first T^e*fillāh*][7]? But there is a teaching: If a man erred and omitted the reference to the New Moon in the evening T^e*fillāh*, we do not require him to repeat it, because he can say it in the morning T^e*fillāh*; [if he omitted it] in the morning, we do not require him to repeat it, because he can say it in the additional T^e*fillāh*; [if he omitted it] in the additional T^e*fillāh*, we do not require him to repeat it, because he can say it in the afternoon!" He replied, "Has it not been reported in this connection: R. Joḥanan declared that this teaching applies only to a Congregation[8]?"

Interval between two T^e*fillōt*.

How long must one wait between T^e*fillāh* and T^e*fillāh*[9]? Rab Huna and Rab Ḥisda [differ]. One said: Until his mind can offer supplication; the other said: Until his mind can offer beseeching

[1] I.e. he said the morning T^e*fillāh* twice, and not the additional.

[2] R. Joḥanan was a very eminent Rabbi, and he clearly intended to imply that R. Jannai did say the additional T^e*fillāh*.

[3] See p. 46.

[4] I.e. they read the additional T^e*fillāh* privately although there were several local Congregations.

[5] Rashi comments: i.e. Rab. Although Rab is usually referred to in this way, here Rabbi must be intended; cf. Hyman, II. p. 785.

[6] It does not refer here to the additional.

[7] See Singer, p. 50.

[8] If he omitted the reference when praying with the Congregation, he does not repeat the T^e*fillāh* because he will hear it said by the Precentor. Some explain that it refers to the Precentor himself, who does not repeat the T^e*fillāh* if he omitted the reference, so as not to trouble the Congregation. In view of this teaching, R. Ḥiyya b. Abba, since he was not praying with a Congregation, was right in repeating the T^e*fillāh*.

[9] If he has to say two.

prayer. He who says: Until his mind can offer supplication [*titḥōnēn*], it is because it is said, "And I supplicated [*wāëtḥannān*] the Lord" (Deut. iii. 23); and he who says: Until his mind can offer beseeching prayer [*titḥōlēl*], it is because it is written, "And Moses besought [*wayy^{e}ḥal*] the Lord" (Exod. xxxii. 11).

Reference to New Moon, if omitted in the evening *T^{e}fillāh*, needs no reparation.

Rab 'Anan said in the name of Rab: If a man erred and omitted the reference to the New Moon in the evening *T^{e}fillāh*, we do not require him to repeat it, because the *Bēt Dīn* only consecrate the new month in the day-time. Amemar said: It is probable that Rab's statement applies to a full month[1]; but in the case of a defective month, we require him to repeat it. Rab Ashē said to Amemar: Since Rab has stated a reason[2], what has it to do whether the month is full or defective! Certainly there is no difference.

May we return unto thee: *The morning* T^{e}fillāh!

[1] The month is "full" when it has 30 days, "defective" when it has 29. When the moon is "full," two days (the concluding day of the old and the first of the new) are observed, and the extra prayer said on both. Therefore if he omitted it one evening, he can say it the next.

[2] Viz. the *Bēt Dīn* consecrate the new month only by day.

CHAPTER V

MISHNĀH I

One must not stand up to say the Tᵉfillāh *except in a serious frame of mind*[1]. *The pious men of old*[2] *used to wait an hour*[3] *and then say the* Tᵉfillāh, *in order to direct their heart to their Father in Heaven. Even when a king greets him, he must not respond; and though a serpent be wound round his heel, he must not interrupt.*

GᴱMĀRĀ

Biblical authority for the teaching of the *Mishnāh*.

Whence is this teaching derived[4]? R. Eleazar said: For the Scriptures state, "She was in bitterness of soul and prayed unto the Lord" (I Sam. i. 10). How is it derived from this verse? Perhaps it was different with Hannah since she was very sore of heart! But said R. Josē b. R. Ḥannina: [Derive it] from the following: "But as for me, in the abundance of Thy lovingkindness will I come into Thy house; I will bow down toward Thy holy Temple in the fear of Thee" (Ps. v. 8). How is it derived from this verse? Perhaps it was different with David, since he afflicted his soul exceedingly in prayer! But said R. Joshua b. Levi: [Derive it] from the following: "Worship the Lord in the beauty of holiness" (*ibid.* xxix. 2)—read not "beauty" [*hadrat*] but "trembling" [*ḥerdat*]. How is it derived from this verse? Perhaps I may indeed tell thee that "in the beauty of holiness" is to be understood literally, as with Rab Judah who used to adorn himself[5] and then pray! But said Rab Naḥman b. Isaac: [Derive it] from the following: "Serve the Lord with fear, and rejoice with trembling" (*ibid.* ii. 11). What means "rejoice with trembling"? Rab Adda b. Mattᵉna said in the name of Rabbah[6]: Where there is rejoicing[7] let there be trembling.

[1] Or, humility; *lit.* "heaviness of head," corresponding to *gravitate mentis*. The opposite is *ḳallūt rōsh*, "lightness of head," levity.

[2] Perhaps identical with the *Wᵉtiḳin*; see p. 55 n. 6.

[3] In silent meditation.

[4] That one may only pray in a serious frame of mind.

[5] I.e. put on his best garments.

[6] *M.* omits: in the name of Rabbah. The correct reading is probably: Rab; cf. Hyman, I. p. 104*b*.

[7] In the worship of God.

Abbai was sitting in the presence of Rabbah, and noticed that he was very merry. He said to him, "It is written, 'Rejoice with trembling'!" He replied, "I have laid the *Tᵉfillīn*[1]." R. Jeremiah was sitting in the presence of R. Zera, and noticed that he was very merry. He said to him, "It is written, 'In all pain[2] there is profit'!" (Prov. xiv. 23). He replied, "I have laid the *Tᵉfillīn*."

Frivolity deprecated.

Mar b. Rabina made a wedding-feast for his son, and noticed that the Rabbis were very merry. He seized a costly goblet[3] worth four hundred *Zūz* and broke it before them, and they became more serious. Rab Ashē made a wedding-feast for his son, and noticed that the Rabbis were very merry. He seized a goblet of white crystal and broke it before them, and they became more serious. The Rabbis said to Rab Hamnuna the Small[4] at the wedding-feast of Mar b. Rabina, "Let the master sing for us." He replied to them, "Woe to us for we are destined to die! Woe to us for we are destined to die!" They said to him, "What can we answer after thee?" He said to them, "Where is the *Tōrāh* and where the religious precept which will protect us[5]?"

Merriment of the Rabbis checked.

fol. 31 a.

R. Joḥanan said in the name of R. Simeon b. Joḥai: It is forbidden that a man's mouth be filled with laughter in this world; because it is written, "Then will our mouth be filled with laughter, and our tongue with singing" (Ps. cxxvi. 2). When? At the time when "They will say among the nations, The Lord hath done great things with these" (*ibid.*). It was said of R. Simeon b. Laḳish that never again was his mouth full of laughter in this world after hearing this teaching from his master R. Joḥanan[6].

A man's mouth must not be filled with laughter.

Our Rabbis have taught: One must not stand up to say the *Tᵉfillāh* immediately after being engaged in a lawsuit or the discussion of a *Hᵃlākāh*[7]; but he may do so after the discussion of a *Hᵃlākāh* which has been decided. What is meant by a *Hᵃlākāh* which has been decided? Abbai said: Like that of R. Zera who stated: The daughters of Israel are very strict with themselves; for if they see even a drop of menstrual flow as small as a mustard

Tᵉfillāh not to be said when the mind is disturbed.

1 And their influence will prevent me from exceeding due bounds.

2 And not in merriment.

3 See p. 182 n. 2.

4 *M.* omits: the Small.

5 From the punishment meted out to the wicked after death.

6 The above passages reflect the condition of mourning in which the Jews considered themselves to be after the overthrow of Temple and State.

7 Because his mind would not be settled.

seed, they wait seven clear days after it. Raba said: Like that of Rab Hosha'ya who stated: A man should act cunningly with his produce, and store it together with the chaff, so that his cattle may eat of it and it become exempt from the tithe[1]. If thou wilt I can say like that of Rab Huna who stated in the name of R. Ze'ira[2]: He who draws blood from an animal destined for a sacrifice is forbidden to make use of it, and [should he use it] he must bring a transgression-offering[3]. The Rabbis act according to our *Mishnāh*[4]; Rab Ashē acted according to the *Bārāitā*[5].

Serious state of mind required.

Our Rabbis have taught: One must not stand up to say the *Tefillāh* from the midst of sorrow, idleness, jocularity, [frivolous] conversation, levity, or idle chatter, but only from the midst of the joy of a religious duty. Similarly a man should not take leave of another from the midst of [frivolous] conversation, jocularity, levity, or idle chatter; but from the midst of a discussion of *Halākāh*. For so we find that the former prophets used to conclude their addresses with words of praise and consolation. So also Mari the son of[6] Rab Huna the son of R. Jeremiah b. Abba taught: A man should not take leave of another except from the midst of a discussion of *Halākāh*, so that he may remember him thereby. Thus, Rab Kahana[7] accompanied Rab Shimi b. Ashē from Pom-Nahara[8] to Be-Sinyata[9] in Babylon. When he arrived there, he said to him, "Is it true what people say that these Babylonian palms are from the time of Adam till now?" He answered, "Thou hast reminded me of something which R. Josē b. R. Ḥannina said, viz.: What means that which is written, 'Through a land that no man passed through, and where no man dwelt' (Jer. ii. 6)? Since no man passed through it, how could anyone dwell there! But it intends to tell us that every land

[1] Corn must be winnowed before it becomes liable to the tithe. If unwinnowed, cattle may feed on it, but it may not be used for human consumption, without the tithe.

[2] *M.*: Ze'iri.

[3] Having committed *me'ilāh* (see Lev. v. 15f.) because, being a non-priest, he utilised something that belonged to the Sanctuary.

[4] I.e. only permit one to pray in a serious frame of mind.

[5] I.e. permitted one to pray after discussing a *Halākāh* which has been decided.

[6] So *M.* correctly. Edd.: grandson of.

[7] *M.*: Huna.

[8] *Lit.* "mouth of the river"; a fertile region near Nehardea; Neubauer, pp. 366f.

[9] *Lit.* "between the palms" is, says Neubauer, *loc. cit.*, probably the first halting-place in Babylonia proper.

concerning which Adam decreed that it should be inhabited has become inhabited, and every land concerning which Adam did not so decree has not been inhabited[1]." Rab Mordecai accompanied Rab Ashē[2] from Hagronya[3] to Be-Kipē[4]; another version: to Be-Dura[5].

The heart must be directed to Heaven.

Our Rabbis have taught: He who prays must direct his heart to Heaven. *Abbā* Saul said: A [Biblical] indication for this matter is: "Thou wilt direct their heart, Thou wilt cause Thine ear to attend" (Ps. x. 17).

R. 'Aḳiba's practice.

There is a teaching: R. Judah said: It was the practice of R. 'Aḳiba, when he said the *T^efillāh* with the Congregation, to shorten [the time in which he said it] and step back[6], so as to avoid troubling the Congregation[7]; but when he said the *T^efillāh* alone, a man might leave him in one corner and find him in another corner. And why so? Because of his bowings and genuflections.

Deductions from Dan. vi. 11.

R. Ḥiyya b. Abba said: A man should always pray in a room which has windows; as it is said, "Now his windows were open in his upper chamber towards Jerusalem" (Dan. vi. 11). It is possible to imagine that a man can pray all the day long; but it has already been clearly stated by Daniel, "And he kneeled upon his knees three times a day and prayed, and gave thanks before his God" (*ibid.*). It is possible to imagine that only when he was taken into captivity, he commenced to pray thus; but it has been said, "As he did aforetime" (*ibid.*). It is possible to imagine that one can pray in any direction he wishes; therefore there is a teaching to state, "Towards Jerusalem" (*ibid.*). It is possible to

[1] He means to imply that Adam decreed that those palms should grow there.

[2] According to Hyman, III. p. 903*a* (see the parallel passage in Sōṭāh 46*b*), this is the correct reading, not Rab Shimi b. Ashē as in edd.

[3] Possibly the town Agranum, situated on one of the tributaries of the Euphrates; Neubauer, p. 347. Wiesner, p. 71, identifies it with the modern Erzerum.

[4] Perhaps identical with the locality of Koufa in Babylon; Neubauer, *loc. cit.* According to Wiesner, *loc. cit.*, it is Mt Capotes near which the Euphrates has its source.

[5] A Babylonian locality in the neighbourhood of the last-mentioned place. There appears to be a lacuna in the text here, relating what happened on that occasion.

[6] See p. 194 n. 4.

[7] By detaining them. They would not resume the Service until the Rabbi had finished his *T^efillāh*, and some of them might want to hurry away to their work.

imagine that a man can include all his prayers in one act of devotion; but it has already been clearly stated by David, "Evening and morning and at noonday" (Ps. lv. 18). It is possible to imagine that one should utter his prayers aloud; but it has already been clearly stated by Hannah, viz. "Her voice could not be heard" (I Sam. i. 13). It is possible to imagine that a man could pray for his own needs and afterwards say the statutory prayers; but it has already been clearly stated by Solomon, viz. "To hearken unto the cry and to the prayer" (I Kings viii. 28)—"cry" means statutory prayer, and "prayer" means personal supplication.

Where personal supplications may be introduced.

One may not offer anything [of personal supplication] after "True and firm[1]"; but after the *T^e^fillāh*, he can say something even like the order of confession for the Day of Atonement[2]. It has been likewise reported: R. Hiyya b. Ashē declared in the name of Rab: Although it has been said that one may pray for his personal needs in the benediction "Who hearkenest unto prayer[3]," if he desires to add after the *T^e^fillāh* even something like the order of [confession for] the Day of Atonement, he may do so.

Deductions from the account of Hannah.

Rab Hamnuna said: How many weighty *H^a^lākōt* there are to be learnt from the passage relating to Hannah! "Now Hannah, she spake in her heart" (I Sam. i. 13)—hence it is deduced that one who prays must direct his heart. "Only her lips moved"—hence, one who prays must pronounce [the words] with his lips. "But her voice was not heard"—hence, it is forbidden to raise the voice when praying. "Therefore Eli thought she had been drunken"—hence, it is forbidden to pray when intoxicated. "And Eli said to her, How long wilt thou be drunken?" (*ibid. v.* 14)—

fol. 31 b.

R. Eleazar said: Hence, if one sees in his neighbour anything that is unseemly, he must rebuke him. "And Hannah answered and said, No, my lord" (*ibid. v.* 15)—'Ulla (another version: R. Josē b. R. Ḥannina) declared: She said to Eli, "Thou art not 'a lord' in this affair, nor does the Holy Spirit rest upon thee, seeing thou hast suspected me of this thing." Some declare that she spoke to him thus: "Thou art not a lord; neither the *Sh^e^kīnāh* nor the Holy Spirit is with thee, for thou hast judged me in the scale of guilt and not in the scale of merit[4]. Dost thou not know

[1] Singer, p. 42, i.e. between the *G^e^'ullāh* and *T^e^fillāh*. See especially p. 56 n. 7. [2] Singer, pp. 258 ff., and compare fol. 17*a*, p. 109.

[3] Singer, p. 49, "Hear our voice."

[4] I.e. thou hast put the worst, not the most favourable, construction on my conduct. Cf. Abot i. 6, Singer, p. 185.

'I am a woman of sorrowful spirit'?" "I have drunk neither wine nor strong drink"—R. Eleazar said: Hence it is deduced that one who is wrongly suspected must clear himself. "Count not thy handmaid for a wicked woman" (I Sam. i. 16)—R. Eleazar said: Hence it is inferred that if a drunken person prays, it is as though he practised idolatry; for it is written here "a wicked woman[1]," and elsewhere it is written, "Certain base fellows[2] are gone out from the midst of thee" (Deut. xiii. 14)—as the reference in this latter passage is to idolatry, so also in the other passage idolatry is intended. "Then Eli answered and said, Go in peace" (I Sam. i. 17)—R. Eleazar said: Hence, if one wrongly suspected another, he must conciliate him; nay more, he must bless him; as it is said, "And the God of Israel grant thy petition" (*ibid.*).

Her prayer for a child.

"And she vowed a vow and said, O Lord of hosts" (*ibid. v.* 11)—R. Eleazar said: From the day that the Holy One, blessed be He, created His universe, there was nobody who called Him "[Lord of] hosts" until Hannah came and gave Him that designation. Hannah said before the Holy One, blessed be He, "Lord of the universe! From all the multitudes of hosts which Thou hast created in Thy universe, is it hard in Thine eyes to grant me even one son?" A parable: To what is the matter like? To a human king who made a feast for his servants. A poor man came and stood at the entrance and said to them, "Give me a morsel of bread"; but they took no notice of him. He pushed his way through and entered the presence of the king, exclaiming, "My lord, the king! From all the feast which thou hast made, is it hard in thine eyes to spare me a morsel of bread?"

Her threat.

"If thou wilt indeed look[3]" (*ibid.*)—R. Eleazar said: Thus spake Hannah before the Holy One, blessed be He, "Lord of the universe! If Thou wilt look, well and good; but if Thou wilt not look, I will go and seclude myself [with another man][4] before Elkanah my husband; and having done so, they will administer to me the waters of the woman suspected of adultery, and Thou wilt surely not make Thy *Tōrāh* a fraud; for it is said, 'Then she shall be cleared, and shall conceive seed'" (Num. v. 28). This is quite right for him who maintains that if [the woman wrongly suspected] was barren, then she will conceive; but according to

[1] *Lit.* daughter of Belial.

[2] *Lit.* sons of Belial.

[3] *Lit.* If looking Thou wilt look.

[4] For the express purpose of arousing her husband's suspicions, though unjustly.

him who maintains [that as the result of her proved innocence], if she usually gave birth in pain she now gives birth with ease, [if she usually brought forth] daughters she now brings forth sons[1], [if she usually brought forth] dark[2] children she now brings forth fair children, [if she usually brought forth] short children she now brings forth tall children—what is there to say[3]? For there is a teaching: "Then she shall be cleared, and shall conceive seed"—this teaches that if she had been barren she now conceives; these are the words of R. Ishmael. R. 'Aḳiba said to him: In that case, all barren women will go and lay themselves under suspicion, and she who has not done wrong [after receiving the waters] will conceive! Nay, it teaches, that if she usually gave birth in pain, she now gives birth with ease; that she will have tall children instead of short, fair instead of dark, two instead of one. But how is "If Thou wilt indeed look" to be explained[4]? The *Tōrāh* speaks according to the language of the sons of man[5].

Her protest.

"[If Thou wilt indeed look] on the affliction of Thy handmaid, and remember me, and not forget Thy handmaid, but wilt give unto Thy handmaid" (I Sam. i. 11). R. Josē b. R. Ḥannina said: Why is "Thy handmaid" repeated thrice? Hannah spake before the Holy One, blessed be He, "Lord of the universe! Three breaches [*bidḳē*] through which death comes[6] hast Thou created in a woman; (another version: Three causes [*dibḳē*] of death), viz.: neglect of the laws concerning menstruation, *Ḥallah* and kindling the Sabbath-lights[7]. Have I transgressed any of them?"

Phrase "seed of men" explained.

"But wilt give Thy handmaid seed of men" (*ibid.*). What means "seed of men"? Rab said: A man among men[8]. Samuel said: Seed which will anoint two men; and who are they? Saul and David. R. Johanan said: Seed equal to two men; and who are they? Moses and Aaron; as it is said, "Moses and Aaron among His priests, and Samuel among them that call upon His name" (Ps. xcix. 6). The Rabbis say: "Seed of men" means seed which will be swallowed up among men[9]. When Rab Dimai came [from

1 See p. 26 n. 5.

2 Considered ugly; see below.

3 What would be the utility of Hannah's ruse?

4 The plan of Hannah was deduced from the use of the infinitive with the finite verb, "If looking Thou wilt look." If the deduction is not drawn, how is the double use of the verb to be accounted for?

5 It is a common idiom, and no inference should be drawn therefrom.

6 I.e. sins for which one is visited with death.

7 See *Mishnāh* Shab. ii. 6, Singer, p. 121.

8 I.e. distinguished.

9 Meaning, an average person, not conspicuous among others.

Palestine] he explained [the words of the Rabbis to mean]: neither tall nor dwarfish nor short, neither dark[1] nor ruddy nor pale, neither too wise nor too foolish.

"I am the woman that stood by thee here" (I Sam. i. 26). R. Joshua b. Levi said: Hence it is deduced that it is forbidden to sit within four cubits of [one engaged in] prayer[2]. **One must not sit near one who prays.**

"For this child I prayed" (*ibid. v.* 27). R. Eleazar said: Samuel was one who decided a *Halākāh* in the presence of his master[3]; as it is said, "And when the bullock was slain, the child was brought to Eli" (*ibid. v.* 25). Because "the bullock was slain," therefore "the child was brought to Eli[4]"! Nay; but Eli said to them, "Call a priest that he may come and slay [the bullock]." Samuel saw them going for a priest to slay it, so he said to them, "Why go searching for a priest to slay it? If the act of slaying is performed by a non-priest it is valid." They brought him before Eli, who asked him, "Whence hast thou this teaching?" He replied, "Is it written, 'The priest shall *slay*'? It is written, 'The priests shall present the blood' (Lev. i. 5). From the receiving of the blood onwards is the function of the priesthood; hence, the act of slaying is valid if performed by a non-priest." Eli said to him, "An excellent teaching hast thou expounded; still thou art one who decided a *Halākāh* in the presence of thy master[5], and whoever does that incurs the penalty of death." Then Hannah came and cried before him, "I am the woman that stood by thee here." He said to her, "Leave me alone that I may punish him, and I will pray that [a son] greater than he be granted thee." She answered him, "For *this* child I prayed." **The infant Samuel's offence.**

"Now Hannah she spake in[6] her heart" (I Sam. i. 13)—R. Eleazar said in the name of R. Josē b. Zimra: [She spoke] about the concerns of her heart. She spake before Him, "Lord of the **Hannah spake "in her heart."**

[1] I have adopted the reading of *M.* אוכם "dark," i.e. ugly, which offers the contrast to "ruddy," i.e. handsome. Edd. read אלם which means "a mute." Rashi explains it as "corpulent," but the word never seems to have that meaning. Some edd. add after it: nor blind.

[2] The ground for this inference is not clear. The explanation offered by the commentators (see Tōsāfōt) is as follows: The word "by thee" עמכה is spelt with a redundant letter ה which has the numerical value of five. Hence it is taken to mean "I was within five [cubits] of thee," because one is not allowed to sit within four cubits of one who prays.

[3] A strictly forbidden action.

[4] What is the connection between the two clauses?

[5] Eli was potentially his teacher, since Samuel's mother had placed him in his charge.

[6] Lit. upon.

universe! In all that Thou hast created in a woman Thou hast created nothing in vain—eyes to see, ears to hear, a nose to smell, a mouth to speak, hands wherewith to do work, feet to walk with, breasts to suckle with. But these breasts which Thou hast placed *upon my heart,* why have I not occasion to suckle with them? Give me a son, that I may suckle with them."

Voluntary fast forbidden on the Sabbath.

R. Eleazar also said in the name of R. Josē b. Zimra: Whoever imposes a fast upon himself on the Sabbath[1], the decree of seventy years is annulled for him[2]; but for all that the penalty for [denying himself] the delight of the Sabbath will be exacted from him. How can he make amends? Rab Naḥman b. Isaac said: Let him observe a fast [in expiation] of his fast.

Hannah and Elijah spoke rebelliously to God.

R. Eleazar also said: Hannah spoke rebelliously to the Most High; as it is said, "She prayed against[3] the Lord" (I Sam. i. 10), which teaches that she spoke rebelliously to the Most High. R. Eleazar also said: Elijah spoke rebelliously to the Most High; as it is said, "For Thou didst turn their heart backward" (I Kings xviii. 37). R. Samuel b. Rab Isaac said: Whence [do we find] that the Holy One, blessed be He, replied and admitted [the plea

fol. 32 a. of] Elijah? For it is written, "[In that day, saith the Lord, will I assemble...] her that I have afflicted" (Micah iv. 6).

Hope for Israel.

Rab Ḥamma b. R. Ḥannina said: Were it not for the following three verses, the feet of the enemies of Israel would give way under them[4]; first, that which is written, "Her that I have afflicted" (*ibid.*); second, that which is written, "Behold as the clay in the potter's hand, so are ye in My hand, O house of Israel" (Jer. xviii. 6); third, that which is written, "I will take away the stony heart out of your flesh, and I will give you a heart of flesh" (Ezek. xxxvi. 26). Rab Pappa said: [It may also be learnt] from this passage: "And I will put My spirit within you, and cause you to walk in My statutes" (*ibid. v.* 27).

[1] The only fast which is permitted on the Sabbath is that of the Day of Atonement. It speaks here of a voluntary fast as, e.g., after a dream of ill omen.

[2] Seventy years is the normal span of human life (Ps. xc. 10) and this will be shortened if one spoils "the day of delight" by fasting. Rashi explains differently in a favourable sense: If one adds to the severity of his fast by choosing the Sabbath day, then should there be a divine decree to his detriment, though it be incurred in extreme youth (seventy years ago), it will be annulled.

[3] I.e. *'al* instead of *el* "unto."

[4] At the thought of the severity of their lot because of their guilt. "Enemies of Israel" is an euphemism for Israel.

R. Eleazar also said: Moses spoke rebelliously to the Most High; as it is said, "And Moses prayed unto the Lord" (Num. xi. 2)—read not "unto [*el*] the Lord" but "against [*'al*] the Lord"; for so the school of R. Eliezer b. Jacob interchange the letters *aleph* and *'ayin*. The school of R. Jannai say: [It may be learnt] from the passage "And Di-Zahab" (Deut. i. 1). What means "And Di-Zahab"? The school of R. Jannai declare: Thus spake Moses before the Holy One, blessed be He, "Lord of the universe! It was because of the silver and gold [*zāhāb*] which Thou didst bounteously give to Israel until they cried, 'It is sufficient' [*dai*], that they were induced to make the calf." The school of R. Jannai said, "A lion growls not in a den full of straw but in a den full of meat[1]." R. Osha'ya said: A parable: [It may be likened] to a man who had a lean cow but of large build. He fed it on horse-beans, and it kicked him. He said to it, "What caused thee to kick me but the horse-beans on which I fed thee!" R. Ḥiyya b. Abba said in the name of R. Joḥanan: A parable: [It may be likened] to a man who had a son. He washed him, anointed him, gave him to eat and drink, tied a purse about his neck, and set him at the entrance of a brothel. How can that son help sinning? Rab Aḥa b. Rab Huna said in the name of Rab Sheshet: That is what people say: "He whose stomach is full increaseth deeds of evil"; as it is said, "When they were fed, they became full, they were filled, and their heart was exalted; therefore have they forgotten Me" (Hosea xiii. 6). Rab Naḥman[2] said: [It may be learnt] from this passage: "Then thy heart be lifted up, and thou forget the Lord thy God" (Deut. viii. 14); and the Rabbis said from the following: "And they shall have eaten their fill, and waxen fat, and turned unto other gods" (*ibid.* xxxi. 20); or if thou wilt, from the following: "But Jeshurun waxed fat and kicked" (*ibid.* xxxii. 15). R. Samuel b. Naḥmani said in the name of R. Jonathan: Whence is it that the Holy One, blessed be He, afterwards admitted [the plea of] Moses? As it is said, "I multiplied unto her silver and gold, which they used for Baal" (Hosea ii. 10).

Moses spoke rebelliously to God.

"And the Lord spake unto Moses, Go, get thee down" (Exod. xxxii. 7). What means "Go, get *thee* down"? R. Eleazar said: The Holy One, blessed be He, spake to Moses, "Moses, get thee down from thy greatness. Have I given thee greatness but for the sake of Israel? And now that Israel has sinned, what art

Exod. xxxii. 7 expounded.

[1] It is plenty that creates the spirit of insubordination.

[2] Some edd. read: Rab Naḥman b. Isaac.

thou to Me?" Immediately the strength of Moses was weakened, and he had not the power to speak[1]. But when He said, "Let Me alone, that I may destroy them" (Deut. ix. 14), Moses said [to himself], "This matter depends upon me." He at once stood up and strengthened himself with prayer and besought mercy [for Israel]. A parable: [It may be likened] to a king who was enraged against his son, and he struck him a violent blow. His friend was sitting in his presence but was afraid to say anything to him. The king exclaimed, "Were it not that my friend were sitting in my presence, I would kill thee." [The friend] said [to himself], "This matter depends upon me." He at once stood up and rescued him.

Exod. xxxii. 10 expounded. "Now therefore *let Me alone*, that My wrath may wax hot against them and that I may consume them; and I will make of thee a great nation" etc. (Exod. xxxii. 10). R. Abbahu[2] said: Were it not explicitly written, it would be impossible to say it; for this teaches that Moses caught hold of the Holy One, blessed be He, like a man who takes hold of his neighbour by his garment, and said before Him, "Lord of the universe! I will not let Thee alone until Thou forgivest and pardonest them."

Exposition continued. "I will make of thee a great nation" etc. R. Eleazar said: Moses spake before the Holy One, blessed be He, "Lord of the universe! If a stool with three legs[3] cannot stand before Thee in the time of Thy wrath, how much less a stool with but one leg[4]! Nay more, I have reason to feel abashed before my ancestors. For now will they say, 'Behold the leader whom He appointed over them! He sought greatness for himself and begged not mercy on their behalf'!"

Exod. xxxii. 11 expounded. "And Moses besought [*wayyᵉḥal*] the Lord his God" (*ibid. v.* 11): R. Eleazar said: This teaches that Moses stood in prayer before the Holy One, blessed be He, until he wore Him out [*heḥᵉlēhū*][5]. Raba said: [Moses besought Him] until He annulled His vow for him; for it is written here *wayyᵉḥal* "and he besought," and elsewhere it is written, "he shall not break [*yaḥēl*] his word" (Num. xxx. 3); and a teacher has said: [He who makes a vow] cannot break it himself, but others can break it on his behalf[6].

1 To defend his own cause.
2 *M.*: Eleazar.
3 The Patriarchs.
4 Moses alone.
5 With his persistent pleading. Thus the verse is rendered "And Moses wore out the Lord."
6 *Wayyᵉḥal* is here rendered "And Moses absolved the Lord [from His vow]."

Samuel[1] said: It teaches that Moses jeopardised himself unto death on their behalf[2]; as it is said, "And if not, blot me, I pray Thee, out of Thy book which Thou hast written" (Exod. xxxii. 32). Raba said in the name of Rab Isaac: It teaches that he called into play [*ḥāl*] the attribute of mercy upon them[3]. The Rabbis say: It teaches that Moses spake before the Holy One, blessed be He, "Lord of the universe! It would be profanation [*ḥullīn*] for Thee to do such a thing." "And Moses besought the Lord." There is a teaching: R. Eliezer the Elder[4] said: This teaches that Moses stood in prayer before the Holy One, blessed be He, until *ăḥīlū* seized him. What means *ăḥīlū*? R. Eleazar said: The fire of the bones. What means "fire of the bones"? Abbai said: *Eshshātā dᵉgarmē*[5].

"Remember Abraham, Isaac and Israel, Thy servants, to whom Thou didst swear by Thine own self" (*ibid. v.* 13). What means "By Thine own self"? R. Eleazar said: Moses spake before the Holy One, blessed be He, "Lord of the universe! If Thou hadst sworn to them by heaven and earth, I might have said that as heaven and earth will be annulled, so will Thine oath be annulled; but now that Thou hast sworn to them by Thy great name, as Thy great name lives and endures for all eternity, so must Thine oath endure for all eternity." Exod. xxxii. 13 expounded.

"And Thou saidst unto them, I will multiply your seed as the stars of heaven, and all this land that I have spoken of will I give unto your seed" (*ibid.*). The phrase "that I have spoken of" should rather be "that Thou hast spoken of"[6]! R. Eleazar said: Up to here we have the words of the disciple, but from here onwards the words of the Master[7]. R. Samuel b. Naḥmani said: All of them are the words of the disciple; but thus spake Moses before the Holy One, blessed be He, "Lord of the universe! The word which Thou saidst unto me, 'Go, speak to Israel,' I went and spoke in Thy name. And now what can I say to them?" Exposition continued.

[1] *M.*: Joḥanan.

[2] Connecting *wayyᵉḥal* with the root *ḥālal* "to be slain."

[3] Wünsche, p. 51 n. 2, thinks that *wayyᵉḥal* is here to be interpreted as *yāḥūlū* in II Sam. iii. 29.

[4] Or, the Great.

[5] The Aramaic equivalent of the Hebrew words for "fire of the bones," i.e. fever.

[6] Since it is Moses who is now speaking, the actual words of God being considered to end with the word "heaven."

[7] According to this interpretation, "And all this land" etc. is God's answer to Moses' reminder "And Thou saidst...heaven."

Moses' argument on behalf of Israel.

"Because the Lord was not able [*y^e^kōlet*]" (Num. xiv. 16). It should have been *yākōl*[1]! R. Eleazar said: Moses spake before the Holy One, blessed be He, "Lord of the universe! Now will the nations of the world say, 'His strength has become weak like that of a woman and He is unable to deliver [His people]'!" The Holy One, blessed be He, said to Moses, "But have they not already seen the miracles and mighty acts which I wrought for Israel by the Red Sea?" He said before Him, "Lord of the universe! They will still be able to say, 'Against one king[2] He was able to stand, but not against thirty-one[3]'!" R. Joḥanan said: Whence is it that the Holy One, blessed be He, afterwards yielded to Moses? As it is said, "And the Lord said, I have forgiven *according to thy word*" (*ibid. v.* 20). The school of R. Ishmael taught: "According to thy word"—the nations of the world will say thus, "Happy the disciple to whom his Master yielded." "But in very deed, as I live" (*ibid. v.* 21)—Raba said in the name of Rab Isaac: This teaches that the Holy One, blessed be He, said to Moses, "Moses, thou hast made Me to survive [in the estimation of the peoples] with thy word."

Praise of God must precede prayer.

R. Simlai expounded: A man should always recount the praise of the Holy One, blessed be He, and thereafter pray [for his needs]. Whence have we this? From Moses; for it is written, "And I besought the Lord at that time, saying" (Deut. iii. 23). Then it is written, "O Lord God, Thou hast begun to show Thy servant Thy greatness, and Thy strong hand; for what god is there in heaven or on earth, that can do according to Thy works, and according to Thy mighty acts?" (*ibid. v.* 24). And after that it is written, "Let me go over, I pray Thee, and see the good land" etc. (*ibid. v.* 25).

(Mnemonic: Deeds, Charity, Offering, Priest, Fast, Lock, Iron[4].)

fol. 32 b. Prayer greater than good deeds.

R. Eleazar said: Greater is prayer than good deeds; for thou hast no one greater in good deeds than Moses, our teacher, nevertheless he was only answered through prayer; as it is said, "Speak no more unto Me of this matter" (*ibid. v.* 26), which is followed by, "Get thee up into the top of Pisgah" (*ibid. v.* 27)[5].

[1] I.e. the feminine form of the word is used in the text.

[2] Pharaoh.

[3] The kings of Canaan.

[4] There follow on here seven teachings of R. Eleazar, and as an aid to the memory (also to prevent any from being lost in oral transmission) a mnemonic is inserted, giving the key-word of each.

[5] It was his prayer that obtained for him permission to view the land of promise.

R. Eleazar also said: Greater is fasting than charity. What is the reason? The former [demands the sacrifice] of the person, the latter of money.

Fasting superior to charity.

R. Eleazar also said: Greater is prayer than sacrifices; as it is said, "To what purpose is the multitude of your sacrifices unto Me?" (Is. i. 11), and it is written, "And when ye spread forth your hands" (*ibid.* v. 15)[1]. R. Joḥanan said: A *Kōhēn* who has committed murder must not lift up his hands[2]; as it is said, "Your hands are full of blood" (*ibid.*).

Prayer greater than sacrifices.

R. Eleazar also said: From the day the Temple was destroyed, the gates of prayer were locked; as it is said, "Yea, when I cry and call for help, He shutteth out my prayer" (Lam. iii. 8). But although the gates of prayer are locked, the gates of tears remain unlocked; as it is said, "Hear my prayer, O Lord, and give ear unto my cry; keep not silence at my tears" (Ps. xxxix. 13). Raba never proclaimed a fast on a cloudy day, because it is said, "Thou hast covered Thyself with a cloud, so that no prayer can pass through" (Lam. iii. 44).

When Temple destroyed, the gates of prayer were locked but not the gates of tears,

R. Eleazar also said: From the day the Temple was destroyed, a wall of iron divides between Israel and their Father in Heaven; as it is said, "And take thou unto thee an iron griddle, and set it for a wall of iron between thee and the city" (Ezek. iv. 3).

and a wall of iron divided between Israel and God.

R. Ḥannin said in the name of R. Ḥannina: Whoever prolongs his prayer, his prayer will not return empty. Whence have we this? From Moses our teacher; as it is said, "And I prayed unto the Lord" (Deut. ix. 26), and it is afterwards written, "[Now I stayed in the mount...forty days and forty nights;] and the Lord hearkened unto me that time also" (*ibid.* x. 10). But it is not so! For R. Ḥiyya b. Abba has said in the name of R. Joḥanan: Whoever prolongs his prayer and calculates on it[3] will eventually come to pain of heart; as it is said, "Hope[4] deferred maketh the heart sick" (Prov. xiii. 12). What is his remedy? Let him occupy himself with *Tōrāh*; as it is said, "But desire fulfilled is a tree of life" (*ibid.*), and "tree of life" is nothing else than *Tōrāh*, as it is said, "It is a tree of life to them that lay hold upon it"

Prayer deliberately lengthened not acceptable to God.

[1] In supplication. Since the text means that having rejected their sacrifices, God will *even* reject their supplications, it follows that prayer is of higher importance than the offering.

[2] To pronounce the priestly benediction.

[3] I.e. anticipates its fulfilment as a reward for its length.

[4] The word for "hope" is here connected with a root meaning "to pray."

(Prov. iii. 18)! There is no contradiction; the latter teaching refers to one who prolongs his prayer and calculates on it, the former to one who prolongs his prayer without calculating on it.

Unanswered prayer should be repeated.

R. Ḥamma b. Ḥannina said: If a man sees that he prays and is not answered he should repeat his prayer; as it is said, "Wait for the Lord; be strong and let thy heart take courage; yea, wait thou for the Lord" (Ps. xxvii. 14).

Four things require effort.

Our Rabbis have taught: Four things require effort, viz.: *Tōrāh*, good deeds, prayer and worldly occupation. Whence is it that *Tōrāh* and good deeds [require effort]? As it is said, "Only be strong and very courageous to observe to do according to all the law" (Josh. i. 7)—"be strong" in *Tōrāh*, and "very courageous" in good deeds. Whence is it that prayer [requires effort]? As it is said, "Wait for the Lord; be strong, and let thy heart take courage; yea, wait thou for the Lord" (Ps. *l.c.*). Whence is it that worldly occupation [requires effort]? As it is said, "Be of good courage, and let us prove strong for our people" etc. (II Sam. x. 12).

Is. xlix. 14 expounded.

"But Zion said, The Lord hath forsaken me, and the Lord hath forgotten me" (Is. xlix. 14). But a woman forsaken is the same as a woman forgotten! R. Simeon b. Laḳish said: The community of Israel spake before the Holy One, blessed be He, "Lord of the universe! Should a man marry a woman after his first wife, he remembers the deeds of the first; but Thou hast forsaken me and forgotten me!" The Holy One, blessed be He, replied, "My daughter, twelve constellations have I created in the firmament[1], and for each constellation I have created thirty[2] hosts, and for each host I have created thirty legions, and for each legion I have created thirty files, and for each file I have created thirty cohorts, and for each cohort I have created thirty camps[3], and in each camp I have suspended three hundred and sixty-five thousand myriads of stars, in accordance with the days of the solar year, and all of them have I only created for thy sake; and yet thou sayest, 'Thou hast forsaken me, Thou hast forgotten me'!"

[1] *M.* adds: corresponding to the twelve tribes.

[2] Wünsche, p. 53 n. 1, suggests that the number 30 is to be connected with the number of days in the month.

[3] The words used here are the Aramaized forms of the Latin military terms: *legio*, *numerus* (רהטון is possibly a corruption of הרטמון = *ἄριθμος*), *cohors*, *castra*; cf. Krauss, pp. 574 f. On this passage see *A. P. A.* I. p. 396 n. 3, and Krauss in *R. E. J.* XXXIX. pp. 57 f.

"Can a woman forget her sucking child ['ūlāh]?" (Is. xlix. 15). The Holy One, blessed be He, said, "Can I forget the burnt-offerings ['ōlōt] of rams and the firstborn of animals which Thou didst offer to Me in the wilderness?" [The community of Israel] spake before Him, "Lord of the universe! Since there is no forgetfulness before the throne of Thy glory, perhaps Thou wilt not forget against me the incident of the Golden Calf!" He replied, "Yea, 'these' will be forgotten" (*ibid.*)[1]. Israel spake before Him, "Lord of the universe! Since there is forgetfulness before the throne of Thy glory, perhaps Thou wilt forget for me the incident at Sinai!" He replied, "Yet 'the I' will I not forget thee" (*ibid.*)[2]. That is the meaning of R. Eleazar's statement in the name of R. Osha'ya: What is that which is written, "Yea, 'these' will be forgotten"? That refers to the incident of the Golden Calf; "Yet 'the I' will I not forget thee"? That refers to the incident at Sinai.

Is. xlix. 15 expounded.

The pious men of old used to wait an hour.

Whence is this? R. Joshua b. Levi said: The Scriptures state, "Happy are they that *dwell* in Thy house" (Ps. lxxxiv. 5). R. Joshua b. Levi also said: He who prays should wait an hour after his prayer[3]; as it is said, "Surely the righteous shall give thanks unto Thy name, the upright shall *dwell* in Thy presence" (*ibid.* cxl. 14)[4]. There is a teaching to the same effect: He who prays should wait an hour before and an hour after his prayer. Whence is it [that he should wait an hour] before his prayer? As it is said, "Happy are they that dwell in Thy house." Whence is it [that he should wait an hour] after his prayer? As it is said, "Surely the righteous shall give thanks unto Thy name; the upright shall dwell in Thy presence."

Meditation before and after prayer.

Our Rabbis have taught: The pious men of old used to wait an hour, pray for an hour, and again wait an hour. Since they spent nine hours in the day in connection with prayer[5], how was

Meditation and the study of *Tōrāh*.

[1] By a change of vowels "Yea these may forget" becomes "Yea 'these' will be forgotten," i.e., the incident where Israel exclaimed "*These* are thy gods" (Exod. xxxii. 4).

[2] R.V. "Yet will I not forget thee," but the word "I" is emphasized in the Hebrew. Hence it is taken to refer to the incident at Sinai when God declared "*I* am the Lord thy God" (Exod. xx. 2). That will not be forgotten by Him.

[3] In silent meditation.

[4] Here the word "dwell" occurs after "they shall give thanks"; but in the former quotation it is followed by "They are ever praising Thee."

[5] There being three statutory Services daily.

their *Tōrāh* kept up, and how was their work done? But since they were pious, their *Tōrāh* was preserved[1] and their work was blessed[2].

Even when a king greets him, he must not respond.

Tᵉfillāh must not be interrupted for an Israelite king,

Rab Joseph said: This teaching applies only to the Israelite kings; but for the kings of other peoples he must stop. Against this is quoted: He who prays [the *Tᵉfillāh*] and sees a highway robber[3] or waggon coming towards him should not interrupt but shorten it and step back! There is no contradiction; for this means where it is possible to shorten, he should shorten, but if not, he should interrupt.

or for a nobleman.

Our Rabbis have taught: It happened that a pious man was saying the *Tᵉfillāh* by the roadside. A nobleman passed and greeted him; but he did not respond. The nobleman waited until he had concluded his prayer; and after he had concluded it, he said to him, "Good for nothing[4]! Is it not written in your *Tōrāh*, 'Only take heed to thyself, and keep thy soul diligently' (Deut iv. 9) and 'Take ye therefore good heed unto yourselves' (*ibid. v.* 15)? When I greeted thee, why didst thou not return my salutation? If I had cut off thy head with a sword, who would have demanded thy blood at my hand?" He replied, "Wait until I shall have conciliated thee with words." And he continued, "If thou hadst been standing before a human king, and thy friend had greeted thee, wouldst thou have responded to him?" "No," he replied. "And if thou hadst responded to him, what would they have done to thee?" He answered, "They would have cut off my head with the sword." He said to him, "May we not use the *à fortiori* argument: If thou standing before a human king, who is here to-day and to-morrow in the grave, actest thus, how much more so I who was standing before the supreme King of kings, the Holy One, blessed be He, Who lives and endures for all eternity?" The nobleman was at once conciliated, and the pious man departed for his house in peace.

fol. 33 a.

[1] Without constant study.

[2] So that they did not have to devote much time to it.

[3] The word *annōs* is not clear. Since the parallel passage in *J. T.* reads the word for "ass," some (e.g. Pinner) connect it with ὄνος. If a Hebrew word, it means "a man of violence." *M.* reads: *hegmōn*, i.e. ἡγεμών.

[4] See p. 144 n. 7.

And though a serpent is wound round his heel, he must not interrupt.

Rab Sheshet said: This teaching applies only to a serpent, but if it be a scorpion he may interrupt[1]. Against this is quoted: If a man fell into a den of lions, we cannot testify concerning him that he is dead[2]; but if he fell into a pit of serpents or scorpions, we can so testify[3]! It is different in this case, because through the pressure[4] they will injure him. R. Isaac[5] said: If he saw oxen[6], he may interrupt; for Rab Osha'ya taught: One should remove himself fifty cubits from an ox which has never injured anybody and as far as he can see it from an ox whose owner has been warned of its tendency to gore. It has been taught in the name of R. Meïr: Even when the ox has its head in the [fodder-]basket, go up to the roof, and remove the ladder from under thee[7]. Samuel said: This applies only to a black ox in the days of *Nīsān*, because Satan then dances between its horns[8].

Tefillāh may be interrupted when there is danger from a scorpion or wild ox.

Our Rabbis have taught: It happened in a certain place that there was a lizard which injured people. They came and informed R. Ḥannina b. Dosa[9]. He said to them, "Show me its hole." They pointed it out to him, and he placed his heel over the mouth of the hole. The lizard came out and bit him, and it died[10]. He put it on his shoulder and brought it to the House of Study. He said to them, "See, my sons, it is not the lizard that kills but sin that kills." At that time the saying originated: "Woe to the man who meets a lizard; but woe to the lizard which R. Ḥannina b. Dosa meets."

R. Ḥannina b. Dosa and the lizard.

1 The latter being more dangerous.

2 So that his widow can remarry, the presumption being that the lions did not devour him and he escaped.

3 Hence the fear of a serpent is as great as that of a scorpion.

4 Of his falling upon them; but normally they do no harm, if left alone.

5 *M.*: R. Isaac b. Judah.

6 Coming towards him while he is saying the *Tefillāh*.

7 I.e. take all possible precautions.

8 I.e. it is liable to become wild.

9 See p. 113 n. 5.

10 According to *J. T.* R. Ḥannina was saying the *Tefillāh* when the lizard bit him. His disciples asked him whether he had been injured, but he replied that he had felt nothing. They found the lizard dead; and the Rabbi's escape was accounted for by the assertion that when a lizard bites a man, if the man reaches water first, the lizard dies; but if the lizard gets there first, the man dies. In Ḥannina's case, a spring of water miraculously opened at his feet, which sealed the fate of the lizard.

MISHNĀH II

We refer to rain in the benediction of "the Revival of the Dead[1]" and the request [for rain] in the benediction of "the Years[2]," and the "Division" in "Thou favourest man with knowledge[3]." R. 'Aḳiba says: One should say the last-mentioned as a fourth benediction by itself. R. Eliezer says: [It is to be included] in the "Thanksgiving[4]."

G^E^MĀRĀ

We refer to rain in the benediction of "the Revival of the Dead."

Reason for location.

Why? Rab Joseph said: Because it is equal to the revival of the dead[5], therefore they fixed it in the benediction of "the Revival of the Dead."

And the request [for rain] in the benediction of "the Years."

Why? Rab Joseph said: Because it is sustenance, therefore they fixed it in the benediction relating to sustenance.

And the "Division" in "Thou favourest man with knowledge."

Why? Rab Joseph said: Because it is wisdom[6], they fixed it in the benediction relating to wisdom. The Rabbis say: Because it refers to the non-holy, therefore they fixed it in the [first] benediction [of the *T^e^fillāh*] for the week-day.

Greatness of knowledge.

R. Ammi said: Great is knowledge, which is placed at the beginning of the benediction said in the week-day [*T^e^fillāh*]. R. Ammi also said[7]: Great is knowledge which is placed between two references to the Divine Name[8]; as it is said, "For a God of knowledge is the Lord" (I Sam. ii. 3). It is forbidden to have mercy upon one who does not possess knowledge; as it is said, "For it is a people of no understanding, therefore He that made them will not have compassion upon them" (Is. xxvii. 11)[9].

1 See Singer, p. 44 bot.
2 *Ibid.* p. 47.
3 *Ibid.* p. 46.
4 *Ibid.* p. 51, "We give thanks."
5 It revives the produce of nature.
6 It requires wisdom to discern between the holy and the profane.
7 *M.*: R. Eleazar said.
8 *Lit.* between two letters.
9 From "it is forbidden" is omitted in *M.* and several early edd.

R. Eleazar said: Great is the Sanctuary which is placed between two references to the Divine Name; as it is said, "...Thou hast made, O Lord, the sanctuary, O Lord..." (Exod. xv. 17). R. Eleazar also said: Every one who possesses knowledge is as though the Sanctuary was built in his days; for "knowledge" is placed between two references to the Divine Name and "Sanctuary" is similarly placed. Rab Aḥa Ḳarḥinaäh[1] retorted: In that case, great is vengeance which is placed between two references to the Divine Name; as it is said, "A God of vengeance, the Lord" (Ps. xciv. 1)[2]! He replied: Quite so, in certain circumstances it is great; and that is what 'Ulla said: Why is "vengeance" mentioned twice in the verse[3]? One for good, the other for evil—for good, as it is written, "He *shone forth* from Mount Paran" (Deut. xxxiii. 2); for evil, as it is written, "O Lord, Thou God, to Whom vengeance belongeth, Thou God, to Whom vengeance belongeth, *shine forth*" (Ps. xciv. 1).

R. 'Aḳiba says: One should say the last-mentioned as a fourth benediction by itself.

Place of the *Habdālāh.*

Rab Shamman b. Abba said to R. Joḥanan, "It is a fact that the men of the Great Assembly[4] instituted for Israel benedictions and prayers, Sanctifications and Divisions; let us see where it was arranged [for the *Habdālāh* to be said]." He replied to him, "At first they fixed it in the *Tᵉfillāh*; when the people became prosperous[5], they arranged for it to be said over the cup of wine[6]; when the people became poor, they again fixed it in the *Tᵉfillāh*; and they said: He who pronounces the 'Division' in the *Tᵉfillāh* must do it again over the cup of wine." It has been similarly reported: R. Ḥiyya b. Abba said in the name of R. Joḥanan: The men of the Great Assembly instituted for Israel benedictions and prayers, Sanctifications and Divisions. At first they fixed

[1] *M.* reads: Adda b. Ahᵃbah. The parallel passage in Sanh. 92*a* reads: Rab Adda; and there is still another reading: Rab Adda of Ḳarṭignin (see p. 191 n. 8).

[2] So the Hebrew literally.

[3] Or, why is the Hebrew word for "vengeance" in the plural?

[4] According to Jewish tradition, the Great Assembly was a body which came into existence in the time of Ezra, received the *Tōrāh* from the prophets (cf. Ābōt I. 1, Singer, p. 184), and initiated many developments in Judaism (see *J. E.* XI. pp. 640ff.). Modern criticism has thrown doubt upon this tradition (see Schürer II. i. pp. 354f.) and the existence of such a body is questioned. But see Abrahams, *Pharisaism and the Gospels*, p. 9.

[5] And could afford wine.

[6] In the *Habdālāh*, Singer, p. 216.

[the *Habdālāh*] in the *Tefillāh*; when the people became prosperous, they arranged for it to be said over the cup of wine; when they again became poor, they fixed it in the *Tefillāh*; and they said: He who pronounces the "Division" in the *Tefillāh* must do it again over the cup of wine. It has been likewise reported: Rabbah and Rab Joseph both declare: He who pronounces the "Division" in the *Tefillāh* must do it again over the cup of wine.

A contrary opinion refuted.

Raba said: We quote against this teaching: If one erred and omitted the reference to rain in the benediction of "the Revival of the Dead" or the request [for rain] in the benediction of "the Years," we make him repeat it; but [if he omitted] the "Division" in "Thou favourest man with knowledge" we do not make him repeat it, because he is able to say it over the cup of wine! Do not say "because he is able to say it over the cup of wine" but "because he says it over the cup of wine." It has been similarly reported: R. Benjamin b. Jephet said: R. Assi[1] asked R. Johanan in Zidon (another version: R. Simeon b. Jacob of Tyre asked R. Johanan), "But I have heard that one who says the 'Division' in the *Tefillāh* must say it again over the cup of wine; or is it not so?" He replied, "Yes, he must say the *Habdālāh* over the cup of wine."

Habdālāh over the cup of wine does not exempt one from saying it in the *Tefillāh*.

The question was raised: How is it with one who says the *Habdālāh* over the cup of wine, does he say it in the *Tefillāh*? Rab Naḥman b. Isaac replied: We draw an *à fortiori* conclusion from the *Tefillāh*: If of the *Tefillāh* where [the *Habdālāh*] was originally instituted they say: He who pronounced the "Division" in the *Tefillāh* must do so again over the cup of wine, how much more so must one who says the *Habdālāh* over the cup of wine, where it was not originally instituted, [say it in the *Tefillāh*]!

Both references preferable.

R. Aḥa[2] the Tall taught in the presence of Rab Huna[3]: He who pronounces the "Division" in the *Tefillāh* is more praiseworthy than he who says it over the cup of wine; but if he says it in both, may blessings alight upon his head. But this is self-contradictory! Thou declarest, "He who pronounces the 'Division' in the *Tefillāh* is more praiseworthy than he who says it over the cup of wine"; hence it is sufficient to say it in the *Tefillāh* alone! And then he teaches, "But if he says it in both,

[1] So *M.* correctly. Edd.: Josē.

[2] *M.*: Ḥiyya.

[3] So *M.* correctly. Edd.: Ḥinnana.

may blessings alight upon his head"; but since he has fulfilled his obligation with the former, he is exempt and [the latter] will be a superfluous benediction, and Rab has declared (another version: R. Simeon b. Laḳish; or R. Joḥanan and R. Simeon b. Laḳish both declare): Whoever utters a superfluous benediction commits a transgression because of [the injunction], "Thou shalt not take the name of the Lord thy God in vain" (Exod. xx. 7)! Understand him therefore to mean: If he pronounced the "Division" in the *T^e^fillāh* and not over the cup of wine, may blessings alight upon his head.

If *Habdālāh* omitted, the prayer must be repeated. fol. 33 b.

Rab Ḥisda[1] asked Rab Sheshet: If a man erred [and omitted the *Habdālāh*] in both, how is it? He replied: If he erred in both, he must start again. Rabina asked Raba: What is the *H^a^lākāh* [if one pronounced the "Division" in the *T^e^fillāh*, must he say it over the cup of wine]? He replied: It is like the Sanctification; although one sanctifies [the Sabbath] in the *T^e^fillāh*, he must do so over the cup of wine; so also with the *Habdālāh*, although he said it in the *T^e^fillāh*, he must do so over the cup of wine.

Where the *Habdālāh* is to be said on a Festival which occurs on the conclusion of the Sabbath.

R. Eliezer said: [It is to be included] in the "Thanksgiving."

R. Zera was riding on an ass, and R. Ḥiyya b. Abin was following him. He said to him, "Is it really so as thou didst state in the name of R. Joḥanan: The *H^a^lākāh* is in agreement with R. Eliezer on a Festival which occurs on the conclusion of the Sabbath?" He replied, "Yes." "The *H^a^lākāh* being so, is it to be inferred that there are some who differ from him[2]? Are there not, indeed, some who differ?" "The Rabbis differ from him." "On which point do the Rabbis differ?" "On the other days of the year[3]." "Do they differ on the question of a Festival which occurs at the conclusion of the Sabbath? Behold R. 'Aḳiba differs[4]!" "Do we, then, act in accordance with R. 'Aḳiba the whole year, that we should now agree and act in accord with his view? Why do we not act in agreement with R. 'Aḳiba the whole year? Because eighteen benedictions were instituted, not nineteen; and so here also, seven benedictions

[1] *M.*: Abbai.

[2] There being no mention in the *Mishnāh* of any opposition to his view.

[3] When a Festival begins with the termination of the Sabbath, they agree with R. Eliezer that the "Division" is included in the "Thanksgiving"; but not when the Sabbath is followed by an ordinary week-day.

[4] In the *Mishnāh* he maintains that the "Division" is not included in any of the benedictions, but is a separate benediction.

were instituted, not eight[1]." [R. Zera] said to him: It has not been reported that the *H^a^lākāh* [is in accord with R. Eliezer], but it has been reported that we incline [towards his view][2]. For it has been reported: Rab Isaac b. Abdemi said in the name of our teacher[3]: The *H^a^lākāh* [is in accord with R. Eliezer]; but some say: We incline [towards his view]. R. Joḥanan said: [The Rabbis] acknowledge [that the *H^a^lākāh* is in agreement with him]. R. Ḥiyya b. Abba said: [R. Eliezer's opinion] is probable. R. Zera said: Take the statement of R. Ḥiyya b. Abba in thine hand[4], because he is most careful to report a teaching exactly as it issued from the mouth of his teacher; like Raḥba of Pombedita[5]. For Raḥba said in the name of R. Judah: The Temple-mount was a double colonnade, and it was a colonnade within a colonnade[6].

Wording of the *Habdālāh* prayer on a Festival.

Rab Joseph said: I know neither the one nor the other[7]; but from Rab and Samuel I know that they instituted a "pearl"[8] for us in Babylon: "Thou, O Lord our God, hast made known unto us the judgments of Thy righteousness; Thou hast taught us to perform the statutes of Thy will. Thou hast caused us to inherit seasons of joy and feasts of free will gifts, and hast given us as an heritage the holiness of the Sabbath, the glory of the appointed time, and the celebration of the festival. Thou hast made a distinction between the holiness of the Sabbath and that of the festival, and hast hallowed the seventh day above the six working days; Thou hast distinguished and sanctified Thy people Israel by Thy holiness. And Thou hast given us," etc.

[1] Viz. the three introductory and three concluding benedictions of the *T^e^fillāh* and the benediction for the Festival. Cf. above fol. 29 *a*, p. 192.

[2] I.e. it is not taught in the Schools as a *H^a^lākāh*, but if a Rabbi is asked for his opinion, he follows R. Eliezer's view.

[3] The reference here is to Rabbi, not Rab.

[4] I.e. note it well.

[5] After the destruction of the Seminary of Nehardea in 259, that of Pombedita sprang into prominence and the town received the name of "Capital of the Exile" (Rōsh. Hash. 23 *b*). It is situated 22 parasangs North of Sura in Babylon, at the mouth [*pōmā*] of the canal Bedita. Neubauer, p. 349.

[6] This is quoted to show how Raḥba reported his teacher *verbatim*. The ordinary word for a colonnade is אצטבא; but since R. Judah used the word סטיו *στοά*, Raḥba also used it in quoting him. On this double colonnade see Derenbourg, *Essai*, p. 51 n., Schürer, II. i. p. 35.

[7] That we "incline" towards R. Eliezer's opinion or that his view is "probable."

[8] A "precious" form of prayer to be used when the Festival occurs on the termination of the Sabbath. Cf. Singer, pp. 227 f.

MISHNĀH III

Whoever says [in his Tefillāh] *"To a bird's nest do Thy mercies extend*[1]*" or "For the good be Thy name remembered*[2]*" or "We give thanks, we give thanks*[3]*," him do we silence.*

GEMĀRĀ

Objection to the prayers cited in the *Mishnāh.*

It is right that we silence him who says, "We give thanks, we give thanks," because he makes it appear as though there were two Powers[4]; and likewise him who says, "For the good be Thy name remembered," the inference being that for the good [may it be remembered] but not for the bad; and we have a Mishnaic teaching: *A man is in duty bound to utter a benediction for the bad even as he utters one for the good*[5]. But why [do we silence him who says], "To a bird's nest do Thy mercies extend"? Two *Amorāīm* in the West[6] differ, viz.: R. Josē b. Abin and R. Josē b. Zebida: one said: Because he causes jealousy between God's creatures[7]; the other said: Because he makes the ordinances of the Holy One, blessed be He, to be simply acts of mercy, whereas they are injunctions[8].

Why Rabbah pretended to approve of such a prayer.

A certain man went down [to the Ark][9] in the presence of Rabbah and said, "Thou hast compassion on a bird's nest; do Thou have compassion and mercy upon us." Rabbah exclaimed, "How this Rabbinical scholar knows how to find favour with his Lord[10]!" Abbai said to him, "Lo, we have learnt in the *Mishnāh*: *We silence him!*" But Rabbah merely wished to test Abbai[11].

[1] The reference is to Deut. xxii. 6 f.

[2] Implying, not for the bad.

[3] Repeating the words; see below in the *Gemārā*.

[4] The dualism—a god of light and a god of darkness—of the Persians.

[5] See fol. 54*a*, p. 348.

[6] I.e. Palestine.

[7] By mentioning birds only.

[8] Which must be obeyed without speculating about their motive. J. Lehmann in *R.E.J.* xxx. pp. 187 ff. suggests that the prayer was originally condemned by the Rabbis because it was Essenic in character. Graetz considers the teaching to be directed against the Gnostics; see his *Gnosticismus und Judentum*, pp. 48 f.

[9] To act as Precentor.

[10] Apparently commending his prayer.

[11] Abbai was his pupil, and Rabbah wished to see whether he knew our *Mishnāh*.

Exaggerated form of praise denounced.

A certain man went down [to the Ark] in the presence of R. Ḥannina. He said[1], "O God, the great, the mighty, the revered, the glorious, the powerful, the feared, the strong, the courageous, the certain, the honoured." R. Ḥannina waited until he had finished. When he had finished, he said to him, "Hast thou exhausted all the praises of thy Lord? What is the use of all those [adjectives]? The three which we do say[2], if Moses our teacher had not used them in the *Tōrāh*[3] and the men of the Great Assembly[4] come and instituted them in the *T^e^fillāh*, we should not have been able to say; and thou dost go on saying all those!" A parable: [It may be likened] to a human king who possessed a million golden *denarii*[5], and people kept praising him as the possessor of [a million *denarii* of][6] silver; is it not an insult to him?

The fear of Heaven.

R. Ḥannina also said: Everything is in the hand of Heaven except the fear of Heaven[7]; as it is said, "And now, O Israel, what doth the Lord thy God require of thee but to fear" (Deut. x. 12). Is, then, the fear of Heaven a small thing[8]? Lo, R. Ḥannina has said in the name of R. Simeon b. Joḥai[9]: The Holy One, blessed be He, has in His treasury nothing but the store of heavenly fear; as it is said, "And the fear of the Lord which is His treasure" (Is. xxxiii. 6)! Yes, in the estimation of Moses it was a small thing; for R. Ḥannina said: A parable: [It may be likened] to a man from whom a large vessel is required; possessing it, it seems to him small; but if he does not possess it, though it be small, it seems to him large.

Wording of prayer must not be duplicated.

[*Who says*], "*We give thanks,*" *him do we silence.*

R. Zera said: Whoever says *Sh^e^ma'*, *Sh^e^ma'*[10] is like him who says "We give thanks, we give thanks" [and is to be silenced]. Against this is quoted: He who reads the *Sh^e^ma'* and repeats the

[1] At the beginning of the first benediction of the *T^e^fillāh*.

[2] "The great, mighty and revered."

[3] Deut. x. 17.

[4] See p. 221 n. 4. The words also occur in Nehem. ix. 32; and Ezra and his colleagues were traditionally the founders of the Great Assembly.

[5] See p. 120 n. 5.

[6] The words in brackets are added by *M.* and the parallel passage in M^e^gillāh 25 *a*.

[7] I.e. God determines whether the person will be tall or short, rich or poor, etc.; but not whether he will be God-fearing or not. That is left to his own choice.

[8] That God should demand nothing else.

[9] *M.*: Lo, R. Joḥanan has said.

[10] This is explained to mean saying the *Sh^e^ma'* verse by verse twice. Blau, *Das altjüdische Zauberwesen*, p. 147, suggests that the original reason for the prohibition is to be sought in the practice of repeating a prayer for superstitious or magical purposes.

words is to be reprimanded. He is to be reprimanded, but not silenced! There is no contradiction. This refers to one who repeats it word by word; but the former refers to him who repeats it verse by verse[1]. Rab Pappa asked Abbai: But perhaps he at first did not direct his mind and finally did so[2]! He replied: Has any- **fol. 34 a.** one intimacy with Heaven[3]? If he did not at first direct his mind [to his prayer], we smite him with a smith's hammer until he does direct his mind[4].

MISHNĀH IV

He who says in his Tᵉfillāh *"The good bless Thee," behold this is the way of error*[5]. *If a man step before the Ark*[6] *and make a mistake [in the* Tᵉfillāh], *another replaces him; and at such a time, one may not decline*[7]. *From where does the latter begin? From the commencement of the benediction where the other erred. He who steps before the Ark should not respond "Amen" after [the benedictions of] the* Kōhᵃnīm[8] *because it might cause him confusion. If there be no other* Kōhēn *there but himself, he does not raise his hands [for the priestly benediction]; but if he is confident that he can raise his hands and return to the* Tᵉfillāh[9], *he is permitted.*

GᴱMĀRĀ

How to treat an invitation to act as Precentor.

Our Rabbis have taught: [If one is invited] to step before the Ark, he should first decline[10]; should he not do so, he is like cooking without salt. But if he decline unduly, he is like cooking spoilt by over-salting. How should he act? The first time [of asking] he declines; the second time he wavers; the third time he stretches his legs and descends [before the Ark].

[1] In this latter case he may be suspected of dualism.

[2] And thus there is no ground of suspicion; so why should he be silenced?

[3] I.e. has anyone the right to address God thoughtlessly as one talks with a familiar friend?

[4] That means, we forcibly impress upon him the necessity of *Kawwānāh*.

[5] The word "error" has been substituted for *Mīnūt* through fear of the Censor. This whole sentence is wanting in the editions of the *Mishnāh* and in *J.T.*

[6] To act as Precentor.

[7] The invitation to officiate; see the *Gᵉmārā*.

[8] See Singer, p. 238*a* (10th ed.) and above, p. 104 n. 3.

[9] Without making a mistake in the prayers.

[10] As a sign of humility, that he is not fit for the sacred duty.

Where excess is bad.

Our Rabbis have taught: There are three things where excess is bad and a small quantity pleasant: leaven, salt and declining an office.

If the Precentor erred in the *Tᵉfillāh.*

Rab Huna said: If he erred in the first three benedictions [of the *Tᵉfillāh*], he commences again at the beginning; if in the middle benedictions, he returns to "Thou favourest man with knowledge[1]"; if in the last [three], he returns to the "Service[2]." Rab Assi said: The middle benedictions have no order[3]. Rab Sheshet quoted in objection: *From where does the latter begin? From the commencement of the benediction where the other erred!* This is a refutation of Rab Huna; but Rab Huna can reply: The middle benedictions are all one benediction[4].

Where personal supplication may be inserted in the *Tᵉfillāh.*

Rab Judah said[5]: A man should never pray for his personal needs in the first three or last three benedictions, but in the middle ones. For R. Ḥannina[6] said: [When saying] the first three benedictions, he is like a slave recounting praise before his master; [when saying] the middle benedictions, he is like a slave begging a reward from his master; [when saying] the last three benedictions, he is like a slave who, receiving a reward from his master, takes his departure and goes away.

On long and short prayers.

Our Rabbis have taught: It happened that a disciple who descended before the Ark in the presence of R. Eliezer unduly prolonged [the prayers]. His disciples said to him, "Our master, what a prolonger he is!" He replied, "Did he prolong more than Moses, our teacher, of whom it is written, 'The forty days and forty nights that I fell down'" (Deut. ix. 25)? It again happened that a disciple who descended before the Ark in the presence of R. Eliezer unduly shortened [the prayers]. His disciples said to him, "What a shortener he is!" He replied, "Did he shorten more than Moses, our teacher; for it is written, 'Heal her now, O God, I beseech Thee'" (Num. xii. 13)[7]? R. Jacob said in the

[1] Singer, p. 46.

[2] *Ibid.* p. 50, "Accept, O Lord our God."

[3] Rashi explains: If he omitted one of the middle benedictions, he can insert it anywhere amongst them when he recalls his omission. Tōsāfōt reject this interpretation and explain: If he omitted one of the middle benedictions and remembers the omission before commencing the concluding benedictions, he goes back to the one omitted and then continues from there, repeating those he had already said.

[4] And should one err in any of them, he goes back to the beginning of the fourth.

[5] *M.* adds: in the name of Rab.

[6] *M.*: Rab Huna.

[7] In the Hebrew, the prayer consists of five monosyllables.

name of Rab Ḥisda: Whoever prays on behalf of another need not mention his name; as it is said, "Heal her now, O God, I beseech Thee," without mentioning Miriam's name.

Where one bows in the *Tefillāh*.

Our Rabbis have taught: These are the benedictions at which a man bends low; at the beginning and end of the "Patriarchs[1]" and at the beginning and end of the "Thanksgiving[2]." Should anyone come to bend low at the end and beginning of every benediction, we tell him not to do so. R. Simeon b. Pazzi said in the name of R. Joshua b. Levi in the name of Bar Ḳappara: The ordinary man [acts] as we have stated; a high priest [bends] at **fol. 34 b.** the end of each benediction; a king at the beginning and end of each benediction. R. Isaac b. Naḥmani said: It was explained to me by R. Joshua b. Levi: The ordinary man [acts] as we have stated; a high priest [bends] at the beginning of each benediction; a king, when once he bends, should not straighten himself [until the end of the *Tefillāh*]; as it is said, "And it was so, that when Solomon had *made an end* of praying all this prayer and supplication unto the Lord, he arose from before the altar of the Lord from kneeling on his knees" (I Kings viii. 54).

Bowing, bending and prostrating defined.

Our Rabbis have taught: "Bowing" means upon the face; as it is said, "Then Bath Sheba bowed with her face to the earth" (*ibid.* i. 31). "Bending" means upon the knees[3]; as it is said, "From kneeling on his knees" (*ibid.* viii. 54). "Prostrating" means spreading out the hands and legs; as it is said, "Shall I and thy mother and thy brethren indeed come to prostrate ourselves to thee to the earth?" (Gen. xxxvii. 10). Rab Ḥiyya b. Rab Huna said: I saw Abbai and Raba just recline on their side[4]. One taught: He who bends the knee in the "Thanksgiving" is praiseworthy; but there is another teaching: Such an one is to be reprimanded! There is no contradiction; one referring to the beginning, the other to the end [of the benediction]. Raba bent the knee at the beginning and end of the "Thanksgiving." The Rabbis asked him, "Why has the master acted so?" He replied, "I saw Rab Naḥman bend the knee, and I saw Rab Sheshet do it.

[1] The first benediction of the *Tefillāh*.

[2] "We give thanks unto Thee," Singer, p. 51, and "Whose name is all-good," p. 53.

[3] Later authorities forbade kneeling in prayer, because it was characteristic of Christian worship. Prostration has also fallen into disuse; but it was practised in the French Synagogues as late as the 13th cent. Abrahams, p. lxxvii.

[4] When prostrating, not spreading out the hands and legs.

Moreover, the teaching: He who bends the knee in the 'Thanksgiving' is to be reprimanded—refers to the 'Thanksgiving' in the *Hallēl*[1]." And the teaching: He who bends the knee in the "Thanksgiving" of the *T^e^fillāh* and in the "Thanksgiving" of the *Hallēl* is to be reprimanded—to what does this refer? To the "Thanksgiving" in the Grace after meals[2].

MISHNĀH V

If one errs while saying the T^e^fillāh, *it is a bad omen for him; and should he be the messenger of the congregation*[3], *it is a bad omen for those who deputed him, since a man's deputy is similar to himself. They declared concerning R. Ḥannina b. Dosa*[4] *that when praying on behalf of the sick, he would say, "This one will live, that one will die." They asked him, "How knowest thou?" He replied, "If my prayer is fluent in my mouth, I know that he is accepted; but if not, I know that he is rejected."*

G^E^MĀRĀ

Error in the first benediction only a bad omen.

To which[5]? R. Ḥiyya[6] stated that Rab Safra said in the name of one attached to the school of Rabbi[7]: To the "Patriarchs[8]." Others refer this [statement of Rab Safra] to the following *Bārāitā*: One who says the *T^e^fillāh* must direct his heart to each benediction; but if unable to do so to each one, he must at least direct his heart to one. To which? R. Ḥiyya stated that Rab Safra said in the name of one attached to the school of Rabbi: To the "Patriarchs."

Scriptural authority for what is narrated of R. Ḥannina b. Dosa.

They declared concerning R. Ḥannina b. Dosa, etc.

Whence is this? R. Joshua b. Levi[9] said: For the Scriptures state, "Peace, peace to him that is far off and to him that is near, saith the Lord that createth[10] the fruit of the lips; and I will heal him" (Is. lvii. 19).

[1] Singer, p. 222 "O give thanks unto the Lord."

[2] *Ibid.* p. 281 "For all this" etc.

[3] The one asked to act as Precentor.

[4] See p. 113 n. 5.

[5] Of the benedictions of the *T^e^fillāh* does the *Mishnāh* refer when it declares that to err therein is a bad omen?

[6] This is probably R. Ḥiyya b. Rab Huna; cf. Hyman II. p. 444*a*.

[7] *M.*: R. Jannai.

[8] The first benediction.

[9] *M.*: R. Ḥiyya b. Abba, said in the name of R. Joḥanan.

[10] *Bōrē'* besides meaning "createth" has also the meaning "is strong"; hence the interpretation here is "If the fruit of the lips [i.e. prayer] is vigorous, fluent, then I will heal him."

R. Ḥiyya b. Abba said in the name of R. Joḥanan: Every prophet prophesied only to marry his daughter to a disciple of the wise, and for him who transacts the affairs of a disciple of the wise and allows him to enjoy his possessions; but as for the disciples of the wise themselves, "No eye hath seen what God, and nobody but Thee[1], will work for him that waiteth for Him" (Is. lxiv. 3)[2]. Glory of the disciples of the wise.

R. Ḥiyya b. Abba also said in the name of R. Joḥanan: Every prophet only prophesied for the days of the Messiah; but as for the world to come, "No eye hath seen what God, and nobody but Thee, will work for him that waiteth for Him." This is at variance with the opinion of Samuel who said: There is no difference between this world and the days of the Messiah, except the servitude of the heathen kingdoms alone; as it is said, "For the poor shall never cease out of the land" (Deut. xv. 11)[3]. Prophets prophesied for the days of the Messiah.

R. Ḥiyya b. Abba also said in the name of R. Joḥanan: Every prophet only prophesied for the penitent; but as for the perfectly righteous, "No eye hath seen what God, and nobody but Thee, will work for him that waiteth for Him." This is at variance with the opinion of R. Abbahu who said: The place which the penitent occupy, the perfectly righteous are unable to occupy; as it is said, "Peace, peace to him that is far off and to him that is near"—"to him that is far off [from God]" first, and then "to him that is near." But R. Joḥanan can reply: What means "To him that is far off"? To him who was far off from transgression from the first; and what means "To him that is near"? To him that was near transgression and has now removed himself therefrom. They prophesied for the penitent.

What is the significance of "No eye hath seen" etc.? R. Joshua b. Levi said: It refers to the wine preserved in the grape from the six days of creation. R. Samuel b. Naḥmani[4] said: It refers to Eden[5], upon which the eye of no creature has gazed. Perhaps thou wilt ask: Where, then, was Adam? In the Garden. But perhaps thou wilt say that the Garden is the same as Eden! Therefore there is a teaching to tell thee, "And a river went out of Eden to water the Garden" (Gen. ii. 10). Hence the Garden and Eden are distinct. What is treasured for the righteous.

[1] I.e. it has not been revealed to any prophet.

[2] *Sic.* R.V. "Neither hath any eye seen a God beside Thee, which worketh for him that waiteth for Him."

[3] Not even in the Messianic era.

[4] Read probably R. Simeon b. Laḳish; cf. *A.P.A.* I. p. 416 n. 4.

[5] Paradise.

R. Ḥannina b. Dosa prays for Rabban Gamaliel's son.

Our Rabbis have taught: It once happened that the son of Rabban Gamaliel was ill. He sent two disciples of the wise to R. Ḥannina b. Dosa to pray on his behalf. When he saw them, he ascended to an upper chamber and prayed on his behalf. On descending he said to them, "Go, the fever has left him." They said to him, "Art thou a prophet?" He replied, "'I am no prophet nor a prophet's son' (Amos vii. 14); but so is my tradition: If my prayer is fluent in my mouth, I know that he is accepted; but if not, I know that he is rejected." They sat down and wrote and noted the time. When they came to Rabban Gamaliel, he said to them, "By the Temple-service! You have neither understated nor overstated [the time]. But thus it happened; at that very hour the fever left him, and he asked us for water to drink."

And for Rabban Joḥanan b. Zakkai's son.

It also happened with R. Ḥannina b. Dosa that he went to study *Tōrāh* with Rabban Joḥanan b. Zakkai. The son of Rabban Joḥanan b. Zakkai fell ill, and he said to him, "Ḥannina, my son! Pray on his behalf that he may live." R. Ḥannina laid his head between his knees, and prayed on his behalf, and he recovered. Rabban Joḥanan b. Zakkai said, "Were Ben Zakkai to press his head between his knees all the day long, no notice would be taken of him." His wife said to him, "Is, then, Ḥannina greater than thou?" He replied, "No; he is like a slave before the King[1], and I like a nobleman before the King."

One should pray in a room which has windows.

R. Ḥiyya b. Abba also said in the name of R. Joḥanan: A man should not pray except in a room which has windows; as it is said, "Now his windows were open in his upper chamber towards Jerusalem" (Dan. vi. 11)[2].

One need not mention the name of him on whose behalf he prays.

R. Jacob b. Iddi said in the name of R. Joḥanan: Whoever prays on behalf of another need not mention his name. Whence have we this? From Moses, our teacher; as it is said, "Heal her now, O God, I beseech Thee" (Num. xii. 13), without mentioning Miriam's name[3].

Impertinent to pray in a valley or to recount one's sins.

Rab Kahᵃna said: I consider him impertinent who prays in a valley[4]. Rab Kahᵃna also said: I consider him impertinent who recounts his sins[5]; as it is said, "Happy is he whose transgression is forgiven, whose sin is pardoned[6]" (Ps. xxxii. 1).

May we return unto thee: *One must not stand.*

[1] The palace-slave keeps constantly entering the presence of the king, whereas the nobleman has to wait for a summons. [2] Repeated from fol. 31 *a*, p. 205.

[3] Some edd. omit this paragraph, which occurs on fol. 34 *a*, p. 229 as the teaching of R. Jacob in the name of Rab Ḥisda.

[4] Where people are constantly passing. One should pray in a secluded spot.

[5] Openly, as though not ashamed of them. [6] *Lit.* covered, i.e. not exposed.

CHAPTER VI

MISHNĀH I

fol. 35 a.

What benediction do we say over fruit? Over the fruit of trees, one says, "[Blessed art Thou, O Lord our God, King of the universe] Who createst the fruit of the tree," except over wine; for over wine one says, "... Who createst the fruit of the vine." Over the fruits of the earth one says: "... Who createst the fruit of the ground," except over bread; for over bread one says, "... Who bringest forth bread from the earth." Over vegetables one says, "... Who createst the fruit of the ground"; but R. Judah declares: "... Who createst divers kinds of herbs."

GᴱMĀRĀ

Biblical authority for the benediction.

Whence is this derived[1]? For our Rabbis have taught: "The fruit thereof shall be holy, for giving praise [*hillūlīm*][2] unto the Lord" (Lev. xix. 24)—this teaches that they require a benediction before and after partaking of them. Hence said R. 'Aḳiba: A man is forbidden to taste anything without previously saying a benediction.

Explanation of the Scriptural verse questioned.

But is the phrase "holy for giving praise" intended to teach that? Surely it is required [to teach as follows:] First, that the All-merciful declares [the owner] must redeem it[3] and then eat it; and second, only those things which require "a song of praise" require redemption, but if they do not require "a song of praise," redemption is unnecessary[4]! This is according to the statement of R. Samuel b. Naḥmani in the name of R. Jonathan who said: Whence is it that we say "a song of praise" only over wine? As

[1] That a benediction is necessary.

[2] The word is in the plural, and being unspecified is considered to mean two. There must accordingly be two praises (i.e. benedictions), one before and one after.

[3] The fruit grown in the fourth year, of which Lev. xix. 24 speaks. That fruit is declared to be "holy" and may not be eaten, unless previously redeemed.

[4] This will be explained as referring only to the fruit of the vineyard. Since these two teachings are drawn from the use of the plural *hillūlīm*, it cannot mean that a benediction is necessary before and after partaking of fruits.

it is said, "And the vine said unto them, Should I leave my wine which cheereth God and man?" (Judges ix. 13). If it cheereth man, how does it cheer God? Hence it is to be inferred that we have "a song of praise" only over wine[1].

The necessity for the benediction established.

It is quite right[2] according to him who teaches "the *planting* of the fourth year[3]"; but according to him who teaches "the *vineyard* of the fourth year" what is there to say[4]? For it has been reported: R. Ḥiyya and R. Simeon b. Rabbi [differ]; one teaches "The vineyard of the fourth year," the other teaches "The planting of the fourth year." According to him who teaches "the vineyard of the fourth year" it is quite right[5] if he argues by analogy of expression[6]; for there is a teaching: Rabbi says: It is stated here, "That it may yield unto you more richly the increase thereof" (Lev. xix. 25), and it is stated elsewhere, "the increase of the vineyard" (Deut. xxii. 9)—as in the latter passage "increase" refers to the vineyard, so also in the former passage it refers to the vineyard; and there thus remains over one *hillūl* to be interpreted as meaning that a benediction is required [when partaking of fruits]. But if he does not resort to this argument from analogy, whence does he derive the necessity for a benediction? And even if he resort to this method of reasoning, we find that a benediction is required after eating[7]; but whence is it that a benediction is necessary before eating? This is no difficulty; for we can use *a fortiori* reasoning—if he is to bless God when he is satisfied, how much more so when he is hungry[8]!

Everything that is enjoyed requires a benediction.

We find this in connection with [the produce of] the vineyard[9]; whence is it [that a benediction is required with] other species? It can be derived from the instance of the vineyard—as the vineyard, a thing that is enjoyed, requires a benediction, so also every-

[1] Only when a drink-offering was brought did the choir of the Levites sing in the Temple; and in this way the wine "cheered" God.

[2] That *hillūlīm* refers to the benediction before and after fruits.

[3] That Lev. xix. 24 refers to all fruit of the fourth year and not to the vine only; consequently the second deduction from *hillūlīm* need not be used to prove that only the vine requires redemption, but can be used to show that a benediction is required when partaking of fruits.

[4] Since the second deduction from *hillūlim* is required to prove that only the vine required redemption, how does he show that a benediction is required when partaking of fruits?

[5] That the second *hillūl* can also show that the benediction is required over fruits.

[6] See p. 18 n. 5.

[7] Cf. Deut. viii. 10.

[8] And he is about to satisfy his hunger.

[9] The reasoning in the preceding paragraph is based on the assumption that Lev. xix. 24 refers to a vineyard.

thing which is enjoyed requires a benediction. But it is possible to object: Why [is a benediction required with the fruit of] the vineyard? Because there is the obligation of the gleanings[1]. Let, then, the instance of corn show [whether this point is material][2]! But why [is a benediction required when partaking of food made from] corn? Because there is the obligation of *Ḥallāh*. Then let the instance of the vineyard show [whether this point is material][3]! The argument has therefore to be reinstated[4], because the feature of the first case is not like that of the second and *vice versa*[5]; but the factor common to both is that each is something which is enjoyed and consequently requires a benediction. Hence everything which is enjoyed requires a benediction.

An objection raised.

How is this[6] the factor common to them both? [That they are both brought upon] the altar is likewise a common factor[7]! Then the olive must also be included because it likewise has this factor of [being brought to] the altar! Does, then, the olive need inclusion because of the factor of the altar? Behold, the expression *kérem* "vineyard" is explicitly written in connection therewith; for it is stated, "And he burnt up the shocks and the standing corn, and also the olive-yards[8]" (Judges xv. 5)! Rab Pappa answered: It is called "a *kérem* of olives" but not *kérem* without qualification. Nevertheless the difficulty remains, "How is this the factor common to them both? [That they are both brought upon] the altar is likewise a common factor."

Necessity of benediction derived from the "seven species."

One can, however, derive [the necessity for a benediction] from "the seven species[9]"—as "the seven species" are things enjoyed and require a benediction, so everything that is enjoyed requires a benediction. But why do "the seven species" [require a bene-

[1] Cf. Lev. xix. 10. Since the gleanings have to be left behind, he must say a benediction over what he enjoys of the vineyard; but the law of gleanings does not apply to other fruits, therefore the inference just drawn is not valid.

[2] The law of gleanings does not apply to corn; and yet a benediction is necessary over bread.

[3] It is not, because *Ḥallāh* does not apply to the vineyard, and yet the latter requires a benediction.

[4] The objections having been disposed of.

[5] Viz. gleanings and *Ḥallāh*.

[6] That they are both enjoyed.

[7] In the drink-offering and meal-offering; hence other fruits do not come in the same category for the purpose of the benediction.

[8] Lit. "vineyard of olives." Since the olive is included because *kérem* is mentioned in connection therewith, the objection that the common factor is the altar lapses.

[9] Cf. Deut. viii. 8.

diction]? Because they are under the obligation of first-fruits[1]. And further, it is right [that a benediction is necessary] after partaking of them, but whence is it [that a benediction is necessary] before partaking of them? That is no difficulty; because it can be derived by *a fortiori* reasoning—if he says a benediction when satisfied, how much more so when hungry! According to him who teaches "the planting of the fourth year" it is quite right [that a benediction is required] for everything that is *planted*; but whence [does he derive the necessity for a benediction] for things not planted, like meat, eggs, fish? It is, however, a generally held opinion that a man is forbidden to enjoy anything of this world without a benediction[2].

To enjoy anything without uttering a benediction is sacrilege.

Our Rabbis have taught: A man is forbidden to enjoy anything of this world without a benediction, and whoever does so commits sacrilege[3]. What is the remedy? Let him go to a Sage. Let him go to a Sage! What can he do for him, seeing that he has done what is forbidden? But, said Raba: [The meaning is,] let him from the first go to a Sage who will teach him the benedictions, so that he should not come to commit sacrilege.

It is like partaking of the holy things of God.

Rab Judah said in the name of Samuel: Whoever enjoys anything of this world without a benediction is as though he had partaken of the holy things of Heaven; as it is said, "The earth is the Lord's, and the fulness thereof" (Ps. xxiv. 1). R. Levi asked: It is written, "The earth is the Lord's and the fulness thereof," and it is written, "The heavens are the heavens of the Lord, but the earth hath He given to the children of men" (*ibid.* cxv. 16)! There is no contradiction; the former passage referring
fol. 35 b. to before the benediction [has been uttered], the latter to after the benediction.

It is like robbing God.

R. Ḥannina b. Pappa said: Whoever enjoys anything of this world without a benediction is as though he robbed the Holy One,

[1] From the common use of "land" in Deut. viii. 8 and *ibid.* xxvi. 2 it is deduced that the law of first-fruit applies only to the "seven species" (see Mᵉnāḥōt 84 *b*). Therefore the necessity for a benediction with things outside this category has still to be proved.

[2] This statement not only answers the question about things which are not planted, but also the question about the factor of "first-fruit" in connection with the seven species.

[3] The word used here, *mā'al*, refers to the offence of utilising property belonging to the Temple by a non-priest. The Universe is regarded as the Divine Temple; but by virtue of the benediction, one becomes consecrated and permitted to partake of its produce.

blessed be He, and the Community of Israel[1]; as it is said, "Whoso robbeth his father or his mother and saith, It is no transgression, the same is the companion of a destroyer" (Prov. xxviii. 24)—"father" is none other than the Holy One, blessed be He; as it is said, "Is not He thy father that hath gotten thee?" (Deut. xxxii. 6); and "mother" is none other than the Community of Israel; as it is said, "Hear, my son, the instruction of thy father, and forsake not the teaching of thy mother" (Prov. i. 8). What means "the companion of a destroyer"? R. Ḥannina b. Pappa said: He is the companion of Jeroboam, the son of Nebat, who corrupted Israel against their Father in Heaven.

Contradictory verses reconciled.

R. Ḥannina b. Pappa asked: It is written, "Therefore will I take back My corn in the time thereof" etc. (Hosea ii. 11), and it is written, "And thou shalt gather in thy corn" etc. (Deut. xi. 14)! There is no contradiction; the latter referring to the time when Israel perform the will of the All-present, the former to when Israel neglect His will.

Duty of earning a livelihood.

Our Rabbis have taught: "And thou shalt gather in thy corn"—what has this teaching to tell us? Since it is written, "This book of the law shall not depart out of thy mouth [but thou shalt meditate therein day and night]" (Josh. i. 8), it is possible to think that these words [are to be understood] as they are written[2]; therefore there is a teaching to say, "And thou shalt gather in thy corn," i.e. conduct at the same time a worldly occupation. These are the words of R. Ishmael. R. Simeon b. Joḥai says: Is it possible for a man to plough at the time of ploughing, sow at seed-time, reap at harvest-time, thresh at the time of threshing, and winnow at the time of wind[3]—what is to become of *Tōrāh*? But when Israel perform the will of the All-present, their work is done by others; as it is said, "And strangers shall stand and feed your flocks," etc. (Is. lxi. 5); and at the time when Israel perform not the will of the All-present, their work has to be done by themselves; as it is said, "And *thou* shalt gather in thy corn." Not that alone, but the work of others will be done by them; as it is said, "And thou shalt serve thine enemy" etc. (Deut. xxviii. 48). Abbai said: Many acted in accord with the teaching of

[1] By omitting to pay to God the benediction due to Him, he withholds the divine blessing from Israel and the fields will not be fruitful.

[2] I.e. taken literally, and consequently no time be devoted to earning a livelihood.

[3] And in addition find leisure for *Tōrāh*.

R. Ishmael[1] and it proved efficacious; but he who acted in accord with R. Simeon b. Joḥai did not find it so. Raba said to the Rabbis: I beg of you not to appear before me during the days of *Nīsān* and *Tishrī*[2], so that you may not be concerned about your maintenance the whole year.

But the study of *Tōrāh* must be our principal concern.

Rabbah b. Bar Ḥannah stated that R. Joḥanan said in the name of R. Judah b. R. El'ai[3]: Come and see that the later generations are not like the former generations. The former generations made their *Tōrāh* their principal concern and their work only occasional, and both flourished in their hand; whereas the later generations made their work their principal concern and their *Tōrāh* only occasional and neither flourished in their hand.

Former generations more scrupulous in giving tithes.

Rabbah b. Bar Ḥannah also stated that R. Joḥanan said in the name of R. Judah b. R. El'ai: Come and see that the later generations are not like the former generations. The former generations used to bring their fruits home by way of the kitchen-garden[4] in order to make them liable to the tithe; whereas the later generations bring their fruits home by way of the roof, or courts, or enclosures in order to exempt them from the tithe. For R. Jannai has said: Produce is not subject to the tithe until it sees the face of the house; as it is said, "I have put away the hallowed things out of my house" (Deut. xxvi. 13). R. Joḥanan said: Even [if it see] a fixed court [it is subject to the tithe]; as it is said, "That they may eat within thy gates and be satisfied" (*ibid. v.* 12).

Except over wine, etc.

Wine has a special benediction.

Why is wine different? Should one say because it is changed [from the grape] into something higher [in value], therefore there is a change in the benediction, but lo, oil which is changed [from the olive] into something higher [in value] has no alteration in the benediction; for Rab Judah said in the name of Samuel, and similarly said R. Isaac in the name of R. Joḥanan: Over olive-oil we pronounce the benediction "...Who createst the fruit of the tree"! The answer is: In this case [of oil, the benediction is unaltered] because none other is possible. What other benediction

[1] Viz. they combined *Tōrāh* with work. Cf. Ābōt ii. 2; Singer, p. 187.

[2] The first and seventh months of the year, corresponding with March—April and September—October, the time of the ripening of corn and the pressing of grapes. By devoting these two months to work, the remainder of the year could safely be given to *Tōrāh*. Raba accordingly agreed with R. Ishmael.

[3] *M.* omits: in the name of, etc.

[4] See Krauss, p. 271, on the word. The meaning is: They bring it straight into the house.

could he say? Should he use the formula "...Who createst the fruit of the olive," the olive itself is called "fruit[1]"! Then let him say "...Who createst the fruit of the olive-tree[2]." But said Mar Zoṭra: Wine nourishes, oil does not. Oil does not nourish? Lo, there is a Mishnaic teaching: He who vows [to abstain] from food may partake of water and salt! And we argue that water and salt are not called "food," but everything else is so called; and we further say that this is a refutation of Rab and Samuel who maintain that we pronounce the benediction "...Who createst various kinds of food" only over the five species[3]. Moreover Rab Huna said: [The quoted *Mishnāh* means,] Whoever declares "Everything that nourishes [I forbid] myself"—hence conclude that oil does nourish[4]! But wine satisfies and oil does not. Does wine satisfy? Lo, Raba used to drink wine the whole of the day preceding Passover to whet his appetite in order to eat the unleavened bread with greater zest! A large quantity whets the appetite, but a little satisfies [hunger]. But does it satisfy at all? For lo, it is written, "And wine that maketh glad the heart of man, making the face brighter than oil, and bread that stayeth man's heart" (Ps. civ. 15)—it is bread, not wine, that is a stay! Nay, wine does both, it satisfies and makes glad, whereas bread is only a stay, but does not cheer. If so, let him utter three benedictions[5]! But men do not fix their meals for its sake[6]. Rab Naḥman b. Isaac[7] asked Raba: How is it if a man did fix his meal on its account[8]? He replied: When Elijah[9] comes, let him say whether such can be fixed for a meal; at present, at least, such a thought does not exist amongst men[10].

[1] There is no special name in Hebrew for the olive-tree as there is for the vine.

[2] This point remaining unanswered, the *Gᵉmārā* proceeds to discover other reasons why wine should have a special benediction.

[3] Viz. wheat, barley, rye, oats and spelt. Rab and Samuel would restrict the term "food," without further qualification, only to these and not, e.g., to oil.

[4] The word "food" in the quoted *Mishnāh* is not used in the technical sense Rab and Samuel would give it, but means anything that nourishes. Since water and salt are alone excluded from this category, oil must be included.

[5] After wine as after bread, i.e. the full Grace after meals; see fol. 37 *a*, p. 250.

[6] Therefore, it cannot be regarded as food, and only one benediction is necessary.

[7] *M.* omits: b. Isaac.

[8] Would three benedictions be necessary?

[9] Who will solve all problems left in doubt.

[10] Viz. to fix a meal on account of wine.

When a benediction is necessary over olive-oil.

It was stated above: "Rab Judah said in the name of Samuel, and similarly said R. Isaac in the name of R. Joḥanan: Over olive-oil we pronounce the benediction '...Who createst the fruit of the tree'." How is this meant[1]? Should I say that he drinks it as a beverage, it does him harm[2]; for there is a teaching: He who drinks the oil of an offering repays its value but not a fifth in addition; but he who anoints himself with the oil of an offering repays its value plus a fifth[3]! But [perhaps it is here meant that] he eats it together with bread. If so, the bread is the principal food and the oil is only accessory; and we have the Mishnaic teaching: This is the general rule: In the case of a food which is the principal thing and together with it something accessory, the benediction is to be uttered over the former, and there is no necessity for a benediction over the latter! But [perhaps what is meant is] he drinks it with *elaiogaron*[4]. (Rabbah b. Samuel said[5]:

fol. 36 a. *Elaiogaron* is the juice of beets; *oxygaron* is the juice of all other kinds of boiled vegetables.) If so, the *elaiogaron* is the principal thing and the oil an accessory; and we have the Mishnaic teaching: This is the general rule: In the case of a food which is the principal thing and together with it is something accessory, the benediction is to be uttered over the former, and there is no necessity for a benediction over the latter! With what are we here dealing[6]? With the case of one who has a sore throat[7]; for there is a teaching: One suffering from a sore throat may not directly mollify it with oil on the Sabbath, but he should put a large quantity of oil into an *elaiogaron* and swallow it. This is evident[8]! But shouldest thou imagine that because he intends it as a cure no benediction at all is necessary, therefore it informs us that since he derives enjoyment from it, he is required to pronounce a benediction[9].

[1] I.e. how is it necessary to have a benediction for oil?

[2] In which case no benediction is required.

[3] See Lev. xxii. 14 according to which the man pays the additional fifth "if he eat of the holy thing," i.e. is nourished thereby. But oil has no beneficial effect on the body, therefore he pays only the value.

[4] *Enigaron*, a corruption of ἐλαιόγαρον, a sauce of oil and garum. See Krauss, p. 72.

[5] *M.*: Rab Judah said in the name of Samuel. The words in round brackets are a gloss to explain the Greek terms.

[6] When it is said oil requires a benediction.

[7] And uses oil as a remedy.

[8] That one may swallow oil added to an *elaiogaron* on the Sabbath; so why is it mentioned?

[9] The fact that it is permitted on the Sabbath proves that legally it is something to be enjoyed, the healing property being only incidental. And further, since the mixture is taken because of the oil, this is the principal

Over wheaten-flour, Rab Judah says: [The benediction is] "...Who createst the fruit of the ground." Rab Naḥman said: It is "...By Whose word all things exist[1]." Raba said to Rab Naḥman: Thou shouldest not differ from Rab Judah, because R. Joḥanan and Samuel agree with him; for Rab Judah said in the name of Samuel, and similarly said R. Isaac in the name of R. Joḥanan: We pronounce over olive-oil the benediction "...Who createst the fruit of the tree"—hence infer that although it has undergone change[2], it still remains essentially the same[3]; and likewise here [with wheaten-flour] although it has undergone change, it still remains essentially the same[4]. Are, however, the two cases analogous? There [with oil], it has not another and higher value; but here it has by being made into bread! But if [the wheaten-flour] have another and higher value, should we no longer use the benediction "...Who createst the fruit of the ground," but say instead "...By Whose word all things exist"? And lo, R. Zera said in the name of Rab Mattᵉna in the name of Samuel: Over raw cabbage and barley-flour we use the benediction "...By Whose word all things exist"; is it not then to be supposed that wheaten-flour requires the benediction "...Who createst the fruit of the ground[5]"? No; wheaten-flour also requires "...By Whose word all things exist." Then he should have specified wheaten-flour, and [we could have argued for ourselves] how much more so barley-flour[6]! If he had specified wheaten-flour, I might have thought that it applies only to wheat, but barley requires no benediction at all; therefore he mentioned it for us. Is, then, [barley-flour] of less value than salt and brine[7]? For there is a teaching[8]: Over salt and brine one says "...By Whose word all things exist." It was necessary[9]; for otherwise it might have entered thy mind to

Benediction over wheaten-flour.

item, the rest being accessory; consequently it is established that there is a circumstance where oil requires a benediction.

1 The point at issue is whether the grinding of the corn into flour alters its nature for the purpose of the benediction. Rab Judah maintains it does not.

2 By being pressed from the olive.

3 And there is no change in the benediction.

4 And the benediction should be "...Who createst the fruit of the ground."

5 If not, why is *barley*-flour specified?

6 Which is inferior to wheaten-flour.

7 That one could imagine barley-flour requires no benediction, whereas salt or brine does!

8 Edd. read incorrectly: A Mishnaic teaching. The quotation is a *Bārāitā*; cf. fol. 40 *b*, p. 268.

9 To specify *barley*-flour above, despite this objection.

say that salt or brine a man is accustomed to convey to his mouth [with his food, and therefore a benediction is required], but since barley-flour is injurious by creating tape-worms no benediction should be uttered at all; therefore he teaches us that since there is some enjoyment therefrom, it is necessary to pronounce a benediction.

Benediction over the palm-heart.

Over the palm-heart[1], Rab Judah said: [The benediction is] "...Who createst the fruit of the ground"; but Samuel said: It is "...By Whose word all things exist." Rab Judah said: It is "...Who createst the fruit of the ground" because it is fruit. Samuel said: It is "...By Whose word all things exist" because in the end it hardens[2]. Samuel said to Rab Judah: Thou keen-witted one[3]! Thy opinion is correct; because over the radish, though it in the end grows hard, we say "...Who createst the fruit of the ground." But it is not so[4]! For people plant radishes for the sake of the tuber, but people do not plant palms for the sake of the heart[5]! Is it, then, [to be assumed] that in every case where men do not plant specifically to obtain that article of food, we do not pronounce the benediction[6] over it? Lo, the caper-bush men plant for the purpose of the caper-blossom; and we have a Mishnaic teaching: In the case of the various kinds of capers, over the leaves and young shoots one says "...Who createst the fruit of the ground," but over the berries and buds[7] "...Who createst the fruit of the tree[8]"! Rab Naḥman b. Isaac said: Men do plant caper-bushes for the sake of the shoots, but not the palm for the sake of the heart; and although Samuel praised Rab Judah[9], the *Hᵃlākāh* is in agreement with Samuel.

[1] "A white, meaty, sweet and tasty substance" in the young palm; Löw, *Aramäische Pflanzennamen*, p. 116.

[2] If not extracted while the palm is young, it becomes part of the tree.

[3] Bacher, *A.B.A.*, p. 51 n. 27 declares that the rendering "Thou keen-witted one" is not beyond dispute, and the expression may refer to his *iron* endurance in study.

[4] There can be no comparison of the two.

[5] When the heart is extracted, the palm withers; therefore it does not bear the same relation to its tree as other fruit does.

[6] *M.* adds: "...Who createst the fruit of the ground."

[7] So Löw, *op. cit.* p. 264. Jastrow translates "caper-flowers." Rashi explains "husks."

[8] From this it is seen that "Who createst the fruit of the ground" is said over the leaves and shoots although the caper is not grown to obtain these; why, then, should that formula not be used for the palm-heart although the palm is not planted for the sake of the heart?

[9] By calling him " n-witted."

Whether caper-berries and buds are fruit.

Rab Judah said in the name of Rab: As for the caper-bush which is still in a state of *'Orlāh* outside the [Holy] Land, one throws away the berries but eats the buds; that is to say, the berries are fruit[1] but not the buds. Against this [deduction] I quote: In the case of the various kinds of capers, over the leaves and their young shoots one says "...Who createst the fruit of the ground," but over the berries and buds "...Who createst the fruit of the tree[2]!" He[3] speaks according to the view of R. 'Aḳiba; for there is a Mishnaic teaching: R. Eliezer[4] says: In the case of the caper-bush, we give tithe of the young shoots and the berries and buds; R. 'Aḳiba says: We only give tithe of the berries because they are fruit[5]. Then let him say that the *Hᵃlākāh* is in agreement with R. 'Aḳiba[6]! If he had said that the *Hᵃlākāh* is in agreement with R. 'Aḳiba, I might have thought that [that is so] even in the Land of Israel; therefore he informs us: Whoever takes a lenient view within the Land, the *Hᵃlākāh* is in accord with him outside the Land, but not within. Then let him say: The *Hᵃlākāh* is in agreement with R. 'Aḳiba outside the Land; for everyone who takes the lenient view within the Land[7], the *Hᵃlākāh* is in accord with him outside the Land! If he had stated that, I might have said: This applies to the tithe of trees which within the Land is a Rabbinical ordinance; but with regard to *'Orlāh*, which within the Land is ordained by the *Tōrāh*, I must suppose that likewise outside the Land we must apply it! Therefore he informs us[8].

Discussion continued.

Rabina found Mar b. Rab Ashē throwing away the berries and eating the caper-buds[9]. He said to him: What is thy opinion—like R. 'Aḳiba's who takes the lenient view[10]? Then let the master act in accord with *Bēt* Shammai who take a still more lenient view[11]. For there is a Mishnaic teaching: In the case of the caper-bush, *Bēt* Shammai say: It constitutes *Kilā'im* in a

[1] And for that reason may not be eaten when in a state of *'Orlāh*.

[2] Hence the buds are regarded as fruit.

[3] I.e. Rab, whose name *M.* includes in the text.

[4] *M.*: Eleazar, incorrectly.

[5] And the buds are not fruit.

[6] If R. 'Aḳiba's view is the correct one.

[7] As R. 'Aḳiba does.

[8] That one may eat the buds outside the Land even when in a state of *'Orlāh*.

[9] I.e. in a state of *'Orlāh*.

[10] That the tithe is only to be given of the caper-berries, and not the buds.

[11] They would also permit the berries to be eaten.

vineyard; but *Bēt* Hillel say: It does not. Both, however, admit that it is subject to *'Orlāh*. This is self-contradictory! Thou declarest, "In the case of the caper-bush, *Bēt* Shammai say: It constitutes *Kilā'īm* in a vineyard"—hence it is a kind of vegetable[1]! It then goes on to state, "Both, however, admit that it is subject to *'Orlāh*"—hence it is a kind of tree[2]! There is no contradiction; for *Bēt* Shammai, being in doubt[3], take the stricter view in both cases[4]. Nevertheless[5] *Bēt* Shammai have a doubt whether it is subject to *'Orlāh*; and we have a Mishnaic teaching: Where there is a doubt [whether a thing is subject to] *'Orlāh*—in the Land of Israel it is prohibited [to be used][6], in Syria it is per-
fol. 36 b. mitted, and outside the Land one may go down and buy it, but he must not see the man gathering it [from the bushes][7]. When R. 'Aḳiba is in opposition to R. Eliezer, we act according to his view[8]; but when *Bēt* Shammai are in opposition to *Bēt* Hillel, [the opinion of the former] is not *Mishnāh*[9].

What constitutes "protection of the fruit."

Thou mayest, however, derive [a conclusion][10] from the fact that [the bud] constitutes a protection of the fruit, and the All-merciful declared, "Ye shall deem it an uncircumcision *with* its fruit[11]" (Lev. xix. 23)—the word "with" meaning to include what is attached to the fruit; and what is that? The protection of the fruit[12]. Raba replied: When do we declare a thing to be the protection of the fruit? When it is so either plucked or attached [to the tree]; but here [the bud is only a protection] when attached, but not when plucked[13]. Abbai quoted in objection: The top-piece of a pomegranate is reckoned in[14] but not the

1 If it were a fruit, it would not constitute *Kilā'īm*.

2 Because vegetables are not subject to *'Orlāh*.

3 As to the category of the caper-bush.

4 And declare it *Kilā'īm* in a vineyard and subject to *'Orlāh*.

5 Here Rabina's question to Mar. b. Rab Ashē is resumed.

6 Because Lev. xix. 23 applies the law only to "the land."

7 He is then in doubt whether the tree is in its fruit three years. Hence, Rabina declares, Mar would be right in eating the berries as well as the buds.

8 Consequently only the berries are to be regarded as fruit, and not the buds; and Mar acted accordingly.

9 I.e. it has no authority. Hence there is no doubt that the caper-bush *is* subject to *'Orlāh*.

10 That even the bud is subject to *'Orlāh*.

11 This is the literal rendering of the Hebrew, the grammatical construction of which is peculiar.

12 The rind, shell, etc.

13 The caper-bud falls from the bush when ripe; hence it cannot be regarded as a protection so that it should be subject to *'Orlāh*.

14 With the fruit to make up the minimum bulk which can contract impurity.

blossom[1]; and since it is stated that the blossom is not reckoned in, conclude that it is not food. And we have a Mishnaic teaching with reference to *'Orlāh*: The skins of the pomegranate and its blossom, and the shells of nuts and the kernels are subject to *'Orlāh*[2]! But, said Raba: When do we declare that a thing constitutes the protection of the fruit? When it is there at the time the fruit has ripened; but the caper-bud is not there at the time the fruit has ripened[3]. But it is not so[4]! For Rab Naḥman has said in the name of Rabbah b. Abbuha: The calyces surrounding dates are forbidden because of *'Orlāh*, since they are the protection of the fruit; and when are they the protection of the fruit? In the early stages [of the fruit's growth], then are they called the protection of the fruit! Rab Naḥman holds the same view as R. Josē; for there is a Mishnaic teaching: R. Josē said: The grape-bud is forbidden[5] because it is fruit; but the Rabbis differ from him[6]. Rab Shimi[7] of Nehardea[8] asked: But do the Rabbis differ from him in the case of other trees[9]? For lo, there is a Mishnaic teaching: From what time must we cease cutting down the trees in the seventh year[10]? *Bēt* Shammai say: All trees, as soon as they produce fruit. *Bēt* Hillel say: Carob-trees when they begin to form chains, vines when they form globules, olive-trees when they bloom, and all other trees when they produce fruit. And Rab Assi[11] said: *Bōser* and *Gārūa'* and the white bean are the same[12]. [The same as] the white bean, dost thou imagine? Nay, the meaning is: The size [of *Bōser* and *Gārūa'*] is like that of the white bean. Whom hast thou heard declaring that the *Bōser* is [to be considered fruit] but not the grape-bud? The Rabbis[13]. It states: "All other trees when they

1 And the blossom bears the same relationship to the pomegranate that the caper-bud does to the berry.

2 If, then, the pomegranate-blossom is subject to *'Orlāh*, so should the caper-bud be.

3 See p. 244 n. 12.

4 That the protection must be attached to the *ripened* fruit.

5 I e. is subject to *'Orlāh*.

6 The *Halākāh* is in agreement with the Rabbis; and since the caper-bud corresponds to the grape-bud, it too should not be subject to *'Orlāh*.

7 *M*. adds: b. Ashē.

8 See p. 74 n. 2.

9 I.e. other than the vine.

10 The year of agricultural rest; cf. Exod. xxiii. 11, Lev. xxv. 4.

11 *M*.: Ashē.

12 I.e. mark the same stage of growth. The *Bōser* is the sour grape, the *Gārūa'* the grape when the stone inside is formed.

13 Who differ from R. Josē.

produce fruit." But, said Raba: When do we say a thing is the protection of the fruit? When, if the protection is removed, the fruit perishes; but here [in the case of the caper] the fruit does not perish if the protecting [bud] is removed. The experiment was made; they removed the blossom of the pomegranate and the fruit withered; they removed the flower of the caper but the caper survived[1]. The *Hᵃlākāh* is according to Mar b. Rab Ashē who threw away the berries and ate the buds; and since these are not regarded as fruit for the purpose of *'Orlāh*, they are likewise not so regarded for the purpose of the benediction. We accordingly utter over them not "...Who createst the fruit of the tree" but "...Who createst the fruit of the ground."

Benediction over pepper.

Over pepper, Rab Sheshet said: [The benediction is] "...By Whose word all things exist"; Raba said: None at all [is required][2]. Raba is consistent with his opinion [expressed elsewhere]; for he has said: If one chews pepper-corns on the Day of Atonement he is free [from guilt][3]; if he chews ginger on the Day of Atonement he is likewise free. It is quoted in objection: R. Meïr has declared: From the statement of Scripture, "Ye shall deem it an uncircumcision with its *fruit*" (Lev. xix. 23), do I not know that a food-bearing tree is intended? Why, then, is there a teaching to tell us "trees for food" (*ibid.*)? To include a tree whose wood and fruit taste alike. And which is that? Pepper; to teach thee that pepper is subject to *'Orlāh*[4], and to teach thee that the Land of Israel lacks nothing; as it is said, "A land wherein thou shalt eat bread without scarceness, thou shalt not lack any thing in it" (Deut. viii. 9)! There is no contradiction[5]; the latter refers to moist [pepper][6], the other to dried. The Rabbis[7] said to Maremar: He who chews ginger on the Day of Atonement is free [from guilt]. But lo, Raba declared: The preserved ginger which comes from India is permitted[8], and we pronounce the benediction "...Who createst the fruit of the ground" over it[9]! There is no contradiction; the latter referring to moist [ginger], the other to dried.

[1] Therefore we cannot argue from one to the other. The remainder of the paragraph reads like a marginal gloss incorporated into the text.

[2] Because it is not regarded as a food.

[3] He has not broken the strict fast enjoined on that day.

[4] Hence pepper is a food.

[5] Between the view of Raba and R. Meïr.

[6] I.e. preserved, over which a benediction is required.

[7] *M.*: Rabina.

[8] To be eaten by Jews although prepared by a Gentile.

[9] Since a benediction is necessary, it must be a food; how, then, could the Rabbis tell Maremar that it may be chewed on the Day of Atonement?

Over *Ḥābīṣ*[1] boiled in a pot and also pounded grain, Rab Judah said: [The benediction is] "...By Whose word all things exist"; Rab Kah^a^na said: It is "...Who createst various kinds of food." With plain pounded grain[2] all agree that "...Who createst all kinds of foods" is the correct benediction, the disagreement arising in connection with pounded grain made like a boiled *Ḥābīṣ*. Rab Judah maintained [that the benediction should be] "...By Whose word all things exist," being of the opinion that the honey is the principal ingredient; whereas Rab Kah^a^na maintained it is "...Who createst various kinds of foods," holding that the flour is the principal ingredient. Rab Joseph said: The view of Rab Kah^a^na seems more probable, because Rab and Samuel both say that a dish which contains one of the five species[3] requires the benediction "...Who createst various kinds of foods." **Benediction over boiled *Ḥābīṣ*.**

It has just been mentioned: "Rab and Samuel both say: A dish which contains one of the five species requires the benediction '...Who createst various kinds of foods'." It has likewise been reported: Rab and Samuel both say: A dish which is of the five species requires the benediction "...Who createst various kinds of foods." It was necessary [to give both these statements]. If we had been taught only the second, I might have said that [that benediction is required] because the dish has the appearance [of one of the five species], but not if mixed with other ingredients; therefore we are informed that a dish which contains it [requires that benediction]. If, on the other hand, we had been taught only the first, I might have said a dish containing any of the five species does [require that benediction], but not rice or millet because these are mixed with other ingredients. Should, however, it have the appearance [of one of the five species], we might say that even with rice or millet we pronounce the benediction "...Who createst various kinds of foods"; therefore we are informed, "A dish which is of the five species requires the benediction '...Who createst various kinds of foods'," to the exclusion of rice and millet; for even if it retain its appearance we do not say that benediction. **Benediction over a dish which contains one of the five species.** **fol. 37 a.**

And over rice and millet do we not bless "...Who createst various kinds of foods"? Lo, there is a teaching: If they brought before a man bread of rice or of millet, he pronounces a benediction **Benediction over rice and millet.**

[1] A mixture of flour, honey and oil beaten into a pulp. It seems to resemble the Arabic *Kunāfeh*, a sweet dish made of wheat-flour fried with clarified butter and honey; cf. Lane, p. 150, *T.A.* I. p. 477 n. 465.

[2] Without honey added. [3] See p. 239.

before and after as with any other cooked dish. And with reference to a cooked dish there is a teaching: Before partaking thereof one should bless "...Who createst various kinds of foods" and after it one benediction which is an abstract of three[1]! [Bread of rice or of millet] is like a cooked dish [in one respect] but unlike a cooked dish [in another]. It is like a cooked dish in so far as there is a benediction before and after partaking thereof. But it is unlike a cooked dish; for over a cooked dish one says at first "...Who createst various kinds of foods," and in the end one benediction which is an abstract of three. [With rice and millet], however, one first says "...By Whose word all things exist" and in the end "...Who createst many living beings with their wants," etc.[2]

The category of rice.

Is not rice a cooked dish[3]? And lo, there is a teaching: The following are cooked dishes[3]: grist, groats, fine flour, split grain, barley-meal and rice! Who said this? R. Johanan b. Nuri; for there is a teaching: R. Johanan b. Nuri says: Rice is a species of corn[3], and through its fermentation [during Passover] one incurs the penalty of excision[4]; but a man can comply with the requirements of the law therewith during Passover[5]. The Rabbis, however, do not agree with him. Do they not? Lo, there is a teaching: He who chews wheat should say the benediction "...Who createst the fruit of the ground"; if he ground it, baked and then boiled it, should the pieces of bread be still whole, before partaking thereof he says "...Who bringest forth bread from the earth[6]" and afterwards he says the three benedictions[7]; but if the pieces are no longer whole[8], he first says "...Who createst various kinds of foods" and afterwards one benediction which is an abstract of three. He who chews rice says the benediction "...Who createst the fruit of the ground"; if he ground it, baked and then boiled it, although the pieces are still whole, he first says "...Who createst various kinds of foods" and afterwards one benediction which is an abstract of three. According to whom [is this teaching]? If I say it is R. Johanan b. Nuri who declared

[1] See fol. 44 *a*, p. 286.
[2] See Singer, p. 290.
[3] I.e. to be regarded as such for the purpose of the benediction.
[4] Cf. Exod. xii. 19.
[5] He may make unleavened cakes of rice.
[6] The benediction over bread.
[7] The full Grace after meals.
[8] A broth is formed.

"Rice is a kind of corn," then one should say "...Who bringest forth bread from the earth" and the three benedictions[1]! Must it not be the Rabbis[2]? This is a refutation of Rab and Samuel[3], and it remains unanswered.

Benediction when wheat is chewed.

The teacher stated: "He who chews wheat should say the benediction '...Who createst the fruit of the ground'." But there is a teaching: [He should say] "...Who createst divers kinds of seeds"![4] There is no contradiction; the latter being the opinion of R. Judah[5], the other of the Rabbis. For our *Mishnāh* teaches: *Over vegetables one says: "...Who createst the fruit of the ground"; but R. Judah declares: "...Who createst divers kinds of herbs."*

The benediction after partaking of rice.

The teacher stated: "He who chews rice says the benediction '...Who createst the fruit of the ground'; if he ground it, baked and then boiled it, although the pieces are still whole, he first says '...Who createst various kinds of foods' and afterwards one benediction which is an abstract of three." But there is a teaching: After partaking thereof no benediction is required! Rab Sheshet said: There is no contradiction: one being the opinion of Rabban Gamaliel, the other of the Rabbis. For there is a teaching: This is the general rule—Any food which belongs to the seven species[6], Rabban Gamaliel says: Three benedictions [are required after partaking thereof], whereas the Rabbis say: One benediction which is an abstract of three.

Benediction after partaking of dates.

It once happened that Rabban Gamaliel[7] and the Elders were reclining in an upper chamber in Jericho; dates were set before them and they ate. Rabban Gamaliel gave permission to R. 'Aḳiba to say Grace[8]. R. 'Aḳiba sat up and said one benediction which is an abstract of three. Rabban Gamaliel said to him, "'Aḳiba, how long wilt thou put thy head between strife!" He replied, "Our master! Although thou sayest thus and thy colleagues say otherwise, thou hast taught us, our master, that where the

[1] Therefore rice cannot be in the same category as wheat.

[2] And according to them the benediction for rice is: "...Who createst various kinds of foods."

[3] Who maintained above that this benediction is restricted to the five species, excluding rice.

[4] *M.* inserts: Rab Huna said.

[5] Who requires a special benediction for each species; see fol. 40 *a*, p. 264.

[6] Enumerated in Deut. viii. 8.

[7] *M.* adds: and R. 'Aḳiba.

[8] Rabban Gamaliel expected R. 'Aḳiba to follow his teaching and say three benedictions.

individual and the many differ, the *H^alākāh* is in accord with the view of the many!"

Benediction after partaking of "the seven species." fol. 37 b.

R. Judah said in his name[1]: Any food which belongs to the seven species and is not a kind of corn, or if a kind of corn it has not been made into bread, Rabban Gamaliel declares three benedictions [are required after partaking thereof], but the Sages declare: Only one benediction[2]. And any food which does not belong to the seven species and is not a kind of corn, for instance, bread of rice or millet, Rabban Gamaliel declares: One benediction which is an abstract of three, but the Sages declare: None at all. According to whom, then, dost thou confirm [the teaching: After partaking of rice one benediction which is an abstract of three is necessary]? According to Rabban Gamaliel. I will quote the latter part of the first teaching, viz.: "If the pieces are no longer whole, he first says '...Who createst various kinds of foods' and afterwards one benediction which is an abstract of three." Whose teaching is this? If Rabban Gamaliel's, since he has just declared that for dates and pounded grain[3] three benedictions are necessary, how much more necessary should they be if the pieces are no longer whole[4]! Nay, it is evident that it must be the Rabbis'[5]. If so, the Rabbis contradict themselves[6]! But it is certainly the view of the Rabbis; and with reference to rice the teaching is: After partaking thereof no benediction is required[7].

Benediction over *Rih^aṭā*.

Raba said: Over the *Rih^aṭā*[8] of the field labourers which contains a large admixture of flour, the benediction is "...Who createst various kinds of food." Why? Because the flour is the principal ingredient. [Over the *Rih^aṭā*] of townspeople which does not contain so much flour, the benediction is "...By Whose word all things exist." Why? Because honey is the principal

[1] The name of Rabban Gamaliel.

[2] *M.* adds: which is an abstract of three.

[3] In the *Bārāitā* above, it is stated "if a kind of corn it has not been made into bread" as, e.g., pounded grain.

[4] Since they were originally bread.

[5] According to them pounded grain only requires one benediction, and similarly boiled bread which is no longer in pieces.

[6] The Rabbis declare above that after "for instance, bread of rice or millet" no benediction is necessary, and here they are made to hold the opinion that one benediction, the abstract of three, is required.

[7] I.e. in the quoted *Bārāitā*, the reading should be "no benediction is required" not "one benediction which is an abstract of three."

[8] A dish resembling the *Ḥābīṣ*, consisting of honey, flour and oil. See *T. A.* I. p. 107.

ingredient. Raba afterwards said: Over both kinds the benediction is "...Who createst various kinds of foods"; because Rab and Samuel both declare: Over any food which contains one of the five species, the benediction is "...Who createst various kinds of foods."

Benediction over *Ḥābīṣ* which contains large pieces of bread.

Rab Joseph said: Over the *Ḥābīṣ* which contains pieces of bread the size of an olive, before partaking thereof the benediction is "...Who bringest forth bread from the earth," and afterwards three benedictions. If it does not contain pieces of bread the size of an olive, before partaking thereof the benediction is "...Who createst various kinds of foods" and afterwards one benediction which is an abstract of three. Rab Joseph said: Whence have I this[1]? There is a teaching: If one[2] were standing and bringing meal-offerings in Jerusalem, he says "Blessed [art Thou, O Lord our God, King of the universe], Who has kept us in life, and hast preserved us, and enabled us to reach this season." If he[3] takes them to eat, he says the benediction "...Who bringest forth bread from the earth"; and it is taught in this connection: They must all be broken into pieces[4] about the size of an olive. Abbai said to him: But according to the *Tannā* of the school of R. Ishmael who declared, "He must crumble [the meal-offerings] until they return to the condition of flour [before eating thereof]," it would then be unnecessary to pronounce the benediction "...Who bringest forth bread from the earth[5]." And if thou sayest that is so[6], lo there is a teaching: If he gathered together from all of them[7] about the size of an olive and ate them, should it be leaven he incurs the penalty of excision[8], and if unleaven, a man can therewith comply with the requirements of the law during Passover[9]! With what are we here dealing? When he rekneaded

[1] That pieces of bread, the size of an olive, require the benediction "...Who bringest forth bread from the earth."

[2] A non-priest. [3] The priest. [4] Cf. Lev. ii. 6.

[5] Since there are no pieces the size of an olive.

[6] I.e. the benediction is unnecessary.

[7] According to Rashi this refers to the crumbs of the meal-offering. But Tōsāfōt object that this cannot be, because it continues "should it be leaven"; and the meal-offering must be unleaven. Consequently it is taken to refer to crumbs of different species, each in itself not the size of an olive.

[8] By eating them on Passover.

[9] When it is his duty to eat unleaven. Consequently these crumbs are together considered to be equivalent to a *piece* of the size of an olive, otherwise he would not be violating the Passover if they were leaven, or fulfil the law of the Passover if unleaven.

the crumbs into a compact mass[1]. In that case, I shall quote the latter part of the *Bārāitā*: That is, only if he eats *them* the time it takes to eat half [a roll][2]. But if he rekneaded them, it should have stated "he eats *it*" not "he eats *them*"! With what are we here dealing? When [the crumbs] are from a whole[3] loaf. How is it then in this matter? Rab Sheshet said: Over *Ḥăbīṣ*, although it does not contain pieces of bread the size of an olive, he blesses "...Who bringest forth bread from the earth." Raba said: This is only so if it has the semblance of bread.

Ṭrōḳnīn subject to Ḥallāh.

Ṭrōḳnīn[4] is subject to *Ḥallāh*. When Rabin came, R. Johanan said: It is exempt from *Ḥallāh*. What is *Ṭrōḳnīn*? Abbai[5] said: Dough baked in a cavity made in the ground.

Ṭārītā and Kuttāḥ exempt from Ḥallāh.

Abbai also said: *Ṭārītā* is exempt from[6] *Ḥallāh*. What is *Ṭārītā*? Some say: A scalded puff-pastry. Others declare it to be Indian bread[7]. Yet others declare it to be bread made into *Kuttāḥ*[8]. R. Ḥiyya taught: Bread made into *Kuttāḥ* is exempt from *Ḥallāh*. But there is a teaching: It is subject to *Ḥallāh*! Yes, but there it mentions the reason, viz.: R. Judah says: The way they are
fol. 38 a. made decides[9]. If he made them into cakes[10], they are subject [to *Ḥallāh*]; but if he made them into "shingles[11]," they are exempt. Abbai asked Rab Joseph: Which benediction is to be said over dough baked in a cavity made in the ground? He said to him: Dost thou consider it to be bread? It is only a thick mass, and the benediction is "...Who createst various kinds of foods." Mar

[1] Therefore we cannot argue from this *Bārāitā* to the case under consideration.

[2] I.e. a piece of bread the size of four eggs. The meaning is, he must not spread the eating of the crumbs over a long space of time; the maximum being the time required to eat half a roll.

[3] *Lit.* large; i.e. a loaf which has not been entirely reduced to crumbs, but only a part of it. If, then, he eats of these crumbs and they are not the size of an olive, he is not required to say the benediction "...Who bringest forth bread from the earth."

[4] טרוקנין which Jastrow considers a corruption of טרקטה, the Latin *tracta*, "a long piece of dough pulled out in making pastry." So Krauss, p. 274.

[5] *M.*: Rab Joseph.

[6] *M.*: is subject to.

[7] Rashi explains: Dough roasted on the spit and covered with oil or eggs and oil. But see *T. A.* I. p. 107.

[8] According to Rashi: Bread baked in the Sun, not an oven. Jastrow explains: A preserve consisting of sour milk, bread-crusts and salt. See also *T. A.* I. p. 472 n. 430.

[9] Whether *Ḥallāh* is necessary.

[10] So that there is the semblance of bread.

[11] I.e. flat boards of dough.

Zoṭra made a meal of it and said the benediction "...Who bringest forth bread from the earth" and [afterwards] the three benedictions[1]. Mar b. Rab Ashē said: A man can comply with the requirements of the law therewith on the Passover. On what ground? We may apply to it the term "bread of affliction" (Deut. xvi. 3).

Benediction over date-honey.

Mar b. Rab Ashē also said: Over the honey of the date-palm we use the benediction "...By Whose word all things exist[2]." What is the reason? Because it is only the moisture [of the tree]. According to whom is this? According to the *Tannā* of the following Mishnaic teaching: In the case of the honey of the date-palm, cider, the vinegar of winter-grapes[3] and other fruit-juices which are brought as an offering, [if a non-priest in error partake thereof] R. Eliezer condemns him to pay the value plus a fifth[4]; but R. Joshua exempts him[5].

Benediction over *Ṭrimmā*.

One of the Rabbis asked Raba: How is it with *Ṭrimmā*[6]? Raba was not sure what he had asked him. Rabina was sitting in the presence of Raba and said [to the questioner]: Dost thou mean a brew of sesame seeds, or of saffron, or of grape-kernels? In the meantime Raba recalled it[7] and he said to him: Thou must surely mean a brew of ground dates; and thou remindest me of something that R. Assi said, viz.: It is permissible to make *Ṭrimmā* from dates brought as an offering, but one must not make strong drink of them. And the *Hªlākāh* is: Over dates made into *Ṭrimmā* we say the benediction "...Who createst the fruit of the tree." On what ground? Because [the dates are considered] as remaining in their original condition [as fruit].

Benediction over *Shattīt*.

Over *Shattīt*[8] Rab said: [The benediction is] "...By Whose word all things exist"; Samuel said: It is "...Who createst various kinds of foods." Rab Ḥisda said: There is no difference of opinion between them; the latter referring to a thick mass, the other to a thin mass. The thick mass is used as food, the thin as a remedy.

[1] He treated it as though it were bread.

[2] Not "...Who createst the fruit of the tree."

[3] Read with *M.*: סתוניות for ספוניות, the grapes which are left unripened in the winter, from which vinegar is made.

[4] Cf. Lev. v. 15 f.

[5] From the payment of the additional fifth, because he does not regard them as fruit. Mar is therefore in agreement with him.

[6] τρῖμμα, a brew of pounded groats and spices. What benediction does it need?

[7] Rabina's question caused Raba to understand what had been asked of him.

[8] Flour of unripe barley mixed with honey.

Rab Joseph[1] quoted in objection: "[R. Judah and R. Josē] both hold that we may stir up a *Shattīt* on the Sabbath and drink Egyptian beer[2]"! If, then, thou thinkest that [the *Shattīt*] is intended as a remedy, is it permitted to compound a remedy on the Sabbath? Abbai said to him: Art thou not of the opinion [that it is permitted to compound a remedy on the Sabbath]? Lo, there is a Mishnaic teaching: All foods may be eaten as a remedy, and likewise all liquids may be drunk! What is there for thee to say[3]? The man intended it as a food [and therefore it may be prepared on the Sabbath]; so here also [in the case of the *Shattīt*] the man intended it as a food. (Another version is: What is there for thee to say? The man intended it as a food, and it became a remedy of itself; so here also [the *Shattīt*] was intended as a food, and it became a remedy of itself[4].)

Discussion continued.

It was necessary to have the statements of Rab and Samuel[5]. For from that [quotation from the *Mishnāh*] I might have said that [only when the *Shattīt*] is intended as a food and becomes a remedy of itself [is a benediction required]; but here, since it was from the outset intended as a remedy, no benediction is at all required[6]. Therefore [from Rab and Samuel's statement] we are informed that since one derives enjoyment therefrom, it is necessary to say a benediction.

For over bread one says: "...Who bringest forth bread from the earth."

Wording of the benediction over bread.

Our Rabbis have taught: What does he say? "...Who bringest forth [*hammōṣī'*] bread from the earth." R. Nehemiah stated: It is "...Who brought forth [*mōṣī'*][7] bread from the earth." Raba said: Nobody disagrees about *mōṣī'* that it has the meaning "brought forth"; as it is said, "God Who brought them forth [*mōṣī'ām*][8] out of Egypt" (Num. xxiii. 22). In what do they

[1] *M.*: Raba. [2] A brew made from roasted wheat; cf. Pᵉsāḥīm 42 *b*.

[3] What becomes of the objection that the *Shattīt* cannot be a remedy since it is not permitted to prepare a remedy on the Sabbath, whereas this may be prepared?

[4] There was nothing more to be done to it to constitute it a remedy; therefore it may be prepared on the Sabbath, although used as a remedy.

[5] Respecting the correct benediction for the *Shattīt*.

[6] Even if eaten as food.

[7] I.e. with the definite article omitted. It is noteworthy that in the other benedictions there is no article. A difference in tense-meaning is here associated with its inclusion or omission.

[8] Not *hammōṣī' ōtām*. The words were spoken by Balaam and refer to a past event.

differ? In the word *hammōṣī'*. The Rabbis hold that *hammōṣī'* means "Who brought forth," for it is written "Who brought thee forth [*hammōṣī'*] water out of the rock of flint" (Deut. viii. 15); and R. Nehemiah holds it means "Who bringeth forth," as it is said, "Who bringeth you out [*hammōṣī'*] from under the burden of the Egyptians" (Exod. vi. 7). The Rabbis explain this verse as follows: Thus spake the Holy One, blessed be He, to Israel, "When I bring you forth, I will do that for you whereby you may know that I am He that *brought you forth*[1] from Egypt; for it is written 'And ye shall know that I am the Lord your God Who brought you out [*hammōṣī'*]'" (*ibid.*).

The Rabbis praised Rab Zᵉbid the father of R. Simeon b. Rab Zᵉbid to R. Zera[2] as being a great man and expert in the benedictions. R. Zera said to them, "Should he come to you bring him to me." On one occasion Rab Zᵉbid paid him a visit. He was handed some bread, and began the benediction [using the word] *mōṣī'*. R. Zera exclaimed, "Is this he of whom they declare he is a great man and expert in the benedictions! It would have been right if he had said *hammōṣī'*; then he would have informed us of the explanation[3] and also intimated that the *Hᵃlākāh* is in accord with the Rabbis. But since he said *mōṣī'*, what does he wish us to infer?" But Rab Zᵉbid acted thus to exclude himself from the divergence of opinion, the *Hᵃlākāh* being in agreement with the Rabbis, viz.: *hammōṣī'*, for it is established in accord with the Rabbis who declare the word to mean "Who brought forth[4]."

Subject continued.

fol. 38 b.

Over vegetables one says: "... Who createst the fruit of the ground"; but R. Judah declares: "... Who createst divers kinds of herbs."

He teaches that vegetables resemble bread [in this respect]: as bread is changed by the fire [in appearance, but the benediction remains unaltered], so also are vegetables changed by the fire [but the benediction is the same]. Rabbanai[5] said in the name of Abbai: This means that the benediction over boiled vegetables is "...Who

Benediction over vegetables.

[1] Accordingly even in Exod. vi. 7 upon which R. Nehemiah relied, *hammōṣī'* has the meaning "Who brought forth."

[2] The text is corrupt, and the translation given seems to follow the correct reading; cf. *D. S. ad loc.* Goldschmidt reads: The Rabbis praised the father of R. Simeon b. Rab Zᵉbid to R. Zera b. Rab.

[3] Of Exod. vi. 7 discussed above.

[4] They give it the sense of the past, because the bread being before the person, it had already been brought forth. I have nevertheless retained the usual rendering "Who bringest forth."

[5] Read: Raba (Hyman III. p. 1095 *a*).

createst the fruit of the ground." (From whence is this derived? Since he taught that vegetables resemble bread[1].)

Conflict of opinion when the vegetables are cooked.

Rab Ḥisda expounded in the name of our teacher—and who is he? Rab: Over boiled vegetables we pronounce the benediction "...Who createst the fruit of the ground"; but our teachers who came down from the land of Israel [to Babylon]—and who are they? 'Ulla in the name of R. Joḥanan—said: Over boiled vegetables we pronounce the benediction "...By Whose word all things exist." I[2] say that any article of food which in its original state[3] requires "...Who createst the fruit of the ground," if cooked requires "...By Whose word all things exist"; and whatever in its original state[4] requires "...By Whose word all things exist," if cooked requires "...Who createst the fruit of the ground." It is quite right that food which in its original state requires "...By Whose word all things exist," if cooked requires "...Who createst the fruit of the ground"; for it is found thus in the instances of cabbage, beet and the pumpkin. But something which in its original state requires "...Who createst the fruit of the ground," if cooked requires "...By Whose word all things exist"—where is such to be found? Rab Naḥman b. Isaac said: There are the instances of garlic and leek.

Discussion continued.

Rab Naḥman expounded in the name of our teacher—and who is he? Samuel: Over boiled vegetables we pronounce the benediction "...Who createst the fruit of the ground"; but our colleagues who came down from the land of Israel—and who are they? 'Ulla in the name of R. Joḥanan—said: Over boiled vegetables the benediction is "...By Whose word all things exist." I say that [their difference of opinion] is taught in the following controversy; for there is a teaching: One complies with the requirements of the law[5] with a wafer which has been soaked or cooked, provided it has not dissolved. These are the words of R. Meïr[6]; but R. Josē says: One complies with the requirements of the law with a wafer which has been soaked, but not with one which has been cooked even if it has not dissolved[7]. It is not so; for it is agreed by all

1 Some authorities omit these words.

2 I.e. Rab Ḥisda in order to harmonise these divergent opinions.

3 Referring to something that is usually eaten raw.

4 Referring to something that is usually cooked, but is eaten raw.

5 To eat unleavened bread on Passover.

6 Accordingly R. Meïr and Samuel agree that cooking does not alter the original nature of the article.

7 R. Josē and R. Joḥanan agree that cooking changes the nature of the article.

that over boiled vegetables the benediction is "...Who createst the fruit of the ground[1]"; and only in this case[2] does R. Josē say so because we require the taste of the unleavened bread, and it is not there [if the wafer is cooked]. Hence, however, even R. Josē admits it[3].

R. Ḥiyya b. Abba said in the name of R. Joḥanan: Over boiled vegetables we pronounce the benediction "...Who createst the fruit of the ground." But R. Benjamin b. Jephet said in the name of R. Joḥanan: Over boiled vegetables the benediction is "...By Whose word all things exist." Rab Naḥman b. Isaac said: 'Ulla confirmed this error according to R. Benjamin b. Jephet[4]. R. Zera asked in astonishment: What has the statement of R. Benjamin b. Jephet to do by the side of that of R. Ḥiyya b. Abba[5]! R. Ḥiyya b. Abba paid careful attention and learnt the teaching from R. Joḥanan his master, but R. Benjamin b. Jephet was not so attentive. Also, R. Ḥiyya b. Abba used to revise his study in the presence of R. Joḥanan his master every thirty days, but R. Benjamin b. Jephet did not do so. Besides, apart from these two reasons[6], there is the incident when lupines were cooked seven times in a pot and eaten as a dessert; they came and questioned R. Joḥanan[7], and he replied, "...Who createst the fruit of the ground[8]." And R. Ḥiyya b. Abba likewise said: I saw R. Joḥanan eat a salted[9] olive, and he pronounced a benediction before and after. This is quite right if thou maintainest that food when cooked is to be regarded as remaining the same; then, before partaking [of the salted olive] the benediction is "...Who createst the fruit of the tree," and afterwards he says one benediction which is an abstract of three. Shouldest thou, however, maintain that cooked food is not to be regarded as remaining the same, it is right that before partaking thereof one should say "...By Whose word all

Discussion continued.

1 And cooking makes no difference to the benediction.

2 The unleavened wafer is exceptional and no general rule can be argued from it.

3 That vegetables are to be considered as unaffected by cooking for the purpose of the benediction.

4 Ascribing to R. Joḥanan the statement that the benediction is "...By Whose word," etc.

5 I.e. Why mention it at all in view of the contradictory report of a more eminent authority?

6 Which show that R. Ḥiyya's version is more trustworthy.

7 About the benediction.

8 Proving that, in his opinion, the cooking made no difference to the benediction.

9 From the standpoint of the benediction, salting is the same as cooking.

things exist"; but what benediction is to be said afterwards? Perhaps "...Who createst many living beings with their wants" etc.[1] Rab Isaac b. Samuel[2] quoted in objection: In the case of herbs wherewith one complies with the requirements of the law on Passover, they or their stalk are legitimate, but not if they have been pickled or cooked or sodden! If thou thinkest they are to be regarded as remaining the same, why not when [these herbs are cooked]? There it is different; because we require the taste of the bitter herbs[3] and it is not there [if they are cooked].

The minimum quantity which requires a benediction. **fol. 39 a.**

R. Jeremiah asked R. Zera, "How could R. Joḥanan pronounce a benediction over a salted olive since, if the stone had been removed, the minimum quantity is wanting[4]?" He replied, "Dost thou think that the quantity equivalent to a large olive is necessary [to constitute the minimum]? About the size of an average olive is sufficient; and there was that quantity, because the olive which they brought to R. Joḥanan was of a large size, so that although the stone was removed, the minimum still remained." For there is a Mishnaic teaching: The olive which they mention [as constituting the minimum] is neither small nor large but an average size, viz.: the kind called *Ēgōrī*[5]. R. Abbahu said: Its name is not *Ēgōrī* but *Ibrōṭī*[6]; and some say *Simrōsī*[7]. Why is it called *Ēgōrī*? Because its oil is stored up [*āgūr*] within it.

Should benediction over cabbage be preferred to that over poultry?

We can say that this is like [the discussion of] the *Tannāīm*. For two disciples were sitting in the presence of Bar Ḳappara, when there were set before him cabbage, Damascene plums and poultry. Bar Ḳappara gave one of the disciples permission to say the benediction. He sat up and said the benediction over the poultry. His companion laughed at him, and Bar Ḳappara became

1 Singer, p. 290. 2 *M.*: Samuel b. Isaac. 3 Cf. Exod. xii. 8.

4 No benediction is required unless the amount of food eaten is the size of an olive. If, therefore, one eats only an olive, he has not partaken of the minimum, since the stone has to be removed.

5 Jastrow adopts the Talmudic derivation which makes this a Hebrew word from the root *agr* "to store," hence "fit for storage, of good quality." It might, however, be the name of a place; see Neubauer, p. 387, who identifies it with Egra in the interior of Babylon. J. Perles, *Zur rabbinischen Sprach- und Sagenkunde*, p. 34, suggests ἄγουρος.

6 *M.*: *Ibrōsī* which Jastrow thinks is a geographical name. Krauss, p. 7, refers to ὡραῖος "fresh"; but see Löw's criticism *ad loc.* Perles, *op. cit.* p. 35, suggests ἀβροτόνινον ἔλαιον.

7 *M.*: *Sibrōsī* which, according to Jastrow, is a geographical name. Wiesner explains it by the Latin *semirudis* "half-ripe" [?]. Krauss, p. 399, regards it as another variant of ὡραῖος. Perles, *loc. cit.*, reads *Imrōsī* which he identifies with *ambrosia*.

angry, saying, "Not with him who uttered the benediction, but with him who laughed, am I angry. If thy companion is like one who has never tasted meat[1], wherefore dost thou laugh at him?" Then he said, "Not with him who laughed am I angry, but with him who uttered the benediction"; and he continued, "If there is no wisdom here, is there no old age here[2]?" It has been taught that both of them did not survive that year[3]. Is it not that they differed in the following point: He who said the benediction thought that for cooked vegetables and poultry it is "...By Whose word all things exist," and therefore what is best liked is to be preferred [for the benediction][4]; but he who laughed thought that for cooked vegetables it is "...Who createst the fruit of the ground" and for poultry "...By Whose word all things exist," and therefore the fruit should be given precedence? No; they both agreed that for cooked vegetables and poultry it is "...By Whose word all things exist"; and here they differed on the following point: One thought that what is best liked is to be preferred [for the benediction], whereas the other thought that the cabbage should receive precedence because it is nourishing[5].

Benediction over turnip-tops.

R. Zera said: When we were at the school of Rab Huna he said to us: For the tops of turnips, if he cut them into large pieces, the benediction is "...Who createst the fruit of the ground"; if into small pieces, it is "...By Whose word all things exist[6]." But when we came to the school of Rab Judah he said: In either case it is "...Who createst the fruit of the ground," because one cuts them up a great deal to sweeten the taste. Rab Ashē said: When we were at the school of Rab Kahᵃna he said to us: For a broth of beet, into which one does not put much flour, the benediction is "...Who createst the fruit of the ground"; for a broth of turnip, into which much flour is put, it is "...Who createst various kinds of foods." Afterwards he said: In either case it is "...Who createst the fruit of the ground," and that they put much flour into it is only done to make it adhere.

[1] He should first have said the benediction over the fruit as being in its natural state. He gave the poultry the preference, as though it were a new luxury for him.

[2] A sarcastic rebuke. If they did not admit their master's superior knowledge, let them at least defer to his riper experience.

[3] They were punished for disrespect towards their teacher.

[4] After the benediction, he partook of the poultry not the vegetables, although the benediction was the same for both.

[5] I.e. more so than the poultry.

[6] Because the semblance of fruit has gone.

Broth of beet beneficial.

Rab Ḥisda said: The broth of beet is pleasant to the heart and good for the eyes, how much more so for the bowels. Abbai said: That is only so when it remains on the stove and makes the sound *Tuk, Tuk*[1]. Rab Pappa said: It is evident to me that the water of the beet is like the beet[2], the water of the turnip like the turnip, and the water of all vegetables like the vegetables themselves. Rab Pappa asked: How is it with dill-water? Is it used to sweeten the taste[3] or to remove the bad smell? Come and hear: Dill, when it gives a taste to the dish, does not come under the law of *T^erūmāh*[4] and does not contract the impurity of foods. Conclude from this that it is used to sweeten the taste! Draw that conclusion.

Benediction over soaked bread.

Rab Ḥiyya b. Ashē said: Over stale bread [which has been placed] in a pot [to soak], the benediction is "...Who bringest forth bread from the earth." This is at variance with R. Ḥiyya[5] who said: This benediction must conclude with [the cutting or breaking of] the bread[6]. Raba retorted: Why is stale bread different, that no [benediction should be pronounced before partaking thereof]? Is it because when the benediction is concluded, it is concluded over a divided loaf? But in the case of [fresh] bread also, when the benediction is concluded, it is likewise concluded over a divided loaf! But, declared Raba: One says the benediction and afterwards breaks [the bread]. The people of Nehardea[7] acted according to R. Ḥiyya, but the Rabbis acted according to Raba. Rabina said: My mother told me, "Thy father acted according to R. Ḥiyya, for R. Ḥiyya maintained that the benediction must conclude with [the breaking of] the bread; but the Rabbis acted according to Raba." The *H^alākāh* is in agreement with Raba who maintained that one should say the benediction and afterwards break the bread.

fol. 39 b. Benediction to be made and then the loaf cut.

Whether benediction is to be made over pieces or whole loaf.

It has been reported: If pieces of bread and whole loaves were set before them, Rab Huna declares that the benediction is to be pronounced over the pieces and it is not necessary over the loaves[8]. R. Joḥanan declared: [To say the benediction over] the whole

[1] An onomatopoeic expression, representing the sound made when the broth is boiling. [2] For the purpose of the benediction.

[3] Then the benediction would be "...Who createst the fruit of the earth"; if the latter alternative, no benediction would be required.

[4] It is then regarded as merely wood and not as a herb; hence its only use is to impart a flavour to a dish.

[5] *M.* adds: b. Abba in the name of R. Joḥanan.

[6] When the bread is soaked, this is impossible.

[7] See p. 74 n. 2.

[8] I.e. when the pieces are larger than the whole loaves.

loaf is the best way to perform the religious duty; but should there be a piece of wheaten-bread and a loaf of barley-bread, all agree that the benediction should be pronounced over the former[1] and is unnecessary over the latter. R. Jeremiah b. Abba said: It is like [the discussion of] the *Tannāīm*, viz.: We take *T^erūmāh* with a whole onion, though small in size, but not with half of a large onion. R. Judah says: Not so, but we take it with the half of a large onion. Do they not differ on the following point: One[2] maintains that which is of greater value is to be preferred, while the other maintains that which is whole is to be preferred? Where there is a priest present[3], there is no difference of opinion that what is of greater value is to be preferred, the disagreement arising where there is no priest[4]. For there is a Mishnaic teaching: Wherever there is a priest present, the *T^erūmāh* is to be taken from the best, but where there is no priest, it is to be taken from that which is most durable; R. Judah says: It is only to be taken from the best. Rab Naḥman b. Isaac said: He who fears Heaven complies with the regulation of the law according to the teaching of both[5]; and who is it [that acts thus]? Mar b. Rabina, for he used to place the piece of bread with the whole loaf and break both.

Discussion continued. A *Tannā* taught in the presence of Rab Naḥman b. Isaac[6]: One should place the piece of bread with the whole loaf and break them both and then say the benediction. Rab Naḥman said to him, "What is thy name?" He replied, "Shalman[7]." He said to him, "Peaceful art thou and peaceful thy teaching, for thou hast restored peace between the disciples." Rab Pappa said: All agree that on Passover one should place the piece together with the whole and break them both. What is the reason? "Bread of affliction" (Deut. xvi. 3) it is written[8].

Procedure on the Sabbath. R. Abba[9] said: On the Sabbath one should break bread over two loaves. What is the reason? "Twice as much bread" (Exod.

[1] Irrespective of its size as compared with the loaf, because its quality is superior.

[2] R. Judah.

[3] To receive the *T^erūmāh*.

[4] In that case, the *T^erūmāh* would have to be stored until it could be handed to a priest, and the half-onion would decay more quickly than a whole one.

[5] Viz. Rab Huna and R. Joḥanan.

[6] *M.*: R. Joḥanan.

[7] *Lit.* peaceful.

[8] The poor man usually has to say his benediction over a piece rather than over a whole loaf; therefore over the unleavened bread, we should use a piece for the benediction.

[9] *M.*: Raba.

xvi. 22) it is written[1]. Rab Ashē said: I saw Rab Kah^a^na take two loaves but only break one[2]. R. Zera used to break off [on the Sabbath a piece of bread to suffice] for the whole of the meal. Rabina said to Rab Ashē: But this must have looked like voracity! He replied: Since he did not act so every day but only now [on the Sabbath] it would not have that appearance. When R. Ammi and R. Assi had occasion to use the bread of *'Ērūb*, they would pronounce over it the benediction "...Who bringest forth bread from the earth," saying, "Since one religious duty[3] is being fulfilled therewith, let us perform still another[4]."

fol. 40 a. On speaking between the benediction and partaking of the food.

Rab[5] declared: [If one broke the bread and pronounced the benediction, and before eating handed a piece to another saying,] "Take it, the benediction has been made; take it, the benediction has been made!" it is unnecessary for him to pronounce it again [before partaking of the bread][6]. [But if before eating he says,] "Bring salt, bring the relish," he must repeat the benediction. R. Joḥanan declared that even if he said, "Bring salt, bring the relish," he likewise need not repeat the benediction[7]. [Should he, however, say,] "Mix food for the oxen! Mix food for the oxen!" the benediction must be repeated. Rab Sheshet declared that even if he said "Mix food for the oxen," he also need not repeat the benediction. For Rab Judah said in the name of Rab: A man must not eat his meal before giving food to his cattle; as it is said, "And I will give grass in thy fields for thy cattle" and then "thou shalt eat and be satisfied" (Deut. xi. 15).

Salt or relish required with bread before the benediction.

Raba b. Samuel said in the name of R. Ḥiyya[8]: The one who is about to break bread is not permitted to do so until they place salt or relish before each person. Raba b. Samuel visited the house of the Exilarch[9]. They set bread before him and he broke

1 Referring to the double portion of manna provided on the Friday for the Sabbath.

2 Because it is stated "they *gathered* twice as much bread," not that they used it all. Hence to hold the two loaves was sufficient.

3 That of the *'Ērūb* (see Glossary, s.v.).

4 Saying a benediction.

5 *M.*: Rabina.

6 It is forbidden to speak between the benediction and the performance of the act for which it had been said. But in this case, the words are not considered an interruption to render the benediction invalid.

7 Because the spoken words were connected with the breaking of the bread, salt being used with the bread over which the benediction is said as salt was required with the meal-offering. Cf. Lev. ii. 13.

8 The correct reading is probably Rabbah b. Samuel...Ḥiyya b. Abba; cf. Hyman, II. p. 438 *b*.

9 The lay head of the Jewish Community in Babylon.

it forthwith[1]. They said to him, "Has the master retracted his teaching?" He replied, "This bread[2] requires no condiment[3]."

Raba b. Samuel also said in the name of R. Ḥiyya: Urine is only completely evacuated in a sitting posture[4]. Rab Kahana said[5]: Where there is loose earth, this is so even when standing[6]; and should there be no loose earth, let him stand on an elevated place and urinate on to a declivity. Another teaching of R. Ḥiyya.

Raba b. Samuel also said in the name of R. Ḥiyya: After every food eat salt, and after every beverage drink water, and thou wilt not come to harm[7]. There is a teaching to the same effect: After every food eat salt, and after every beverage drink water, and thou wilt not come to harm. There is another teaching: Who has partaken of any food without eating salt or drunk any beverage without drinking water will be troubled during the day with a bad odour in his mouth and at night with croup. Use of salt and water beneficial.

Our Rabbis have taught: He who makes his food float in water[8] will not suffer with indigestion. How much [should he drink]? Rab Ḥisda said: A cupful to a loaf. A similar teaching.

Rab Mari said in the name of R. Joḥanan: He who makes it a habit to eat lentils once in thirty days keeps croup away from his house; but not every day. What is the reason[9]? Because it is bad for the breath of the mouth. Lentils should be eaten once in thirty days. R. Mari also said in the name of R. Joḥanan: He who makes it a habit to eat mustard once in thirty days keeps illnesses away from his house; but not every day. What is the reason? Because it is bad for heart-weakness. Similarly with mustard. Rab Ḥiyya b. Ashē said in the name of Rab: He who makes it a habit to eat small fish will not suffer with indigestion; more than that, small fish make a man's whole body fruitful[10] and strong. Small fish beneficial to health. Rab Ḥamma b. R. Ḥannina said: He who makes it a habit to use black cumin will not suffer with pain of Black cumin also healthy.

1 Not waiting for salt.

2 Being fresh and tasty.

3 This last word is rendered by Rashi and others "delay" (sc. for salt). But Jastrow establishes the meaning "condiment."

4 Rashi explains: When standing, he fears his clothes will be splashed and consequently he restrains himself.

5 *M.* omits these words here and inserts them after "even when standing."

6 There is then no cause for this fear, the loose earth absorbing the urine.

7 Through illness.

8 I.e. he drinks a large quantity of water at his meal.

9 That he should not eat lentils every day.

10 *Lit.* cause it to be fruitful and multiply, i.e. stimulate sexual vigour.

the heart. It is quoted in objection: Rabban Simeon b. Gamaliel says: Black cumin is one of the sixty deadly poisons, and he who sleeps to the east of his store [of cumin], his blood is on his own head[1]! There is no contradiction; the latter referring to its odour, the other to its taste. The mother of R. Jeremiah used to bake bread for him and sprinkle [black cumin] upon it, and then scrape it off[2].

But R. Judah declares: "...Who createst divers kinds of herbs."

R. Judah requires a special benediction for each species.

R. Zera (another version: R. Ḥinnana b. Pappa) said: The *Hᵃlākāh* is not in accord with R. Judah[3]. R. Zera (another version: R. Ḥinnana b. Pappa) also said: What is R. Judah's reason[4]? The Scriptures state, "Blessed be the Lord day by day" (Ps. lxviii. 20)—are we to bless Him by day and not by night! Nay, it means to tell thee: Day by day give Him the appropriate blessing[5]; so here also, for every species of food give Him an appropriate benediction.

God will increase the knowledge of them who desire to know *Tōrāh*.

R. Zera (another version: R. Ḥinnana b. Pappa) also said: Come and see that the attribute of the Holy One, blessed be He, is not like that of the human being. The attribute of the human being is to support the empty vessel[6] but not the full; but the Holy One, blessed be He, is not so—He supports the full vessel, not the empty[7]. As it is said, "And He said, If hearing, thou wilt hear" (*sic*! Exod. xv. 26)—i.e. if thou wilt hear [once], thou wilt hear again[8]; but if not, thou wilt not hear. Another explanation is: If thou wilt hear the old, thou wilt also hear the new[9]; but should thine heart turn aside [from the *Tōrāh*], thou wilt never again hear.

1 The west wind will carry the odour to him with fatal results.

2 She allowed the flavour of the cumin to penetrate into the bread, but would not permit it to remain because the smell was injurious.

3 *M.* omits this sentence.

4 That he requires a special benediction for vegetables and not merely "...Who createst the fruit of the ground."

5 I.e. a special form of praise for the Sabbath, Passover, etc.

6 The ignorant.

7 See Bacher, *A. P. A.* II. p. 518 n. 3 who compares Matt. xiii. 12 "For whosoever hath, to him shall be given."

8 Referring to *Tōrāh*.

9 Add to thy knowledge.

MISHNĀH II

If one said the benediction "...Who createst the fruit of the ground" over fruits of the tree, he has complied with the requirements of the law. If, over fruits of the earth, he said "...Who createst the fruit of the tree," he has not so complied. If over all of them he said "...By Whose word all things exist," he has complied with the requirements of the law.

GEMĀRĀ

Who is it that teaches that the main feature about the tree is the earth[1]? Rab Naḥman b. Isaac said: It is R. Judah; for there is a Mishnaic teaching: If the water-supply dried up[2] or the tree was cut down, one brings [the first-fruits to Jerusalem] but does not make the declaration[3]. R. Judah says: He both brings [the first-fruits] and makes the declaration[4].

Why benediction "fruit of the ground" is valid with fruits of the tree.

If, over fruits of the earth, etc.

This is evident! Rab Naḥman b. Isaac said: It is only necessary for R. Judah who declares that wheat is a kind of tree; for there is a teaching: The tree from which Adam ate was—so says R. Meïr—the vine, because thou hast nothing which brings lamentation upon man as does wine; as it is said, "And he drank of the wine, and was drunken" (Gen. ix. 21). R. Nehemiah says: It was the fig-tree, for by the very thing that they were disgraced were they restored; as it is said, "And they sewed fig-leaves together" (*ibid.* iii. 7). R. Judah said: It was wheat, because a child does not know to call "Father, mother" before it has tasted wheat[5]. It may enter thy mind to say that since R. Judah maintains that wheat is a kind of tree, the benediction over it should be "...Who createst the fruit of the tree"! Therefore we are

What was the tree from which Adam ate?

1 Because according to the *Mishnāh*, the benediction "...Who createst the fruit of the ground" is allowed over fruits of the tree.

2 So that the field lost its fertility.

3 See Deut. xxvi. 5–10. The declaration concludes with "And now, behold, I have brought the first of the fruit of the land which Thou, O Lord, hast given me." But since the water-supply has ceased or the tree which grew the fruit been cut down, the land will no longer yield him fruits and therefore the declaration ought not to be made.

4 Since the land remains, he requires the declaration to be made; accordingly he holds that the ground is the main feature of the tree.

5 A child reaches the age when it eats bread before it can speak. This is intended to explain the name "tree of knowledge" (Gen. ii. 17).

informed that we say the benediction "...Who createst the fruit of the tree" only where, if thou takest away the fruit, a stem

fol. 40 b.

remains which again produces; but where, if thou takest away the fruit, there is no stem to produce again fruit[1], we do not say the benediction "...Who createst the fruit of the tree" but "...Who createst the fruit of the ground."

If over all of them he said "...By Whose word all things exist," etc.

Whether the form of the benediction as instituted by the Rabbis must be adhered to.

It has been reported: Rab Huna said: Except bread and wine[2]; but R. Joḥanan said: Even bread and wine. Let us say that this is like [the following controversy of] the *Tannāīm*: If one sees bread and exclaims, "How fine is this bread; blessed be the All-present Who created it," he has complied with the requirements of the law[3]. If he sees a fig and exclaims, "How fine is this fig, blessed be the All-present Who created it," he has likewise complied. These are the words of R. Meïr; but R. Josē says: Whoever changes the form which the Sages assigned to the benedictions has not fulfilled his obligation. Let us say that Rab Huna is in agreement with R. Josē[4] and R. Joḥanan with R. Meïr[5]! Rab Huna could tell thee: I am even in agreement with R. Meïr; for R. Meïr only speaks above of a case where one mentions the name of bread, but where he does not mention the name of bread, even R. Meïr admits [that the man's words do not constitute a valid benediction][6]. R. Joḥanan, on the other hand, could tell thee: I am in agreement even with R. Josē; for R. Josē only disagrees above because the man used a form of benediction which the Rabbis had not ordained, but if he had said "...By Whose word all things exist" which the Rabbis had ordained, even R. Josē admits [that it would be valid].

Is the benediction valid if not Hebrew?

Benjamin the shepherd used to double the bread[7] and say "Blessed be the Lord of this bread[8]." Rab said: He thereby complied with the requirements of the law. But Rab has declared: A benediction which contains no mention of the Divine

[1] E.g. wheat. [2] These have special benedictions; see p. 233.

[3] This is valid as a benediction and he may proceed to eat.

[4] Since they both demand the precise benediction.

[5] Who are content so long as praise is offered to God.

[6] If the man had merely said, "Blessed be the All-present Who has created this" and not "this bread," it would not have sufficed for R. Meïr. Hence he agrees with Rab Huna who is not satisfied with "...By Whose word," etc. because it makes no mention of the bread.

[7] I.e. break a piece and place salt or relish in between; cf. Lane, p. 148. On the various explanations of the phrase, which is literally "to wrap the bread," see *T. A.* III. p. 51. [8] These words are Aramaic, not Hebrew.

Name is no benediction[1]! What Benjamin did say was "Blessed be the All-merciful, the Lord of this bread." But lo, we require three benedictions! What means, then, "he has complied with the requirements of the law" as stated by Rab? He has complied so far as the first benediction is concerned[2]. What does he intend to teach us? That [it is valid] although he said it in a non-holy tongue[3]! We have already learnt: The following may be said in any language: The portion of the *Sōṭāh*[4], the declaration concerning the tithe[5], the *Shᵉma'*, *Tᵉfillāh* and the Grace after meals[6]! [Nevertheless Rab's statement] was necessary; for it might have entered thy mind to say that this[7] only applies when one utters the benediction in a non-holy language exactly as the Rabbis ordained it in the holy tongue; but should he not say it in the non-holy language exactly as the Rabbis ordained it in the holy tongue, I am to declare that he has not [complied]. Therefore he informs us [that the benediction is valid even when the wording does not exactly conform to the Hebrew original].

Whether a benediction must contain reference to God as King.

It was stated above: "Rab said: A benediction which contains no mention of the Divine Name is no benediction." But R. Joḥanan has said: A benediction which contains no reference to the Divine Kingship[8] is no benediction! Abbai said: Rab's opinion seems more probable; for there is a teaching[9]: [It is written] "I have not transgressed any of Thy commandments, neither have I forgotten" (Deut. xxvi. 13)—"I have not transgressed," i.e. by omitting the benediction, "neither have I forgotten," i.e. to mention Thy Name thereby; but he does not teach here [that it is necessary to refer to] the Kingship. (R. Joḥanan, however, explains: "Neither have I forgotten," i.e. to mention Thy Name and Kingship thereby[10].)

1 And there is no mention of it in Benjamin's benediction of which Rab approved.

2 Benjamin's formula is acceptable as a substitute for the first of the three benedictions.

3 The language having been Aramaic.

4 The priest's address to the woman suspected of adultery; see Num. v. 21 f.

5 Cf. Deut. xxvi. 13-15.

6 Since we have this teaching concerning the Grace after meals, permitting it to be said in any language, what was the purpose of Rab's remark?

7 That the benediction not in Hebrew is valid.

8 Viz. "King of the Universe." Derenbourg, *R. E. J.* xiv p. 27, suggests that stress was laid upon the Divine Kingship in every benediction as a sort of protest against the rule of the Roman tyrants.

9 *M.*: a Mishnaic teaching.

10 This sentence is omitted in *M.* and some edd.

MISHNĀH III, IV

III. *Over anything whose growth is not from the earth, one says "...By Whose word all things exist." Over vinegar, fruit which falls unripe from the tree and locusts, one says "...By Whose word all things exist." R. Judah declares: No benediction is to be pronounced over anything which comes under the category of a curse*[1].

IV. *If there were several kinds of food before him, R. Judah says: Should there be among them one of the seven species*[2], *he pronounces the benediction over that. The Sages declare: He may say it over whichever of them he pleases.*

G^EMĀRA

Benediction over food which does not grow from the earth.

Our Rabbis have taught: Over anything whose growth is not from the earth, e.g. the flesh of cattle, beasts, birds and fish, one says "...By Whose word all things exist." Over milk, eggs and cheese, one says "...By Whose word." Over bread which has become mouldy, wine over which a film has formed, and cooked food which has gone bad[3], one says "...By Whose word." Over salt, brine, morils and truffles, one says "...By Whose word." That is to say that morils and truffles are not grown from the soil. There is, however, a teaching: He who vows not to eat fruits grown from the earth is forbidden to eat the fruits of the earth but is allowed morils and truffles; if he declares, "All that is grown from the earth shall be forbidden me," he is also prohibited from eating morils and truffles! Abbai replied: These grow from the earth but do not derive their nutriment therefrom. But lo, the *Mishnāh* reads: *Anything whose* growth *is not from the earth!* Read, "Anything which does not derive nutriment from the earth."

Over fruit which falls unripe from the tree [*nōb^elōt*].

The meaning of *nōb^elōt*.

What are *nōb^elōt*? R. Zera and R. El'a [differ in their explanation]. One says: They are the fruit scorched by the sun; the other says: They are dates blown from the tree by the wind. Our *Mishnāh* states: *R. Judah declares: No benediction is to be pronounced over anything which comes under the category of a curse.* That is quite right according to him who says *nōb^elōt*

[1] All the things so far mentioned come within this category.

[2] See next folio, p. 271.

[3] *Lit.* whose form has passed.

means "Fruit scorched by the sun," for that may be called a kind of curse; but according to him who says it means "Dates blown from the tree by the wind," how is this a kind of curse? [R. Judah's statement refers] to the remainder[1].

Another version: It is quite right according to him who says *nōbᵉlōt* means "Fruit scorched by the sun" that over it we pronounce the benediction "...By Whose word"; but according to him who says [it means] "Dates blown from the tree by the wind" the benediction "...By Whose word" should rather be "...Who createst the fruit of the tree[2]"! Nay, everybody agrees that *nōbᵉlōt* without further qualification means "Fruit scorched by the sun"; where they differ is with reference to *nōbᵉlōt tᵉmārāh*. For there is a Mishnaic teaching: Those fruits with which, in case of doubt as to the tithe[3], the law deals leniently are: *Shīṭīn*, *Rīmīn*, *'Uzrādīn*[4], *Bᵉnōt Shūaḥ*, *Bᵉnōt Shiḳmāh*, *Gofnīn*, *Niṣpāh* and *Nōbᵉlōt Tᵉmārāh*. *Shīṭīn*, Rabbah b. Bar Ḥannah said in the name of R. Joḥanan, are a species of figs. *Rīmīn* are lote[5]. *'Uzrādīn* are crab-apples. *Bᵉnōt Shūaḥ*, Rabbah b. Bar Ḥannah said in the name of R. Joḥanan, are white figs. *Bᵉnōt Shiḳmāh*, Rabbah b. Bar Ḥannah said in the name of R. Joḥanan, are sycamore-figs. *Gofnīn* are late grapes. *Niṣpāh* is the caper-bush. *Nōbᵉlōt Tᵉmārāh*—R. El'a and R. Zera [differ in their explanation]—One says "Fruit scorched by the sun"; the other says "Dates blown from the tree by the wind." It is quite right according to him who says [it means] "Fruit scorched by the sun," that is what he teaches, viz. "Those fruits with which, in case of doubt as to the tithe, the law deals leniently"—it is the doubt that exempts them [from the tithe], but if there is certainty[6], then they are subject. But according to him who says it means "Dates blown from the tree by the wind," how can they be subject [to the tithe] in the case of certainty, since they are public property[7]? With what are we here dealing? With a case

Meaning of *nōbᵉlōt tᵉmārāh*.

1 Of the things enumerated in the *Mishnāh*, viz. vinegar and locusts.

2 Because they need not necessarily be spoilt as the scorched fruits are.

3 I.e. if he purchased these fruits from a person of whom he is not certain that he gave the tithe, it is unnecessary for the buyer to give a tithe.

4 According to Löw, *Aramäische Pflanzennamen*, pp. 287 f. the correct reading is '*Uzrārin*.

5 For כנדי read כינרי with the 'Ārūk, i.e. χόνναρος.

6 That no tithe had been taken.

7 Fruit fallen from the tree can be claimed by the poor and is not subject to the tithe.

where he has arranged them for storage; for R. Isaac[1] stated that R. Joḥanan said in the name of R. Eliezer b. Jacob: Gleanings, forgotten sheaves, and the produce of the corner of the field[2], if he[3] arranged them for storage, they become subject to the tithe.

fol. 41 a. Others say: It is quite right according to him who maintains it[4] means "Dates blown from the tree by the wind"—then that is why he mentions here [in our *Mishnāh*] *nōb^elōt* without further specification[5] and there [in the Mishnaic quotation] he calls it [*nōb^elōt*] *t^emārāh*. But according to him who says [*nōb^elōt t^emārāh*] means "Fruit scorched by the sun," let him teach in both passages[6] either *nōb^elōt t^emārāh* or *nōb^elōt* without further specification! The question [remains unanswered].

IV. *If there were several kinds of food before him*, etc.

Statement of the *Mishnāh* elucidated. 'Ulla said: The difference of opinion arises when the benediction is the same for them; for R. Judah holds that one of the seven species is to be given preference, whereas the Rabbis hold that the kind which is best liked should be given preference. Where, however, the benediction is not the same, all agree that he should first say it over that which he likes best and then say it over the others.

The inference disputed. Against this is quoted: If radishes and olives were before him, he pronounces the benediction over the radishes and he is exempt from saying it over the olives[7]! With what are we here dealing? With the case where the radishes are the principal item[8]. If so, I will quote the continuation: R. Judah says: He pronounces the benediction over the olive, because it belongs to the seven species! Does not R. Judah agree with the Mishnaic teaching: *In the case of a food which is the principal thing and together with it is something accessory, the benediction is to be uttered over the former and there is no necessity for a benediction over the latter*[9]? Shouldest thou declare that here also R. Judah is not in agree-

[1] *M.*: R. Isaac b. Eleazar said in the name of R. Eliezer b. Jacob.

[2] Cf. Lev. xix. 9f., xxiii. 22, Deut. xxiv. 19.

[3] The poor who collected the fruits.

[4] The term *Nōb^elōt T^emārāh* in the Mishnaic quotation.

[5] In the sense "Fruit scorched by the sun."

[6] In our *Mishnāh* and in the Mishnaic quotation.

[7] But it has just been mentioned he says the benediction first "over that which he likes best and then...over the other."

[8] And he only eats the olives to remove the sharp taste of the radishes; in that case, the second benediction is unnecessary.

[9] Cf. fol. 44 *a*, p. 284. If R. Judah accepts this teaching, how can he demand a benediction for the olive which is only accessory to the radish?

ment, lo there is a teaching: R. Judah says: If the olive is only there on account of the radish, he pronounces the benediction over the radish and it is unnecessary over the olive! We certainly deal here with the case where the radish is the principal item; and where R. Judah and the Rabbis differ is in another matter. The text is defective and should read thus: If radishes and olives were before him, he says the benediction over the former and it is unnecessary over the latter. Of what does it speak here? When the radish is the principal item; but should that not be so, all agree that he says the benediction over one and then over the other. Where there are two species, the benediction for which is the same, he says the benediction over any one he pleases. R. Judah says: He utters it over the olive, because it is one of the seven species.

Two conflicting opinions on the question.

R. Ammi and R. Isaac Nappāḥā[1] are at variance over this matter[2]. One declares that the difference of opinion arises when the benediction is the same, for R. Judah holds that one of the seven species is to be given preference, whereas the Rabbis hold that the kind which is best liked is to be given preference. Where, however, the benediction is not the same, all agree that he says the benediction over one and then over the other. The second [Rabbi] declares that there is difference of opinion even where the benediction is not the same. It is quite right according to him who declares that there is difference of opinion where the benediction is the same; that is clear. But according to him who declares that they disagree where the benediction is not the same, in what do they differ? R. Jeremiah said: In which is to come first; for Rab Joseph (another version: R. Isaac) said: Whatever is given precedence in the Scriptural verse must take precedence for the benediction; as it is said, "A land of wheat and barley, and vines and fig-trees and pomegranates, a land of olive-trees and honey" (Deut. viii. 8)[3].

Deut. viii. 8 sets standards of measure.

This teaching, however, conflicts with the statement of R. Ḥanan[4] who said: This whole verse only speaks of "standards[5]." "Wheat"—for there is a Mishnaic teaching: Whoever enters a plague-infected house with his garments upon his shoulders, his sandals and rings in his hand, he and they immediately become

[1] I.e. the smith. [2] Viz. the dispute between R. Judah and the Rabbis.

[3] The seven species are enumerated in this verse.

[4] Some edd. read: Ḥanin.

[5] And therefore the order in which they are mentioned does not matter. The *Talmūd* goes on to explain what is meant by "standards."

unclean[1]. If he was clothed in his garments, his sandals upon his feet and his rings upon his finger, he immediately becomes unclean, but they remain undefiled until he tarries there a sufficient time to eat a *p^erās*[2] of wheaten-bread[3], but not barley-bread, reclining and eating it with a relish. "Barley"—for there is a Mishnaic teaching: The bone [of a dead person or animal] the size of barley defiles by touch and carrying, but does not defile in a tent[4]. "Vine"—it requires a fourth [of a *Lōg*] of wine for a Nazirite[5]. "Fig-tree"—to carry as much as a dried fig [from a private to a public court or *vice versa*] constitutes a breach of the Sabbath. "Pomegranate"—as we have the Mishnaic teaching:
fol. 41 b. The vessels of house-owners[6] have the standard size of a pomegranate[7]. "A land of olive-trees"—R. Josē b. R. Ḥannina said: [This means], a land where the standard for everything is the size of the olive. The standard for *everything*, dost imagine? Lo, there are the others just mentioned[8]! Nay, [the meaning is], a land where the standard for most things is the size of the olive. "Honey"—one must have eaten as much as a large date on the Day of Atonement [to have incurred the penalty for breaking the fast]. But the other [Rabbi][9]? [He asks]: Are these standards explicitly stated in this verse? No, they are ordained by the Rabbis, and this verse serves only as a support.

Another reference to this verse.

Rab Ḥisda and Rab Hamnuna were sitting at a meal, when dates and pomegranates were set before them. Rab Hamnuna took and pronounced the benediction over the dates first. Rab Ḥisda said to him, "Does not the master agree with the statement of Rab Joseph (another version: R. Isaac), viz.: That which is given precedence in the verse (Deut. viii. 8) must precede for the benediction?" He replied, "'Dates[10]' is the second word

[1] Cf. Lev. xiv. 46. Since he is not wearing the things, they become defiled at once. As for his actual garments, they do not become defiled (requiring washing) unless he "lieth or eateth" there; cf. *v.* 47.

[2] A loaf equal in size to four eggs.

[3] Barley-bread, being coarser, would take longer to eat. Hence "wheat" sets a standard of time in connection with the contracting of defilement.

[4] By its presence alone, without actual contact.

[5] To constitute a breach of his vow. Cf. Num. vi. 3.

[6] As contrasted with those of an artisan, which are exposed for sale.

[7] I.e. a piece that size, if broken off, renders the vessel immune against defilement; and when actually defiled, a breakage of that extent makes the vessel immediately clean.

[8] Wheat, barley, etc.

[9] I.e. Rab Joseph who explains Deut. viii. 8 differently; what does he make of this explanation of R. Ḥanan?

[10] Represented in the text by "honey."

after 'land,' 'pomegranate' the fifth word after 'land'[1]." Rab Ḥisda said to him, "Would that we had iron feet so that we could always [follow and] listen to thee!"

Whether benediction is required over food brought in the course of a meal.

It has been reported: If they set before them figs and grapes in the middle of a meal, Rab Huna declared that they require a benediction before partaking thereof but not after. Similarly said Rab Naḥman: They require a benediction before partaking thereof but not after. But Rab Sheshet said: They require a benediction both before and after, because there is nothing which requires a benediction before partaking thereof which does not require one after it, bread offered as a dessert[2] being alone excepted. This is at variance with the statement of R. Ḥiyya who said: [The benediction over] bread exempts all other articles of food, and that over wine exempts all other kinds of beverage [from the necessity of another benediction]. Rab Pappa said: The *Hᵃlākāh* is—Articles of food which are brought in connection with the meal[3], in the course of the meal, require a benediction neither before nor after; if they are not brought in connection with the meal[4], in the course of the meal, they require a benediction before but not after; if brought after the meal, they require a benediction before and after.

Why benediction over bread does not make one over wine unnecessary.

They asked Ben Zoma: Why is it said, "Articles of food brought in connection with the meal, in the course of the meal, require a benediction neither before nor after"? He replied: Because [the benediction over] the bread makes it unnecessary. If so, let the bread make [a benediction] unnecessary also for the wine! It is different with wine, because it necessitates a benediction for itself[5].

fol. 42 a.

A meal requires Grace after it.

Rab Huna ate thirteen rolls[6], three to a *Ḳab* in size, and said no Grace. Rab Naḥman said to him, "Is there still hunger!" But everything which others fix as a meal requires Grace.

1 The word "land" occurs twice in the verse, and "honey" stands nearer to the second word "land" than "pomegranate" does to the first. For that reason it may be given precedence.

2 Served with spices, nuts, honey, etc.

3 According to Rashi, that means the relish eaten with the bread; but Tōsāfōt explain it to refer to foods like meat, fish, which ordinarily figure in the meal.

4 I.e. do not ordinarily form part of the meal, e.g. nuts, fruit.

5 As, e.g., when used for ritual purposes, even though he does not then regard it as a beverage.

6 Of dessert-bread; see above.

Whether bread-dessert requires *hammōṣī'*.

Rab Judah was holding the wedding-feast for his son in the house of Rab Judah b. Ḥ^abiba[1]. They set before him bread as dessert; and when it came, he heard them say *hammōṣī'*. He said to them, "What is the *ṣiṣi*[2] I hear? Perhaps it is the benediction *hammōṣī'* that you have said?" They replied, "It is; for there is a teaching: R. Mona said in the name of R. Judah: We do pronounce *hammōṣī'* over bread-dessert, and Samuel declared that the *H^alākāh* is in agreement with R. Mona." He said to them, "The *H^alākāh* is not in agreement with him." It is reported that they said to him, "But lo, the master has himself declared in the name of Samuel: The bread-wafers used as dessert may be utilised as an *'Ērūb* and we say the benediction *hammōṣī'* over them!" [He replied,] "It is different there [with the *'Ērūb*] because one makes a meal of them; but here where one does not make a meal of them, no [benediction is necessary]."

Food may be eaten until the table is removed.

Rab Pappa went on a visit to the house of Rab Huna b. Rab Nathan. After they had finished their meal, they set before them several things to eat. Rab Pappa took of them and ate. They said to him, "Does not the master hold that if one has finished [his meal], he must not eat anything further[3]?" He replied, "This has only been said when the table has been cleared."

But if food is specially sent, after the table is removed, it may be eaten.

Raba[4] and R. Zera went on a visit to the house of the Exilarch. After the tray had been taken away from before them, there was sent to them from the Exilarch's house a gift [of fruit][5]. Raba ate it, but R. Zera did not. The latter said to him, "Does not the master hold that if the table has been cleared, it is forbidden to eat?" He replied, "We depend upon the Exilarch's tray[6]."

Anointing the hands with oil before saying Grace after meals.

Rab said: He who is accustomed [to anoint his hands] with oil [after finishing a meal], the oil impedes him[7]. Rab Ashē said: When we were at the school of Rab Kah^ana, he said to us, "For instance we are accustomed to the use of oil, and the oil impedes us." But the *H^alākāh* is in agreement with none of these teachings, but with that which Rab Ḥiyya b. Ashē said in the name of Rab, viz.: There are three actions which have to be performed with

[1] *M.*: the house of Rab Ḥ^abiba.

[2] The sibilant syllables of *hammōṣī'*...*hā'āreṣ*.

[3] Until he has said Grace after meals and then pronounce a fresh benediction.

[4] *M.*: Rabbah.

[5] On this gift, see *T. A.* III. p. 21.

[6] And so long as he keeps sending food, the meal is not at an end.

[7] The anointing of the hands, not the clearing of the table, is the signal that the meal is finished.

dispatch: the putting on of hands[1] must be followed immediately by the act of slaughtering; the *Tᵉfillāh* must follow immediately on the *Gᵉʾullāh*[2]; and the Grace after meals must follow immediately on the washing of the hands[3]. Abbai[4] declared: We also add[5]: A benediction [immediately alights upon him who entertains] disciples of the wise[6]; as it is said, "The Lord hath blessed me for thy sake" (Gen. xxx. 27); or, if thou wilt, from this passage, as it is said, "The Lord blessed the Egyptian's house for Joseph's sake" (*ibid.* xxxix. 5).

MISHNĀH V, VI

V. *If a man said the benediction over wine before the meal, he is exempt from saying it over the wine after the meal. If he said it over the dainty[7] served before the meal, he is exempt from saying it over the dainty served after the meal. If he said it over the bread, he is exempt from saying it over the dainty; over the dainty, he is not exempt from saying it over the bread.* Bēt *Shammai declare: Nor from saying it over a cooked dish.*

VI. *If men were sitting [at the meal], each one says Grace for himself. If they were reclining[8], one may say it for all. If wine* **fol. 42 b.** *is set for them in the course of the meal, each one says the benediction for himself; after the meal, one may say it for all. The same one says the benediction over the perfume, although they do not bring the perfume until after the meal.*

GᴱMĀRĀ

Rabbah b. Bar Ḥannah said in the name of R. Joḥanan: The *Mishnāh* teaching[9] applies only to Sabbaths and Festivals, for then a man arranges his meal with wine[10]; but on other days of the year, a

The *Mishnāh* refers to Sabbaths and Festivals.

[1] Cf. Lev. i. 4. [2] See pp. 55 f.

[3] It refers to the "latter waters"—the washing at the end of the meal; and this is the right signal that the meal is finished.

[4] *M.*: Rab Ashē.

[5] As another instance of something immediately following on something else. [6] See fol. 63 *b*.

[7] Hors d'œuvre; see *T. A.* I. p. 472 n. 428. Rashi mentions that it often took the form of poultry or fish; it would then correspond to the *gustatio* of the Romans; cf. *T. A.* III. p. 259 n. 284; *D. C. A.* p. 385.

[8] See p. 278.

[9] In the first sentence of the *Mishnāh*, about the benediction over wine.

[10] I.e. he knows beforehand he will linger at the table and drink several cups.

benediction is to be said over each cup of wine. It has been similarly reported: Rabbah b. Mari[1] said in the name of R. Joshua b. Levi: The teaching applies only to Sabbaths and Festivals and the time when one comes from the bath-house and the meal after blood-letting, for then a man arranges his meal with wine; but on the other days of the year, a benediction is to be said over each cup of wine.

The correct and incorrect procedure. Rabbah b. Mari visited the house of Raba on a week-day, and noticed him pronounce the benediction [over the wine] before the meal and again after it; and he said to him, "That is correct, and so also said R. Joshua b. Levi." Rab Isaac b. Joseph visited the house of Abbai on a Festival and noticed that he pronounced the benediction over each cup. He said to him, "Does not the master agree with the opinion of R. Joshua b. Levi?" He replied, "It only just occurred to me[2]."

Whether benediction over wine in course of the meal renders one unnecessary after the meal. The question was asked: How is it if wine is brought in the course of the meal[3]—does it make the benediction over the wine after the meal unnecessary? Shouldest thou wish to quote our *Mishnāh: If a man said the benediction over wine before the meal, he is exempt from saying it over the wine after the meal*—this is because both of them are for drinking; but here, since one[4] is for steeping and the other for drinking, it is not so; or perhaps that makes no difference? Rab said: He is exempt [from repeating the benediction]; but Rab Kahᵃna said: He is not. Rab Naḥman said: He is exempt; but Rab Sheshet said: He is not. Rab Huna, Rab Judah and all the pupils of Rab say: He is not[5]. Raba quoted against Rab Naḥman: *If wine is set for them in the course of the meal, each one says the benediction for himself; after the meal, one may say it for all[6]!* He replied: This is what he means to say[7], If no wine was set for them in the course of the meal, only after it, then one may say the benediction for all.

[1] *M.*: Rab Mari.

[2] To drink an additional cup of wine, it not being his usual practice. For that reason he repeated the benediction.

[3] And not before the meal, as stated in the *Mishnāh.*

[4] The wine during the meal is chiefly used for dipping into it.

[5] *M.* omits "not."

[6] Hence it seems to follow that although a benediction is said over wine brought during the meal, a further benediction is required for the wine brought after the meal. This contradicts Rab Naḥman and the others who say "he is exempt."

[7] In the last clause of the quoted *Mishnāh.*

If he said it over the bread, he is exempt from saying it over the dainty; over the dainty, he is not exempt from saying it over the bread. Bēt *Shammai declare: Nor from saying it over a cooked dish.*

Question about *Bēt* Shammai's view.

The question was asked: Are *Bēt* Shammai in disagreement with the first clause of this teaching, or is it perhaps with the second clause? They are in disagreement with the first clause[1]; for the first *Tannā* declares: *If he said it over the bread, he is exempt from saying it over the dainty*, so how much more [is it unnecessary for him to say a benediction] over a cooked dish; then *Bēt* Shammai come to declare that not only does [the benediction over] the bread not exempt that over the dainty, but it does not even exempt that over a cooked dish! Or is it perhaps with the second clause that *Bēt* Shammai disagree? For it teaches: [Having said the benediction] *over the dainty, he is not exempt from saying it over the bread;* it is [the benediction over] the bread from which he is not exempt, but he is exempt from that over the cooked dish; and then *Bēt* Shammai come to say: He is not even exempt from that over the cooked dish! The question [remains unanswered].

VI. *If men were sitting [at the meal], each one says Grace for himself.*

When one may say Grace for all.

If they were reclining, then yes[2]; but if they were not reclining, no! Against this I quote the following: If ten were journeying by the way, although they all partake of one loaf, each of them says Grace for himself; should they sit down to eat, although each eats of his own loaf, one may say Grace for all. Note that he here states "they sit," i.e. although they are not reclining! Rab Naḥman b. Isaac said: [This *Bārāitā* refers to the case where] for instance men say, "Let us go and eat our meal in a certain place[3]."

Uncertainty of Rab's pupils on the question.

When Rab died, his disciples followed his cortège. On their return they said, "Let us go and have our meal by the River Danaḳ[4]." After they had eaten, they sat on and the question was asked: Does our *Mishnāh* intend that only when they recline [does

[1] Some edd. omit these words.

[2] One can say Grace for all; to recline makes the meal more formal and unites the diners into one party.

[3] If such words were spoken, then whether they sit or recline, they form a party and one can say Grace for all.

[4] According to Neubauer, p. 341 n., Danaḳ is a contraction of d^{e}Anaḳ "the river of Anaḳ" near Sura. This is supported by the reading of *M.*: בנהר אנק.

one say the benediction for all] and not if they sit; or is it perhaps that where people say, "Let us go and eat our meal in a certain place" this is to be regarded the same as reclining? They were unable [to answer the question]. Rab Adda b. Ahᵃbah stood up, fol. 43 a. turned the torn part of his garment[1] to the rear and made a fresh tear, exclaiming, "Rab has died and we have not learnt [the regulations of] the Grace after meals!" In the meanwhile an Elder came and pointed out the disagreement between our *Mishnāh* and the *Bārāitā*[2], and taught them: When men say, "Let us go and eat our meal in a certain place," it is the same as if they had reclined.

If they were reclining, one may say Grace for all.

Reclining at a meal.

Rab said: This teaching applies only to bread for which reclining is necessary, but for wine reclining is not necessary. R. Joḥanan, however, said: Even for wine likewise reclining is needed. (Another version: Rab said: This teaching applies only to bread where it is beneficial to recline, but with wine it is not beneficial to recline. R. Joḥanan, however, said: Even with wine it is likewise beneficial to recline.) Against this teaching is quoted: What is the procedure of reclining[3]? The guests enter and seat themselves upon stools and chairs until all are assembled. Then water is brought to them, and each washes one hand[4]. Wine is set for them, and each says the benediction for himself. They thereupon ascend [the couch] and recline, and water is brought before them; and although each one has washed one hand, he again washes both hands[5]. Wine is brought to them[6], and although each has said the benediction for himself, one may now say it for all! According to one version of Rab's statement, viz.: "This teaching applies only to bread for which reclining is necessary, but for wine reclining is not necessary," the first part [of this *Bārāitā*] is in disagreement[7]! It is different with guests, because it is their intention to move their position[8]. And according to the other version of

[1] A sign of mourning is to rend the garments; see Oesterley and Box, p. 332.

[2] See the preceding paragraph.

[3] Büchler, *Der galiläische 'Am hā'āreṣ*, pp. 134 ff., explains that it is not an ordinary meal that is here referred to, but that of a company of *Ḥᵃbērim* (see Glossary, s.v.).

[4] Which will hold the preliminary cup of wine.

[5] Because he will touch food with both hands.

[6] This is the wine before the meal, the other was only introductory.

[7] Because it states "Wine is set for them and each says the benediction for himself." But if reclining is not necessary for wine, let one say it for all!

[8] They have not yet formed themselves into one party.

Rab's statement, viz.: "This teaching applies only to bread where it is beneficial to recline, but with wine it is not beneficial to recline," the latter part [of the *Bārāitā*] is in disagreement[1]! It is different there, because while it is beneficial to recline for the bread, it is at the same time beneficial to recline for the wine.

If wine is set for them in the course of the meal.

Reason for the regulation of the *Mishnāh.*

Ben Zoma was asked: Why is it stated: *If wine is set for them in the course of the meal, each one says the benediction for himself; after the meal, one may say it for all*? He replied: Because the gullet is not empty[2].

The same one says the benediction over the perfume, etc.

Who has the privilege of saying Grace.

Since he teaches, *The same one says the benediction over the perfume*, it is to be inferred that there may be somebody more worthy than he; why, then, [is it his privilege]? Because he is the first to wash his hands at the conclusion of the meal. This supports the statement of Rab; for Rab Ḥiyya b. Ashē said in the name of Rab: He who is the first to wash his hands at the conclusion of the meal has the privilege of saying Grace. Rab and R. Ḥiyya were sitting at table in the presence of Rabbi. Rabbi said to Rab, "Arise, wash thy hands." R. Ḥiyya noticed that Rab was trembling[3], and said to him, "O son of princes[4]! See it is for the privilege of saying Grace after meals that Rabbi tells thee [to wash]."

When the benediction should be said over perfume.

R. Zera said in the name of Raba b. Jeremiah[5]: From what time may we say the benediction over the smell [of the perfume][6]? From the time its column of smoke ascends. R. Zera said to Raba b. Jeremiah, "But one has not yet smelt it!" He replied, "According to thy reasoning, one says the Grace before meals but has not yet eaten! His intention is to eat, and so here likewise it is his intention to smell."

[1] Because it states "Wine is brought to them and...one may say it for all." But if reclining is not beneficial with wine, let each say it for himself!

[2] If one said the benediction for all during the meal, some of the diners may not be able to respond "Amen," since there is food in their mouth; cf. fol. 51 *a*, p. 325.

[3] Rab was afraid that he was told to wash because his hands were dirty. He must have been quite a youth when this happened; hence his nervousness.

[4] See p. 86 n. 8.

[5] *M.*: Another version: Rabbah b. Jeremiah.

[6] "The Egyptians take great delight in perfumes; and often fumigate their apartments"; Lane, p. 142. But perfumes do not seem to have been used after a meal, although the guest before departing was perfumed; *ibid.* p. 208. Cf. *T. A.* I. p. 690 n. 281, III. p. 63.

The benediction over perfume.

R. Ḥiyya b. Abba[1] b. Naḥmani stated that Rab Ḥisda said in the name of Rab (another version: Rab Ḥisda said in the name of Z^e'iri): Over all kinds of perfumes the benediction is "...Who createst fragrant woods," excepting musk which comes from a species of animal and its benediction is "...Who createst various kinds of spices." Against this teaching is quoted: We only say "...Who createst fragrant woods" over the balsam-trees of the house of Rabbi[2] and the balsam-trees of the Emperor's palace and over the myrtle-tree wherever it comes from! This refutation [remains unanswered].

Benediction over balsam-oil and fragrant woods.

Rab Ḥisda asked Rab Isaac[3], "What is the benediction over balsam-oil?" He replied, "Thus said Rab Judah: It is '...Who createst the oil of our land'." Rab Ḥisda said to him, "Leave out Rab Judah, because the land of Israel is very dear to him; what is the benediction generally?" He replied, "Thus said R. Joḥanan: It is '...Who createst fragrant oil'." Rab Adda b. Ah^abah said: Over costum the benediction is "...Who createst fragrant woods," but not over the oil in which it is steeped. Rab Kah^ana said: [That is the benediction] even for the oil in which it is steeped, but not the oil with which it is ground. The men of Nehardea[4] said: [That is the benediction] even for the oil in which it is ground.

fol. 43 b. Benediction over flowers.

Rab Giddel said in the name of Rab: Over jasmine[5] the benediction is "...Who createst fragrant woods." Rab Ḥananel said in the name of Rab: Over sea-rush the benediction is "...Who createst fragrant woods." Mar Zoṭra said: What is the Scriptural authority[6]? "She had brought them up to the roof, and hid them with the stalks of flax[7]" (Josh. ii. 6). Rab M^esharsh^eya said: Over the garden-narcissus the benediction is "...Who createst fragrant woods," but over the wild narcissus "...Who createst fragrant herbs." Rab Sheshet said: Over violets the benediction is "...Who createst fragrant herbs." Mar Zoṭra[8] said: He who smells the citron or quince should say "Blessed be He Who setteth a beautiful fragrance in fruits." Rab Judah said: He who goes out during

[1] *M.*: Rabbah.

[2] Who lived in princely style.

[3] *M.*: Joseph.

[4] See p. 74 n. 2.

[5] For סמלק "jasmine," Krauss, p. 385, reads סמבק *sambucus* "the elder-tree."

[6] For regarding these as "wood."

[7] *Lit.* flax of wood.

[8] *M.*: Raba.

the days of *Nīsān* and sees the trees budding should say "Blessed be He Who has caused nothing to be lacking in His Universe and created therein beautiful creations and beautiful trees wherefrom men may derive pleasure."

Biblical basis for benediction over a fragrant smell. Rab Zoṭra b. Ṭobiah said in the name of Rab: Whence is it learnt that one should pronounce a benediction over a fragrant smell? As it is written, "Let every soul[1] praise the Lord" (Ps. cl. 6). From what is it that the soul, but not the body, derives enjoyment? Say it is a fragrant smell.

Fragrance of the young men of Israel. Rab Zoṭra b. Ṭobiah also said in the name of Rab: The young men of Israel will in the future give forth a sweet fragrance like Lebanon; as it is said, "His branches shall spread, and his beauty shall be as the olive-tree, and his fragrance as Lebanon" (Hosea xiv. 7).

God has made every occupation agreeable in the eyes of those who follow it. Rab Zoṭra b. Ṭobiah also said in the name of Rab: What means that which is written, "He hath made everything beautiful in its time" (Eccles. iii. 11)? It teaches that the Holy One, blessed be He, makes every occupation agreeable in the eyes of those who follow it. Rab Pappa said: Hence the proverb, "Hang the heart of a palm-tree around a sow, and it will act as usual[2]."

Protection against evil spirits. Rab Zoṭra b. Ṭobiah also said in the name of Rab: [Walking by the light of] a torch is equal to two[3]; by moonlight is equal to three. The question was asked: Is the light of the torch equal to two, including himself; or perhaps it is equal to two excluding himself? Come and hear: [It is stated,] "By moonlight is equal to three." That is quite right if thou sayest it means including himself, well and good; but if thou sayest it means excluding himself, why are four necessary? For lo, the teacher has said: To a single person an evil spirit appears and injures him; to two it appears but does not injure them; to three it does not appear at all! Certainly it is to be concluded that the expression "torch-light is equal to two" means including himself. Draw that conclusion.

Shaming a fellow-creature publicly a serious offence. Rab Zoṭra b. Ṭobiah also said in the name of Rab (another version: Rab Ḥanna b. Bizna in the name of R. Simeon Ḥᵃsida; still another version: R. Joḥanan said in the name of R. Simeon b. Joḥai): It were better for a man to cast himself into the midst of a fiery furnace rather than cause the face of his fellow-creature

[1] So the Hebrew literally.

[2] Cf. the proverb "The sow loves bran better than roses." On the palm-heart, see p. 242 n. 1.

[3] Walking together, as protection against the evil spirits of the night.

to blanche in public[1]. Whence is this derived? From Tamar; as it is said, "When she was brought forth" etc. (Gen. xxxviii. 25)[2].

Whether benediction over oil precedes that over myrtle.

Our Rabbis have taught: If they set before him oil and myrtle[3], *Bēt* Shammai declare: He first says the benediction over the oil and then over the myrtle; *Bēt* Hillel declare: He first says the benediction over the myrtle and then over the oil. Rabban[4] Gamaliel said: I will decide—Oil we use for its fragrance and for anointing, whereas we use the myrtle only for its fragrance and not for anointing[5]. R. Joḥanan said: The *H^alākāh* is in accord with him who decided. Rab Pappa visited the house of Rab Huna b. Rab Iḳa[6]; they set before him oil and myrtle. He took and made the benediction first over the myrtle and then over the oil. Rab Huna said to him: Does not the master hold that the *H^alākāh* is in accord with the words of him who decided? He replied: Thus said Raba: The *H^alākāh* is in accord with *Bēt* Hillel. But it was not so, and he only did this to extricate himself.

Order of benedictions over oil and wine.

Our Rabbis have taught: If oil and wine are set before him, *Bēt* Shammai declare: He should take hold of the oil in his right hand and the wine in his left, say the benediction over the oil and then over the wine; *Bēt* Hillel declare: He should take hold of the wine in his right hand and the oil in his left, say the benediction over the wine and then over the oil. And he should rub the oil upon the head of the attendant[7]; but if the attendant be a disciple of the wise, he should rub it upon the wall, because it is a disgrace for a disciple of the wise to go into the street perfumed.

Eight things a disgrace to a disciple of the wise.

Our Rabbis have taught: Six[8] things are a disgrace to a disciple of the wise: He should not go out into the street perfumed; nor go out alone at night; nor go out with patched sandals; nor converse with a woman in the street; nor recline in the company of *'Ammē hā'āreṣ*; nor be the last to enter the House of Study. Some declare that he should also not walk with a big stride, nor walk with an erect carriage.

1 By putting him to shame. To cause the blood to rush from the face is deemed equal to shedding blood.

2 She did not mention Judah's name.

3 At the end of the meal, the oil to anoint his hands stained by food, and the myrtle as perfume.

4 *M.* adds: Simeon b.

5 Hence precedence should be given to oil.

6 *M.*: Ḥannah b. Rab.

7 Being a disciple of the wise himself, he may not go out perfumed.

8 *M.*: eight.

He should not go out into the street perfumed. R. Abba b. R. Ḥiyya b. Abba said in the name of R. Joḥanan[1]: This refers to a place where people are suspected of pederasty. Rab Sheshet said: They mean only with his garment [perfumed], but on his body [it is permitted] because it removes [the odour of] perspiration. Rab Pappa said: [To perfume] his hair is like [perfuming] his garment; but some declare that it is like [perfuming] his body[2]. To go into the street perfumed.

He should not go out alone at night, because of the suspicion [it may arouse]; and they mean only where he has no fixed hour [for going out at night], but if he have a fixed hour, it will be well known that he goes out as is his usual custom[3]. To go out alone at night.

He should not go out with patched sandals. This supports the statement of R. Ḥiyya b. Abba who said: It is a disgrace for a disciple of the wise to go out with patched sandals[4]. But it is not so; for R. Ḥiyya b. Abba went out thus! Mar Zoṭra b.[5] Rab Naḥman said: It means with a patch on top of a patch, and it refers only to the legging; but as for the sole, we have no objection. And even in the case of the legging, it means only when walking by the way; but as for wearing such in the house, we have no objection. It further refers to the days of Summer, but in the days of Winter we have no objection[6]. To wear patched sandals.

He should not converse with a woman in the street. Rab Ḥisda said: Even if it be his wife[7]. There is a teaching to the same effect: Even if it be his wife, or his daughter, or his sister, because everybody is not well acquainted with his female relations. To converse with a woman in the street.

He should not recline in the company of *'Ammē hā'āreṣ*. What is the reason? He may perhaps be induced to be drawn after them. To associate with *'Ammē hā'āreṣ*.

He should not be the last to enter the House of Study; because such an one is called "a transgressor[8]." Last to enter the House of Study.

Some declare he should not walk with a big stride. For the teacher has said: A big stride takes away one five hundredth part of the light of a man's eyes. What is the remedy for it? He may restore it [by drinking the wine of] Sanctification on the [Sabbath] night. To walk with a big stride.

[1] *M.* omits: in the name of R. Joḥanan.
[2] And is permissible.
[3] And there will be no suspicion.
[4] This sentence is omitted in some edd.
[5] *M.* omits: Mar Zoṭra b.
[6] The mud will not make the patch so noticeable.
[7] Cf. Ābōt i. 5, Singer, p. 185.
[8] The reading is doubtful; several commentators have "idle."

To walk with erect carriage.

He should not walk with an erect carriage. For the teacher has said: He who walks with an erect carriage, even a distance of four cubits, is as though he pushed against the feet of the *Sh^e^kīnāh*[1]; for it is written, "The whole earth is full of His glory" (Is. vi. 3).

fol. 44 a.

MISHNĀH VII

If they set before him salted food first and with it bread, he says the benediction over the salted food and this makes it unnecessary over the bread, because the bread is something accessory to it. This is the general rule: In the case of a food which is the principal thing and together with it is something accessory, the benediction is to be uttered over the former and there is no necessity for a benediction over the latter.

G^E^MĀRĀ

The fruits of Gennesareth.

Is there any salted food which is the principal thing and the bread accessory? Rab Aḥa b. Rab 'Awira said in the name of Rab Ashē[2]: They refer to one who eats the fruits of Gennesareth[3]. Rabbah b. Bar Ḥannah said: At the time we were following R. Joḥanan to eat the fruits of Gennesareth, when we were a hundred in number we used each to take ten for him, and when we were ten we used each to take a hundred for him; and a basket of the capacity of three *Sāōt* could not hold a hundred of them. But he ate them all and swore that he had tasted no food. No food, dost imagine? But say, [He meant that he had eaten no] satisfying meal. R. Abbahu ate so many of them that a fly would glide down his face[4]. R. Ammi and R. Assi ate so many of them that their hair fell out. R. Simeon b. Laḳish ate so many of them that he began to rave. R. Joḥanan reported this to the household of the Prince, and R. Judah the Prince sent officials after him and brought him to his house.

[1] I.e. acted in a haughty manner towards God.

[2] *M.*: 'Ulla in the name of R. Assi. The correct reading is probably Aḥa b. Iwya in the name of Rab Assi. Cf. *D. S. ad loc.*

[3] Famed for its fertility; Josephus, *Wars*, III. x. 8. According to Tōsāfōt, these fruits were excessively sweet, so that after eating them, one required something salted to restore the appetite.

[4] It made the flesh so smooth and sleek.

When Rab Dimai came [from Palestine] he said: Jannaeus the king[1] had a city on the king's mountain[2] from which they obtained sixty myriad basins of salted fish[3] for the hewers of the fig-trees from one Sabbath-eve to the next[4]. When Rabin came he said: Jannaeus the king had a tree on the king's mountain from which they took down forty *Sāōt* of young pigeons[5] monthly from three broods. When R. Isaac came he said: There was a city in the land of Israel named Gofnit[6] in which were eighty pairs of brothers of a priestly family married to eighty pairs of sisters of a priestly family[7]; and the Rabbis searched from Sura to Nehardea[8] and could not find [a similar case] with the exception of the daughters of Rab Ḥisda who were married to Rammi b. Ḥamma and Mar ‘Uḳba b. Ḥamma; but although the women belonged to a priestly family, the men did not.

Two wonderful cities in Palestine.

Rab said: A meal without salt is no meal[9]. R. Ḥiyya b. Abba said in the name of R. Joḥanan: A meal without some acrid substance[10] is no meal.

Salt necessary at a meal.

MISHNĀH VIII

If one ate grapes, figs or pomegranates, he says after them the three benedictions. These are the words of Rabban Gamaliel; but the Sages declare: One benediction which is an abstract of three. R. ‘Aḳiba says: Even if one eats [nothing but] boiled vegetables

[1] See p. 190 n. 9.

[2] According to Wiesner, p. 100, it is Mt Ephraim; but this is very unlikely. See the long discussion by Büchler in *J. Q. R.* XVI. pp. 180–192, from which it appears that no one locality is intended but a whole district in Judea.

[3] Büchler, *ibid.* p. 188 n. 2, understands the word to mean "confectionery"; but this is disputed by Krauss, *Antoninus und Rabbi*, p. 25 n. 1.

[4] The workers were so numerous that so huge a quantity of food was required for them.

[5] To be used as offerings in the Temple. Cf. Büchler, *Priester und Cultus*, pp. 188 f. and *J. Q. R.* XVI. pp. 189 f.

[6] Or Gofnin. Identified with the Biblical Ophni (Josh. xviii. 24) and the modern Jifna, about five hours' journey from Jerusalem; Neubauer, p. 157. This, however, is questioned; see *Encyc. Biblica*, col. 3515.

[7] I.e. the entire family consisted in each case of two brothers and two sisters who intermarried.

[8] See p. 74 notes 1 and 2.

[9] Cf. "The world could not endure without salt, pepper and spice," Sōferīm xv. 8. The Greeks and Romans also used much salt at their meals; Wiesner, p. 101 and *T. A.* I. p. 499 n. 657.

[10] E.g. bitter herbs.

and makes a meal of it, he pronounces thereover the three benedictions. If one drinks water to slake his thirst, he says the benediction "...By Whose word all things exist"; R. Ṭarphon says: "...Who createst many living beings and their wants."

GᴱMĀRĀ

Why Rabban Gamaliel requires three benedictions after grapes, etc.

What is Rabban Gamaliel's reason[1]? Because it is written, "A land of wheat and barley and vines and fig-trees and pomegranates" (Deut. viii. 8), and it is written, "A land wherein thou shalt eat bread without scarceness" (*ibid. v.* 9), and it is written "And thou shalt eat and be satisfied, and bless the Lord thy God" (*ibid. v.* 10)[2]. And the Rabbis[3]? [The reference to] the "land"[4] interrupts the subject-matter[5]. But for Rabban Gamaliel likewise [the reference to] the "land" interrupts the subject-matter[6]! He requires that to exclude the case of one who chews wheat[7].

Benedictions over the five species.

R. Jacob b. Iddi said in the name of R. Ḥannina: Over any food which belongs to the five species[8], before partaking thereof one says the benediction "...Who createst various kinds of foods," and afterwards one benediction which is an abstract of three.

Benedictions over the seven species.

Rabbah b. Mari said in the name of R. Joshua b. Levi: Over any food belonging to the seven species[9], before partaking thereof one says the benediction "...Who createst the fruit of the tree," and afterwards one benediction which is an abstract of three.

Wording of the one benediction which is an abstract of three.

Abbai asked Rab Dimai: What is the one benediction which is an abstract of three? He replied: For the fruit of the tree it is[10]: "[Blessed art Thou, O Lord our God, King of the universe,] for the tree and the fruit of the tree and for the produce of the field; for the desirable, good and ample land which Thou didst give as an heritage unto our fathers, that they might eat of its

[1] That he requires three benedictions.

[2] Each of these three verses offers the basis of a benediction.

[3] What answer do they make to Rabban Gamaliel's reason?

[4] In *v.* 9.

[5] I.e. *v.* 10 has no connection with *v.* 8; therefore one benediction is sufficient.

[6] Why does he not draw the same inference as the Sages?

[7] The reference in *v.* 9 is to "bread," and according to Rabban Gamaliel, it is inserted lest without it, connecting *v.* 10 with *v.* 8, it be thought that even if one chewed wheat in its raw state, he must say the three benedictions. Hence *v.* 9 is inserted to show that the wheat must be made into "bread" before the benedictions are necessary.

[8] Wheat, barley, rye, oats and spelt.

[9] See p. 271.

[10] Cf. Singer, pp. 287 f.

fruits and be satisfied with its goodness. Have mercy, O Lord our God, upon Israel Thy people, upon Jerusalem Thy city, upon Thy Sanctuary and altar. Rebuild Jerusalem, Thy holy city, speedily in our days; lead us up thither and make us rejoice in its rebuilding[1]; for Thou art good and beneficent unto all." For the five species it is: "[Blessed...universe] for the sustenance and the nourishment, and for the produce of the field[2]," etc. And the benediction is concluded: "[Blessed art Thou, O Lord,] for the land and for the sustenance[3]."

Its conclusion in the case of fruit.

In the case of fruit[4] how should the benediction conclude? When Rab Dimai came he said: Rab concluded on the New Moon thus, "Blessed [art Thou, O Lord] Who sanctifiest Israel and the beginnings of the months[5]." So how should it be concluded in this case of fruit? Rab Ḥisda said: "[Blessed art Thou, O Lord,] for the land and its fruits." R. Joḥanan said: "For the land and for the fruits[6]." R. 'Amram[7] said: There is no contradiction, Rab Ḥisda's wording being customary with us [in Babylon] and R. Joḥanan's with them [in Palestine]. Rab Naḥman b. Isaac objected: They eat and we make the benediction[8]! Nay, the wording should be reversed; Rab Ḥisda said: "For the land and for the fruits" and R. Joḥanan said: "For the land and its fruits."

fol. **44 b.** Benedictions for eggs and meat.

Rab Isaac b. Abdemi said in the name of our teacher[9]: Over an egg and various kinds of meat, before partaking thereof one says the benediction "...By Whose word all things exist" and afterwards "...Who createst many living beings" etc.; but not over vegetables[10]. R. Isaac declared: Even over vegetables, but not over water. Rab Pappa said: Even over water. Mar Zoṭra acted in accord with Rab Isaac b. Abdemi, and Rab Shimi b. Ashē[11] in accord with R. Isaac. (A mnemonic for thee is: One in

[1] *M.* adds (similarly Singer, p. 288): May we eat of the fruits of the land, and be satisfied with its goodness, and bless Thee for it in holiness and purity.

[2] Cf. *ibid.* p. 287.

[3] *Ibid.* p. 289.

[4] These words are omitted in some edd. and in *M.*

[5] An indication that each detail should be specified. According to Pinner (in his edition of this Tractate), this statement about Rab Dimai is misplaced and should be inserted in fol. 49 *a*, bot. See p. 316.

[6] So Singer, p. 289 top.

[7] *M.*: Naḥman.

[8] If the Babylonians used the formula "For the land and *its* [i.e. Palestine] fruits," they utter a benediction over something they have not enjoyed. Therefore they say "and for *the* fruits," wherever grown.

[9] The reference is to Rabbi not Rab; cf. on fol. 30 *b*, p. 200 n. 5.

[10] I.e. after vegetables "...Who createst many living beings" is unnecessary.

[11] *M.*: Ḥiyya.

accord with two and two in accord with one[1].) Rab Ashē said: When I think of it, I act in accord with them all[2].

Things which require a benediction before but not after.

We have a Mishnaic teaching: Everything that requires a benediction after it requires one before it; but there are things which require a benediction before but not after. This is quite right for Rab Isaac b. Abdemi, since it is to exclude vegetables, and for R. Isaac to exclude water; but for Rab Pappa what is it to exclude? It excludes the commandments[3]. But for the sons of the West[4] who on removing the *Tᵉfillīn* say the benediction, "[Blessed art Thou, O Lord our God, King of the universe] Who didst sanctify us with Thy commandments and commanded us to observe Thy statutes," what is it to exclude? Fragrant odours.

Nourishment of the egg.

R. Jannai said in the name of Rab[5]: Any food [whose minimum standard is the size of] an egg, the egg is superior to it [as nourishment]. When Rabin came he said: Better is a light-roasted[6] egg than six measures of fine flour. When Rab Dimai came he said[7]: Better is a light-roasted egg than six [measures of fine flour] and a hard-baked egg than four. Of a boiled egg [it is said], any food [whose minimum is the size of] an egg, the egg is superior to it [as nourishment] with the exception of meat.

R. 'Aḳiba says: Even if one eats boiled vegetables, etc.

Cabbage-stalks a nourishment.

Is there any boiled vegetable which is to be regarded as nourishment? Rab Ashē said: It refers to cabbage-stalks.

Foods beneficial and harmful.

Our Rabbis have taught: Milt is good for the teeth but bad for the bowels; horse-beans are bad for the teeth but good for the bowels. All raw vegetables make the complexion pale; anything not fully grown makes the body shrink; every living being[8] restores the soul and everything near to the soul[9] restores the soul. Cabbage [is good] as nourishment and beet as a remedy; but woe to the body[10] through which vegetables keep constantly passing[11].

[1] I.e. the Rabbi with one part to his name (Zoṭra) acted in accord with the Rabbi who had two parts to his name (Isaac b. Abdemi).

[2] By saying a benediction after everything, even water.

[3] Before the performance of which, but not afterwards, a benediction is required; e.g. the laying of *Tᵉfillīn*.

[4] Palestine.

[5] *M.*: Rab Zera.

[6] *Lit.* rolled; i.e. on hot coals.

[7] *M.* reads: Better is a light-roasted egg than six hard-baked, and one hard-baked than four boiled. Any food, etc.

[8] *Lit.* soul; i.e. something that has been alive and is eaten whole; e.g. small fish.

[9] I.e. the part of the animal near the vital organs.

[10] *Lit.* house.

[11] When vegetables are a frequent and principal article of diet.

The master said above, "Milt is good for the teeth but bad for the bowels." What is the remedy? Let him chew it and then throw it away. "Horse-beans are bad for the teeth but good for the bowels." What is the remedy? Let him boil them well and swallow them. "All raw herbs make the complexion pale." R. Isaac said: This refers only to the first meal after blood-letting. R. Isaac also said: It is forbidden to converse with him who has eaten [raw] herbs before the fourth hour of the day[1]. For what reason? Because of the evil odour. R. Isaac also said: It is forbidden for a man to eat raw herbs before the fourth hour of the day. Amemar, Mar Zoṭra and Rab Ashē were sitting [at table], and they set before them raw herbs before the fourth hour. Amemar and Rab Ashē ate, but not so Mar Zoṭra. They said to him, "What is thy opinion? Is it because R. Isaac declared: It is forbidden to converse with him who has eaten [raw] herbs before the fourth hour of the day on account of the evil odour? Behold we have eaten, and still thou talkest with us!" He replied, "I agree with the other statement of R. Isaac, viz.: It is forbidden for a man to eat raw herbs before the fourth hour of the day." Subject continued.

"Anything not fully grown makes the body shrink." Rab Ḥisda said: Even a young kid worth a *Zūz*; and it only refers to that which is not a fourth [of its full natural size], but if it be a fourth, we have no objection. "Every living being restores the soul." Rab Pappa said: Even the small fishes from the swamps. "Everything near to the soul restores the soul." Rab Aḥa b. Jacob said: This is the neck. Raba[2] said to his attendant, "When thou bringest me a piece of meat, take the trouble and obtain it from a place near to where the benediction is pronounced[3]." "Cabbage is good as nourishment and beet as a remedy." Is the cabbage good as food but not as a remedy? Lo, there is a teaching: Six things cure a man from his sickness and their remedy is [an efficacious] remedy, viz.: Cabbage, beet, a decoction of dry poley[4], the maw, the womb and the large lobe of the liver! But say: Cabbage is good also as nourishment[5]. "Woe to the body through which vegetables keep constantly passing." But it is not so! For lo, Raba[6] said to his attendant, "If thou seest vegetables in the Subject continued.

[1] See p. 6 n. 5.

[2] *M.*: Rab.

[3] When the animal is slaughtered; the reference being to the neck which is cut across.

[4] We must read יבשין "dry" for דבש "honey," as in the parallel passage, fol. 57 *b*, p. 378.

[5] Besides as a remedy.

[6] *M.*: Rab.

market, never ask me, With what wilt thou wrap thy bread?" Abbai said: [It means vegetables] without meat; and Raba said: Without wine[1]. It has been reported: Rab said: [It means vegetables] without meat; Samuel said: Without wood[2]; and R. Joḥanan said: Without wine. Raba asked Rab Pappa the brewer, "We break [the harmful effects of vegetables] by means of meat and wine; but you who do not use much wine, how do you break it?" He replied, "With chips of wood[2]." For example, Rab Pappa's[3] wife, when cooking it, broke [its harmful effects] with eighty twigs of Persian trees.

Harmful effects of salted fish.

Our Rabbis have taught: A small salted fish sometimes kills on the seventh, the seventeenth and twenty-seventh, and some say the twenty-third[4] day. This applies only to the case where it has been roasted but not roasted [thoroughly]; but if it has been well-roasted, there is no objection. And when it has been well-roasted, it only applies to the case where one does not drink beer after it; but if he drinks beer after it, there is no objection.

If one drinks water to slake his thirst, etc.

What does this intend to exclude[5]? Rab Iddi b. Abin said: fol. 45 a. To exclude him whom a piece of food chokes[6].

R. Ṭarphon says: "... Who createst many living beings and their wants."

Raba b. Rab Ḥanan[7] said to Abbai (another version: to Rab Joseph): How is the *H^a^lākāh*? He replied: Go and see how the people act[8].

May we return unto thee: *What benediction do we say!*

1 Only then are they injurious.

2 I.e. well-cooked over a fire of wood.

3 *M.*: Joseph's.

4 *M.*: 28th, i.e. day of salting, if eaten then.

5 Since the *Mishnāh* adds the words "to slake his thirst."

6 And he drinks water to relieve himself; then no benediction is required.

7 *M.*: Rabbah b. Rab Ḥanin.

8 The general practice is to say "...By Whose word" and then "...Who createst many living beings."

CHAPTER VII

MISHNĀH I, II

I. *Three who ate together are under the obligation of* Zimmūn. *One who has eaten* D^e^mai[1], *or the first tithe*[2] *from which* T^e^rūmāh *has been taken*[3], *or the second tithe*[4] *or food belonging to the Sanctuary which had been redeemed, and the attendant who has eaten food the size of an olive and the Samaritan may be included for* Zimmūn. *One who has eaten of the untithed, or the first tithe from which* T^e^rūmāh *has not been taken, or the second tithe or food belonging to the Sanctuary which had not been redeemed, and the attendant who has eaten less than the size of an olive, and the idolator*[5] *may not be included for* Zimmūn.

II. *Women, slaves and minors may not be included. How much* [*must one have eaten at the meal*] *to be included for* Zimmūn? *The size of an olive. R. Judah says: The size of an egg.*

G^E^MARĀ

Whence is this derived[6]? Rab Assi said: Because the Scriptures state, "O magnify ye the Lord with me[7], and let us exalt His name together" (Ps. xxxiv. 4). R. Abbahu said: From the following, "For I will proclaim the name of the Lord; ascribe ye[8] greatness unto our God" (Deut. xxxii. 3). Biblical basis for *Zimmūn*.

[1] Produce from which it is uncertain whether the tithe has been given. For the law of the tithe, see Lev. xxvii. 30 ff.

[2] Due to the Levites; cf. Num. xviii. 21.

[3] The Levite had to give a tenth of his tithe to the priest, known as the *T^e^rūmāh* of the tithe; cf. Num. xviii. 26.

[4] Cf. Deut. xiv. 22 ff. This was a tithe of the produce after the Levite had received his tithe, and had to be eaten in Jerusalem or redeemed by its equivalent in money being spent there.

[5] The original reading was probably "heathen" and altered to "idolator" to satisfy the Censor.

[6] That three who eat together should say Grace with *Zimmūn*.

[7] The unspecified plural "ye" denotes two and "me" the third.

[8] "I" is one and "ye" two, making a total of three.

Tone of voice in which responses and translation of the lections should be uttered.

Rab Ḥanan b. Abba[1] said: Whence is it that he who responds "Amen" must not raise his voice above him who pronounces the benediction? As it is said, "O magnify ye the Lord with me[2], and let us exalt His name together." R. Simeon b. Pazzi said: Whence is it that the translator is not permitted to raise his voice above that of the reader[3]? As it is said, "Moses spoke, and God answered him by a voice" (Exod. xix. 19)—there was no need to say "by a voice"; what, therefore, does the teaching "by a voice" tell us? By a voice [equal to that] of Moses. There is a similar teaching: The translator is not permitted to raise his voice above that of the reader; and if the translator is not able to pitch his voice as loud as the reader, then the reader should lower his voice and read.

Whether two may arrange *Zimmūn*.

It has been reported: If two ate together, Rab and R. Joḥanan differ in opinion—One declares that if they wish to arrange *Zimmūn* they may do so; but the other declares that if they wish to do so, they may not. There is, however, the Mishnaic teaching: *Three who ate together are under the obligation of* Zimmūn—three, yes; two, no[4]! There [in the case of three] it is obligatory, but here [with two] it is voluntary. Come and hear: Three who ate together are under the obligation of *Zimmūn* and are not permitted to divide themselves up[5]. [Hence it is to be inferred that] three can and two cannot make *Zimmūn*! It is different there, because they originally [being three in number] laid upon themselves the obligation[6]. Come and hear: The attendant who was waiting upon two men should eat with them[7], even if they did not give him permission[8]. If he waited upon three, he should only eat with them when they give him permission! It is different there, because it is proper for them to be placed under the obligation of *Zimmūn* from the outset of the meal[9]. Come and hear: Women may arrange *Zimmūn* for themselves and slaves for themselves; but women, slaves and minors may not include each other,

fol. 45 b.

[1] *M.*: Raba.
[2] I.e. with a voice equal to mine.
[3] In the ancient Synagogues, the Scriptural lesson read in Hebrew was followed by a translation in the Aramaic vernacular; cf. Oesterley and Box, pp. 46 ff.
[4] This contradicts the opinion that two may, if they wish it.
[5] But if two may arrange *Zimmūn*, why may not one leave?
[6] Whereas if they separate, it would be only voluntary with two.
[7] The minimum quantity of food which necessitates the saying of Grace.
[8] In order to make a third for *Zimmūn*.
[9] By the attendant joining with them, even uninvited.

should they desire *Zimmūn*[1]. And although a hundred women are like two men[2], yet it teaches "Women arrange *Zimmūn* for themselves and slaves for themselves[3]"! It is different there, because there are many persons[4]. If so, I will quote the sequel: "Women and slaves may not include each other, should they desire *Zimmūn*"—why not? Are they not many persons! It is different there, because [there is the fear] of licentiousness.

It is to be concluded that it was Rab who said above, "If they[5] wish to arrange *Zimmūn*, they may not"; for Rab Dimai b. Joseph said in the name of Rab: If three ate together, and one of them went out into the street, they call to him [that they desire to include him for *Zimmūn*, and should he consent, even in his absence] they may reckon him in for *Zimmūn*. The reason [why they can have *Zimmūn* without him is] that they called to him; hence if they did not call to him, they are not [to have *Zimmūn*][6]. It is different there, because from the outset [by being three] they placed upon themselves the obligation of *Zimmūn*[7]. Nay, it is to be concluded that it was R. Joḥanan who said above, "If they[5] wish to have *Zimmūn*, they may not"; for Rabbah b. Bar Ḥannah said in the name of R. Joḥanan: If two ate together, one of them may comply with the requirements of the law by means of the Grace said by the other; and we ask the question: What does he intend to inform us? For we have the teaching: If a man heard [Grace said by another], although he does not make the responses, he has complied with the requirements of the law! And R. Zera said: He means to tell us that there can be no Grace with *Zimmūn* between the two of them. Thus it is to be concluded [that R. Joḥanan is the author of the above statement]. Raba b. Rab Huna said to Rab Huna[8]: But the Rabbis who come from the West declare: If [two] wish to have *Zimmūn* Discussion continued.

[1] Edd. read here "And lo, even a hundred women," which should probably be omitted. See *D. S. ad loc.*

[2] In that there is no obligation for *Zimmūn*, but it is purely voluntary.

[3] This speaks as though it were obligatory for women; and if a hundred women are equal to two men in this respect, then it should be obligatory for two men!

[4] There are at least three women so that the number required by Ps. xxxiv. 4 is forthcoming, which is not the case with two men.

[5] I.e. two.

[6] And accordingly Rab teaches that two men may not arrange *Zimmūn*.

[7] By being three originally, the obligation remains; but if there were only two, they could voluntarily arrange *Zimmūn*. Hence Rab cannot be the author of the statement in question.

[8] *M.*: Rabbah said to Rab Huna.

they may! Is it not to be supposed that they heard this from R. Johanan[1]? No, they heard it from Rab before he went down to Babylon.

On including an absent person for *Zimmūn*.

It was stated above: "Rab Dimai b. Joseph said in the name of Rab: If three ate together and one of them went into the street, they call to him and include him for *Zimmūn*." Abbai said: That is only if they called to him and he makes the responses[2]. Mar Zotra said: This teaching only applies to three; but with ten [they cannot include him] unless he comes back[3]. Rab Ashē objected: On the contrary, the reverse is more probable, because nine look like ten, but two do not look like three[4]! But the *Halākāh* is in agreement with Mar Zotra. What is the reason? Since it is necessary to mention the Divine Name, which is not customary with less than ten. Abbai said: We have it by tradition that if two ate together, it is a meritorious act on their part to separate[5]. There is a teaching to the same effect: If two ate together, it is a meritorious act on their part to separate. Of what does it speak here? When both of them are learned[6]; but if one is learned and the other illiterate, the former says Grace and the other fulfils his obligation [by listening].

On interrupting a meal for *Zimmūn*.

Raba stated: The following have I said and it has been similarly reported[7] in the name of R. Zera: If three ate together, one should interrupt his meal for the other two[8], but two need not interrupt their meal for one. They need not? Lo, Rab Pappa, i.e. he and another, interrupted the meal for *Abbā* Mar, his son! Rab Pappa is different, because he acted within the bounds of strict justice[9].

***Zimmūn* necessary whenever three eat together.**

Judah b. Maremar, Mar b. Rab Ashē and Rab Aha of Difti[10] dined together, and there was not one amongst them who was more distinguished than his associates to say Grace for them. They sat on and said[11]: The *Mishnāh* teaches: *Three who ate*

1 Who was a Palestinian teacher, whereas Rab was a Babylonian.

2 I.e. he is within hearing distance.

3 When ten or more dine together, "our God" is added in the introduction to the Grace; see Singer, p. 279.

4 The absence of one is not so noticeable in the former case.

5 So that each may say Grace for himself.

6 *Lit.* scribes.

7 *M.* adds: In the West [i.e. Palestine].

8 Who have finished and wish to say Grace with *Zimmūn*.

9 I.e. he did more than was necessary to pay honour to his son.

10 See p. 48 n. 2.

11 This is the reading of certain commentators. Edd.: They sat on and were asked.

together are under the obligation of Zimmūn. That must refer only to where there is an eminent man present[1], but where they are all equal, it is preferable to separate for the purpose of the Grace. Thereupon each said Grace for himself; but when they came before Maremar, he said to them: The duty of Grace you have fulfilled, but not the duty of *Zimmūn*; and should you say, "Let us go back and have Grace with *Zimmūn*," there cannot be a *Zimmūn* retrospectively.

Response to be made by one who has not joined in the meal.

If one comes in and finds them saying Grace, what response does he make? Rab Zebid said, "Blessed be His name, yea, continually to be blessed for ever and ever[2]." Rab Pappa said: He responds with "Amen." There is no disagreement here; the former refers to where he finds them saying, "Let us say Grace," the other to where he finds them saying "Blessed." If he finds them saying "Let us say Grace," he responds "Blessed be His name" etc., and if he finds them saying "Blessed," he responds "Amen."

Responding "Amen" after one's own benediction.

One taught: He who responds "Amen" after his own benedictions is praiseworthy; but another taught: He is to be reprimanded. There is no contradiction; the former refers to "Who...rebuildest Jerusalem[3]," the latter to the other benedictions.

Responding "Amen" after the third benediction of the Grace.

Abbai responded ["Amen" to his benediction "Who...rebuildest Jerusalem"] with a loud voice for the day-labourers to hear and stand up[4], because "Who art kind and dealest kindly[5]" is not ordained by the *Tōrāh*[6]. Rab Ashē used to make that response softly, so that the day-labourers should not hold "Who art kind and dealest kindly" in contempt[7].

fol. 46 a. Who has the privilege of saying Grace before and after the meal.

R. Zera was ill. R. Abbahu went in to visit him, and took [a vow] upon himself, "If the little one with the scorched legs[8] recovers, I will make a joyous day for the Rabbis." He did recover, and R. Abbahu made a feast for all the Rabbis. When it was time to commence the meal, he said to R. Zera, "Let the master

1 To lead in the Grace; cf. fol. 47 *a*, p. 302.

2 Cf. Singer, p. 280, top.

3 See Singer, p. 282, and note that the formula ends with "Amen."

4 To return to their work, not waiting for the remainder of the Grace.

5 The benediction in Singer, p. 283.

6 Which only requires three benedictions, Singer, pp. 280–282.

7 By omitting it.

8 A nickname of R. Zera, perhaps because he was very short. See Rashi to Bab. Meṣīa' 85 *a*. The *Talmūd* (*loc. cit.*) narrates an incident wherein R. Zera's legs were scorched during an act of self-immolation. See *A. P. A.* III. p. 7 n. 2 where it is suggested that the truer reading is to be found in Sanh. 37 *a*, viz. "The scorched one (i.e. dark complexioned) with short legs."

begin for us[1]." He replied, "Does not the master hold with R. Joḥanan's statement, 'The master of the house should break the bread'?" He commenced for them. When the time came to say Grace after meals, he said to R. Zera, "Let the master say Grace for us." He replied, "Does not the master hold with the statement of Rab Huna of Babylon, 'The one who breaks bread should say Grace after meals'?" With whose opinion was R. Abbahu in agreement? With that which R. Joḥanan said in the name of R. Simeon b. Joḥai: The master of the house breaks bread so that he may do so with a good will[2], and the guest says Grace so that he may bless his host. What benediction does he use? "May it be Thy will that the master of this house may not be put to shame in this world nor confounded in the world to come." Rabbi added to this: "And may he prosper in all his possessions[3]; may all his and our possessions be successful and near to the city[4]; may not Satan have power over the works of his hands nor over ours; and may there not leap before him or us any thought of sin, transgression or iniquity from now and for evermore."

Extent of the *Zimmūn* benediction.

Up to where is the benediction of *Zimmūn*[5]? Rab Naḥman said: Until "We will bless[6]"; but Rab Sheshet said: Until "[Blessed art Thou, O Lord,] Who givest food unto all[7]." Let us say [that their difference is] like that of the *Tannāīm*; for one taught: The Grace after meals [may be said by] two or three; and there is another teaching: Three or four[8]. They hold that

[1] By saying Grace before meals and breaking the bread.

[2] *Lit.* with a fine eye.

[3] I.e. landed property. There is a variant "in all his works" which Bacher prefers; cf. *A. T.* II. p. 464 n. 4.

[4] In which he dwells, so that he can keep constantly in touch with them and it be unnecessary for him to face the perils of a journey.

[5] If one interrupts his meal to enable the other two to say Grace with *Zimmūn*, at what point may he resume? So explain Tōsāfōt. According to Rashi it means: How much has to be said in addition to the usual Grace because of the *Zimmūn*?

[6] I.e. "We will bless Him of Whose bounty we have partaken," to which the response is made "Blessed be He of Whose bounty" etc., Singer, p. 279.

[7] The end of the first benediction, *ibid.* p. 280. Tōsāfōt object to Rashi's explanation (see note 5 above) that this benediction is an essential part of the Grace even for an individual, so how could it be only included when there is *Zimmūn*?

[8] This is the translation required by the explanation of Tōsāfōt; viz., Grace can be said by two or three, in the case where one of the diners is acquainted with one benediction and the other person or persons with the

everybody admits that "Who art kind and dealest kindly" is not ordained by the *Tōrāh*[1]. Are we, then, not to suppose that they differ on the following point: He who says, "[The Grace may be said by] two or three" holds that [the benediction of *Zimmūn* extends] until "Who givest food unto all"; and he who says "Three or four" holds that it extends until "We will bless"? No; Rab Naḥman reconciles [the two conflicting versions] according to his opinion, and so does Rab Sheshet. Rab Naḥman reconciles them according to his opinion—Everybody agrees that [the *Zimmūn* benediction extends] until "We will bless"; that is quite right for him who said "Three or four," but as for him who said "Two or three," he could tell thee that we are here dealing with the Grace of the day-labourers; for the teacher has said: Such an one opens with "Who feedest" and includes "Who ...rebuildest Jerusalem" in the benediction of "the land[2]." Rab Sheshet reconciles them according to his opinion—Everybody agrees that [the *Zimmūn* benediction extends] until "Who givest food unto all"; that is quite right for him who said "Two or three," but he who said "Three or four" is of the opinion that "Who art kind and dealest kindly" is ordained by the *Tōrāh*[3].

The fourth benediction not ordained by the *Tōrāh*.

Rab Joseph said: Thou mayest know that "Who art kind and dealest kindly" is not ordained by the *Tōrāh* because day-labourers may omit it[4]. Rab Isaac b. Samuel b. Marta said in

remaining two. Each says what he knows, and all thereby fulfil their obligation. Or it can be said by three or four; i.e. one may be acquainted with the *Zimmūn* formula and the first benediction, and two others with one benediction each, or each one of the four with one portion. According to Rashi, the text should be rendered: The Grace after meals consists of two [benedictions, viz. when two eat together and there is no *Zimmūn*] or of three [benedictions, viz. when three eat together. This is on the supposition that the *Zimmūn* formula extends to the end of the first benediction]; and there is another teaching: It consists of three [benedictions, viz. when two eat together] or four [benedictions, viz. when the *Zimmūn* formula is added]. Apart from the objection mentioned in the preceding note, Tōsāfōt point out that the numerals "two, three, four" are grammatically to be connected with a masculine noun (viz. men) and not a feminine word (viz. benedictions).

[1] I.e. the fourth benediction in Singer, p. 283, which is not to be considered in this connection.

[2] They compress the second and third benedictions into one; thus, when two labourers say Grace, they say two benedictions, and when three, they say three.

[3] This fourth benediction is accordingly an essential part of the Grace, and gives something to a fourth man to say, even though the *Zimmūn* formula includes the first benediction.

[4] But they cannot ignore an ordinance of the *Tōrāh*.

the name of Rab[1]: Thou mayest know that "Who art kind and dealest kindly" is not ordained by the *Tōrāh*, because it opens with "Blessed"[2] and does not conclude with "Blessed"; according to the teaching: One commences all benedictions with "Blessed" and concludes them with "Blessed," excepting the benediction over fruits, commandments[3], one benediction which follows immediately on another, and the last benediction of the reading of the *Sh^ema'*. In some of these instances one opens with "Blessed"
fol. 46 b. but does not conclude with it; and in others one concludes with "Blessed" but does not commence with it. Since one opens the benediction "Who art kind and dealest kindly" with "Blessed" but does not conclude with it, the inference is that it is a benediction by itself. Rab Naḥman b. Isaac said: Thou mayest know that "Who art kind and dealest kindly" is not ordained by the *Tōrāh*, because they omit it in the house of a mourner[4]; according to the teaching: What do they say in the house of a mourner[5]? "Blessed...Who art kind and dealest kindly[6]." R. 'Aḳiba said, "Blessed be the true Judge." Is, then, "Who art kind and dealest kindly" to be said but not "The true Judge"? Nay, the meaning is, "Who art kind and dealest kindly" is also to be said.

Grace to be said in the house of a mourner.

Mar Zoṭra visited the house of Rab Ashē whom some bereavement had befallen[7]. [In the Grace after meals] he opened with the benediction[8]: "Who art kind and dealest kindly, true God and Judge, Who judgest with righteousness and in judgment takest [the souls of men unto Thyself], Who rulest in Thy world, doing therein according to Thy will, for all Thy ways are judgment and all is Thine. We are Thy people and Thy servants, and in all circumstances it is our duty to give thanks unto Thee and to bless Thee. O Thou Who repairest the breaches in Israel, mayest Thou also repair this breach in Israel, granting us life."

1 *M.* reverses the authors of this and the preceding sentences.

2 If it were ordained by the *Tōrāh*, it would be connected with what precedes, and would not require "Blessed" as its opening word.

3 See, e.g., the benedictions to be said before putting on the *Tallīt* and *T^efillīn*; Singer, pp. 14, 16.

4 But they cannot ignore an ordinance of the *Tōrāh*.

5 *M.*: In the benediction of a mourner.

6 See Singer, pp. 282 f., bottom of the pages.

7 *M.* adds: through his son.

8 Cf. Singer, p. 283, bot.

To where does he return[1]? Rab Zᵉbid said in the name of Abbai: He returns to the commencement[2]; but the Rabbis say: To the place where he made the interruption[3]. The *Hᵃlākāh* is—He returns to the place where he made the interruption.

Method of saying the *Zimmūn* formula.

The Exilarch said to Rab Sheshet, "Although you are old[4] Rabbis, the Persians are more expert than you in the etiquette of a meal. When there are two couches, the more important guest reclines first and the other above him; when there are three, the chief guest reclines in the centre, the next important above him and the third below him." Rab Sheshet said to him, "But should the chief guest wish to converse with him [who is above him], he would have to straighten himself and sit up to do so!" The Exilarch replied, "It is otherwise with the Persians, because he would communicate with him by gesture[5]."

Etiquette of a meal among the Persians.

[Rab Sheshet asked the Exilarch], "With whom do [the Persians] commence to wash previous to the meal?" He replied, "With the chief guest." "Does, then, the chief guest watch his hands[6] until all the others wash?" He replied, "They immediately set a tray before him." "With whom do they commence to wash at the conclusion of the meal?" He answered, "With the person of least importance." "Then the chief guest sits with his hands stained until they all wash!" He replied, "They do not remove the tray from before him until they set water before him."

Subject continued.

Rab Sheshet said [to the Exilarch]: I know a teaching, viz.: What is the procedure of reclining? When there are two couches, the more important person reclines first, and the other below him.

Custom among the Jews.

[1] According to Rashi, the question refers to the man who stopped his meal in order to be included for *Zimmūn* with two others. Since, in Rab Sheshet's view, he joins with them up to the end of the first benediction, where should he resume his Grace? According to Tōsāfōt, it refers to the man who is leading the Grace with *Zimmūn*. After the others have responded "Blessed be He of Whose bounty we have partaken, and through Whose goodness we live," where does he go on?

[2] On Rashi's interpretation, to the beginning of the first benediction; but on that of Tōsāfōt, he repeats his own formula with an addition, viz. "We will bless Him of Whose bounty we have partaken and through Whose goodness we live."

[3] According to Rashi, he starts the second benediction; according to Tōsāfōt, he resumes the response of the others: "Blessed be He of Whose bounty" etc. Cf. Singer, p. 280, line 2 of Hebrew.

[4] Rashi omits the word "old."

[5] It is apparently to be understood that Persian etiquette forbade speaking at table; cf. *T.A.* III. p. 7. Jews also observed silence during a meal; see *ibid.* p. 267 n. 400.

[6] I.e. do nothing.

When there are three couches, the chief person reclines first, the next important above him, and the third below him. They begin the washing previous to the meal with the chief guest. As for the washing at the conclusion of the meal, when there are five, they commence with the chief guest; but when there are a hundred[1] they commence with the person of least importance until they reach the last five, and then they commence with the principal guest. To whom the water after the meal returns[2], [the privilege of saying] Grace likewise returns. This supports the statement of Rab; for Rab Ḥiyya said in the name of Rab: He who washes his hands first at the end of a meal is delegated to say Grace.

Rab at the table of Rabbi.

Rab and R. Ḥiyya were sitting at table in the presence of Rabbi. Rabbi said to Rab, "Arise, wash thy hands." R. Ḥiyya noticed that Rab was trembling[3] and said to him, "O son of princes! See, it is for the privilege of saying Grace after meals that Rabbi tells thee [to wash]."

fol. 47 a. Matters in which one does not give another precedence.

The Rabbis have taught: We do not honour a man on a road or bridge[4], or with [washing] the hands stained [in the course of the meal][5]. Rabin and Abbai were journeying along a road; the ass of Rabin went in front of Abbai's, and he did not say to him, "Let the master go [first]." Abbai said [to himself], "Since this young Rabbi has come from the West[6], he has grown very conceited." When he reached the entrance of the Synagogue, Rabin said to him, "Let the master enter [first]." He retorted, "And up to now have I not been master[7]!" He replied, "Thus spake R. Joḥanan: We only honour a man [by making way for him] in the case of a door which has a *M^e^zūzāh*." "If there is a *M^e^zūzāh*, one does; but if there is no *M^e^zūzāh*, one does not? Then, in the case of a Synagogue or House of Study which has no *M^e^zūzāh*, there also one should not honour a man [by making way for him]!" "Nay, [the meaning is,] A door which is liable to have a *M^e^zūzāh* affixed[8]."

When one may begin eating at a meal.

Rab Judah the son of Rab Samuel b. Shelat said in the name of Rab: Those who recline at table are not permitted to eat anything until he who breaks bread partakes thereof. Rab Safra sat

[1] Not literally, but a large number.
[2] Of these five.
[3] See fol. 43 *a*, p. 279 n. 3; and on "Son of princes," p. 86 n. 8.
[4] By making way for him.
[5] By giving him the opportunity to wash first.
[6] He had studied under R. Joḥanan in Palestine.
[7] So far Rabin had not made way for him.
[8] The Synagogue, not being a fixed abode, did not require a *M^e^zūzāh*.

there and said, "To taste" was said [by Rab, not "to eat"]. What is to be deduced therefrom? That a man is in duty bound to repeat [a statement] in the exact language of his teacher[1].

Some points in connection with the meal.

Our Rabbis have taught: Two may wait upon each other with a dish, but three may not. The one who breaks bread puts forth his hand first[2]; but if he wishes to show respect to his teacher or his superior[3], he has the power to do so. Rabbah b. Bar Ḥannah was marrying his son into the family of Rab Samuel[4] b. Rab Ḳaṭṭina. He sat beforehand and taught his son[5]: He who is to break the bread is not permitted to do so until the response "Amen" has been completed by all. Rab Ḥisda said: By the majority. Rammi b. Ḥamma asked him, "What difference does the majority make since the benediction has not been completed[6], the minority having not yet completed it?" He replied, "I declare that whoever makes the response 'Amen' unduly [prolonged] acts in error[7]."

How the response "Amen" should not be made.

Our Rabbis have taught: In responding "Amen" one should not make the word hurriedly pronounced[8] or cut short[9] or an "orphan[10]"; nor should he hurl the benediction from his mouth[11]. Ben 'Azzai says: Whoever responds with an "orphan Amen," his sons will be orphaned, with a "hurried Amen" his days will be hurried[12], with a "cut short Amen" his days will be cut short. But whoever prolongs the "Amen," his days and years will be prolonged for him.

Whether one who is not present at the commencement of the meal may be included for *Zimmūn*.

Rab and Samuel were sitting at a meal. Rab Shimi b. Ḥiyya came and hurriedly ate his food. Rab said to him, "What is thine intention—to join with us [in saying Grace with *Zimmūn*]? We

[1] Cf. above, fol. 33 *b*, p. 224.

[2] To pick his portion from the dish. On the Oriental mode of dining, cf. Lane, p. 148, *T. A.* III. pp. 26 ff.

[3] *M.* adds: "in wisdom," i.e. by waiving his right to the first choice.

[4] *M.*: Daniel.

[5] The regulations connected with the breaking of the bread, since the honour was given to a bridegroom.

[6] The response is considered part of the benediction.

[7] I.e. if he allows much time to elapse between saying the benediction and breaking the bread; therefore Rab Ḥisda is satisfied if the majority say "Amen."

[8] I.e. "'men."

[9] I.e. "Ame-."

[10] I.e. saying "Amen" without having heard the benediction to which it is the response.

[11] As though it were something he was glad to be rid of.

[12] Meaning, he will die suddenly.

have concluded the meal[1]." Samuel said to him, "If they brought me mushrooms or Abba[2] pigeons, should we not eat[3]?"

Most distinguished person has the privilege of saying Grace.

Rab's disciples were sitting at a meal, and Rab[4] entered. They said, "A great man has come who will say Grace for us." He said to them, "Are you of opinion that a great man must say Grace? No, one who was at the main part of the meal should say Grace." But the *Hᵃlākāh* is—The most important person says Grace, although he arrived at the end of the meal.

One who has eaten Dᵉmai, etc.

Why one who has eaten *Dᵉmai* may be included.

But he had no right [to eat it][5]! If he so choose, he can renounce his possessions and become a poor man, and then he would have the right [to eat it]; for we have a Mishnaic teaching: We may feed the poor and soldiers[6] on *Dᵉmai*. But Rab Huna has said: It has been taught: *Bēt* Shammai declare that we may not feed the poor and soldiers on *Dᵉmai*[7].

The first tithe from which Tᵉrūmāh *has been taken.*

Why the *Mishnāh* mentions the case of one who partakes of the first tithe of which *Tᵉrūmāh* has been taken.

This is evident[8]! No; it is necessary to state it for the case where [the Levite] anticipated with the ears of corn and separated therefrom the *Tᵉrūmāh* of the tithe before [the priest] had separated the great *Tᵉrūmāh*[9]. This is in accord with R. Abbahu who said in the name of R. Simeon b. Laḳish: The first tithe, which [the Levite] anticipated and separated from the ears, is exempt from the great *Tᵉrūmāh*; as it is said, "Ye shall set apart of it a gift for the Lord, even a tithe of the tithe" (Num. xviii. 26)—i.e. "a tithe of the tithe" I tell thee [to set apart], but not a great *Tᵉrūmāh* or a *Tᵉrūmāh* of a tithe of a tithe. Rab Pappa said to Abbai: In that case, even if [the Levite] anticipated [and separated

[1] Before Rab Shimi entered, and therefore he could not join in Grace with them.

[2] Rab's name. The *Talmūd* mentions here their favourite dishes.

[3] Therefore the meal cannot be considered as ended, and Rab Shimi may be included for Grace.

[4] Some edd. read "Rab Aḥa" incorrectly.

[5] And he obtains the privilege of joining with *Zimmūn* by means of something that is forbidden.

[6] I.e. billeted troops.

[7] But the *Hᵃlākāh* is not in agreement with *Bēt* Shammai.

[8] Since the first tithe from which *Tᵉrūmāh* has been taken is allowable, it is obvious that one who has eaten it may be included for *Zimmūn*. Why does the *Mishnāh* mention it?

[9] This great *Tᵉrūmāh* was due to the priest; cf. Num. xviii. 8 ff., and should be separated from the produce before the tithe is taken. If, however, the order had been reversed, it would not invalidate a man from being included for *Zimmūn*.

his tithe] from the corn-heap[1], it would likewise [be exempt from the great *Terūmāh*]! He replied: To meet thy objection the Scriptures state, "Out of all your tithes[2] ye shall set apart" (Num. xviii. 29). **fol. 47 b.**
What, however, seest thou[3]? The latter is corn but the other is not[4].

The second tithe or food belonging to the Sanctuary which had been redeemed.

This is evident[5]! With what are we here dealing? For instance, if he paid its value but not the additional fifth[6]; hence he informs us that [not having paid] the additional fifth does not prevent him [from being included for *Zimmūn*].

The attendant who has eaten food the size of an olive.

Why the attendant may be included.

This is evident[7]! Perhaps thou mayest argue that the attendant has no fixed place[8]; therefore we are informed [that he is to be included].

The Samaritan may be included for Zimmūn.

Why the Samaritan may be included.

Why should he be? He is nothing better than an *'Am hā'āreṣ*, and there is a teaching: *'Ammē hā'āreṣ* are not to be included for *Zimmūn*! Abbai said: It refers to a Samaritan who is a *Ḥābēr*. Raba said: Thou mayest even suppose that it refers to a Samaritan who is an *'Am hā'āreṣ*, and we are here dealing with the *'Am hā'āreṣ* so designated by the Rabbis who disagree in this matter with R. Meïr. For there is a teaching: Who is an *'Am hā'āreṣ*? Whoever does not eat his non-holy food[9] in a condition of ritual purity—these are the words of R. Meïr; but the Sages say: Whoever does not properly tithe his fruits. These Samaritans, however, do properly apportion the tithe, for they are careful to observe what is written in the *Tōrāh*[10]. The teacher has said: The commandments

Definition of *'Am hā'āreṣ*.

1 Before the corn is ground.

2 The Biblical text reads: "Out of all that is given you" not "all your tithes."

3 In drawing a distinction between the ears and the corn-heap.

4 According to Deut. xviii. 4 "the first-fruits *of the corn*" were the portion of the priest; therefore the *Terūmāh* would be due from the corn-heap, but not from the ears which are no longer called "corn."

5 Since the Temple-property had been redeemed, why should he not be included?

6 See Lev. v. 16.

7 Since he has eaten sufficient to necessitate Grace.

8 With the other diners, since he is continually going backward and forward and should not be included with them.

9 I.e. his every-day sustenance.

10 The Samaritans were the people of mixed origin with whom the Assyrians had repopulated North Palestine after driving the Israelite inhabitants into exile. In course of time they came to look upon themselves as a part of the Jewish people and claimed the right to share in the rebuilding of the Temple. When this right was contested, they broke away and formed a separate Community, taking with them the Pentateuch.

to which the Samaritans adhere they observe more scrupulously than the Israelite.

Subject continued.

Our Rabbis have taught: Who is an *'Am hā'āreṣ*? Whoever does not read the *Sh^e^ma'* evening and morning—these are the words of R. Eliezer; but R. Joshua says: Whoever does not lay *T^e^fillīn*. Ben 'Azzai says: Whoever has no *Ṣīṣīt* on his garment[1]. R. Nathan says: Whoever has no *M^e^zūzāh* on his door. R. Nathan[2] b. Joseph says: Whoever has sons and does not rear them to the study of *Tōrāh*. Others declare: Even if one has studied *Tōrāh* and *Mishnāh* but has not ministered to the disciples of the wise[3], he is an *'Am hā'āreṣ*. Rab Huna said: The *H^a^lākāh* is in accord with the last mentioned.

Concerning Rab M^e^nashya b. Taḥlifa.

Rammi b. Ḥamma refused to include for *Zimmūn* Rab M^e^nashya b. Taḥlifa who taught *Sifrā*, *Sifrē*[4] and the *H^a^lākāh*. When Rammi b. Ḥamma departed this life, Raba said: He only died because he refused to include Rab M^e^nashya b. Taḥlifa for *Zimmūn*. But there is a teaching: Others declare: Even if one has studied *Tōrāh* and *Mishnāh* but has not ministered to the disciples of the wise, he is an *'Am hā'āreṣ*[5]! It is different with Rab M^e^nashya b. Taḥlifa because he did minister to the Rabbis, but Rammi b. Ḥamma failed to make careful inquiry about him. Another version is: Rab M^e^nashya heard the teachings from the mouth of the Rabbis and studied them, and therefore was like a Rabbinical scholar.

One who has eaten of the untithed, or the first tithe, etc.

Exclusion of one who has eaten of the untithed, etc.

[If he has eaten of] the untithed, it is evident [that he should not be included]! No; it was necessary to state it because of the untithed which is so designated by the Rabbis. How is this meant? As referring to that which grows in an unperforated pot[6].

[1] *M.* adds: And a *M^e^zūzāh* on his door.

[2] Some edd. read: Jonathan. *M.* has Nathan.

[3] And thus derived the teachings from their lips.

[4] Halakic commentaries on Leviticus, and Numbers and Deuteronomy respectively.

[5] And in the view of Rammi b. Ḥamma, Rab M^e^nashya came within this class.

[6] According to D^e^māi v. 10, that which grows in a perforated pot, placed in the ground, is legally like that which grows in the ground. But if something grows in an unperforated pot, is that to be considered as growing in the soil and subject to the tithe? The Rabbis say it is, and one who eats of this untithed should not be included for *Zimmūn*.

The first tithe from which Tᵉrūmāh *has not been taken.*

That is evident! No; it is necessary [to mention it] for the case where [the Levite] anticipated [the priest by taking the tithe] from the corn-heap[1]. Thou mayest argue that it is as Rab Pappa said to Abbai[2]. Therefore we are informed that it is as Abbai answered him[3].

Exclusion of one who has eaten that from which *Tᵉrūmāh* has not been taken.

The second tithe or food belonging to the Sanctuary which had not been redeemed.

This is evident! No; it is necessary [to mention it] for the case where it has been redeemed but not according to the *Hᵃlākāh.* With "the second tithe," for instance, where he redeemed it with uncoined silver, whereas the All-merciful declared, "Thou shalt bind up the money in thy hand" (Deut. xiv. 25)—i.e. money which has a stamp upon it[4]. With "food belonging to the Sanctuary" for which [for instance] he had given a piece of land in exchange but he had not redeemed with money; whereas the All-merciful declared, "He shall add the fifth part *of the money* of thy valuation unto it, and it shall be assured to him" (Lev. xxvii. 19)[5].

Exclusion of one who has eaten of the second tithe, etc.

And the attendant who has eaten less than the size of an olive.

That is evident[6]! But since he taught the first clause relating to food the size of an olive, he also teaches the latter clause relating to food less than the size of an olive.

Exclusion of the attendant.

And the idolator[7] may not be included for Zimmūn.

That is evident! With what are we here dealing? With a proselyte who has been circumcised but not undergone immersion; for R. Zera said in the name of R. Joḥanan[8]: He is certainly not to be regarded as a proselyte until he has been circumcised and undergone immersion, and so long as he has not undergone immersion he is still a non-Jew.

Exclusion of an idolator.

[1] See fol. 47 *a*, bot., and top of fol. 47 *b*, p. 303.

[2] That the tithe should be exempt from the great *Tᵉrūmāh* and permissible to be eaten, and therefore such an one should be included for *Zimmūn.*

[3] That it is subject to the great *Tᵉrūmāh*, and one is forbidden to eat of the tithe unless this *Tᵉrūmāh* is separated; and hence, he who eats thereof should not be included.

[4] The word for "Thou shalt bind" (וצרת) is here connected with צורה "stamp, image."

[5] This is the reading of the Biblical text, which the *Talmūd* does not quote verbally, but as follows: "And he shall give the money, and it shall be assured to him."

[6] Because anybody who eats less than the size of an olive is exempt from saying the Grace.

[7] See p. 291 n. 5.

[8] *M.*: For R. Ḥiyya b. Abba said.

II. *Women, slaves and minors may not be included for* Zimmūn.

Inclusion of an infant.

R. Josē[1] said: An infant lying in the cradle may be included for *Zimmūn*. But lo, there is our Mishnaic teaching: *Women, slaves and* minors *may not be included!* R. Josē is in agreement with the statement of R. Joshua b. Levi who said: Although they declare that an infant lying in the cradle may not be included for *Zimmūn*, yet we may consider him an addition to make up a quorum of ten[2].

Inclusion of a slave to make a quorum in Synagogue.

R. Joshua b. Levi also said: Nine [free] men and a slave may be reckoned together for a quorum[3]. Against this is quoted: It happened that R. Eliezer went into a Synagogue and did not find ten there, so he freed his slave and with him completed the requisite number. Since he freed him he was [included], but had he not freed him, he would not! Two had been required [to complete the quorum], so he freed one slave and fulfilled the obligation [of having ten] with the other. But how could he act thus? For, lo, Rab Judah declared: Whoever frees his slave transgresses a command of the *Tōrāh*; as it is said, "Of them shall ye take your bondmen *for ever*" (Lev. xxv. 46)! For the purpose of fulfilling a religious duty it is different. But it is fulfilling a religious duty through the means of a transgression[4]! The fulfilling of a religious duty which affects the many[5] is different.

Meritorious to be among the first ten in Synagogue.

R. Joshua b. Levi also said: A man should always go early to the Synagogue so that he may have the merit of being counted with the first ten; for even if a hundred come after him, he receives upon himself the reward of them all. The reward of them all, dost imagine? Nay, he means to say, he is given a reward equal to them all.

Inclusion of the Ark in Synagogue quorum.

Rab Huna said: Nine and the Ark[6] may be reckoned together for a quorum. Rab Naḥman asked him: Is the Ark a man! But,

[1] *M.*: Ashē; and Rashi's reading is: Assi. [2] See p. 294 n. 3.

[3] To hold a Congregational service for which a minimum of ten males over the age of 13 is required.

[4] And that is forbidden.

[5] And not the individual. Since the freeing of the slave enables nine men to have a Congregational service, it is permitted.

[6] I.e. the chest in the Synagogue where the Scrolls of the Law are deposited. See Oesterley and Box, p. 338. According to Azulay (quoted by Goldschmidt, p. 171) וארון "and the Ark" is really the initial letters of four words: ואחד רואה ואינו נראה "And One Who sees but is invisible," referring to the Divine Presence in the Synagogue. There may be here a reference to the custom of giving a minor a Scroll of the Law to hold, and thereby including him in the quorum; cf. Löw, *Lebensalter*, p. 208 and p. 409 n. 46.

said Rab Huna, since nine look like ten, they may be reckoned together. Another version is: When they are gathered together[1]; another version is: When they are scattered.

Inclusion of the Sabbath for *Zimmūn*. R. Ammi said: Two and the Sabbath[2] may be reckoned together for *Zimmūn*. Rab Naḥman asked him: Is the Sabbath a man! But, said R. Ammi, two disciples of the wise who sharpen [their minds] one against the other with the study of *Hᵃlākāh* may be reckoned together [for *Zimmūn*]. Rab Ḥisda declared: For instance, I and Rab Sheshet. Rab Sheshet declared: For instance, I and Rab Ḥisda.

When a minor may be included for *Zimmūn*. R. Joḥanan said[3]: A minor who develops puberty prematurely may be included for *Zimmūn*. There is a teaching to the same effect: A minor who shows signs of puberty[4] is to be included, but if he does not show such signs[5] he is not to be included; we are, however, not to be very particular with a minor[6]. But this is self-contradictory! Thou sayest: If he shows signs of puberty he is [to be included], but if not, he is not; and then it continues, "We are, however, not to be very particular with a minor"! What does this mean to include? Surely it is to include the boy who **fol. 48 a.** develops puberty prematurely. But the *Hᵃlākāh* is not in agreement with any of these teachings, but with that which Rab Naḥman said: A minor who understands to Whom we say Grace is to be included for *Zimmūn*.

How Rabbah tested fitness of minors. Abbai and Raba[7] were sitting in the presence of Rabbah. He asked them, "To Whom do we say Grace[8]?" They replied, "The All-merciful." "And where does the All-merciful dwell?" Raba pointed upwards to the ceiling; Abbai went outside and pointed towards the heavens. Rabbah said to them, "Both of you are

1 I.e. when the nine are seated close together, without actually counting them, it is not possible to notice that there is one short. Therefore, including the presence of the Ark, the Congregational service may be held. The alternative version supposes that it is easier to detect the absence of one when the nine are seated close together.

2 Pineles (quoted by Goldschmidt, *loc. cit.*) thinks that שבת is the initial letters of שונים בדברי תורה "[Two] who study words of *Tōrāh* [together]."

3 *M.*: Rab Hisda said in the name of R. Joḥanan.

4 *Lit.* who produced two hairs.

5 Although he has reached the age of puberty, i.e. 13 years.

6 He may be included whether he shows signs of puberty or not.

7 *M.*: Rab b. R. Ḥanan. *D.S.* thinks the correct reading is Raba b. R. Ḥanan which is accepted by Hyman, iii. p. 1041 a, and Bacher, *A. B. A.* (2nd ed.) add. p. 12.

8 They were boys, and Rabbah wished to apply the test mentioned in the preceding paragraph.

Rabbis; for that is what the proverb says, 'Every pumpkin is known by its stem[1]'."

On making up ten for Grace.

Rab Judah b. Rab Samuel b. Shelat said in the name of Rab: If nine ate corn-food and one ate vegetables, they are to be reckoned together[2]. R. Zera[3] said, "I asked Rab Judah, 'How is it with eight or seven[4]?' He replied, 'It makes no difference.' Concerning six there was[5] no need for me to ask." R. Jeremiah said to him, "Well hast thou done in not asking [about six]. What is the reason there[6]? Because there is a majority [who have eaten corn-food]." But here also [with six] there is a majority! But R. Zera was of opinion that we require a clearly recognisable majority[7].

King Jannaeus and Simeon b. Sheṭaḥ.

King Jannaeus and his Queen were dining together, and since he had put the Rabbis[8] to death, he had nobody to say Grace for them. He said to his wife, "Would that we had somebody to say Grace for us." She said to him, "Swear to me that if I bring thee such a man, thou wilt not harm him." He swore to her; and she brought him her brother, Simeon b. Sheṭaḥ[9]. The king gave him a seat between himself and her, and said to him, "See how much honour I pay thee." He replied, "It is not thou that honourest me, but it is the *Tōrāh* that brings me honour; for it is written, 'Extol her, and she will exalt thee; she will bring thee honour when thou dost embrace her' (Prov. iv. 8)[10]." The king said to him, "Thou seest they[11] do not accept any lordship[12]!" He was handed a cup of wine to say Grace. He said, "How shall I word

[1] I.e. one can usually detect in the young what they will be like later. From their answers Rabbah foresaw that they would become learned men.

[2] To say the formula for ten; see p. 318.

[3] *M.*: Huna.

[4] Who ate corn-food and two or three who ate vegetables.

[5] Edd. insert the word "certainly" which the commentators find difficulty in explaining. *M.* omits it.

[6] That it is allowed with seven and three.

[7] Which is apparent with seven and three but not with six and four.

[8] Viz. the Pharisees of whom Alexander Jannaeus was a bitter opponent.

[9] Who was a leader of the Pharisaic party and had been in hiding.

[10] In *J.T.*: For it is written in the Book of Ben Sira, "Exalt her and she will raise thee and make thee to sit among great men." No such verse occurs in Ecclesiasticus. The first clause is from Prov. iv. 8 and the second is a reminiscence of Ecclus. xi. 1. The earlier part of the incident between Simeon b. Sheṭaḥ and Jannaeus, especially the cause of the former's flight, is differently told in *J.T.*

[11] The Pharisees.

[12] Since Simeon b. Sheṭaḥ denied that the king had the power to honour him, Jannaeus took this as evidence that the Pharisees were disloyal to the throne. Some edd. read: The king said to her, "Thou seest he [i.e. Simeon] does not accept lordship." He meant to point out to the Queen that her attempt to bring about a rapprochement between him and the Pharisees was futile.

the Grace[1]? 'Blessed be He of Whose bounty Jannaeus and his companions have eaten'?" He drank the cup of wine. They gave him another cup of wine and then he said Grace.

What constitutes a meal for the purpose of Grace.

R. Abba b. R. Ḥiyya b. Abba said[2]: Simeon b. Sheṭaḥ who did this[3] acted so on his own account[4]. For thus said R. Ḥiyya b. Abba in the name of R. Joḥanan: Nobody can cause others to have complied with the requirements of the law[5] until he has eaten corn-food of the size of an olive. Against this is quoted: Rabban Simeon b. Gamaliel says: If one has ascended [the couch] and reclined with them, even though he has not dipped with them except the smallest quantity[6] and has not eaten with them except a single dried fig, he is to be reckoned with them [for Grace]! Yes, he may be reckoned with them, but he is unable to cause others to comply with the requirements of the law until he has eaten corn-food of the size of an olive. It has been similarly reported: Rab Ḥanna[7] b. Judah said in the name of Raba: Even if he has not dipped with them except the smallest quantity and **fol. 48 b.** has not eaten with them except a single dried fig, he is to be reckoned with them, but as for causing others to comply with the requirements of the law, that he cannot do until he has eaten corn-food of the size of an olive. Rab Ḥanna b. Judah said in the name of Raba: The *Hᵃlākāh* is—If he has eaten a single cabbage-leaf and drunk a cup of wine, he is to be reckoned with them; but as for causing others to comply with the requirements of the law, that he cannot do until he has eaten corn-food of the size of an olive.

Who instituted the benedictions of the Grace after meals.

Rab Naḥman said: Moses instituted for Israel the benediction "Who feedest[8]" at the time the manna descended for them. Joshua instituted for them the benediction of "the land[9]" when they entered the land [of Canaan]. David and Solomon instituted [what follows] until[10] "Who...rebuildest Jerusalem[11]." David instituted "[Have mercy, O Lord our God] upon Israel Thy people, upon Jerusalem Thy city," and Solomon[12] instituted "and upon

1 Since he had eaten nothing.
2 Some edd. add "in the name of R. Joḥanan" incorrectly.
3 Viz. said Grace after only having had a cup of wine and no solid food.
4 None of the Rabbis agree with him.
5 By saying Grace on their behalf.
6 Of bread into the dish.
7 *M.*: Huna.
8 The first benediction of the Grace; Singer, p. 280.
9 The second benediction; *ibid.* pp. 280 f.
10 This is the reading of *M.*; edd. omit "until."
11 The third benediction; *ibid.* pp. 281 f.
12 When he built the Temple.

the great and holy House." The benediction "Who art kind and dealest kindly[1]" was instituted in Jabneh[2] in connection with the slain of Bethar[3]; for Rab Matt^e^na said: On the day the slain of Bethar were allowed burial, there was instituted in Jabneh the benediction "Who art kind and dealest kindly"—"Who art kind," because the bodies did not decompose[4]; "and dealest kindly," because they were allowed burial.

Order of the benedictions.

Our Rabbis have taught: The following is the order of the Grace after meals: The first benediction is "Who feedest"; the second, the benediction of "the land"; the third, "Who...rebuildest Jerusalem"; the fourth, "Who art kind and dealest kindly." On the Sabbath, one begins and ends with consolation and refers to the sanctity of the day in the middle[5]. R. Eliezer says: If he wishes to include [the reference to the Sabbath] in the "consolation," he may do so; in the benediction of "the land," he may do so; in the benediction instituted by the Sages in Jabneh, he may do so. The Sages, however, say: He should only include it in the "consolation." Then the Sages agree with the first *Tannā*[6]! There is a point of difference between them, viz.: the *post factum*[7].

Basis for the Grace in the *Tōrāh*.

Our Rabbis have taught: Whence do we derive the Grace after meals from the *Tōrāh*? As it is said, "And thou shalt eat and be satisfied and bless" (Deut. viii. 10)—this refers to the benediction "Who feedest"; "the Lord thy God" (*ibid.*)—to the benediction of *Zimmūn*; "for the land" (*ibid.*)—to the benediction of "the land"; "the good" (*ibid.*)—to "Who...rebuildest Jerusalem," for so it states "That goodly hill-country and Lebanon" (*ibid.* iii. 25); "which He hath given thee" (*ibid.* viii. 10)—to "Who art kind and dealest kindly." I have here only the Grace after meals; whence do we derive the Grace before meals? Thou canst reason

[1] The fourth benediction; *ibid.* pp. 283 f.

[2] See p. 111 n. 1.

[3] The town of Bethar, near Sepphoris, was the scene of the last stand of the Jews against the Romans in 135 C.E. The name is probably derived from the Latin *vetera* (sc. *castra*); cf. Krauss, p. 153.

[4] During the long period in which the Jews could not bury their dead.

[5] The benediction of consolation is the third, beginning "Have mercy"; see Singer, p. 281 for the Sabbath formula.

[6] Why is their opinion separately stated if it agrees with that of the first *Tannā*?

[7] See p. 96 n. 2. In the view of the Rabbis, if the man included the reference to the Sabbath in a benediction other than the "Consolation," he must restart at the commencement. The first *Tannā*, on the other hand, only requires it in the "Consolation" *ab initio*, but if he included it in another benediction, *post factum* it is to be allowed.

by *a fortiori* argument—if a man should bless God when satisfied, how much more so when he is hungry[1]!

Another version.

Rabbi says[2]: "And thou shalt eat and be satisfied and bless" refers to the benediction "Who feedest," but the benediction of *Zimmūn* is derived from "Magnify the Lord with me" (Ps. xxxiv. 4)[3]; "for the land"—to the benediction of "the land"; "the good"—to "Who...rebuildest Jerusalem," for so it states "That goodly hill-country and Lebanon"; the benediction "Who art kind and dealest kindly" was instituted in Jabneh. I have here only the Grace after meals; whence do we derive the Grace before meals? There is a teaching to state, "Which He hath given thee"—i.e. as soon as He hath given thee[4].

Still another version respecting Grace before meals.

R. Isaac said: [This reasoning] is unnecessary. Behold it states, "And He will bless thy bread and water" (Exod. xxiii. 25)—read not "And He will bless" [*ūbērak*] but "And bless thou" [*ūbārēk*]. When is it called "bread[5]"? Before one eats it[6].

Yet another version.

R. Nathan[7] said: [This reasoning] is unnecessary. Behold it states, "As soon as ye are come into the city, ye shall straightway find him, before he go up to the high place to eat; for the people *will not eat until he come, because he doth bless the sacrifice; and afterwards they eat* that are bidden" (I Sam. ix. 13)[8]. Why all this[9]? [10]Because women are garrulous. Samuel[11] said: The women did it in order to gaze upon Saul's beauty; for it is written, "From his shoulders and upward he was higher than any of the people" (*ibid.* v. 2). R. Johanan said: [The women did it] because one reign must not encroach upon another even a hair's breadth[12].

[1] See fol. 35 *a*, p. 234.

[2] Some edd. incorrectly insert here: "It [i.e. the *a fortiori* argument] is unnecessary."

[3] See fol. 45 *a*, p. 291.

[4] I.e. even before enjoying His gift, before partaking thereof, offer Him a benediction.

[5] Over which the benediction has to be said.

[6] Hence Grace before meals is required by the *Tōrāh*.

[7] *M.* adds: b. Assi. *D. S.* thinks the correct reading is R. Nathan b. R. Joseph.

[8] From this passage it is clear that Grace before meals is necessary.

[9] Why did the women of whom Saul inquired the way to Samuel's house give him such a long and involved reply?

[10] *M.* inserts: Rab said: Hence it is derived that women, etc.

[11] I.e. the *Āmōrā* of that name.

[12] As soon as Saul would meet Samuel, the latter's rule of the people would come to an end; and as the predestined hour had not arrived yet, the women detained Saul until the ordained time.

Basis for the benediction over *Tōrāh.*

I have here only the benediction for meals; whence is the benediction over *Tōrāh* derived? R. Ishmael said: By *a fortiori* reasoning—for temporal life[1] one says a benediction; how much more so for the life of the world to come[2]! R. Ḥiyya b. Naḥmani[3], the disciple of R. Ishmael, says in the name of R. Ishmael: [This reasoning] is unnecessary; for it states, "For the good land which He hath *given* thee" (Deut. viii. 10) and elsewhere it is stated, "And I will *give* thee the tables of stone, and the law and the commandments," etc. (Exod. xxiv. 12)[4].

One must bless God for the bad as well as the good.

R. Meïr said: Whence is it that as one blesses for the good so should he bless for the bad[5]? There is a teaching to state, "Which the Lord thy God hath given unto thee" (Deut. xxvi. 11)—He is thy Judge in every circumstance wherein He judgeth thee, whether it be with the attribute of goodness or the attribute of punishment[6]. R. Judah b. Batyra said: [This reasoning] is unnecessary; for it states, "Good" (Deut. viii. 7) and "the good" (*ibid. v.* 10)[7]—"good" i.e. *Tōrāh*, as it is said "For I give you *good* doctrine" (Prov. iv. 2); "the good" i.e. the rebuilding of Jerusalem, as it is said "That *goodly*[8] hill-country and Lebanon" (Deut. iii. 25)[9].

The proper wording of the Grace.

There is a teaching: R. Eliezer[10] says: Whoever does not say "a desirable, good and ample land" in the benediction of "the land" and "the kingdom of the house of David" in "Who...rebuildest Jerusalem" has not complied with the requirements of the law. Naḥum the Elder says: He must mention the Covenant[11] in the blessing of "the land." R. Josē says: He must mention the *Tōrāh* therein[12]. P^elemo says: He must refer to the Covenant

[1] Dependent upon food.

[2] Dependent upon the knowledge and practice of *Tōrāh*. *M.* reads: for eternal life.

[3] *M.*: Abba.

[4] From the common use of the verb "to give," a *G^ezērāh Shāwāh* (see p. 18 n. 5) is drawn—if a benediction is required for the land (cf. the second paragraph of the Grace) given by God, likewise is a benediction required for the *Tōrāh* given by Him.

[5] Cf. fol. 54 *a*, p. 348.

[6] R. Meïr's explanation is based upon the teaching of the Rabbis that *JHWH* "the Lord" is the Deity in His attribute of mercy, and *Ĕlōhīm* "God" represents Him as Judge. In Deut. xxvi. 11 both names occur.

[7] In the first passage the definite article is wanting.

[8] *Lit.*: the good.

[9] As a benediction is required for the latter, so also for the former.

[10] *M.* omits "Eliezer" and hence intends R. Judah the Prince as the author.

[11] Sc. of circumcision; see Singer, p. 280, "As well as for Thy covenant which Thou hast sealed in our flesh."

[12] *Ibid.* "Thy Law which Thou hast taught us."

before the *Tōrāh*, because the latter was given with a three-fold covenant but the former with a thirteen-fold covenant[1]. R. Abba[2] **fol. 49 a.** says: One must mention thanksgiving therein at the commencement and conclusion[3], and he who shortens [the Grace] must not omit more than one of them; for whoever omits more than one of them is to be reprimanded. Whoever concludes the benediction of "the land" with the words "[Blessed art Thou, O Lord,] Who givest lands as a heritage," or the benediction "Who...rebuildest Jerusalem" with the words "Who savest Israel" is a boor. And whoever does not include a reference to the Covenant and the *Tōrāh* in the benediction of "the land" and a reference to the kingdom of the house of David in the benediction "Who...rebuildest Jerusalem" has not complied with the requirements of the law. This supports the teaching of R. El'ai who stated that R. Abba b. Aḥa[4] said in the name of our master: Whoever omits the reference to the Covenant and the *Tōrāh* in the benediction of "the land" and to the kingdom of the house of David in the benediction "Who...rebuildest Jerusalem" has not complied with the requirements of the law.

Whether the fourth benediction requires a reference to God as King.

Abbā Josē b. Dostai[5] and the Rabbis disagree, one declaring that "Who art kind and dealest kindly" requires a reference to the [Divine] Kingship[6], the other declaring that it does not. He who contends that it requires a reference to the Kingship is of opinion that this benediction was ordained by the Rabbis[7], and he who contends that it does not is of opinion that the benediction is ordained by the *Tōrāh*[8].

[1] *Tōrāh* was given to Israel in three places—Sinai, Mt Gerizim and the plains of Moab, in each of which localities a covenant was entered into; cf. Deut. xxvii. 11 ff., xxviii. 69. In the passage dealing with the law of circumcision, Gen. xvii, the word for "covenant" occurs 13 times.

[2] Rab is here intended.

[3] It opens with "We thank Thee," etc., Singer, p. 280 and concludes "For all this...we thank and bless Thee," *ibid.* p. 281.

[4] So *J. T.* probably correctly (see Hyman, I. p. 15 a). Edd.: Jacob b. Aḥa. *M.*: that R. Aḥa said in the name of the Rabbis. "Our master" here means Rab.

[5] *M.*: R. Dosa.

[6] In the opening sentence, viz. "King of the Universe"; cf. Singer, p. 283 top.

[7] See the discussion on fol. 46 *a*, pp. 297 f. If it is held that this benediction is Rabbinic, then it is distinct from what precedes (which is from the *Tōrāh*), and being a separate benediction requires the reference to the Kingship, because without it a benediction is not complete. Cf. above, fol. 40 *b*, p. 267.

[8] And not being a separate benediction, it does not require a reference to the Kingship.

The conclusion of the third benediction.

Our Rabbis have taught: How should one conclude the benediction of the rebuilding of Jerusalem? R. Josē b. R. Judah says[1]: "Who savest Israel." Is one to say "Who savest Israel" and not "Who...rebuildest Jerusalem[2]"? Nay, [it means,] one also says "Who savest Israel." Rabbah b. Rab Huna visited the house of the Exilarch. [When saying Grace,] the latter opened with one and concluded with two[3]. Rab Ḥisda asked: What advantage is there in concluding with two? Moreover there is a teaching: Rabbi says: We should not conclude with two!

Whether the conclusion of a benediction may contain two references.

It has just been stated: "Rabbi says: We should not conclude with two." Levi quoted against Rabbi, "For the land and for the food[4]"! It means, "The land which yields food[5]." "For the land and for the fruits[6]"! It means "The land which yields fruits." "Who hallowest Israel and the seasons[7]"! It means, "Israel who sanctify the seasons." "Who sanctifiest Israel and the beginnings of the months[8]"! It means, "Israel who hallow the beginnings of the months." "Who hallowest the Sabbath, Israel and the seasons[7]"! This is an exception. Why is it different[9]? Here it is one idea, but there it is two, each distinct from the other. What is the reason that we do not conclude with two? We must not perform commandments in bundles[10]. How is it, then, in this matter? Rab Sheshet said: If one opens with "Have mercy...upon Israel Thy people," he concludes with "Who savest Israel"; if one opens with "Have mercy...upon Jerusalem Thy city," he concludes with "Who...rebuildest Jerusalem." Rab Naḥman[11] said: Even if one opens with "Have mercy...upon Israel Thy people," he should conclude with "Who...rebuildest Jerusalem"; because it is said, "The Lord doth build up Jerusalem, He gathereth together the dispersed of Israel" (Ps. cxlvii. 2)—when "doth the

[1] *M.*: R. Joshua says.

[2] This is the reading of *M.* Edd.: "and not refer to the rebuilding of Jerusalem."

[3] When saying the third benediction, he omitted either "upon Israel Thy people" or "upon Jerusalem Thy city," but concluded "Who savest Israel and...rebuildest Jerusalem."

[4] The conclusion of the second benediction, which contains two items.

[5] Hence they are really one idea.

[6] See Singer, p. 289 top.

[7] *Ibid.* p. 229 bot.

[8] *Ibid.* p. 226 bot.

[9] In being permitted, whereas "Who savest Israel and...rebuildest Jerusalem" is not.

[10] I.e. we must have a separate benediction for each religious act.

[11] *M.* adds: b. Isaac.

Lord build up Jerusalem"? At the time that "He gathereth together the dispersed of Israel[1]."

R. Zera[2] said to Rab Ḥisda, "Let the master come and teach." He replied, "[The regulations concerning] Grace after meals have I not learnt, so shall I teach!" R. Zera asked him, "How is that?" He replied, "When I visited the house of the Exilarch and said the Grace after meals, Rab Sheshet stretched his neck over me like a serpent[3]." "But why?" "Because I made no reference to the Covenant, the *Tōrāh* or the Kingship." "And why didst thou not mention them?" "In accord with the statement of Rab Ḥananel in the name of Rab, viz.: If one has not referred to the Covenant, the *Tōrāh* and the Kingship, he has complied with the requirements of the law—'the Covenant' because it does not apply to women; 'the *Tōrāh* and the Kingship' because they apply neither to women nor slaves." "And thou didst abandon all these *Tannāīm* and *Ămōrāīm*[4] and act according to the view of Rab[5]!"

Rab Hisda's difficulty with the form of the Grace.

Rabbah b. Bar Ḥannah said in the name of R. Joḥanan: The benediction "Who art kind and dealest kindly" requires a reference to the Kingship. What does he intend to tell us—that a benediction which contains no reference to the Kingship has not the name of benediction? But R. Joḥanan has already told us this once[6]! R. Zera[7] said: He means to say that it needs two references to the Kingship, one for its own sake[8] and one for "Who...rebuildest Jerusalem." If so, three are required—one for its own sake, one for "Who...rebuildest Jerusalem" and one for the benediction of "the land"; for, why should not the benediction of "the land" have one? Because it is a benediction which is connected with the preceding[9]. Then "Who...rebuildest Jerusalem" should likewise not require one because it is a benediction which is connected with the preceding! Strictly speaking, even "Who...rebuildest Jerusalem" does not require one; but since it mentions the kingdom of the house of David, it is not proper to omit a reference to

The fourth benediction.

[1] Therefore it is the rebuilding of Jerusalem which should be the constant prayer, since the rest depends upon that.

[2] *M.*: Ze'ira.

[3] To express astonishment.

[4] Who require these references to be included.

[5] That is why Rab Sheshet showed astonishment.

[6] See fol. 40 *b*, p. 267.

[7] *M.*: Ze'ira.

[8] To constitute it a benediction.

[9] Therefore the reference to the Kingship at the beginning of the first benediction governs this one also.

the [Divine] Kingship. Rab Pappa said: This is what R. Zera meant to say: It requires two references to Kingship besides the one for its own sake[1].

Omission of reference to Sabbath etc. in the Grace, and its reparation.

R. Zera sat behind Rab Giddel and Rab Giddel sat before Rab Huna; he sat and said: If one erred and omitted to mention the reference to the Sabbath [in the Grace after meals][2], he says "Blessed be He Who has given Sabbaths for rest to His people Israel in love for a sign and a covenant. Blessed [art Thou, O Lord,] Who sanctifiest the Sabbath." Rab Huna asked Rab Giddel: Who said that? Rab. Again he sat and said: If one erred and omitted to mention the reference to the Festival[3], he says, "Blessed be He Who has given Festivals to His people Israel for rejoicing and a memorial. Blessed...Who sanctifiest Israel and the seasons." He asked him: Who said that? Rab. Again he sat and said: If one erred and omitted to mention the reference to the New Moon he says, "Blessed be He Who has given beginnings of the month to His people Israel for a memorial"; but I do not know whether he adds the words "and for rejoicing" or not, whether he adds a conclusion to the benediction or not, or whether it is his own or his master's[4].

If error is made in the Grace. **fol. 49 b.**

Giddel b. Minjomi was standing[5] before Rab Naḥman. Rab Naḥman made a mistake [in the Grace] and returned to the commencement. He asked him, "Why did the master do so?" He replied, "Because Rab Shela[6] has said in the name of Rab: If one erred, he should return to the commencement." "But Rab Huna has declared in the name of Rab: If one erred, he should say 'Blessed be He Who has given' [etc.]"! He said to him, "Was it not reported in this connection: Rab M^e^nashya b. Taḥlifa said in the name of Rab: This teaching only applies if he has not commenced the benediction 'Who art kind and dealest kindly'; but if he has commenced it, he must return to the beginning?"

1 In addition to the opening formula, "Blessed art Thou...King of the Universe" (Singer, p. 283 line 1) we have "our Father, our King" (*ibid.* line 2) and "O King Who art kind" (line 4).

2 In the third benediction; Singer, p. 281.

3 *Ibid.* p. 282.

4 Pinner (in his edition of this Tractate) suggests to insert here the following from fol. 44 *a*: When Rab Dimai came he said: Rab concluded on the New Moon thus, "Blessed...Who sanctifiest Israel and the beginnings of the month." See p. 287.

5 *M.*: sitting.

6 Viz. Shela b. Abina; cf. Hyman, III. p. 1112 b.

Omission of reference to the New Moon in the *Tefillāh* and Grace respectively.

Rab Iddi b. Abin said in the name of Rab 'Amram, in the name of Rab Naḥman, in the name of Samuel[1]: If one erred and omitted the reference to the New Moon in the *Tefillāh*[2] we make him repeat it; in the Grace after meals[3] we do not make him repeat it. Rab Abin[4] asked Rab 'Amram, "Why is the *Tefillāh* different from the Grace after meals in this respect?" He replied, "To me also that was a difficulty and I put the question to Rab Naḥman, who told me, 'I have not heard the reason from the master, Samuel'; but let us see: With regard to the *Tefillāh* which is an obligation, we make him repeat it; but with regard to the Grace after meals, where one can eat or not eat just as he pleases, we do not make him repeat it." "But now, on the Sabbaths and Festivals, when there is no question of his not eating[5], then also, if he erred, he should repeat it!" He replied, "Quite so; for Rab Shela said in the name of Rab: If he erred, he must recommence at the beginning." "But Rab Huna declared in the name of Rab: If one erred, he says 'Blessed be He Who has given'[6]!" "Has it not been reported in that connection: 'This teaching only applies if he has not commenced the benediction "Who art kind and dealest kindly"; but if he has started it, he recommences at the beginning'?"

How much [must one have eaten at the meal] to be included for Zimmūn*?*

How much must one have eaten to be included for *Zimmūn*?

That is to say, R. Meïr considers it to be the size of an olive and R. Judah the size of an egg. But we have been told the reverse; for there is a Mishnaic teaching: And so, he who went from Jerusalem and recalled that he had with him holy flesh[7], if he has passed Ṣofim[8], he burns it where he is; but if not, he turns back and burns it before the Temple with some of the wood piled on the altar. How much [of the holy flesh must one have to make such a return necessary]? R. Meïr says: In either case[9] the size of an egg; but R. Judah says: In either case the size of

[1] *M.* omits: in the name of Samuel.

[2] See Singer, p. 50.

[3] *Ibid.* p. 282.

[4] *M.*: Rab Iddi b. Abin.

[5] It is obligatory to have three full meals on those days.

[6] See the preceding paragraph.

[7] I.e. flesh of a sacrifice which must not be eaten outside Jerusalem.

[8] Mt Scopus, on the North outskirt of Jerusalem.

[9] Viz. holy flesh or leaven, of which the quoted *Mishnāh* also treats; i.e. if when on his way to Jerusalem for the festival of Passover, he recalls that he has left leaven in his house.

an olive[1]! R. Joḥanan said: The statement must be reversed[2]. Abbai said: There is certainly no necessity to reverse it; for here[3] they differ in the interpretation of Scripture: R. Meïr holds, "And thou shalt eat" (Deut. viii. 10)—i.e. eating; "and thou shalt be satisfied"—i.e. drinking; and "eating" means the minimum quantity of the size of an olive. R. Judah, on the other hand, holds, "And thou shalt eat and be satisfied"—i.e. eating wherein is some satisfaction; and what is that? That is the minimum quantity of the size of an egg. But in the other case[4], they differ in reasoning: R. Meïr holds that his return must be equal to his defilement—as his defilement[5] is only possible by means of something of the minimum size of an egg, so must his return be necessitated by holy flesh of the minimum size of an egg. R. Judah, however, holds that his return must be equal to his prohibition[6]—as his prohibition is with something of the minimum size of an olive, so must his return be necessitated by holy flesh of the minimum size of an olive.

MISHNĀH III

How do we [say Grace] with Zimmūn*? With three persons [at table], one says "We will bless [Him of Whose bounty we have partaken]"; with three and himself, he says "Bless ye [Him of Whose bounty]" etc. With ten, one says "We will bless our God [of Whose bounty]" etc.; with ten and himself, he says "Bless ye...," and that is the same whether there be ten or ten myriads*[7]*. With a hundred, one says "We will bless the Lord our God..."; with a hundred and himself, he says "Bless ye [the Lord our God]" etc. With a thousand, one says "We will bless the Lord our God, the God of Israel..."; with a thousand and himself, he says "Bless ye...." With ten thousand, one says "We will bless the Lord our*

1 The standards required here, so far as the two Rabbis are concerned, are the reverse of those mentioned in our *Mishnāh*.

2 In the quoted *Mishnāh*, the minimum of the olive must be ascribed to R. Meïr and *vice versa*.

3 On the question of Grace after meals.

4 Of the holy flesh.

5 Nothing less than the size of an egg can cause defilement.

6 To eat leaven on Passover less than the size of an olive does not constitute a breach of the law.

7 This is R. 'Aḳiba's view which has been adopted. See Singer, p. 279. What follows is the opinion of R. Josē.

God, the God of Israel, the God of hosts, Who is enthroned above the Cherubim, for the food of which we have partaken"; with ten thousand and himself, he says "Bless ye...." As he blesses, exactly so do they respond after him: "Blessed be the Lord our God, the God of Israel, the God of hosts, Who is enthroned above the Cherubim, for the food of which we have partaken." R. Josē of Galilee says: According to the numerical size of the assembly do they determine the form of the benediction; as it is said, "Bless ye God in full assemblies, even the Lord, ye that are from the fountain of Israel" (Ps. lxviii. 27). *R. 'Aḳiba said: What do we find in the Synagogue? Whether many or few, one says "Bless ye the Lord[1]." R. Ishmael says: "Bless ye the Lord Who is to be blessed."*

GᴱMĀRA

Samuel said: A man should never exclude himself from the general body[2]. But there is our Mishnaic teaching: *With three and himself, he says "Bless ye"*! He means to say "Bless ye also"; but in any case "We will bless" is preferable. But Rab Adda b. Ahᵃbah declared: The school of Rab say: We have the teaching: Six people [who eat together] should divide themselves up[3], and so up to ten[4]. That is quite right if thou sayest "We will bless" is preferable, and therefore they are to be divided up; but if thou sayest "Bless ye" is preferable, why should they be divided up[5]? Is it not, then, to be concluded that "We will bless" is preferable? Draw that conclusion. There is a teaching to the same effect[6]: Whether one says "Bless ye" or "We will bless," we should not take him to task on that account[7]; but punctilious people do[8].

"We will bless" preferred to "Bless ye." fol. 50 a.

Also, from the form of benediction used by a man it may be recognised whether he is a disciple of the wise or not. How is this? Rabbi declares: [If he says] "And through Whose goodness [we live]," he is a disciple of the wise; but if "And from

The proper wording.

1 E.g. in the benediction over the *Tōrāh*, Singer, p. 68; and the formula does not vary with the size of the Congregation.

2 By, e.g., saying "Bless ye" not "We will bless." See fol. 30 *a*, p. 196.

3 Into two parties of three, so that each arranges *Zimmūn*.

4 Ten should not be divided up, because ten are required for the addition of "our God" to the formula.

5 If the six are divided into two parties of three, there will not be four for the formula "Bless ye."

6 Viz. that in our *Mishnāh*, the phrase "Bless ye" means "Bless ye also."

7 Because both phrases include the speaker.

8 On the word נוקרן, see Krauss, p. 357, and Löw's note *in loc.*

Whose goodness[1]," he is a boor. Abbai said to Rab Dimai: But it is written, "And from Thy blessing let the house of Thy servant be blessed for ever" (II Sam. vii. 29)! With a petition it is different[2]. With a petition likewise it is written, "Open thy mouth wide[3], and I will fill it" (Ps. lxxxi. 11)! This is written in connection with words of *Tōrāh*[4].

Subject continued. There is a teaching: Rabbi declares: If one says "Through Whose goodness we live" he is a disciple of the wise; if he says "[Through Whose goodness] they live" he is a boor. The Rabbis of Neharbel[5] taught the reverse[6]; but the *Hᵃlākāh* is not in agreement with them.

Subject continued. R. Joḥanan declared: [If he says] "We will bless Him of Whose bounty we have partaken" he is a disciple of the wise; if he says "[We will bless] the One of Whose bounty we have partaken" he is a boor[7]. But Aḥa b. Raba[8] said to Rab Ashē: But we say: "[We will bless] the One Who has performed for our fathers and for us all these miracles[9]"! He replied: Here it is obvious that it is the Holy One, blessed be He, Who performed the miracles. R. Joḥanan declared: [If he says] "Blessed be He of Whose bounty we have partaken" he is a disciple of the wise; but if he says "[Blessed be He] for the food of which we have partaken," he is a boor[10]. Rab Huna b. Rab Joshua said: This refers only to three, where the Divine Name is not mentioned; but with ten, where the Name is mentioned, the matter is clear[11]. As our *Mishnāh* teaches: *As he blesses, exactly so do they respond*

1 Because "from" implies only part of the Divine goodness, as though we were not entirely dependent upon His goodness.

2 We must be humble in asking for the Divine blessing and not, as it were, demand the whole of it; therefore the use of "from" is justifiable. But in the Grace we make a declaration, and so "from" is out of place.

3 In asking for the Divine blessing, i.e. ask for much and there is no need to be humble in petitioning God.

4 This request is for spiritual things, not material good.

5 According to Neubauer, p. 395, it is a contraction of Nahr Bull, a Babylonian town on the river Divalah. Wiesner, p. 109, identifies it with Nahr Obolla, a tributary of the Euphrates near ancient Basra.

6 Their objection to "*we* live" was that it excluded the rest of mankind, whereas "they" means humanity generally.

7 Because this formula might be referred to the host, not God.

8 *M.* omits: b. Raba.

9 In the Passover Ritual.

10 By specifying "food," it might be thought that he is referring to the host; but we have to thank God for much else beside food.

11 With ten the formula is "Blessed be our God"; therefore it cannot possibly be understood of the host.

after him: "Blessed be the Lord our God, the God of Israel, the God of hosts, Who is enthroned above the Cherubim, for the food of which we have partaken[1]."

Whether ten or ten myriads.

Authorship of our *Mishnāh*. This is self-contradictory! Thou sayest: *Whether ten or ten myriads*, implying that they are the same[2]; and then it continues: *With a hundred, one says; With a thousand, one says; With ten thousand, one says!* Rab Joseph said: There is no contradiction, the latter being the statement of R. Josē of Galilee, the other of R. 'Aḳiba. For the *Mishnāh* declares: *R. Josē of Galilee says: According to the numerical size of the assembly do they bless; as it is said, "Bless ye God in full assemblies."*

R. 'Aḳiba said: What do we find in the Synagogue?

***Halākāh* in agreement with R. 'Aḳiba.** What does R. 'Aḳiba make of the verse quoted by R. Josē of Galilee? He requires that for the following teaching: R. Meïr says: Whence is it derived that even the embryos in their mothers' womb sang the song at the Red Sea? As it is said, "Bless ye God in full assemblies[3], even the Lord, ye that are from the fountain of Israel" (Ps. lxviii. 27). And the other[4]? He derives it from the word "fountain"[5]. Raba said: The *Halākāh* is in agreement with R. 'Aḳiba. Rabina and Rab Ḥamma b. Buzi visited the house of the Exilarch. [When about to say Grace] Rab Ḥamma stood up and looked about to see whether there were a hundred people present. Rabina said to him: It is unnecessary; thus said Raba: The *Halākāh* is in agreement with R. 'Aḳiba[6].

Grace in the house of the Exilarch. Raba said: When we dine at the house of the Exilarch, we say Grace in threes[7]. But they should have said Grace in tens[8]! If the Exilarch had heard, he would have been angry[9]. But they

[1] Here "food" is mentioned; but no exception can be taken because the Deity is explicitly referred to.

[2] For the purpose of the *Zimmūn* formula.

[3] Meaning everybody present, without exception, even the unborn babes.

[4] R. Josē, whence does he derive this teaching, since he uses "full assemblies" as in the *Mishnāh*?

[5] As implying the womb.

[6] So that ten or ten myriads have the same formula.

[7] The assembly being very large and the meal prolonged, when three who sit together finish, they say Grace quietly between themselves.

[8] So as to add "our God" to the formula.

[9] If they had said Grace in parties of ten, it would have been more conspicuous and a louder tone of voice would have been required. The Exilarch might then have noticed what they were doing and regard it as a slight that they had not waited for him to say Grace.

could have fulfilled their duty by means of the Grace said by the Exilarch! Since everybody made the responses in a loud voice, it could not be heard.

Zimmūn when one finishes his meal before the others.

Rabbah Tospaäh said: If three were dining together, and one finishing before the others says Grace for himself, they fulfil the obligation of *Zimmūn* with him, but not he with them; because the *Zimmūn* cannot be retrospective[1].

R. Ishmael says.

Benediction over the *Tōrāh*.

Rafram b. Pappa visited the Synagogue of Abi Gibar[2]. He stood up, read in the Scroll and exclaimed, "Bless ye the Lord"; he then stopped and did not say "Who is to be blessed." They all shouted "Bless ye the Lord Who is to be blessed." Raba said: Thou black pot[3]! What hast thou to do with this controversy? Moreover, everybody acts in accord with the opinion of R. Ishmael.

MISHNĀH IV, V

IV. *Three who have eaten together are not permitted to separate [before Grace], and similarly with four or five. Six may divide themselves [into two parties for* Zimmūn*] up to ten. But ten may not divide themselves up, [and similarly] up to twenty.*

V. *If two parties eat in the same room, should some of one party be visible to some of the other party, they may be reckoned together for* Zimmūn[4]*; but if not, each party arranges* Zimmūn *for itself. We may not say the benediction over wine until water has been added to it*[5]*. These are the words of R. Eliezer; but the Sages say: The benediction may be pronounced [over wine without dilution].*

G^E^MĀRĀ

Three who dine together may not separate before Grace has been said.

What does he wish to tell us[6]? We have already learnt in the *Mishnāh*: *Three who ate together are under the obligation of* Zimmūn[7]! He means to inform us the same as that which R.

[1] And include one who has already said Grace.

[2] *M.*: Gobar. An uncertain locality. Wiesner, p. 110, conjectures that it is Edessa on the ground that its ruler had the title of Abgar.

[3] Uncomely scholar (Jastrow).

[4] E.g., if there were five in each party, they could add "our God" to the formula.

[5] It was also the practice of the Greeks and Romans to dilute their wine. See *D. C. A.* pp. 384 f.

[6] In the first sentence of *Mishnāh* IV.

[7] See fol. 45 *a*, p. 291.

Abba said in the name of Samuel: Three who sat down to eat together, although they have not yet partaken of food, are not permitted to separate [before saying Grace]. Another version: R. Abba[1] said in the name of Samuel: This is what he teaches [in our *Mishnāh*]: Three who sat down to eat together, although each partakes of his own loaf, are not permitted to separate [before saying Grace]. Or also [he means to inform us] the same as that which Rab Huna said: Three persons who came together from three parties[2] are not permitted to separate [before saying Grace]. Rab Ḥisda said: This only applies to those who came together from three different parties, each of which consists of three men[3]. Raba said: This only refers to the case where the original parties **fol. 50 b.** did not at the outset include these [three men] in their own place for *Zimmūn*[4]; but if they had done so, then the necessity for *Zimmūn* has passed from these men[5]. Raba said: Whence do I state this? For we have the Mishnaic teaching: A [defiled] couch, half of which has been stolen or lost or has been divided between brothers or partners, becomes clean[6]; but if it is restored, it can from that time onwards contract defilement. From that time onwards it may contract defilement, but not retrospectively[7]. Infer from this that since it has been divided, the defilement has passed from it. So here also[8], since the parties had included these men for *Zimmūn*, it passes from them.

V. *If two parties eat in the same room*, etc.

It has been taught: If there be an attendant between them[9], he unites them [for *Zimmūn*][10].

We may not say the benediction over wine.

Benediction over undiluted wine.

Our Rabbis have taught: Until water has been added, we do not say the benediction "...Who createst the fruit of the vine"

1 *M.*: Raba.

2 I.e. three parties which have had the meal but not yet said Grace.

3 Consequently the three who have come together were originally under the obligation of *Zimmūn*.

4 If, e.g., each party had consisted of four persons, and one of each party came together, then these three men must have *Zimmūn* for themselves.

5 I.e. each party started to say Grace and after the *Zimmūn* formula had been said, one man left. Should three of these come together, they cannot finish their Grace with *Zimmūn*.

6 An incomplete article cannot contract defilement.

7 The original defilement does not return when the article is made whole.

8 In the circumstance described in note 5 above.

9 I.e. one attendant serving both parties.

10 Even though one party be not visible to the other.

over the wine, but "...Who createst the fruit of the tree"; and we may wash the hands therewith[1]. From the time that water has been added, the benediction is "...Who createst the fruit of the vine," and we may not wash the hands therewith. These are the words of R. Eliezer; but the Sages say: In either case the benediction is "...Who createst the fruit of the vine," and we may not wash the hands therewith. In agreement with whom is that which Samuel said: A man may fulfil all his needs with bread[2]? With whom? With R. Eliezer[3]. R. Josē b. R. Ḥannina said: The Sages agree with R. Eliezer that over a cup of wine intended for the Grace we do not say the benediction until water is added. What is the reason? Rab Osha'ya answered: We require a commandment to be performed with the choicest[4]. But what is the use [of undiluted wine] according to the Rabbis? R. Zera said: It may be used for a beverage made of caryota[5].

Foodstuffs must be carefully handled.

Our Rabbis have taught: Four things are said concerning bread—we may not place raw meat upon bread; we may not pass a cup full of wine over bread; we may not throw bread; we may not rest a dish upon bread[6]. Amemar, Mar Zoṭra and Rab Ashē dined together, and dates and pomegranates were placed before them. Mar Zoṭra took [some of the fruit] and threw it before Rab Ashē as his portion. The latter said to him, "Does not the master agree with that which has been taught: One may not throw articles of food?" [He replied], "That refers to bread." "But there is a teaching: Just as one may not throw bread, so one should not throw any article of food!" He replied, "But there is a teaching: Although one may not throw bread, other articles of food may be thrown!" There is, however, no contradiction, one referring to that which becomes repugnant [by throwing], the other to that which does not become repugnant.

1 In the same way that the juice of fruits may be used for that purpose.

2 If, e.g., his hands are stained and he has nothing else with which to wipe them, he may rub them with a piece of bread. The Greeks also wiped their hands with bread, but the Romans had water passed round for the purpose; *D. C. A.* p. 384.

3 Since he allowed undiluted wine for washing the hands. The Rabbis object because it involves spoiling foodstuff, and for the same reason they would object to bread being used for cleaning the hands.

4 And undiluted wine in ancient times was very strong and was improved by the addition of water; see *D.C.A.* p. 384.

5 A species of date, the brew of which was used for medicinal purposes.

6 So as not to spoil it.

Use of foodstuff in connection with a marriage.

Our Rabbis have taught: We may let wine[1] run through pipes before a bride and bridegroom[2], and throw before them roasted ears of corn and nuts in the Summer[3] but not in Winter; but we may not throw cakes[4] before them in Summer or Winter.

If one put food into his mouth without a benediction.

Rab Judah said: If one forgot and put food into his mouth without a benediction, he should push it on one side [in his mouth] and say the benediction. Another taught: He should swallow it; there is another teaching: He should spit it out; there is still another teaching: He should push it aside [in his mouth]. There is no contradiction; the teaching that he should swallow it refers to liquids; that he should spit it out refers to something that will not become repugnant; and that he should push it on one side refers to something which would become repugnant. But also with something which would not become repugnant let him push it on one side and say the benediction! Rab Isaac Ḳaskᵉsaāh[5] explained [why that is not so] in the presence of R. Josē b. Abin, in the name of R. Joḥanan[6]: Because it is said, "My mouth shall be *filled* with Thy praise" (Ps. lxxi. 8)[7]. fol. 51 a.

May the benediction be said after the food has been eaten?

Rab Ḥisda was asked: If one has eaten or drunk without having said the benediction[8], may he say it afterwards? He answered: Shall one who has eaten garlic so that the smell is diffused eat more garlic so that its smell be more diffused[9]? Rabina said: Consequently, even if he has finished the meal, he may go back and say the benediction! For there is a teaching: If one has had immersion and ascended [from the water], as he ascends he should say "Blessed...Who hast sanctified us with Thy commandments and commanded us concerning immersion." But the two cases are not parallel; for there [in the instance of immersion], the man

1 *M.* adds: and oil.

2 Usually explained as a symbol of prosperity. But see Büchler's exhaustive article in *M.G.W.J.* XLIX. pp. 12 ff. where he shows that it was done to pay honour to any distinguished person, for the purpose of diffusing a pleasant odour. Cf. Josephus, *Antiq.* VIII. iv. 1.

3 The streets being then dry, the corn and nuts will not be spoilt by mud.

4 Because these would be spoilt even when the streets are dry.

5 This surname is uncertain. *M.* reads Sakkāāh, perhaps "the sack-maker"; and there are other variants quoted by *D. S.*, "of Ctesiphon" and "of Circesium."

6 *M.* omits: in the name of R. Joḥanan.

7 I.e. when saying the benediction, the mouth should (if possible) not contain food.

8 Referring to Grace before meals or the benediction over wine.

9 I.e. having done one wrong (not saying the benediction) shall he commit another (omit it altogether)?

was not at the outset fit [to pronounce a benediction][1]; but here [in the instance of the benediction] the man was fit at the outset [to say it], and since it was deferred it must remain so.

Properties of asparagus-beverage.

Our Rabbis have taught: Asparagus-beverage[2] is beneficial for the heart, good for the eyes and how much more so for the digestive organs; so if one grows addicted to it, it is beneficial for the whole of his body; but if he becomes intoxicated therewith, it is harmful to his whole body. Since he teaches that it is beneficial for the heart, it is to be inferred that we are here dealing with [a brew] with wine; and he teaches, "How much more so for the digestive organs." But there is a teaching: For the heart, eye and milt it is beneficial, but injurious to the head, bowels and piles! The teaching above refers to old wine[3]; according to the Mishnaic teaching: [If one says] "I vow to abstain from wine because it is injurious to the bowels," and they tell him "But is not old wine beneficial for the bowels?" and he remains silent, then he is forbidden to drink new wine but is permitted to drink of the old. Draw that inference[4].

How it should be drunk.

Our Rabbis have taught: Six things are said of the asparagus-beverage: One should only drink it undiluted and full[5]; one receives it with the right hand but drinks it [holding it] with the left; one must not talk after drinking it; one must not stop in the course of drinking; one must only return the cup to him who handed it to him; he should expectorate after drinking it; and one must not support it except with its own kind[6]. But there is a teaching: One should not support it except with bread! There is no contradiction, the latter referring to [a brew] with wine, the other to [a brew] with beer. One teacher states: For the heart, eyes and milt it is beneficial but injurious to the head, bowels and

1 The cause of the immersion being impurity; and one may not say a benediction when in a condition of defilement.

2 The Greek word ἀσπάραγος, which is not identical in meaning with what is now called "asparagus." It is the name given to the young shoots of various plants (see Krauss, pp. 93 f.). Brecher, *Das Transcendentale...im Talmud*, p. 181 n. 127, connects the word with the Latin *purgans* and renders "Purgiertrank"; but this is improbable. The beverage referred to here is the "heart" of the cabbage brewed with wine or beer. By "beer" is intended a brew of figs or dates.

3 At least three years old (Rashi).

4 That we are here dealing with asparagus brewed with wine, not beer.

5 Viz. from a full cup.

6 I.e. if it is brewed with beer made from figs, he should only eat figs; if from dates, he should only eat dates.

piles; whereas there is another teaching: It is beneficial for the head, bowels and piles but injurious to the heart, eyes and milt! There is no contradiction; the latter referring to [a brew] with wine, the other to [a brew] with beer. One teacher states: If he expectorates after drinking it he will be smitten [with illness]; and there is another teaching: If he does not expectorate after drinking it he will be smitten! There is no contradiction; the latter referring to [a brew] with wine, the other to [a brew] with beer. Rab Ashē said: Now that thou maintainest that one who does not expectorate after drinking it will be smitten [with illness], the spittle should be emitted even in the presence of a king[1].

What the angel Suriel told R. Ishmael b. Elisha.

R. Ishmael b. Elisha[2] said: Three things Suriel[3], the Prince of the Presence, related to me: Do not take thy shirt in the morning from the hand of the attendant and put it on[4]; do not let thy hands be washed by one who has not washed his own; and do not return the cup of asparagus-beverage except to him who handed it to thee, because a band of demons (another version: a company of angels of destruction) lies in wait for a man, saying, "When will he commit one of these acts and be trapped?"

What the Angel of Death told R. Joshua b. Levi.

R. Joshua b. Levi said: Three[5] things did the Angel of Death tell me: Do not take thy shirt in the morning from the hand of the attendant and put it on; do not let thy hands be washed by him who has not washed his own[6]; and do not stand before women when they return from being with a dead person, because I leap and go before them with my sword in my hand[7], and I have permission to destroy. But if one met [such women], what is the remedy? Let him move four cubits from his place; or if there is a river let him cross it; or if there is another road let him proceed along it; or if there is a wall let him stand behind it[8]; but if

[1] Because the duty to preserve the body in a healthy condition is more important than the honouring of a king.

[2] *M.*: Simeon b. Eleazar. But see what is related of the supernatural communication to Ishmael b. Elisha on fol. 7 *a*, p. 35.

[3] *M.* omits the name.

[4] But take it thyself.

[5] *M.*: seven.

[6] *M.* adds here; Return [the cup of] asparagus-beverage only to him who handed it to thee; do not enter alone a Synagogue in which children are not being taught, because I store my weapon there; when any [disturbance] is happening in the city, do not walk in the middle of the road but on the side; when there is peace in the city do not walk along the side of the public road but in the middle.

[7] Since death entered the world through woman, the angel of death accompanies her (Wünsche, p. 63 n.).

[8] *M.* reads: let him stand behind it, turn his face to the wall and say.

not, let him turn his face away and say, "And the Lord said unto Satan, The Lord rebuke thee, O Satan" (Zech. iii. 2) until they have passed him by.

The cup of wine used for the Grace.

R. Zera said in the name of R. Abbahu (another version: it was taught in a *Bārāitā*): Ten things are said with reference to the cup used for the Grace after meals: It requires washing and rinsing, undiluted [wine] and must be full, crowning and covering[1]; he takes it with both hands and places it in the right hand, raises it a handbreadth from the floor[2] and gazes at it. Some also say: He sends it as a present to his household[3]. R. Joḥanan said: We only observe four of those rules: washing, rinsing, undiluted [wine] and [the cup] must be full. It has been taught: Washing refers to the inside [of the cup], rinsing to the outside.

Subject continued.

R. Joḥanan said: Whoever says the benediction over a full cup will be granted a boundless inheritance; as it is said, "And full with the blessing of the Lord; possess thou the sea and the south" (Deut. xxxiii. 23). R. Josē b. R. Ḥannina said: He will be worthy to inherit two worlds, this world and the world to come. "Crowning"—Rab Judah used to crown it with disciples[4]. Rab Ḥisda used to crown it with small cups[5]. R. Ḥanan said: And with undiluted [wine][6]. Rab Sheshet said: Until the benediction of "the land[7]." "Covering" [the head]—Rab Pappa used to wrap himself [in his *Ṭallīt*], sit down [and say the Grace][8]. Rab Assi[9] used to spread a cloth over his head. "He takes it with both hands"—R. Ḥinnana b. Pappa said: What is the Scriptural authority? "Lift up your hands in holiness[10], and bless ye the Lord" (Ps. cxxxiv. 2). "And he places it in his right"—R. Ḥiyya b. Abba said in the name of R. Joḥanan: The earlier [Rabbis] asked:

1 These terms will be explained in the next paragraph.

2 Viz. if he is lying on cushions or a low couch and the food is placed on the floor; otherwise he raises it a handbreadth from the table.

3 To his wife to drink, who would not be dining with her husband when visitors were present.

4 I.e. make them sit round about the cup.

5 To make the cup of benediction conspicuous.

6 The word for "and with undiluted wine" seems out of place and yields no sense. The commentators find it difficult to explain. *M.* omits it, reading: R. Ḥanan said in the name of Rab Sheshet.

7 The wine must remain undiluted up to that point in the Grace, and then water is added.

8 The words in brackets are added by *M.*

9 *M.*: Ashē.

10 I.e. for a holy purpose—the benediction. R.V. "to the Sanctuary."

May the left hand support the right? Rab Ashē said: Since the earlier [Rabbis] raised this question without having it decided, we must act according to the stricter view[1]. "He raises it a hand- fol. 51 b. breadth from the floor"—R. Aḥa b. R. Ḥannina said[2]: What is the Scriptural authority? "I will lift up the cup of salvation and call upon the name of the Lord" (Ps. cxvi. 13). "He gazes at it"—so that his thoughts may not wander. "He sends it as a present to his household"—so that his wife may be blessed.

Rab Naḥman's wife and the cup of Grace.

'Ulla visited the house of Rab Naḥman; he wrapped the bread[3] and said Grace and gave the cup of benediction to Rab Naḥman. Rab Naḥman said to him, "Let the master send the cup of benediction to Jalta[4]." He replied, "Thus spake R. Joḥanan: The fruit of a woman's body is only blessed through the fruit of a man's body[5]; as it is said, 'He will also bless the fruit of thy body' (Deut. vii. 13)—it is not said 'the fruit of her body' but 'the fruit of thy body'." There is a teaching to the same effect: R. Nathan says: Whence is it that the fruit of a woman's body is only blessed through the fruit of a man's body? As it is said, "He will also bless the fruit of thy body"—it is not said "the fruit of her body" but "the fruit of thy body." Meanwhile Jalta heard [that the cup of benediction had not been sent to her]. She arose in anger, went to the wine-cellar and broke four hundred flasks of wine. Rab Naḥman said to him, "Let the master send her another cup." 'Ulla sent it to her [with the message], "All this measure of wine belongs to the benediction[6]." She sent back the reply, "From pedlars comes gossip, from rags come vermin[7]."

The cup of ill-luck.

Rab Assi[8] said: One must not speak over the cup of benediction. Rab Assi[8] also said: We may not say the benediction over a cup of ill-luck[9]. What means "a cup of ill-luck"? Rab Naḥman b.

[1] And not support the cup with the right and left.

[2] *M.*: R. Ḥinnana said.

[3] See p. 266 n. 7.

[4] Rab Naḥman's wife.

[5] Therefore it was more important for the man to drink the cup of benediction than for a woman.

[6] He meant that not only the wine in the cup of benediction, but the whole flask from which it is poured, brings a blessing; and the cup he was sending her contained such wine.

[7] A proverb which Jalta quoted to imply that from such a man as 'Ulla nothing good could be expected.

[8] *M.*: Ashē.

[9] *Lit.* punishment.

Isaac said: A second cup[1]. There is a teaching to the same effect: He who drinks [cups of wine] of an even number should not say Grace; because it is said, "Prepare to meet thy God, O Israel" (Amos iv. 12)[2]; but such an one is not fitly prepared.

Grace must be said sitting.

R. Abbahu said (another version: it was taught in a *Bārāitā*): He who eats while walking should say Grace standing; but he who eats standing should sit to say Grace; and when he reclines at the meal, he should sit up to say Grace. The *Halākāh* in every case is: He sits and says Grace.

May we return unto thee: *Three who ate!*

1 The allusion is here to the idea that even numbers were inauspicious and under the influence of evil spirits.

2 I.e. prepare to meet Him by avoiding everything that is inauspicious.

CHAPTER VIII

MISHNĀH I—VIII

I. *The following are the points of variance between* Bēt *Shammai and* Bēt *Hillel in connection with the meal*[1]. Bēt *Shammai say: [On a Sabbath or Festival] one pronounces the benediction over the day and then over the wine; but* Bēt *Hillel say: He pronounces the benediction over the wine and afterwards over the day.*

II. Bēt *Shammai say: We wash the hands and then fill*[2] *the cup; but* Bēt *Hillel say: We fill the cup and then wash the hands.*

III. Bēt *Shammai say: One wipes his hands with a napkin which he lays upon the table; but* Bēt *Hillel say: [He lays it] upon the bolster [of his couch].*

IV. Bēt *Shammai say: [After the meal] they clear up*[3] *and then we wash the hands [prior to Grace]; but* Bēt *Hillel say: We wash the hands and then they clear up.*

V. Bēt *Shammai say: [The order of benedictions is*[4]*] light, food, spices and* Habdālāh[5]*; but* Bēt *Hillel say: Light, spices, food and* Habdālāh. Bēt *Shammai say: The wording*[6] *is "... Who created the light of fire"; but* Bēt *Hillel say: It is "... Who createst the lights of the fire."*

VI. *We may not say the benediction over the light or spices of gentiles, over the light or spices of the dead*[7]*, nor over the light or spices of idolatry. Nor do we say the benediction over the light until one can make use of its illumination.*

VII. *If one ate and forgot to say Grace,* Bēt *Shammai declare he should return to his place and say it; but* Bēt *Hillel declare he may say it wherever [the omission] is remembered by him. And*

[1] See p. 278 n. 3.

[2] *Lit.* mix, sc. with water. See p. 322.

[3] The floor by the couch upon which the diner had been reclining or the table at which he had been sitting.

[4] At the meal on the conclusion of the Sabbath or Festival.

[5] On the use of spices and light in the *Habdālāh* ceremony, see Abrahams, pp. clxxxii f.

[6] Of the benediction over light.

[7] The *turibula* and *faces* used by the Romans at a funeral; *D.C.A.* p. 103.

what length of time may elapse in which he can say Grace? A sufficient time for the food in the stomach to be digested.

VIII. *If wine is brought to them after the food and there is* [*only sufficient for*] *one cup,* Bēt *Shammai declare he says the benediction over the wine and then over the food; but* Bēt *Hillel declare he says the benediction over the food and then over the wine. One may make the response "Amen" after an Israelite who pronounces a benediction*[1], *but not after a Samaritan who pronounces a benediction until he has heard the whole of the benediction.*

GEMĀRĀ

Relative order of benedictions over the wine and the Sabbath or Festival.

Our Rabbis have taught: The points of variance between *Bēt* Shammai and *Bēt* Hillel in connection with the meal are: *Bēt* Shammai say: [On a Sabbath or Festival] one pronounces the benediction over the day and then over the wine, because the day causes the wine to be brought[2] and because he has already hallowed the day[3] before the wine was brought. But *Bēt* Hillel say: One pronounces the benediction over the wine and then over the day, because the wine causes the Sanctification to be said[4]. Another reason is: The benediction over the wine is constant but that over the day is not constant, and when we have that which is constant and not constant, the former takes precedence[5]. The *Halākāh* is in agreement with *Bēt* Hillel. Why is this other reason necessary? Shouldest thou say that there [*Bēt* Shammai offer] two reasons but here [*Bēt* Hillel offer] only one, therefore here also we have two reasons. "The benediction over the wine is constant but that over the day is not constant, and when we have that which is constant and not constant, the former takes precedence. The *Halākāh* is in agreement with *Bēt* Hillel." All this is obvious, for a *Bat Ḳōl* had issued forth[6]! If thou wilt I can say [that this controversy] preceded the *Bat Ḳōl*[7]; or if thou wilt I can say it
fol. 52 a. followed after the *Bat Ḳōl*, but R. Joshua it was who said: We pay no attention to a *Bat Ḳōl*[8].

1 Although he has not heard the whole of it.

2 For the *Ḳiddūsh* which is not said on a non-holy day.

3 By the special prayers inserted into the Service.

4 If there were no wine or bread for Grace before meals, the *Ḳiddūsh* would be omitted.

5 See p. 176 n. 1.

6 And proclaimed that when *Bēt* Shammai and *Bēt* Hillel differ, the *Halākāh* is in agreement with the latter. See 'Ērūbīn 13 *b*.

7 Consequently it was necessary to make the above statement.

8 When it interferes with a discussion of *Halākāh*; see Bab. Meṣīa' 59 *b*.

Which benediction is of greater importance.

Do *Bēt* Shammai, however, hold that the benediction over the day is of greater importance[1]? Lo, there is a teaching: On entering his house at the conclusion of the Sabbath, he says the benediction over the wine, the light and the spices and after that says the *Habdālāh*; and should he have only one cup [of wine], he leaves it until after the meal and combines all [the benedictions] afterwards[2]. But how is it shown that this teaching emanates from *Bēt* Shammai; perhaps it is from *Bēt* Hillel? That cannot enter thy mind; because it states "light and afterwards spices," and from whom hast thou heard that opinion? *Bēt* Shammai; for there is a teaching: R. Judah said: *Bēt* Shammai and *Bēt* Hillel do not differ that the benediction over food comes first and *Habdālāh* afterwards; in what do they differ? About light and spices—*Bēt* Shammai declare: Light and afterwards spices, whereas *Bēt* Hillel declare: Spices and afterwards light. But how is it shown that this teaching emanates from *Bēt* Shammai as interpreted by R. Judah; perhaps it is from *Bēt* Hillel as interpreted by R. Meïr[3]? That cannot enter thy mind[4]; for it states here in our *Mishnāh*: Bēt *Shammai say: [The order of benedictions is] light, food, spices and* Habdālāh; *but* Bēt *Hillel say: Light, spices, food and* Habdālāh; and there in the *Bārāitā* it states: "Should he have only one cup [of wine], he leaves it until after the meal and combines all [the benedictions] afterwards[5]." Conclude therefore that it emanates from *Bēt* Shammai as interpreted by R. Judah.

Nevertheless there is a difficulty[6]! *Bēt* Shammai hold that the advent of a [holy] day is different from its conclusion; for with

1 By giving it precedence over the benediction over wine.

2 I.e. after the meal, over the cup of wine he says Grace, the benediction over the wine, light, spices and *Habdālāh*, the last-named corresponding to "the benediction of the day." Consequently "the benediction of the day" comes last and not first as was stated above.

3 On the next folio, p. 337, it is stated that according to R. Meïr, the point at issue is not the order of light and spices, but the benediction over the food; consequently the quoted *Bārāitā* could be *Bēt* Hillel's teaching.

4 To connect the *Bārāitā* with our *Mishnāh*.

5 The *Mishnāh* places the benediction over food, according to both Schools, in the middle, whereas the *Bārāitā* allows it to come first. We have, therefore, to depend upon the difference of the two Schools in the version of R. Judah, viz. the order of light and spices, according to which the *Bārāitā* agrees with *Bēt* Shammai.

6 According to the *Mishnāh*, *Bēt* Shammai require the benediction over the day before that over the wine; but according to the *Bārāitā* (which it is concluded emanates from *Bēt* Shammai) the benediction over the wine precedes the *Habdālāh*.

its advent the more we anticipate it the better[1]; but with its conclusion the later we defer it the better[2], so that it may not seem to us a burden.

Procedure when there is only one cup of wine.

Do *Bēt* Shammai hold that the Grace after meals requires a cup of wine? For our *Mishnāh* teaches: *If wine is brought to them after the food and there is only sufficient for one cup,* Bēt *Shammai declare: He says the benediction over the wine and then over the food*[3]. Is it not to be supposed that he says the benediction [over the wine] and then drinks it? No; he says the benediction and leaves it [undrunk for the Grace]. But the teacher has said: He who says a benediction must taste! He does taste [but leaves the greater part]. But the teacher has said: If he tasted it, he disqualifies it [for another benediction]! He tastes it with his hand[4]. But the master has said: The cup of benediction requires a measure [of a fourth of a *Lōg*]; and lo, he made it less than that measure! He originally had more than the required measure. But it states: "There is only sufficient for one cup"! There was not sufficient for two cups, but more than enough for one. But R. Ḥiyya has taught: *Bēt* Shammai declare: He says the benediction over the wine and drinks it, and after that says Grace! Nay, there are two *Tannāīm* who differ as to the teaching of *Bēt* Shammai[5].

II. Bēt *Shammai say: We wash the hands and then fill the cup,* etc.

Order of washing the hands and filling the cup.

Our Rabbis have taught: *Bēt* Shammai say: We wash the hands and then fill the cup; for if thou sayest that we fill the cup first, there is a fear lest the liquid which is on the outside of the cup may contract defilement on account of his hands and in its turn defile the cup[6]. But the hands can defile the cup[7]! The hands

[1] The advent is marked by the benediction over the day, therefore it should come first, and it is to that the *Mishnāh* refers.

[2] The conclusion is marked by the *Habdālāh* and should come last. Since the *Bārāitā* refers to the conclusion of the holy day, it does not conflict with the *Mishnāh*.

[3] The *Bārāitā* stated: "Should he have only one cup of wine, he leaves it until after the meal and combines all [the benedictions] afterwards," i.e. wine is required for Grace. But according to the *Mishnāh*, if wine is brought to the man after he has eaten, so that he has not yet said a benediction over wine, he does so over this cup, drinks it and then says Grace; therefore wine is not essential for the Grace.

[4] I.e. dips his finger in the wine, which he then puts to his mouth.

[5] According to the *Tannā* of the *Mishnāh*, i.e. R. Judah, *Bēt* Shammai require wine for Grace; but R. Ḥiyya understands them as not requiring it.

[6] Liquid is the conductor of defilement for food; cf. Lev. xi. 34.

[7] Without the medium of a liquid; so why this fear?

are [only unclean in] the second degree[1], and [anything unclean in] the second degree cannot make a third [unclean grade] with things non-holy except through the medium of a liquid. But *Bēt* Hillel declare: We fill the cup and then wash the hands; for if thou sayest that we wash the hands first, there is a fear lest the moisture on the hands may contract defilement on account of the cup [which might be ritually unclean] and in its turn defile the hands. But the cup can defile the hands[2]! A vessel[3] cannot make a man contract defilement. But it can defile the liquid which it contains! We are dealing here with a vessel whose exterior has been defiled by liquid, that is to say whose interior is ritually clean but the exterior unclean; for there is a Mishnaic teaching: If a vessel's exterior has been defiled by liquid, the exterior is unclean but the interior, edge, brim and handle are clean. If, however, the interior is defiled, then the whole of it becomes unclean. **fol. 52 b.**

Point of difference between the two Schools.

What is the point of difference between them? *Bēt* Shammai hold that it is forbidden to use a vessel whose exterior has become defiled by liquid for fear of the spillings[4], but there is no need to fear lest the moisture of the hand will contract defilement through the cup. *Bēt* Hillel, on the other hand, hold that it is permitted to use a cup whose exterior has become defiled by a liquid, saying that spillings are not frequent; but there is reason to fear lest the moisture on the hand contract defilement on account of the cup. Another reason is that the meal follows immediately on the washing of the hands. Why this other reason? Thus said *Bēt* Hillel to *Bēt* Shammai: According to you who maintain that it is forbidden to use a cup whose exterior has been defiled because of the fear of spillings, even so it is better [to wash the hands last] because the meal follows immediately on the washing of the hands[5].

III. Bēt *Shammai say: One wipes his hands*, etc.

Where the napkin is to be placed.

Our Rabbis have taught: *Bēt* Shammai say: One wipes his hands with a napkin which he lays upon the table; for if thou sayest that [he lays it] upon the bolster, there is a fear lest the moisture on the napkin may contract defilement on account of the bolster and this in turn may render the hands ritually unclean[6].

[1] Contracting defilement from something else.

[2] Even if the hands are not moist.

[3] Unless it be unclean in the first degree.

[4] From the interior of the cup on to the exterior and thereby increase the possibility of the hand contracting defilement.

[5] And the hands are then clean for the meal.

[6] Should he wipe his hands during the meal.

But the bolster can defile the napkin! One vessel cannot cause another vessel to contract defilement. But the bolster can make the man unclean! A vessel[1] cannot cause a man to contract defilement. But *Bēt* Hillel say: [He lays it] upon the bolster; for if thou sayest that [he lays it] upon the table, there is a fear lest the moisture on the napkin may contract defilement on account of the table and in its turn defile the food. But the table can defile the food which is upon it! We deal here with a table [unclean] in the second degree[2], and [anything unclean in] the second degree cannot make a third [unclean grade] with things non-holy except through the medium of a liquid.

The point of difference between the two Schools.

What is the point of difference between them? *Bēt* Shammai hold that it is forbidden to use a table [unclean in] the second degree through fear of those who are eating *T^erūmāh*[3]; but *Bēt* Hillel hold that it is permitted to use a table unclean in the second degree, because those who eat *T^erūmāh* are careful[4]. Another reason is: The washing of the hands for non-holy food is not ordained by the *Tōrāh*. Why this other reason? Thus said *Bēt* Hillel to *Bēt* Shammai: Should you ask what difference is there that in the case of food we are concerned [about defilement][5] but in the case of the hands we have no concern? Even so [our view] is better because the washing of the hands for non-holy food[6] is not ordained by the *Tōrāh*; therefore it is preferable that the hands should be defiled, since that has no basis in the *Tōrāh*, rather than food should be defiled, for which there is a basis in the *Tōrāh*.

IV. Bēt *Shammai say: [After the meal] they clear up*, etc.

Order of clearing the room and washing the hands before Grace.

Our Rabbis have taught: *Bēt* Shammai say: They clear up and then we wash the hands [before Grace]; for if thou sayest that we wash the hands first, the consequence may be that thou wilt spoil some food[7]. (*Bēt* Shammai do not hold that the washing of the hands comes first. What is the reason? On account of the pieces of bread[8].) But *Bēt* Hillel say: If the attendant is a

[1] See p. 335 n. 3. [2] See p. 335 n. 1.

[3] Which belongs to the class of holy things and can be defiled by a table unclean in the second degree.

[4] To protect themselves against defilement.

[5] *Bēt* Hillel's reason was the desire to protect the food from defilement.

[6] And *Bēt* Shammai are concerned to protect the hands from defilement.

[7] The water may splash on to it, and it is forbidden to spoil food; cf. fol. 50 *b*, p. 324.

[8] Which may be spoiled by being splashed upon. The words in brackets are omitted by *M.* and are probably an interpolation.

disciple of the wise, he takes those pieces of bread which are of the size of an olive and leaves the pieces which are less than that size[1]. This supports the statement of R. Joḥanan who said: Pieces of bread which are less than the size of an olive may be destroyed by the hand.

The point of difference between the two Schools.

What is the point of difference between them? *Bēt* Hillel hold that it is forbidden to employ as an attendant one who is an *'Am hā'āreṣ*[2], whereas *Bēt* Shammai hold that such may be employed. R. Isaac[3] b. R. Ḥannina said in the name of Rab Huna: Throughout our Chapter, the *Halākāh* is in agreement with *Bēt* Hillel except in this point where it is in agreement with *Bēt* Shammai. R. Osha'ya, however, teaches the reverse, that here also the *Halākāh* is in agreement with *Bēt* Hillel.

V. Bēt *Shammai say: [The order of benedictions is] light, food,* etc.

The order of the benedictions.

Rab Huna b. Judah[4] visited the house of Raba[5] and noticed that he said the benediction over the spices first. He said to him: Note that *Bēt* Shammai and *Bēt* Hillel do not differ on the question of the light; for our *Mishnāh* teaches: Bēt *Shammai say: [The order is] light, food, spices and* Habdālāh; *but* Bēt *Hillel say: Light, spices, food and* Habdālāh[6]! Raba answered after him[7]: These are the words of R. Meïr; but R. Judah says: *Bēt* Shammai and *Bēt* Hillel do not differ that [the benediction over] food comes first and *Habdālāh* last. In what do they differ? In [the order of] light and spices; for *Bēt* Shammai say: First [the benediction] over the light and then the spices, but *Bēt* Hillel say: First over the spices and then the light. And R. Joḥanan said: People act in agreement with the view of *Bēt* Hillel as interpreted by R. Judah[8].

1 Consequently there is no need to fear that bread will be spoilt by the water, since the crumbs do not count.

2 Therefore the attendant will know that the larger pieces have to be removed, and the washing of the hands can safely be done before the table is cleared.

3 This, not Josē as in edd., is probably the correct reading. Cf. *D. S. ad loc.*

4 *M.* omits: b. Judah.

5 *M.*: Rab.

6 Why, then, did Raba say the benediction over spices before over the light?

7 I.e. continued the teaching of the *Mishnāh* which must be supplemented as follows.

8 Hence Raba acted aright in saying the benediction over the spices first.

Bēt *Shammai say: The wording is "... Who created* [bārā'] *the light* [mᵉ'ōr] *of fire*" etc.

Wording of the benediction over the *Habdālāh* light.

Raba said: Everybody agrees about *bārā'* that it means "he created." In what do they differ? About the word *bōrē'*[1]; *Bēt* Shammai hold that *bōrē'* means "he will create[2]," but *Bēt* Hillel hold that *bōrē'* has also the same meaning as *bārā'*. Rab Joseph quoted in objection[3]: "I form the light and create [*bōrē'*] darkness" (Is. xlv. 7); "He formeth the mountains and createth [*bōrē'*] the wind" (Amos iv. 13); "He that created [*bōrē'*] the heavens and stretched them forth" (Is. xlii. 5)! But, said Rab Joseph, everybody agrees that *bārā'* and *bōrē'* mean "he created." Wherein do they differ? About *mᵉ'ōr* and *mᵉ'ōrē* ["light" and "lights"] for *Bēt* Shammai hold there is only one light in fire, but *Bēt* Hillel hold there are many[4]. There is a teaching to the same effect: *Bēt* Hillel said to *Bēt* Shammai: There are many lights in fire.

VI. *We may not say the benediction over the light or spices of gentiles.*

Light and spices of gentiles may not be used for the purpose of *Habdālāh*.

It is quite right [that we do not use] the light [of a gentile] because it has not "rested[5]"; but why not the spices? Rab Judah said in the name of Rab: We are here dealing with [spices used] at the banquet of gentiles[6], because the assumption is that the banquet of gentiles is dedicated to idolatry. But since he teaches in the sequel: *We may not say the benediction over the light or spices of idolatry*, it is to be inferred that in the first part of the statement we are not dealing with idolatry[7]! R. Ḥannina of Sura[8] said: [In the sequel] he merely states the reason: What is the reason that we do not say a benediction over the light or spices of the gentiles? Because the assumption is the banquet of gentiles is dedicated to idolatry.

[1] The word used by *Bēt* Hillel. It is the participle of the verb.

[2] Or, he continues to create.

[3] To *Bēt* Shammai that *bōrē'* can mean "he will create." In all the following passages the participle refers to the past.

[4] Rashi explains: coloured lights, as red, white, green. "[*Bēt*] Hillel considered the different colours of bodies to be due to different sorts of light: whilst [*Bēt*] Shammai attributed colour to the object coloured, and not to the light by means of which we see it" (S. Brodetsky in *J. R.* II. p. 66).

[5] I.e. by its light forbidden work has been done on the Sabbath.

[6] Throughout this passage some edd. read "Samaritans," for fear of the Censor.

[7] Therefore the objection to "the spices of the gentiles" cannot be on the ground of idolatry.

[8] *M.*: Rab Ashē. On Sura, see p. 74 n. 1.

Our Rabbis have taught: We say a benediction over the light which rested but not if it has not rested. What means "rested" and "not rested"? If we would say that it has not rested because of work [which has been done on the Sabbath by its illumination], even if it be work which is permitted[1], there is a teaching: We may say the benediction over the light used [on the Sabbath] by a woman in confinement or an invalid! Rab Naḥman b. Isaac[2] said: What means "rested"? It rested from work which is a transgression [on the Sabbath]. There is a teaching to the same effect: We may at the conclusion of the Sabbath say the benediction over [the light of] a lantern which has been burning the whole day[3]. **The light must have "rested." fol. 53 a.**

Our Rabbis have taught: We may make the benediction over a light kindled by a gentile from an Israelite or kindled by an Israelite from a gentile, but not over a light kindled by a gentile from a gentile. Why is [the light kindled] by a gentile from a gentile different that one may not [say the benediction over it]? Because it has not "rested." If so, the light kindled by an Israelite from a gentile may likewise not have "rested"! And shouldest thou say that the light which is prohibited ceases to exist[4] whereas the other is quite a different one and came into being in the hand of the Israelite, there is the teaching: Who causes a flame to issue into the public way [on the Sabbath][5] has incurred guilt; but why has he incurred guilt? What he has taken up he has not set down, and what he has set down he has not taken up[6]! There is certainly also a prohibition [about the light kindled by an Israelite from a gentile][7], but when he says the benediction he does so over the additional part which is permitted[8]. If so, a **Which light may and may not be used.**

[1] E.g. attending to a sick person. [2] *M.* omits: b. Isaac.

[3] Provided it was lit before the advent of the Sabbath; but if kindled on the Sabbath, one may not use it for the benediction.

[4] I.e. the flame is not to be considered as continuous and the same, but as consisting of a succession of flashes, each distinct. Consequently it may be thought that the prohibited light ceases with the termination of the Sabbath, and the flame then becomes permissible for the purpose of the benediction.

[5] The circumstance referred to here is: A man puts oil in a vessel and places it in the public way, and by means of a torch which he holds while in the private domain, sets light to it.

[6] The flame of the burning oil is distinct from the torch which ignited it; and the law only considers an infraction of the Sabbath the carrying of the *same thing* from the private to the public way or *vice versa*. Since then, in that circumstance, the man is deemed guilty of an infraction of the law, the ignited oil must be considered identical with the torch.

[7] Viz. the original torch of the gentile which may have been used for work on the Sabbath. [8] The light kindled by the Israelite.

light kindled by a gentile from a gentile should also be allowed! Really that is so; but there is a fear because of the first gentile[1] and the first torch[2].

Subject continued. Our Rabbis have taught: Were one walking [at the conclusion of the Sabbath] outside the town and saw a light, if the majority [of the inhabitants] are gentiles, he should not say the benediction [over that light], but if the majority are Israelites, he may say it. This is self-contradictory! Thou sayest, "If the *majority* are gentiles, he should not say the benediction," hence if they are half [gentiles] and half [Israelites] he may say it. Then it continues, "If the *majority* are Israelites, he may say it," hence if they are half and half, he may not say it! It is quite right that even if they are half and half, he should also say the benediction; but since he taught the first clause "If the majority are gentiles," he also adds "If the majority are Israelites[3]."

When a torch held by a child may be used. Our Rabbis have taught: Were one walking [at the conclusion of the Sabbath] outside the town and saw a child holding a torch, he makes inquiries; if the child is an Israelite, he says the benediction [over the lighted torch], but if a gentile, he does not. Why is a child specified? It is the same even with an adult! Rab Judah said in the name of Rab[4]: We are here dealing with a point of time near to the setting of the sun[5]; so if it were an adult, it is obvious that he must certainly be a gentile[6]. But in the case of a child, one might say it is an Israelite and it is by chance that he is holding [the torch].

What constitutes a light for the benediction. Our Rabbis have taught: Were one walking [at the conclusion of the Sabbath] outside the town and saw a light, if it is as thick as the opening of a furnace he says the benediction over it[7], but if it is not, he does not say the benediction over it. One taught: We do say the benediction over the light of a furnace; but there is another teaching: We do not say the benediction over it! There is no contradiction; because the latter refers to the beginning [of its kindling], the other subsequently[8]. One taught: We do

[1] Who may have kindled his light on the Sabbath, which is forbidden.

[2] Which may have been ignited on the Sabbath. If, however, the light of the gentile had not been kindled on the Sabbath, it would be allowed.

[3] This clause is only inserted for completeness and is not to be pressed for any deductions.

[4] *M.*: Rab said.

[5] I.e. very soon after sunset.

[6] Because a Jew would not be found holding a torch then, since it is a forbidden act on the Sabbath.

[7] It is then worthy of being considered an illumination.

[8] When it is in full blaze and gives forth illumination.

say the benediction over the light of an oven or stove; but there is another teaching: We do not say the benediction over it! There is no contradiction; because the latter refers to the beginning [of its kindling], the other subsequently. One taught: We do say the benediction over the light of a Synagogue or House of Study; but there is another teaching: We do not say the benediction over it! There is no contradiction; the latter referring to a case where there is a distinguished person[1] present, the other to a case where there is no distinguished person present. But if thou wilt I can say that both refer to where a distinguished person is present, and still there is no contradiction; the one referring to where there is a beadle[2], the other to where there is no beadle. Or if thou wilt I can say that both refer to where there is a beadle, and still there is no contradiction; the one referring to where there is moonlight[3] and the other to where there is no moonlight.

Whether one says the benediction for all in the Synagogue.

Our Rabbis have taught: If they were sitting in the House of Study [at the conclusion of the Sabbath] and light is brought to them, *Bēt* Shammai declare that each one says the benediction for himself; but *Bēt* Hillel declare that one says the benediction for all, because it is said, "In the multitude of people is the King's glory" (Prov. xiv. 28)[4]. It is quite right that *Bēt* Hillel explain the reason [for their view]; but what is the reason of *Bēt* Shammai? They hold that it will cause an interruption in the House of Study[5]. There is a teaching to the same effect: Those who belonged to the school of Rabban Gamaliel used not to exclaim *Marpē'*[6] in the House of Study because of the interruption it causes.

[1] In whose honour the light had been kindled; and since it is not an ordinary illumination it cannot be used for the benediction.

[2] Who may be having his meal there, and consequently the light is for illumination and the benediction may be said.

[3] By whose light the beadle could have his meal; therefore the illumination is in honour of a distinguished visitor and cannot be used for the benediction.

[4] I.e. the religious devotion of a Congregation is better than that of an individual.

[5] All those studying would have to stop to listen, perhaps in the middle of a difficult passage; whereas each could say the benediction when most convenient for him.

[6] An exclamation meaning "healing," when somebody sneezed. *J. T.* Chap. vi, has the Greek word *ἴησις* in place of the Hebrew *marpē'*. See *J. E.* II. p. 255. In Tōsiftā Shab. viii. 5, it is denounced as a superstitious custom. On the Eastern etiquette in the event of one sneezing, see Lane, p. 210.

We may not say the benediction over the light or spices of the dead.

Benediction not said over light and spices of the dead.

What is the reason? The light which is kindled [for the dead] is in its honour[1] and the spices are used to remove the odour[2]. Rab Judah said in the name of Rab[3]: Over a light which they carry before [the corpse] by day or by night[4] no benediction is to be made[5]; but we may say it over a light which is only carried before it at night[6].

Which spices and oil may not be used.

Rab Huna said: We may not say the benediction over spices used in a privy[7] or the oil which is used to remove the dirt[8]. That is to say that the benediction [for spices] is not to be pronounced over anything which is not used for the purpose of smelling. Against this is quoted: If one enters a perfumer's shop and smells the odour, even though he sit there all day he only pronounces the benediction once; but if he keeps going in and out, he pronounces it each time. But here [the perfume] was not for smelling[9] and still he says the benediction! Yes, it is there for smelling, so that people should smell it and come to buy.

When benediction not said over a fragrant odour.

Our Rabbis have taught: Were one walking outside the town and smelt a fragrant odour, if the majority [of the inhabitants] are gentiles, he must not pronounce a benediction; but if the majority are Israelites, he does. R. Josē said: Even if the majority are Israelites he must likewise not pronounce a benediction, because the daughters of Israel use incense for purposes of sorcery[10]. But do all of them burn incense for sorcery? Some for sorcery and some also to perfume their garments; hence it will be found that the majority [in the town] do not use it for smelling, and where the majority do not use it for smelling, the benediction is

[1] And not as illumination.

[2] And not for smelling.

[3] *M.*: Rab said.

[4] I.e. at the burial of an eminent person to pay him honour. This was the Roman custom; cf. *D. C. A.* p. 103.

[5] If the funeral takes place at the conclusion of the Sabbath.

[6] Because it is used as illumination.

[7] Because it is used as a disinfectant and not for smelling.

[8] On the hands after a meal, the oil being mixed with spices. In the case of the oil, it means that the benediction is not "Who createst fragrant wood" but "Who createst fragrant oil"; see fol. 43 *a*, p. 280.

[9] I.e. the perfume is not there for one to smell but to be sold.

[10] In 'Ērūbīn 64 *b*, the Rabbis deplore that the Jewish women are addicted to sorcery. Hillel declared: "The more women, the more witchcraft"; Ābōt ii. 8; Singer, p. 188. Roman writers also refer to this fact; cf. Radin, *Jews among the Greeks and Romans*, p. 325. For the Talmudic references, see Blau, *Das altjüdische Zauberwesen*, pp. 23 ff.

not to be pronounced. R. Ḥiyya b. Abba said in the name of R. Joḥanan: He who walks on the Sabbath-eve in Tiberias[1] and at the conclusion of the Sabbath in Sepphoris[2] and smells a fragrant odour should not pronounce the benediction because the presumption is that it is only being used to perfume garments.

Our Rabbis have taught: If one were walking in a street where idolatry [is practised] and takes pleasure in smelling the odour [of incense] he is a sinner.

Nor do we say the benediction over the light until one can make use of its illumination. **fol. 53 b.**

When a light is regarded as illumination.

Rab Judah said in the name of Rab: The phrase "until one can make use of its illumination" does not mean that one must actually use it, but if one who stands near to it can use its light, then even those who are at a distance [may say the benediction]. Similarly said Rab Ashē[3]: We have learnt that one at a distance [may say the benediction]. Against this is quoted: If he had a light hidden in his bosom or in a lantern or saw a flame but made no use of its light or used its light without seeing its flame, he must not say the benediction until he sees the flame and makes use of its light! It is quite right that one uses the light without seeing the flame, for it may happen to stand in a corner; but how is it possible to see the flame without using its light? Is it not when it is far off? No, it refers to when it keeps growing dimmer.

Glowing coals may be used for the purpose of the benediction.

Our Rabbis have taught: We may say the benediction over glowing coals, but not over dying coals[4]. What is to be understood by glowing coals? Rab Ḥisda said: When one puts a chip of wood to them and it ignites. The question was asked: Is the word for dying coals spelt *'ōmᵉmōt* or *'ōmᵉmōt*[5]? Come and hear: For Rab Ḥisda[6] b. Abdemi quoted, "The cedars in the garden of God could not darken [*'āmam*] it" (Ezek. xxxi. 8)[7].

How near one must be to the light.

Raba said: [The statement of the *Mishnāh* means] one must actually use the illumination[8]. And how [near must he be to the light]? 'Ulla said[9]: Sufficient for one to be able to distinguish

[1] See p. 46 n. 6.

[2] Sepphoris is identified by the *Talmūd* (Mᵉgillāh 6 *a*) with Ḳiṭron (Judges i. 30); but it is improbable. Josephus (*Vita*, § 67) places it in Galilee. It is now identified with the village of Sefuriyeh, five miles N.W. of Nazareth.

[3] *M.*: Assi.

[4] Which give out no light.

[5] There is a difference in the initial letter.

[6] *M.*: Isaac.

[7] Hence the correct spelling is *'ōmᵉmōt*.

[8] Before pronouncing the benediction.

[9] *M.* omits: 'Ulla said.

between an *as* and a *dupondium*[1]. Hezekiah said: Sufficient for one to be able to distinguish between the stamp[2] of a Tiberian coin and a Sepphorian coin. Rab Judah said the benediction over the light in the house of Ada the waiter[3]. Raba[4] said it over the light in the house of Guria[5] b. Ḥamma. Abbai said it over the light in the house of Bar Abbuha[6]. Rab Judah said in the name of Rab: One does not go looking for a light[7] as we do for other commandments. R. Zera said: At first I used to go about [searching for a light] but since I heard the statement of Rab Judah in the name of Rab, I also do not go searching for it; but should it chance to me of its own accord, I say the benediction[8].

VII. *If one ate and forgot to say Grace*, etc.

Whether one must return to the place where he ate to say Grace.

Rab Z^e^bid[9] (another version: Rab Dimai b. Abba) said: The dispute is only in the case of one who has forgotten; but if he omitted it intentionally, all agree that he must return to his place and say Grace. This is obvious, because the *Mishnāh* states "and *forgot*"! Thou mayest, however, argue that the same thing applies[10] to one who omitted it intentionally and the statement "he forgot" is only intended to show the extreme view of *Bēt* Shammai; therefore he informs us[11]. There is a teaching: *Bēt* Hillel said to *Bēt* Shammai: According to your words, he who ate at the top of the Temple Mount and forgot and descended without saying Grace must return to the top and say it! *Bēt* Shammai replied to *Bēt* Hillel: According to your words, if one left a purse at the top of the Temple Mount, should he not go up to fetch

1 Roman coins, the *as* being half the value of the other.

2 *M^e^lōzmā*, according to Jastrow (so also Krauss) a corruption of νόμισμα. Rashi gives it the meaning "a weight."

3 Which was at some distance from Rab Judah's house. This was in conformity with his view in the last paragraph but one.

4 *M.*: Rabbah; but the reading of edd. is preferable, because it follows on Raba's statement in this paragraph.

5 *M.*: Goda. His house was near Raba's, so that the latter could use the light.

6 *M.*: Ḥabo.

7 So as to say the benediction.

8 We have here reflected a state of poverty where artificial light was rare in a house. See fol. 2 *b*, p. 3 n. 6.

9 *M.*: Judah b. Abin, and omits: another version, etc. According to *D. S.* the correct reading is Rab Iddi b. Abin.

10 I.e. the two Schools differ.

11 That according to *Bēt* Hillel also, he must return to his place if he omitted Grace deliberately.

it? For his own purpose[1] he may go up; how much more so for the honour of Heaven! There were two disciples; one acted in error according to the view of *Bēt* Shammai[2] and found a purse of gold, and the other acted deliberately according to the view of *Bēt* Hillel[3] and a lion devoured him.

What happened to Rabbah b. Bar Ḥannah.

Rabbah b. Bar Ḥannah was journeying with a caravan; he ate but forgot to say Grace. He said [to himself], "How shall I act? If I tell them I have forgotten to say Grace, they will answer, 'Say it now; for wherever thou utterest a benediction it is to the All-merciful thou dost utter it.' It is better that I tell them I have lost a golden dove." He said to them, "Wait for me, because I have lost a golden dove." He went back, said Grace and found a golden dove. Why exactly a dove? Because the Community of Israel is likened to a dove; for it is written, "The wings of the dove are covered with silver, and her pinions with the shimmer of gold" (Ps. lxviii. 14). Just as a dove only escapes with the aid of its wings, so Israel is only delivered through the aid of the commandments.

And what length of time may elapse, etc.

How long it takes for food to be digested.

What is the length of time for food to be digested? R. Joḥanan said: As long as he is not hungry. R. Simeon b. Laḳish said: As long as he is thirsty on account of the food he has eaten. Rab Jemar b. Shelamya said to Mar Zoṭra (another version: Rab Jemar b. Shezbi to Mar Zoṭra): Did R. Simeon b. Laḳish say that? For lo, R. Ammi declared in the name of R. Simeon b. Laḳish: What is the length of time for food to be digested? Sufficient time for a person to walk four *Mīl*! There is no contradiction, one referring to a heavy meal, the other to a light meal[4].

Responding to a benediction the whole of which has not been heard.

VIII. *If wine is brought to them*, etc.

That is to say an Israelite may respond although he has not heard the whole of the benediction. But since he has not heard it, how can he fulfil his obligation[5]? Ḥiyya b. Rab[6] said: [It

[1] *Lit.* honour.

[2] I.e. although he omitted the Grace by accident, he acted according to the stricter view of *Bēt* Shammai and was rewarded.

[3] He left his table previous to Grace deliberately having to go somewhere else, with the intention of saying it there.

[4] In the opinion of Rashi, this means a walk of four *Mīl* for a heavy meal; but Tōsāfōt explain four *Mīl* for a light meal.

[5] This is meant of one who was among the diners. He must hear the Grace said in order to comply with the requirements of the law.

[6] *M.*: Ḥiyya b. Shela.

refers to a man] who has not eaten with them[1]. Similarly said Rab Naḥman in the name of[2] Rabbah b. Abbuha: It refers to a man who has eaten with them. Rab[3] said to his son Ḥiyya, "My son, snatch [the cup of wine] and say Grace[4]"; and similarly said Rab Huna to his son Rabbah[5], "Snatch [the cup of wine] and say Grace." That is to say, he who says Grace is superior to him who just responds "Amen"[6]; but lo, there is a teaching: R. Josē says: Greater is he who responds "Amen" than he who says Grace! R. Nᵉhorai[7] said to him: By Heaven it is so. Thou canst prove it; for behold the common soldiers go down to open the fight but the veterans go down to win the victory[8]. This matter is discussed by the *Tannāim*; for there is a teaching: Both he who says the benediction and he who responds "Amen" are implied[9], only he who says the benediction is more quickly [rewarded] than he who responds "Amen."

Responding to benediction made by children in school.

Samuel asked Rab: Should one respond "Amen" after the children in school[10]? He replied: We make the response "Amen" after everybody except school-children, because they only utter [the benediction] for the purpose of learning it. This rule applies when it is not the time that they read the *Haftārāh*; but should it be the time when they read the *Haftārāh*, one does make the response.

Whether anointing the hands with oil is essential before Grace.

Our Rabbis have taught: The oil prevents the Grace [from being said][11]—these are the words of R.[12] Zilai; but R. Ziwai says: It does not prevent it. R. Aḥa says: Good oil prevents

1 He entered the room while Grace was being said.

2 *M.* omits: Rab Naḥman in the name of.

3 *M.*: Raba.

4 He meant, be eager to have the privilege of saying Grace for the whole company.

5 *M.* omits: Rabbah.

6 Otherwise why did Rab and Rab Huna give such advice to their sons?

7 *M.* omits the name, thus making R. Judah the Prince the author.

8 The "common soldier" is here the one who starts the Grace, the "veteran" he who rounds it up with the responses. *M.* omits the second "go down." The translation would then be: The common soldiers go down to do the fighting and the officers claim the victory.

9 In Nehem. ix. 5 which refers to those who "stand up and bless" and those who respond "Blessed be Thy glorious name." According to the Rabbis, this latter phrase was used in the Temple as the equivalent of "Amen"; cf. fol. 63 *a*, p. 416.

10 Who are learning the benedictions.

11 I.e. removing the food-stains from the hand by means of oil is an essential preliminary to the Grace.

12 *M.* inserts here: R. Meïr, which yields no sense. According to *D. S.* the probable reading is: R. Ziwai, the son-in-law of R. Meïr says.

it. R. Zohᵃmai says: Just as one who is dirty is unfit for the Temple-service, so are dirty hands unfit for the Grace. Rab Naḥman b. Isaac said: I know neither Zilai nor Ziwai nor Zohᵃmai; but I know the following teaching: Rab Judah said in the name of Rab (another version: it is taught in a *Bārāitā*): "Sanctify yourselves" (Lev. xi. 44)—i.e. the washing before the meal[1]; "and be ye holy" (*ibid.*)—i.e. the washing after the meal; "for holy" (*ibid.*)—i.e. the oil; "I am the Lord your God[2]"—i.e. the Grace.

May we return unto thee: *The following are the points of variance!*

[1] *Lit.* "the first water"—"the latter water."

[2] The Hebrew text omits "the Lord your God." There is some confusion between Lev. xi. 44 and *ibid.* xx. 7.

CHAPTER IX

fol. 54 a.

MISHNĀH I—V

I. *He who beholds a place where miracles have been wrought for Israel says, "Blessed [art Thou, O Lord our God, King of the Universe] Who wroughtest miracles for our fathers in this place." [He who beholds] a place from which idolatry has been uprooted says, "Blessed... Who hast uprooted idolatry from our land."*

II. *For shooting stars, earthquakes, thunders, storms and lightnings he says, "Blessed... Whose strength and might fill the world." For mountains, hills, seas, rivers and deserts he says, "Blessed... Who hast made the creation." R. Judah states: He who beholds the ocean*[1] *says, "Blessed... Who hast made the ocean," but only when he beholds it at intervals. For rain and good tidings he says, "Blessed... Who art good and dispensest good." For bad tidings he says, "Blessed be the true Judge."*

III. *He who has built a new house or bought new vessels says, "Blessed... Who hast kept us in life, hast preserved us and enabled us to reach this season." One says the benediction for a calamity apart from any attendant good, and for good fortune apart from any attendant evil; but he who supplicates concerning that which is past utters a vain prayer. If his wife is pregnant and he says, "May it be Thy will that my wife bear a son," behold that is a vain prayer. If he were on the way, and hearing a cry of lamentation in the city, exclaims, "May it be Thy will that it be not within my house," behold that is a vain prayer.*

IV. *He who enters a town*[2] *should offer prayer twice, once on entering and once on leaving. Ben 'Azzai says: Four times, twice on entering and twice on leaving. He gives thanks for what is past and supplicates for what is yet to be.*

V. *A man is in duty bound to utter a benediction for the bad even as he utters one for the good*[3]*; as it is said, "And thou shalt*

[1] *Lit.* great sea.

[2] A fortified town is here intended in which is a military governor, who is usually a tyrant and does not rule justly.

[3] It has been suggested that this exhortation is directed against Sadducean teaching; cf. Lehmann in *R. E. J.* xxxi. pp. 31 ff.

love the Lord thy God with all thy heart, and with all thy soul, and with all thy might" (*Deut.* vi. 5)—*"with all thy heart," i.e. with thy two impulses, with the good and the evil impulse*[1]; *"with all thy soul," i.e. even if He take thy soul; "with all thy might," i.e. with all thy wealth. Another explanation of "with all thy might* [meʾōdékā]*"—with whatever measure* [middāh] *He metes out to thee, do Thou return Him thanks* [mōdéh].

A man should not behave with levity towards the Eastern Gate [*of the Temple*], *since it is directed towards the Holy of Holies. Nor may one enter the Temple Mount with his staff, his sandal, his wallet, and with the dust upon his feet; nor may he use it as a short cut, and to expectorate* [*on the Temple Mount is forbidden*] a fortiori.

At the conclusion of every benediction in the Sanctuary they used to say "For ever[2]*"; but when the* Mīnīm[3] *perverted the truth and declared that there is only one world, it was ordained that the wording should be "From everlasting to everlasting*[4]*." It was further ordained that a man should greet his friends by mentioning the Divine Name*[5]; *as it is said, "And behold, Boaz came from Bethlehem, and said unto the reapers, The Lord be with you; and they answered him, The Lord bless thee"* (*Ruth* ii. 4); *and it is said, "The Lord is with thee, thou mighty man of valour"* (*Judges* vi. 12); *and it is said, "And despise not thy mother when she is old"* (*Prov.* xxiii. 22)[6]; *and it is said, "It is time for the Lord to work; they have made void Thy law"* (*Ps.* cxix. 126). *R. Nathan says:* [*This means,*] *They have made void Thy law, because it is time for the Lord to work.*

1 The idea of two is derived from the spelling of the word for "heart"—לבבך instead of לבך; see *A. P. A.* II. p. 15 n. 3.

2 *Lit.* for *a* world.

3 Some edd. read "Sadducees"; and they are intended here as they denied the future life. See p. 100.

4 *Lit.* "from the world to the world"—two worlds.

5 Viz. the Tetragrammaton *JHWH*, usually rendered "the Lord" which the Jews pronounced *Ădōnāi*. Wiesner, pp. 118 f., conjectures that this is directed against the Samaritans who substituted for *JHWH* the word *ha-Shēm* "the Name." Hence by using the word *Ădōnāi* in his salutation, it would be recognised that it was a Jew, not a Samaritan, who was speaking.

6 The application of this verse to the subject-matter will be explained on fol. 63 *a*, p. 417.

GᴱMĀRĀ

Benediction on beholding a place where a miracle had been wrought.

Whence have we this[1]? R. Joḥanan said: Because the Scriptures state, "And Jethro said, Blessed be the Lord Who hath delivered you" etc. (Exod. xviii. 10). Do we say a benediction for the miracle wrought on behalf of the many but not for the miracle wrought on behalf of an individual? Lo, there was the man who was journeying by 'Eber Jamina[2] when a lion attacked him, and a miracle was wrought for him and he was rescued. He came before Raba who told him: Whenever thou reachest that spot, say "Blessed...Who hast wrought a miracle for me in this place." And Mar b. Rabina was passing through the valley of 'Arabot[3] and thirsted for water; a miracle was wrought for him and a well was created and he drank. On another occasion, he was passing through the market-place of Maḥoza[4] when a wild camel attacked him, and the wall was cleft for him and he went through it. Whenever he came to 'Arabot he said the benediction "Blessed...Who hast wrought for me a miracle in 'Arabot and with the camel"; and whenever he came to the market-place of Maḥoza he said, "Blessed...Who hast wrought for me a miracle with the camel and in 'Arabot." They answer[5]: In the case of a miracle wrought on behalf of the many, everybody is obliged to utter the benediction[6]; but in the case of a miracle wrought on behalf of an individual, only he[7] is obliged to say it.

One must praise God when beholding places of historical importance.

Our Rabbis have taught: He who beholds the fords of the [Red] Sea, or the fords of the Jordan, or the fords of the valleys of Arnon, or the hail-stones in the descent of Bet Ḥoron[8], or the stone which Og, king of Bashan, sought to cast upon Israel[9], or the stone upon

1 That a benediction is required when one beholds a place where a miracle occurred. According to Rashi the reading is: Whence is it that we have to say a benediction for a miracle?

2 *M.*: 'Ēber Jardēnā; i.e. "the other side of the Jordan." Rashi explains: A district to the S. of the Euphrates. Wiesner, p. 120, connects 'Ēber with the Babylonian river Chabor; hence the phrase means: the right, or N. bank of the Chabor.

3 The district between the Chabor and the canal of Is; Wiesner, p. 121.

4 A town on the Tigris, identified with the fortified Maogamalcha; Neubauer, pp. 356 f.

5 The question above whether a benediction is to be said for the miracle which happens to an individual.

6 Even if he had not experienced it himself.

7 Isaac Alfasi (the medieval Talmudist) reads: He, his son and his grandson.

8 See Josh. x. 11.

9 *M.* and some edd. read: Moses.

which Moses sat when Joshua fought against Amalek[1], or [the pillar of salt of] Lot's wife[2], or the wall of Jericho which was swallowed up in its place—over all these one must give thanks and praise before the All-present.

Miracle at the fords of Arnon.

It is quite right with the fords of the [Red] Sea; for it is written, "And the children of Israel went into the midst of the Sea upon the dry ground" (Exod. xiv. 22). [It is quite right with] the fords of the Jordan; for it is written, "And the priests that bare the ark of [the covenant of][3] the Lord stood firm on dry ground in the midst of the Jordan, while all Israel passed over on dry ground, until all the nation were passed clean over the Jordan" (Josh. iii. 17). But the fords of the valleys of Arnon—whence is it [that a benediction is necessary]? For it is written, "Wherefore it is said in the book of the Wars of the Lord, Et and Heb in the rear[4] and the valleys of Arnon" etc. (Num. xxi. 14). It has been taught: "Et and Heb in the rear" were two lepers who journeyed in the rear of the camp. When the Israelites were to pass through [the valleys of Arnon], the Amorites came and made **fol. 54 b.** caves for themselves in which they hid, saying, "When the Israelites pass here we will kill them." But they knew not that the Ark was journeying before Israel and was lowering the rocks in front of them; so when the Ark reached [the spot where the Amorites were in hiding], the rocks clave together, killing them, and their blood descended into the valleys of Arnon. When Et and Heb came and saw blood issuing from between the rocks, they went and told the Israelites and uttered a song. That is what is written, "And he poured out the valleys that incline toward the seat of Ar and lean upon the border of Moab" (*ibid.* *v.* 15)[5].

Miracle of the hail-stones.

"Hail-stones" *abnē elgābīsh.* What are *abnē elgābīsh*? It has been taught: They are stones which remained suspended [in the air] for the sake of a man[6] and descended for the sake of a man.

1 See Exod. xvii. 12. 2 See Gen. xix. 26.

3 This word, occurring in the Hebrew text, is omitted in edd. *M.* inserts it.

4 R.V. "Vaheb in Suphah"; marg. "in storm."

5 The first word is read *āshad* instead of *éshed*, "the slopes of," in the Biblical text. As rendered here, the verse means that the hills on the Ar side of the valley inclined towards the hills on the Moab side, so that the Amorites were crushed in between. Wiesner, p. 122, points out that this *Aggādāh* seems to have been known to the author of the Vulgate: Unde dicitur in libro bellorum Domini: Sicut fecit in Mari rubro, sic faciet in torrentibus Arnon. Scopuli torrentium *inclinati sunt* ut requiescerent in Ar, et recumberent in finibus Moabitarum.

6 "For the sake of a man" in Hebrew *'al gab ish.*

They remained suspended for the sake of a man, viz.: Moses; for it is written, "Now the *man* Moses was very meek" (Num. xii. 3), and it is written, "And the thunders and hail ceased[1], and the rain poured not upon the earth" (Exod. ix. 33). They descended for the sake of a man, viz. Joshua; for it is written, "Take thee Joshua the son of Nun, a *man* in whom is spirit" (Num. xxvii. 18), and it is written, "And it came to pass, as they fled from before[2] Israel, while they were at the descent of Beth-horon, that the Lord cast down great stones" (Josh. x. 11).

Fate of Og, king of Bashan.

"The stone which Og, king of Bashan, sought to cast upon Israel." A tradition has been handed down in this connection: Og said, "What is the extent of Israel's camp? Three *Parsāh*. I will go and uproot a mountain of the size of three *Parsāh*, and cast it upon them so that I will kill them." He went and uprooted a mountain of the size of three *Parsāh* and carried it upon his head; but the Holy One, blessed be He, sent ants which bored a hole through it so that it sank about his neck. As he sought to draw it off, his teeth were extended on both sides, so that it was impossible to extricate himself. That is what is written, "Thou hast broken the teeth of the wicked" (Ps. iii. 8); and it is in accord with the statement of R. Simeon b. Laḳish who said: What means that which is written, "Thou hast broken the teeth of the wicked"? Read not "Thou hast broken" [*shibbartā*] but "Thou hast prolonged" [*shirbabtā*]. What was the height of Moses? Ten cubits[3]. He took an axe ten cubits long, jumped to a height of ten cubits and struck Og on his ankle[4] and killed him.

Why Moses sat on a stone.

"The stone upon which Moses sat"; for it is written, "But Moses' hands were heavy; and they took a stone, and put it under him, and he sat thereon" (Exod. xvii. 12). [Had not Moses a cushion or bolster upon which to sit? But thus spake Moses: Since Israel are now enduring hardship, I too will endure hardship with them[5].]

Pillar of Lot's wife.

"Lot's wife"; as it is said, "But his wife looked back from behind him and she became a pillar of salt" (Gen. xix. 26)[6]. It

[1] I.e. they were descending but stopped half-way.

[2] The *Talmūd* inserts here "the children of" which is not in the Biblical text.

[3] About 15 feet.

[4] Which was accordingly 45 ft. from the ground.

[5] The words in brackets are not in edd., but are added by *M*. They are to be found in the Meḳīltā *ad loc.* (ed. Friedmann, p. 54 *b*), Ta'anīt 11 *a*.

[6] The existence of this salt-pillar is referred to in the Apocrypha, Wisdom of Solomon, x. 7. Josephus (*Antiq.* I. xi. 4) claims to have seen it. Edd. insert here: And the wall of Jericho which was swallowed up; as it is written, "And the wall fell down flat" (Josh. vi. 20). But it disturbs the connection and is dealt with in the following paragraph.

is quite right with all these miracles[1]; but that of Lot's wife was a punishment[2]! [On beholding it] one should say "Blessed be the true Judge[3]." But it mentions above thanksgiving and praise! It has been taught: For Lot and his wife we say two benedictions—for his wife one says, "Blessed be the true Judge"; and for Lot one says, "Blessed...Who rememberest the righteous." R. Joḥanan said: Even at the time of His wrath, the Holy One, blessed be He, remembers the righteous; as it is said, "And it came to pass, when God destroyed the cities of the Plain, that God remembered Abraham, and sent Lot out of the midst of the overthrow" (Gen. xix. 29).

Miracle of Jericho's wall.

"And the wall of Jericho which was swallowed up." And the wall of Jericho which was swallowed up! Lo, it fell! As it is said, "And it came to pass when the people heard the sound of the horn, that the people shouted with a great shout, and the wall *fell* down flat" (Josh. vi. 20). Since its breadth and height were equal, it must in consequence have been swallowed up [in the earth][4].

Four classes of people from whom thanksgiving is due.

Rab Judah said in the name of Rab[5]: Four classes of people must offer thanksgiving: They who go down to the sea, who journey in the desert[6], the invalid who recovers and the prisoner who has been set free. "They who go down to the sea"—whence have we this? For it is written, "They that go down to the sea in ships... these saw the works of the Lord...He raised the stormy wind... They mounted up to the heaven, they went down to the deeps... They reeled to and fro, and staggered like a drunken man...They cried unto the Lord in their trouble, and He brought them out of their distresses. He made the storm a calm...Then were they glad because they were quiet...Let them give thanks unto the Lord for His mercy, and for His wonderful works to the children of men" (Ps. cvii. 23–31). "They who journey in the desert"—whence have we this? For it is written, "They wandered in the wilderness in a desert way; they found no city of habitation...Then they cried unto the Lord...and He led them by a straight way... Let them give thanks unto the Lord for His mercy" (*ibid. vv.*

[1] That a benediction should be said on beholding their site.

[2] And a benediction would be out of place.

[3] Usually said on hearing bad news.

[4] For if it had fallen on its side, the obstacle would have remained the same. But the Bible states "the people went up into the city, every man straight before him," i.e. with nothing in the way. Consequently the wall must have sunk into the ground.

[5] *M.* and some edd. omit "in the name of Rab."

[6] And return in safety.

4–8). "The invalid who recovers"—whence have we this? For it is written, "Crazed because of the way of their transgression, and afflicted because of their iniquities, their soul abhorred all manner of food...They cried unto the Lord in their trouble...He sent His word and healed them...Let them give thanks unto the Lord for His mercy" (Ps. cvii. 17–21). "The prisoner who has been set free"—whence have we this? For it is written, "Such as sat in darkness and in the shadow of death...because they rebelled against the words of God...Therefore He humbled their heart with travail...They cried unto the Lord in their trouble...He brought them out of darkness and the shadow of death...Let them give thanks unto the Lord for His mercy" (*ibid. vv.* 10–15).

The form of benediction.

What benediction should he utter? Rab Judah said, "Blessed ...Who bestowest lovingkindnesses[1]." Abbai said: It is necessary for him to offer his thanksgiving in the presence of ten; for it is written, "Let them exalt Him in the assembly of the people" etc. (*ibid. v.* 32). Mar Zoṭra said: Two of them must be Rabbis; as it is said, "And praise Him in the seat of the elders" (*ibid.*). Rab Ashē[2] retorted: Say that they must all be Rabbis! But is it written, "In the assembly of elders"? No, it is written, "In the assembly of the people." Then say[3]: [He must offer thanksgiving] in the presence of ten ordinary persons and two Rabbis! The question [remains unanswered].

Thanksgiving offered by another on one's behalf.

Rab Judah was ill and recovered. Rab Ḥanna[4] of Bagdat[5] and other Rabbis went in to visit him. They said to him, "Blessed be the All-merciful Who has given thee back to us and has not given thee to the dust." He said to them, "You have exempted me from the obligation of thanksgiving." But lo, Abbai said: He must offer thanksgiving in the presence of ten! There were ten present. But it was not he who offered thanksgiving! It was not necessary, because he responded "Amen" after them.

People who require guarding.

Rab Judah said: Three require guarding[6], viz.: an invalid, a bridegroom and a bride. In a *Bārāitā* it is taught: An invalid[7], woman in confinement, bridegroom and bride. Some say: Also a mourner[8]; and others add: Also disciples of the wise at night[9].

[1] For the modern form, see Singer, p. 148.

[2] *M.*: Raba.

[3] *M.* assigns this remark to Rabina.

[4] *M.*: Huna.

[5] Perhaps the modern Eski Bagdad in Babylon; Neubauer, p. 360.

[6] Against evil spirits.

[7] *M.* omits.

[8] On the belief that women in childbirth are liable to attack by evil spirits, cf. Frazer, *Folklore of the Old Testament*, III. pp. 472 ff.; for bridegroom and bride, I. pp. 520 ff.; and for mourners, III. pp. 236, 298 ff.

[9] Whom the evil spirits tempt to lapses from morality.

Three things which it is meritorious to prolong. fol. 55 a.

Rab Judah also said: There are three things which, if one prolong, lengthen his days and years; viz. Who prolongs his prayer, his stay at table and in the privy. "Who prolongs his prayer"—is that a virtue? And lo, R. Ḥiyya b. Abba said in the name of R. Joḥanan: Whoever prolongs his prayer and calculates on it will eventually come to pain of heart; as it is said, "Hope deferred maketh the heart sick" (Prov. xiii. 12)[1]. And R. Isaac said: Three things cause the sins of a man to be remembered; viz. [passing under] a wall threatening to fall[2], calculating on prayer and surrendering one's case against a man to Heaven[3]! There is no contradiction; the latter refers to where one calculates [on the prolongation of his prayer], the other to where he does not calculate upon it. So how should one act? He makes many supplications. "He who prolongs his stay at table"—perhaps a poor man will come and he will give him [some food]; for it is written, "The altar of wood three cubits high...and he said unto me, This is the table that is before the Lord" (Ezek. xli. 22). He opens with "altar" and concludes with "table"! R. Joḥanan and R. Eleazar both say: So long as the Temple was in existence, the altar used to atone for Israel, but now a man's table atones for him[4]. "He who prolongs his stay in the privy"—is that a virtue? Lo, there is a teaching: Ten things cause a man piles[5]: Eating the leaves of reeds, the leaves of the vine, the sprouts of the vine, the palate[6] of an animal[7], the backbone of a fish, salted fish which has not been sufficiently cooked, to drink the lees of wine, to wipe oneself [after evacuation] with lime, potters' clay, or pebbles with which another has wiped himself; and some add: Also unduly to strain oneself in the privy! There is no contradiction; the latter refers to one who stays and strains, the other to one who stays long but does not strain. It is like the incident where a certain

[1] See fol. 32 *b*, p. 215.

[2] Because it is tempting Providence.

[3] Thereby showing over-confidence in his innocence.

[4] When he has the poor as his guests. Cf. "Let the poor be the members of thy household"; Ābōt i. 5, Singer, p. 185. Although this is the interpretation required by the context, Bacher (following Epstein) thinks that the dictum originally referred to the ritualistic purity of the daily meals; cf. *A. P. A.* I. p. 225 n. 2.

[5] Wünsche renders: Zehn Dinge bringen den Menschen zu den Unteren (d.i. unter die Erde); but this is improbable.

[6] *Lit.* threshing sledge. According to Rashi: all parts of the animal which are rough and indented.

[7] *M.* adds: without salt.

matron[1] said to R. Judah b. R. El'ai, "Thy face is like that of pig-rearers and usurers[2]." He replied, "On my faith! Both [occupations] are forbidden me; but there are twenty-four privies from my lodging-place to the House of Study, and whenever I go there I test myself in all of them."

Three things which shorten life.

Rab Judah also said[3]: Three things shorten a man's days and years: To be given a Scroll of the *Tōrāh* from which to read [a portion in the Synagogue] and decline to read; to be handed the cup of benediction to say Grace and decline; and to give oneself an air of superiority[4]. "To be given a Scroll of the *Tōrāh* from which to read and decline to read"—for it is written, "For that is thy life and the length of thy days" (Deut. xxx. 20). "To be handed the cup of benediction to say Grace and decline"—for it is written, "I will bless them that bless thee" (Gen. xii. 3)[5]. "To give oneself an air of superiority"—for R. Ḥamma b. R. Ḥannina[6] said: Why did Joseph die before his brothers[7]? Because he gave himself superior airs.

Three things for which one should pray.

Rab Judah also said in the name of Rab: For three things it is necessary to offer supplication: A good king, a good year, and a good dream. "A good king"—for it is written, "The king's heart is in the hand of the Lord as the water-courses" (Prov. xxi. 1). "A good year"—for it is written, "The eyes of the Lord thy God are always upon it, from the beginning of the year even unto the end of the year" (Deut. xi. 12). "A good dream"—for it is written, "Wherefore cause Thou me to dream[8] and make me to live" (Is. xxxviii. 16).

Three things which God proclaims.

R. Joḥanan said: There are three things which the Holy One, blessed be He, Himself proclaims, viz.: famine, plenty and a good leader. "Famine"—for it is written, "The Lord hath called for a famine" (II Kings viii. 1). "Plenty"—for it is written, "I will call for the corn and will increase it" (Ezek. xxxvi. 29). "A good

1 In the parallel passage (Nᵉdārīm 49 *b*) it is not a matron but a *Mīn*. To refer to indelicate matters like this in conversation between the sexes is common in the East. Cf. Lane, p. 473.

2 I.e. fresh and healthy-looking.

3 *M.* adds: in the name of Rab.

4 The last phrase might also mean, to occupy a position of authority.

5 And the one who says Grace blesses his host.

6 *M.*: R. Ḥiyya said.

7 This is deduced from Exod. i. 6, "And Joseph died and (sc. then) all his brethren."

8 *Sic.* R.V. "Recover Thou me." The root of the word is identical with the letters in the word for "dream."

leader"—for it is written, "And the Lord spoke unto Moses, saying, See I have called by name Beṣalel, the son of Uri" etc. (Exod. xxxi. 1 f.).

R. Isaac said: We must not appoint a leader over the Community without first consulting them; as it is said, "See, the Lord hath called by name Beṣalel, the son of Uri" (*ibid.* xxxv. 30). The Holy One, blessed be He, asked Moses, "Is Beṣalel acceptable to thee?" He replied, "Lord of the universe, if he is acceptable to Thee, how much more so to me!" He said to him, "Nevertheless, go and tell the people." He went and asked Israel, "Is Beṣalel acceptable to you?" They answered, "If he is acceptable to the Holy One, blessed be He, and to thee, how much more so to us!" **Community must be consulted about the appointment of its leader.**

R. Samuel b. Naḥmani said in the name of R. Jonathan: He was called Beṣalel because of his wisdom; for at the time that the Holy One, blessed be He, said to Moses, "Go, tell Beṣalel, 'Make for Me a tabernacle, an ark and vessels[1]'," Moses went and inverted the order, saying to him, "Make an ark and vessels and a tabernacle[2]." He replied, "Moses, our teacher, it is the way of the world for a man to build a house and afterwards furnish it; but thou sayest, 'Make for Me an ark, vessels and a tabernacle'! Where shall I place the vessels which I make? Perhaps thus spake the Holy One, blessed be He, unto thee, 'Make a tabernacle, an ark and vessels'." Moses replied, "Perhaps thou wert in the shadow of God[3] and thou knowest this." **Explanation of Beṣalel's name.**

Rab Judah said in the name of Rab: Beṣalel knew how to combine the letters[4] with which the heavens and earth had been created; for it is written here, "And He hath filled him with the spirit of God, in *wisdom* and in *understanding* and in *knowledge*" (Exod. xxxv. 31), and it is written elsewhere, "The Lord by *wisdom* founded the earth; by *understanding* He established the heavens" (Prov. iii. 19) and "By His *knowledge* the depths were broken up" (*ibid.* v. 20). **Beṣalel's wisdom.**

R. Joḥanan said: The Holy One, blessed be He, only gives wisdom to him who has wisdom; as it is said, "He giveth wisdom unto the wise, and knowledge to them that know understanding" **God gives wisdom only to the wise.**

[1] That is the order in Exod. xxxi. 7 f.

[2] Thus in Exod. xxv. 10 the Ark is mentioned; *ibid.* *vv.* 23 and 31 we have the table and candlestick, i.e. "the vessels"; and in xxvi. 1 the tabernacle.

[3] *Beṣēl ēl*, hence Beṣalel.

[4] Knowledge derived from the mystic art. See Abelson, *Jewish Mysticism*, pp. 100 f. and Ginsburg, *The Kabbalah*, pp. 153 ff.

(Dan. ii. 21). Rab Taḥlifa the Palestinian[1] heard this and repeated it in the presence of R. Abbahu. He said to him: You learn it from there; but I learn it from the following, for it is written, "In the hearts of all that are wise-hearted I have put wisdom" (Exod. xxxi. 6)[2].

Teachings about dreams.

Rab Ḥisda said: [There is no reality in] any dream without a fast[3]. Rab Ḥisda also said: An uninterpreted dream is like an unread letter[4]. Rab Ḥisda also said: Neither a good nor a bad dream is fulfilled in every detail. Rab Ḥisda also said: A bad dream is preferable to a good dream[5]. Rab Ḥisda also said: When a dream is bad, the pain it causes is sufficient [to prevent its fulfilment], and when the dream is good, the joy it brings is sufficient. Rab Joseph said: As for a good dream, even in my own case[6], its cheerfulness frustrates it [so that it is not realised]. Rab Ḥisda also said: A bad dream is worse than scourging; as it is said, "God hath so made it that men should fear before Him" (Eccles. iii. 14), and Rabbah b. Bar Ḥannah said in the name of R. Joḥanan: This refers to a bad dream[7].

Every dream contains an improbable element.

"The prophet that hath a dream, let him tell a dream; and he that hath My word, let him speak My word faithfully. What hath the straw to do with the wheat? saith the Lord" (Jer. xxiii. 28). What connection has "straw and wheat" with a dream? But said R. Joḥanan in the name of R. Simeon b. Joḥai: Just as one cannot have wheat without straw, similarly it is impossible for a dream to be without something that is vain. R. Berekiah said: A dream, though it be fulfilled in part, is never completely realised. Whence is this learnt? From Joseph; for it is written, "And behold the sun and the moon and eleven stars bowed down to me"

1 *Lit.* son of the West.

2 It was always considered preferable to find authority for an opinion in the Pentateuch than in other parts of the Bible.

3 The original is obscure, and the reading of *M.* בלא should be adopted instead of ולא. The 'Ārūk gives it a reverse meaning: Every dream has some reality, except that which one dreams while fasting. Against this interpretation is the commonly held idea that a full stomach prevents dreams (cf. p. 90 n. 8), and that a morning-dream (when the stomach is empty) has great significance. See next folio, p. 363.

4 Has no effect for good or evil, because it depends upon the interpretation, as will be explained later.

5 Because it leads to searching of heart and contrition.

6 He was blind, and consequently his joy would be less than that of one possessed of sight.

7 Most of the statements in this paragraph seem to have the purpose of belittling the importance of dreams.

(Gen. xxxvii. 9); but at that time his mother[1] was no longer living. R. Levi said: A man should always wait up to twenty-two years for [the fulfilment of] a good dream. Whence is this learnt? From Joseph; for it is written, "These are the generations of Jacob. Joseph, being seventeen years old" etc. (*ibid.* v. 2)[2], and it is written, "And Joseph was thirty years old when he stood before Pharaoh" (*ibid.* xli. 46). From seventeen to thirty—how many years is it? Thirteen; add the seven years of plenty and two of famine[3], hence we get twenty-two. **fol. 55 b.**

Good man not shown a good dream.

Rab Huna said: A good man is not shown a good dream[4] and a bad man is not shown a bad dream[5]. There is a teaching to the same effect: Throughout David's lifetime he never saw a good dream, and throughout Aḥitophel's lifetime he did not see a bad dream. But lo, it is written, "There shall no evil befall thee" (Ps. xci. 10), and Rab Ḥisda said in the name of Rab Jeremiah b. Abba: [These words mean,] neither bad dreams nor evil thoughts will trouble thee[6]! Nay; the good man sees no evil dream, but others dream about him. And since he sees no [dream] himself, is that an advantage? For lo, R. Zeʿira[7] said: Whoever abides seven days without a dream is called evil; as it is said, "He shall abide satisfied, he shall not be visited by evil" (Prov. xix. 23). Read not *sābēaʿ* "satisfied" but *shébaʿ* "seven"[8]! Nay, this is what he means to say: The good man sees a dream but [the next morning] he does not know what he has seen[9].

How a bad dream may be nullified.

Rab Huna b. Ammi[10] stated that R. Pedat said in the name of R. Joḥanan: He who sees a dream and his soul is depressed[11]

[1] Represented in the dream by "the moon."

[2] At that age he had the dream.

[3] When his brothers bowed before him; cf. Gen. xlv. 6.

[4] If he dreams at all, it is a bad dream. For the reason see p. 358 n. 5.

[5] His dreams are good, so that he may enjoy this world, since he will be debarred from the joys of the next world.

[6] *M.* and some edd. insert here: "Neither shall any plague come nigh thy tent" (*ibid.*)—i.e. thou shalt not find thy wife in doubt whether she be menstrual when thou returnest from a journey. The words disturb the connection.

[7] The parallel passage (fol. 14 *a*, p. 90) reads: R. Jonah in the name of R. Zera. *M.*: R. Zera in the name of R. Jannai. The correct reading is probably R. Jannai [II] said in the name of R. Zera. Cf. *D. S. ad loc.* and Hyman, II. p. 765 a.

[8] See p. 90 n. 9.

[9] And without interpretation it can have no effect.

[10] *M.* omits: b. Ammi. According to Hyman, III. p. 1009 a, the correct reading is Ḥanan b. Ammi.

[11] Because it was a bad dream.

should go and have it interpreted in the presence of three. He should have it interpreted! But Rab Ḥisda has said: An uninterpreted dream is like an unread letter[1]! Nay, but say: He should have it turned into good in the presence of three. He should assemble three men and say to them, "I have seen a good dream"; and they should say to him, "Good it is and may it be good. May the All-merciful turn it to good; seven times may it be decreed concerning thee from Heaven that it should be good, and may it be good." Then they should recite three verses in which the word *hāpak* "turn" occurs, three in which *pādāh* "redeem" occurs, and three in which *shālōm* "peace" occurs. Three verses in which "turn" occurs—"Thou didst *turn* for me my mourning into dancing; Thou didst loose my sackcloth and gird me with gladness" (Ps. xxx. 12); "Then shall the virgin rejoice in the dance, and the young men and the old together; for I will *turn* their mourning into joy, and will comfort them, and make them rejoice from their sorrow" (Jer. xxxi. 12); "Nevertheless the Lord thy God would not hearken unto Balaam; but the Lord thy God *turned* the curse into a blessing unto thee" (Deut. xxiii. 6). Three verses in which the word "redeem" occurs—"He hath *redeemed* my soul in peace so that none came nigh me" (Ps. lv. 19); "And the *redeemed* of the Lord shall return and come with singing unto Zion...and sorrow and sighing shall flee away" (Is. xxxv. 10); "And the people said unto Saul, Shall Jonathan die, who hath wrought this great salvation in Israel?...So the people *rescued* [*pādāh*] Jonathan, that he died not" (I Sam. xiv. 45). Three verses in which the word "peace" occurs—"*Peace, peace*, to him that is far off and to him that is near, saith the Lord that createth the fruit of the lips; and I will heal him" (Is. lvii. 19); "Then the spirit clothed Amasai, who was chief of the captains: Thine are we, David, and on thy side, thou son of Jesse; *peace, peace* be unto thee, and *peace* be to thy helpers; for thy God helpeth thee" (I Chron. xii. 18); "Thus ye shall say, All hail! and *peace* be both unto thee, and *peace* be to thy house, and *peace* be unto all that thou hast" (I Sam. xxv. 6).

If one has forgotten his dream.

Amemar, Mar Zoṭra and Rab Ashē were sitting together; they said: Let each one of us relate something which the others have not heard. One of them commenced and said: He who has seen a dream and knows not what he has seen, let him stand before the *Kōh^a^nīm* at the time that they spread their hands [to pronounce

[1] See p. 358.

the priestly benediction] and utter the following[1]: "Lord of the universe! I am Thine and my dreams are Thine; a dream have I dreamed and I know not what it is. Whether I dreamed concerning myself, or my fellows dreamed concerning me, or I dreamed concerning others, if they be good dreams, strengthen and fortify them [and may they be fulfilled][2] like the dreams of Joseph; but if they require to be remedied, heal them as the waters of Marah [were healed] by the hands of Moses our teacher, as Miriam [was healed] from her leprosy[3], as Hezekiah from his illness, and like the waters of Jericho [sweetened] by the hands of Elisha. And as Thou didst turn the curse of the wicked Balaam into a blessing, so do Thou turn all my dreams for me into good." He should conclude [his prayer] simultaneously with the *Kōhanīm*, so that the Congregation responds "Amen." But if not[4], let him say the following: "Thou majestic One in the heights, Who abidest in might, Thou art peace and Thy name is peace. May it be Thy will to grant us peace."

How the Evil Eye may be averted.

The next commenced and said: He who enters a town[5] and is afraid of the Evil Eye[6], let him take his right thumb in his left hand and his left thumb in his right hand and say the following: "I, A the son of B, come from the seed of Joseph against whom the Evil Eye had no power; as it is said, 'Joseph is a fruitful vine, a fruitful vine by a fountain' (Gen. xlix. 22)[7]. Read not *'ălē 'ayin* 'by a fountain' but *'ōlē 'ayin* 'overcoming the [Evil] Eye'." R. Josē b. R. Ḥannina said: It may be derived from the verse: "And let them[8] grow [*weyidgū*] into a multitude in the midst of the earth" (*ibid.* xlviii. 16); i.e. as the fishes [*dāgīm*] in the sea are covered by the water and the Evil Eye cannot have power over them, in similar manner the Evil Eye has no power over the

[1] The prayer which follows was included in the Prayer Book to be recited by the entire Congregation, whether they had dreamed or not, during the Priestly Benediction by the *Kōhanīm* in the Synagogue; but the modern editions omit it and it is falling into disuse.

[2] *M.* adds the words in brackets.

[3] Some authorities and the Prayer Book insert here: as Naaman from his leprosy.

[4] I.e. if he cannot finish together with them. But instead of these words, some authorities read: "When [at the conclusion of the benediction] the *Kōhanīm* turn their faces [from the people to the Ark]." On this ceremony, see *J. E.* III. pp. 244 ff.

[5] *M.*: a house.

[6] See p. 131 n. 4. Here it seems to mean the sensual passion. On this method of charming away the Evil Eye, see Feldman, *The Jewish Child*, p. 193.

[7] In the parallel passage (fol. 20 *a*, p. 131) it is: R. Abbahu said: Read not.

[8] The sons of Joseph.

seed of Joseph. Should he, however, be afraid of his own Evil Eye, let him gaze upon the wing of his left nostril.

Invalid should not announce his illness on the first day.

The third of them commenced and said: He who is ill should not disclose the fact on the first day so as not to cause himself bad luck, but after that he may disclose it. As when Raba fell ill, on the first day he did not disclose it, but after that he said to his attendant, "Go, announce that Raba is ill. Let him who loves me pray on my behalf, and let him that hates me rejoice over my plight; for it is written, 'Rejoice not when thine enemy falleth, and let not thy heart be glad when he stumbleth; lest the Lord see it and it displease Him, *and He turn away His wrath from him*' (Prov. xxiv. 17 f.)."

Dreams influenced by angels and evil spirits.

When Samuel had a bad dream, he used to say, "The dreams speak falsely" (Zech. x. 2); but when he had a good dream, he used to say, "Do the dreams speak falsely? For lo, it is written, 'I [God] do speak with him in a dream' (Num. xii. 6)." Raba asked: It is written, "I do speak with him in a dream," and it is written, "The dreams speak falsely"! There is no contradiction; the former being through an angel, the latter through an evil spirit.

Fulfilment of a dream depends upon its interpretation.

R. Bizna b. Zabda stated that R. 'Aḳiba said in the name of R. Panda, in the name of R. Naḥum, in the name of R. Biryam, in the name of an Elder—and who is he? R. Banaäh[1]: There were twenty-four interpreters of dreams in Jerusalem. I once had a dream and went to consult them all; but the interpretation each gave me differed from that of the others. Nevertheless all their interpretations were realised in me; to fulfil that which was said "All dreams follow the mouth [of the interpreter][2]." Is there such a Scriptural passage as "All dreams follow the mouth[3]"? Yes; and it is like the statement of R. Eleazar who said: Whence is it that all dreams follow the mouth? As it is said, "And it came to pass, as he interpreted to us, so it was" (Gen. xli. 13). Raba said: That is only so if he interprets it from the content of the dream; as it is said, "To each man according to his dream he did interpret" (*ibid. v.* 12). "When the chief baker saw that the interpretation was good" (*ibid.* xl. 16)—how did he know

[1] *M.*: R. Bizta stated that R. Zera said in the name of R. 'Uḳba...R. Pabna ...R. Tanḥum...R. Parna...who is he? R. Nehorai.

[2] Bacher considers הפה "the mouth" to have been originally 'הפ, abbreviation for הפתרונות "the interpretations." See *R. E. J.* XXVII. pp. 141 ff.

[3] This question is asked because "That which was said" is a formula to introduce a Biblical quotation.

this[1]? R. Eleazar said: This teaches that each of them was shown the dream and interpretation of the other.

Types of dreams which are fulfilled. R. Joḥanan said: If one wakes up and a verse comes to his mouth[2], it is to be regarded as a minor prophecy. R. Joḥanan also said: Three types of dream are fulfilled—a morning dream, a dream which his friend has about him, and a dream interpreted in the midst of a dream. Some add: Also a dream which is repeated; as it is said, "And for that the dream was doubled unto Pharaoh twice" (Gen. xli. 32).

Dream results from one's thoughts. R. Samuel b. Naḥmani said in the name of R. Jonathan: A man is only shown[3] [in a dream what emanates] from the thoughts of his heart; as it is said, "As for thee, O king, thy thoughts came into thy mind upon thy bed" (Dan. ii. 29). Or if thou wilt I can say from this passage, "That thou mayest know the thoughts of thy heart" (*ibid. v.* 30). Raba[4] said: Thou mayest know this from the fact that a man is never shown [in a dream] a golden date-palm or an elephant entering the eye of a needle[5].

fol. 56 a. Example of the Roman Emperor. The Roman Emperor said to R. Joshua b. R. Ḥannina[6], "You declare that you are wise. Tell me what I shall see in my dream." He replied, "Thou wilt see the Persians enslaving thee, despoiling thee, and making thee pasture unclean animals with a golden crook." The Emperor reflected upon it the whole day and in the night saw it [in a dream][7].

Example of King Shapor. King Shapor said to Samuel, "You declare that you are very wise. Tell me what I shall see in my dream." He replied, "Thou wilt see the Romans come and take thee captive and make thee grind date-stones[8] in a golden mill." The king reflected upon it the whole day and in the night saw it [in a dream][9].

[1] I.e. how did the baker know about the butler's dream and its interpretation? The Bible does not mention that he had been told but that he *saw*.

[2] Spontaneously. Or it may refer to hearing a chance verse quoted, e.g. by school-children, this being regarded as a kind of oracle; cf. *T. A.* III. p. 228, and for some examples from Rabbinic literature, *ibid.* p. 353 n. 229. It may be compared with the practice of opening the Bible in haphazard manner to find in the page a helpful reference.

[3] *M.*: Raba said: Whence is it that a man is only shown, etc.

[4] *M.*: Rab Joseph.

[5] Because he never thinks of such things.

[6] The parallel passage (B^e^kōrōt 8 *b*) has Ḥ^a^nanyah, correctly.

[7] The mention of R. Joshua b. Ḥ^a^nanyah in connection with the Persian-Roman Wars would be an anachronism. For "Persians" we should probably read "Parthians"; and we may have here a reminiscence of the defeat of Trajan in 116 C.E.

[8] Used as fodder for camels.

[9] There is no historical record of Shapor I having been taken prisoner by Rome.

Bar Hedja the interpreter of dreams and Abbai and Raba.

Bar Hedja was an interpreter of dreams. When one paid him a fee, he interpreted [the dream] favourably; but if no fee was given him, he interpreted it unfavourably. Abbai and Raba had a dream; Abbai gave him a *Zūz* but Raba gave him nothing. They said to him: We were made to read in our dream the words "Thine ox shall be slain before thine eyes" (Deut. xxviii. 31). To Raba he said: Thy business will fail, and thou wilt have no desire to eat because of the grief of thy heart. To Abbai he said: Thy business will prosper, and thou wilt have no desire to eat because of the joy of thy heart. They said to him: We were made to read in our dream the words "Thou shalt beget sons and daughters, but they shall not be thine, for they shall go into captivity" (*ibid. v.* 41). To Raba he replied in an unfavourable sense. To Abbai he said: Thy sons and daughters will be many, and thy daughters will marry [husbands in distant parts of] the world, so that they will seem to thee as though they had gone into captivity. [They said to him: In our dream] we were made to read the words "Thy sons and thy daughters shall be given unto another people" (*ibid. v.* 32). To Abbai he said: Thy sons and daughters will be many; thou wilt say [they should marry] thy relatives, but [thy wife] will say they [should marry] her relatives, and she will compel thee to give them to her relatives, and it will seem [as though they had been given] to another people. To Raba he said: Thy wife will die, and thy sons and daughters will come under the control of another wife. For Raba[1] said in the name of R. Jeremiah b. Abba in the name of Rab: What means that which is written, "Thy sons and thy daughters shall be given unto another people"? This refers to a stepmother. [They said to Bar Hedja]: We were made to read in our dream the words "Go thy way, eat thy bread with joy" (Eccles. ix. 7). To Abbai he said: Thy business will prosper and thou wilt eat and drink and read Scriptural verses from the joy of thy heart. To Raba he said: Thy business will fail, thou wilt slaughter [cattle] but not eat, and thou wilt drink and read Scriptural verses to banish thy dread. We were made to read the words "Thou shalt carry much seed out into the field, and shalt gather little in for the locust will consume it" (Deut. xxviii. 38). To Abbai he gave an interpretation from the first half of the verse; to Raba from the latter half. We were made to read the words "Thou shalt have olive-trees throughout all thy borders, but thou

[1] The parallel passage (J^e^bāmōt 63 *b*) reads Rab Ḥanan b. Raba; and *M.* omits: in the name of R. Jeremiah...is written.

shalt not anoint thyself with the oil, for thine olives shall drop off" (Deut. xxviii. 40). To Abbai he gave an interpretation from the first half of the verse; to Raba from the latter half. We were made to read the words "And all the peoples of the earth shall see that the name of the Lord is called upon thee, and they shall be afraid of thee" (*ibid. v.* 10). To Abbai he said: Thy fame will go forth as the Principal of the College and the fear of thee will be widespread in the world. To Raba he said: The king's treasury will be broken into and thou wilt be arrested as one of the thieves, and everybody will draw an inference from thee[1]. The next day the king's treasury was broken into, and they came and arrested Raba.

They said [to Bar Hedja]: We saw [in a dream] lettuce upon the mouth of a jar. To Abbai he said: Thy business will be doubled like the lettuce. To Raba he said: Thy business will be bitter like the lettuce. They said to him: We saw [in a dream] meat upon the mouth of a jar. To Abbai he said: Thy wine[2] will be sweet and everybody will come to buy meat and wine of thee. To Raba he said: Thy wine will be sour and everybody will come to buy meat to eat therewith. They said to him: We saw [in a dream] a jug hanging upon a date-palm. To Abbai he said: Thy wares will be exalted like the palm. To Raba he said: Thy wares will be sweet as dates[3]. They said to him: We saw [in a dream] a pomegranate sprouting on the mouth of a jar. To Abbai he said: Thy wares will be high-priced like the pomegranate. To Raba he said: Thy wares will be stale [and taste] like the pomegranate. They said to him: We saw [in a dream] a jug fall into a well. To Abbai he said: Thy wares will be sought as one says, "A piece of bread fell into a well and cannot be found[4]." To Raba he said: Thy wares will go bad and thou wilt cast them into a well. They said to him: We saw [in a dream] a young ass standing by the side of our pillow and braying. To Abbai he said: Thou wilt become the President of the College and an *Āmōrā* will stand by thee. To Raba he said: The words "the firstling of an ass" (Exod. xiii. 13) have been erased from thy *Tᵉfillīn*[5]. Raba said to him: I have myself seen that the

[1] They will say that if Raba is suspected, surely suspicion will fall on us. Thus "they shall be afraid of thee."

[2] Both Abbai and Raba dealt in wine.

[3] Rashi explains: sweet to the buyer because of its cheapness.

[4] A proverbial expression quoted from Shab. 66 *b*.

[5] Exod. xiii. 11 ff. is one of the four passages written on the parchment contained in the phylacteries.

words are there. He replied: The letter *wāw* in the word *ḥªmōr* "ass" has certainly been erased from thy *Tᵉfillīn*[1].

Later on Raba went to him alone and said: I dreamt that the outer door fell. He replied: Thy wife will die[2]. He said: I dreamt that my back and front teeth fell out. He replied that his sons and daughters would die. He said: I dreamt of two doves flying. He replied: Thou wilt divorce two wives[3]. He said: I dreamt of two turnip-tops. He replied: Thou wilt receive two blows[4]. That day Raba went and sat in the House of Study the whole day[5]. He found there two blind men quarrelling with each other. Raba went to part them, and they struck him twice. They raised [their sticks] to give him another blow; but he cried, "That's enough! I only dreamt of *two*!"

Finally Raba came and gave [Bar Hedja] a fee, and said to him: I dreamt of a wall falling. He replied: Thou wilt acquire a boundless estate. He said to him: I dreamt that Abbai's house collapsed and its dust covered me. He replied: Abbai will die and his [Office as Principal of the] College will revert to thee. He said to him: I dreamt that my house collapsed and everybody came to take each a brick. He replied: Thy teachings will be scattered throughout the world. He said to him: I dreamt that my head was split open and my brains fell out. He replied: The stuffing will fall out of thy bolster. He said to him: I dreamt that I was made to read the *Hallēl* of Egypt[6]. He replied: Many miracles will happen to thee.

Fate of Bar Hedja.

[Once Bar Hedja] went with Raba on a boat; he said [to himself], "Why should I accompany a man to whom miracles will happen[7]?" As he descended [from the boat] a book[8] of his fell. Raba found it and saw written therein, "All dreams follow the mouth [of the interpreter]." He exclaimed, "Thou rascal! It

1 *M.* adds: Raba looked and saw that it was erased. The word *ḥªmōr* should be here spelt without the *wāw*. The Scribe wrongly inserted the letter and then erased it.

2 The wife, being the mistress of the house, is compared to the door which makes it secure.

3 On the comparison of a wife (or beloved) to a dove, cf. Cant. v. 2.

4 The turnip-top, resembling a stick, suggested a blow.

5 Thinking that there he would be safe from the fulfilment of the interpretation.

6 As read on the Passover-night to celebrate the miracles performed in Egypt.

7 He was afraid the boat would sink and Raba miraculously escape, but not he.

8 I.e. a book on dreams, as the sequel shows.

rested with thee [whether my dreams were auspicious or not], and thou didst cause me all this pain. I forgive thee everything except [what thou didst say about][1] the daughter of Rab Ḥisda[2]. May it be His will that this fellow be handed over into the power of the Government and it have no mercy on him!" Bar Hedja said, "What can I do? There is a tradition that the curse of a wise man, even when undeserved, comes to pass; and how much more so that of Raba who has justification for uttering a curse!" He said [to himself] "I will go into exile[3]; for a teacher has said, 'Exile[4] atones for sins'." He went into exile among the Romans, and sat down at the door of the king's treasury[5]. The wardrobe-keeper had a dream and said to him: I dreamt that a needle entered my finger. Bar Hedja said, "Give me a *Zūz*"; but he refused, so he gave him no reply. Then the wardrobe-keeper said: I dreamt that decay[6] seized two of my fingers. He said, "Give me a *Zūz*"; but he refused and received no answer. He said to him: I dreamt that decay seized my whole hand. He replied: Decay has seized all the [king's] silken garments. The king's household heard of this and they brought the wardrobe-keeper to put him to death. He said to the king, "Why me? Take him who knew but spoke not." They took Bar Hedja, and he said to him, "Because of the *Zūz* [which I refused thee], destruction has come upon the king's silken garments." They tied two cedars **fol. 56 b.** with a rope, bound one foot to one cedar and the other foot to the other cedar, and then released the rope. When he was decapitated each tree bounded back to its original position, and his body fell in two.

R. Ishmael interprets his nephew's dreams.

Ben Dama, the son of Ishmael's sister, asked R. Ishmael: I dreamt that both my cheekbones fell out. He replied: Two Roman nobles planned to do thee harm but they died[7]. Bar Ḳappara said to Rabbi[8]: I dreamt that my nose fell off. He replied: The divine wrath has departed from thee[9]. He said to him: I dreamt that both my hands were cut off. He replied: Thou wilt not be dependent upon the work of thy hands. He said to him: I dreamt that both my legs were amputated. He replied: Thou wilt ride upon a horse.

1 *M.* inserts: my sons and daughters and.
2 Raba's wife whose death was foretold.
3 *M.* adds: Perhaps it will bring me expiation.
4 *M.* adds: half.
5 Reading *d^ebē* for *d^erēsh*; cf. Jastrow, p. 526 b and *T. A.* I. p. 525 n. 51.
6 Rashi gives the word the meaning "worm."
7 The cheekbone indicated the mouth which spoke the plot.
8 *M.* inserts: Simeon.
9 The Hebrew word for "nose" also has the meaning "anger."

He said to him: I dreamt that somebody told me, "Thou wilt die in *Ădār* and not behold *Nīsān*." He replied: Thou wilt die in honour [*idrūtā*] and not fall into the power of temptation [*nissāyōn*].

R. Ishmael interprets the dreams of a *Mīn*.

A certain *Mīn* said to R. Ishmael[1]: I dreamt that I poured oil upon olives. He replied that he had outraged his mother[2]. He said to him: I dreamt that I plucked a star. He replied: Thou hast stolen the son of an Israelite. He said to him: I dreamt that I swallowed a star. He replied: The son of an Israelite thou didst sell and eat up the proceeds. He said to him: I dreamt that my eyes kissed one another. He replied that he had outraged his sister. He said to him: I dreamt that I kissed the moon. He replied that he had outraged the wife of an Israelite. He said to him: I dreamt that I walked in the shade of a myrtle. He replied that he had outraged a betrothed maiden. He said to him: I dreamt there was a shadow over me and yet it was beneath me. He replied that he had gratified an unnatural lust. He said to him: I dreamt that ravens came to my bed. He replied: Thy wife has been unfaithful with many men. He said to him: I dreamt that doves came to my bed. He replied: Many women hast thou defiled. He said to him: I dreamt that I held two doves and they flew away. He replied: Thou didst marry two women and parted from them without a document of divorce. He said to him: I dreamt that I was shelling eggs. He replied: The dead hast thou stripped. He said to him, "I am guilty of all these acts with the exception of the last which is not [true]." Just then a woman came and said to him, "That cloak which thou art wearing belonged to so-and-so who died and thou didst strip him of it." He said to him: I dreamt that I was told, "Thy father has left thee property in Cappadocia[3]." He asked, "Hast thou property in Cappadocia?" He replied, "No." "Hast thy father been to Cappadocia?" "No," he answered. "In that case *Kappa* means 'a beam' and *Deka* 'ten.' Go, examine the beam which heads number ten, for it is full of coins[4]." He went and found it full of coins.

[1] *M.*: Simeon b. Joseph; but *D.S.* thinks the true reading to be R. Ishmael b. R. Josē, which is adopted by Bacher, *A. T.* I. p. 257 n. 6.

[2] When the interpretation refers to a moral delinquency, the reply is in the third person.

[3] A district in Asia Minor.

[4] In this version, the name is regarded as a combination of the Aramaic *Ḳōfā* "a beam," and the Greek δέκα "ten." But there is another version in the Palestinian *Talmūd*, Ma'ᵃsēr Shēnī, IV. 55 *b*, where it is considered to be made up of κάππα "twenty" and δόκοι "beams." See Krauss, p. 559.

R. Ḥannina said: Who dreams of a well will see peace; as it is said, "And Isaac's servants digged in the valley, and found there a well of living water" (Gen. xxvi. 19)[1]. R. Nathan[2] said: He will find *Tōrāh*; as it is said, "Whoso findeth me findeth *life*" (Prov. viii. 35), and it is written here "a well of *living* water[3]." Raba said: [It means] life literally.

Dreams explained.

R. Ḥanan[4] said: There are three [types of dreams which indicate] peace—a river, bird and pot. "A river"—for it is written, "Behold I will extend peace to her like a river" (Is. lxvi. 12). "A bird"—for it is written, "As birds hovering, so will the Lord of hosts protect Jerusalem" (*ibid.* xxxi. 5). "A pot"—for it is written, "Lord, Thou wilt establish[5] peace for us" (*ibid.* xxvi. 12). R. Ḥannina said: But it must be a pot in which there is no meat; for it is said[6], "They chop them in pieces, as that which is in the pot, and as flesh within the caldron" (Micah iii. 3)[7].

Dreams which indicate peace.

R. Joshua b. Levi said: Who dreams of a river should on rising say, "Behold I will extend peace to her like a river" (Is. lxvi. 12), before another verse occurs to him, viz.: "For distress will come in like a river" (*ibid.* lix. 19). Who dreams of a bird should on rising say, "As birds hovering so will the Lord of hosts protect" (*ibid.* xxxi. 5), before another verse occurs to him, viz.: "As a bird that wandereth from her nest, so is a man that wandereth from his place" (Prov. xxvii. 8). Who dreams of a pot should on rising say, "Lord, Thou wilt establish [*shāpat*] peace for us" (Is. xxvi. 12), before another verse occurs to him, viz.: "Set on [*shāpat*] the pot, set it on" (Ezek. xxiv. 3). Who dreams of grapes should on rising say, "I found Israel like grapes in the wilderness" (Hos. ix. 10) before another verse occurs to him, viz.: "Their grapes are grapes of gall" (Deut. xxxii. 32). Who dreams of a mountain should on rising say, "How beautiful upon the mountains are the feet of the messenger of good tidings" (Is. lii. 7), before another verse occurs to him, viz.: "For the mountains will I take up a weeping and wailing" (Jer. ix. 9). Who dreams of a horn should on rising say, "And it shall come to pass in that

Quoting Scripture to confirm the favourable interpretation of a dream.

[1] "Living" water being a symbol of peace.

[2] Read probably R. Jonathan; cf. *A. P. A.* I. p. 64 n. 2.

[3] By the argument *Gezērāh Shāwāh* (see p. 18 n. 5) it is deduced that it was *Tōrāh* that Isaac discovered.

[4] *M.*: Ḥannina.

[5] The word here used, *shāpat*, is commonly used in the sense of setting a pot on the fire.

[6] For שנינו read שנאמר.

[7] Hence "flesh within the caldron" denotes strife, not peace.

day, that a great horn shall be blown" (Is. xxvii. 13), before another verse occurs to him, viz.: "Blow ye the horn of Gibeah" (Hos. v. 8). Who dreams of a dog should on rising say, "But against any of the children of Israel shall not a dog whet his tongue" (Exod. xi. 7), before another verse occurs to him, viz.: "Yea, the dogs are greedy" (Is. lvi. 11). Who dreams of a lion should on rising say, "The lion hath roared, who will not fear?" (Amos iii. 8), before another verse occurs to him, viz.: "A lion is gone up from his thicket" (Jer. iv. 7). Who dreams of shaving should on rising say, "And [Joseph] shaved himself and changed his raiment" (Gen. xli. 14), before another verse occurs to him, viz.: "If I be shaven, then my strength will go from me" (Judges xvi. 17). Who dreams of a well should on rising say, "A well of living waters" (Cant. iv. 15), before another verse occurs to him, viz.: "As a cistern welleth with her waters, so she welleth with her wickedness" (Jer. vi. 7). Who dreams of a reed should on rising say, "A bruised reed shall he not break" (Is. xlii. 3), before another verse occurs to him, viz.: "Behold, thou trustest upon the staff of this bruised reed" (*ibid.* xxxvi. 6).

Interpretation of dreams.

Our Rabbis have taught: Who dreams of a reed [*ḳānēh*] may hope for wisdom; as it is said, "Get [*ḳᵉnēh*] wisdom" (Prov. iv. 5). Who dreams of reeds may hope for understanding; as it is said, "With all thy getting get understanding" (*ibid. v.* 7)[1]. R. Zera said: A pumpkin [*ḳārā*], a palm-heart [*ḳōrā*], wax [*ḳīrā*] and a reed [*ḳanyā*] are all auspicious in a dream[2]. There is a teaching[3]: Nobody is shown a gourd [in a dream] except him who is a fearer of Heaven with all his strength[4]. Who dreams of an ox should on rising say, "His firstling bullock, majesty is his" (Deut. xxxiii. 17), before another occurs to him, viz.: "If an ox gore a man" (Exod. xxi. 28).

Dreaming of an ox.

Our Rabbis have taught: Five things are said in connection with the ox: Who [dreams that he] eats of its flesh will grow rich; that an ox had gored him, he will have sons who will contend with[5] each other in *Tōrāh*; that it bit him, sufferings will come upon him; that it kicked him, a long journey is destined for him;

1 The word "get" is repeated, hence the plural "reeds."

2 Because of the resemblance of the words to "reed" which has a favourable interpretation.

3 *M.*: Rab Joseph taught.

4 Because of the resemblance of the word for "gourd" with "My eyes *fail* with looking upward" (Is. xxxviii. 14).

5 *Lit.* gore.

that he rode upon it, he will ascend to greatness. But there is a teaching: [One who dreams of] riding upon an ox will die! There is no contradiction, the former referring [to a dream wherein] he rides upon the ox, the latter to when the ox rides on him.

Dreams about animals, etc.

Who dreams of an ass may hope for salvation[1]; as it is said, "Behold thy king cometh unto thee; he is triumphant and victorious, lowly, and riding upon an ass" (Zech. ix. 9). Who dreams of a cat in a place where the word for it is *Shunnārā*, a beautiful song [*shīrāh nāāh*] will be composed in his honour; [but where the word for it is] *Shinnārā*, a change for the worse [*shinnūi ra'*] is in store for him[2]. Who dreams of grapes, if they are white, both in their season and out of season, they are a good omen; if they are black, in their season they are a good omen, but out of season a bad omen[3]. Who dreams of a white horse, whether standing still or galloping, it is a good omen for him; if it is roan, should it be standing still, it is a good omen; should it be galloping, it is a bad omen. Who dreams of Ishmael, his prayer will be heard[4]; but only of Ishmael the son of Abraham, and not of an ordinary Arab[5]. Who dreams of a camel, death had been decreed upon him by Heaven, but he has been delivered therefrom. R. Ḥamma[6] b. R. Ḥannina said: What is the Scriptural authority for this? "I will go down with thee into Egypt; and I will also surely bring thee up again" (Gen. xlvi. 4)[7]. Rab Naḥman b. Isaac[8] said: It may be derived from the following, "The Lord also[9] hath put away thy sin; thou shalt not die" (II Sam. xii. 13). Who dreams of Phineas, a miracle will be wrought for him[10]. Who dreams of an elephant [*pīl*], miracles [*pelā'ōt*] will be wrought for him;

1 *M.*: the Messiah.

2 *M.* reads: Where the word for it is *Shunnārā*, a change for the worse is in store for him; where the word for it is *Shūrānā*, a beautiful song will be composed in his honour.

3 *M.* adds: He should offer up supplication. If [he dreamt] that he had eaten them, he is assured that he is a son of the world to come.

4 Cf. Gen. xxi. 17.

5 The Arabs were descended from Ishmael.

6 *M.*: Abba.

7 "Surely bring up," in Hebrew *gam 'ālōh*, which suggests *gāmāl* "camel."

8 *M.* omits: b. Isaac.

9 The word "also," *gam*, is connected with γάμμα, with the meaning of "camel." In place of this verse there is a variant in which Ps. lii. 7 is quoted; Bacher, *A. B. A.* (2nd ed.) add. p. 13.

10 In Sanh. 82 *b* it is related of Phineas that when interceding for Israel, he overcame the opposition of the ministering angels and wrought wonders for his people.

of elephants, miracles upon miracles will be performed for him. But there is a teaching: To dream of all kinds of animals is a good omen with the exception of the elephant and ape! There is no

fol. 57 a. contradiction; the former referring to animals which are bridled, the latter to those which are not bridled. Who dreams of the name "Huna," a miracle will be wrought for him[1]; of "Ḥannina, Ḥᵃnanya, Johanan," miracles will be wrought for him. Who dreams of a *Hespēd*[2], from Heaven will pity and redemption be vouchsafed him. This only applies [to him who sees in his dream the word *Hespēd*] in writing[3]. [Who dreams] that he makes the response "May His great name be blessed" is assured that he is a son of the world to come. [Who dreams] that he recites the *Shᵉma'* is meet that the *Shᵉkīnāh* should rest upon him[4], but his generation is not worthy of it. Who dreams that he lays the *Tᵉfillīn* may hope for greatness; as it is said, "And all the peoples of the earth shall see that the name of the Lord is called upon thee, and they shall fear thee" (Deut. xxviii. 10)[5]; and there is a teaching: R. Eliezer the Great says: This refers to the *Tᵉfillīn* worn on the head. Who dreams that he is saying the *Tᵉfillāh*, it is a good omen for him; but this applies only when he does not conclude it[6].

Dreaming of sexual inter-course. Who dreams of having intercourse with his mother may hope for understanding[7]; as it is said, "Yea, thou wilt call understanding 'mother'" (Prov. ii. 3)[8]. [Who dreams] of having intercourse with a betrothed maiden may hope for *Tōrāh*; as it is said, "Moses commanded us a law [*Tōrāh*], an inheritance of the congregation of Jacob" (Deut. xxxiii. 4)—read not *mōrāshāh* "an inheritance" but *mᵉ'ōrāsāh* "betrothed maiden." Who dreams of having had intercourse with his sister may hope for wisdom; as it is said, "Say unto wisdom, thou art my sister" (Prov. vii. 4). Who dreams

[1] Because the name contains the letter N, the initial of the word *nēs*, "miracle." The other names mentioned have the letter more than once.

[2] Funeral oration. The first two letters of the word are connected with *ḥūs* "to have pity" and the last two with *pādāh* "to redeem."

[3] And does not dream of attending a funeral oration.

[4] *M.* adds: like Moses our teacher.

[5] See fol. 6 *a*, p. 29.

[6] I.e. he wakes up before the *Tᵉfillāh* is ended.

[7] Suetonius, *Julius Caesar*, § 7, relates that Caesar had such a dream, and it was interpreted to mean that he was destined for high rank. (Wiesner, p. 128.)

[8] The textual rendering is "Yea if thou wilt call for understanding." But *im* "if" is read as *ēm* "mother."

of having had intercourse with a married woman is assured that he is a son of the world to come; but this applies only if he was not acquainted with her and did not think of her during the evening.

Dreaming of wheat and barley and fruits.

R. Ḥiyya b. Abba said[1]: Who dreams of wheat will see peace; as it is said, "He maketh thy borders peace; He giveth thee in plenty the fat of wheat" (Ps. cxlvii. 14). Who dreams of barley, his iniquities will depart[2]; as it is said, "Thine iniquity is taken away, and thy sin expiated" (Is. vi. 7). R. Zera said: I never went up from Babylon to the Land of Israel without dreaming of barley[3]. Who dreams of a well-laden vine, his wife will not miscarry; as it is said, "Thy wife shall be as a fruitful vine" (Ps. cxxviii. 3). [Who dreams] of a choice vine may hope for the Messiah; as it is said, "Binding his foal unto the vine and his ass' colt unto the choice vine" (Gen. xlix. 11)[4]. Who dreams of the fig, his *Tōrāh* will be preserved within him; as it is said, "Whoso keepeth the fig-tree shall eat the fruit thereof" (Prov. xxvii. 18)[5]. Who dreams of pomegranates, if small, his business will bear fruit like the pomegranate; if large, his business will grow like the pomegranate; if split open, should he be a disciple of the wise, he may hope for *Tōrāh*; as it is said, "I would cause thee to drink of spiced wine, of the juice of my pomegranate" (Cant. viii. 2); but should he be an *'Am hā'āreṣ*, he may hope for commandments [to perform], as it is said, "Thy temples [*raḳḳāh*] are like a pomegranate split open" (*ibid.* iv. 3). What means *raḳḳāh*? Even the illiterate [*rēḳānīm*] amongst thee will be full of commandments as a pomegranate [is full of seeds]. Who dreams of olives, if small, his business will be fruitful and multiply and endure like olives. But this applies only to [dreaming of] the fruit; if [he dreamt] of olive-trees, then he will have numerous offspring; as it is said, "Thy children like olive-plants, round about thy table" (Ps. cxxviii. 3). Some say that he who dreams of the olive, a good name will proceed from him; as it is said, "The Lord called thy name a leafy olive-tree, fair and goodly fruit" (Jer. xi. 16). Who dreams of olive-oil may hope for the light of *Tōrāh*; as it is said, "That they bring unto thee pure olive-oil beaten for the

1 *M.* omits.

2 *Se'ōrīm* "barley" suggests *sār 'āwōn* "iniquity has departed."

3 It was popularly thought that a visit to the Holy Land brought expiation for sin. See p. 375 n. 2.

4 This verse having a Messianic significance.

5 The *Tōrāh* is compared to the fig-tree, 'Ērūbīn 54 *a*, bot.

light" (Exod. xxvii. 20). Who dreams of palms, his iniquities will be ended[1]; as it is said, "The punishment of thine iniquity is accomplished, O daughter of Zion" (Lam. iv. 22).

Various dreams interpreted. Rab Joseph said: Who dreams of a goat, the year will be blessed for him; of goats, years will be blessed for him; as it is said, "And there will be goat's milk enough for thy food" (Prov. xxvii. 27). Who dreams of the myrtle[2], his business undertakings will prosper; and if he has no business undertakings, an inheritance will fall to his lot from some other place. 'Ulla said (another version: It was taught in a *Bārāitā*): This only applies when he sees [the myrtle] on its stem. Who dreams of a citron, will be honoured before his Maker; as it is said, "The fruit of goodly trees, branches of palm-trees" (Lev. xxiii. 40). Who dreams of a palm-branch has but one heart for his Father in Heaven. Who dreams of a goose may hope for wisdom[3]; as it is said, "Wisdom crieth aloud in the street" (Prov. i. 20); and he who [dreams of having] intercourse with it will become the Principal of a Seminary. Rab Ashē said: I dreamt of seeing one and having intercourse with it, and I ascended to greatness[4]. Who dreams of a cock may hope for a son, of cocks may hope for sons, of hens[5] may hope for a beautiful rearing [of his children] and rejoicing. Who dreams of eggs, his petition remains in suspense[6]; if broken, his petition has been granted. Similarly is it with nuts and cucumbers and all glass vessels and all such breakable articles. [Who dreams] that he entered a town, his desires will be fulfilled for him; as it is said, "And He led them unto their desired haven" (Ps. cvii. 30). Who dreams of shaving his head, it is a good omen for him[7]; [of shaving] his head and beard, [it is a good omen] for him and all his family. [Who dreams] that he is sitting in a small boat, a good name will proceed from him; if in a big boat, then from him and all his family; but that only applies when it is sailing high

[1] *Tᵉmārīm* "palms" suggests *tammū mōrīm* "finished are the rebels (i.e. sinners)."

[2] Which has numerous leaves.

[3] Among the Romans the goose was deemed a wise animal (Wiesner, p. 128).

[4] He became Principal of the Seminary in Sura.

[5] *Tarnᵉgōl* "hen" suggests the interpretation that follows.

[6] Rashi explains that while the egg-shell remains unbroken, one is doubtful of its contents. Pinner suggests that the interpretation may be due to resemblance between the Aramaic words for "egg" and "petition"; and as when the egg is broken it is finished with, that suggests a petition granted. The Rev. A. Newman writes, "A spherical body, like an egg, cannot stand firm. Hence, as the egg is unstable, so is the fulfilment of the petition uncertain."

[7] See p. 370.

on the seas. Who dreams that he is performing the functions of nature, it is a good omen for him; as it is said, "He that is bent down shall speedily be loosed[1]" (Is. li. 14). But that only applies if he does not [dream of] wiping himself. Who dreams of ascending to the roof will ascend to greatness; of descending, he will descend from greatness. Abbai and Raba both say: Since he has ascended, he has ascended[2]. Who dreams of rending his garments, the Divine decree will be rent for him. Who dreams of standing naked, if in Babylon he will stand without sin; but if in the Land of Israel, [he will stand] naked without commandments[3]. Who dreams that he has been arrested by the police[4], the Divine protection will be vouchsafed him. [If he dreamt] that they placed him in neck-chains[5], the Divine protection will be doubly vouchsafed him; but this applies only to a neck-chain, not to a common cord. Who dreams of walking into a pool[6] will be appointed Principal of a Seminary; into a forest[7], he will be made the head of the Collegiates.

Dreams which signify promotion to the headship of the Seminary.

Rab Pappa and Rab Huna b. Rab Joshua had a dream. Rab Pappa [dreamt that he] walked into a pool and was appointed the Principal of a Seminary, and Rab Huna b. Rab Joshua that he walked into a forest and was made the head of the Collegiates. Another version is: They both [dreamt that they] walked into a pool; but Rab Pappa, who was wearing a drum[8] around his neck, was made Principal of the Seminary, whereas Rab Huna b. Rab Joshua, who had no drum around his neck, was made the head of the Collegiates. Rab Ashē said: I [once dreamt that I] walked into a pool, with a drum around my neck, and I made a noise therewith[9].

[1] The Hebrew words for "bent down" and "excrement" are somewhat similar in sound.

[2] And will not be deposed.

[3] The interpretation is explained by two Talmudical statements: "Who dwells in the Land of Israel abides sinless" (Kᵉtūbōt 111 *a*) and "Who dwells outside the Land of Israel is as though he worshipped idols" (*ibid.* 110 *b*). Therefore naked in Babylon means without the sins one would expect there; and naked in Palestine means without having fulfilled the commandments which distinguish Jewish life there from that elsewhere.

[4] And is securely guarded by them.

[5] Indicating additional precautions.

[6] Where there are large and small reeds, figurative of students of different ages.

[7] Where all the trees are full-grown, representing mature students.

[8] A drum was carried in the East before a man of eminence and beaten to attract attention and secure respectful salutation.

[9] He was subsequently appointed Principal of the Seminary in Sura.

Dreaming of blood-letting.

A *Tannā* taught in the presence of Rab Naḥman b. Isaac[1]: Who dreams of blood-letting, his sins will be pardoned him[2]. But there is a teaching: His sins are set in order for him! What means "set in order"? Set in order so as to be pardoned.

Dreaming of a serpent.

A *Tannā* taught in the presence of Rab Sheshet: Who dreams of a serpent, his sustenance will be provided him; if it bit him, his sustenance will be doubled for him; if he killed it, his sustenance is lost. Rab Sheshet said to him: [When he dreams of killing the serpent], how much more likely is it that his sustenance will be doubled! But it is not so; and it was Rab Sheshet who dreamt that he saw a serpent and killed it[3].

Dreaming of liquids.

A *Tannā* taught in the presence of R. Joḥanan[4]: To dream of any kind of liquids is a good omen, with the exception of wine. Some [dream they] drink it and it is a good omen for them, and some do so and it is a bad omen for them. There are some who [dream they] drink it and it is a good omen for them, as it is said, "Wine that maketh glad the heart of man" (Ps. civ. 15); and there are some who [dream they] drink it and it is a bad omen for them, as it is said, "Give strong drink unto him that is ready to perish, and wine unto the bitter in soul" (Prov. xxxi. 6). R. Joḥanan said to the *Tannā*: Teach that in the case of a disciple of the wise, it is always a good omen; as it is said, "Come, eat of my bread, and drink of the wine which I have mingled" (*ibid.* ix. 5).

fol. 57 b.

R. Joḥanan said: If one wakes up and a verse comes to his mouth, it is to be regarded as a minor prophecy[5].

Dreaming of kings, the Scriptures, etc.

Our Rabbis have taught: There are three kings [to dream of whom has significance]. Who dreams of David may hope for piety; of Solomon, may hope for wisdom; of Ahab, he should be concerned about punishment. There are three prophets [to dream of whom has significance]. (Who dreams of the Book of Kings may hope for greatness;)[6] of Ezekiel, may hope for wisdom; of Isaiah, may hope for consolation; of Jeremiah, he should be concerned about punishment. There are three major books of the Hagiographa [to dream of which has significance]. Who dreams of the Book of Psalms may hope for piety; of Proverbs, may hope for

1 *M.* omits: b. Isaac.
2 Sins are described as crimson, Is. i. 18.
3 He accordingly wished to give it a favourable interpretation.
4 *M.*: Rab Naḥman.
5 Repeated from fol. 55 *b*, p. 363.
6 This sentence is out of place, and is omitted by *M.*

wisdom; of Job, he should be concerned about punishment. There are three minor books of the Hagiographa [to dream of which has significance]. Who dreams of the Song of Songs may hope for piety; of Ecclesiastes, may hope for wisdom; of Lamentations, he should be concerned about punishment; and he who dreams of the Scroll of Esther, a miracle will be wrought for him. There are three Sages [to dream of whom has significance]. Who dreams of Rabbi[1] may hope for wisdom; of R. Eleazar b. 'Azariah[2], may hope for wealth; of Ishmael b. Elisha[3], he should be concerned about punishment. There are three disciples of the wise[4] [to dream of whom has significance]. Who dreams of Ben 'Azzai[5] may hope for piety; of Ben Zoma, may hope for wisdom; of Aḥēr[6], he should be concerned about punishment.

Classes of dreams which are a good omen, and their exceptions.

To dream of any species of animal is a good omen with the exception of the elephant, monkey and long-tailed ape[7]. But a teacher has said: Who dreams of an elephant, a miracle will be wrought for him! There is no contradiction; the latter refers to where it is bridled and the other to where it is not bridled[8]. To dream of any kind of metal-tool is a good omen, with the exception of the hoe, the mattock and the axe; but this applies only when he sees them with their handles. To dream of any kind of fruit is a good omen with the exception of unripe dates. To dream of any kind of vegetables is a good omen with the exception of turnip-heads. But Rab[9] said: I did not become rich until I dreamt of turnip-heads! When he saw them, he saw them on their stem. To dream of any kind of colour is a good omen with the exception of blue. To dream of any kind of birds is a good omen with the exception of the owl, the horned owl and the bat[10].

(The body; The body; Essence; Restore; Enlarge—mnemonic[11].)

1 I.e. Judah the Prince; but *M.* reads "R. 'Aḳiba."

2 He was very rich; see fol. 27 *b*, p. 181.

3 He suffered martyrdom under the Romans. See p. 35 n. 2.

4 They are not called "Sages" because they had not received ordination as Rabbis.

5 He was renowned as an ascetic; cf. Graetz, *Gnosticismus und Judentum*, pp. 71 f.

6 *Lit.* "another," the name given to Elisha b. Abuya who became a heretic. See Ḥagīgāh 15 *a*, ed. Streane, pp. 83 ff.

7 Read with *M. ḳippōf* for *ḳippōd.*

8 See fol. 56 *b*, p. 372.

9 *M.* adds: Ashē.

10 It is very doubtful whether the last word *ḳūrpᵉrāi* means "bat." *M.* omits it here, but precedes this sentence with: To dream of any kind of reptile is a good omen with the exception of the mole (*ḳūpᵉdāi*).

11 See p. 214 n. 4.

Things which do and do not benefit the body. Three things enter the body without its deriving any benefit therefrom; melilot[1], date-berries and unripe dates. Three things do not enter the body, but it derives benefit therefrom: washing, anointing and regular motions [*tashmīsh*]. Three things are of the essence of the world to come: the Sabbath, the sun and *tashmīsh*. *Tashmīsh* of what? Are we to suppose *tashmīsh* of the bed[2]? That weakens! No; *tashmīsh* of the orifices. Three things restore a man's [tranquillity of] mind: melodious sound, sight and smell. Three things enlarge a man's mind[3]: a beautiful home, a beautiful woman and beautiful utensils.

(Five and six and ten—mnemonic.)

Five things a sixtieth of something else. Five things are a sixtieth part of something else: fire, honey, the Sabbath, sleep and a dream. Fire is a sixtieth part of *Gēhinnōm*; honey a sixtieth of manna; the Sabbath a sixtieth of the world to come; sleep a sixtieth of death; a dream the sixtieth of prophecy.

Six favourable symptoms in an invalid. Six things are a favourable symptom in an invalid: sneezing, perspiration, abdominal motion, seminal emission, sleep and a dream. "Sneezing"—for it is written, "His sneezings flash forth light" (Job xli. 10). "Perspiration"—for it is written, "In the sweat of thy face shalt thou eat bread" (Gen. iii. 19). "Abdominal motion"—for it is written, "He that is bent down shall speedily be loosed; and he shall not go down dying into the pit" (Is. li. 14). "Seminal emission"—for it is written, "Seeing seed, he will prolong his days" (*ibid.* liii. 10). "Sleep"—for it is written, "I should have slept, then had I been at rest" (Job iii. 13). "A dream"—for it is written, "Thou didst cause me to dream[4] and make me to live" (Is. xxxviii. 16).

Remedies for sickness. Six things cure an invalid from his sickness and their remedy is an [efficacious] remedy, viz.: cabbage, beet, a decoction of dried poley, the maw, the womb and the large lobe of the liver[5]. Some add: Also small fish; more than that, small fish make a man's whole body fruitful and strong[6].

Ten things harmful to an invalid. Ten things cause an invalid to relapse and his sickness becomes worse, viz.: to eat the flesh of the ox, fat meat, roast meat, poultry, roasted egg; also shaving, and partaking of cress, milk, cheese; and bathing. Some add: Also nuts; others add: Also cucumbers.

[1] A kind of clover used as a relish.
[2] I.e. sexual intercourse, the meaning which the word usually has.
[3] Meaning, put him into a cheerful frame of mind.
[4] See p. 356 n. 8.
[5] See fol. 44 *b*, p. 289.
[6] See fol. 40 *a*, p. 263 n. 10.

The school of R. Ishmael taught: Why are they called "cucumbers" [*ḳishshūīm*]? Because they are injurious [*ḳāshīm*] to the body like swords. But it is not so! For lo, it is written, "And the Lord said unto her, Two nations are in thy womb" (Gen. xxv. 23)—read not *gōyīm* "nations," but *gē'īm* "lords"; and Rab Judah said in the name of Rab: These are Antoninus and Rabbi[1] from whose table radish, lettuce and *cucumbers* were never absent either in Summer or Winter! There is no contradiction; the large ones [are injurious], the small ones [beneficial].

Dreaming of matters connected with a house.

Our Rabbis have taught: [If one dreams] there is a corpse in the house, there will be peace in the house; that he was eating and drinking in the house, it is an auspicious omen for the house; that he took a vessel from the house, it is an inauspicious omen for the house. Rab Pappa explained [the "vessel" to refer to] a shoe or sandal. Everything that the corpse takes away [if seen in a dream] is auspicious with the exception of a shoe or sandal[2]; and everything that the corpse gives is auspicious with the exception of dust and mustard[3].

[*He who beholds*] *a place from which idolatry has been uprooted.*

Benediction over a place from which idolatry has been uprooted.

Our Rabbis have taught: (Who sees a statue of Hermes says, "Blessed...Who hast shown long-suffering to those who transgress Thy will[4]"). [If he sees] a place from which idolatry has been uprooted, he should say, "Blessed...Who hast uprooted idolatry from our land; and as it has been uprooted from this place, so may it be uprooted from all places of Israel. And do Thou turn the heart of those who serve idols to serve Thee." But if this is outside the Land [of Israel], it is unnecessary to say "And do Thou turn the heart of those who serve idols to serve Thee," because most of them are gentiles. R. Simeon b. Eleazar said: The benediction should also be uttered outside the Land, because they will in the future become converted; as it is said, "For then will I turn to the peoples a pure language" (Zeph. iii. 9).

Benedictions to be said in Babylon.

Rab Hamnuna expounded: Who sees the wicked Babylon should utter five benedictions. If he sees Babylon, he says "Blessed... Who hast destroyed wicked Babylon." If he sees the palace of

[1] Often mentioned together in the *Talmūd* as being intimate friends. Antoninus is often identified with Marcus Aurelius. See *J. E.* i. pp. 656 f. The latest and most exhaustive investigation of the material is by Krauss, *Antoninus und Rabbi*, who identifies him with Avidius Cassius, a famous general of Marcus Aurelius and Procurator of Judea.

[2] Indicating a journey.

[3] Indicating a grave and what grows upon it.

[4] This sentence is omitted by *M.* and some edd. It occurs again below.

Nebuchadnezzar, he says "Blessed...Who hast destroyed the palace of Nebuchadnezzar." If he sees the den of lions or the fiery furnace, he says "Blessed...Who hast performed miracles for our fathers in this place." If he sees a statue of Hermes, he says "Blessed... Who hast shown long-suffering to those who transgress Thy will." If he sees a place [in Babylon] from which dust is being taken away[1], he says "Blessed...Who sayest and doest, Who doth decree and fulfil." When Raba saw asses carrying this dust, he struck them upon the back with his hand and exclaimed, "Run, ye righteous, to perform the will of your Master." When Mar b. Rabina came to Babylon, he took up some earth in his mantle and cast it out, to fulfil that which was said, "I will sweep it with the besom of destruction" (Is. xiv. 23). Rab Ashē said: I had not heard that of Rab Hamnuna, but from my own mind I said all those benedictions.

fol. 58 a. The curse pronounced over Babylon and Samaria.

R. Jeremiah b. Eleazar said: When Babylon was cursed, her neighbours were cursed; but when Samaria was cursed, her neighbours were blessed. When Babylon was cursed, her neighbours were cursed; for it is written, "I will also make it a possession for the bittern, and pools of water" (*ibid.*)[2]. When Samaria was cursed, her neighbours were blessed; for it is written, "Therefore I will make Samaria a heap in the field, a place for the planting of vineyards" (Micah i. 6).

Benediction on beholding a crowd of Israelites.

Rab Hamnuna also said: Who beholds crowds of Israelites should say "Blessed...Who art wise in secrets[3]"; but [on beholding] crowds of idolaters he says, "Your mother shall be ashamed" etc. (Jer. l. 12). The Rabbis have taught: Who sees crowds of Israelites should say "Blessed...Who art wise in secrets," because their minds differ and their faces differ. Ben Zoma saw a crowd on top of the ascent of the Temple Mount and said, "Blessed... Who art wise in secrets, and blessed...Who hast created all these to serve me[4]."

Adam's toil to maintain himself.

[Ben Zoma] used to say: How much labour Adam must have expended before he obtained bread to eat! He ploughed, sowed, reaped, piled up the sheaves, threshed, winnowed, selected [the ears], ground, sifted [the flour], kneaded and baked, and after

[1] Possibly referring to the debris of the ruins to be used as building material elsewhere. But cf. *T. A.* I. p. 289 n. 171.

[2] It was to become perpetual ruins, and thus an eyesore to bordering States; whereas Samaria was to become a vineyard plantation.

[3] Knowing what is in the heart of each one.

[4] To attend to my wants, as explained in the next paragraph.

that he ate; whereas I get up in the morning and find all this prepared for me. And how much labour must Adam have expended before he obtained a garment to wear! He sheared, washed [the wool], combed, spun, wove, and after that he obtained a garment to wear; whereas I get up in the morning and find all this prepared for me. All artisans[1] attend and come to the door of my house, and I get up and find all these things before me.

Difference between a good and bad guest.

He used to declare: What does a good guest say? "How much trouble has my host taken on my behalf! How much meat he set before me! How much wine he set before me! How many cakes he set before me! And all the trouble he took was only for my sake." But what does the bad guest say? "What trouble has my host taken? I ate one piece of bread; I ate one slice of meat; I drank one cup of wine; and whatever trouble my host experienced was only for the sake of his wife and children." What does one say concerning a good guest? "Remember that thou magnify his work, whereof men have sung" (Job xxxvi. 24); and of a bad guest it is written, "Men do therefore fear him; he regardeth not any that are wise of heart" (*ibid.* xxxvii. 24).

Definition of "a crowd.'

"And the man was an old man in the days of Saul, stricken in years among men" (I Sam. xvii. 12). Raba (other versions: Rab Zebid, Rab Osha'ya)[2] said: This refers to Jesse, the father of David, who went out with a crowd, came in with a crowd and expounded [*Tōrāh*] with a crowd. 'Ulla said: We have received a tradition that there is no crowd in Babylon. It has been taught: A crowd must not consist of less than sixty myriads.

Benedictions on beholding Sages and kings.

Our Rabbis have taught: Who beholds the Sages of Israel should say, "Blessed...Who hast imparted of Thy wisdom to them that fear Thee"; but [on beholding] the wise men of other peoples, he says "Blessed...Who hast given of Thy wisdom to Thy creatures[3]." Who beholds the kings of Israel should say, "Blessed...Who hast imparted of Thy glory to them that fear Thee"; but [on beholding] the kings of other peoples he says, "Blessed...Who hast imparted of Thy glory to Thy creatures[3]." R. Joḥanan said: A man should always bestir himself to run to meet the kings of Israel; and not only the kings of Israel, but even to meet the kings of other peoples, for if he is worthy, he will distinguish between the kings of Israel and of other peoples[4].

[1] The text reads "peoples"; but the emendation אומניות for אומות yields better sense. *M.* omits the sentence.

[2] *M.*: Rab in the name of R. Abbahu.

[3] Some edd. read: to flesh and blood.

[4] Cf. fol. 9 *b*, p. 56 and 19 *b*, pp. 127 f.

Rab Sheshet and the *Mīn.*

Rab Sheshet was blind. Everybody went to greet a king, and Rab Sheshet arose and went with them. A certain *Mīn* met him and said, "Pitchers [go] to the river, where [go] the potsherds[1]?" He replied, "Come, see how I know things better than thou[2]." The first troop of soldiers passed by, and when a shout arose, the *Mīn* said to him, "Now the king is coming." Rab Sheshet answered, "He is not coming yet." A second troop passed, and when a shout arose, the *Mīn* said to him, "Now the king is coming." Rab Sheshet answered, "He is not coming." A third troop passed, and while there was silence, Rab Sheshet said to him, "Now certainly the king is coming." The *Mīn* asked him, "Whence hast thou this?" He replied, "Earthly kingship is like the Kingship of Heaven, of which it is written, 'Go forth, and stand upon the mount before the Lord. And behold, the Lord passed by, and a great and strong wind rent the mountains, and broke in pieces the rocks before the Lord; but the Lord was not in the wind; and after the wind an earthquake; but the Lord was not in the earthquake; and after the earthquake a fire; but the Lord was not in the fire; and after the fire a still small voice' (I Kings xix. 11 f.)." When the king arrived, Rab Sheshet began and uttered the benediction for him. The *Mīn* said to him, "For one whom thou seest not thou dost pronounce a benediction!" And what happened to that *Mīn*? Some say that his associates put his eyes out; others declare that Rab Sheshet set his eyes upon him and he became a heap of bones.

Story of R. Shela.

R. Shela flogged a certain man who had had intercourse with a gentile[3] woman; so he went and laid a charge against him before the king, saying, "There is a certain Jew who judges without the king's consent." The king sent an official for him [to appear]. When R. Shela came he was asked, "For what reason didst thou flog this person?" He replied, "Because he had intercourse with a she-ass." They said to him, "Hast thou witnesses?" He answered, "Yes." Elijah[4] came in human guise and gave evidence. They said to him, "In that case, his punishment is death." He said to them, "From the day we were exiled from our land, we have no power to inflict the death-sentence; but you do with him as you

1 A proverbial expression meaning, as it is useless to take a piece of broken earthenware to draw water, so is it useless for a blind man to go to witness a procession.

2 Although blind.

3 Some edd., fearing the Censor, read "Egyptian."

4 See p. 7 n. 5.

please." While they were considering the case, R. Shela commenced saying, "Thine, O Lord, is the greatness and the power" etc. (I Chron. xxix. 11). They asked him, "What is it thou art saying?" He replied, "I am saying, 'Blessed be the All-merciful Who has made earthly kingship like the Kingship of Heaven and has given you power and love of justice'." They said, "The honour of the kingship is very dear to him." They thereupon handed to him the staff[1] and said to him, "Do thou act as judge." When he went out, the man said to him, "Does the All-merciful perform a miracle for such liars!" He replied, "Thou evil-doer! Are not they called 'asses'? For it is written, 'Whose flesh is as the flesh of asses' (Ezek. xxiii. 20)."

Story continued.

[R. Shela] perceived that the man was going to tell them that he called them asses. He said [to himself], "That man is a pursuer, and the *Tōrāh* has stated, If one seeks to kill thee, do thou kill him first[2]"; so he smote him with the staff and killed him. He then said, "Since a miracle was wrought for me with this verse, I will expound it." [He went to the House of Study and expounded][3]: "Thine, O Lord, is the greatness"—that refers to the work of Creation; for so it is stated, "Who doeth great things past finding out" (Job ix. 10). "And the power"—that refers to the Exodus from Egypt; as it is said, "And Israel saw the great work" etc. (Exod. xiv. 31). "And the glory"—that refers to the sun and moon which stood still for Joshua; as it is said, "And the sun stood still, and the moon stayed" (Josh. x. 13). "And the victory" [*nēsaḥ*]—that refers to the overthrow of Rome[4]; for so it is stated, "And their life-blood [*nēsaḥ*] is dashed against My garments" (Is. lxiii. 3). "And the majesty"—that refers to the battle at the valleys of Arnon; as it is said, "Wherefore it is said in the book of the Wars of the Lord: Vaheb in Suphah, and the valleys of Arnon" (Num. xxi. 14)[5]. "For all that is in heaven and earth"—that refers to the war of Sisera; as it is said, "They fought from heaven, the stars in their courses fought against Sisera" (Judges v. 20). "Thine is the kingdom, O Lord"—that refers to the war of Amalek; for so it is stated, "The hand upon the throne of the Lord, the Lord will have war with Amalek from generation to

1 I.e. they give him the right to inflict punishment.

2 Deduced from Exod. xxii. 1.

3 *M.* adds these words.

4 This is probably the original reading, which has been corrupted for the sake of the Censor. *M.* reads "the wicked kingdom" and some edd. have "Babylon."

5 See fol. 54 *a*, *b*, p. 351.

generation" (Exod. xvii. 16). "And Thou art exalted"—that refers to the war of Gog and Magog[1]; for so it is stated, "Behold I am against thee, O Gog, chief prince of Meshech and Tubal" (Ezek. xxxviii. 3). "As head above all"—Rab Ḥanan b. Raba said in the name of Rab[2]: Even the waterman[3] is appointed by Heaven. In a *Bārāitā* it is taught in the name of R. 'Aḳiba: "Thine, O Lord, is the greatness"—that refers to the division of the Red Sea. "And the power"—that refers to the smiting of the first-born. "And the glory"—that refers to the giving of the *Tōrāh*. "And the victory"—that refers to Jerusalem. "And the majesty"—that refers to the Temple.

fol. 58 b. On beholding houses of Israelites and idolaters.

Our Rabbis have taught: Who sees the houses of Israelites when inhabited says, "Blessed...Who dost set the boundary of the widow[4]"; [but when he sees them] in ruins he says, "Blessed be the true Judge." [Who beholds] the houses of idolaters when they are inhabited says, "The Lord will pluck up the house of the proud" (Prov. xv. 25); [but when he sees them] in ruins he says, "O Lord, Thou God, to Whom vengeance belongeth, Thou God to Whom vengeance belongeth, shine forth" (Ps. xciv. 1).

Philanthropy of Rab Ḥanna b. Ḥ^{a}nilai.

'Ulla and Rab Ḥisda were journeying along the road. When they reached the entrance of the house of Rab Ḥanna b. Ḥ^{a}nilai, Rab Ḥisda broke down and sighed. 'Ulla asked him, "Why dost thou sigh? For lo, Rab has said: A sigh breaketh half the body of a man; as it is said, 'Sigh therefore, thou son of man, with the breaking of thy loins,' etc. (Ezek. xxi. 11); and R. Joḥanan[5] has said: It even breaks the whole body; as it is said, 'And it shall be, when they say unto thee, Wherefore sighest thou? that thou shalt say, Because of the tidings, for it cometh; and every heart shall melt' etc. (*ibid.* v. 12)." He answered him, "How should I not sigh [on beholding] a house in which there were sixty[6] cooks by day and sixty cooks by night and they baked for each person what he desired. Nor did he[7] ever take his hand away from his purse, thinking that perhaps there may come a poor man, the son of respectable people, and while he is reaching for his purse,

[1] See p. 41 n. 4.

[2] "Name of Rab" is the reading of the parallel passage, Bab. Bat. 91 *b*, and is to be adopted. Cf. Hyman, II. p. 469 a. Edd.: R. Joḥanan.

[3] A very lowly office, filled by one of the lowest class.

[4] After the destruction, Jerusalem was compared to a widow; Lam. i. 1.

[5] *M.*: Nathan.

[6] "Sixty" is often used in the *Talmūd* not literally, but to denote an indefinite number.

[7] Rab Ḥanna b. Ḥ^{a}nilai.

he would be put to shame. Moreover it had four doors open to the four directions, and whoever entered hungry came out sated. He used also to cast wheat and barley outside during the years of drought, so that anybody who was ashamed to take it by day came and took it by night. And now that it is fallen into ruins, shall I not sigh?" He said to him, "Thus spake R. Joḥanan: From the day the Temple was destroyed, a decree was issued that the houses of the righteous should be destroyed; as it is said, 'In mine ears said the Lord of hosts: Of a truth many houses shall be desolate, even great and fair, without inhabitant' (Is. v. 9). Also said R. Joḥanan[1]: The Holy One, blessed be He, will restore them to habitation; as it is said, 'A Song of Ascents. They that trust in the Lord are as Mount Zion' (Ps. cxxv. 1)—just as the Holy One, blessed be He, will restore Mount Zion to habitation, so will He restore the houses of the righteous to habitation." He perceived that his mind was still not at rest, so he said to him, "It is enough for the slave to be like his master[2]."

On beholding the graves of Israelites.

Our Rabbis have taught: Who beholds the graves of Israel says[3]: "Blessed...Who formed you in judgment, Who nourished you in judgment, sustained you in judgment, and gathered you in judgment, and will hereafter raise you in judgment." Mar b. Rabina concluded the benediction in the name of Rab Naḥman[4]: "And knowest the number of you all in judgment, and will hereafter restore you to life and cause you to survive. Blessed...Who quickenest the dead." [Who beholds] the graves of idolaters says, "Your mother shall be sore ashamed" (Jer. l. 12).

Seeing a friend after some lapse of time.

R. Joshua b. Levi said: Who sees his friend after [an interval of] thirty days says, "Blessed...Who hast kept us in life, and hast preserved us, and enabled us to reach this season." After [an interval of] twelve months he says, "Blessed...Who quickenest the dead." Rab said: The dead is only forgotten from the heart after twelve months[5]; as it is said, "I am forgotten as a dead man out of mind; I am like a lost vessel" (Ps. xxxi. 13)[6].

[1] *M.*: Rab Naḥman said; and *D.S.* mentions another variant, Rab Naḥman b. Isaac.

[2] I.e. why should Rab Ḥanna's house meet with a better fate than the Temple which had been destroyed?

[3] What follows is included in the Burial Service; see Singer, p. 319.

[4] *M.* adds: b. Isaac.

[5] *M.* inserts here: What is the Scriptural authority for this? Rab Aḥa b. Rab Jacob said.

[6] If an article was lost and not found within twelve months, it was deemed irrecoverable.

Fate of Rab Ḥannina b. Rab Iḳa.

Rab Pappa and Rab Huna b. Rab Joshua were journeying along the road and met Rab Ḥannina b. Rab Iḳa. They said to him, "Since we have seen thee, we will offer two benedictions on thine account: 'Blessed...Who impartest Thy wisdom to them that fear Thee' and 'Blessed...Who hast kept us in life' etc." He replied, "I also, since I have seen you, deem you to be in my eyes like the sixty myriads of the house of Israel and say three benedictions on your account: the two you have uttered and also 'Blessed...Who art wise in secrets[1].'" They said to him, "Art thou as wise as all that?" They set their eyes on him and he died[2].

Beholding men with deformities.

R. Joshua b. Levi said: Who beholds men smitten with a leprous eruption says, "Blessed...Who variest the forms of Thy creatures." It is quoted in objection: Who beholds a negro, a red-spotted or white-spotted person, a hunchback, dwarfed or dropsical person says, "Blessed...Who variest the forms of Thy creatures"; but [on beholding] a person with an amputated limb, or blind, or flat-headed, or lame, or smitten with boils or a leprous eruption he says, "Blessed be the true Judge"! There is no contradiction; the former refers to one suffering thus from his mother's womb, the other to one suffering thus after birth. This is also proved from the fact that he teaches that [the man afflicted with leprous eruption] is like the person with an amputated limb[3]. Deduce from this [that the leper referred to in the *Bārāitā* is one who became diseased after birth].

Benedictions on beholding elephant, ape, or beautiful works of creation.

Our Rabbis have taught: Who beholds an elephant, or monkey or long-tailed ape says, "Blessed...Who variest the forms of Thy creatures[4]." If he beholds beautiful works of creation and fine trees he says, "Blessed...to Whom it is thus in Thy universe."

Shooting stars.

II. *For shooting stars* [Zīḳīn].

What means *Zīḳīn*? Samuel said: *Kōkᵉbā di-Shᵉbīṭ*[5]. Samuel also said: The paths of heaven are as familiar to me as the streets

1 The benediction to be said on beholding a "crowd" of Israelites; see the preceding folio.

2 They were apparently annoyed by his excessive praise in comparing them with the sixty myriads of the house of Israel and suspected him of sarcasm. He would in that case have used the Divine Name in the benediction disrespectfully.

3 Which obviously happened after birth.

4 Wiesner (p. 136) sees here a trace of the idea that the souls of the wicked are made to inhabit the bodies of such animals. Cf. Sanh. 109 *a*.

5 Rashi explains this to mean "shooting stars." Other commentators hazard "comet." The 'Ārūk translates *Zīḳīn* "comets" and *K. di-S.* "shooting stars." They both probably mean "shooting stars." On this astronomical passage, see Brodetsky, *J. R.* II. pp. 167 ff.

of Nehardea[1], with the exception of the *Kōkᵉbā di-Shᵉbīṭ*, for I know not what that is. There is a tradition that it never passes through the constellation of Orion, for if it did the world would be destroyed. But we see that it does pass through! It is its brightness that passes through, and so it seems as though it does actually pass through. Rab Huna b. Rab Joshua[2] said: It is the Veil [*Vīlōn*] which is rent and rolled up, so that the light of the heaven [*Rᵉḳīa‘*] appears[3]. Rab Ashē said: A star disappears from one side of Orion and [the beholder] sees a companion star [appear] on the other side and is bewildered; and thus it seems as though it had passed through [the constellation][4].

Orion and the Pleiades.

Samuel asked: It is written "Who maketh the Bear, Orion and the Pleiades" (Job ix. 9) and it is written "That maketh the Pleiades and Orion" (Amos v. 8)! How is that[5]? Were it not for the heat of Orion, the world could not exist because of the coldness of the Pleiades, and were it not for the coldness of the Pleiades, the world could not exist because of the heat of Orion[6]. There is also a tradition: Were it not that the tail of the Scorpion was placed in the Fire-River[7], nobody who had been stung by a scorpion could live. That is what the All-merciful said to Job, "Canst thou bind the chains of the Pleiades, or loose the bands of Orion?" (Job xxxviii. 31).

Legend about the constellation of the Bear.

What means *Kīmāh* [the Pleiades]? Samuel said: About a hundred [*kᵉmē'āh*] stars; some say: Which are gathered together, but others say: Which are scattered. What means *‘Āsh* [the Bear]? Rab Judah said: *Jūtā*[8]. What is *Jūtā*? Some say: The tail of a ram; others say: The head of a calf. But the more probable view is that of him who said, "The tail of a ram"; for it is written, "And the ‘Ajish will be comforted for her children" (*ibid.* v. 32)[9]. Hence it seems as if something is lacking [in the tail]

1 See p. 74 n. 2. 2 *M.*: b. Judah.

3 There are "seven heavens of which the first, *Vīlōn*, was merely a 'curtain' which was withdrawn by day and replaced by night, thus alternately exposing and hiding the Sun, which, together with the moon, planets, and stars, was fixed to the second, *Rᵉḳia‘*." Brodetsky, *loc. cit.* p. 171.

4 It is merely an error of perspective (Brodetsky).

5 That the order is reversed.

6 They thus counteract each other's intensity; and that is why the same order is not retained in the two passages.

7 A mythical river mentioned in Dan. vii. 10. It is perhaps meant to denote the Milky Way; see *J. E.* IV. p. 249.

8 Wiesner identifies this with Ὑάδες, the Hyades, a group of seven stars.

9 R.V. "Or canst thou guide the Bear with her sons." But the legend that follows requires *tanḥēm* to be read as *tinnāḥēm*.

fol. 59 a. and it has the appearance of having been torn away [from the star]; and the reason that the *'Ajish* follows the *Kīmāh* is that it says to it, "Give me back my children." For when the Holy One, blessed be He, sought to bring the flood upon the world, He took two stars from the Pleiades[1] and thus brought the flood upon the world; and when He sought to stop it, He took two stars from the Bear and stopped it. But He should have restored [the original stars]! "A pit cannot be filled with its own clods[2]"; or also, "An accuser cannot become a defender[3]." Then He should have created two other stars! "There is nothing new under the sun" (Eccles. i. 9). Rab Naḥman said: The Holy One, blessed be He, will hereafter restore them; as it is said, "And the 'Ajish will be comforted for her children."

And for earthquakes.

What is an earthquake? What is an earthquake? Rab Ḳaṭṭina said: A subterranean rumbling. Rab Ḳaṭṭina was journeying by the way, and when he reached the entrance of the house of a necromancer a rumbling noise broke forth. He said, "Does the necromancer know what this rumbling is?" The latter called to him, "Ḳaṭṭina, Ḳaṭṭina! Why should I not know? When the Holy One, blessed be He, remembers His children who dwell in misery among the nations of the world, He causes two tears to descend to the Ocean, and the sound is heard from one end of the world to the other; and that is the rumbling." Rab Ḳaṭṭina said, "The necromancer lies and his words are false; for in that case, there should be one rumbling noise followed by another[4]!" But it is not so; there is really one rumbling noise followed by another, and the reason that Ḳaṭṭina did not acknowledge the necromancer's statement was that people should not be led astray after him. Rab Ḳaṭṭina himself explained [that the phenomenon was due to God] clapping His hands; as it is said, "I will also smite My hands together, and I will satisfy My fury" (Ezek. xxi. 22). R. Nathan says: The rumbling is due to His sighing; as it is said, "I will satisfy My fury upon them, and I will be eased" (*ibid.* v. 13). The Rabbis say: He treads upon the firmament; as it is said, "He giveth a noise, as they that tread grapes, against all the inhabitants of the earth" (Jer. xxv. 30). Rab Aḥa b. Jacob[5] said: He presses

[1] To let the floods through. [2] See p. 11.

[3] A proverbial expression. The two stars, having been instruments of destruction, cannot be used to bring reparation.

[4] For the *two* tears.

[5] *M.* omits: b. Jacob.

His feet beneath the Throne of Glory; as it is said, "Thus saith the Lord, the heaven is My throne, and the earth is My footstool" (Is. lxvi. 1).

And for thunders.

What is thunder? Samuel said: The clouds in a whirl; as it is said, "The voice of Thy thunder was in the whirlwind; the lightnings lighted up the world, the earth trembled and shook" (Ps. lxxvii. 19). The Rabbis say[1]: The clouds pouring water one into the other; as it is said, "At the sound of His giving a multitude of waters in the heavens" (Jer. x. 13). Rab Aḥa b. Jacob said: It is a mighty lightning-flash which strikes against a cloud and the latter is shattered into hail-stones. Rab Ashē said: The clouds are hollow[2] and a blast of wind comes and blows across their mouths, so it is like a blast across the mouth of a jar. The most probable view is that of Rab Aḥa b. Jacob, that the lightning strikes, the clouds are made to rumble and rain descends. **What is thunder?**

And for storms.

What is a storm? Abbai said: A hurricane; and further said Abbai: There is a tradition that a hurricane never happens during the night. But we have seen it occurring! It must have commenced in the daytime. Abbai likewise said: There is a tradition that a hurricane does not last two hours; to fulfil that which was said, "Trouble shall not rise up the second time" (Nahum i. 9). But we have seen it lasting [longer than that]! It stopped in between[3]. **What is a storm?**

For lightnings one says, "Blessed... Whose strength and might fill the world."

What is lightning? Raba said: A flash. Also said Raba[4]: A single flash, a white flash, a green flash, and clouds which rise in the western corner and come from the south corner, and two clouds which rise one opposite the other, are all inauspicious. What is to be deduced therefrom? That one should offer supplication. This applies only to the night[5], but in the morning there is no significance in them. Rab Samuel b. Isaac said: There is no significance in morning-clouds; for it is written, "Your goodness is as a morning cloud" (Hosea vi. 4). Rab Pappa[6] said to Abbai: But there is a proverbial expression, "If on opening the door [in the morning] there is rain, set down thy sack, O ass-driver, and **What is lightning?**

[1] *M.*: Rab said.
[2] I.e. not full of water.
[3] It was not continuous.
[4] *M.*: Rab said.
[5] *D. S.* adopts the reading of the Paris MS: to the whole of the day.
[6] *M.*: Raba.

lie on it[1]"! There is no contradiction; for this refers to [a sky] covered with heavy clouds, whereas the former refers to [a sky] covered with light clouds.

On seeing the rainbow.

R. Alexander said in the name of R. Joshua b. Levi: Thunder was only created to break the pride of the heart; as it is said, "God hath so made it that men should fear before Him" (Eccles. iii. 14). Also said R. Alexander in the name of R.[2] Joshua b. Levi: Who sees the rainbow should prostrate himself upon his face; as it is said, "As the appearance of the bow that is in the cloud...and when I saw it, I fell upon my face" (Ezek. i. 28). In the West[3] they curse one who acts thus, because it has the appearance as though he worships the rainbow; but he should certainly pronounce a benediction. What is the benediction? "Blessed...Who remembrest the Covenant." It has been taught in a *Bārāitā*: R. Ishmael, the son of R. Joḥanan b. Baroḳa says: [The benediction is, "Blessed...] Who art faithful with Thy Covenant and fulfillest Thy word." Rab Pappa said: Let us therefore say both: "Blessed...Who remembrest the Covenant, art faithful with Thy Covenant and fulfillest Thy word."

For mountains and hills...he says, "Blessed... Who hast made the Creation."

Question against the *Mishnāh* answered.

Is it then to be supposed that all the other things hitherto mentioned do not belong to the work of Creation? For lo, it is written, "He maketh[4] lightnings for the rain" (Ps. cxxxv. 7)! Abbai said: Connect them all and learn them together[5]. Raba said: In the former instances he pronounces two benedictions: "Blessed...Whose strength fills the world and Who hast made the Creation"; but here "...Who hast made the Creation" is applicable, but "Whose strength fills the world" is not applicable[6].

Seeing the firmament in its purity.

R. Joshua b. Levi said: Who sees the firmament in its purity[7] says, "Blessed...Who hast made the Creation." When is this? Abbai[8] said: When it has rained the whole night and in the morning a north wind comes and clears the sky[9]. This is at variance

[1] I.e. do not carry the corn to market, because the morning rain will make the fields fertile and wheat will be cheap.

[2] *M.*: Joḥanan. [3] Palestine. [4] I.e. created.

[5] This is explained by Raba's statement which follows.

[6] Mountains and hills are stationary and in fixed places, whereas thunder, etc. occur throughout the world.

[7] I.e. perfectly unclouded. [8] *M.*: 'Ulla.

[9] It is stated in Jōmā 21 *b*, "When the wind blows towards the North [i.e. a South wind]...there is abundant rain; when the wind blows from the North...there is little rain." Prov. xxv. 23 reads in R.V. "The North wind

with the statement of Rafram b. Pappa who said in the name of Rab Ḥisda: Since the Temple was destroyed, the firmament has never been seen in its purity; as it is said, "I clothe the heavens with blackness, and I make sackcloth their covering" (Is. l. 3).

fol. 59 b. Seeing the heavenly bodies.

Our Rabbis have taught: He who sees the sun [starting] on its new circuit or the moon in its strength, or the stars in their courses, or the planets in their order says, "Blessed...Who hast made the Creation." And when is it [that the sun starts on its new circuit]? Abbai said: Every twenty-eight years when the cycle begins again, and the Spring equinox falls in Saturn on the night of the third day of the week, which is the beginning of the fourth day[1].

R. Judah states: He who beholds the ocean says, "Blessed...Who hast made the ocean," but only when he beholds it at intervals.

Benediction on seeing the Euphrates and Tigris.

At intervals of what length? Rammi b. Abba said in the name of R. Isaac: Of thirty days. Also said Rammi b. Abba in the name of R. Isaac: Who sees the Euphrates up to the Babylonian bridge says, "Blessed...Who hast made the Creation"; but nowadays since the Persians have altered it[2], [that benediction is only to be said] from Bē Shapor[3] onwards. Rab Joseph said: From Ihi Dᵉḳira[4] onwards. Further said Rammi b. Abba: Who sees the Tigris from the bridge of Shaporstan[5] says, "Blessed...Who hast made the Creation."

Why [is the Tigris called] *Ḥiddeḳel* (Gen. ii. 14). Rab Ashē said: Its waters are sharp [*ḥad*] and swift [*ḳal*][6]. Why [is the Euphrates called] *Pᵉrāt*? Because its waters are fruitful [*pārāh*] and multiply. Rab said: The reason why the inhabitants of Maḥoza[7] are so shrewd is because they drink the waters of the Tigris; the reason why they are red-spotted is because they indulge in sexual intercourse in the daytime; and the reason why their eyes are unsteady is because they dwell in dark houses[8].

bringeth forth rain"; but it is noteworthy that the Vulgate (in which there is evidence of Jewish influence) renders: Ventus aquilo *dissipat* plurias (Wiesner, p. 144).

[1] I.e. between Tuesday and Wednesday.

[2] Diverting the course by numerous canals for irrigation.

[3] The town of Sipphara; Neubauer, p. 336.

[4] The town of Hit. Dᵉḳira is connected by Wiesner (p. 147) with *ḳirā* "wax," and is so-named because of its naphtha wells. Cf. *T. A.* I. p. 17.

[5] This is the reading of *M.* and equals "Shapor's land." Edd.: Shᵉbistānā.

[6] A similar explanation is given by Josephus, *Antiq.* I. i. 3.

[7] See p. 350 n. 4.

[8] Shaded to keep out the sun's glare.

For rain and good tidings he says, "Blessed... Who art good and dispensest good."

Benediction for rain.

But is the benediction for rain "Who art good and dispensest good"? For lo, R. Abbahu has said (another version: It was taught in a *Bārāitā*): From what time do we say the benediction over rain? From the time the bridegroom goes forth to meet his bride[1]; and what is the wording of the benediction? Rab Judah said: "We give thanks unto Thee for every drop which Thou hast caused to descend for us"; and R. Joḥanan concluded it thus: "Though our mouths were full of song as the sea...we could not sufficiently thank Thee, O Lord our God" etc. until "shall prostrate itself before Thee[2]. Blessed art Thou, O Lord, to Whom abundant thanksgivings are due." Is it "abundant thanksgivings" and not "all thanksgivings"? Raba declared: I say "God of thanksgivings." Rab Pappa said: Let us therefore say both: "Abundant thanksgivings and God of thanksgivings." Still there is a contradiction[3]! No, there is not; [the formula in the *Mishnāh*] applies when he heard [that it had been raining], the other when he actually sees it. But if he heard [that it had been raining] it is good tidings, and our *Mishnāh* states: *For good tidings one says, "Blessed... Who art good and dispensest good*[4]"! Nay, they both refer to when he actually sees it; and there is no contradiction, [the formula in the *Mishnāh*] applying when little rain fell, the other when there was a heavy downpour. Or if thou wilt I can say that both refer to a heavy downpour; and there is no contradiction, [the formula in the *Mishnāh*] applying to a landowner[5], the other to one who is not. If he be a landowner, does he say the benediction "Who art good and dispensest good"? For lo, our *Mishnāh* teaches: *He who has built a new house or bought new vessels says, "Blessed... Who hast kept us in life, preserved us and caused us to reach this season."* [If, however, the house had been built or the vessels bought] for himself and others, he says "Who art good and dispensest good[6]"! There is no contradiction; one

[1] A figurative expression. The first rain is absorbed in the soil and requires no benediction. But when the fallen drops [the bridegroom] begin to rebound towards the falling drops [the bride], then it is required.

[2] This passage is now included in the Sabbath Morning Service; Singer, pp. 125 f.

[3] On the form of benediction for rain.

[4] Therefore it was unnecessary for the *Mishnāh* to specify "For rain and good tidings," since the latter includes the former.

[5] Who has especially to be thankful for rain.

[6] It follows from this that the landowner's benediction should be "Who

refers to where there is a partnership, the other to where there is no partnership. And there is a teaching: The summary of the matter is: Over things of his own he says "Blessed...Who hast kept us in life and preserved us" etc.; over things which belong to him and another he says "Blessed...Who art good and dispensest good."

But in a case where there is not another [sharing] with him, does he not use the benediction "Who art good and dispensest good"? Lo, there is a teaching: Should they announce to him "Thy wife has given birth to a son," he says "Blessed...Who art good and dispensest good[1]"! Even here, his wife [shares the joy] with him, because she has a preference for a son[2]. Come and hear: If his father dies and he is his heir, he first says, "Blessed be the true Judge" and then "Blessed...Who art good and dispensest good"! Here also there are brothers who share the inheritance with him[3]. Come and hear: If the wine is changed [for a better kind during the meal] there is no necessity to utter another benediction; but if he changed his place[4] [and other wine is brought to him] he should utter a further benediction; and Rab Joseph b. Abba said in the name of R. Joḥanan[5]: Although it has been stated that if the wine is changed another benediction is unnecessary, still he says, "Blessed...Who art good and dispensest good"! Here also there are the other members of the company who drink with him.

Form of benediction when the good is shared with others.

III. *He who has built a new house or bought new vessels*, etc.

Rab Huna said: This only applies if he has not similar vessels, but if he has similar vessels[6] there is no need for him to say a benediction. R. Joḥanan declared: Even if he has similar vessels, he must say the benediction. From this it is to be deduced that if he bought and then made a further purchase, all agree that there is no necessity for a benediction[7]. Another version: Rab

When a benediction is necessary on acquiring new vessels.

fol. 60 a.

hast kept us in life" not "Who art good," since presumably he is the sole owner of the field.

[1] The child is his own, and yet he says the benediction to be uttered over something that is shared. [2] See p. 26 n. 5.

[3] According to the Biblical law, the entire heritage could not pass to one son. [4] Went elsewhere to finish his meal.

[5] M. omits: Joseph...Joḥanan, reading: And Rab said.

[6] I.e. by inheritance or presentation, not by purchase.

[7] In respect to the second purchase. This deduction clearly follows from Rab Huna's view, and also from R. Joḥanan's, because he only requires the benediction after the purchase when the articles the man possesses have not been bought.

Huna said: This only applies where he did not buy and make a further purchase; but if he bought and made a further purchase, there is no necessity for a benediction[1]. R. Joḥanan said: Even if he bought and made a further purchase, it is necessary to say the benediction. From this it is to be deduced that if he possesses vessels[2] and purchases more, all agree that he must say the benediction[3]. Against this is quoted: If he built a new house and he has not a similar one, or bought new vessels without possessing the like, he must say a benediction; but if he has the like, he need not say the benediction. These are the words of R. Meïr; R. Judah says: In either case, a benediction is necessary! It is quite right according to the first version; for then Rab Huna agrees with R. Meïr and R. Joḥanan with R. Judah. According to the latter version, however, it is right that Rab Huna agrees with R. Judah, but with whom is R. Joḥanan in agreement[4]? Neither with R. Meïr nor R. Judah[5]! R. Joḥanan can reply to thee: It is obvious that according to R. Judah, if a man made a purchase and then a fresh purchase, he also must say a benediction [for the latter][6]; but the point of variance [between R. Judah and R. Meïr] is where the man already possessed the article[2] and made a fresh purchase, to show the extreme view taken by R. Meïr; for even if he made a purchase, already possessing a similar article, there is no necessity for a benediction, how much more unnecessary is it if he purchased and then made a fresh purchase. But let the conflict of opinion [in the *Bārāitā* between R. Meïr and R. Judah] be in the case where the man bought an article and then purchased another and no benediction is necessary[7], to show the extreme view taken by R. Judah[8]! It is preferable to take the extreme view on the side of leniency.

The *Mishnāh* illustrated.

One says the benediction for a calamity apart from any attendant good.

How is this? For instance, if a freshet swept his field[9], although

1 Because a benediction is only required after the first purchase.

2 I.e. by inheritance or presentation, not by purchase.

3 Even Rab Huna who demands a benediction after the first purchase, irrespective of the fact whether the man possesses similar articles.

4 In requiring a benediction after a second purchase.

5 Because R. Judah only requires a benediction after a *first* purchase when a similar article is in the man's possession.

6 Thus agreeing with R. Joḥanan.

7 For the second purchase according to R. Meïr.

8 Who demands a benediction for the second purchase, and consequently R. Joḥanan would not be in agreement with him.

9 Doing damage to fences and crops.

it may be [eventually] beneficial inasmuch as the land is covered with alluvium and improves [in fertility], still for the time being it is a calamity.

And for good fortune apart from any attendant evil.

The *Mishnāh* illustrated.

For instance, if he found treasure trove, although it is bad for him because the king will hear and deprive him thereof, still for the time being it is good for him.

If his wife is pregnant and he says, "May it be Thy will that my wife bear a son," behold that is a vain prayer.

Prayer in connection with an unborn child.

Then prayer [in such circumstances] is of no avail! Rab Joseph[1] quoted in objection: "And afterwards she bore a daughter and called her name Dinah" (Gen. xxx. 21). What means "and afterwards"? Rab said[2]: After Leah passed judgment on herself, saying, "Twelve tribes are destined to issue from Jacob—six have issued from me and four from the handmaids, that makes ten; if this child [which is expected from me] be a male, my sister Rachel will not even be like one of the handmaids[3]." Immediately [the child in the womb] was changed to a daughter; as it is said, "And she called her name Dinah [judgment]"! We may not quote a miraculous event [against the *Mishnāh*]. Or if thou wilt I can say that the incident of Leah occurred within forty days [of conception], according to the teaching: During the first three days [of the conjugal act] a man may pray that [his seed] should not become abortive; from the third to the fortieth day he may pray that a male-child shall be born to him; from the fortieth day to the third month he may pray that it should not be a monstrosity[4]; from the third to the sixth month he may pray that it should not be a premature birth; from the sixth to the ninth month he may pray that it should issue in safety. But is it of any avail to pray [during the first forty days that it should be a male child]? For lo, R. Isaac b. R. Ammi[5] has said: If it is the man who first emits seed his wife bears a daughter; but if the woman first emits seed she gives birth to a son; as it is said, "If a woman emits seed[6] and bare a male child" (Lev. xii. 2)! With what are we here dealing? For instance, if they both emit seed simultaneously.

[1] *M.*: Abba. [2] *M.* omits: Rab said.

[3] Each of whom had given birth to two sons.

[4] *Sandāl*, the technical term for which is "sympodia"; cf. Feldman, *The Jewish Child*, p. 134.

[5] *M.*: R. Isaac of the School of R. Ammi; the reference being to R. Isaac b. Redifa; cf. *A. P. A.* III. p. 720 n. 8. [6] R.V. "conceive seed."

If he were on the way.

Hillel's confidence.

Our Rabbis have taught: It happened that Hillel the Elder was returning from a journey and heard a cry of lamentation in the city and said, "I am confident that it is not in my house"; and to him the Scriptural verse applies, "He shall not be afraid of evil tidings; his heart is steadfast, trusting in the Lord" (Ps cxii. 7). Raba[1] said: Whenever thou expoundest this verse, it is to be explained from the first clause to the second and from the second to the first. It is to be explained from the first clause to the second, thus: "He shall not be afraid of evil tidings." Why? "His heart is steadfast, trusting in the Lord." It is to be explained from the second clause to the first, thus: "His heart is steadfast, trusting in the Lord"; [therefore] "he shall not be afraid of evil tidings."

Sinful to show fear.

A certain disciple was following R. Ishmael b. R. Josē in the market-place of Zion. The latter noticed that he was afraid and said to him, "Thou art a sinner; for it is written, 'The sinners in Zion are afraid' (Is. xxxiii. 14)." He replied, "But it is written, 'Happy is the man that feareth alway' (Prov. xxviii. 14)!" He said to him, "This is written in connection with words of *Tōrāh*[2]."

Harmful to be afraid.

R. Judah b. R. Nathan took up [his cloak] and followed Rabbi in the market-place of Tiberias. The latter noticed that he was afraid and sighed; so he said[3], "That fellow wants sufferings to befall him; for it is written, 'For the thing which I did fear is come upon me, and that which I was afraid of hath overtaken me' (Job iii. 25)." [He replied,] "But lo, it is written, 'Happy is the man who feareth alway'!" "That is written in connection with words of *Tōrāh*."

IV. *He who enters a town should offer prayer twice.*

Prayers on entering and leaving a town.

Our Rabbis have taught: On entering, what does he say? "May it be Thy will, O Lord our God, that Thou cause me to enter this town in peace." Having entered, he says, "I give thanks before Thee, O Lord my God, for that Thou hast caused me to enter this town in peace." On desiring to depart, he says, "May it be Thy will, O Lord my God and God of my fathers, that Thou cause me to depart from this town in peace." Having left he says, "I give thanks before Thee, O Lord my God, for that Thou hast caused me to depart from this town in peace; and as Thou hast caused

[1] *M.*: Rabbah.

[2] It is good always to fear lest one neglect the study and practice of *Tōrāh*.

[3] This is the reading of *M.* adopted by Hyman, I. p. 121 b. Edd.: Judah b. Nathan...followed Rab Hamnuna; he sighed so Rab Hamnuna said.

me to depart in peace, so do Thou conduct me in peace, uphold me in peace, and direct my steps in peace, and deliver me from every enemy and ambush by the way. [Let me obtain grace, loving-kindness, and mercy in Thine eyes and in the eyes of all who behold me. Blessed art Thou, O Lord, Who hearkenest unto prayer][1]." Rab Mattᵉnah said: This prayer only applies to a town where they do not administer justice and sentence to death[2]; but in a town where they do administer justice and sentence to death, there is no need for such a petition. Another version is: Rab Mattᵉnah said: Even in a town where they administer justice and sentence to death [the prayer is necessary]; because sometimes there may not chance to be anybody to plead in his favour[3].

Prayers on entering and leaving a bath-house.

Our Rabbis have taught: Who enters a bath-house says, "May it be Thy will, O Lord my God, to deliver me from this and anything similar, and may no disgrace or iniquity befall me; but should any disgrace or iniquity befall me, may my death be an atonement for all my sins." Abbai said: Let not a man speak thus, so as not to open his mouth to Satan[4]. For said R. Simeon b. Laḳish, and it has been similarly taught in the name of R. Josē: A man should never open his mouth to Satan. Rab Joseph said[5]: What is the Scriptural authority? For it is written, "We should have been as Sodom, we should have been like unto Gomorrah" (Is. i. 9). What did the prophet answer them? "Hear the word of the Lord, ye rulers of Sodom" (*ibid.* v. 10). When he leaves [the bath-house], what does he say? R. Aḥa said[6]: "I give thanks before Thee, O Lord my God, because Thou hast delivered me from the fire." R. Abbahu entered a bath-house, and its floor gave way beneath him. A miracle occurred, and he stood upon a pillar and rescued a hundred and one men with one arm[7]. He exclaimed, "This is what R. Aḥa meant[8]."

Prayer before cupping.

Who goes in to have himself cupped should say, "May it be Thy will, O Lord my God, that this operation be a cure for me, and do Thou heal me for Thou art a faithful Healer and Thy cure is certain, since it is not the way of human beings to cure, but

[1] The words in brackets are added by *M.* See Singer, p. 310.
[2] Where there is no protection of the law and he is liable to attack.
[3] Should he be arrested on a charge of which he is innocent.
[4] See fol. 19 *a*, p. 126.
[5] *M.* omits.
[6] For "R. Aḥa said," there is a variant (see *D. S. ad loc.*) "Our Rabbis have taught" which is adopted by Bacher, *A. P. A.* III. p. 115 n. 4.
[7] *M.* adds: and 101 with the other. In the parallel passage, Kᵉtūbōt 62 *a*, "and rescued" etc. is omitted.
[8] I.e. that thanksgiving should be offered up when leaving the bath-house.

thus are they accustomed[1]." Abbai declared: Let not a man speak thus; for there is a teaching of the school of R. Ishmael: [It is written,] "Only he shall pay for the loss of his time, and shall cause him to be *thoroughly healed*" (Exod. xxi. 19); from this [it follows] that a physician is given permission [by God] to cure. When he rises [from the cupping], what does he say? R. Aḥa[2] declared, "Blessed be He Who heals without pay."

fol. 60 b. Prayers on entering and leaving a privy.

Who enters a privy says[3], "Be honoured, ye honoured and holy Beings who minister to the Most High! Give glory to the God of Israel; leave me while I enter and do my will, then shall I come unto you." Abbai said: Let not a man speak thus[4], lest they leave him and depart; but let him say, "Guard me, guard me, help me, help me, support me, support me, wait for me, wait for me until I enter and come out, for such is the way of human beings." When he comes out, he says, "Blessed...Who hast formed man in wisdom and created in him many orifices and vessels. It is revealed and known before the throne of Thy glory, that if one of these be opened, or one of those closed, it would be impossible [to exist and][5] to stand before Thee." How is it to be concluded? Rab said, "[Blessed art Thou, O Lord,] Who healest the sick." Samuel said: Does Abba[6] regard the whole world as sick[7]? Nay, [the conclusion of the benediction should be: "Blessed...] Who healest all flesh." Rab Sheshet said: [It should conclude: "Blessed...] Who doest wondrously." Rab Pappa said: Let us therefore say both: "Who healest all flesh and doest wondrously."

Prayer on retiring to rest.

Who goes in to sleep upon his bed says from "Hear, O Israel" to "And it shall come to pass, if ye shall hearken diligently"; then he says[8]: "Blessed...Who makest the bands of sleep to fall upon mine eyes, and slumber upon mine eyelids, and givest light to the apple of the eye. May it be Thy will, O Lord my God, to suffer me to lie down in peace and place my portion in Thy *Tōrāh*; and do Thou accustom me to the performance of the commandments and not to transgression; and bring me not into the power of sin, iniquity, temptation or contempt; and let the good impulse

1 Sc. to perform the operation of cupping. Abbai's view on the value of the physician's services is endorsed in Ecclus. xxxviii. 1 ff.

2 *M.*: Raba, which Bacher prefers; cf. *A. P. A. loc. cit.*

3 Addressing the angels who are supposed to accompany him.

4 Referring to the words "leave me" which *M.* inserts here.

5 Inserted by *M.* and found in the Prayer Book. See Singer, p. 4.

6 The name of Rab.

7 Since everybody has occasion to use this prayer.

8 Cf. Singer, p. 293.

have dominion over me but not the evil impulse; and do Thou deliver me from evil occurrence and sore diseases; and let not evil dreams and lustful thoughts trouble me; and let my bed be perfect before Thee, and give light to mine eyes lest I sleep the sleep of death. Blessed art Thou, O Lord, Who givest light to the whole world in Thy glory."

Prayers to be said on waking up.

When he awakens he says: "O my God, the soul which Thou hast given me is pure. Thou didst create it within me, Thou didst breathe it into me, Thou preservest it within me, and Thou wilt take it from me, but wilt restore it unto me hereafter. So long as the soul is within me, I will give thanks unto Thee, O Lord my God and God of my fathers, Sovereign of all worlds, Lord of all souls. Blessed art Thou, O Lord, Who restorest souls unto dead bodies[1]."

Morning benedictions.

When he hears the cry of the cock let him say: "Blessed...Who hast given the cock intelligence to distinguish between day and night[2]." When he opens his eyes let him say: "Blessed...Who openest the eyes of the blind." When he straightens himself and sits up let him say: "Blessed...Who loosest them that are bound." When he has clothed himself let him say: "Blessed...Who clothest the naked." When he raises himself let him say: "Blessed...Who raisest up them that are bowed down." When he descends [from the bed] to the ground let him say: "Blessed...Who spreadest forth the earth above the waters." When he walks let him say: "Blessed...Who hast made firm the steps of man." When he has tied up his shoes let him say: "Blessed...Who hast supplied my every want." When he has fastened his girdle let him say: "Blessed...Who girdest Israel with might." When he spreads the cloth upon his head let him say: "Blessed...Who crownest Israel with glory[3]." When he wraps himself with the *Ṣīṣīt* let him say: "Blessed...Who hast sanctified us by Thy commandments and hast commanded us to enwrap ourselves in the fringed garment." When he places the *Teffīlīn* upon his arm let him say: "Blessed... Who hast sanctified us by Thy commandments, and hast commanded us to lay the *Teffīlīn*"; upon the head let him say: "Blessed...Who hast sanctified us by Thy commandments, and hast commanded us concerning the precept of the *Teffīlīn*." When he has washed his hands let him say: "Blessed...Who hast sanctified us by Thy commandments and commanded us concerning

[1] See Singer, p. 5. [2] On this benediction, see Abrahams, p. xvi.

[3] These benedictions are no longer said after each act, but are all included in the Morning Service; see Singer, pp. 5 f.

the washing of the hands." When he has washed his face let him say: "Blessed...Who removest the bands of sleep from mine eyes and slumber from mine eyelids. May it be Thy will, O Lord my God, to accustom me to Thy *Tōrāh* and cause me to cleave to Thy commandments, and lead me not into the power of sin, iniquity, temptation or contempt; and subdue my will that it be subservient to Thee; and keep me far from an evil man and evil companion; and cause me to cleave to the good impulse and a good companion in Thy universe; and let me obtain this day, and every day, grace, favour and mercy in Thine eyes and in the eyes of all who behold me; and bestow lovingkindnesses upon me. Blessed art Thou, O Lord, Who bestowest lovingkindnesses upon Thy people, Israel[1]."

V. *A man is in duty bound*, etc.

Resignation to the Divine Will.

What means: *A man is in duty bound to utter a benediction for the bad even as he utters one for the good?* Are we to suppose that as for the good he says the benediction "...Who art good and dispensest good," he is to make the same benediction for the bad? For lo, our *Mishnāh* teaches: *For good tidings he says "Who art good and dispensest good"* and *For bad tidings he says "Blessed be the true Judge"*! Raba said: It is only necessary that he should receive [the bad] with gladness. R. Aḥa[2] said in the name of R. Levi: What is the Scriptural authority? "I will sing of mercy and justice; unto Thee, O Lord, will I sing praises" (Ps. ci. 1)—if it be mercy[3], I will sing; and if it be justice[4], I will sing. R. Samuel b. Naḥmani[5] said: It may be derived from the following: "In the Lord, I will praise His word; in God, I will praise His word" (*ibid.* lvi. 11)[6]—"In the Lord, I will praise His word" refers to His attribute of goodness; "In God, I will praise His word" refers to His attribute of retribution. R. Tanḥum[7] said: It may be derived from the following: "I will lift up the cup of salvation and call upon the name of the Lord" (*ibid.* cxvi. 13) [and] "I found trouble and sorrow, but I called upon the name of the Lord" (*ibid.* *vv.* 3 f.). The Rabbis say: It may be derived from the following: "The Lord gave, and the Lord hath taken away; blessed be the name of the Lord" (Job i. 21).

1 See Singer, pp. 6 f.

2 *M.*: Zera.

3 And good befalls me.

4 And for my sins misfortune happens.

5 *M.*: Ishmael b. Nathan.

6 In the Bible text, the words "Lord" and "God" are transposed. On the interpretation of the Divine Names, see p. 312 n. 6.

7 *M.*: Ḥannina.

Example of R. 'Aḳiba.

Rab Huna stated that Rab said[1] in the name of R. Meïr, (and it has been similarly taught in the name of R. 'Aḳiba): A man should always accustom himself to say, "Whatever the All-merciful does, He does for the best[2]." As when R. 'Aḳiba was journeying by the way, he came to a certain town and asked for hospitality, but it was refused him; so he exclaimed, "Whatever the All-merciful does is for the best." He went and spent the night in the field, having with him a cock, an ass and a lamp[3]. A gust of wind came and extinguished the lamp, a cat came and ate the cock, and a lion came and devoured the ass; but he exclaimed, "Whatever the All-merciful does is for the best." That same night a band of robbers came and captured the town[4]. He thereupon said to them[5], "Did I not tell you that whatever the Holy One, blessed be He, does is all for the best!"

fol. 61 a.

Words should be few before God.

Rab Huna stated that Rab said[1] in the name of R. Meïr: A man's words should always be few before the Holy One, blessed be He; as it is said, "Be not rash with thy mouth, and let not thy heart be hasty to utter a word before God; for God is in heaven, and thou upon earth, therefore let thy words be few" (Eccles. v. 1).

Man's two impulses.

Rab Naḥman b. Rab Ḥisda expounded: What means that which is written, "Then the Lord God formed man" (Gen. ii. 7), the word *wayyīṣer* "and He formed" being spelt with two letters *yod*? The Holy One, blessed be He, created two impulses[6], one good and the other evil. Rab Naḥman b. Isaac objected: Therefore since the word *wayyīṣer* is not mentioned in connection with the animal[7] it has no evil impulse, and yet we see it injuring and biting and kicking! Nay [the double *yod* is to be explained] according to the statement of R. Simeon b. Pazzi who said: Woe to me because of my Creator [*Yōṣᵉrī*][8], and woe to me because of my impulse [*Yiṣrī*][9]. Or [it may be explained] according to the statement of R. Jeremiah b. Eleazar who said: The Holy One, blessed be He,

1 *M.* omits: that Rab said.

2 Cf. Romans viii. 28.

3 The lamp so as to study by night, the ass to ride upon, and the cock to awaken him at dawn.

4 The lamp and the animals might have betrayed his presence to the robbers.

5 The captives presumably, he being bereft of all his possessions remaining unmolested.

6 In Hebrew *Jēṣer*, the initial letter being *yod*.

7 Instead there is *'āsāh* "he made," Gen. i. 25.

8 If I follow my evil impulse.

9 Which excites evil desires that must be suppressed.

made Adam with two faces[1]; as it is said, "Behind and before hast Thou formed me" (Ps. cxxxix. 5)[2].

Creation of Eve.

"And the rib, which the Lord God had taken from the man, made He a woman" (Gen. ii. 22). Rab and Samuel [comment upon this]: One declared that it was a face [from which Eve was made]; the other declared that it was a tail[3]. It is right according to him who says that it was a face; that is what is written, "Behind and before hast Thou formed me[4]." But according to him who said it was a tail, what means "Behind and before hast Thou formed me"? It is [to be explained] according to the statement of R. Ammi who said: "Behind[5]" refers to the work of creation, "before" to retribution[6]. It is right that "behind" may refer to the work of creation, for Adam was not created until the eve of the Sabbath; but that "before" refers to retribution—retribution for what? Are we to suppose the punishment of the serpent-incident? Lo, there is a teaching: Rabbi says: With [the award of] greatness we begin with the most important; but with a curse, we begin with the least important. With greatness we begin with the most important—for it is written, "And Moses spoke unto Aaron, and unto Eleazar and unto Ithamar, his sons that were left, Take the meal-offering that remaineth" etc. (Lev. x. 12). With a curse we begin with the least important—first the serpent was cursed, then Eve and then Adam[7]! Nay, the retribution in connection with the flood [is referred to]; for it is written, "And He blotted out every living substance which was upon the face of the ground, both man and cattle" (Gen. vii. 23)[8].

Subject continued.

It is quite right according to him who says that [Eve was created from] a face; that is what is written *wayyīṣer* "And He formed," spelt with a double *yod*. But according to him who said that it was from a tail, what means *wayyīṣer*? It is [to be explained]

[1] One in front and one behind (cf. the Latin Janus), so that he was split in two when Eve was created from him.

[2] *Ṣartānī* "Thou hast hemmed me in" is connected here with *ṣūrāh* "an image."

[3] I.e. a rib protruding from the body like a tail.

[4] With two faces, as explained above.

[5] "Behind" also means "last," i.e. the last to be created, after the animals.

[6] "Before" can also mean "first," i.e. the first to be punished, before the animals.

[7] Since Adam was punished last, the interpretation of Ps. cxxxix. 5 by R. Ammi cannot apply to the serpent-incident.

[8] Here "man" is mentioned before "cattle."

according to the statement of R. Simeon b. Pazzi who said: Woe to me because of my Creator and woe to me because of my impulse. It is quite right according to him who says that it was a face; that is what is written, "Male and female created He them" (Gen. v. 2)[1]. But according to him who said it was a tail, what means "Male and female created He them"? It is [to be explained] according to R. Abbahu who asked: It is written "Male and female created He them," and it is written, "For in the image of God made He man" (*ibid.* ix. 6). How is this? At first He planned to create two, but in the end only one was created. It is quite right according to him who says it was a face; that is what is written, "He closed up the place with flesh instead thereof" (*ibid.* ii. 21). But according to him who said it was a tail, what means "He closed up the place with flesh instead thereof"? R. Jeremiah (other versions: Rab Zᵉbid; Rab Naḥman b. Isaac) said: That was only necessary in the place of the wound[2]. It is quite right according to him who said it was a tail; that is what is written, "And He made [*lit.* built]" (*ibid. v.* 22)[3]. But according to him who said it was a face, what means "He made"? It is [to be explained] according to R. Simeon b. Mᵉnasya who expounded: What means, "And the rib which the Lord God had taken from the man, made He [*bānāh*] a woman"? It teaches that the Holy One, blessed be He, plaited her hair and brought her [adorned] to Adam; for so in the sea-towns[4] they call plaits *binyātā*[5].

Another explanation of "And He made [*lit.* built]"—Rab Ḥisda said (another version: It was taught in a *Bārāitā*): This means that the Holy One, blessed be He, fashioned Eve like a store-building; as the store is narrow above and broad below so as to receive the fruits, similarly is a woman narrow above and broad below so as to receive the child. "And He brought her unto the man" (*ibid.*). R. Jeremiah b. Eleazar said[6]: This means that the Holy One, blessed be He, constituted Himself Adam's "best man"; hence the *Tōrāh* teaches a rule of conduct, viz.: that an eminent man should accompany one of less importance as "best man," and it will not injure [his dignity]. **The female form.**

1 I.e. with a male and female countenance.

2 Where the tail-like rib was removed, flesh had to be substituted.

3 It would be more natural to say "He built" a rib, than a face, into a woman.

4 See p. 32 n. 8.

5 The point of the explanation is that the word for "plaits" also means "tents, dwelling-places"; cf. *T. A.* I. p. 278 n. 87.

6 *M.* omits the name.

A man should not walk behind a woman.

According to him who said [Eve was made from] a face, which of them[1] went in front? Rab Naḥman b. Isaac said: It is more probable that the masculine countenance went in front; for there is a teaching: A man should never walk behind a woman along the road, even his own wife[2]. Should a woman meet him on a bridge he should let her pass by on the side; and whoever crosses a stream behind a woman will[3] have no portion in the world to come.

Nor gaze at her.

Our Rabbis have taught: He who pays money to a woman counting it from his hand into hers for the sake of gazing at her, even if he possess *Tōrāh* and good deeds like Moses our teacher, he will not escape the punishment of *Gēhinnōm*; as it is said, "Hand to hand[4] the evil man shall not be unpunished" (Prov. xi. 21)—he shall not escape the punishment of *Gēhinnōm*.

Manoah acted wrongly.

Rab Naḥman said: Manoah was an *'Am hā'āreṣ*; for it is written, "And Manoah went *after* his wife" (Judges xiii. 11). Rab Naḥman b. Isaac[5] retorted: But that is likewise true of[6] Elisha; for it is written, "And he arose and followed her" (II Kings iv. 30)—here also he actually walked behind her! Nay; [it means that Elisha] followed her words and advice, and so also [in the instance of Manoah] he followed her words and advice. Rab Ashē said: With reference to what Rab Naḥman said, viz. that Manoah was an *'Am hā'āreṣ*, he had not even learnt [the Scriptures which are taught] in an elementary school; as it is said, "And Rebekah arose, and her damsels, and they rode upon the camels, and followed the man" (Gen. xxiv. 61)—they went behind the man, not in front of him.

What a man should avoid.

R. Joḥanan said[7]: A man should walk behind a lion rather than behind a woman, behind a woman rather than behind an idolater, behind an idolater rather than behind a Synagogue when the Congregation is at prayer[8]. But this last is only meant when he is not carrying a load; should he, however, be carrying a load,

[1] The masculine and feminine countenance.

[2] In the Orient, wives always walk behind as a mark of inferiority; but here the reason is rather that the man's passion should not be inflamed.

[3] *M.*: not escape the punishment of *Gēhinnōm*.

[4] R.V. "Though hand join to hand"; R.V. marg. "My hand upon it."

[5] *M.* omits: Naḥman b.

[6] The text inserts here: "Elkanah, for it is written, 'And Elkanah went after his wife'; and of." There is no such verse in the Bible; nor is Elkanah mentioned in the subsequent discussion.

[7] *M.*: Rab Naḥman said (another version: R. Joḥanan; and some say it was taught in a *Bārāitā*).

[8] See fol. 8 *b*, p. 48.

there is no objection. It is only meant when there is no other entrance; but should there be another entrance, there is no objection. It is further only meant when he is not riding upon an ass; but should he be riding upon an ass, there is no objection. It is likewise only meant when he is not wearing *Tᵉfillīn*; but if he is wearing *Tᵉfillīn*, there is no objection.

Rab said: The evil impulse is like a fly and dwells between the two entrances of the heart; as it is said, "Dead flies make the ointment of the perfumers fetid and putrid" (Eccles. x. 1). Samuel said: It is like a kind of wheat [*ḥiṭṭāh*]; as it is said, "Sin [*ḥaṭṭ'āt*] croucheth at the door" (Gen. iv. 7)[1]. The evil impulse.

Our Rabbis have taught: There are two reins in man, one prompting him to good, the other to evil. It is probable that the good is on the right side and the bad on the left; for it is written, "A wise man's understanding is at his right hand; but a fool's understanding at his left" (Eccles. x. 2). Man's dual nature.

Our Rabbis have taught: The reins prompt [the thought], the heart exercises intelligence, the tongue pronounces, the mouth completes [the words]. The gullet lets in and brings out all kinds of food[2], the windpipe produces voice, the lungs absorb all kinds of liquids, the liver arouses anger, the gall lets a drop fall upon it and stills it, the milt produces laughter, the large intestine grinds [food], the maw induces sleep and the nose awakens. Should the organ which induces sleep arouse from sleep, or should the organ which arouses from sleep induce sleep, the person pines away. It has been taught: Should both of them induce sleep or arouse from sleep simultaneously, one immediately dies. Functions of the human organs. **fol. 61 b.**

There is a teaching: R. Josē of Galilee says[3]: The good impulse controls the righteous; as it is said, "My heart is wounded within me" (Ps. cix. 22)[4]. The evil impulse controls the wicked; as it is said, "Transgression speaketh to the wicked, in the midst of the heart, There is no fear of God before his eyes" (*ibid.* xxxvi. 2). Both impulses control average people; as it is said, "Because He standeth at the right hand of the needy, to save him from them Control of the impulses.

[1] Schechter suggests that this latter interpretation is probably connected with the legend that the tree of knowledge grew wheat (above fol. 40 *a*, p. 265). Cf. *Aspects of Rabbinic Theology*, p. 256 n.

[2] "The Talmudic idea is based on the curious physiological notion that the food passed from the oesophagus first into the large intestine where the food was supposed to be crushed as in a mill, and thence only, through various organs, into the stomach proper"; Edersheim, *Life and Times*, II. p. 23 n.

[3] *M.*: The School of R. Josē of Galilee taught.

[4] By "heart" is to be understood "the evil impulses of the heart."

that judge his soul" (Ps. cix. 31)[1]. Raba said, "The average people are, for instance, ourselves." Abbai said to him, "The master does not leave life for any creature[2]!" Raba also said: The universe was only created for the completely wicked or the completely righteous[3]. Raba said: Let a man know himself whether he is completely righteous or not. Rab said[4]: The universe was only created for Ahab the son of Omri and for R. Ḥannina b. Dosa—for Ahab the son of Omri, this world[5]; and for R. Ḥannina b. Dosa, the world to come[6].

"*And thou shalt love the Lord thy God*" (Deut. vi. 5).

The love of God.

There is a teaching: R. Eliezer says: If it is stated "With all thy soul," why is it stated "With all thy might"? And if it is stated "With all thy might," why is it stated "With all thy soul"? But should there be a man whose body is dearer to him than his money[7], therefore it is stated "With all thy soul[8]"; and should there be a man whose money is dearer to him than his body, therefore it is stated "With all thy might." R. 'Aḳiba says: "With all thy soul" [means,] even if He take thy soul[9].

R. 'Aḳiba and Pappos b. Judah.

Our Rabbis have taught: Once the wicked[10] government decreed that Israel should no longer occupy themselves with *Tōrāh*. There came Pappos b. Judah and found R. 'Aḳiba attracting great assemblies and studying *Tōrāh*. He said to him, "'Aḳiba, art thou not afraid of the wicked government?" He replied, "I will tell thee a parable: To what is the matter like? To a fox who was walking along the bank of the stream and saw some fishes gathering together from one place to another. He said to them, 'From what are you fleeing?' They answered, 'From nets which men are bringing against us.' He said to them, 'Let it be your pleasure to come up on the dry land, and let us, me and you, dwell together even as my fathers dwelt with your fathers.' They replied, 'Art

1 "Them that judge [i.e. control] his soul," in the plural, indicating two impulses.

2 If a man like Raba describes himself as "average," what can ordinary people be!

3 For the former, this world because they have no share in the world to come; for the latter, the world to come because they usually have to endure sufferings here.

4 *M.*: Raba also said.

5 Who possessed abundant gold and silver; see I Kings xx. 3.

6 His poverty was proverbial; cf. above fol. 17 *b*, p. 113.

7 By "might" is understood "wealth."

8 I.e. with thy very self, thy body.

9 I.e. thy life to prove thy love of God.

10 Some edd. read "Grecian" because of the Censor. Rome is meant.

thou he of whom they tell that thou art the shrewdest of animals? Thou art not clever but a fool! For if we are afraid in the place which is our life-element, how much more so in a place which is our death-element!' So also is it with us: Now while we sit and study *Tōrāh*, in which it is written, 'For that is thy life, and the length of thy days' (Deut. xxx. 20), we are in such a plight, how much more so if we go and neglect it!"

They are both arrested.

It is related that but a few days passed when they arrested R. 'Aḳiba and bound him in prison, and they arrested Pappos b. Judah and bound him by his side. 'Aḳiba said to him, "Pappos, who brought thee here?" He replied, "Happy art thou, R. 'Aḳiba, inasmuch as thou hast been arrested on account of the *Tōrāh*! But woe to me, Pappos, who has been arrested on trivial grounds!"

Martyrdom of R. 'Aḳiba.

When they brought R. 'Aḳiba out to execution, it was the time for reading the *Shema'*; and though they were combing his flesh with iron combs, he kept receiving upon himself the yoke of the Kingdom of Heaven[1]. His disciples said to him, "Our master, thus far[2]!" He answered them, "Throughout my life I have been troubled about this verse, '[And thou shalt love the Lord thy God...] and with all thy soul' which means: Even if He take thy life. For said I, 'When will it be in my power to fulfil it?' But now that the opportunity is mine, shall I not fulfil it?" He prolonged the word *éḥād*[3] until his soul left [the body] with the word *éḥād* [on his lips]. A *Bat Ḳōl* issued forth and announced, "Happy art thou, R. 'Aḳiba, that thy soul went out with the word *éḥād*!" The ministering angels spake before the Holy One, blessed be He, "Such *Tōrāh*, and such a reward? 'From men, by Thy hand, O Lord, from men' etc. (Ps. xvii. 14)[4]." He replied to them, "Their portion is in this life" (*ibid.*). A *Bat Ḳōl* issued forth and announced, "Happy art thou, R. 'Aḳiba, for thou art destined for the life of the world to come!"

A man should not behave with levity towards the East Gate [of the Temple], since it is directed towards the Holy of Holies, etc.

Where and when the *Mishnāh* applies.

Rab Judah said in the name of Rab[5]: This is only meant from *Ṣōphīm*[6] inwards, and only applies to one who can see [the Temple].

[1] I.e. continued the recital of the *Shema'*.

[2] Although suffering such agonies, you still say the *Shema'*!

[3] "One" in "Hear, O Israel," etc.

[4] I.e. is this the fate due to such a man? He should have met his death at Thy hand and not at the hands of torturers.

[5] *M.* omits: in the name of Rab.

[6] See p. 317 n. 8. Past Mt Scopus, one has no view of the Temple.

It has been similarly reported: R. Abba b. R. Ḥiyya b. Abba said: Thus declared R. Joḥanan[1]: This is only meant from *Ṣōphīm* inwards, and only applies to one who can see [the Temple] and when there is no barrier [between him and it], and at the time when the *Shᵉkīnāh* rests [upon the Sanctuary][2].

On exercising the natural functions and the direction of the Temple.

Our Rabbis have taught: He who wishes to exercise his natural functions, if in Judea he should not face East or West[3] but North or South; if in Galilee, he should only face East or West. R. Josē, however, permits it [in any direction] because he used to say that the prohibition only applies to one who can see [the Temple], when there is no barrier, and at the time when the *Shᵉkīnāh* rests [upon the Sanctuary]. But the Sages prohibit it. Then the Sages agree with the first *Tannā*[4]! The question of the side divides them[5].

Another teaching.

There is another teaching: He who wishes to exercise his natural functions, if in Judea he must not face East or West, but North or South; but in Galilee, North and South are prohibited, East or West is permitted. R. Josē, however, permits it [in any direction], because he used to say that the prohibition only applies to one who can see [the Temple]. R. Judah says: It is prohibited while the Temple is standing; but when the Temple is no longer standing it is permitted. R. 'Aḳiba prohibits it in all circumstances. Then R. 'Aḳiba agrees with the first *Tannā*! The question of outside the [Holy] Land is between them[6].

The subject continued.

Rabbah[7] had bricks set up for him facing East and West[8]. Abbai went and put them facing North and South[9]; but Rabbah[7] proceeded to put them right, exclaiming, "Who is it that is troubling me? I agree with R. 'Aḳiba's view when he declared that it is prohibited in all circumstances."

fol. 62 a. What R. 'Akiba learnt from R. Joshua.

There is a teaching: R. 'Aḳiba said: Once I went into a privy behind R. Joshua and learnt from him three things. I learnt that we should not evacuate East or West, but North or South. I learnt

[1] *M.*: R. Abbahu in the name of Rabina b. Ḥiyya b. Abba in the name of R. Abba in the name of R. Joḥanan.

[2] I.e. the Temple is still in existence.

[3] So as not to expose himself towards the Temple.

[4] Why, then, is their opinion mentioned separately?

[5] Viz. the side of Judea and Galilee which is not in a line with the Temple. The first *Tannā* prohibits it even in these localities, whereas the Sages permit it.

[6] 'Aḳiba takes the stricter view and extends the prohibition beyond Palestine.

[7] *M.*: Raba. He lived in Babylon.

[8] So that he faced N. or S.

[9] To find out whether he adhered to R. 'Aḳiba's opinion.

that we should not expose ourselves standing but sitting. I also learnt that we should not wipe ourselves with the right hand but with the left[1]. Ben ‘Azzai said to him, "Wert thou so impudent with thy master?" He replied, "It was a matter of *Tōrāh* and I wished to learn."

What Ben ‘Azzai learnt from R. ‘Aḳiba.

There is a teaching: Ben ‘Azzai said: I once went into a privy behind R. ‘Aḳiba and learnt from him three things. I learnt that we should not evacuate East or West, but North or South. I learnt that we should not expose ourselves standing but sitting. I also learnt that we should not wipe ourselves with the right hand but with the left. R. Judah said to him, "Wert thou so impudent with thy master?" He replied, "It was a matter of *Tōrāh* and I wished to learn."

Rab Kahᵃna and Rab.

Rab Kahᵃna went and hid himself under Rab's bed and heard him converse [with his wife] and laugh and have intercourse. Rab Kahᵃna said to him, "Abba's[2] mouth is like that of one who has never sipped a dish[3]." Rab exclaimed, "Kahᵃna, art thou here? Go out; for it is not proper!" He replied, "It is a matter of *Tōrāh* and I wished to learn[4]."

Why the left hand must only be used to wipe the body.

Why should we not wipe with the right hand but only with the left? Raba said: Because the *Tōrāh* was given with the right hand; as it is said, "At His right hand was a fiery law unto them" (Deut. xxxiii. 2). Rabbah b. Bar Ḥannah said[5]: Because it is near the mouth[6]. R. Simeon b. Laḳish said: Because he binds the *Tᵉfillīn* with it. Rab Naḥman b. Isaac said: Because he points to the accents of the *Tōrāh* with it[7]. It is like [the discussion of] the *Tannāīm*. R. Eliezer says: Because he eats with it. R. Joshua says: Because he writes with it. R. ‘Aḳiba said: Because he points to the accents of the *Tōrāh* with it.

Modesty in a privy.

R. Tanḥum b. Ḥᵃnilai said: Whoever is modest in a privy is delivered from three things: from serpents, scorpions and evil spirits[8]; some say: Also his dreams will be such that his mind

[1] The Moslems have a similar practice, and do not touch food with the left hand. Cf. Lane, p. 150 n. 2.

[2] Rab's name.

[3] I.e. Rab behaved as though it were an entirely new experience to him.

[4] "Die alten kannten die Prüderie nicht und verhandelten über eheliche Pflichten mit dem grössten Freimut"; *T.A.* II. p. 466 n. 366.

[5] *M.* adds: in the name of R. Joḥanan.

[6] I.e. it is used for conveying food to the mouth; see Lane, p. 148.

[7] When reading from the Scroll.

[8] The Moslems also believe that evil spirits haunt such places, and offer a prayer before entering; cf. Lane, p. 229.

will be set at ease. There was a privy in Tiberias[1] which if two people entered, even by day, they came to harm. R. Ammi and R. Assi entered it separately and no harm befell them. The Rabbis said to them, "Were you not afraid?" They answered, "We were taught a charm[2]: a charm for the privy is modesty and silence; a charm against sufferings is silence and prayer." Abbai reared a lamb to accompany him into the privy[3]. But he should have reared a goat[4]! A satyr may be changed into a goat. Before Raba was appointed Principal [of the Seminary], the daughter of Rab Ḥisda[5] used to rattle a nut in a flask for him[6]; but afterwards when he ruled [over the Seminary] she made an aperture for him [in the wall] and placed her hand upon his head[7].

On performing the natural functions in a place other than a privy.

'Ulla said: Behind a fence one may ease himself immediately[8]; but in an open place[9] [he may do it] so long as he can break wind without anybody hearing it. Issi b. Nathan[10] taught as follows: Behind a fence [he may ease himself] so long as he can break wind without anybody hearing, but in an open place so long as nobody sees him. Against this [latter teaching] is quoted: They[11] may go out from the entrance of the olive-press and ease themselves behind a fence[8], and they remain in a state of ritual purity! They take a more lenient view in connection with [those who supervise] ritual purity[12]. Come and hear: [It has been taught:] To what distance may they[11] go and remain clean? So long as one can see them[13]! It is different with food-stuffs whose purity [must be supervised], because the Rabbis take a more lenient view in such a case. Rab Ashē asked: What means "so long as nobody sees him," as stated by Issi b. Nathan? So long as his neighbour cannot see the exposed part of the body, but he may see the man himself.

[1] See p. 46 n. 6.

[2] Read with Jastrow *ḳiblē* "charm" instead of *ḳabbālāh* "a tradition."

[3] As a protection against evil spirits.

[4] The evil spirits often assume the form of a goat. The word "satyrs" in Is. xiii. 21 is literally "he-goats." See R.V. marg.

[5] Raba's wife.

[6] When he went into the privy, to frighten away the evil spirits. Cf. Frazer, *Folklore in the Old Testament*, III. pp. 446 ff.

[7] As a more effective protection, because owing to his exalted position he was particularly liable to attack.

[8] Even if people are about.

[9] *Lit.* valley; where there is no fence.

[10] The more correct reading is Assi b. Nathan; see *D. S. ad loc.*

[11] Those who are appointed to supervise the production of olive-oil and see that it does not contract defilement in the process.

[12] So that they may not be long absent from their watch.

[13] This contradicts Issi b. Nathan who requires him to be out of sight in an open place.

A certain funeral-orator who went down [to deliver an address] in the presence of Rab Naḥman said, "How modest was [the deceased] in his habits!" Rab Naḥman said to him, "Didst thou ever go into a privy with him that thou knowest whether he was modest or not? For there is a teaching: He only is called modest who is so in a privy." But what had Rab Naḥman to care about in this matter? Because there is a teaching: As the dead are called to account [for their deeds], so are the funeral-orators[1] and they who respond ["Amen"] after them called to account.

Criterion of modesty.

Our Rabbis have taught: Who is modest? He who relieves himself at night in the same place where he relieves himself by day[2]. But it is not so! For lo, Rab Judah said in the name of Rab: A man should always accustom himself [to perform his natural functions] morning and evening[3] so that it will be unnecessary for him to go far [and find a secluded spot]. And further, Raba used to go as far as a *Mīl* by day; but at night he would say to his attendant, "Prepare for me a place in the street of the town." Similarly used R. Zera to say to his attendant, "See whether there is anybody behind the Seminary, as I wish to relieve myself"! Read not [in the *Bārāitā*] "in the same place," but read "in the same manner that he relieves himself by day[4]." Rab Ashē said: Even if thou retainest the words "the same place" [there is no contradiction, because it means,] it is only necessary [to proceed] to a corner[5].

Subject continued.

It was stated above: "Rab Judah said in the name of Rab: A man should always accustom himself [to perform his natural functions] morning and evening, so that it will be unnecessary for him to go far [and find a secluded spot]." There is a teaching to the same effect: Ben 'Azzai says: Rise early and go out, and act likewise after dusk so that thou needest not go a distance; feel the need and then sit down, but do not sit down and then [wait to] feel the need, for whoever does so, even should they practise sorcery in Aspamia[6] it will befall him. But should he through forgetfulness act thus, what is his remedy? On rising, let him say

Habits recommended.

[1] Who attribute to the dead virtues they do not possess.

[2] He is careful, even at night, to retire to a secluded spot.

[3] I.e. before dawn and after dusk.

[4] I.e. he observes the rules laid down in fol. 23 *b*, pp. 152 f.

[5] "Same place" accordingly means "the same kind of place," viz. where there is privacy.

[6] A place-name used in the *Talmūd* to express extreme distance. It denotes several different places; cf. Krauss, pp. 90 f.

as follows, "Not to me, not to me[1]; no *Taḥīm* and no *Taḥtīm*[2]; not these and not from these[3]; no charms of a sorcerer and no charms of a sorceress."

fol. 62 b. Some maxims.

There is a teaching: Ben 'Azzai says: Lie upon any couch but not on the floor; sit upon any seat except a beam[4]. Samuel said: Sleeping at dawn is like a steel edge to iron[5]; evacuation at dawn is like a steel edge to iron. Bar Ḳappara used to sell proverbs for *denarii*: "While thou art hungry, eat; while thou art thirsty, drink; while the cauldron is still hot, pour out[6]." "When the horn is sounded in [the market of] Rome[7], O son of a fig-seller, sell thy father's figs[8]." Abbai said to the Rabbis: When you pass through the alleys of a town to go into the country, look neither to the one side nor the other, lest women be sitting there, and it is not proper to gaze at them.

The privy in the Temple-court.

Rab Safra entered a privy. R. Abba came and emitted a sound at the door[9]. Rab Safra said to him, "Let the master enter." After leaving, R. Abba said to him, "So far thou hast not brought in the demon; but thou hast received the tradition about the demon[10]. Have we not learnt thus in the *Mishnāh*: There was an open fire-place there [in the Temple-court], and a splendid privy; and this was its splendid feature: if it was found locked, it was known that somebody was in there, but if it was found open, it was known that it was vacant[11]. Hence infer that it is not proper [to speak in a privy]! But Rab Safra thought that it was dangerous[12]; for there is a teaching[13]: Rabban Simeon b. Gamaliel says: If the

1 Sc. may their spells come.

2 Obscure words of doubtful meaning. Rashi explains them to be the name of the magic practices.

3 I.e. not all their spells nor part of them. Another possible translation is: May they have no use or effect, neither the charms of a sorcerer nor the charms of a sorceress.

4 In the first case there is the danger of serpents; in the latter, of falling off.

5 I.e. healthy and strengthening.

6 Meaning, do not put the matter off. The proverb is here applied to relieving oneself; this should be done as soon as the need is felt.

7 That selling is to commence.

8 If the father is away, the son should not wait for his return, but sell his father's goods. Hence the teaching of the proverb is also: Do not procrastinate.

9 He cleared his throat as a signal, to find out whether anybody was there.

10 One should not speak in a privy, and by so doing Rab Safra exposed himself to the attack of the demon (*lit.* goat); see the preceding fol., p. 410.

11 The necessity for speaking in such a place was thus obviated.

12 For anyone to delay relieving himself, and for that reason had asked R. Abba to enter.

13 Cf. fol. 25 *a*, p. 161.

fecal discharge is kept back it causes dropsy, and if the fluid in the urinary duct is kept back it causes jaundice. R. Eleazar[1] entered a privy; a certain Roman[2] came and pushed him. R. Eleazar got up and went out; and a serpent came and tore out the [Roman's] gut. R. Eleazar applied to him the verse: "Therefore will I give a man under thee" (Is. xliii. 4)—read not *ādām* "a man" but *Ĕdōm* "an Edomite[3]."

Saul's modesty.

"And he said to kill thee, but it spared thee" (I Sam. xxiv. 11)[4]. "And he said"! It ought to be "And I said"; "but it spared"! It ought to be "but I spared." R. Eleazar said: Thus spake David to Saul, "According to the *Tōrāh*, thou art liable to be put to death, because thou art a pursuer; and the *Tōrāh* declares that if one comes to kill thee, kill him first[5]. But the modesty which is manifest in thee has spared thee." In what did [Saul's modesty] consist? For it is written, "And he came to the sheep-cotes[6] by the way, where was a cave; and Saul went in to cover his feet" (*ibid. v.* 4). It has been taught that it was a fence within a fence and a cave within a cave. "To cover"—R. Eleazar said: This teaches that he covered himself like a booth[7].

Why David could get no heat.

"Then David arose, and cut off the skirt of Saul's robe privily" (*ibid. v.* 5). R. Josē b. R. Ḥannina[8] said: Whoever deals contemptuously with garments will in the end derive no benefit from them; as it is said, "Now King David was old and stricken in years; and they covered him with clothes but he could get no heat" (I Kings i. 1).

David's sin in numbering the people.

"If it be the Lord that hath stirred thee up against me, let Him accept an offering" (I Sam. xxvi. 19). R. Eleazar said[9]: Thus spake the Holy One, blessed be He, to David, Thou callest Me a "stirrer-up," behold I will cause thee to stumble in a matter which even school-children know; for it is written, "When thou takest the sum of the children of Israel, according to their number, then shall they give every man a ranson for his soul unto the Lord...that there be no plague among them, when thou numberest them" (Exod. xxx. 12). Immediately "Satan stood up against Israel" (I Chron. xxi. 1); for it is written, "He stirred up David

[1] *M.*: Eliezer.
[2] Many edd. read "Persian" for fear of the Censor.
[3] *Ĕdōm* being considered the prototype of Rome.
[4] R.V. "And some bade me kill thee; but [mine eye] spared thee."
[5] See on fol. 58 *a*, p. 383 n. 2.
[6] *Lit. fences* of the sheep.
[7] The noun "booth" is derived from the verb "to cover."
[8] *M.* omits: R. Josē b.
[9] *M.* omits.

against them, saying, Go, number Israel and Judah" (II Sam. xxiv. 1). But when he numbered them, he took no ransom from them; and it is written, "So the Lord sent a pestilence upon Israel from the morning even to the time appointed" (*ibid. v.* 15). What means "the time appointed"? Samuel[1] the Elder, the son-in-law of R. Ḥannina, said in the name of R. Ḥannina: From the time of slaying the continual offering until the time of the sprinkling of the blood. R. Joḥanan said: [It means] precisely until noon.

Death of Abishai.

"And He said to the angel that destroyed the people, It is enough [*rab*]" (*ibid. v.* 16). R. Eleazar said: Thus spake the Holy One, blessed be He, to the angel, Take for me the chief [*rab*] among them, so that through him I can punish them for their sins[2]. At that moment Abishai b. Zeruiah died, who was equal [in worth] to the majority of the *Sanhedrin*.

What God beheld.

"And as he was about to destroy, the Lord beheld, and He repented Him" (I Chron. xxi. 15). What did He behold? Rab said: He beheld our father Jacob; for it is written, "And Jacob said when he *beheld* them" (Gen. xxxii. 3). Samuel said: He beheld the ashes of [the sacrifice substituted for] Isaac; as it is said, "God will provide[3] Himself the lamb" (*ibid.* xxii. 8). R. Isaac the Smith[4] said: He beheld the money of the atonement; as it is said, "And thou shalt take the atonement money from the children of Israel" etc. (Exod. xxx. 16). R. Joḥanan said: He beheld the Temple; for it is written, "In the mount where the Lord is seen" (Gen. xxii. 14). R. Jacob b. Iddi and R. Samuel b. Naḥmani[5] differ in this matter; one declaring that He beheld the atonement money, the other declaring that He beheld the Temple. The more probable view is that of him who said that He beheld the Sanctuary; because it is said, "As it is said to this day, In the mount where the Lord is seen."

Nor may one enter the Temple Mount with his staff...; nor may he use it as a short cut [ḳoppendāriā].

Using a Synagogue as a short cut.

What means *ḳoppendāriā*? Raba said: A short cut, as the word implies[6]. But Rab Ḥanna[7] b. Adda said in the name of Rab Samma b. R. Mari: It is as people say, "Instead of going round the row

1 *M.*: R. Ishmael.

2 It being thought that the death of a righteous man brings expiation for the sins of a community.

3 *Lit.* behold.

4 *M.* omits: the smith.

5 *M.*: Ishmael b. Naḥman.

6 It is the equivalent of the Latin [*via*] *compendiaria*.

7 *M.*: Huna.

of houses[1], I will go through it" Rab Naḥman said in the name of Rabbah b. Abbuha: If one enters a Synagogue not for the purpose of making it a short cut, he may use it in that manner. R. Abbahu said: If it was originally a public path[2], it is permitted [as a short cut for all]. R. Ḥelbo said in the name of Rab Huna: Who enters a Synagogue to pray is allowed to use it as a short cut; as it is said, "But when the people of the land shall come before the Lord in the appointed seasons, he that entereth by the way of the north gate to worship shall go forth by the way of the south gate" (Ezek. xlvi. 9).

And to expectorate on the Temple Mount is forbidden a fortiori.

Rab Bebai said in the name of R. Joshua b. Levi[3]: Whoever expectorates on the Temple Mount in this time[4] is as though he expectorates into the pupil of his eye[5]; as it is said, "And Mine eyes and My heart shall be there *perpetually*" (I Kings ix. 3). Raba said: Expectoration is allowed in a Synagogue, because it is analogous to [the wearing of] a shoe—just as [the wearing of] a shoe is prohibited on the Temple Mount but is permitted in a Synagogue, so is expectoration forbidden on the Temple Mount but permitted in a Synagogue. Rab Pappa said to Raba (other versions: Rabina to Raba; Rab Adda b. Mattena to Raba): Why should one derive it [by analogy] from a shoe; let him derive it from the short cut! He replied: The *Tannā* derives it from the shoe, and thou sayest [it should be derived] from the short cut—how can that be? For there is a teaching: A man must not enter the Temple Mount with his staff in his hand, his shoe upon his foot, and his money tied up in his cloth or in his money-bag thrown over his shoulder, nor may he make it a short cut; and [the prohibition of] expectoration is derived *a fortiori* from the shoe—as in the case of a shoe which is not in itself contemptible the *Tōrāh* declares, "Put off thy shoes from off thy feet" (Exod. iii. 5), must not expectoration, which is in itself contemptible, be all the more forbidden! R. Josē b. Judah[6] says: [This reasoning] is unnecessary; for it is stated, "For none might enter within the king's gate clothed with sackcloth" (Esther iv. 2)—and is there not here an *a fortiori* deduction: If it is thus with sackcloth which is not a disgusting thing in the presence of human beings, must not expectoration, which is disgusting in the presence of the supreme

Expectoration in the Synagogue.

[1] In Aramaic *maḳḳap-nā dārē*; hence *ḳoppendāriā*.
[2] Before the Synagogue was built thereon.
[3] *M.*: in the name of R. Issi.
[4] I.e. after its destruction.
[5] Euphemistically for "the eye of God."
[6] *M.* omits: b. Judah.

King of kings, be all the more prohibited! [Rab Pappa] answered: This is the position I take up: Let us derive a strict conclusion[1] from the instance [of the shoe] and also from the instance [of the
fol. 63 a. short cut]; and I say that with reference to the Temple Mount where [the wearing of] a shoe is forbidden, let one derive [the prohibition against expectoration] from a shoe; but with reference to the Synagogue[2] where one is permitted [to wear] shoes, instead of deriving permission [to expectorate, by analogy] from a shoe, let him derive a prohibition [against expectoration, by analogy] from the short cut! But, answered Raba: [The Synagogue] is analogous to his own house—as a man is concerned about anybody using his house as a short cut but is not concerned about expectoration or [the wearing of] shoes, so also with the Synagogue, as a short cut it is prohibited, but expectoration and [the wearing of] shoes are allowed.

At the conclusion of every benediction in the Sanctuary they used to say "For ever," etc.

"Amen" not used in the Temple.

Why all this[3]? Because the response "Amen" was never made in the Sanctuary. Whence is it that "Amen" was never used as a response in the Sanctuary? As it is said, "Stand up and bless the Lord your God from everlasting to everlasting" (Nehem. ix. 5), and it continues, "And let them say: Blessed be Thy glorious Name, that is exalted above all blessing and praise" (*ibid*)[4]. It is possible to think that all benedictions should have one praise[5]; therefore there is a teaching to state, "Above all[6] blessing and praise"—for each benediction give Him praise.

It was further ordained that a man should greet his friends by mentioning the Divine Name, etc.

Inclusion of God's name in a greeting.

What means "And it is said[7]"? Shouldest thou argue that Boaz mentioned [the Divine Name in his salutation] of his own accord[8], come and hear: "The Lord is with thee, thou mighty

1 I.e. a prohibition.

2 Some edd. wrongly read: Sanctuary.

3 And not the simple response "Amen."

4 And they were not to respond "Amen."

5 This is capable of two interpretations: (1) If there is a series of benedictions, one response after the last, and not after each, is sufficient. So Rashi. (2) That one and the same formula of praise is to be used after all benedictions, and not a wording distinctive for each.

6 I.e. every.

7 Why does the *Mishnāh* (see p. 349) add the quotation from Judges vi. 12 after that from Ruth ii. 11?

8 And it is not to be taken as a general rule; therefore the *Mishnāh* quotes another instance.

man of valour" (Judges vi. 12). Shouldest thou argue that it was an angel that spake to Gideon[1], come and hear: "Despise not thy mother[2] when she is old" (Prov. xxiii. 22). And it is stated, "It is time for the Lord to work; they have made void Thy Law" (Ps. cxix. 126). Raba said: This verse is to be explained from the first clause to the second, and from the second to the first. It is to be explained from the first clause to the second, thus: "It is time for the Lord to work"; why? Because "they have made void Thy Law." It is to be explained from the second to the first, thus: "They have made void Thy Law"; why? Because "It is time for the Lord to work."

Scattering and collecting knowledge of *Tōrāh*.

There is a teaching: Hillel the Elder says: When people collect [learning], do thou scatter; when they scatter [learning], do thou collect[3]. If thou seest a generation to which *Tōrāh* is dear, do thou scatter; as it is said, "There is that scattereth, and yet increaseth" (Prov. xi. 24); but if thou seest a generation to which *Tōrāh* is not dear, do thou collect; as it is said, "It is time for the Lord to work; they have made void Thy Law."

Some teachings of Bar Ḳappara.

Bar Ḳappara expounded[4]: "If goods are cheap, hasten[5] and buy them." "In a place where there is no man, be a man[6]." Abbai said: Infer from this that where there is a man, do not be a man[7]. This is evident! No, it is necessary for the case where the two of them are of equal standing[8]. Bar Ḳappara expounded: Which is a brief Scriptural passage upon which all the principles of the *Tōrāh* depend? "In all thy ways acknowledge Him, and He will direct thy paths" (*ibid.* iii. 6). Raba said: Even for a matter of

[1] I.e. the quotation is not a greeting but the message which the angel was commanded to communicate; therefore this verse cannot be used to support the teaching that the Divine Name must be mentioned in a salutation.

[2] By "thy mother" is here meant the great men of the past. Follow in their ways; so that even if Boaz used the Name of his own accord, act likewise.

[3] I.e. when people are eager to study *Tōrāh*, impart thy knowledge to them; but when they are indifferent, do thou continue to study. On the wording of this saying, cf. *A.T.* i. p. 6 n. 2. A metaphor from agricultural life is employed, "scattering" referring to the sowing of seed, and "gathering" to the harvest; cf. *T.A.* ii. p. 578 n. 299.

[4] What follows are proverbs; cf. top of fol. 62 *b*, p. 412.

[5] Reading with the 'Ārūk *ḳephōṣ* instead of *ḳebōṣ* "collect" sc. money.

[6] Cf. Hillel's maxim in Āḇōt ii. 6, Singer, pp. 187 f.

[7] I.e. when there is already somebody to teach the people, do not compete with him. Thus Bar Ḳappara's statement is linked on to the preceding paragraph.

[8] But if the teacher is inferior to himself, he should displace him.

transgression[1]. Bar Ḳappara expounded: A man should always teach his son a clean and light trade[2]. Which is such? Rab Ḥisda[3] said: Needle-stitching[4].

Some teachings of Rabbi.

There is a teaching: Rabbi[5] says: A man should never multiply friends[6] in his house; as it is said, "There are friends that one hath to his own hurt" (Prov. xviii. 24). There is a teaching: Rabbi says: Let not a man appoint a steward over his house; for if Potiphar had not appointed Joseph steward over his house, he would not have experienced the incident [of his wife's temptation]. There is a teaching: Rabbi says: Why does the section of the Nazirite adjoin the section of the woman suspected of adultery[7]? To tell thee that whoever sees such a woman in her disgrace should separate himself from wine[8].

Fate of the man who withholds his offerings and tithes.

Hezekiah b. R. Parnak said in the name of R. Parnak[9] in the name of R. Joḥanan: Why does the section of the woman suspected of adultery adjoin the section of the offerings and tithes? To tell thee that whoever has offerings and tithes and does not hand them to the priest will in the end require the services of a priest in the matter of his wife; as it is said, "And every man's hallowed things shall be his[10]" (Num. v. 10) and next to it is, "If any man's wife go aside" (*ibid.* v. 12). Not only that, but in the end he will be in need of the offerings and tithes[11]; as it is said, "And every man's hallowed things shall be his[12]." Rab Naḥman b. Isaac[13] said: Should he duly hand them over, in the end he will

[1] I.e. even if engaged upon something forbidden, think of Him, then "He will direct (*lit.* straighten) thy paths." There are some who explain that the transgression refers only to the violation of a religious rite, as, e.g., the desecration of the Sabbath for the purpose of saving life. Some MSS (cf. *D. S. ad loc.*) insert here the proverb: The thief on the point of breaking into [a house] calls on God [for help].

[2] On this subject, see my *Ancient Jewish Proverbs*, Chap. v.

[3] *M.*: Judah.

[4] An Aramaised form of τριμίτιον "stitching with three-fold thread"; Krauss, p. 589, *T. A.* I. p. 569 n. 317.

[5] There is a variant: R. Meïr, which is perhaps to be preferred. See *D. S. ad loc.*, *A.T.* II. p. 17 n. 4.

[6] Wiesner, p. 157, points out that the word for "friends" is not *ōhᵉbim* but *rē'im*, which rather means "acquaintances."

[7] Numb. v. and vi.

[8] Drunkenness often leading to adultery.

[9] Some edd. omit: in the name of R. Parnak.

[10] The priest's.

[11] He will have need of the poor-tithe.

[12] I.e. if he withholds them from the priest, he will require them himself because of his poverty.

[13] *M.*: Raba.

grow rich; as it is said, "Whatever any man giveth the priest, it shall be his" (Num. v. 10)—i.e. much wealth shall be his.

Remember God in trouble.

Rab Huna b. Berekiah said in the name of R. Eleazar ha-Ḳappar: Whoever associates the name of Heaven with his trouble[1], his substance will be doubled for him; as it is said, "And the Almighty be thy treasure, and precious[2] silver unto thee" (Job xxii. 25). R. Samuel b. Naḥmani said: His sustenance will fly to him like a bird; as it is said, "And precious silver unto thee."

Relaxation from *Tōrāh* detrimental.

[3]R. Ṭabi said in the name of Josiah: Whoever relaxes from words of *Tōrāh* will have no strength to stand in the day of trouble; as it is said, "If thou faint in the day of adversity, thy strength is small indeed" (Prov. xxiv. 10). R. Ammi[4] b. Mattenah said in the name of Samuel: Even [if he relax from] a single commandment; as it is said, "If thou faint"—i.e. in any single instance.

Ḥananyah and the Palestinian Rabbis.

Rab Safra said: R. Abbahu related that when Ḥananyah[5], the nephew of R. Joshua, went to the Diaspora[6], he used to intercalate the years[7] and fix the new moons outside the [Holy] Land. They sent two disciples of the wise to him, R. Josē b. Kippar, and the grandson of Zechariah b. Ḳabuṭal. When he saw them, he asked, "Why have you come?" They answered, "To study *Tōrāh* have we come." He issued a proclamation[8], "These men are the famous men of the generation and their fathers ministered in the Temple; as we have learnt: Zechariah b. Ḳabuṭal says, 'Often have I read from the Book of Daniel before [the High Priest][9]'." Ḥananyah began to declare certain things unclean, and they pronounced them clean; he forbade certain things, and they declared them permissible. He thereupon proclaimed concerning them, "These men are worthless and men of no standing [and their fathers defiled the High Priesthood][10]." They said to him, "Thou hast already built up [our reputation here] and thou canst not pull down; thou hast already raised a fence and thou canst

[1] I.e. blesses God for the bad as well as the good.

[2] "Precious," *tō'āfōt*, is here connected with the Aramaic root *'āf* "to double"; hence "and silver will be doubled unto thee." In what follows, it is connected with the Hebrew root *'ūf* "to fly"; hence "and silver will fly unto thee."

[3] *M.* inserts: R. Samuel b. Mattenah stated that.

[4] *M.*: Ṭabi.

[5] This, and not Ḥannina, is the correct form of the name. Cf. *D. S. ad loc.*

[6] The Jewish Community of Babylon.

[7] See p. 63 n. 1. The arrangement of the Calendar was only permitted in Judea; Sanh. 11 *b*.

[8] Being flattered that they had come to him for tuition.

[9] On the night of the Day of Atonement when the High Priest was not allowed to sleep. Cf. Jōmā 18 *b*.

[10] Added by *M.*

not make a breach." He said to them, "Why, when I declare something unclean, do you pronounce it clean, and when I forbid you permit?" They said to him, "Why dost thou intercalate years and fix new moons outside the [Holy] Land?" He replied, "Did not 'Aḳiba b. Joseph act similarly[1]?" They said to him, "Keep R. 'Aḳiba out of it, because he left not his equal in the land of Israel[2]." He said to them, "I also have not left my equal in the land of Israel." They said to him, "The kids which thou didst leave behind have grown into goats with horns; and they have sent us to thee, saying to us, 'Go, tell him in our name[3]; if he obeys, well and good; but if not, let him be excommunicated.

fol. 63 b. Tell also our brethren in the Diaspora[4]; if they obey, well and good; but if not, let them ascend a mountain[5], let Aḥiyyah[6] build an altar and Ḥᵃnanyah play the harp[7], and let them all repudiate [their Judaism], declaring that they have no lot with the God of Israel'." Immediately all the people broke forth into loud weeping and said, "God forbid! We have a lot with the God of Israel." Why all this? Because it is said, "For out of Zion shall go forth the law, and the word of the Lord from Jerusalem" (Is. ii. 3).

A question answered. It is quite right that Ḥᵃnanyah declared something unclean and they pronounced it clean; that is merely taking the stricter view. But how could he declare anything unclean and they pronounce it clean? For lo, there is a teaching: If a Sage declares anything unclean, his colleague is not allowed to pronounce it clean; and if he declares it forbidden, his colleague is not allowed to pronounce it permissible! They thought [to act thus] so that the people may not be led by him.

Expositions of *Tōrāh* by Rabbis who visited Jabneh. Our Rabbis have taught: When our Rabbis entered the vineyard of Jabneh[8], there were present R. Judah, R. Josē, R. Nehe-

[1] It is mentioned in the *Talmūd* (Jᵉbāmōt 122 *a*) that he had done so in Nehardea.
[2] When he went to Babylon.
[3] Sc. to desist from usurping the right to fix the Calendar.
[4] To be guided by the authorities in Judea and not by Ḥᵃnanyah.
[5] To worship on a "high place" like the heathens.
[6] The lay head of the Babylonian Jews.
[7] He belonged to the Levites who were Temple-musicians.
[8] The name given to the Seminary in that town. See p. 111. "Vineyard" is usually explained in a figurative sense; but Krauss is of the opinion that the school was originally an actual vineyard; cf. *T. A.* iii. p. 340 n. 45 a. In the *Midrāsh* to Cant. ii. 5, there is another version of this incident with several differences. The place was not Jabneh but Usha; and in addition to the Rabbis mentioned here, there were R. Meïr, R. Simeon b. Joḥai and R. Eliezer b. Jacob. Bacher regards the version in the *Midrāsh* as the more authentic account; *A. T.* ii. p. 54 n. 6.

miah and R. Eliezer[1], the son of R. Josē of Galilee. They all began to expound *Tōrāh* in honour of the hospitality [which had been extended to them]. R. Judah, the chief of orators[2] in every place, began with the honour of the *Tōrāh* and expounded: "Now Moses used to take the tent and pitch it without the camp" (Exod. xxxiii. 7). Can we not use here an *a fortiori* argument: If of the Ark of God, which was never more than twelve *Mīl*[3] distant, the *Tōrāh* declares, "Everyone that sought the Lord went out unto the tent of meeting, which was without the camp" (*ibid.*), how much more so[4], the disciples of the wise who go from city to city and from province to province to study *Tōrāh*!

[5]"And the Lord spoke unto Moses face to face" (*ibid. v.* 11). R. Isaac said: The Holy One, blessed be He, spake unto Moses, "Moses, I and thou will discuss aspects[6] of *Hᵃlākāh*." Another version: Thus spake the Holy One, blessed be He, unto Moses, "In the same manner that I have shown thee a cheerful countenance, do thou likewise show Israel a cheerful countenance, and restore the tent to its place." "And he would return into the camp" etc. (*ibid.*). R. Abbahu said: The Holy One, blessed be He, spake to Moses, "Now will they say, The Master is angry[7] and the disciple is angry[8]; what will become of Israel? If thou wilt restore the tent to its place [within the camp], well and good; but if not, Joshua the son of Nun, thy disciple, will minister in thy stead." That is what is written, "And he would return into the camp[9]." Raba said: Nevertheless the word did not go forth from Him in vain; as it is said, "But his minister Joshua, the son of Nun, a young man, departed not out of the tent" (*ibid.*).

Exod. xxxiii. 11 expounded.

Further did R. Judah begin with the honour of the *Tōrāh* and expound: "Attend and hear; this day thou art become a people unto the Lord thy God" (Deut. xxvii. 9). But was it on that day that the *Tōrāh* had been given to Israel[10]? Was that not the completion of forty years! But it is intended to teach thee that every

Exposition of Deut. xxvii. 9.

1 This reading of the Paris MS (cf. *D. S. ad loc.*) is to be preferred to that of edd.: Eleazar.

2 He is given this title in Shab. 33 *b* and Mᵉnāḥōt 103 *b*. On its significance, see *A.T.* II. p. 193 n. 6.

3 That being the extent of the camp.

4 Should it be said that they "sought the Lord."

5 *M.* inserts: Further did R. Judah begin and expound.

6 *Lit.* faces.

7 Because of the Golden Calf.

8 Since he had removed the tent outside the camp.

9 Sc. with the tent.

10 Since it was the reception of the *Tōrāh* which constituted Israel a nation.

day is the *Tōrāh* endeared to them who study it as on the day that it was given on Mount Sinai. R. Tanḥum b. R. Ḥiyya, of the town of Acco, said: Thou mayest know from this that should a man recite the *Sh^e^ma'* morning and evening, but omit it a single evening, he is like one who has never recited it at all.

Tōrāh only acquired in a class.

"Attend [*haskēt*]"—i.e. "form classes[1]" and occupy yourselves with *Tōrāh*, because *Tōrāh* is only acquired in a class. This is in accord with the statement of R. Josē b. R. Ḥannina who said: What means that which is written, "A sword is upon the boasters [*baddīm*] and they shall become fools" (Jer. l. 36)? A sword is upon the enemies of the disciples of the wise[2] who sit separately [*bad wā-bad*] and study *Tōrāh*. Not only so, but they become foolish; for it is written here "And they shall become fools" and in another passage it is written, "For that we have done foolishly" (Num. xii. 11)[3]. If thou wilt I can quote the following: "The princes of Zoan are become fools" (Is. xix. 13).

One must be prepared to suffer for *Tōrāh*.

Another explanation of "Attend [*haskēt*] and hear, O Israel" (Deut. xxvii. 9)—i.e. submit to blows [*katt^e^tū*] on behalf of the words of *Tōrāh*; according to the statement of R. Simeon b. Laḳish who said: Whence is it learnt that the words of *Tōrāh* endure only with him who would suffer death on its behalf? As it is said, "This is the law: when a man dieth in a tent" (Num. xix. 14)[4]. Another explanation of "Attend [*haskēt*] and hear, O Israel": Be silent [*has*] and then discuss [*kattēt*]; according to the statement of Raba who said: A man should always study *Tōrāh* first and afterwards meditate thereon.

Prov. xxx. 33 expounded.

The school of R. Jannai said: What means that which is written, "For the churning of milk bringeth forth curd, and the wringing of the nose bringeth forth blood; so the forcing of wrath bringeth forth strife" (Prov. xxx. 33)? With whom dost thou find the cream of *Tōrāh*? With him who spat out for its sake the milk which he sucked from his mother's breast[5]. "And the wringing of the nose bringeth forth blood"—a disciple with whom his master is the first time angry[6] but he remains silent [under the rebuke] is worthy to distinguish between impure and pure blood[7]. "So the forcing

[1] *Haskēt* is made into two words: *'ăsū kittōt*.

[2] Euphemism for the disciples themselves.

[3] This verse and Is. xix. 13 which follows are only quoted to establish the meaning of the word "become fools" in Jer. l. 36.

[4] For "tent" in the sense of a School of *Tōrāh*, see p. 102 n. 2.

[5] I.e. he began its study in his earliest years.

[6] The same Hebrew word means "nose" and "anger."

[7] I.e. whether blood-stains are menstrual and defiling or not.

of wrath bringeth forth strife"—a disciple with whom his master is the first and second time angry but he remains silent [under the rebuke] is worthy to distinguish between suits involving money and suits involving life. For there is a Mishnaic teaching: R. Ishmael says: Who wishes to grow wise should study money-suits, for there is no branch of *Tōrāh* more [complex] than these; they are like a well[1].

To ask questions necessary in study of *Tōrāh*.

R. Samuel b. Naḥmani said: What means that which is written, "If thou hast done foolishly in lifting up thyself, or if thou hast planned devices [*zāmam*], lay thy hand upon thy mouth" (Prov. xxx. 32)? Everyone who makes himself foolish[2] for the sake of words of *Tōrāh* will in the end be lifted up; but if he muzzles [*zāmam*] his mouth[3], he will have to put his hand to his mouth[4].

Meritorious to entertain disciples of the wise.

R. Nehemiah began [to speak] in honour of the hospitality and expounded: What means that which is written, "And Saul said unto the Kenites, Go, depart, get you down from among the Amalekites, lest I destroy you with them; for ye showed kindness to all the children of Israel, when they came up out of Egypt" (I Sam. xv. 6)? Can we not use here an *a fortiori* argument: If Jethro[5], who only befriended Moses for his own honour, is treated with so much consideration, how much more so one who entertains a disciple of the wise in his house, giving him to eat and drink, and allowing him to enjoy his possessions!

Subject continued.

R. Josē began [to speak] in honour of the hospitality and expounded: "Thou shalt not abhor an Edomite, for he is thy brother; thou shalt not abhor an Egyptian, because thou wast a stranger in his land" (Deut. xxiii. 8). Can we not use here an *a fortiori* argument? If the Egyptians are not to be abhorred, who only befriended the Israelites for their own needs—as it is said, "And if thou knowest any able men among them, then make them rulers over my cattle" (Gen. xlvii. 6)—how much more so, one who entertains a disciple of the wise in his house, giving him to eat and drink, and allowing him to enjoy his possessions!

The blessing of Obed-Edom.

R. Eliezer, the son of R. Josē of Galilee, began [to speak] in honour of the hospitality and expounded: "And the Lord blessed

[1] Very deep.

[2] By asking his teacher questions concerning what he does not understand, thus exposing his ignorance.

[3] And he is afraid to ask questions.

[4] Being unable to answer when a question is put to him. Cf. Hillel's maxim: Nor can a shame-faced man learn (Ābōt ii. 6; Singer, p. 187).

[5] Who is described as a Kenite in Judges i. 16.

Obed-Edom and all his house...because of the Ark of God" (II Sam. vi. 11 f.). Can we not use here an *a fortiori* argument? If the Ark which neither ate nor drank, but which Obed-Edom swept and besprinkled[1], brought him a blessing, how much more so one who entertains a disciple of the wise, giving him to eat and drink, and allowing him to enjoy his possessions! What was the blessing wherewith He blessed him? R. Judah b. Z^e^bida said: It refers to Ḥamot[2] and her eight daughters-in-law who each bore six children

fol. 64 a. at one birth; as it is said, "Peullethai the eighth son" (I Chron. xxvi. 5), and it is written "For God blessed him" (*ibid.*), "All these were the sons of Obed-Edom, they and their sons and their brethren, able men in strength for the service; threescore and two of Obed-Edom" (*ibid. v.* 8)[3].

"Sinai" and "the uprooter of mountains."

R. Abin the Levite[4] said: Whoever forces fate[5], fate will force him; but whoever yields to fate, fate yields to him. So was it with Rabbah and Rab Joseph; for Rab Joseph [was nicknamed] "Sinai[6]" and Rabbah "the uprooter of mountains[7]." The time needed them[8]; so [the electors] sent [a message] there[9], "Of 'Sinai' and 'the uprooter of mountains,' which should be given preference?" They returned answer, "'Sinai' should be preferred, because all stand in need of an owner of wheat[10]." Nevertheless Rab Joseph did not accept the offer, because the Chaldeans[11] told him, "Thou wilt reign only two years[12]." Rabbah ruled two and twenty years[13], and then Rab Joseph two and a half; but all the years that Rabbah ruled he never called a cupper to his house[14].

[1] I.e. probably with wine and oil to perfume the air; cf. Büchler in *M.G.W.J.* XLIX. p. 33 and Josephus, *Antiq.* VIII. iv. 1.

[2] The wife of Obed-Edom.

[3] In order to explain the total of 62, the *Talmūd* reasons as follows: Obed-Edom had 8 sons, and then God blessed him, i.e. with six at one birth, making a family of 14. Then each of the eight daughters-in-law had six sons, thus bringing the aggregate to 62.

[4] *M.* omits: the Levite.

[5] *Lit.* the hour.

[6] Because he was learned in *Tōrāh*.

[7] Meaning, skilled in dialectics.

[8] One of them was required to fill the vacant position as the Principal of the Seminary at Pombedita.

[9] To the Rabbis of Palestine.

[10] For such a position, depth of knowledge was more necessary than keen argumentative powers.

[11] Astrologers.

[12] And then die.

[13] Rabbah was Principal 309—330, and was succeeded by Rab Joseph who died in 333.

[14] I.e. he never gave himself superior airs. If he needed blood-letting, instead of calling the cupper to his house, he went to him.

R. Abin the Levite also said: What means that which is written, "The Lord answer thee in the day of trouble; the name of the God of Jacob set thee up on high" (Ps. xx. 2)? The God of Jacob, but not the God of Abraham and Isaac! From this we learn that the owner of a beam should go in with the heaviest part of it[1].

Ps. xx. 2 discussed.

R. Abin the Levite also said: Whoever partakes of a meal at which a disciple of the wise is present is as though he partakes of the lustre of the *Shᵉkīnāh*; as it is said, "And Aaron came, and all the elders of Israel, to eat bread with Moses' father-in-law before God" (Exod. xviii. 12). Did they eat before God? Was it not before Moses that they ate? But it means to tell thee that whoever partakes of a meal at which a disciple of the wise is present is as though he partakes of the lustre of the *Shᵉkīnāh*.

To partake of a meal at which a disciple of the wise is present is like partaking of the *Shᵉkīnāh*.

R. Abin the Levite also said: One who takes leave of his friend should not say to him, "Go in peace" but "Go to peace"; because in the case of Jethro who said to Moses "Go to peace" (Exod. iv. 18), the latter advanced and prospered; but in the case of David who said to Absalom "Go in peace" (II Sam. xv. 9), the latter went and was hanged.

The phrases "Go in peace" and "Go to peace."

R. Abin the Levite also said: One who takes leave of the dead should not say to him, "Go to peace" but "Go in peace"; as it is said, "But thou shalt go to thy fathers in peace" (Gen. xv. 15).

Subject continued.

R. Levi b. Ḥiyya said[2]: He who goes out from the Synagogue and enters the House of Study to occupy himself with *Tōrāh* is worthy to receive the presence of the *Shᵉkīnāh*; as it is said, "They go from strength to strength, every one of them appeareth before God in Zion" (Ps. lxxxiv. 8).

From the Synagogue to the House of Study.

R. Ḥiyya b. Ashē said in the name of Rab[3]: The disciples of the wise have rest neither in this world nor in the world to come; as it is said, "They go from strength to strength, every one of them appeareth before God in Zion."

Disciples of the wise have no rest in both worlds.

R. Eleazar said in the name of R. Ḥannina: The disciples of the wise increase peace in the world; as it is said, "And all thy children shall be taught of the Lord; and great shall be the peace of thy children" (Is. liv. 13). Read not *bānayik* "thy children"

Prayer for peace.

[1] If, e.g., a builder wishes to set up a beam as part of a scaffold, he should put the thicker end into the ground, since it will be a stronger support. Similarly when praying, one relies most on the patriarch Jacob who is less remote from us in time than the others.

[2] *M.*: R. Ḥiyya b. Abba said in the name of R. Joḥanan.

[3] *M.*: R. Levi said.

but *bōnayik* "thy builders[1]." "Great peace have they that love Thy law; and there is no stumbling for them" (Ps. cxix. 165). "Peace be within thy walls, and prosperity within thy palaces" (*ibid.* cxxii. 7). "For my brethren and companions' sakes, I will now say, Peace be within thee" (*ibid. v.* 8). "For the sake of the house of the Lord our God, I will seek thy good" (*ibid. v.* 9). "The Lord will give strength unto His people; the Lord will bless His people with peace" (*ibid.* xxix. 11)[2].

May we return unto thee: *He who beholds!* And finished is the Tractate *B^e^rākōt.*

[1] By "builders" are meant the religious leaders.

[2] The Tractate ends on the note of peace, as does the *T^e^fillāh*, Singer, p. 54.

ADDITIONAL NOTES

P. 70. The alteration of "evil" into "all things" is due to a reluctance to ascribe "evil" as a creation to God. Thus Maimonides points out that darkness is not a creation, but the absence of light (A. Newman). He describes it as a "negative property" which "requires no agent"; *Guide*, Part III, Chap. x.

P. 80, l. 1. "I have never been worthy [to hear the reason]." The rendering given by Bertinoro (commentator on the *Mishnāh*, died 1510) is: I have never succeeded [in convincing my colleagues].

P. 100, last paragraph. "Rab Joseph taught in the presence of Raba: 'And thou shalt write them'" etc. Rashi comments: "Let the writing be perfect," on the same principle that Rab Obadiah explained "and ye shall teach" (see p. 101 n. 2). Rab Josiah's deduction may have been drawn from reading *ūk^e^sabtām* "and thou shalt write them" as *ūk^e^sōb t. m.*, the last two letters being regarded as the initials of *T^e^fillīn* and *M^e^zūzāh*, i.e. "write [the paragraphs of the *Sh^e^ma'* in] the *T.* and *M.*" (A. Newman).

P. 108, n. 6. On the identification of Rabbi's friend, see p. 379, n. 1.

P. 109, l. 16. "The leaven that is in the dough." On this phrase, see Abrahams, *Pharisaism and the Gospels*, pp. 51 ff.

Pp. 299 f. Compare with the Jewish custom that of the Romans: "The couch at the right of the table was called the upper couch; that at the left, the lower; and that between, the middle couch. With few exceptions each couch was made to accommodate three persons; the diner rested on his left arm on a cushion at the side nearer the table, and stretched his feet out toward the right. Hence, the first on the upper couch had what was called 'the highest place.' The one next was said to recline 'below' him, because lying on the side toward which the first person extended his feet; the man at the outer end of the lower couch was said to be 'at the foot,' *imus*"; A. Mau, *Pompeii, Its Life and Art*, p. 257.

P. 386, n. 5. Epstein, in *M.G.W.J.* LXIII. pp. 15 ff., argues that *Zīḳīn* means "storms," and the word in the *Mishnāh* [*Rūḥōt*] rendered "storms" is a gloss.

GLOSSARY

ABBĀ (Aram. father). Title of affection given to a number of Rabbis. Equivalent of πατήρ in Matt. xxiii. 9. (Cf. Schürer, II. i. p. 316.) According to Kohler (*J.Q.R.* XIII. pp. 567 ff.), it was originally the title given to the head of an Essene community.

ĂDĀR (Heb. borrowed fom Babylon). The twelfth month of the year.

AGGĀDĀH, AGGADTĀ [in Heb. HAGGĀDĀH] (Aram. narration). The name given to the portions of Rabbinic literature not included under *H^a^lākāh*. It embraces homiletic expositions of the Bible, folklore, history, legend, etc. On the origin of the term, see Bacher in *J.Q.R.* IV. pp. 406 ff. On the types of *Aggādāh*, see Mielziner, p. 57 and Schürer, II. i. pp. 339 ff.

'AM HĀ'ĀREṢ pl. 'AMMĒ HĀ'ĀREṢ (Heb. people of the earth). The opposite of the *Ḥābēr* (q.v.) and denotes the Jew who was careless about the performance of certain ceremonial obligations—particularly the laws of tithe and Levitical purity (cf. fol. 47*b* of our Tractate). The remarks of Schürer, II. ii. pp. 8 ff. must be read with caution, his views having been severely criticised by Jewish scholars, notably Büchler, *Der galiläische 'Am hā'āreṣ*. See also Montefiore, Hibbert Lectures, pp. 497 ff.

ĀMŌRĀ pl. ĂMŌRĀĪM (Aram. speaker). (1) Attendant of the *Tannā* who expounded at length the teaching, a summary of which the latter had given him in a low voice. (2) Name given to the Talmudical Rabbis who lived after the redaction of the *Mishnāh*.

BA'AL ḲERĪ pl. BA'ALĒ ḲERĀYĪN (Heb. one whom a mishap had befallen). A man who has experienced nocturnal pollution by the emission of semen.

BĀRĀITĀ (Aram. that which is outside.) A teaching of the *Tannāīm* not included in the *Mishnāh*, generally introduced by "Our Rabbis have taught" or "There is a teaching."

BAT ḲŌL (Heb. daughter of a voice). A heavenly voice giving utterance to a divine pronouncement. The Rabbinic material on the subject has been collected by E. A. Abbott, *From Letter to Spirit*, Book II and Appendix IV. See also *J. E.* II. pp. 588 ff.

BĒT (Heb. the house of). School; used especially of *Bēt* Shammai and *Bēt* Hillel, the two Schools which preserved and developed the teachings of those authorities.

BĒT DĪN (Heb. house of judgment). The Jewish court of law. See Schürer, II. i. pp. 169 ff.

'ĒRŪB (Heb. mixture). The act by means of which the legal fiction of continuity is established. In our Tractate we have reference only to *'Ērūb Teḥūmin*; viz. by depositing food sufficient for two meals before the advent of the Sabbath in a place which is the limit a person may travel on the day of rest (i.e. 2000 cubits, about 1000 yards), that spot is regarded as the man's temporary abode, and he may continue his journey from there a similar distance. See Schürer, II. ii. pp. 121 f., *J. E.* V. p. 204. On Rabbinical legal devices, see Raffalovich in the *Jewish Review*, Vol. IV., and the Appendix by Schechter in Montefiore's Hibbert Lectures.

GĒHINNŌM (Heb. valley of Hinnōm). In Greek, Gehenna. Originally the name of a valley, South of Jerusalem, where the horrors of Moloch worship were practised. It then became used as the name of the place where the wicked, after death, suffer the penalties of their misdeeds. See *J. E.* v. pp. 582 ff.

G^eMĀRĀ (Aram. completion, or traditional teaching). The discussion of the *Mishnāh* which forms the body of the *Talmūd*.

G^e'ULLĀH (Heb. redemption). Name given to the section of the liturgy between the *Sh^ema'* and the *T^efillāh* (Singer, pp. 42–44). To unite the *G^e'ullāh* with the *T^efillāh* is to follow the benediction "Blessed...Who hast redeemed Israel" immediately with "O Lord, open Thou my lips."

HABDĀLĀH (Heb. division). Form of prayer to mark the termination of the Sabbath or Festival: (1) Included in the *T^efillāh* (Singer, p. 46); (2) A separate service in which a cup of wine, spices and light are used (Singer, pp. 216 f.; Oesterley and Box, pp. 378 ff.).

ḤĀBĒR (Heb. associate). A member of the Jewish religious party which rigorously submitted to the Levitical laws of tithe and purity. Opposite of the *'Am hā'āreṣ*. See the literature quoted under that term; also *J. E.* VI. pp. 121 ff.

HAFṬĀRĀH (Heb. dismissal). Reading from the Prophets which follows the lection from the Pentateuch in the Synagogue. See Schürer, II. ii. p. 81, *J. E.* VI. pp. 135 f.

HAGGĀDĀH s.v. *Aggādāh*.

H^aLĀKĀH pl. H^aLĀKŌT (Heb. way, custom). (1) The legal sections of the *Talmūd*; opposite of *Aggādāh*. (2) Decision arrived at after a discussion on a point of law; hence, the rule of conduct to adopt. See Schürer, II. i. pp. 330–339.

ḤALLĀH (Heb. rounded cake). Piece of dough, one twenty-fourth of the whole in the case of an individual and a half of that in the case of a baker, set apart as the priest's due from any of the five species of grain (wheat, barley, spelt, oats and rye) which was being kneaded (Num. xv. 17–21). After the destruction of the Temple, the piece was separated and burnt. See Schürer, II. i. pp. 241 f., *J. E.* VI. pp. 174 f.

HALLĒL (Heb. praise). Psalms recited on Festivals and the New Moon (Singer, pp. 219–224). "The *Hallēl* of Egypt" consists of Ps. cxiii to Ps. cxviii; and "to complete the *Hallēl*" means to include Ps. cxv. 1-11 and Ps. cxvi. 1-11. "The great *Hallēl*" is the name given to Ps. cxxxvi.

ḲAB (Heb.). Measure of capacity, one sixth of a *S^eāh*, equal to 2197 cubic centimetres.

KAWWĀNĀH (Heb. root, to be firm). (1) Intention; i.e. the religious duty must be performed with the deliberate thought of its proper fulfilment. (2) Attention; i.e. concentration of the mind, devoutness of heart.

ḲIDDŪSH (Heb. sanctification). Form of prayer to mark the inauguration of the Sabbath or Festival: (1) Included in the *T^efillāh* (Singer, pp. 116 f., 229); (2) A separate service with the cup of wine (*ibid.* pp. 124, 230 f., 243 f.; Oesterley and Box, pp. 374 ff.).

KIL'ĀĪM (Heb. two kinds). Term for the forbidden mixture of seeds or stuffs. (Cf. Lev. xix. 19; Deut. xxii. 9–11.)

KŌHĒN pl. KŌH^aNĪM (Heb. priest). In Temple times, a descendant of Aaron who officiated in the Sanctuary. After the destruction of the Temple, the distinctiveness of the *Kōhēn* was preserved by certain privileges (e.g. he was the first to be called to the Reading of the *Tōrāh*) and disabilities (e.g. he must not defile himself by contact with the dead, except in the case of his nearest relatives).

LŌG (Heb.). A liquid measure equal to the contents of, or the space occupied by, six eggs; about 549 cubic centimetres.

LŪLĀB (Heb. palm-branch). The branch of the palm which, bound together with myrtle branches and branches of the willow, is used on the Festival of Tabernacles (Lev. xxiii. 40). See Oesterley and Box, pp. 399 ff.

M^eGILLĀH (Heb. scroll). Name given especially to the Book of Esther read on the Feast of Pūrīm. See Oesterley and Box, pp. 407 ff.

MĒT MIṢWĀH (Heb. corpse which is a religious obligation). The dead body of a person who has no relatives to attend to its burial. The duty of interment devolves upon whoever discovers it, even the High Priest.

M^eZŪZĀH (Heb.). A piece of parchment, inscribed with Deut. vi. 4–9, xi. 13–21, affixed to the doorpost. For a fuller description, see Oesterley and Box, pp. 454 f.

MIDRĀSH (Heb. exposition.) Originally the deduction of an idea or practice from the Scriptures. It was then used in a narrower sense to denote the Aggadic exegesis of the Bible, and particularly the collections of such homilies and expositions. See Oesterley and Box, pp. 77 ff.

MIḲWÉH (Heb. gathering, sc. of water). Name given to the ritual bath of purification, containing at least forty *Sāōt* of running water.

MĪL (Greek μίλιον or Latin *mille* sc. *passus*). A measure of distance, equal to 2000 cubits, about 1000 yards.

MĪN pl. MĪNĪM (perhaps Heb. species, sect). A heretic, especially the early Jewish-Christian. The passages in Rabbinic literature referring to the *Minīm* are collected and discussed in R. T. Herford, *Christianity in Talmud and Midrash*.

MISHNĀH (Heb. repetition, teaching by repetition). The corpus of Jewish law redacted by R. Judah the Prince.

NĪSĀN (Heb. borrowed from Babylon). First month of the year.

'ORLĀH (Heb. foreskin). The fruit of trees which must not be eaten during the first three years of planting (Lev. xix. 23).

PĀRĀSHĀH (Heb. separation). A section of Scripture; a paragraph. The weekly lection from the Pentateuch.

PARSĀH (perhaps the Greek παρασάγγης). A measure of distance; Persian mile, about 4000 yards.

RAB (Heb. great, master). (1) Title of the Babylonian *Ămōrāīm*. (2) Name by which Abba Arika is usually quoted.

RABBAN (Heb. master). Title of respect given to four of the *Tannāīm*: Gamaliel I and II, Simeon b. Gamaliel and Joḥanan b. Zakkai. On others who sometimes receive this title, see Schürer, II. i. p. 316, note 27.

RABBI (Heb. my master). (1) Title of the *Tannāīm* and Palestinian *Ămōrāīm*. (2) Name by which R. Judah the Prince is usually quoted.

S^eĀH pl. SĀŌT (Heb.). Measure of capacity, equal to six *Ḳabs*; about 13,184 cubic centimetres.

S^eMŪKĪN (Heb. connected). The law of Biblical exegesis which is based on the fact that two passages are found together in the text and are therefore to be connected in interpretation. See Mielziner, pp. 177 ff.

SH^e^KĪNĀH (Heb. abiding). The Divine Presence as manifested on earth; the Spirit of God immanent in the world. See Oesterley and Box, pp. 217 ff., Abelson, *Immanence of God in Rabbinic Literature*, Chaps. IV–XII.

SH^e^MA' (Heb. hear). Collection of Scriptural passages (Deut. vi. 4–9, xi. 13–21, Num. xv. 37–41) to be recited morning and night.

ṢĪṢIT (Heb. fringes). Fringes attached to the corners of a garment as ordained in Num. xv. 37–41. For a description, see Oesterley and Box, pp. 450 ff.

SUKKĀH (Heb. booth). Booth, with a roof of branches and leaves, in which the Israelite was commanded to dwell during the Festival of Tabernacles (Lev. xxiii. 34). See Oesterley and Box, pp. 397 ff.

ṬALLĪT (Heb.). A cloak with "fringes" worn during the time of prayer. See Oesterley and Box, pp. 450 ff.

TALMŪD (Heb. learning). Name given to that branch of Rabbinic literature which comprises the *Mishnāh* and *G^e^mārā*.

TANNĀ pl. TANNĀĪM (Aram. one who teaches by repetition). (1) A teacher of Rabbinic law. (2) Title given to the Rabbis named in the *Mishnāh* and *Bārāitā*.

T^e^FILLĀH pl. T^e^FILLŌT (Heb. prayer). From meaning "prayer" in general, the word is used to denote the important section of the liturgy which must be said standing, viz. the Eighteen benedictions of the week-day service (Singer, pp. 44–54), and the corresponding forms for Sabbaths and Festivals (*ibid.* pp. 115–119, 136–142, 159–166, 175 f., 225 f., 227–229, 233–242, 245–254, 256–268).

T^e^FILLĪN (Aramaised form of the Heb.). Phylacteries worn on the forehead and left arm during the morning prayer of a week-day, although in Talmudic times they were worn throughout the day. They consist of two "cases" attached to leather thongs. Each case contains parchment inscribed with Exod. xiii. 1–10, 11–16; Deut. vi. 4–9, xi. 13–21. For a fuller description, see Oesterley and Box, pp. 447 ff. and the article (with illustrations) in *J. E.* x. pp. 21 ff.

T^e^RŪMĀH (Heb. [portion of offering] lifted off, separated). Portion of the crops and produce generally set aside as the priest's due. It consisted principally of wheat, wine and oil.

TŌRĀH (Heb. instruction). Used in a wide sense to denote the whole body of Jewish teaching as contained in the Scriptures and the traditions connected therewith. It is also employed to mean the Pentateuch, as distinct from the Prophetical books. On the Rabbinic conception of *Tōrāh*, see Oesterley and Box, Chap. VII, R. T. Herford, *Pharisaism*, and Schechter, *Aspects of Rabbinic Theology*, Chaps. VIII–XI.

ZIMMŪN (Heb. arrangement, designation). Arrangement whereby three or more men who take their meal in common say Grace together with introductory responses. He who leads the prayer commences, "Let us say Grace," to which the others respond, "Blessed be the name of the Lord from this time forth and for ever." The leader says, "With the sanction of those present, we will bless Him of Whose bounty we have partaken." To this, the response is "Blessed be He of Whose bounty we have partaken, and through Whose goodness we live," which is repeated by the leader (Singer, pp. 279 f.).

ZUZ (Heb.). A coin, the equivalent of the silver *denarius* and worth about 7*d.*

INDEX I

RABBINICAL AUTHORITIES CITED

[Abbreviations: BA = Babylonian *Āmōrā*; c. = *circa* "about"; DS = the reading adopted by Rabbinovicz; l. = *lege* "read"; M = the reading of the Munich MS; PA = Palestinian *Āmōrā*; s.l. = *sic lege* "read thus"; s.v. = *sub voce* "under the term"; T = *Tannā*. ? denotes a doubtful reading and ! an incorrect reading. The number following a name indicates the century in which the Rabbi flourished. Rabbinic chronology offers numerous perplexities, owing to the fact that the *Talmūd* gives no dates. With a few exceptions, it is not possible to state the year of birth or death. Much confusion is also caused by the same name sometimes denoting more than one Rabbi. The modern works which have been chiefly consulted are: the articles in *J.E.*, Bacher's books on the *Aggādāh*, and the Hebrew works of Weiss and Hyman.]

(*The reference is to the pagination of the Talmudic text.*)

Abba I (BA 3–4) 11 b 14 a 19 b 22 a [M] 24 b 28 b 49 a 50 a 60 a [M] 61 b [M] 62 b
Abba II (PA 4–5) 9 a [!] 39 b
Abbā Benjamin s.v. Benjamin
Abbā Josē b. Dostai s.v. Josē b. Dostai
Abbā Mar b. Pappa s.v. Mar b. Pappa
Abbā Saul s.v. Saul
Abba b. Abba, the father of Samuel (BA 2–3) 18 b 30 a
Abba b. Aḥa (PA 3) 22 a [s.l.] 25 b [M s.l.] 49 a [s.l.]
Abba [Ărīkā] b. Aibu s.v. Rab
Abba b. Ḥinnana, or Ḥannina (PA 3–4) 30 a [M s.l.] 56 b [M]
Abba b. Ḥiyya b. Abba (PA 4) 5 a 14 a [M s.l.] 43 b 48 a 61 b
Abba b. Kahᵃna (PA 3–4) 3 b 6 b
Abba b. Mari 5 a [M ! l. Raba b. Mari]
Abba b. Zabda (PA 3) 11 a 16 b
Abbahu (PA 3–4) 6 b 8 a 9 b 10 a 14 a, b 20 a 24 b 32 a 34 b 39 a 44 a 45 a 46 a 47 a 51 a, b 55 a 58 a [M] 59 b 60 a 61 a, b [M] 62 b 63 a, b
Abbahu b. Zuṭarti (BA) 12 b. This is the only place in the *Talmūd* where this Rabbi is mentioned
Abbai (BA 279–338) 5 a 6 a, b 7 a 8 a, b 9 b 10 b 11 b 14 b 17 a, b [M] 19 b 20 a, b 21 a 22 b 23 a, b 25 a, b 27 b 28 b 29 a, b 30 b 31 a 32 a 33 a [M] 33 b 34 b 35 b 36 b 37 b 38 a, b 39 a 40 b 42 a, b 44 a, b 45 a, b 46 b 47 a, b 48 a 49 b 50 a 53 b 54 b 56 a 57 a 59 a, b 60 a, b 61 b 62 a, b 63 a
Abbai b. Abin (BA 4) 29 b
Abdan [or Abidan = Abba Judan] (PA 3) 27 b
Abin or Rabin (PA 4) 7 a 22 a 27 b 30 a 37 b 44 a, b 47 a 49 b
Abin the Levite (PA 4) 64 a
Abin [or, Rabin] b. Adda (BA 4) 6 a, b
Abina (PA 3) 4 b [!] 7 a 30 a
Abṭalion (T 1 B.C.) 19 a
Adda b. Ahᵃbah (BA 3) 5 b 8 b 20 a, b 21 b 22 a 24 b 33 a [M] 42 b 43 a 50 a
Adda b. Mattᵉna I (BA 3) 30 b
Adda b. Mattᵉna II (BA 4) 23 a 62 b
Aḥa I (T 2) 2 b 13 b 53 b 60 a
Aḥa II (PA 4) 3 b 47 a [!] 50 a [M] 59 a [M] 60 b
Aḥa Ărīkā ["the tall," i.e. Aḥa b. Pappa] (PA 3) 33 a

Aḥa of Difti (BA 5) 45 b
Aḥa Ḳarḥināāh (BA 4) 33 a
Aḥa b. Abba b. Aḥa [!] 25 b l. Abba b. Aḥa
Aḥa b. Adda (BA 4) 8 a [M]
Aḥa b. 'Awira [!] 44 a l. Aḥa b. Iwya
Aḥa b. Bizna [!] 3 b l. Ḥanna b. Bizna
Aḥa b. Ḥannina (PA 3) 5 a 8 a, b 9 a 51 b
Aḥa b. Ḥiyya b. Abba [!] 14 a l. Abba b. Ḥiyya b. Abba
Aḥa b. Huna (BA 4) 23 a 32 a
Aḥa b. Iwya (BA 3) 44 a [s.l.]
Aḥa b. Jacob (BA 3) 13 b 22 a [?] 27 a 44 b 58 b [M] 59 a
Aḥa b. Raba (BA 4–5) 6 a 50 a
Aḥai (B 6, post-Amoraic period) 2 b 13 b [M] 25 b [!]
Aḥēr s.v. Elisha b. Abuya
Aḥi (PA 3–4) 14 a
Ahilai (BA 3–4) 25 b [M s.l.]
'Aḳabya b. Mahalalel (T 1–2) 19 a
'Aḳiba [b. Joseph] (T c. 50–132) 8 b 9 a, b 13 a, b 22 a 23 a 27 b 28 a, b 29 a 31 a, b 33 a, b 35 a 36 a, b 37 a 44 a, b 46 b 49 b 50 a 55 b 57 b [M] 58 a 60 b 61 b 62 a 63 a
Alexander (PA 3) 17 a 59 a
Amemar (BA 4–5) 12 a 25 a 30 b 44 b 50 b 55 b
Ammi (PA 3–4) 3 b 6 b 8 a 9 b 11 b 14 a 16 a 17 a 20 b 22 b [M] 27 a, b [M] 30 b 33 a 39 b 41 a 44 a 47 b 53 b 61 a 62 a
Ammi b. Mattenah (BA 3?) 63 a. Only place in the *Talmūd* where he is mentioned
'Amram (BA 4) 44 a 49 b
'Anan (BA 3) 30 b
Aphes (PA 3) 18 b
Ashē (BA 352–427) 3 b 4 a 5 a 6 a, b 9 b 12 a 13 b 17 b 18 a 23 a 24 a, b 26 a 29 a 30 a, b 31 a 36 b [M] 39 a, b 42 a 44 a [!], b 45 b 46 b 47 b [M] 50 a, b 51 a, b [M] 52 b [M] 53 b 54 b 55 b 57 a, b 58 b 59 a, b 61 a 62 a
Ashyan (PA 3) 14 a
Assi I (BA 3) 6 a [M s.l.] 9 b [M!] 18 a 23 a [M s.l.] 34 a 36 b 38 a 44 a [s.l.] 45 a 47 b [?] 51 a, b 53 b [M]
Assi II (PA 3–4) 4 b [M s.l.] 6 b 8 a 14 a 16 a 20 b 22 b 24 b 27 a, b 29 a, b 30 b 33 a [M s.l.] 39 b 44 a 62 a
Assi b. Nathan (BA 3) 62 a [DS]
'Awira (BA 4) 20 b

Bali (BA 4) 25 b
Bannaāh (T 2–3) 55 b
Bar Ḳappāra (T 2–3) 13 a, b 24 a 34 a 39 a 56 b 62 b 63 a
Bebai I (BA 3–4) 6 b
Bebai II (PA 4) 62 b
Bebai b. Abbai (BA 4) 6 a, b [?] 8 b 29 a
Bebai b. Naḥman [!] 6 b [M]
Ben 'Azzai [= Simeon b. 'Azzai] (T 2) 6 b 18 a 21 b 22 a 47 a, b 54 a 57 b 62 a, b
Ben Dama [= Eleazar b. Dama] (T 2) 56 b
Ben Zoma [= Simeon b. Zoma] (T 2) 6 b 12 b 41 b 43 a 57 b 58 a
Benjamin (T 2) 5 b 6 a
Benjamin b. Japhet (PA 3) 33 a 38 b
Berekiah (PA 4) 55 a
Berona (BA 3) 9 b
Bēt Hillel s.v. Hillel
Bēt Shammai s.v. Shammai
Biryam [?] 55 b
Bizna b. Zabda [!] 55 b

Dimai (BA 4) 6 b 21 b 22 a 27 b [M] 31 b 44 a, b 50 a
Dimai b. Abba (BA ?) 53 b
Dimai b. Joseph (BA 3) 45 b
Dimai b. Lewai (BA 4) 27 b
Dostai b. Mattun (T 2) 7 b

El'ai I (T 2) 22 a
El'ai II (PA 3–4) 9 b 22 a 25 b [M] 40 b 49 a
Eleazar ha-Ḳappār (T 2) 63 a
Eleazar Ḥisma (T 1–2) 27 b [s.l.]
Eleazar b. Abina (PA 4) 4 b [M s.l.]
Eleazar b. 'Azariah (T 1–2) 9 a 11 a 12 b 15 a, b 27 b 28 a 30 a, b 57 b
Eleazar b. Ḥanok (T 1–2) 19 a
Eleazar b. Josē (PA 5) 27 b
Eleazar [b. Pedat] (PA 3) 3 b [M] 4 b [!] 5 a [M] 5 b [M s.l.] 6 b 7 a, b 9 b 10 a [M] 11 b 12 b 16 a, b 17 a, b 19 a 20 b

21 a 22 b 25 b 27 b 28 a 30 b 31 a, b 32 a, b 33 a 36 a [M !] 55 a, b 62 b 64 a
Eleazar b. Ṣadoḳ (T 1) 19 b 29 b
Eleazar b. Shammua' (T 2) 22 a [M]
Eliezer [b. Hyrcanus, also called the Great or Elder] (T 1–2) 2 a, b 3 a 4 a 5 b [!] 6 a, b [?] 7 b [!] 9 a, b 10 a [!] 11 b 13 a, b [M] 16 b 19 a 21 b 25 b 28 b 29 a, b 32 a 33 a, b 34 a 36 a, b 38 a, 47 b 48 b 50 a, b 57 a 61 b 62 a, b [M]
Eliezer b. Jacob (T 1–2) 10 b 32 a 40 b
Eliezer b. Josē of Galilee (T 2) 63 b
Elisha b. Abuya (T 1–2) 57 b
Ezekiel (BA 3) 11 a

Gamaliel I (T 1) 28 b
Gamaliel II (T 1–2) 2 a 4 b 8 b 9 a 16 a, b 18 a 27 b 28 a, b 34 b 37 a, b 43 b 44 a 53 a
G^eniba (BA 3) 25 a 27 a
Giddel (BA 3) 20 a 21 b 43 b 49 a
Giddel b. Minyomi (BA 3) 49 a

Ḥ^alafta b. Saul (T 2–3) 29 a
Ḥamma of Nehardea (BA 4) 22 b
Ḥamma b. Buzi (BA 4) 50 a
Ḥamma b. Ḥannina (PA 3) 5 b 15 b 32 a, b 40 a 55 a 56 b
Hamnuna I (BA 3) 10 a 11 b 17 a 22 b 31 a 41 b 57 b 58 a
Hamnuna II (BA 3–4) 24 b 25 a 60 a [?]
Hamnuna Zoṭi (BA 4) 17 a 31 a
Hamnuna b. Joseph (BA 4) 24 a. Only place in the *Talmūd* where he is mentioned
Ḥanan (T 2) 10 b 41 a [?] 51 a 56 b
Ḥanan b. Abba [also b. Raba or Rabbah] (BA 3) 45 a 58 a
Ḥanan b. Ammi (BA 4) 55 b [s.l.]
Ḥanan b. Raba s.v. Ḥanan b. Abba
Ḥananel (BA 3) 43 b 49 a
Ḥ^ananyah b. Gamaliel s.v. Ḥannina b. Gamaliel
Ḥ^ananyah, nephew of R. Joshua (T 1–2) 63 a, b
Ḥanna of Bagdat (BA 3) 54 b
Ḥanna b. Adda (BA ?) 62 b
Ḥanna b. Bizna (BA 3–4) 3 b [M s.l. 7 a 43 b
Ḥanna b. Ḥ^anilai (BA 3–4) 58 b
Ḥanna b. Judah (BA 4) 48 a, b
Ḥanna b. Rab [?] 43 b [M]
Ḥannin (PA 4) 4 b [M] 8 a [M] 32 b 41 a [?]
Ḥannina (T 2) 2 b
Ḥannina of Sura (BA 5) 52 b
Ḥannina, nephew of R. Joshua [!] l. Ḥ^ananyah
Ḥannina b. Dosa (T 1) 17 b 33 a 34 b 61 b
Ḥannina b. Gamaliel (T 1–2) 22 a
Ḥannina [b. Ḥamma] (PA 3) 5 b 8 a 17 a 22 a 24 a 27 b 28 b 32 b 33 b 34 a 44 a 51 b [M] 56 b 60 b [M] 62 b 64 a
Ḥannina b. Iḳa s.v. Ḥinnana b. Iḳa
Ḥannina [or, Ḥinnana] b. Pappa (PA 3–4) 5 a 23 a 35 b 40 a 51 a
Ḥelbo (PA 4) 6 b 12 a 29 a 62 b
Hezekiah (PA 4) 53 b
Hezekiah b. Ḥiyya (PA 3) 18 b
Hezekiah b. Parnak (PA 4) 63 a
Hillel (T died 10) 60 a 63 a
Bēt Hillel 10 b 11 a 16 a 23 a, b 36 a, b 43 b 51 b 52 a, b 53 a, b
Hillel b. Samuel b. Naḥmani (PA 4) 28 b [s.l.]
Ḥinnana 33 a l. Huna
Ḥinnana b. Iḳa (BA 4) 25 b 58 b
Ḥinnana b. Pappa s.v. Ḥannina b. Pappa. [On the form of the name, cf. *A. P. A.* II. p. 513, n. 2]
Ḥisda (BA 218–309) 5 a 8 a 10 b 12 a 15 a, b 17 a 19 a [M] 20 b 22 a, b 23 b 24 a, b 25 a 26 a 27 a 29 b 30 a, b 33 a 34 a 38 a, b 39 a 40 a 41 b 43 a, b 44 a, b 47 a, b 49 a 50 a 51 a 53 b 55 a, b 56 a 58 b 59 a 61 a 62 a 63 a
Ḥisda b. Abdemi 53 b l. Isaac b. Abdemi
Ḥiyya (PA 3–4) 13 b 14 a 16 b 17 a 18 a 23 b 24 a 26 a 29 b [M] 30 a [M] 33 a [M] 34 b 35 a 37 b 39 a, b 40 a [!] 41 b 43 a 46 b 52 a 55 a [M]
Ḥiyya b. Abba (PA 3–4) 5 a, b 13 b 14 a [M], b 15 a 22 a 25 b [M] 29 b 30 b 31 a 32 a, b 33 a, b 34 b 38 b 39 a [M]

40 a [s.l.] 43 b 44 a 47 b [M] 48 a, b [M] 51 a 53 a 54 b 57 a 64 a [M]
Ḥiyya b. Abba b. Naḥmani 43 a s.v. Ḥiyya b. Rabbah b. Naḥmani
Ḥiyya b. Abin (BA 4) 6 a 27 b [!] 30 a 33 b
Ḥiyya b. Ammi (BA 4) 8 a
Ḥiyya b. Ashē (BA 3) 11 b 14 b 27 b [M s.l.] 31 a 39 a 40 a 42 a 43 a 46 b 64 a
Ḥiyya b. Huna (BA 4) 34 b
Ḥiyya b. Naḥmani (T 2) 48 b
Ḥiyya b. Rab (BA 3) 12 a 14 b 16 a [M] 30 a 53 b
Ḥiyya b. Rab of Difti (BA 3) 8 b
Ḥiyya b. Rabbah b. Naḥmani (BA 4) 43 a [s.l.]
Ḥiyya b. Shela [!] 53 b [M]
Hosha'ya s.v. Osha'ya
Huna I (BA 216–297) 5 a, b 6 a, b 7 b 9 b 11 b 21 b 22 a 24 a 25 a, b 26 a 27 a 28 b 29 b 30 b 31 a 33 a [M s.l.] 34 a 35 b 37 a 39 a, b 40 b 41 b 42 a, b 45 b 46 a 47 a, b 48 a [M] 49 a, b 50 a 52 b 53 a, b 55 b 59 b 60 a, b 61 a 62 b
Huna II (BA 3) 24 b
Huna b. Adda (BA ?) 62 b [M]
Huna b. Ammi 55 b l. Ḥanan b. Ammi
Huna b. Berekiah (BA ?) 63 a. Only place in the *Talmūd* where he is mentioned
Huna b. Ḥinnana [or, Ḥannina] 30 a l. Abba b. Ḥannina
Huna b. Ika (BA 4) 43 b
Huna b. Joshua (BA 4) 22 b 50 a 57 a 58 b
Huna b. Judah (BA 4–5) 8 a 26 a 48 a [M], b [M] 52 b 58 b [M]
Huna b. Nathan (BA 4) 42 a

Iddi b. Abin (BA 4) 14 a 44 b 49 b 53 b [s.l. ?]
Ila b. Samuel b. Marta (BA 3–4) 13 b. Only place in the *Talmūd* where he is mentioned
Isaac (T 2) 13 b 48 b
Isaac of Ḳarṭignin (PA ?) 29 a
Isaac Ḳaskᵉsāāh (PA 4) 51 a
Isaac Nappāḥā ["the smith"] (PA 3–4) 41 a 62 b
Isaac b. Abdemi I (PA 3) 30 b 33 b 44 b
Isaac b. Abdemi II (BA 3) 53 b [M s.l.]
Isaac b. Adda [or, Iddi] (BA 3) 4 a
Isaac [b. Aḥa, the Halakist] (PA 3–4) 7 b 10 b 13 b 23 b 24 a 26 a 27 a 33 a 35 b 36 a 40 b 41 a, b 43 a 44 b 48 b 55 a 59 b
Isaac b. Ammi (BA 4) 60 a [?]
Isaac b. Ashyan (BA 3) 14 a
Isaac b. Eleazar [identified with Isaac Nappāḥā] 40 b [M]
Isaac b. Ḥannina (BA 3) 52 b [s.l.]
Isaac b. Joseph (PA 3–4) 9 a 11 b 42 b
Isaac b. Judah (BA 3–4) 33 a [M]
Isaac b. Naḥmani (PA 3) 34 b
Isaac [b. Phineas, the Aggadist] (PA 3–4) 4 a 5 a, b 6 a, b 7 b 10 b 18 b 19 a 32 a 44 a 55 a 61 a [M] 62 b [M] 63 b
Isaac b. Rab [!] 4 a [M]
Isaac b. Rᵉdifa (PA 4) 60 a [M]
Isaac b. Samuel [?] 3 a [!] 38 b [?]
Isaac b. Samuel b. Marta (BA 3–4) 3 a [M s.l.] 13 b [M] 25 b 46 a
Ishmael b. Elisha [the High Priest; see p. 35, n. 2] 7 a 51 a 57 b
Ishmael [b. Elisha] (T 1–2) 11 a 31 b 35 b 48 b 49 b 50 a 56 b [?] 63 b
School of: 19 a 32 a 37 b 57 b 60 a
Ishmael b. Joḥanan b. Baroḳa (T 2) 59 a
Ishmael b. Josē (T 2) 27 b 56 b [DS] 60 a
Ishmael b. Naḥman [!] 62 b [M]
Ishmael b. Nathan [!] 60 b [M]
Issi b. Nathan [!] 62 a l. Assi b. Nathan
Iwya (BA 4) 28 b

Jacob (BA 3–4) 11 a 29 b 30 a 34 a
Jacob b. Aḥa (PA 4) 23 a 49 a [!]
Jacob b. Bat Samuel (BA 4; see p. 103, n. 4) 25 b
Jacob b. Iddi (PA 3) 4 a 5 a 11 a [M] 29 b 44 a 62 b
Jannai I (T and PA 2–3) 22 a 30 b 35 b 44 b
School of: 9 a 32 a 34 b [M] 63 b
Jannai II (PA 3) 55 b [DS]
Jannai, brother of Ḥiyya b. Abba (PA 3) 21 b
Jemar b. Shᵉlamya (BA 4) 53 b

Jemar b. Shezbi (BA 5) 53 b
Jeremiah (PA 4) 13 b 24 a 30 b 38 b 40 a 41 a 48 a 61 a
Jeremiah of Difti (BA 4) 25 a [M s.l.]
Jeremiah b. Abba I (BA 3) 27 a, b 55 b 56 a
Jeremiah b. Abba II (BA 3–4) 39 b
Jeremiah b. Eleazar (PA 3) 58 a 61 a
Johanan ha-Sand^{e}lār ["the sandal-maker"] (T 2) 22 a
Johanan b. ha-Horanit (T 1) 11 a
Johanan [b. Nappaha] (PA 180–279) 4 a, b 5 a, b 6 b 7 a, b 8 a 9 b 10 a, b 11 b 12 a, b 13 b 14 a, b 15 a 16 a, b 17 a, b 18 a 20 a 21 a, b 22 b 23 a 24 b 25 a, b 26 a 28 a, b 29 b 30 b 31 a, b 32 a, b 33 a, b 34 b 35 b 36 a 37 b 38 b 39 a, b 40 a, b 42 b 43 a, b 44 a, b 45 a, b 46 a 47 a, b 48 a, b 49 a, b 50 a 51 a, b 52 b 53 a, b 54 a, b 55 a, b 57 a, b 58 a, b 59 a [M], b 60 a 61 a, b 62 a [M], b 63 a 64 a [M]
Johanan b. Nuri (T 1–2) 37 a
Johanan b. Zakkai (T 1) 17 a 28 b 34 b
Jonah (PA 4) 14 a
Jonathan [b. Eleazar] (PA 3) 6 b [?] 7 a 8 a [M] 9 b [M s.l.] 18 a 23 a 25 a 32 a 35 a 55 a, b 56 b [s.l.]
Jonathan [or, Nathan] b. Joseph (T 2) 22 a 47 b [s.l.] 48 b [s.l.]
Josē of Galilee (T 1–2) 49 b 50 a 61 b
Josē b. Abba s.v. Joseph b. Abba
Josē b. Abin (PA 4) 12 b 13 a 22 a 33 b 51 a
Josē b. Dostai (T 2) 28 a 49 a
Josē b. Eliakim (T ?) 9 b. Only place in the *Talmūd* where he is mentioned
Josē [b. H^{a}lafta] (T 2) 2 b 3 a 4 a, b [!] 7 a [!] 15 a, b 16 b 19 a 22 a 25 a 33 a [!] 36 b 38 b 40 b 47 b 48 b 53 a, b 60 a 61 b 62 b [M] 63 b
Josē b. Hannina (PA 3) 6 a 8 a 10 b 20 a 22 b 26 a, b 30 b 31 a, b 41 b 50 b 51 a 52 b [!] 55 b 62 b 63 b
Josē b. Judah (T 2) 49 a 62 b
Josē b. Kippar (T 2) 63 a
Josē b. Z^{e}bida (PA 4) 12 b [M] 13 a 22 a 33 b
Josē b. Zimra (PA 3) 7 a [s.l.] 10 b 31 b
Joseph b. Abba (BA 3–4) 11 b 59 b
Joseph [b. Hiyya] (BA died 333) 3 b 6 a [M] 7 a 8 b 9 a 11 a, b [M] 12 b 13 a, b 14 b 15 b 17 b 19 a 21 a, b 22 a, b 24 a 25 a, b 28 a, b 29 b 32 b 33 a, b 36 b 37 b 38 a 41 a, b 43 a [M] 45 a 46 a 50 a 52 b 55 a, b [M] 56 b [M] 57 a 59 b 60 a 64 a
Joseph b. Minyomi (BA 4) 23 a
Joseph b. N^{e}hunya (BA 3) 23 b 24 a. Only references to him in the *Talmūd*
Joseph b. Raba (BA 4) 13 b
Joshua [b. H^{a}nanyah] (T 1–2) 2 b 3 b 9 a, b 10 b 13 b [M] 16 a 25 b 27 b 28 a, b 29 a, b 38 a 47 b 49 a [M] 52 a 56 a [s.l.?] 62 a
Joshua b. Hannina [!] 56 a [!]
Joshua b. Iddi (BA 4–5) 4 a
Joshua b. Karhah (T 2) 7 a 13 a 14 b
Joshua b. Levi (PA 3) 3 b [?] 4 b 5 b 6 b 7 a 8 a, b 9 a 10 a, b 13 b 19 a 21 b 22 a, b 24 b 26 a, b 27 a 28 a, b 29 a, b 30 a, b 31 b 32 b 34 a, b 42 b 44 a 47 b 51 a 56 b 58 b 59 a 62 b
Josiah I (T 2) 13 b 22 a
Josiah II (PA 3) 15 b 27 b 63 a
Josiah III (BA 4) 15 b [s.l.]
Judah of Difti [!] 25 a l. Jeremiah of Difti
Judah G^{e}lust^{e}rāā (?) 22 a. Only reference to him in the *Talmūd*
Judah, brother of Sala H^{a}sida (BA 3) 5 b 29 b
Judah ha-Nāsī' ["the Prince"; usually referred to as "Rabbi"] (T 135–220) 3 b 13 a, b 16 b 17 a [M] 24 a 27 b 29 b [M] 30 a, b 33 b 34 b 35 a 43 a 44 a, b 46 a, b 48 b 49 a 50 a 53 b [M] 56 b 57 b 60 a [M] 61 a 63 a
Judah b. Abin [!] 53 b [M]
Judah b. Ammi (PA 4) 19 b [M s.l.]
Judah b. Ashē [!] 19 b [!]
Judah b. Baba (T 2) 27 a
Judah b. Batyra I (T 1) 22 a
Judah b. Batyra II (T 1) 48 b
Judah [b. El'ai = *R.* Judah] (T 2) 2 b 8 b 13 a, b 14 a 15 a, b 18 a 19 a, b 20 b 21 b 22 a, b 26 a, b 27 a 28 a 30 a, b 31 a 33 b 35 a, b 37 a, b 39 b 40 a, b

41 a 42 a 45 a 49 b 52 a, b 54 a 55 a 59 b 60 a 61 b 62 a 63 b
Judah [b. Ezekiel = *Rab* Judah] (BA 220–299) 5 b 8 b 10 a, b 11 b 12 a 13 b 17 b 19 a, b 20 a 21 a 23 a, b 24 a, b 25 a, b 26 a [M] 27 a, b 29 a 30 b 34 a 35 a, b 36 a, b 39 a 40 a 42 a, b 43 a, b 47 b 50 b 51 a 52 b 53 a, b 54 b 55 a 57 b 58 b 59 b 61 b 62 a 63 a [M]
Judah b. Gamaliel (PA 3) 22 a
Judah b. Ḥ^{a}biba (PA 3) 12 b 42 a
Judah b. Ḥiyya (PA 3) 18 b
Judah b. Maremar (BA 5) 45 b
Judah b. M^{e}nasya (PA ?) 10 a
Judah b. Nathan (BA 4) 60 a. Only place in the *Talmūd* where he is mentioned
Judah b. Pazzi (PA 3) 21 b
Judah b. Samuel b. Shelat (BA 3) 47 a 48 a
Judah [or, Judan] b. Simeon b. Pazzi (PA 4) 9 b 15 a, b
Judah b. Z^{e}bida (PA 3) 12 b 63 b

Kah^{a}na I (PA 3) 42 b 62 a
Kah^{a}na II (BA 3) 14 b 36 b
Kah^{a}na III (BA 3–4) 19 b 31 a 39 a, b 42 a
Kah^{a}na IV (BA 4–5) 24 a. [In the following passages, where Kah^{a}na is named, there is no data for identification: 27 a 34 b 40 a 43 a]
Ḳaṭṭina (BA 3) 59 a

Levi (PA 3) 4 a 10 b 28 b 35 a 55 b 60 b 64 a
Levi b. Ḥamma [!] 5 a l. Levi b. Laḥma
Levi b. Ḥiyya (PA ?) 64 a
Levi b. Laḥma (PA ?) 5 a [M s.l.]
Levi b. Samuel b. Naḥmani [!] 28 b l. Hillel b. S. b. N.
Levi [b. Sisi] (T 2–3) 18 b 30 a 49 a

Manni (PA 4) 10 b
Mar b. Ashē (BA 5) 26 a 36 a, b 38 a 45 b
Mar b. Pappa (BA 4) 45 b
Mar b. Rabina (BA 4) 4 b 17 a 25 b 30 b 31 a 39 b 54 a 57 b 58 b
Mar ‘Uḳba s.v. ‘Uḳba
Mar ‘Uḳba b. Ḥamma s.v. ‘Uḳba b. Ḥ.
Mar Zoṭra s.v. Zoṭra
Mar Zoṭra b. Naḥman s.v. Zoṭra b. N.
Maremar (BA 5) 30 a 36 b 45 b
Mari I (BA 3) 40 a 42 b [M]
Mari II (BA 4) 24 a
Mari b. Bat Samuel (BA 3–4; see p. 103, n. 4) 16 a
Mari b. Huna b. Jeremiah b. Abba (BA 4) 26 a 31 a [s.l.]
Matt^{e}na (BA 3) 10 a 11 b 15 a 36 a 48 b 60 a
Meïr (T 2) 2 b 3 a 7 a 9 b 10 a 13 a, b 14 a 15 a, b 17 a 22 a, b 33 a 36 b 38 b 40 a, b 47 b 48 b 49 b 50 a 52 a, b 60 a, b 61 a 63 a [DS]
Menaḥem (PA 3) 8 a
M^{e}nashya b. Taḥlifa (BA 3) 47 b 49 b
M^{e}sharsh^{e}ya (BA 4) 43 b
M^{e}yasha, grandson of R. Joshua b. Levi (PA 3) 23 a 24 b
Mona (T 2) 42 a
Mordecai (BA 5) 31 a

Naḥman b. Ḥisda (BA 4) 61 a
Naḥman b. Isaac (BA died 356) 2 b [M] 4 b 5 b 6 a, b 8 a 11 a 13 b [M !] 14 a [M] 22 a 23 b 24 a 25 a 27 a [M] 28 a 29 b 30 b 31 b 32 a [?] 33 a 35 b 36 a 38 b 39 b 40 a 42 b 44 a 46 b 49 a [M] 51 b 53 a, b 56 b 57 a 58 b [M] 61 a 62 a 63 a
Naḥman [b. Jacob] (BA died 320) 4 b 13 b 21 a 22 a, b 23 a, b 25 a [M], b 27 a, b 29 a 32 a [?] 34 b 35 b [M] 36 a, b 38 b 41 b 42 a, b 43 b [M] 44 a [M] 46 a 47 b 48 a, b 49 a, b 51 b 53 a [M], b 56 b [M] 57 a [M] 58 b 59 a 61 a 62 a, b
Naḥum (T 2) 55 b
Naḥum the Elder (T 1) 48 b
Naḥum of Gimzo [or, Gam Zū] (T 1) 22 a
Nathan (T 2) 3 b 6 b [M] 8 a [?] 12 a 47 b 48 b [?] 51 b 54 a 56 b [?] 58 b [M] 59 a
Nathan b. Abishalom (T 2) 22 a
Nathan b. Assi [!] 48 b [M]

Nathan b. Joseph s.v. Jonathan b. J.
Nathan b. Mar 'Uḳba (BA ?) 13 b. Only reference to him in the *Talmūd*
Nathan b. Ṭobi (PA 3) 28 a
Neḥemiah (T 2) 23 b [M] 24 a [M] 38 a 40 a 63 b
Neḥemiah b. Joseph (BA 4) 24 a [M]
Nehorai (T 2) 53 b 55 b [M]
Neḥunya b. ha-Ḳanah (T 1–2) 28 b

Obadiah (BA 4) 15 b
Osha'ya [or, Hosha'ya] I (PA 3) 3 b 11 a 29 b 32 a, b 33 a 52 b
Osha'ya [or, Hosha'ya] II (BA 3–4) 15 b [!] 22 b 31 a 32 a [M] 50 b 58 a

Panda [?] 55 b. Only reference to him in the *Talmūd*; name uncertain
Pappa (BA 300–375) 6 b 8 a, b 11 a, b [M] 14 b 16 a 18 a 19 a 20 a 22 b 23 a [M] 24 a 25 a 32 a 33 b 35 a 39 a, b 41 b 42 a 43 b 44 b 45 b 47 a, b 49 a 51 a 57 a, b 58 b 59 a, b 60 b 62 b
Pappa b. Aḥa b. Adda (BA 4) 29 b
Pappos b. Judah (T 2) 61 b
Parnak (PA 3) 63 a
Pedat [b. Eleazar] (PA 3) 11 b 55 b
Pelemo (T 2) 48 b

Rab (BA 154–247) 3 a 5 b 6 a [M] 7 a, b 10 b 11 a, b 12 a, b 13 b 14 a, b 16 b 17 a, b 19 b 20 a 21 a [M], b 25 a, b 26 a [M] 27 a, b 29 a, b 30 a [M], b 31 a, b 33 a, b 34 a [M] 35 b 36 a, b 37 a, b 38 a, b 40 a, b 42 a, b 43 a, b 44 a, b 45 a, b 46 a, b 47 a 48 a 49 a, b 52 b 53 a, b 54 b 55 a 56 a 57 b 58 a, b 59 a [M] 60 a, b 61 a, b 62 a, b 64 a
School of: 25 a 50 a
Rab b. Shaba (BA 4) 14 a [!] 19 b
Raba (BA 279–352) 3 b 5 a 6 a, b 8 a, b 9 a [M s.l.] 10 b [?] 11 b 12 b 13 b 14 a [M], b [M] 15 a, b 16 a 17 a 19 b 20 b 22 b 23 a, b 24 a 25 a, b 26 a 27 b 28 b 29 a 30 a 31 a 32 a, b 33 a, b 34 b 35 a, b 36 a, b 37 b 38 a, b [s.l.] 39 a, b 42 a, b 43 b 44 b 45 a [M], b 47 b 48 a, b 50 a, b 52 b 53 b 54 a, b [M] 55 b 56 a, b 57 a, b 58 a 59 a, b 60 a, b 61 b 62 a, b 63 a, b
Raba [or, Rabbah] b. Ḥanan (BA 4) 45 a 48 a [s.l.]
Raba b. Ḥannina [!] 12 a [M]
Raba b. Huna [!] 45 b l. Rabbah b. Huna
Raba b. Isaac [!] 10 b [M]
Raba b. Ishmael [!] 29 a [M]
Raba b. Jeremiah (BA 3) 43 a
Raba [or, Rabbah] b. Mari (PA 3) 5 a [DS] 42 b 44 a
Raba b. Samuel (BA 4) 22 b 40 a [!]
Raba b. Shaba (BA 4) 14 a [M s.l.] 19 b
Raba b. 'Ulla [!] 11 b [M] l. Rabbah b. 'Ulla
Rabbah Tospaäh (BA 5) 50 a
Rabbah b. Abbuha (BA 3) 21 a 36 b 53 b 62 b
Rabbah b. Bar Ḥannah (PA 3) 12 a [!] 13 b 14 b [M] 23 a 24 b 25 a 35 b 40 b 42 b 44 a 45 b 47 a 49 a 53 b 55 a 62 a
Rabbah b. Ḥinnana Saba (BA 3 ?) 12 a, b
Rabbah b. Huna (BA died 322) 12 a [M s.l.] 25 a 45 b [s.l.] 49 a 53 b
Rabbah b. Isaac (BA 3) 10 b [DS]
Rabbah b. Mari s.v. Raba b. M.
Rabbah [b. Naḥmani] (BA 270–330) 12 b 14 a, b 15 a [M s.l.] 19 b [M] 22 b 25 b [M] 29 b 30 b 33 a, b 42 a [M] 45 b [M] 48 a 53 b [M] 60 a [M] 61 b 64 a
Rabbah b. Samuel (BA 3) 29 a 35 b 40 a [s.l.]
Rabbah b. Shela (BA 4) 2 b 8 a 10 a
Rabbah b. 'Ulla (BA 4) 11 b [s.l.] 12 a
Rabbanai [!] 38 b l. Raba
Rabbanai, brother of Ḥiyya b. Abba s.v. Jannai, brother of Ḥ. b. A.
Rabbi s.v. Judah ha-Nāsī'
Rabin s.v. Abin
Rabin b. Adda s.v. Abin b. A.
Rabin b. Zuṭarti [!] 12 b [M]
Rabina I (PA 3–4) 6 b [M] 14 a 15 a 18 a 20 b 23 a 25 a 26 a 33 b 36 a, b [M] 38 a 39 b 40 a [M] 51 a 62 b
Rabina II (BA 5) 24 b 36 b [M] 39 b 50 a 54 b [M]
Rabina b. Ḥiyya b. Abba [!] 61 b [M]
Rafram b. Pappa I (BA 3–4) 8 a 24 a [M] 26 a 59 a

Rafram b. Pappa II (BA 4) 15 a [M] 50 a
Raḥbah (BA 3–4) 18 a 33 b
Rammi b. Abba (BA 3–4) 59 b
Rammi b. Ḥamma (BA 3–4) 44 a 47 a, b
Resh Laḳish s.v. Simeon b. Laḳish

Ṣadoḳ (T 1–2) 27 b
Safra (PA 3–4) 16 b 34 b 47 a 62 b 63 a
Saḥorah (BA 3–4) 5 a 26 a
Samma b. Mari (BA ?) 62 b. Only reference to him in the *Talmūd*
Samuel (BA 175–254) 8 b 10 b 11 b 12 a 13 b [M] 14 a 17 a, b 18 b 19 a, b 20 a 21 a 23 b 24 a 25 a 27 b 29 a 30 a 31 b 32 a 33 a, b 34 b 35 a, b 36 a, b 37 a, b 38 a, b 42 a 44 b 47 a 48 b 49 b 50 a, b 53 b 55 b 56 a 58 b 59 a 60 b 61 a 62 b 63 a
Samuel ha-Ḳāṭōn (T 1–2) 28 b 29 a
Samuel Saba [son-in-law of Ḥannina b. Ḥamma] (PA 3) 62 b. Only reference to him in the *Talmūd*
Samuel b. Isaac (PA 4) 14 b 31 b 38 b [M] 59 a
Samuel b. Judah (BA 3) 14 b
Samuel b. Ḳaṭṭina (BA 3) 47 a
Samuel b. Matt^enah [!] 63 a [M]
Samuel b. Naḥmani (PA 3) 7 a 9 b 17 a 18 b 23 a 32 a 34 b [?] 35 a 55 a, b 60 b 62 b 63 a, b
Saul (T 2) 31 a
Shammai, *Bēt* 10 b 11 a 23 a, b 36 a, b 42 a, b 43 b 47 a 51 b 52 a, b 53 a, b
Shamman [or, Simeon] b. Abba (PA 3–4) 21 b 33 a
Shela I (T 2–3) 58 a
Shela II (BA 3) 15 b
Shela b. Abina (BA 3) 49 b [s.l]
Sh^emaya (T 1 B.C.) 19 a
Shesha b. Iddi (BA 4) 4 a [M] 17 b 24 a
Sheshet (BA 3–4) 6 b 8 a 12 b 14 a 16 a 17 a 23 a, b 24 a 25 a 30 a 32 a 33 a 34 a, b 36 b 37 a, b 40 a 41 b 42 b 43 b 46 a, b 47 b 49 a 51 a 57 a 58 a 60 b
Shimi of Nehardea (BA 3) 36 b
Shimi b. Ashē (BA 4) 31 a 36 b [M] 44 b
Shimi b. Ḥiyya (BA 3) 44 b [M] 47 a
Shimi b. 'Uḳba (BA 3) 10 a. Only reference to him in the *Talmūd*
Simeon ha-Pāḳōlī ["the cotton dealer"] (T 1) 28 b
Simeon Ḥ^asīdā (T 2–3) 3 b 7 a 43 b
Simeon b. Abba s.v. Shamman b. A.
Simeon b. Abishalom (PA ?) 7 b
Simeon b. 'Azzai s.v. Ben 'Azzai
Simeon b. Eleazar (T 2–3) 25 b 30 a 51 a [M] 57 b
Simeon b. Gamaliel (T 2) 8 b [M] 16 b 17 b 18 a 25 a, b 40 a 43 b [M] 48 a 62 b
Simeon b. Jacob of Tyre (PA 3) 33 a
Simeon b. Joḥai (T 2) 5 a, b 7 b 8 b 9 a 10 a 14 b 16 a [M] 28 a 31 a 33 b 35 b 43 b 46 a 55 a
Simeon b. Joseph [!] 56 b [M]
Simeon b. Laḳish (PA 3) 3 b [M] 5 a 7 a 8 a 9 b 10 b 11 b 19 a 31 a 32 b 33 a 34 b [s.l.] 44 a 47 a 53 b 54 b 60 a 62 a 63 b
Simeon b. M^enasya (T 2–3) 61 a
Simeon b. Pazzi (PA 3) 10 a 34 a 45 a 61 a
Simeon b. Rabbi (T 2–3) 13 b 35 a
Simeon b. Sheṭaḥ (T 1 B.C.) 48 a
Simeon b. Z^ebid (PA 3) 38 a
Simeon b. Zoma s.v. Ben Zoma
Simlai (PA 3) 32 a
Symmachus (T 2) 13 b

Ṭabi (BA 3–4) 15 b 63 a
Taḥlifa Ma'^arābā (PA 3) 55 a
Tanḥum [b. Ḥ^anilai] (PA 3) 6 b 28 b 29 a, b 55 b [M] 60 b 62 a
Tanḥum b. Ḥiyya of Acco (PA 3) 63 b
Ṭarphon (T 1–2) 10 b 11 a 44 a 45 a
Theodosius (T 1) 19 a

'Uḳba [Mar] I (BA 3–4) 10 b 29 b
'Uḳba [Mar] II (PA 3) 10 a 15 b [M]
'Uḳba [Mar] b. Ḥamma (BA 3) 44 a
'Uḳba [Rab] (PA 3) 55 b [M]
'Ulla [b. Ishmael] (PA 3–4) 8 a 9 b 14 b 25 a 27 b 28 b 31 b 33 a [M] 38 b 41 a 44 a [M!] 51 b 53 b 57 a 58 a, b 59 a [M] 62 a

Zakkai (T 2) 25 b
Z^e^bid (BA 4) 23 a 25 b 38 a 45 b 46 b 53 b 58 a 61 a
Ze'era [!] 28 a [M] 31 a [!] 55 b [!]
Ze'iri (PA 4) 18 b 22 a 31 a [M s.l.] 43 a 49 a [M]
Zera (PA 4) 3 b 4 a 5 a 6 b 9 a, b 13 b [M] 14 a 16 b 22 a 23 a 24 b 27 b 28 a 29 b 30 b 31 a 33 b 36 a 38 a, b 39 a, b 40 a, b 42 a 43 a 44 b [M] 45 b 46 a 47 b 48 a 49 a 50 b 51 a 53 b 55 b [s.l.] 56 b 57 a 60 b [M] 62 a
Zeriḳa (BA 3–4) 3 b 11 b
Zilai (?) 53 b
Ziwai (?) 53 b
Zohmai (?) 53 b. Only reference to these three in the *Talmūd*
Zoṭra [Mar] (BA 5) 5 a 6 b 8 a 23 a 25 a 26 a 29 a 30 a 35 b 38 a 43 b 44 b 45 b 46 b 50 b 53 b 54 b 55 b
Zoṭra [Mar] b. Naḥman (BA 4) 43 b
Zoṭra [R.] (T 2) 13 b
Zoṭra b. Ṭobiah (BA 3) 7 a 43 b

INDEX II

SCRIPTURAL AND LITURGICAL

A. OLD TESTAMENT

(The versification of the Hebrew Bible is followed. Where it differs from that of the English Version, the latter is given within square brackets.)

GENESIS

i. 5 ...... 2, 172
i. 25 ...... 401 n.
i. 28 ...... 61 n.
ii. 7 401
ii. 10 231
ii. 14 391
ii. 17 ...... 265 n.
ii. 21 403
ii. 22 ...... 402, 403
iii. 7 265
iii. 19 378
iv. 7 405
v. 2 403
vii. 23 402
ix. 6 403
ix. 21 265
ix. 23 167
xii. 3 356
xv. 8 40
xv. 13 53
xv. 14 53
xv. 15 425
xvii. 4 ...... 81 n.
xvii. 5 81
xvii. 15 81
xviii. 1 177
xix. 26 ...... 351 n., 352
xix. 27 ...... 31, 174
xix. 29 353
xxi. 17 ...... 371 n.
xxii. 8 414
xxii. 14 414
xxiii. 3 117
xxiii. 4 117
xxiv. 61 404
xxiv. 63 174
xxv. 23 379
xxv. 24 26
xxv. 27 ...... 102 n.
xxv. 33 40
xxvi. 19 369
xxvii. 36 40
xxvii. 41 40
xxviii. 11 174
xxviii. 15 14
xxix. 35 40
xxx. 21 395
xxx. 27 275
xxxi. 4 49
xxxii. 3 [2] 414
xxxii. 8 [7] 14
xxxv. 10 80
xxxvii. 2 359
xxxvii. 9 359
xxxvii. 10 229
xxxvii. 19 ...... 61 n.
xxxvii. 21 40
xxxviii. 25 282
xxxix. 5 275
xl. 16 362
xli. 12 362
xli. 13 362
xli. 14 370
xli. 32 363
xli. 46 359
xlv. 6 ...... 359 n.
xlvi. 2 ...... 80 n., 81
xlvi. 4 371
xlvii. 6 423
xlvii. 29 ...... 119 n.

xlviii. 16 ...... 131, 361
xlix. 11 373
xlix. 22 ...... 131, 361

EXODUS

i. 6 ...... 356 n.
i. 7 39
iii. 5 415
iii. 6 ...... 39, 87 n.
iii. 14 54
iv. 18 425
vi. 7 255
ix. 33 352
xi. 2 53
xi. 4 ...... 11, 13 n.
xi. 7 370
xii. 2 63
xii. 8 ...... 51, 258 n.
xii. 9 ...... 125 n.
xii. 10 52
xii. 11 51
xii. 12 51
xii. 19 ...... 248 n.
xii. 22 ...... 51 n.
xii. 29 ...... 53 n.
xii. 33 ...... 53 n.
xii. 36 ...... 53, 54
xii. 37 ...... 39 n.
xiii. 13 365
xiv. 22 351
xiv. 31 383
xv. 16 14
xv. 17 221
xv. 26 ...... 20, 264
xvi. 8 132
xvi. 21 177
xvi. 22 261
xvii. 12 ...... 351 n., 352
xvii. 16 384
xviii. 10 350
xviii. 12 425
xix. 15 ...... 134 n.
xix. 16 ff. 33
xix. 19 292
xx. 2 ...... 217 n.
xx. 7 223
xx. 8 133
xx. 10 ...... xxiii.
xx. 18 34
xx. 24 28
xxi. 6 ...... 28 n.
xxi. 19 398
xxi. 26 f. ...... 22 n.
xxi. 28 370
xxi. 29 ...... 177 n.
xxii. 1 [2] ...... 383 n.
xxii. 17 [18] 139
xxii. 18 [19] 139
xxiii. 11 ...... 245 n.
xxiii. 25 311
xxiv. 11 112
xxiv. 12 ...... xxiv, 19, 312
xxv. 10 ...... 357 n.
xxv. 17 ...... 197 n.
xxv. 23 ...... 357 n.
xxv. 31 ...... 357 n.
xxvi. 1 ...... 357 n.
xxvii. 20 374
xxx. 12 413
xxx. 16 414
xxxi. 1 f. 357
xxxi. 6 358
xxxi. 7 f. ...... 357 n.
xxxii. 4 ...... 217 n.
xxxii. 7 211
xxxii. 10 212
xxxii. 11 ...... 201, 212
xxxii. 13 ...... 63, 213
xxxii. 32 213
xxxiii. 7 421
xxxiii. 11 421
xxxiii. 13 37
xxxiii. 14 ...... 35, 40
xxxiii. 16 37
xxxiii. 19 38
xxxiii. 20 38
xxxiii. 23 39
xxxiv. 7 38
xxxiv. 28 ...... 112 n.
xxxiv. 29 f. 39
xxxiv. 30 39
xxxv. 30 357
xxxv. 31 357

LEVITICUS

i. 4 ...... 275 n.
i. 5 209
ii. 6 ...... 251 n.

ii. 13 ...... 22, 262 n.
v. 5 ...... 21 n.
v. 15 f. ...... 204 n., 253 n.
v. 16 ...... 303 n.
vii. 15 ff. ...... 1 n.
x. 12 402
xi. 34 ...... 334 n.
xi. 44 347
xii. 2 395
xii. 2 ff. ...... 13 n.
xiii. 46 ...... 23 n., 163
xiv. 37 ff. ...... 163 n.
xiv. 46 ...... 272 n.
xiv. 47 ...... 272 n.
xix. 9 f. ...... 270 n.
xix. 10 ...... 235 n.
xix. 19 ...... 127 n.
xix. 23 ...... 244, 246
xix. 24 ...... 233 f.
xix. 25 234
xix. 26 66
xix. 36 ...... 78 n.
xx. 7 ...... 347 n.
xx. 27 ...... 140 n.
xxi. 1 ff. ...... 127 n.
xxii. 4 ff. ...... 1 n.
xxii. 7 ...... 2 f.
xxii. 14 ...... 240 n.
xxii. 32 138
xxiii. 22 ...... 270 n.
xxiii. 32 48
xxiii. 40 374
xxv. 4 ...... 245 n.
xxv. 35 ff. ...... 78 n.
xxv. 46 306
xxvii. 19 305
xxvii. 30 ff. ...... 291 n.

NUMBERS

v. 10 ...... 418, 419
v. 11 ff. 124
v. 12 418
v. 21 f. ...... 267 n.
v. 23 101
v. 28 ...... 207 f.
vi. 3 ...... 272 n.
vi. 7 129
vi. 24 ff. ...... 104 n.
vi. 26 134
xi. 2 211
xii. 3 352
xii. 6 362
xii. 8 39
xii. 11 422
xii. 13 ...... 228, 232
xiv. 16 214
xiv. 20 214
xiv. 21 214
xiv. 27 ...... 28 n., 138 n.
xv. 31 161
xv. 34 xxiii
xv. 38 ...... 55 n., 79
xv. 39 79
xv. 41 79
xvi. 21 138
xviii. 8 ff. ...... 302 n.
xviii. 21 ...... 291 n.
xviii. 26 ...... 291 n., 302
xviii. 29 303
xix. 14 422
xxi. 14 ...... 351, 383
xxi. 15 351
xxiii. 8 36
xxiii. 22 ...... 78, 254
xxiv. 6 102
xxiv. 9 79
xxiv. 16 36
xxvii. 18 352
xxviii. 5 94
xxviii. 7 ...... 177 n.
xxviii. 14 94
xxx. 3 [2] 212
xxxii. 3 48
xxxiii. 3 53
xxxiii. 38 ...... 45 n.

DEUTERONOMY

i. 1 211
iii. 23 ...... 201, 214
iii. 24 214
iii. 25 ...... 214, 310, 312
iii. 26 214
iii. 27 214
iv. 7 30
iv. 8 30
iv. 9 ...... 139 ff., 218
iv. 10 ...... 139 ff.
iv. 15 218

iv. 34 30
v. 12 133
vi. 4 ...... 29, 83, 85, 86 f., 97, 99, 103
vi. 5 ...... 349, 406
vi. 6 ...... 19 n., 83 f., 97, 99
vi. 7 ...... 2, 16, 19 n., 67, 105, 132 n., 136
vi. 8 ...... 132 n.
vi. 9 ...... 100 f., 132 n.
vii. 13 329
viii. 5 23
viii. 7 ...... 23, 312
viii. 8 ...... 235 n., 236 n., 249 n., 271 f., 286
viii. 9 ...... 246, 286
viii. 10 ...... 134, 135, 234 n., 286, 310 f., 312, 318
viii. 14 211
viii. 15 255
ix. 14 ...... 39, 212
ix. 25 228
ix. 26 215
x. 2 ...... 48 n.
x. 10 215
x. 12 226
x. 17 ...... 134, 226 n.
xi. 12 356
xi. 14 237
xi. 15 262
xi. 18 85
xi. 19 ...... 85 n., 101
xi. 21 44
xiii. 14 [13] 207
xiv. 22 ff. ...... 291 n.
xiv. 25 305
xv. 11 231
xvi. 1 53
xvi. 3 ...... 80, 253, 261
xvi. 6 52
xvii. 6 120
xvii. 11 128
xviii. 4 ...... 143 n., 303
xxii. 1 128
xxii. 6 f. ...... 225 n.
xxii. 9 ...... 143 n., 234
xxii. 11 ...... 127 n.
xxii. 13 ff. ...... 68 n.
xxii. 29 140
xxiii. 1 [xxii. 30] 140
xxiii. 4 [3] 183
xxiii. 6 [5] 360
xxiii. 8 [7] 423
xxiii. 13 [12] 164
xxiii. 14 [13] 164
xxiii. 15 [14] 163, 167
xxiv. 16 38
xxiv. 19 ...... 270 n.
xxvi. 2 ...... 236 n.
xxvi. 5 ff. ...... 265 n.
xxvi. 11 312
xxvi. 12 238
xxvi. 13 ...... 238, 267
xxvi. 13–15 ...... 267 n.
xxvi. 14 ...... 106 n.
xxvi. 17 29
xxvi. 18 29
xxvi. 19 30
xxvii. 9 ...... 100, 103, 421 f.
xxvii. 11 ff. ...... 313 n.
xxviii. 10 ...... 29, 365, 372
xxviii. 31 364
xxviii. 32 364
xxviii. 38 364
xxviii. 40 365
xxviii. 41 364
xxviii. 48 237
xxviii. 66 158
xxviii. 69 [xxix. 1] 22, 313 n.
xxx. 20 ...... 356, 407
xxxi. 20 211
xxxii. 3 ...... 135, 291
xxxii. 6 237
xxxii. 15 211
xxxii. 18 26
xxxii. 24 20
xxxii. 32 369
xxxii. 47 161
xxxiii. 2 ...... 29, 221, 409
xxxiii. 4 372
xxxiii. 17 370
xxxiii. 23 328
xxxiii. 29 30
xxxiv. 4 123
xxxiv. 5 ...... 45 n.

JOSHUA

i. 7 216
i. 8 ...... 82 n., 237
ii. 6 280

iii. 17 351
vi. 20 ...... 352 n., 353
x. 11 ...... 350 n., 352
x. 13 383
xv. 11 ...... 111 n.
xviii. 24 ...... 285 n.

JUDGES

i. 16 ...... 423 n.
i. 30 ...... 343 n.
v. 20 383
vi. 12 ...... 349, 417
vii. 19 9
viii. 33 79
ix. 13 234
xiii. 11 404
xiv. 3 79
xv. 5 235
xvi. 17 370

I SAMUEL

i. 10 ...... 202, 210
i. 11 ...... 207 f.
i. 13 ...... 206, 209
i. 14 206
i. 15 ...... 26 n., 206
i. 16 207
i. 17 207
i. 25 209
i. 26 209
i. 27 209
ii. 1 ff. 191
ii. 2 60
ii. 3 220
vii. 17 64
ix. 2 311
ix. 13 311
xii. 23 77
xiv. 45 360
xv. 6 423
xvii. 12 381
xxii. 8 77
xxii. 19 ...... 78 n.
xxiv. 4 [3] ...... 150 n., 413
xxiv. 5 [4] 413
xxiv. 11 [10] 413
xxv. 6 360
xxvi. 19 413
xxviii. 6 ...... 78 n.
xxviii. 15 78
xxviii. 19 78
xxx. 17 11

II SAMUEL

iii. 3 ...... 13 n., 14 n.
iii. 29 ...... 213 n.
vi. 11 f. 424
vii. 10 43
vii. 29 320
ix. 13 ...... 13 n.
x. 12 216
xii. 11 41
xii. 13 371
xv. 9 425
xvi. 23 12
xx. 23 12
xxi. 6 78
xxiii. 20 119
xxiv. 1 414
xxiv. 15 414
xxiv. 16 414
xxiv. 17 ...... 61 n.

I KINGS

i. 1 413
i. 31 229
ii. 46 ...... 47 n.
vii. 21 ...... 188 n.
viii. 191
viii. 28 ...... 28, 206
viii. 35 197
viii. 44 197
viii. 48 197
viii. 54 229
ix. 3 415
xiv. 9 66
xviii. 2 60
xviii. 28 ...... 158 n.
xviii. 36 f. 33
xviii. 37 ...... 54, 210
xix. 11 f. 382
xx. 3. ...... 406 n.

II KINGS

iii. 11 43
iii. 12 61
iv. 9 ...... 64, 65

iv. 10 ...... 62 n., 64
iv. 27 65
iv. 30 404
viii. 1 356
xvii. 30 ...... 27 n.
xviii. 4 ...... 62 n.
xviii. 16 ...... 62 n.

ISAIAH

i. 9 ...... 126, 397
i. 10 ...... 126, 397
i. 11 215
i. 15 215
i. 18 ...... 376 n.
i. 28 47
ii. 3 420
ii. 22 89
iii. 14 34
iii. 18 ff. ...... 157 n.
v. 9 385
v. 16 77
v. 18 161
vi. 3 284
vi. 6 18
vi. 7 373
x. 13 183
xiii. 3 49
xiii. 21 ...... 410 n.
xiv. 23 380
xix. 13 422
xxvi. 12 369
xxvi. 20 36
xxvii. 11 220
xxvii. 13 370
xxxi. 5 369
xxxii. 7 ...... 62 n.
xxxii. 9 112
xxxiii. 6 226
xxxiii. 14 396
xxxv. 10 360
xxxvi. 6 370
xxxvii. 35 63
xxxviii. 1 61
xxxviii. 2 ...... 25, 62
xxxviii. 3 ...... 62, 63
xxxviii. 14 ...... 370 n.
xxxviii. 16 ...... 356, 378
xxxviii. 17 64
xlii. 3 370
xlii. 5 338
xliii. 4 413
xliii. 18 80
xliii. 19 80
xlv. 7 ...... 70, 338
xlvi. 12 113
xlvii. 2 157
xlvii. 3 158
xlviii. 18 f. 27
xlix. 8 43
xlix. 14 216
xlix. 15 217
l. 2 30
l. 3 391
l. 10 30
li. 14 ...... 375, 378
lii. 7 369
liii. 10 ...... 21, 378
liv. 1 58
liv. 13 425
lvi. 7 34
lvi. 11 370
lvii. 19 ...... 230 f., 360
lix. 19 369
lxi. 5 237
lxii. 8 29
lxiii. 3 383
lxiv. 3 [4] 231
lxvi. 1 389
lxvi. 12 369

JEREMIAH

ii. 6 204
iv. 7 370
iv. 19 62
vi. 7 370
vii. 16 174
ix. 9 [10] 369
x. 10 91
x. 13 389
xi. 16 373
xii. 14 44
xvii. 21 f. xxiii
xviii. 6 210
xxiii. 7 f. 80
xxiii. 28 358
xxiii. 29 142
xxv. 30 ...... 6, 388
xxvii. 22 159

xxxi. 3 71
xxxi. 12 360
xxxii. 18 23
xxxiii. 11 ...... 33, 34
xlix. 6 183
l. 12 .. ... 380, 385
l. 36 422

EZEKIEL

i. 7 65
i. 28 390
iv. 3 215
v. 13 388
viii. 16 ...... 32 n.
xvi. 7 157
xvi. 63 77
xviii. 24 190
xx. 25 161
xxi. 11 [6] 384
xxi. 12 [7] 384
xxi. 22 [17] 388
xxi. 30 [25] 120
xxiii. 20 ...... 167, 383
xxiv. 3 369
xxiv. 17 ...... 68, 105
xxxi. 8 343
xxxvi. 26 210
xxxvi. 27 210
xxxvi. 29 356
xxxviii. 3 384
xli. 22 355
xlvi. 9 415

HOSEA

ii. 9 [7] 37
ii. 10 [8] 211
ii. 11 [9] 237
v. 8 370
vi. 3 31
vi. 4 389
ix. 10 369
xi. 10 31
xiii. 6 211
xiv. 7 [6] 281

JOEL

iii. 1 [ii. 28] ...... 90 n.

AMOS

iii. 8 370
iv. 12 ...... 149, 330
iv. 13 338
v. 2 18
v. 8 387
vii. 14 232
viii. 10 106
ix. 14 183

MICAH

i. 6 380
iii. 3 369
iv. 6 210
vi. 5 36

NAHUM

i. 9 389

HABAKKUK

i. 13 42

ZEPHANIAH

iii. 9 379
iii. 18 186

ZECHARIAH

iii. 2 328
ix. 9 371
x. 2 362

MALACHI

ii. 5 76
iii. 16 28

PSALMS

i. 57
i. 1 57
ii. 57, 58
ii. 1 41
ii. 11 202

ii. 12 57
iii. 58
iii. 1 ...... 41, 58
iii. 2 [1] 41
iii. 8 [7] 352
iv. 5 [4] 18, 19
v. 4 [3] 33
v. 8 [7] 202
vii. 12 [11] 35
x. 5 42
x. 17 205
xii. 9 [8] 32
xiv. 1 79
xvii. 14 ...... 26, 407
xix. 15 [14] 17, 56, 57
xx. 2 [1] 425
xxiv. 1 236
xxvi. 6 94
xxvii. 13 14
xxvii. 14 216
xxix. 189, 191
xxix. 2 202
xxix. 3 190
xxix. 11 ...... 29, 426
xxx. 6 [5] 36
xxx. 12 [11] 360
xxxi. 6 [5] 18
xxxi. 13 [12] 385
xxxii. 1 232
xxxii. 6 ...... 45 f.
xxxiv. 4 [3] 291, 292, 311
xxxiv. 15 [14] 34
xxxv. 10 162
xxxv. 13 77
xxxvi. 2 [1] 405
xxxvii. 1 42
xxxvii. 33 42
xxxix. 3 [2] 20
xxxix. 13 [12] 215
xlvi. 9 [8] 41
li. 17 [15] 17, 56
lii. 7 [5] ...... 371 n.
lv. 18 [17] 132, 206
lv. 19 [18] 44, 360
lvi. 11 [10] 400
lvii. 1 58
lvii. 9 [8] 12
lxiii. 5 [4] 107
lxiii. 6 [5] 107
lxvi. 12 33
lxvi. 20 22
lxviii. 13 [12] 54
lxviii. 14 [13] 345
lxviii. 15 [14] 101
lxviii. 20 [19] 264
lxviii. 21 [20] 45
lxviii. 27 [26] 319, 321
lxix. 14 [13] 43
lxxi. 8 325
lxxii. 5 ...... 56, 195
lxxvii. 19 [18] 389
lxxxi. 11 [10] 320
lxxxii. 1 28
lxxxiv. 5 [4] 217
lxxxiv. 8 [7] 425
lxxxv. 14 [13] 90
lxxxvi. 2 13
lxxxvii. 2 46
xc. 10 ...... 210 n.
xci. 10 359
xcii. 3 [2] 76
xciv. 1 ...... 221, 384
xciv. 12 ...... 21 f.
xciv. 17 ...... 122 n.
xcix. 6 208
ci. 1 400
cii. 1 ...... 65, 174
ciii. 1 59
ciii. 2 59
ciii. 20 f. 59
civ. 1 59
civ. 15 ...... 239, 376
civ. 29 59
civ. 35 ...... 57, 59
cvi. 23 63
cvi. 30 ...... 31, 174
cvii. 4–8 353
cvii. 10–15 354
cvii. 17–21 354
cvii. 23–31 353
cvii. 30 374
cvii. 32 354
cix. 22 405
cix. 31 406
cxi. 8 58
cxi. 10 111
cxii. 1 46
cxii. 7 396
cxv. 16 236
cxv. 17 ...... 19 n., 122 n.

cxvi. 3 f. 400
cxvi. 13 ...... 329, 400
cxix. 18 xxxvii
cxix. 28 186
cxix. 46 13
cxix. 62 ...... 9, 13
cxix. 126 ...... 349, 417
cxix. 147 10
cxix. 148 9
cxix. 165 426
cxxii. 7 426
cxxii. 8 426
cxxii. 9 426
cxxv. 1 385
cxxv. 5 123
cxxvi. 2 203
cxxviii. 2 47
cxxviii. 3 373
cxxx. 1 65
cxxxiv. 2 328
cxxxv. 7 390
cxxxvi. 25 17
cxxxix. 5 402
cxl. 14 [13] 217
cxli. 2 33
cxliv. 14 113
cxlv. 17
cxlv. 9 37
cxlv. 14 18
cxlv. 16 17
cxlvi. 8 76
cxlvii. 2 314
cxlvii. 14 373
cxlix. 5 19
cxlix. 6 19
cl. 6 ...... 162, 281

PROVERBS

i. 8 237
i. 20 374
ii. 3 372
iii. 6 ...... xxix, 417
iii. 12 ...... 21, 22
iii. 18 216
iii. 19 357
iii. 20 357
iv. 2 ...... 20 f., 312
iv. 5 370
iv. 7 370
iv. 8 308
vi. 23 23
vii. 4 372
vii. 9 10
viii. 34 ...... 44 f.
viii. 35 ...... 44, 45, 369
ix. 5 376
xi. 21 404
xi. 24 417
xii. 21 42
xiii. 12 ...... 215, 355
xiv. 23 203
xiv. 28 341
xiv. 31 119
xv. 1 111
xv. 25 384
xvi. 6 23
xvii. 5 118
xvii. 10 37
xvii. 26 37
xviii. 22 45
xviii. 24 418
xix. 17 119
xix. 23 ...... 90, 359
xxi. 1 356
xxi. 21 23
xxi. 27 148
xxi. 30 ...... 127 f.
xxiii. 5 20
xxiii. 15 14
xxiii. 17 42
xxiii. 22 ...... 349, 417
xxiii. 23 23
xxiii. 25 125
xxiv. 10 419
xxiv. 17 f. 362
xxv. 23 ...... 390 n.
xxvii. 8 369
xxvii. 11 14
xxvii. 18 373
xxvii. 27 374
xxviii. 4 42
xxviii. 14 396
xxviii. 24 237
xxx. 15 f. 100
xxx. 32 423
xxx. 33 422
xxxi. 6 376
xxxi. 26 58

JOB

i. 21 400
ii. 13 ...... 31 n.
iii. 13 378
iii. 22 46
iii. 25 396
v. 7 20
ix. 9 387
ix. 10 383
xiii. 15 61
xiv. 21 120
xiv. 22 120
xviii. 4 26
xxii. 25 419
xxxvi. 5 44
xxxvi. 24 381
xxxvii. 24 381
xxxviii. 31 387
xxxviii. 32 387
xli. 10 [18] 378

CANTICLES

ii. 14 158
iv. 1 158
iv. 3 373
iv. 4 198
iv. 15 370
v. 2 ...... 366 n.
viii. 2 373

RUTH

ii. 4 349

LAMENTATIONS

i. 1 ...... 384 n.
i. 4 186
iii. 8 215
iii. 40 21
iii. 44 215
iv. 22 374

ECCLESIASTES

i. 9 388
i. 15 173
iii. 11 281
iii. 14 ...... 358, 390
iv. 17 ...... 149 f.
v. 1 [2] 401
v. 6 [7] 62
vii. 1 110
vii. 26 45
viii. 1 60
ix. 5 119
ix. 7 364
x. 1 405
x. 2 405
xii. 13 34

ESTHER

ii. 22 ...... 7 n.
iv. 2 415

DANIEL

ii. 21 358
ii. 29 363
ii. 30 363
iii. 21 ...... 130 n.
v. 28 ...... 127 n.
vi. 11 [10] 205, 232
vii. 10 ...... 387 n.
ix. 17 40
ix. 21 18
x. 13 18

NEHEMIAH

iv. 15 [21] 4
iv. 16 [22] 4
ix. 5 ...... 346 n., 416
ix. 7 81
ix. 32 ...... 226 n.

I CHRONICLES

i. 27 81
iii. 1 ...... 14 n.
v. 1 40
xii. 18 360
xvii. 9 43
xvii. 21 ...... 29 f.
xxi. 1 413
xxi. 15 414

xxiii. 15 39
xxiii. 17 39
xxvi. 5 424
xxvi. 8 424
xxvii. 34 12
xxix. 11 383

II CHRONICLES

vi. 32 197
xxviii. 18 ...... 144 n.
xxx. 2 ...... 63 n.
xxxii. 30 ...... 62 n.

B. APOCRYPHA

ECCLESIASTICUS

xi. 1 ...... 308 n.
xxxviii. 1 ff. ...... 398 n.

WISDOM OF SOLOMON

x. 7 ...... 352 n.

C. NEW TESTAMENT

MATTHEW

iii. 4 ...... 113 n.
iii. 16 ...... 8 n.
v. 22 ...... 144 n.
vi. 19 ...... 122 n.
vi. 34 ...... 30 n., 54 n.
xiii. 12 ...... 264 n.
xiv. 25 ...... 6 n.
xxii. 30 ...... 112 n.
xxiii. 9 ...... 427 n.

MARK

v. 9 ...... 27 n.
vi. 48 ...... 6 n.

ACTS

xiii. 33 ...... 57 n.

ROMANS

viii. 28 ...... 401 n.

I CORINTHIANS

v. 7 ...... 109 n.

D. LITURGY

אדיר במרום 361
אדני שפתי 17, 56
אהבה רבה ...... 71 ff.
אהבת עולם 71
אלהי נצור 110
אלהי נשמה 399
אלהי עד שלא נוצרתי 109
אלו פינו מלא שירה 392
אמת ואמונה 76
אמת ויציב 72, 76, 91, 92, 136, 206
אני שלך וחלומותי שלך 361
אשר בדברו מעריב ערבים ...... 74 f.
אשר יצר את האדם 398
אשר יצר אתכם בדין 385
אשרי 17
אתה חוננתנו ...... 193, 220 ff.

בורא מאורי האש 331, 338
ברכות השחר ...... 399 f.
ברכת הכהנים ...... 72 f., 215, 361 f.
ברכת המינים ...... 189 ff.

האל הקדוש 77
הבדלה ...... 173 f., 180, 221 ff., 331, 333, 337–344
הבינגו ...... 8 n., 104, 192, 197
המלך המשפט 77
המעביר שנה מעיני 400
המפיל חבלי שנה ...... 398 f.
השכיבנו 17, 50, 57

והערב נא 72
ותודיענו 224
ותן טל ומטר 174, 193, 220, 222

יהי רצון...שתחדש 108
יהי רצון...שתצילני 108
יהיו לרצון ...... 17, 56 f.
יוצר אור ...... 66, 70 ff.
יעלה ויבא ...... 194, 200 f.

מודים 138, 192
משיב הרוח 174, 193, 220, 222

על המחיה 287
על העץ ועל פרי העץ ...... 286 f.

פרשת ציצית 79, 91

צדוק הדין 126

קדוש ...... 133, 179 f., 223, 283
קדושה 138
קדיש ...... 8, 138 f.

רצה 72

שהחינו 251, 348, 385

תפלת הדרך ...... 196, 396 f.

See also Index III, ss.vv. "Amen," Benedictions, Grace, *Hallēl*, *Sh^ema'*, *T^efillāh*, *Zimmūn*.

INDEX III

GENERAL

Aaron, 208
Āb, ninth day of, 114 f.
Abbott, E. A., quoted, 427 n.
Abelson, J., quoted in notes, xxxiv, 19, 34, 60, 139, 357, 430
Abi Gibar (place), 322
Abishai, death of, 414
Abraham, 31, 40, 53, 81
Abrahams, I., quoted in notes, xxxi, xxxiii, 8, 17, 27, 189, 221, 229, 331, 399, 426
Absalom, 41, 58, 425
Adam, 204 f., 265, 380 f., 402 f.
Aeolian Harp, 11
Aged, respect for the, 48
Aggādāh, character of the, xxxii ff.
Agrippa I, 127 n.
Ahab, 60, 406
Aḥitophel, 11, 12, 113, 359
Alexander Jannaeus, 190, 285, 308
Alfasi, Isaac, 350 n.
"Altar of Atonement," 23
'Am hā'āreṣ, 181 n., 282 f., 303 f., 337, 404
"Amen," response of, 292, 295, 301, 332, 346, 416
Ammonites, 183
Angel of Death, 18, 122, 327
Angelology, 6, 18, 109, 122, 327, 398, 407
Animals, consideration for, 262
Antoninus, 379
Aphorisms, rabbinical, 111 f.
Arab, 32
'Arabot (place), 350
Aramaean woman, bed of, 49
Arnon, miracle at the fords of, 351
As (Roman coin), 344
Asmaktā, xxxvi, 272
Aspamia (place), 411
Asparagus-beverage, 326 f.
Astrologers, 424
Astronomical references, 216, 386 ff.
Avidius Cassius, 379 n.
Azulay, H., quoted, 306 n.

Ba'al Ḳ^eri, and his prayers, 134 ff., 148; and study of *Tōrāh*, 139 ff., 146 ff.; purification of, 141, 143, 147, 171
Babylon, 26 n., 44, 46 n., 65 n., 204, 379 f., 391, 419
Bacher, W., quoted in notes, passim
Bagdat (place), 354
Balaam, 36
Bar Hedja, interpreter of dreams, 364 ff.
Bat Ḳōl, 8, 78, 113, 332, 407
Baths (ritual), 131
Bear, constellation of the, 387 f.
Be-Dura (place), 205
B^eḥirtā (Tractate), 177, 178
Be-Kipē (place), 205
Benediction, validity depends upon correct conclusion, 74 f.; must contain the Divine Name, 75, 267, and reference to the Divine Kingship, 75, 267, 313, 315; transgression if superfluous, 223; necessity for, on partaking of food, 233 ff.; minimum quantity of food necessitating, 258; precedence of, 258 f., 270 ff., 282, 332 f., 337; interruption of, before partaking of food, 262; language of, 266 f.; inclusion of the word "Blessed," 298; before food, if omitted, 325
Benediction to be said, before reading of *Tōrāh*, 71 f., 135 f., 312; by priestly guard in the Temple, 74; over liquors, 74; fruits, 233; wine,

233 f., 238 f.; bread, 233, 254 f., 260 f., 266; vegetables, 233, 255 ff.; "seven species," 235, 249 f., 270 f.; "five species," 239, 247; olive-oil, 239 f.; wheaten-flour, 241; the palm-heart, 242; capers, 242 f.; pepper, 246; *Ḥābiṣ*, 247, 251; rice and millet, 247 ff.; *Rihᵃtā*, 250 f.; date-honey, 253; *Ṭrimmā*, 253; *Shattīt*, 253 f.; turnips, 259; fruits, 265; things not grown from the earth, 268; bread-dessert, 273 f.; perfumes, 280; fragrant woods, 280; flowers, 280; after partaking of fruit, 285 f.; water, 286; on removing the *Tᵉfillīn*, 288; on beholding historical sites, 348, 350, 380; natural phenomena, 348; on acquiring new articles, 348; on escaping from danger, 354; on beholding places from which idolatry has been uprooted, 379; a crowd of Israelites, 380; sages and kings, 381; houses of Israelites, 384; deformed persons, 386; a rainbow, 390; the heavenly bodies, 391; rain and hearing good tidings, 392; on entering and leaving a town, 396 f., and a bath-house, 397; before blood-letting, 397; on entering and leaving a privy, 398

Benedictions, the "Eighteen," s.v. *Tᵉfillāh*; of *Habdālāh*, see Index II D, s.v.; of the *Shᵉma'*, 66, 70–73; of Grace after meals, 309 ff.

Benevolence, 23

Bᵉrākōt (Tractate), xxviii

Bᵉruriah (R. Meïr's wife), 57, 58

Beṣalel, 357

Be-Shapor (place), 391

Be-Sinyata (place), 204

Bēt Dīn, 123, 124, 201

Bēt Pᵉrās, 127

Bethar (place), 310

Beverages, 253 f.

Bible, use of, in the *Talmūd*, xxxv f.

Blau, L., quoted in notes, 48, 49, 55, 152, 226, 342

Blood-letting, 276, 289, 397 f., 424

Boaz, 416

"Book of Remedies," 62

Bowing, in prayer, 76, 189, 229

Bread, "breaking of," 260 ff.; must be carefully handled, 324

Brecher, G., quoted, 326 n.

Bridegroom, felicitation of, 32, 33 f., 325; and his religious obligations, 67 f., 103, 105, 114; in danger from evil spirits, 354

Brodetsky, S., quoted in notes, 36, 338, 386, 387

Büchler, A., quoted in notes, 14, 72, 157, 278, 285, 325, 424, 427

Burckhardt, J. L., quoted, 68 n.

Burial, 46, 93, 116, 120, 342

Caesarea, 83 n.

Calendar, Jewish, 63, 419 f.

Cappadocia, 368

Carob-tree, 113 n.

Carthage, 191 n.

Cat, black, in magic, 27

Catullus, quoted, 159 n.

Cemetery, etiquette in, 118 f.

Censor, alterations in text for the, 37, 48, 113, 227, 291, 338, 382, 383, 406, 413

Charity, 31, 384 f.; dependence upon, 32 f.

"Chastenings of love," 21–24

Childlessness, 23 f.

Children, procreation of, a religious duty, 61

Chileab, 13 f.

Cock, power of darkness, 27, 36 f.

Compendiaria (via), 414 f.

Conduct, rules of, 48, 263, 281 f., 327, 403, 408 f., 410 ff.

Confession, on Day of Atonement, 109

Conybeare, F. C., quoted, xxxiv

Cortège, accompanying a, 118

Croup, 45, 263

Cucumbers, as diet, 378 f.

"Cup of ill-luck," 329 f.

Cupping, s.v. Blood-letting

Curse, power of pronouncing a, 367

Danaḳ (river), 277

Daniel, 205; Book of, 419

David, 10, 11, 13, 14, 41, 57, 59, 113, 119 n., 202, 208, 309, 359, 413, 425

Day, division of, by Jews, 2 n., 6 n.
Dead, honouring the, 10, 118 f.; do they know what transpires on earth? 119–123; speaking evil of the, 123; taking leave of the, 425. See also Resurrection
Death, 18, 19, 45, 59
Decalogue, in the Ritual, 72 f.
Defilement, ritual, 127 f., 272, 334 ff.
Delitzsch, F., quoted, xxvii, 47 n.
Demonology, 19 f., 27, 327. See also Evil Spirits
Denarius (Roman coin), 120, 226
Dérek Éreṣ (Tractate), 141 f.
Derenbourg, J., quoted in notes, 190, 224, 267
D^{e}rāsh, xxxvi
Deuteronomy, Book of, 139 f.
Dietetics, 239, 260, 263, 288 ff., 378 f.
Difti (place), 48, 165, 294
Digestion, 345
Dinah, 395
Diocletian, 128 n.
Disciples, rabbinical, 18, 65, 77, 114, 123, 137, 151, 160, 178 f., 182, 183, 231, 275, 282 ff., 304, 307, 319 f., 354, 373, 376, 421–426
Doeg, 113
Domestic habits, 3 f., 15. See also Conduct, rules of
Dōr^{e}shē Ḥ^{a}mūrōt, 158
Dōr^{e}shē R^{e}shūmōt, 158 n.
Dreams, xxxv, 61, 90, 182, 356, 358–377, 378, 379, 409
Drunkenness, 418
Dualism, 225
Dūmāh (Angel), 122
Dupondium (Roman coin), 344

Earthquake, how caused, 388
'Eber Jamina (place), 350
Eden and the Garden, 231
Edersheim, A., quoted, 72 n., 405 n.
'Ēduyyōt (Tractate), 183
Egg, as diet, 288
Egypt, deliverance from, 16, 53, 80, 87, 92, 136
Egyptian beer, 254
Egyptians, 54
Elaiogaron, 240
Elbogen, I., quoted in notes, 17, 56, 65, 188
Eli, 209
Elijah, 7, 18, 32, 33, 43, 54, 60, 196, 210, 239, 382
Elisha, 43, 60, 64, 113, 404
Elkanah, 207, 404 n.
Epstein, J. N., quoted, 426 n.
'Ērūb, 262, 274
Essenes, 55 n., 94 n., 225 n., 427
Euphemisms, 8, 18, 70, 94, 125, 130, 186, 210, 415, 422
Euphrates, 391
Eve, creation of, 402 f.
Evil Eye, xxxiv, 26 n., 131, 361 f.
Evil Spirits, xxxiv, 8 f., 19 f., 27, 281, 354, 362, 409 f., 412
Excommunication, 123 ff.
Exilarch, 262, 274, 299, 314, 321
Ezra, 14, 145 f., 221 n.

Fasting, 31, 89, 110, 210, 215, 272
Feldman, W. M., quoted, 361 n., 395 n.
"Fence" round the *Tōrāh*, 15, 144
Fire, analysis of, 338
"Fire-River," 387
Fish, as diet, 263, 289, 355, 378
Frazer, J. G., quoted in notes, 26, 354, 410
Friedmann, M., quoted, xxxii, 352 n.
Funeral Oration, 31, 107, 126, 411. See also Burial
Funk, S., quoted, 49 n.

Gabriel (Angel), 18
Galilee, 408
Garden of Eden, name for Paradise. 108, 188
Gehazi, 65, 113
Gēhinnōm, 49, 58, 101, 123, 188, 378, 404
Gēmaṭriyyā, 45 n.
Gennesareth, the fruits of, 284
G^{e}ullāh, s.v. *T^{e}fillāh*
G^{e}zērāh Shāwāh, 18 n., 52, 101
Gimzo (place), 144 n.
Ginsburg, C. D., quoted, 357 n.
Gnostics, 225 n.
Gobeans, 114
God, conception of, in the *Aggādāh*, xxxiii; mourns destruction of the

Temples, 7, 8; man's dependence upon, 17, 30; attributes of, 20, 39, 59 f., 264; chastens whom He loves, 21; His gifts through suffering, 22 f.; attends the Synagogue, 28, 30; wears *Tᵉfillīn*, 29; prays, 34 f.; anger of, 35 f., 212; mercy of, 35, 61; and problem of reward and punishment, 38; trust in, 61, 396; unity of, 86; called "Ancient of Days," 112; defends honour of scholars, 123; honouring of, precedes all else, 127 ff.; why He favours Israel, 134; should be blessed in adversity, 225, 312, 400 f.; His commands to be obeyed without question, 225; fear of, left to free will, 226; the earth His Sanctuary, 236; the Hebrew names for, 312 n.; gives wisdom only to the wise, 357; submission to, 400; was Adam's "best man," 403; love of, 406. See also Israel
Gofnit (place), 285
Gog and Magog, 41, 58, 80, 384
Golden Calf, 217
Goldschmidt, W. L., quoted in notes, 29, 35, 102, 187, 255, 306, 307
Grace before and after meals, 97, 99 f., 104, 116 f., 131 f., 133 f., 135 f., 147, 230, 248 ff., 267, 274 f., 277–330, 344 f. See also *Zimmūn*
Graetz, H., quoted, xxvi, 225 n., 377 n.
"Great Assembly," xxiii, 221, 226
Greek, *Shᵉma'* read in, 83 n.
Greeks, 7 n., 285 n., 322 n., 324 n.
Grenfell and Hunt, quoted, 152 n.
Guest, duties of a, 381

Ḥābēr, 181 n.
Hafṭārāh, 346
Hagronya (place), 205
Hᵃlākāh, character of the, xxix ff.
Ḥallāh, 156, 208, 235, 252
Hallēl, 17, 51, 88, 89, 230, 366
Hannah, 60, 191, 202, 206 ff.
Healing, by touch, 24
Heretics, 37, 58, 73, 189 f., 227 n., 349, 368, 382
Herford, R. T., quoted in notes, vi, xxxiii, 113, 122, 189, 429, 430
Hermes, Statue of, 379 f.
Herod II, 127 n.
Hezekiah, 25, 60–63, 188
Holy of Holies, 197
Ḥoni *Hammᵉ'aggēl*, 124 f.
Honouring one's fellow-creatures, 128
Horse, a light sleeper, 10 n.
Hospitality, 64, 65, 355
House of Study, 8, 46, 102, 112 f., 151, 180, 182, 184 f., 187, 219, 282 f., 341, 383, 425; in Heaven, 122
Hyades (stars), 387 n.
Hyman, A., quoted in notes, passim

Idolatry, 338
Ihi Dᵉḳira (place), 391
Imitatio Dei, xxxiii, 35 n.
Immersion, s.v. Purification; for proselytes, 305
Impulses, of man, 19, 398 f., 400, 401 f., 405
Incantations, 152 n., 226 n., 411 f.
India, 246
Indigestion, 263
Isaiah, 60 f.
Ishbosheth, 13
Israel, people of, 8, 29, 35, 36, 58, 210 ff., 216 f., 237, 281, 345, 388

Jabneh (place), 111, 189, 190, 310, 311; "vineyard" of, 420
Jacob, 14, 81, 425
Jalta (Rab Naḥman's wife), 329
Jastrow, M., quoted in notes, passim
Jericho, 249, 353
Jeroboam, 237
Jerusalem, 7, 56, 177, 197
Jēṣer Ra', 19, 131, 399, 401, 405
Jēṣer Ṭōb, 19, 398, 400, 405
Jethro, 423, 425
Job, Book of, 110
John Hyrcanus, 190
Joseph, 131, 356, 358 f., 361
Josephus, quoted in notes, xxiv, 62, 284, 325, 343, 352, 391, 424
Joshua, 15, 309, 352
Julius Caesar, 372 n.
Justice, administration of, 28, 397

Kallāh, 27 n.

Karbāltā, 130
Kawwānāh, 83 ff., 97, 99, 103, 114, 200, 205, 227, 230
Kᵉrētī and *Pᵉlētī*, 12
Kᵉrūm, 32
King, honouring a, 56, 127, 218, 381 f.
"Kiss of Death," 45
Kneeling, during prayer, 229
Knowledge, greatness of, 220 f.; pursuit of, 422 f.
Kōhēn, 104 n., 127 n., 129, 215, 227, 360 f.
Koḥl, 121
Kohler, K., quoted, 427
Ḳōl wā-Ḥōmer, 22 n., 100
Koran, quoted, 55 n., 95 n.
Krauss, S., quoted in notes, passim

Labour, dignity of, 46, 418
Lane, E. W., quoted in notes, passim
Laughter, deprecated, 203
Lauterbach, J. Z., quoted, 158 n.
Law, the Oral, xxiii f.
Leah, 40, 395
Lection, from Pentateuch, 47 f., 292
Lehmann, J., quoted, 225 n., 348 n.
Lentils, as food, 263
Lewysohn, L., quoted, 32 n.
Lightning, 389
Liturgy, see Index II D
Lizard, 219
Locust, 113
Loewe, H., quoted, 159 n.
Lot's wife, 352 f.
Löw, I., quoted in notes, 242, 258, 269, 319
Löw, L., quoted, 306 n.
Lūlāb, 198

Maʿᵃsēh Merkābāh, 139
Maḥoza (place), 350, 391
Maimonides, quoted, xxviii, 1 n., 426 n.
Male children, importance attached to, 26, 208, 393
Manoah, 404
Manna, 177
Marcus Aurelius, 108 n., 379 n.
Marpē', 341
Marriage, 45, 67 f., 105, 176 f.
Martyrdom, R. 'Aḳiba's, 407
Mata Mᵉḥasya (place), 114
"Matriarch," title of, 107
Matun (woman's name), 131
Mau, A., quoted, 426 n.
Meals, time of, 3 ff.; etiquette of, 154, 274 ff., 299 ff.; regulations concerning, 331–337. See also Washing hands
Medes, etiquette of, 49
Medical references, 45, 161, 240, 242, 263, 289, 326 f., 355, 378, 413
Mᵉgillāh, 88, 98, 198
Mᵉʿīlāh, 204 n.
Mᵉkiltā, quoted, 352 n.
Mephibosheth, 13
Mercy-seat, 197
Merit, ancestral, 38, 61
Merriment, excessive, deprecated, 203
Messiah, 80, 231
Mēt Miṣwāh, 129
Mᵉzūzāh, 131 f., 300, 304
Michael (angel), 18
Mielziner, M., quoted in notes, xxv, 18, 22, 96, 141, 427, 429
Miḳwēh, 131
Milky Way, 387 n.
Mīn, s.v. Heretics
Minḥāh, 33, 178
Minor, religious obligations of a, 98, 131, 133, 291, 306 f.
Miracles, 14 f., 350 ff.
Mishnāh, origin of the, xxv f.
Mnemonics, 214, 287 f., 377, 378
Moment, duration of a, 36
Montefiore, C. G., quoted, xxxi, 427
Moses, 11 f., 37 ff., 53, 54, 63, 112 n., 208, 211–214, 215, 226, 228, 309, 352, 357, 421, 425
Mourner's Grace after meals, 298; danger from Evil Spirits, 354
Mourning customs, 68, 105 f.
Mustard, 263

Naḥmanides, quoted, xxxiv
Names, significance of, 41
"Nazarene, the," 113
Nazirite, 129 n., 272
Nebuchadnezzar's palace, 380
Necromancer, 388
Neharbel (place), 320

Nehardea (place), 74, 199, 245, 260, 280, 285, 387, 420 n.
Nèshef, meaning of, 10 f.
N^etinim, 114 n.
Neubauer, A., quoted in notes, passim
New Year's Eve, 120 f.
Newman, A., quoted in notes, 94, 374, 426
Night, division of, by Jews, 6 n.; watches of the, 6, 9

Obed-Edom, 424
Oesterley and Box, quoted in notes, passim
Og, king of Bashan, 352
Oil, anointing hands with, 274, 346
Okteriël (name of God), 35
Omens, 158, 159, 230, 389. See also Dreams
Oriental customs, 3, 15, 26, 27, 31, 64 n., 68 n., 70, 95, 131, 155 n., 279 n., 341 n., 356 n., 375 n., 404 n., 409 n.
Orion, constellation of, 387
'Orlāh, 243 ff.
"Oven of the Serpent," 125
Oxygaron, 240

Palestine, 23 n., 91, 159, 197, 243, 246, 284 f., 375 n.
Parables, 41, 53, 69, 80, 207, 211, 212, 226, 406
Parthians, 363 n.
Paschal offering, 51 f.
Passover, 239, 248, 251, 256, 258, 261, 320
"Patriarch," title of, 107
Peace, 425 f.
Penitence, 231
Perfumes, 279 f., 282 f., 342
Perles, J., quoted, 87 n., 258 n.
Persians, 49, 171, 225 n., 299, 363, 391
P^eshāṭ, xxxvi
Pharisees, xxiv, 190 n., 308 n.
Physician, 397 f.
Physiological references, 395, 405
Pig, 163
"Pillar of salt," the, 352 f.
Pinneles, H. M., quoted, 307 n.
Pinner, E. M., quoted in notes, 218, 287, 316, 374
Plagues, 18, 23 f., 271 f.
Pleiades, 387 f.
Poisons, 263 f.
Pombedita (place), 186 n., 224, 424 n.
Pom-Nahara (place), 204
Poverty, 3 n., 157 n., 221, 344 n.
Prayer, Rabbinic conception of, xxxi; not allowed in ruins, 7 f.; by the roadside, 7 f., 218; abbreviated, 8, 189; laws regulating, 25, 205 f., 232; in Synagogue, 28; fix a place for, 30 f., 43; forbidden at rear of Synagogue, 32, 404 f.; importance of Statutory Services, 33; congregational, 43, 193; one must not rely on one's merits when praying, 63; in a lowly place, 65; must precede morning meal, 66; for one's neighbour, 77; language of, 83 f.; must precede one's private affairs in the morning, 89 f.; some specimens of, 92, 107–110, 160, 195; washing before, 95; meditation the equivalent of speech, 134 f.; mind must not be distracted during, 152; demeanour during, 158 f.; in House of Study, 187; devotion during, 187; direction of body during, 189, 197; personal supplications, 194, 206, 228; must not be perfunctory, 194 f., 200; necessary at dawn and sunset, 195; in a place of danger, 195; when setting out on a journey, 196; should be worded in the plural, 196; should be preceded by praise, 214; greater than good deeds, 214, and sacrifices, 215; if lengthy, 215, 228, 355; should be repeated if unanswered, 216; meditation before and after, 217; types of, condemned, 225 f.; words must not be duplicated, 226 f.; a good omen, if fluent, 230, 232. See also Benedictions, *Kawwānāh*, Liturgy, *Sh^ema'*, Synagogue, *T^efillāh*
Precentor, 65 n., 104, 138, 190, 193 f., 200 n., 225, 227 f., 230
Predecessors, superiority of, 130
Priests and the *T^erūmāh*, 1–5, 418 f.; ritual in the Temple, 72 f., 209

Privy, 46, 49, 150 ff., 161, 170 f., 355 f., 398, 408 ff.
Prophets, 231
Proselyte, 114, 124, 183, 305
Proverbs, 11, 25, 45, 46, 211, 219, 281, 308, 329, 365, 382, 388, 389, 412, 417, 418 n.
Psalms, 17, 41, 57, 58
Purification, by immersion, 140–148

Quorum, for congregational prayer, 28, 30, 43, 306

Rabbinovicz, R., xxix; quoted in notes, passim
Rachel, 191
Radin, M., quoted, 342 n.
Raffalovich, I., quoted, 427
Rainbow, 390
Rainfall, in Palestine, 120 n.
Rashi, quoted in notes, passim
Reclining, at meal, 278
Resurrection, taught in the *Tōrāh*, 100
Reuben, 40
Reward and punishment, 38
Rice, category of, 247 ff.
Righteous, the, 42, 406
Romans, 6 n., 41 n., 267 n., 275 n., 285 n., 322 n., 324 n., 331 n., 342 n., 363, 367, 374 n., 413
Rome, 383, 406 n., 412; Jews of, 125
Ruins, 7 f.
Ruth, 41

Sabbath, 4, 31, 116 f., 210, 240, 254, 261 f., 272, 339, 378
Sadducees, xxiv, 37 n., 100 n., 190, 348 n., 349 n.
Salt, 3, 5, 22, 228, 239, 241, 262 f., 285
Salutation, 34, 82, 87 ff., 111; should include the Divine Name, 349, 416 f.; on leaving a friend, 425
Samaria, 380
Samaritans, 291, 303 f., 332, 349 n.
Samuel, 64, 78, 209
Sanhedrin, 11, 12, 111 n., 145 n., 414
Sarah, 81, 191
Saturn, 391
Saul, 58, 78, 113, 208, 311, 413
Schechter, S., quoted in notes, passim
Scholars, honouring of, 123 ff.
Schorr, O. H., quoted, 35 n., 102 n.
Schürer, E., quoted in notes, passim
Scopus, Mt, 317, 407 f.
Scroll of the Law, 47, 152, 169 f., 356
Sᵉgan ha-Kōhᵃnim, 72 n.
Sᵉmūkīn, 58, 139
Sennacherib, 183
Sepphoris, 343
Septuagint, quoted, 20 n.
Shapor I, 363
Shapor II, 49 n.
Shaporstan (place), 391
Shᵉkīnāh, 26, 28, 37, 112, 179, 206, 284, 372, 408, 425
Shᵉma', time of recital in the evening, 1–17, 51; Scriptural authority for reading, 2; must precede the *Tᵉfillāh*, 16 f.; should be read on one's bed, 18, 398; overcomes the evil impulse, 19; has protective power, 19; time of recital in the morning, 55; if read out of proper time, 66; posture when reading, 67 ff., 86; exemption from, by bridegroom, 67 f., 103, 105; interrupting the reading to greet a person, 82, 87 ff.; its sections, 82, 91 f.; language in which it may be read, 83 f., 267; must be read audibly, 83 f., 95 ff.; word *ēḥād* must be distinctly pronounced, 86; first sentence sufficient at night, 87; evening recital: Palestinian custom, 91; order of its sections, 92 f.; *Tᵉfillīn* worn during the reading, 93 f.; washing the hands before, 94 f.; two paragraphs included in the *Tᵉfillīn*, 100 f.; clear enunciation of its words necessary, 101 f.; law when error made during the reading of, 102; when read by workmen, 103; bridegroom may read it, if he so desires, 106, 114; reading merits the world to come, 107; mourner exempted from, 116 ff.; burial at the time of, 126; during funeral oration, 126 f.; exemption of women, slaves and minors, 131; how recited by a *Ba'al Kᵉrī*, 134, 141, 148; procedure in

case of doubt, 136 f.; recital near excrement, 148; recital in bed when not alone, 155 f.; recital when naked, 160, 161, 166 f.; recital in filthy surroundings, 160 ff.; forbidden in presence of a naked person, 167; procedure when setting out on a journey, 198; whoever omits it is an *'Am hā'āreṣ*, 304; recited by R. 'Aḳiba at his martyrdom, 407; omission to recite, 422
Shimei, 47
Shōfār, 198
Shooting-stars, 386 f.
Sifrā debē Rab, 71, 93 n., 119
Sifrē, 129 n.
Silence, value of, 31, 410
Sin, 14, 58, 77, 219
Singer, S., Authorised Hebrew Prayer Book, quoted in notes, passim
Slaves, 105 ff., 131, 291 ff., 306
Sleep, 378, 405, 412
Sneezing, significance during prayer, 159; exclamation for, 341; symptom in an invalid, 378
Solomon, 47, 59, 62, 191, 309
Sorcery, 412; Jewish women addicted to, 342
Soul, 60, 399
Spirits, conversing, 120 f., 123
Stepmother, 364
Storms, 389
Streane, A. W., quoted, 377 n.
Study, purifying effect of, 102. See also Disciples, House of Study, *Tōrāh*
Suetonius, quoted, 372 n.
Sufferings, removed by *Tōrāh*, 20; submission under, 21; medium of divine gifts, 22, 113
Sukkāh, 69
Sun-worshippers, 32, 37
Sura (place), 74, 285, 338
Suriel (Angel), 327
Synagogue, efficacy of prayer in, 8, 28; attendance at, 15, 30, 44, 46; where situated, 26 n.; God attends, 28, 30; leave slowly and hasten to, 31; forbidden to pray at the rear of, 32; in Tiberias, 46, 200; passing behind during prayer, 48 f., 404 f.; precentor's platform in, 65 n.; procedure in, 137 f.; early attendance meritorious, 306; quorum for service in, 306 f.; illumination in, 341; making a "short cut" of, 414 f.; House of Study greater than, 425

Talmūd, origin of, xxiii ff.; characteristics of, xxvi f.; first editions of, xxix; use of the Bible in, xxxv f.
Targūm, 20 n., 47, 48, 102 n.
Taylor, C., quoted, 15 n.
Tefillāh, follows the *Shema'*, 16 f.; to be joined with the *Ge'ullāh*, 16 f., 55 f., 275; its introductory and concluding sentences, 17, 57; should be said before one's bed, 25 f.; position of feet during, 65; bowing in the course of, 76, 189, 229; wording during the ten days of Penitence, 77; when read by workmen, 103 f.; its recital merits the world to come, 107; mourner exempted from, 116 ff.; during funeral oration, 126; obligation of women, slaves and minors to say, 131 f.; to be said by a *Ba'al Ḳerī*, 135, 148; procedure in case of doubt, 137; repetition with the Congregation, 137; interruption of, to make responses, 138 f.; procedure when there is filth in the room, 148, 162; when nature needs to be relieved, 149, 160; body must be covered when saying, 161; *terminus ad quem* in the morning, 172, 175 ff.; omission to say, and its reparation, 172 f.; instituted by the Patriarchs, 174 f.; correspondence with the daily offerings, 174 f.; *terminus ad quem* in the afternoon, 178; on the Sabbath, 178 ff., 191; *terminus ad quem* in the evening, 180; whether obligatory in the evening, 180 ff.; *terminus ad quem* of the Additional, 185; when two *Tefillōt* clash, 185; partaking of food before saying the Additional, 186; a daily obligation, 189; to what the Benedictions correspond, 189 f.; its origin, 190; on the

New Year, 191; on fast days, 191; the abstract of, 192; omissions from, 193 f., 200, 317; when journeying, 197 f.; laws regulating the Additional, 199; must be said in a serious frame of mind, 202 ff.; not to be interrupted for greetings, 218; interruption in case of danger, 219; precentor's error in, 227 f.; personal petition added to, 228; to err in, a bad omen, 230; may be said in any language, 267

Tᵉfillīn, 29 f., 39, 68, 85, 93, 100 f., 105, 116, 118, 131 f., 150–155, 161–170, 203, 288, 304, 365 f.

Temple, 7, 8, 65 n., 72, 215, 224, 234 n., 407 f., 416

Temple Mount, 349, 380, 414 f.

Tᵉrūmāh, 1–5, 96 ff., 260, 261, 291, 302 f., 336

Thanksgiving, from whom due, 353 f.

Thompson, R. C., quoted, 27 n.

Thunder, how caused, 389 f.

Tiberias, 46, 200, 343, 396, 410

Tigris, 391

Tithe, 204, 238, 243, 267, 269 f., 291, 302 f., 305, 418

Tōrāh, transmission of, xxiii ff.; rules of exposition, xxv; not to be discussed in the presence of a corpse, 10; "fence" round the, 15, 144; overcomes the evil impulse, 19; removes sufferings, 20; gift to Israel, 20 f.; obtained through sufferings, 22; expiates sin, 23; and the *Shᵉkīnāh*, 28 f.; merit of study, 31; service of, 43; study more important than Synagogue attendance, 46; benediction before study of, 71 f., 135 f.; teaches the Resurrection, 100; brings purification, 102; must be studied and practised for its own sake, 109, 111 f.; imposes duties, 113; honouring the Scroll of, 118, 170; its study when person is unclean, 141 ff., 148; study in unclean surroundings, 162 f.; reward of study, 187; requires effort, 216; study of, should be combined with a worldly occupation, 237 f.; introduction of children to, 304; basis of, 417; how to be studied, 422 f.; devotion to, 422

Tōsāfōt, quoted in notes, passim

Trajan, 363 n.

Twilight, defined, 5

Ūrim and *Tummīm*, 12, 78

Usha (place), 145

Vegetables, as diet, 289 f.

Visiting the sick, 61

Vulgate, quoted, 351 n., 391 n.

Washing hands, before prayer, 94 f.; before and after meals, 124, 275, 278 f., 299 f., 331, 334 ff.

Watcher of corpse, 117 f.

Water, as beverage, 263

Weiss, I. H., quoted, xxiv, xxv, 14 n.

Wᵉtīḳin, 55, 166, 172, 202 n.

Wiesner, I., quoted in notes, passim

Wine, 177, 179 f., 221, 239, 265, 272, 275 ff., 290, 322–334, 393

Woman, 64, 157 f., 210, 283, 311, 327, 342, 354, 403 f., 412; her religious obligations, 112, 131 ff., 291 ff., 306

Workmen, and their prayers, 103 f., 295

World to come, 23, 112, 187, 188, 378, 406, 425

Wünsche, A., quoted in notes, 27, 58, 213, 216, 327, 355

Zimmūn, 116 f., 291–330

Made in the USA
Monee, IL
12 August 2022

11466377R00291